RESEARCH HANDBOOK ON INTELLECTUAL PROPERTY AND COMPETITION LAW

Research Handbook on Intellectual Property and Competition Law

Edited by
Josef Drexl

Director, Max Planck Institute for Intellectual Property, Competition and Tax Law, Munich, Germany

Edward Elgar
Cheltenham, UK • Northampton, MA, USA

Published by
Edward Elgar Publishing Limited
The Lypiatts
15 Lansdown Road
Cheltenham
Glos GL50 2JA
UK

Edward Elgar Publishing, Inc.
William Pratt House
9 Dewey Court
Northampton
Massachusetts 01060
USA

A catalogue record for this book
is available from the British Library

Library of Congress Control Number: 2008932899

ISBN 978 1 84542 047 5 (cased)

Typeset by Cambrian Typesetters, Camberley, Surrey
Printed and bound in Great Britain by MPG Books Ltd, Bodmin, Cornwall

Contents

Contributors

Steve Anderman, BA (CUNY), JD (Yale), MSc London, Professor of Law at the University of Essex, UK.

Robert D. Anderson, Counsellor, Intellectual Property Division, WTO Secretariat, responsible for government procurement and competition policy issues.

Emanuela Arezzo, Dott. (LUISS), LL M (Erasmus University Rotterdam), Research Fellow at the Libera Università Internazionale degli Studi Sociali (LUISS) Guido Carli in Rome.

Josef Bejček, JUDr., CSc, Professor at Faculty of Law, Masaryk University, Brno, former dean of Masaryk University Faculty of Law, Brno (1995–2001).

Beatriz Conde Gallego, Dr. iur. (Munich), LL M (Würzburg), Research Fellow at the Max Planck Institute for Intellectual Property, Competition and Tax Law, Munich.

Josef Drexl, Dr. iur. (Munich), LL M (Berkeley); Director of the Max Planck Institute for Intellectual Property, Competition and Tax Law, Munich, Honorary Professor of Law at the University of Munich.

Stefan Enchelmaier, Dr. iur. (Bonn), LL M (Edinburgh), MA (Oxon.), Professor of Law at the University of York.

Gustavo Ghidini, Professor of Intellectual Property Law at the Università Statale di Milano and at the Libera Università Internazionale degli Studi Sociali (LUISS) Guido Carli in Rome; attorney in Milan.

Warren S. Grimes, BA (Stanford), JD (Michigan), Irving D. and Florence Rosenberg Professor of Law, Southwestern Law School, Los Angeles, California, USA.

Christian Handke, BA (London), MA (Linköping), Junior Lecturer at the Erasmus University Rotterdam.

Andreas Heinemann, Dr. jur. (Munich), Dipl.-Ök. (Hagen), DIAP (ENA, Paris), Professor of Law at the University of Zurich.

Clifford A. Jones, JD (Okla.); M.Phil., Ph.D. (Cantab.), Levin College of Law, University of Florida, USA.

Olav Kolstad, Dr. jur., Professor at the Department of Private Law, University of Oslo.

Annette Kur, Dr. iur., Research Fellow at the Max Planck Institute for Intellectual Property, Competition and Tax Law, Munich, Associate Professor at the University of Stockholm.

Mark-Oliver Mackenrodt, LL M (NYU), Research Fellow at the Max Planck Institute for Intellectual Property, Competition and Tax Law, Munich.

Mark R. Patterson, BSEE (Ohio State), MS (Ohio State), JD (Stanford), Professor of Law, Fordham University School of Law, New York, NY, USA.

Ole-Andreas Rognstad, Dr. jur., Professor of Law at the University of Oslo, Department of Private Law.

Junko Shibata, Assistant Professor of Law at the University of Kagawa.

Paul Stepan, Mag. rer.soc.oec., Assistant for Cultural Economics and Creative Industries at the Erasmus University Rotterdam.

Ruth Towse, BA Political Economy (Reading, UK), MSc (Econ) (LSE), Ph.D. (Rotterdam), Reader in Cultural Industries at the Erasmus University, Rotterdam and Bournemouth University, UK.

Hanns Ullrich, Dr. iur. (Berlin), M.C.J. (N.Y.U.), Emeritus Professor of Competition Law, Intellectual Property Law, Universität der Bundeswehr München, Professor at the European University Institute (EUI) in Florence (2003–6).

Abbreviations

ABA	American Bar Association
aff'd	affirmed
AG	Advocate General (ECJ)
AIDA	*Annali italiani del diritto d'autore*
Alb. L.J. Sci. & Tech.	*Albany Law Journal of Science and Technology*
All E.R.	All England Reports
AMA	Antimonopoly Act (Japan)
Am. Econ. Rev.	*American Economic Review*
Antitrust Bull.	*Antitrust Bulletin*
Antitrust L.J.	*Antitrust Law Journal*
ASCAP	American Society for Composers, Authors and Publishers
B. E. J. Econ. Anal. & Pol'y	*The Berkeley Electronic Journal of Economic Analysis and Policy*
BER	Block Exemption Regulation (EC)
Berkeley Tech. L.J.	*Berkeley Technology Law Journal*
BGH	Bundesgerichtshof (German Federal Supreme Court)
BIOS	biological open source lines
Boston U. L.J.Rev.	*Boston University Law Journal Review*
BT-Drucks.	Bundestags-Drucksache (documents of the German Parliament)
Bull. WHO	*Bulletin of the World Health Organization*
CAFC	US Court of Appeals for the Federal Circuit
Cal. L. Rev.	*California Law Review*
Can. Bus. L.J.	*Canadian Business Law Journal*
Cardozo Art & Enter. L.J.	*Cardozo Arts and Entertainment Law Journal*
C.D.E.	*Cahiers de Droit Européen*
CDPA	Copyright, Designs and Patents Act (UK)
CDR	Community Design Regulation; compact disc recordable
cert.	certiorari
CFI	Court of First Instance
Ch.	Chapter
CII	computer-implemented invention
Cir.	US Circuit Court of Appeals

C.M.L. Rev.	*Common Market Law Review*
Col. J. L. & Arts	*Columbia Journal of Law and the Arts*
Col. L. Rev.	*Columbia Law Review*
COM	European Commission
Comp. L. Rev.	*Competition Law Review*
Comp. Pol'y Newsletter	*Competition Policy Newletter*
CRi	*Computer und Recht International*
C.T.L.R.	*Computer and Telecommunication Law Review*
D.	US District Court
D.C. Cir.	US Court of Appeals for the District of Columbia
DG	Directorate General (European Commission)
Dir. Aut.	*Il Diritto d'autore*
Dir. Inf.	*Il Diritto dell'informazione e dell'informatica*
DMCA	US Digital Millennium Copyright Act
DoJ	US Department of Justice
DRM	digital rights management
E.B.L.R.	*European Business Law Review*
EC	European Community; Treaty establishing the European Community (as amended by the Treaty of Nice 2001)
ECJ	European Court of Justice
ECLR	*European Competition Law Review*
Econ. J.	*Economic Journal*
ECR	European Court Reports
EEA	European Economic Area
EEC	European Economic Community
EIPR	*European Intellectual Property Review*
E.L. Rev.	*European Law Review*
Emory L.J.	*Emory Law Journal*
EPC	European Patent Convention
EPEC	European Policy Evaluation Consortium
EPO	European Patent Office
EPOR	European Patent Office Reports
EU	European Union
EuZW	*Europäische Zeitschrift für Wirtschaftsrecht*
EWS	*Europäische Zeitschrift für Wirtschafts- und Steuerrecht*
F.	Federal Reporter (US)
Fed. Cir.	US Court of Appeals for the Federal Circuit
Fordham Intell. Prop., Media & Enter. L.J	*Fordham Intellectual Property, Media & Entertainment Law Journal*

Fordham Int'l L.J.	*Fordham International Law Journal*
Fordham L. Rev.	*Fordham Law Review*
Foro It.	*Il Foro italiano*
FRAND conditions	fair, reasonable and non-discriminatory conditions
F. Suppl.	Federal Supplement (US)
FTC	US Federal Trade Commission
GATT	General Agreement on Tariffs and Trade
Geo. L.J.	*Georgetown Law Journal*
Global Econ. J.	*Global Economy Journal*
GRUR	*Gewerblicher Rechtsschutz und Urheberrecht*
GRUR Int.	*Gewerblicher Rechtsschutz und Urheberrecht Internationaler Teil*
Harv. J. L. & Pub. Pol'y	*Harvard Journal of Law and Public Policy*
Harv. J. L. & Tech.	*Harvard Journal of Law and Technology*
Harv. L. Rev.	*Harvard Law Review*
Hastings L.J.	*Hastings Law Journal*
H.L.	House of Lords
ICTSD	International Center for Trade and Sustainable Development
IIC	*International Review of Intellectual Property and Competition Law*
IJIO	*International Journal of Industrial Organization*
Inf. Econ. & Pol'y	*Information Economics and Policy*
Int'l J. L. & Econ.	*International Journal of Law and Economics*
IP	intellectual property
IPQ	*Intellectual Property Quarterly*
IPR(s)	intellectual property right(s)
J. Cultural Econ.	*Journal of Cultural Economics*
J. Econ. Persp.	*Journal of Economic Perspectives*
J. Econ. Surv.	*Journal of Economic Surveys*
JFTC	Japan Fair Trade Commission
J. Ind. Econ.	*Journal of Industrial Economics*
J.I.E.L.	*Journal of International Economic Law*
J. Inf. Techn. Th. & Appl.	*Journal of Information Technology Theory and Application*
JITE	*Journal of Institutional and Theoretical Economics*
J. Leg. Stud.	*Journal of Legal Studies*
J. L. & Econ.	*Journal of Law and Economics*
J. L. Econ. & Org.	*Journal of Law, Economics and Organization*
J. Pat. & Trademark Off. Soc'y	*Journal of the Patent and Trademark Office Society*

J. Pol'y Anal. & Manag.	*Journal of Policy Analysis and Management*
J. Polit. Econ.	*Journal of Political Economy*
JZ	*Juristen-Zeitung*
K.C.L.J.	*King's College Law Journal*
L.Ed.	Lawyer's Edition
Leg. Iss. Econ. Integr.	*Legal Issues of Economic Integration*
Marquette Intell. Prop. L. Rev.	*Marquette Intellectual Property Law Review*
Minn. L. Rev.	*Minnesota Law Review*
N.Y.U. Ann. Surv. Am. L.	*New York University Annual Survey of American Law*
N.Y.U. L. Rev.	*New York University Law Review*
OECD	Organization for Economic Co-operation and Development
OECD J. Comp. L. & Pol'y	*OECD Journal of Competition Law and Policy*
OEM	original equipment manufacturer
OHIM	Office for Harmonisation in the Internal Market
OJ	Official Journal (EC, EU)
Okla. Bar J.	*Oklahoma Bar Journal*
Pacific Rim L. & Pol'y J.	*The Pacific Rim Law and Policy Journal*
PD	Proposed Directive (EC)
PTO	US Patent and Trademark Office
Q. J. Econ.	*Quarterly Journal of Economics*
RAND conditions	reasonable and non-discriminatory conditions
RAND J. Econ.	*RAND Journal of Economics*
RERCI	*Review of Economic Research on Copyright Issues*
Res. in L. & Econ.	*Research in Law and Economics*
Rev. Ind. Org.	*Review of Industrial Organization*
Riv. Dir. Ind.	*Rivista di Diritto Industriale*
RIW	*Recht der internationalen Wirtschaft*
RPC	Reports of Patent Cases (UK)
Rutgers Comp. & Tech. L.J.	*Rutgers Computer and Technology Law Journal*
Rutgers L.J.	*Rutgers Law Journal*
R&D	research and development
S. Cal. L. Rev.	*Southern California Law Review*
S.Ct.	Supreme Court Reporter
SIAE	Società Italiana degli Autori ed Editori
SIEC	significant impediment to effective competition

SLC	substantial lessening of competition
SME	small and medium-sized enterprise
SPC	supplementary protection certificate
SSNIP	Small but Significant Non-transitory Increase in Price
Sw. U. L. Rev.	South Western University Law Review
Temp. J. Sci. Tech. & Envtl. L.	*The Temple Journal of Science, Technology and Environmental Law*
Tex. Intell. Prop. L.J.	*Texas Intellectual Property Law Journal*
Tex. L. Rev.	*Texas Law Review*
Topics in Econ. Anal. & Pol'y	Topics in Economic Analysis and Policy
TRIPS	Agreement on Trade-related Aspects of Intellectual Property Rights
TT	technology transfer
TTBER	Technology Transfer Block Exemption Regulation No. 772/2004 (EC)
U. Balt. L. Rev.	*University of Baltimore Law Review*
UCC	Uniform Commercial Code (US)
UCD	Unregistered Community Design
U. Chi. L. Rev.	*University of Chicago Law Review*
UCLA L. Rev.	*University of California at Los Angeles Law Review*
UMTS	Universal Mobile Telecommunications System
UNCTAD	United Nations Conference on Trade and Development
U. Pa. L. Rev.	*University of Pennsylvania Law Review*
U. Pitt. L. Rev.	*University of Pittsburgh Law Review*
US	United States
U.S.	United States Reports (Supreme Court)
USC	United States Code
USCA	United States Code Annotated
U.S.P.Q.	United States Patent Quarterly
v.	versus
Va. L. Rev.	*Virginia Law Review*
Vand. L. Rev.	*Vanderbilt Law Review*
Wash. U. L.Q.	*Washington University Law Quarterly*
WIPO	World Intellectual Property Organization
WL	Westlaw
W.L.R.	Weekly Law Reports
WRP	*Wettbewerb in Recht und Praxis*
Wm. and Mary L. Rev.	*William and Mary Law Review*
WTO	World Trade Organization

WuW	*Wirtschaft und Wettbewerb*
Yale J. Reg.	*Yale Journal on Regulation*
Yale L.J.	*Yale Law Journal*
Y.E.L.	*Yearbook of European Law*
ZEuP	*Zeitschrift für Europäisches Privatrecht*
ZEuS	*Zeitschrift für Europäische Studien*
ZHR	*Zeitschrift für das gesamte Handelsrecht*
ZWeR	*Zeitschrift für Wettbewerbsrecht (Journal of Competition Law)*

Preface

The application of competition law to intellectual-property-related cases may well be regarded as one of the most complex and critical fields of competition policy. Whereas in the past intellectual property and competition were mostly considered as contradictory concepts, it is today widely admitted that both fields of law, intellectual property and competition law, are meant to promote complementary goals, namely innovation based on dynamic concepts of competition. Still it largely remains disputed whether and under which conditions competition law may intervene and restrain the use of an intellectual property right. At this very moment this dispute also seems to be mirrored by transatlantic disagreement. In September 2007 the European Court of First Instance upheld the decision of the Commission to order Microsoft *inter alia* to provide competitors with interoperability information on its operating system despite possible intellectual property rights involved. Thomas Barnett, Deputy Assistant Attorney General of the Antitrust Division of the US Department of Justice, reacted immediately and accused the Court of 'harming consumers by chilling innovation and discouraging competition'.

Concern about expanding and possibly 'anti-competitive' intellectual property rights, blocking patents and patent ambush cases, network effects, especially in information technology industries, and the growing need for standardization compel those practising in these areas of law to request more fundamental research on the interface of intellectual property and competition law. Such research, however, in both economic theory and legal studies, is still in a stage of infancy. Economics can well explain and advise how markets work when it comes to price and output, but the field still lacks operational models for intervention in order to guarantee that the use of very roughly hewn IP systems does not harm the delicate dynamics of competition and, ultimately, consumer welfare. Meanwhile lawyers have to struggle with the growing number of IP-related competition law cases and discuss the most appropriate ways to draw the line between the exclusivity of the right and competition law intervention with a view to enhancing innovation.

This *Handbook*, bringing together 18 chapters by lawyers and economists from different countries, responds to this need for further research. All the contributions are the result of a research project organized and financed by the Max Planck Institute for Intellectual Property, Competition and Tax Law in Munich, Germany. The project ran for several years. A first meeting took place in 2003 at Kloster Seeon (Bavaria), where initial papers were discussed in the framework of a smaller group. This group decided to develop such a handbook by inviting more authors to write articles on subtopics in the field according to their preference. A second meeting then took place at the Munich Institute in September 2006. All papers had been distributed among the participants beforehand. Each member of the group presented and criticized the paper of another member. After two days of intensive discussion the participants were sent home to work on their papers. The result of this work is published in this book.

Given the scheme of the research project, the reader should not expect to find detailed information on what the state of the law is on each and every subissue at the interface of intellectual property and competition law. In contrast, the book is meant to be a source of inspiration on a high academic level and enhance further discussion and research. Given the timing, the authors were not able to include the decision of the Court of First Instance in *Microsoft*. Still quite a number of chapters dealing with the underlying economic and legal issues of this case may now be read through the lens of this decision and turn out to be very useful for future research.

The *Handbook* is divided into six parts. The first part deals with overall policies and economic theory. The first three chapters focus on the European situation, but, by searching for new approaches to competition policy addressing IP-related cases, they undoubtedly have a broader reach. *Olav Kolstad* presents a concept for protecting dynamic competition by balancing effects on allocative, productive and dynamic efficiencies in the most appropriate manner possible. Under Article 81 of the EC Treaty, and based on an analysis of the case law, he argues in favour of taking into account the effects of an agreement on innovation in the context of Article 81(1), whereas productive efficiency would only be considered in the framework of Article 81(3). While Kolstad sees the *IMS Health* judgment of the European Court of Justice (ECJ) as in line with the protection of dynamic competition, my own contribution and that by Andreas Heinemann are clearly inspired by a critical view of this judgment. Dealing with the issue of refusal to license, *IMS Health* is critical to how we have to view the relationship between the exclusivity of a right and competition. Rejecting the view of some economists that the costs of intervention in the use of an IPR will never be outweighed by what can be won, I, *Josef Drexl*, advocate a thorough evaluation of the effects of a given behaviour on innovation in the relevant market as a basis for intervention. In this sense I recommend that the European Commission develop a 'more economic approach to IP and competition', protecting the process of dynamic competition in relevant markets, covering all fields of competition enforcement. In a similar vein and in response to the ECJ in *IMS Health*, *Andreas Heinemann* sketches a competition policy that relies on the concept of the contestability of markets. He presents a consistent theory according to which competition policy should intervene when IPRs create entry barriers; he also explains when competition law enforcers should accept the exclusivity of the IP right. *Mark-Oliver Mackenrodt* provides a concise picture of the economics of network effects. Against this backdrop he further develops ideas on the role of IP rights in network industries. Although the author refrains from discussing case law, the user of this book will certainly find much inspiration in his chapter for dealing with many cases, including *Microsoft*.

The second part deals with contractual relationships. *Steve Anderman* presents a comprehensive analysis of the European regulatory regime for licensing under the revised EU Technology Transfer Block Exemption Regulation (TTBER) of 2004 in view of a policy for the enhancement of innovation. The European TTBER does not apply to patent pools. This is where *Hanns Ullrich* comes in with his critical assessment of how the Commission plans to address patent pool arrangements as set out in the European Technology Transfer Guidelines. The author's thorough analysis questions many assumptions about patent pools accepted so far in both the US and the EU. *Mark Patterson* looks closer at field-of-use restrictions in licensing agreements, which generally enjoy generous treatment by competition agencies in the US and the EU. Yet as an explicit warning addressed to Europeans, he criticizes practice in the US that even allows restrictions of use that is not part of the specific scope of exclusivity of the IP right. *Junko Shibata* then takes us to Japan and explains how practice there manages to develop the necessary control of the use of IPRs although the Japanese Antimonopoly Act seems to exempt intellectual property from its application.

Part 3 of the book deals with unilateral restraints based on IPRs. Here, *Beatriz Conde Gallego* compares the law in the US and the EU with regard to refusals to license. This field has definitely been the focal point of the debate on intellectual property and competition law in recent years. Whereas many, especially in the US, might argue that in the EU the law goes too far by accepting a duty to license under certain conditions, the author points out that the analysis has so far focused too much on the freedom of the right-holder not to license and on her incentives to innovate. The author advocates a different approach, which is based on the idea of complementary goals of IPRs and competition and the effects a given IPR exercises on the relevant market. The following two articles by *Clifford Jones* and *Warren Grimes* react to the recent US Supreme Court decision in *Illinois Tool Works*, which repealed an earlier judgment that, in applying Section 2 of the Sherman Act, inferred a presumption of significant market power from the existence of a patent. Whereas it may be considered conventional wisdom that patents do statistically rather rarely lead to market dominance, *Clifford Jones*, in criticizing the Supreme Court, demonstrates that such departure from earlier case law can by no means be explained by more recent legislation cutting back the patent-abuse doctrine under the Patent Act. He makes a strong argument that such a policy of taking back antitrust enforcement may be most detrimental at times when IP protection becomes more expansionist as a consequence of successful rent-seeking. *Warren Grimes* assesses the harmful effects on competition of tying the sale of additional products to the patented product and criticizes the Supreme Court in *Illinois Tool Works* for having completely refrained from giving guidance on how to handle tying cases. This critique is integrated into a most interesting analysis of the policy of different antitrust enforcers in the US regarding IP-related cases. The author criticizes the politicized Antitrust Division of the Department of Justice in particular, which in several cases has successfully convinced the courts to relax antitrust rules on IPRs.

In Part 4 *Josef Bejček* takes us to merger law. He reviews how effects on innovation can be best taken into account in an analytical way so as to promote dynamic efficiency when IPRs play a role in merger control cases. He thereby prefers a long-term evaluation of the beneficial effects to an analysis that focuses on short-term gains in consumer welfare.

The three chapters in Part 5 remind us that competition policy considerations play a major role in designing well-functioning IP laws and, conversely, that IP laws as such do not always promote innovation and dynamic competition. *Annette Kur* takes a fresh look at the spare-parts discussion in European design law. She explains why such protection by itself produces anti-competitive results and should therefore be repealed, as is now proposed by the European Commission in the face of resistance by the car industry. *Gustavo Ghidini* and *Emanuela Arezzo* analyse the interplay of copyright law and patent law with regard to the protection of computer programs. The authors reject the conventional wisdom according to which patent law, in contrast to copyright law, will hamper the dynamic development of the software industry. In the light of the competition goal, they highlight the obvious deficiencies of copyright law, such as, the lack of control over the grant of protection, the excessive term of protection and, maybe most importantly, the lack of any rules on solving the conflict between the prior right-holder and the follow-on innovator. Especially when it comes to European law on refusals to license, copyright has so far been the most important IP right. This contrasts with academic debate, which focuses on innovation theories without giving due account to the fact that the major goal of copyright to promote creativity and not innovation. In order to correct this imbalance, the book includes a comprehensive review by *Christian Handke*, *Paul Stepan* and *Ruth Towse* of the economic literature on copyright.

Finally, Part 6 of the book turns to cross-border aspects of the interface between IP and competition policy. The first two chapters deal with the issue of whether more consistency can be achieved in applying the rules on free movement of goods on the one hand and the competition rules of the EC

Treaty on the other hand. *Stefan Enchelmaier* thus explores the bilateral relationships in the triangle of protecting competition, guaranteeing free movement of goods and protecting intellectual property. Although EC competition law and the free-movement principles may pursue similar goals and respond to similar problems, he recommends caution in considering further harmonization of the two sets of rules with regard to intellectual property, such as streamlining the principle of European exhaustion with the application of Article 81 EC. In contrast, it is the very premise of the chapter by *Ole-Andreas Rognstad* that more harmonization of the two sets of rules is possible and should accordingly be implemented in the case law. At the end of the book, *Robert Anderson* explores the possibilities of developing more precise international rules on the application of competition law to IP-related cases in the framework of the TRIPS Agreement, whereby he takes into account the pros and cons of such a development for developing countries in particular.

A number of people were extremely helpful in making the publication of this book possible. In addition to the authors, who demonstrated close cooperation throughout the course of the project, I would like to express my gratitude to the staff at the Max Planck Institute. In addition to the two authors, Mark-Oliver Mackenrodt and Stefan Enchelmaier, who has by now become a professor at the University of York, Rupprecht Podszun and Nadine Klass were very helpful in reviewing the drafts of the contributions. Allison Felmy carried the heaviest burden by reviewing the English of the many non-native speakers. Delia Zirilli managed the complex communication process at the reviewing stage. Last but not least, this book would not have come into existence without the support of the publisher. From the very beginning, Luke Adams supported the idea of having such a *Handbook* on behalf of the publisher. I would like to thank Luke for his patience and his sharing of enthusiasm over the last several years.

Munich, November 2007 Josef Drexl

PART 1

OVERARCHING POLICIES AND ECONOMIC THEORIES

1 Competition law and intellectual property rights – outline of an economics-based approach

Olav Kolstad

1 Competition law and IP law – in conflict or pursuing a common aim?

From a competition law point of view intellectual property rights (IPRs) may be viewed as a means to reduce competition. An IPR gives the right holder a right hindering others from offering the protected product to the market in competition with the IPR holder. An IPR may also be used to restrict competition between licensees given the right to produce a protected product. EC Treaty Articles 81 and 82 protect the market mechanism from anti-competitive conduct. If national legislation on IPRs gives the right holders the possibility to restrict competition, the logical response from the EC competition rules is to censor anti-competitive conduct based on IPRs.

The relationship between EC Treaty Articles 81 and 82 and IP law is not necessarily one of conflict. It can be argued that competition law and IP law share the same economic objectives. If the two sets of rules are interpreted against the background of a common aim, possible conflicts between competition law and IP law can be reduced. In section 2, I will outline a theoretical framework for an economics-based analysis of the common goal of competition and IP law. In section 3, I will apply the theoretical framework developed in section 2 in the interpretation of Articles 81 and 82.

2 The theoretical framework – an outline

2.1 The efficiency goal of Articles 81 and 82

It is well established that EC competition law has an economic goal. The economic goal of Articles 81 and 82 is the protection and promotion of effective competition leading to effective market performance. Articles 81 and 82 do not protect competition for its own sake, but because efficient markets offer a diversity of products at the lowest price. It is in the interest of society that competition, as the driving force behind the market mechanism, should lead to efficient market performance. Further, it is in the interest of consumers that competition put pressure on suppliers forcing them to share the surplus resulting from efficient performance with consumers in the form of lower prices, and put pressure on suppliers to invest in research and development to promote innovations.

In a world with scarce resources, a vital question is how to put the available resources to the best use for society as a whole, without wasting them. In a market economy the market mechanism has the task of allocating given resources to the best use. In a market context, the benchmark for good use is consumer preferences. The price system allocates resources to the production of products consumers demand.

A more efficient allocation of resources can increase economic welfare up to a certain point. In a perfect world the market mechanism would lead to Pareto optimality. The use of resources will be Pareto-efficient when it is not possible to change the situation to make at least one person better off without making one person worse off.[1] If it is possible to make one person better off without making anyone worse off, it is possible to realize a Pareto improvement. As one approaches the Pareto optimum, the gains realized with each Pareto improvement will decline.

Even though an efficient allocation of resources is important, it is not allocative efficiency that over time contributes the most to economic welfare. In the long run, the state of technology is not given, and to have economic growth one must find new ways to use resources in a more efficient manner. One must in other words come up with new knowledge and innovative products.

It is a generally accepted and well-substantiated point of view that innovation is the main source of increases in economic welfare. While it can be said to be relatively clear how the market mechanism through the price system contributes to an efficient allocation of resources in the short run, it is not equally clear how the market mechanism contributes to innovation. But it is quite clear that there is a direct connection between the functioning of the market mechanism and the incentives the market players have to innovate.

Competition policy and competition laws have as their primary aim to protect competition to secure the efficient functioning of the market mechanism. The focus has in practice been to protect the functioning of the price system or the price mechanism, to secure an efficient allocation of resources in the short run. Competition rules have in other words focused on efficiency in a static perspective, on allocative efficiency. This may be illustrated by the Commission's description of the object of Article 81(1) in its Guidelines on the application of Article 81(2):[2] 'The objective of Article 81 is to protect

---

1 Van den Bergh, Roger J. and Peter D. Camesasca (2001), *European Competition Law and Economics – A Comparative Perspective*, London: Sweet & Maxwell, p. 64.

2 Communication from the Commission – Notice – Guidelines on the application of Article 81(3) of the Treaty, OJ 2004 No. C 101, p. 97, para. 13.

competition on the market as a means of enhancing consumer welfare and of ensuring an efficient allocation of resources'.

Innovations or dynamic efficiency have not been given the same focus in the enforcement of the competition rules. But it seems that today it is generally accepted that it is relevant to take into consideration dynamic efficiency as a part of the efficiency goal when interpreting Articles 81 and 82.

Static and dynamic efficiency are two dimensions of the efficiency goal.[3] Competition as the driving force of the market mechanism furthers both static and dynamic efficiency. But competition does not necessarily maximize both static and dynamic efficiency. It can be shown that in market structures with many small suppliers competing fiercely, resources will be allocated in an efficient way, but that fierce competition between many small suppliers will limit the capital available for innovation. In more concentrated markets, on the other hand, the suppliers will have greater possibility and incentives to invest in R&D, and more concentrated markets may thus be more innovative.[4] This does not mean that inventors should be protected against competition and given a monopoly. IP right holders must be pressed to further technological improvements and innovations. To do this there must be a certain degree of competition on the market. But economic theory can tell us that market structure has an influence on dynamic efficiency, and that has implications for the regulation of market conduct.

If concentrated markets further dynamic efficiency to a greater extent than markets with many small suppliers, this could lead to the conclusion that static and dynamic efficiency are two dimensions of the efficiency goal in conflict with one another. But the key issue is not to maximize static and dynamic efficiency, respectively, but to maximize the sum of both static and dynamic efficiency. If the overriding goal is an efficient use of society's scarce resources, the task is to find the interpretation of Articles 81 and 82 that gives the best overall result. This must be reflected in the notion of competition under Articles 81 and 82. The challenge is to develop an analytical framework that includes the effects on dynamic competition and dynamic efficiency in the analysis of conduct alleged to be contrary to Articles 81 and 82. This is especially important for the analysis of conduct based on IPRs. IPRs promote innovations and technological progress, and if this is not recognized in competition law analysis one risks prohibiting conduct that may have a positive effect on dynamic efficiency. When assessing whether conduct based on IPRs is

---

3 A third efficiency dimension is efficient use of the resources inside the production entities, through product-specific and plant-specific economies.

4 For an analysis of market structure and technological innovation, see Scherer, F.M. and David Ross (1990), *Industrial Market Structure and Economic Performance*, Boston: Houghton Mifflin, pp. 613–60.

contrary to Articles 81 and 82, the effects of the conduct on both static and dynamic efficiency must be taken into account. Only if the sum is negative is the conduct contrary to the efficiency goal of Articles 81 and 82.

2.2 *Dynamic efficiency as a common goal for competition law and IP law*

The rules on IPRs are not based on an explicit economic rationale to the same extent as competition rules, and the aims of intellectual property law are, in legal discussion and case law, usually expressed in terms other than economic. At first glance it could thus appear that economic welfare analysis does not have the same relevance as a source for arguments when interpreting rules on intellectual property as when interpreting Articles 81 and 82. But it is clear that intellectual property rules have as one of their aims the furtherance of innovations. This goal can be described as the promotion of dynamic efficiency in an economic sense. If economic analysis can establish dynamic efficiency as a common goal for IP law and competition law, the common theoretical framework could form the basis for an analysis of conduct based on IPRs under Articles 81 and 82.

IPRs are 'a legally enforceable power to exclude others from using a resource (with no need to make contracts with would-be users of the resource forbidding their use)'.[5] The economic value of an intellectual property is realized in the market. IPRs protect the right holder from others taking over and reaping the rewards from his or her intellectual or marketing efforts, that is from free-riding on these efforts. An inventor invests time and resources in R&D activity hoping that the result will be an invention that will have an economic value exceeding the investments. An author is only able to invest time and effort in writing if the book in the end will give him an income. A trade mark owner will only invest in promoting a trade mark if this gives added value to the products sold under the trade mark. The investments are 'sunk' investments once they are spent. To warrant making the investments, the investor, that is, the inventor, author or trade mark owner, must expect that once commercialization occurs, product prices can be held above 'production' and marketing costs for sufficiently long for the discounted present value of the profits to exceed the value of the front-end investment.[6]

Knowledge has the characteristics of a public good. If an innovator is not given some kind of exclusivity to his or her innovation, the knowledge can be multiplied and spread with only insignificant costs. If others are allowed to use the knowledge for free, the innovator will not be able to recoup the often large

---

[5] Landes, William M. and Richard A. Posner (2003), *The Economic Structure of Intellectual Property Law*, Cambridge, Mass.: Harvard University Press, p. 12.

[6] Scherer and Ross, *supra* note 4, at 622.

investments connected with R&D activities. From society's point of view the most efficient use of knowledge, when it is produced, is to spread it to all who can use the knowledge at a price that covers the distribution costs. But this static view will have serious consequences for the incentives to innovate. The incentives to innovate will in a world without some kind of protection against unauthorized use of innovations be small. IPRs give the innovator the exclusive right to utilize the new knowledge an innovation results in, and this gives potential innovators economic incentives to innovate. R&D activities are connected with large investments. To recoup the investments and to earn an acceptable rate of return on the investments, exclusivity regarding the utilization of new knowledge is a prerequisite. Thus, IPRs give incentives to invest in the production of intellectual property. Further, IPRs make it possible to raise funds to invest in such activity.

Intellectual property protects new knowledge and information. Without the 'production' of new knowledge and new information there will be no technical progress and limited economic growth. Thus from an economic point of view the object of IP laws is to further technical and other progress for the benefit of society, and for the benefit of consumers who profit from new products, more efficient production processes and greater product differentiation.

If efficient use of resources in the long term is a goal of IPRs, the rationale behind these rights should be to strike the right balance between static and dynamic efficiency. IPRs give innovators the opportunity to reap a 'monopoly' profit for a period. This guarantees that innovators have the motivation and the possibility for further innovations. But the scope and duration of the protection IPRs give should not exceed what is necessary to secure the optimal rate of innovations. If the protection is too far-reaching, this will lead to unnecessary allocative losses to the detriment of consumers.

When regulating the exercise of IPRs in intellectual property law, for instance the duration of IPRs, the rule maker thus has to balance the gains IPRs give society by encouraging creation and dissemination of new knowledge against the costs – the reduction in competition and higher prices – that IPRs lead to. This balancing approach is, if explained in economic terms, the same approach used under competition law when regulating the exercise of IPRs. Dynamic efficiency is a common aim for both competition rules and intellectual property rules, and the regulation of the exercise of IPRs under the two sets of rules can be based on a similar balancing approach.

The Commission is also of the opinion that competition law and IP law share the same objectives. This is expressed in the theory of complementarity advocated by the Commission in its Guidelines on technology transfer:[7]

---

[7] Guidelines on the application of Article 81 of the EC Treaty to technology transfer agreements, OJ EC 2004 No. C 101, p. 2, para. 7.

> The fact that intellectual property laws grant exclusive rights of exploitation does not imply that intellectual property rights are immune from competition law intervention. Articles 81 and 82 are in particular applicable to agreements whereby the holder licenses another undertaking to exploit his intellectual property rights. Nor does it imply that there is an inherent conflict between intellectual property rights and the Community competition rules. Indeed, both bodies of law share the same basic objective of promoting consumer welfare and an efficient allocation of resources. Innovation constitutes an essential and dynamic component of an open and competitive market economy. Intellectual property rights promote dynamic competition by encouraging undertakings to invest in developing new or improved products and processes. So does competition by putting pressure on undertakings to innovate. Therefore, both intellectual property rights and competition are necessary to promote innovation and ensure a competitive exploitation thereof.

2.3 *Are competition law and IP law complementary?*

It follows from the theory of complementarity that since competition law and IP law share the same objectives there will be no conflict between the two bodies of law. In my opinion one cannot conclude from complementarity regarding objectives that there will be no conflict of norms and no conflicts between competition law and IP law. Despite the fact that dynamic efficiency is a common goal for competition law and IP law, competition law and IP law are not fully complementary for two reasons.

First, competition law has traditionally focused primarily on static competition and the allocation of resources and not taken into account the effects of conduct on dynamic competition and dynamic efficiency. Even if competition law and IP law share dynamic efficiency as a common goal, the supremacy of static efficiency in practice has created a conflict.

Second, even if the goals of IP laws can be described in economic terms, this does not mean that the goals of IP laws have transformed into economic goals. There are still goals that are not economic in character. To use a term used in competition law to characterize non-economic goals, IP law is based on 'populistic' goals in addition to economic goals.[8] To the extent that IP laws have goals differing from the goals of competition law, there is a conflict between the two areas of law. It is only possible to develop a common frame of analysis if the goals are common. Differing goals could be used to argue that it is not possible to reconcile IP law and competition law. A conflict between IP law and competition rules must in that case be solved by formal rules giving either IP law or competition law primacy over the other.

The two sets of law are thus not fully complementary. The expansion of IPRs in the last few decades has in my opinion deepened the conflict. This

---

[8] On populistic goals in antitrust policy, see Bork, Robert H. (1978), *The Antitrust Paradox*, New York: Basic Books, pp. 5–8.

expansion is generally not justified by economic considerations, but by the interests of the innovator as a private property right owner. This development has to a certain extent been counteracted by a development whereby IP laws have incorporated to a greater extent the goal of economic efficiency. To some extent one can say that IP laws have absorbed elements of competition policy. As a result of this, the focus has changed from 'property' towards 'exclusivity'. Such absorption does of course reduce the conflict potential both on a policy level and on the norm level. But this adjustment of IP law and policy to the goals of competition rules has not eliminated conflicts between the two areas of law.

2.4 An analytical tool based on dynamic efficiency – the concept of dynamic competition

Although, as I contend, there is in practice a potential for conflict in the interface between IP law and competition law, the concept of dynamic competition creates a common ground for competition and IP law that can be used to develop an analytical framework for the competition-law analysis of conduct based on IPRs that will reduce the conflict potential. The competition rules accept that to further dynamic efficiency new knowledge has to be protected by IPRs. But conduct based on IPRs can have negative effects on competition and the competition rules can be considered as a second tier of regulation governing the exercise of IPRs.[9] Thus Articles 81 and 82 inevitably have to strike a balance between static and dynamic efficiency if IP law authorizes conduct that goes beyond what is necessary to further innovations and dynamic efficiency, at the expense of allocative efficiency.

Static and dynamic efficiency are abstract concepts. In practice it is difficult to measure the quantitative effects of an agreement or conduct on static or dynamic efficiency, and it will in addition not be possible to anticipate the effects of an agreement or unilateral conduct on the market. It is in any event not the role of Articles 81 and 82 to sum up the anticipated effects on static and dynamic efficiency and allow or prohibit an agreement or conduct based on the anticipated net result. Articles 81 and 82 protect the process of competition, not efficient market results as such. It is the undertakings that are the addressees of Articles 81 and 82, and the prohibitions are directed towards their conduct in the market place. The efficiency goal must thus be quantified and put into concrete operation in the interpretation of Articles 81 and 82, and a concept of dynamic competition must be developed that reflects the market processes leading to innovations and increased dynamic efficiency. When a

---

9 Anderman, Steven D. (1998), *EC Competition Law and Intellectual Property Rights – The Regulation of Innovation*, Oxford: Clarendon, p. 5.

concept of dynamic competition is developed, the economic rationale of IPRs must be taken into account, and conduct that is the result of IP law must be recognized as pro-competitive to the extent that it lies within the common economic rationale of IP law and competition law.

One reason for the rather modest role dynamic efficiency has played in competition-law analysis may be that the theoretical framework for a dynamic analysis is not developed to the same extent as the theoretical framework for a static efficiency analysis. Where the model for perfect competition gives a seemingly clear starting point for the analysis of effects on competition and static efficiency, and where the theory on workable competition implements the theoretical framework, economic theory has not come up with clear answers regarding dynamic efficiency. To develop a concept of dynamic competition it is a prerequisite that economic theory develop an analytical tool that can be used in the competition analysis under Articles 81 and 82. Economic theory must identify how different types of market conduct contribute to static and dynamic efficiency, respectively.

The theory of complementarity advocated by the Commission argues that competition law and IP law do not only share common goals, but that competition as the driving force behind the market mechanism also furthers innovations. Competition is thus a means to further both static and dynamic efficiency. Competition does so by putting pressure on competitors to innovate. 'Therefore, both intellectual property rights and competition are necessary to promote innovation and ensure a competitive exploitation thereof.'[10] The Commission establishes in its theory of complementarity a concept of dynamic competition in which IPRs play a role: intellectual property rights promote dynamic competition by encouraging undertakings to invest in developing new or improved products and processes.

If conduct based on an IPR reduces the incentives to invest in R&D activities, it seems to follow from the Commission's concept of dynamic competition that the conduct should be viewed as a restriction on dynamic competition. In addition, the concept of dynamic competition seems to have a static dimension. It is the view of the Commission that competition furthers innovation 'by putting pressure on undertakings to innovate'. Holders of IPRs must face competition in the market to have an incentive to compete for new markets. The Commission's concept of dynamic competition seems to fit well with the theoretical framework outlined above, and will in the following be used to illustrate how the theoretical framework may be put into quantifiable terms in the application of Articles 81 and 82 to conduct based on IPRs.

---

[10] TT Guidelines, *supra* note 7, para. 7.

3 Applying the theoretical framework in the legal analysis

3.1 Introduction

Competition law is not applied economics. Economic and legal theories will play an important role in describing how the theoretical framework can be applied when assessing different types of conduct. But the prerequisite for the use of the theoretical framework outlined above is that the existing case law open up for an analysis where dynamic competition and dynamic efficiency are given a more important role. It is easy to agree with the Commission when it states in its TT Guidelines that '[i]n assessing licensing agreements under Article 81, the existing analytical framework is sufficiently flexible to take due account of the dynamic aspects of technology licensing'.[11] But the, in my opinion, unanswered question is how the 'dynamic aspects' of allegedly anti-competitive conduct should be brought into the analysis under Articles 81 and 82.

In this section, I will flesh out the theoretical framework outlined in section 2. This I will do on the basis of the case law of the Court of Justice. I will not argue that the Court of Justice has used an economic approach in its analysis of conduct based on IPRs. Rather, I will show how such an economic approach could be fitted into the existing framework for competition analysis under Articles 81 and 82.

3.2 Existence, exercise and special subject matter

The Court of Justice has consistently held that the 'existence' of an IPR is not in breach of Article 81(1) or Article 82, but that an improper 'exercise' of an IPR may be in breach of the two prohibitions.[12] If the 'existence' of an IPR is not in conflict with Articles 81 and 82, this implies that certain types of conduct 'inherent' in the IPR are not contrary to the competition rules. This is the 'specific subject matter' of the IPR, an expression used by the Court of Justice synonymously with 'existence'.[13]

From the case law, it is hard to find guidance on where the line between 'existence' and 'exercise' is to be drawn. Since an IPR does not exist 'in itself', as a physical property, it can be said to exist in conduct the right holder can base on his or her IPR. In other words: the existence of an IPR has little value to the holder if he is not able to exercise the right. IPRs are thus valuable because they enable the holder to exercise rights which prevent third

---

11 TT Guidelines, *supra* note 7, para. 9.

12 See for instance Case 262/81, *Coditel v. Ciné Vog* ('*Coditel II*'), [1982] ECR 3381.

13 Case 238/87, *Volvo v. Veng*, [1988] ECR 621.

parties from committing infringing acts. Since 'existence' in reality consists of different types of conduct making it possible for the right holder to realize the economic value of the IP, it is not possible to define 'existence' based on an analysis of 'existence' as a concept of its own.

That the existence of an IPR is not in itself contrary to Articles 81 and 82 implies that there are certain kinds of conduct inherent in an IPR that, even if the conduct restricts competition in a static sense, are not contrary to Articles 81 and 82. Thus there must be other effects of an IPR that outweigh the negative impact of an IPR on allocative efficiency. This effect must be, it may be argued, the impact of IPRs on dynamic efficiency. If the positive effect on dynamic efficiency is larger than the negative effects of the conduct on allocative efficiency, conduct based on an IPR does not violate the competition rules.

Interpreted this way the distinction between 'existence' and 'exercise' is a way to express the fact that Articles 81 and 82 have to strike a balance between static and dynamic efficiency. An IPR 'exists' in the sense that the conduct resulting from the IPR is part of the 'specific subject matter' of the IPR, if the conduct makes a positive contribution to an efficient use of resources. Based on an economic analysis it can be shown that IPRs contribute to dynamic efficiency, and that their existence is not contrary to the competition rules. Competition policy is not concerned with the granting of intellectual property rights, because competition policy acknowledges the need to grant inventors some kind of protection to further dynamic efficiency. Thus there is as a starting point no conflict between the rules that confer IPRs and competition law. But it is not possible based on a general analysis to list types of conduct 'inherent' in an IPR or that is a part of an IPR's 'specific subject matter', that is, conduct that in general will contribute to dynamic competition and outweigh the negative effects on static competition. Further, not all kinds of 'exercise' of IPRs are contrary to Articles 81 and 82, but the Court of Justice gives scant guidance on how to distinguish legal from illegal exercise. As a consequence, the effect of an agreement must be analysed in the individual case to decide whether the impact on static and dynamic competition in sum is positive or negative.

The economic approach outlined in section 2 seems to fit in well with the dichotomy between existence and exercise of IPRs drawn by the Court of Justice, introduced in 1966 in *Consten and Grundig* and maintained in its later case law. The distinction between 'existence' and 'exercise' thus seems to prepare the ground for an interpretation of Articles 81 and 82 in which dynamic competition and dynamic efficiency play a more central role.

3.3 Article 81 and the analysis of dynamic competition

3.3.1 A concept of dynamic competition must be developed under Article 81(1) Article 81(1) prohibits agreements between undertakings, decisions by associations of undertakings and concerted practices 'which have as their object or effect the prevention, restriction or distortion of competition'. The objective assigned to Article 81(1) is to prevent undertakings, by restricting competition between themselves or with third parties, from reducing the welfare of the final consumer of the products in question.[14] If allocative efficiency were the sole goal of Article 81(1), the prohibition would be limited to banning conduct that restricts competition in a static sense, which is competition between suppliers of existing products. But dynamic competition, that is, the endeavour to uncover new knowledge, is also relevant under Article 81. The question is how the substantive analysis of the dynamic aspects of competition should be carried out when analysing the effects of an agreement or concerted practice on competition.

3.3.2 Article 81(1) and dynamic competition The Court of Justice has not in its case law developed a coherent analytical tool for the analysis of the effects of an agreement on dynamic competition. This does not mean that the Court of Justice has ignored the dynamic aspects of technology licensing and other agreements. I will in the following use two important examples in which it can be argued that the Court of Justice brought dynamic competition into the analysis. Based on these two cases I will outline how dynamic competition can be assessed under Article 81(1).

EXAMPLE 1: NUNGESSER An important case regarding licensing agreements is *Nungesser*.[15] The case concerned plant breeders' rights, but the principles set out in the judgment are not limited to this type of right, but also apply to other kinds of 'manufacturing' licences involving the licensing of patents and know-how.[16]

In its so-called *Maize Seeds* decision, which led to the *Nungesser* judgment, the Commission had taken the view that an exclusive licensing agreement must by its very nature be treated as an agreement prohibited by Article 81(1).[17] In their support for the applicant, the German and British Governments claimed that this interpretation was 'incompatible with the terms of Article [81] of the Treaty and conflicts with a sensible competition policy'.[18] Not every exclusive

---

[14] Case T-168/01, *GlaxoSmithKline Services v. Commission*, [2006] ECR II-2969, para. 118.

[15] Case 258/78, *Nungesser v. Commission*, [1982] ECR 2015.

[16] Jones, Alison and Brenda Sufrin (1994), *EC Competition Law*, Oxford: Oxford University Press, pp. 705 and 708.

[17] European Commission Decision of 21 September 1978, Case IV/28824 – *Maize Seeds*, OJ 1978 No. L 286, p. 23.

[18] Case 258/78, *Nungesser v. Commission*, [1982] ECR 2015, para. 45.

licence of an industrial or commercial property right, whatever its nature, could be regarded as an agreement prohibited by Article 81(1), which could only be implemented between the parties in a given case if the conditions in Article 81(3) were satisfied.

In its assessment, the ECJ distinguished between open exclusive licences and exclusive licences with absolute territorial protection.[19] An open licence 'relates solely to the contractual relationship between the owner of the right and the licensee, whereby the owner merely undertakes not to grant other licences in respect of the same territory and not to compete himself with the licensee in that territory'.

Thus, an open exclusive licence does not give protection against competition from parallel importers or licensees assigned other territories selling to customers in the territory of the licensee. Exclusive licences with absolute territorial protection, on the other hand, 'eliminate all competition from third parties, such as parallel importers or licensees from other territories'.[20]

The ECJ found that the agreement in question was an open licence, and on this basis examined whether the agreement restricted competition. Regarding the effects of the agreement, the German Government argued that 'the protection of agricultural innovations by means of breeders' rights constitutes a means of encouraging such innovations and the grant of exclusive rights for a limited period, is capable of providing a further incentive to innovative efforts'.[21] Further, the German Government argued that if exclusive licences were prohibited this would 'be prejudicial to the dissemination of knowledge and techniques in the Community'.[22]

The German Government thus used the contribution of exclusive rights and licensing agreements to dynamic efficiency as arguments in an assessment under Article 81(1). The Court of Justice accepted the argument. If a licensee could not be protected from competition from other licensees this would be 'damaging to the dissemination of a new technology and would prejudice competition in the Community between the new product and similar existing products'.[23]

The ECJ found that an open exclusive licence was not incompatible with Article 81(1) in itself. That the Court of Justice accepts the argument that a licensing agreement giving territorial protection does not have an anti-competitive object shows that the Court is willing to take into consideration the effects of an agreement on dynamic competition under Article 81(1). An open

---

19 *Ibid.*, at para. 53.
20 *Ibid.*
21 *Ibid.*, at para. 55.
22 *Ibid.*
23 *Ibid.*

exclusive licence gives protection against competition from the licensor and against others receiving licences in the designated territory, but not protection from parallel importers and licensees from other territories. The Court seems to accept that a restriction of static competition between the licensor and the licensees and between the licensees, that is, a restriction of intra-brand competition, may be outweighed by the positive effects that the clauses giving territorial protection have on dynamic competition.

The ECJ then examined the effect of the agreement on third parties. The Court referred to its case law, where it had consistently held that absolute territorial protection granted to a licensee to control and prevent parallel imports resulted in a separation of national markets contrary to the creation of a single market and Article 81. On this basis the Court found the exclusive licence contrary to Article 81(1) in so far as the contract restricted competition from third parties on the German market.

It seems clear from the judgment that 'the single market imperative' was decisive when the Court ruled that the territorial protection given the licensee was contrary to Article 81(1). The ECJ is thus not willing to take dynamic efficiency into consideration if an agreement clearly harms the creation of a single market. On the other hand, the Court of Justice accepts that exclusive licences that do not harm the creation of a single market must be assessed on the basis of their effects, even if they clearly restrict static competition. In *Nungesser* the ECJ thus shows that it is open for analysis under Article 81(1) in which competition *for* markets is taken into consideration, and that competition *for* markets can be allowed even if it restricts competition *in* the market.

EXAMPLE 2 – PRONUPTIA The decision of the Court of Justice in *Pronuptia*[24] clearly indicates that dynamic efficiency is a part of an Article 81(1) analysis. In a referral to the Court of Justice under Article 234 of the EC Treaty, the German Federal Supreme Court (*Bundesgerichtshof, BGH*) asked the ECJ whether Article 81(1) was applicable to franchise agreements that have as their object the establishment of a special distribution system whereby the franchisor provides to the franchisee, in addition to goods, certain trade names, trade marks, merchandising materials and services.

The Court of Justice did not assess the compatibility of franchise agreements with Article 81(1) on a general basis, but only on the basis of the provisions of the agreement before the referring court, so as 'to make its reply as useful as possible to the Bundesgerichtshof'.[25] Despite this assessment on the facts, the Court's interpretation of Article 81(1) gives guidance on the method

24 Case 161/84, *Pronuptia*, [1986] ECR 353.

25 *Ibid.*, at para. 14.

used to assess the effects of franchise agreements and, as the analysis will show, on a method used to balance static and dynamic competition.

The Court of Justice started its analysis by listing the positive effects of franchise agreements in general. The Court stressed that franchise agreements do not establish a method of distribution, but are a way for an undertaking to derive financial capital from its expertise without investing its own capital. Through franchise agreements a franchisor can allow others to use an established business name and successful business methods. In return the franchisees pay royalties. Both the business name and knowledge of the business methods used can be classified as intellectual property protected by the rules on trade marks or know-how. It can be argued that the development of new trade marks and business methods furthers dynamic competition. This is also acknowledged expressly by the Court of Justice in the *Hag II* judgment:[26]

> Trade mark rights are, it should be noted, an essential element in the system of undistorted competition which the Treaty seeks to establish and maintain. Under such a system, an undertaking must be in a position to keep its customers by virtue of the quality of its products and services, something which is possible only if there are distinctive marks which enable customers to identify those products and services. For the trade mark to be able to fulfil this role, it must offer a guarantee that all goods bearing it have been produced under the control of a single undertaking which is accountable for their quality.

The judgment in *Pronuptia* can thus be understood as dealing with dynamic efficiency under Article 81. Even if trade marks differ from IPRs that more clearly protect innovations, such as patents or copyrights, the Court's analysis in *Pronuptia* has general relevance regarding the analysis of dynamic competition and dynamic efficiency.

As a starting point for the analysis the ECJ states that a system of distribution franchisees does not interfere with competition. This is in line with its judgments in which it confirms that the 'specific subject matter' of IPRs is not contrary to the competition rules. In order for a franchise system to work, two conditions must be met. Provisions that are essential for these two conditions to be met are, in the opinion of ECJ, not contrary to Article 81(1).

First, the franchisor must be able to protect his know-how against unauthorized use, especially by competitors. Provisions essential to protect intellectual property in the form of know-how in a franchise agreement will thus not constitute a restriction on competition for the purposes of Article 81(1).[27] This is true even if the contract clauses limit the franchisee's freedom to start a competing business for a reasonable time after the expiry of the agreement.

---

26 Case 10/89, *CNL-SUCAL v. Hag* ('*Hag II*'), [1990] ECR I-3711.
27 *Ibid.*, at para. 16.

Second, the franchisor must be able to protect the identity and reputation of the network bearing his business name or symbol.[28] In other words, the franchisor can take steps to protect the value of his trade mark, even if this restricts the freedom of the franchisees, without infringing Article 81(1). The franchisor may thus put an obligation on the franchisees not to deviate from the business methods developed by the franchisor and to use the know-how provided. Further, the franchisees can be instructed to sell the goods covered by the contract only from premises that ensure uniform presentation in conformity with the franchisor's specifications. This may reduce competition between the franchisees, but it secures the value of the franchisor's intellectual property right. For the same reason the franchisor can restrict the franchisees' ability to assign their franchise to undertakings not approved by the franchisor. Finally, a provision to obtain the approval of the franchisor for all advertising will also be regarded as essential for the maintenance of the network's identity.

In *Pronuptia* the Court applies what resembles a balancing approach to assessing franchising agreements, where the positive dynamic aspects of franchise agreements in general justify clauses that restrict static competition.

TAKING ACCOUNT OF DYNAMIC COMPETITION UNDER ARTICLE 81(1) Inspired by the two judgments of the ECJ, one can, in my opinion, argue that the Court accepts taking the effects of an agreement on dynamic competition into consideration when assessing whether the agreement restricts competition contrary to the prohibition in Article 81(1). It can be argued that the Court in *Nungesser* accepted that a restriction of static competition may be necessary to further dynamic competition. In *Pronuptia* the Court accepted that the positive effects of franchise agreements on dynamic competition may justify restrictions on static competition.

On this basis it may be argued that the analysis of the Court of Justice of dynamic competition may be further developed based on the analytical framework outlined in section 2. The effects of an agreement on dynamic competition must be assessed and recognized in full under Article 81(1). If an agreement contributes to dynamic competition this must be weighed against restrictions in static competition and allocative efficiency losses under Article 81(1).

In legal writing the *Nungesser* and *Pronuptia* cases have been cited as examples of cases dealing with ancillary restraints.[29] In *Métropole Télévision*, the Court of First Instance (CFI) gave the following explanation of the concept

---

[28] *Ibid.*, at para. 17.

[29] See for instance Whish, Richard (2003), *Competition Law*, Oxford: Oxford University Press, pp. 118 *et seq.*

of ancillary restraints: 'In Community competition law the concept of an ancillary restriction covers any restriction which is directly related and necessary to the implementation of a main operation'.[30] If a restriction can be classified as ancillary to a main operation, 'the compatibility of that restriction with the competition rules must be examined with that of the main operation'.[31] It follows from this that 'if the main operation does not fall within the scope of the prohibition laid down in Article [81(1)] of the Treaty, the same holds for the restrictions directly related and necessary for that operation'.[32] If the main operation is contrary to Article 81(1), the ancillary restrictions will also be caught by the prohibition (but may be exempted according to Article 81(3)).

In *Nungesser* and *Pronuptia* the clauses in question were necessary for agreements that, in the opinion of the Court of Justice, did not interfere with competition. In *Hag II* the Court even said that trade marks were 'an essential element in the system of undistorted competition'. If these clauses are viewed as ancillary restraints, the 'main operation' of the agreements assessed in the two cases, that is, the system of franchise distribution agreements and open exclusive licences regarding plant breeders' rights, thus did not fall within the scope of Article 81(1). It seems clear from the reasoning of the Court that the 'main operation' did not fall within Article 81(1) because of the effects the agreements in question normally had on dynamic competition.

IPRs are essential for dynamic competition. But *Nungesser* and *Pronuptia* were not about the 'existence' of IPRs. The question was whether concrete clauses in agreements regulating the exercise of IPRs were contrary to Article 81(1). Agreements regulating the exercise of IPRs may have positive effects on dynamic competition. But even if one says that agreements that have as their 'main operation' regulating the exercise of IPRs are not contrary to Article 81(1), or rather the target of Article 81(1), the effects of individual clauses in such agreements nevertheless must be assessed under Article 81(1). That was also what the Court did in *Nungesser* and *Pronuptia.* But if a clause is defined as an ancillary restraint to a 'main operation', there will be, as the Court of First Instance (CFI) pointed out in *Métropole Télévision*, no real balancing of the positive effects of the clause in question. Rather, the focus of the assessment is whether the ancillary restraint represents a proportional means to further the 'main operation'.

The 'main operation' of an agreement regulating the exercise of IPRs is the sum of the individual clauses in the agreement. Since the 'main operation' is

---

[30] Case T-112/99, *Metropole Télévision (M6) v. Commission*, [2001] ECR II-2459, para. 104.

[31] *Ibid.*, at para. 115.

[32] *Ibid.*, at para. 116.

to have positive effects on dynamic efficiency it must in each individual case be assessed whether the agreement really furthers dynamic competition, and whether the dynamic gains justify the restraints of static competition. A more realistic approach to the dynamic aspects of such agreements will thus be to recognize that the effects on dynamic competition must be assessed in the individual case. Abstract effects on dynamic competition cannot justify finding 'the main object' of an agreement to be outside Article 81(1). Each agreement must be assessed on its own merits, and restrictions on static competition must be justified after balancing the concrete effects on static and dynamic competition.

It can be asked whether the introduction of a balancing approach under Article 81(1) in reality represents the introduction of a rule of reason under Article 81(1). In *Métropole Télévision*, the applicants argued that a rule of reason must be applied under Article 81(1). The CFI expressly rejected this suggestion:[33]

> According to the applicants, as a consequence of the existence of a rule of reason in Community competition law, when Article [81(1)] of the Treaty is applied it is necessary to weigh the pro and anti-competitive effects of an agreement in order to determine whether it is caught by the prohibition laid down in that article. It should, however, be observed, first of all, that contrary to the applicants' assertions the existence of such a rule has not, as such, been confirmed by the Community courts. Quite to the contrary, in various judgments the Court of Justice and the Court of First Instance have been at pains to indicate that the existence of a rule of reason in Community competition law is doubtful.

According to the system of Article 81, the pro- and anti-competitive effects of an agreement could only be weighed against each other under Article 81(3): 'It is only in the precise framework of that provision that the pro and anti-competitive aspects of a restriction may be weighed. . . . Article [81(3)] of the Treaty would lose much of its effectiveness if such an examination had to be carried out already under Article [81(1)] of the Treaty'.[34]

Following the structure of Article 81, the 'dynamic aspects' of an agreement will first be relevant under the 'counterfactual' assessment in Article 81(3). Strictly following the structure of Article 81 would mean that all agreements involving IPRs would be contrary to Article 81(1) if they restrict competition in a static sense. When assessing licensing agreements, the sole focus under Article 81(1) would be whether the agreement in question restricts inter-brand or intra-brand competition. In a static perspective it would for instance not be relevant to take into account that licensing agreements secure the inventor from free-riding.

---

33 *Ibid.*, at para. 72.
34 *Ibid.*, at para. 74 (citations omitted).

Article 81(3) focuses on whether efficiency gains may outweigh the allocative efficiency losses resulting from a restriction in competition, and whether the consumers get a fair share of the efficiency gains. Neither the Court of Justice nor the Court of First Instance has gone into great detail regarding the content of the different types of efficiency gains covered by Article 81(3), first condition, or how they relate to each other. The Commission names the gains relevant under the first condition laid out in Article 81(3) 'efficiency gains', or 'efficiencies'.[35] A term that may be used to describe all factors relevant for this first condition is 'productive efficiency'.[36]

Productive efficiency is achieved when known technology is used in a better way to improve existing products or production processes. Classical examples of such efficiency are economies of scale and economies of scope. In the context of Article 81(3), the focus is whether an agreement results in productive efficiency by making it possible for the parties to co-ordinate their common use of their production facilities so as to use them in a more efficient manner. Competition will also give the parties to the agreement incentives to produce more efficiently, but this is not the focus of Article 81(3). On the contrary, the pressure that competition puts on the suppliers involved to enhance their productivity in production is already reduced as a consequence of the agreement. The restriction of competition that makes an agreement fall within Article 81(1) will, viewed separately, reduce the incentive that competition gives the suppliers to produce as efficiently as possible to reduce cost. Article 81(3) makes it possible to take into account productive efficiencies resulting from the agreement that outweigh the x-inefficiency and the allocative efficiency losses resulting from the agreement. But this shows that Article 81(3) is not focused on whether processes 'outside' the parties to the agreement could lead to a more efficient use of resources. Productive efficiency gains relevant under Article 81(3) are the result of better use of the resources 'inside', or within the production facilities of the co-operating undertakings.

Dynamic efficiency is the production of new knowledge leading to innovations. The pressure to innovate comes from the market, or from 'outside' the parties to an agreement that restricts competition, but if the pressure from static competition is too strong this may influence negatively the possibility to invest in R&D. An agreement reducing competition may have positive effects on the processes leading to innovations, in other words, have positive

---

35 Guidelines on the application of Article 81(3), *supra* note 2, paras 48–82.

36 Odudu, Okeoghene (2006), *The Boundaries of EC Competition Law – The Scope of Article 81*, Oxford: Oxford University Press, p. 138.

effects on dynamic competition. But this is not the result of another use of the production facilities of the parties. It is a result of clauses allowing the parties to restrict competition on the market in a way that guarantees that the value of an IPR is not reduced.

Whether an agreement that restricts competition has positive effects on dynamic efficiency must be assessed on the basis of the effects of the agreement on the processes in the market that are of importance to dynamic efficiency: in short, on dynamic competition. This analysis must be carried out together with the analysis of the effects in the market on static competition, and cannot be viewed separately as a gain related to the market result. The effects of an agreement on dynamic competition must thus be analysed under Article 81(1).

To the extent that dynamic competition and dynamic efficiency have been taken into account in the analysis in the case law on agreements under Article 81, the case law has been focused on positive effects on dynamic efficiency. On the other hand, the Court of Justice has not taken proper account of the negative effects agreements may have on dynamic competition. An R&D agreement may lead to reduced investments in R&D activities because the participants do not need to fear that the competitors participating in the joint venture will increase their investments in R&D activities, and thus to reduced dynamic competition. Further, a licensing agreement may also lead to dynamic efficiency losses, for instance through restrictive grant-back clauses that hinder licensees in coming up with new inventions based on the protected knowledge. Agreements having negative effects on innovative processes represent a restriction of competition contrary to Article 81(1).

Both negative and positive effects of an agreement or concerted practice on dynamic competition should thus be taken into account under Article 81(1). All effects of an agreement or concerted practice on competition as a process would thus be assessed under Article 81(1).

3.3.3 What is left for Article 81(3)? If positive and negative effects on dynamic competition are relevant under Article 81(1), what is then left for Article 81(3) and the alternative 'technical progress'?

Article 81(3) prescribes an efficiency enquiry. It follows from Article 81(3) that a conduct that restricts competition and thus has a negative impact on allocative efficiency contrary to the prohibition in Article 81(1) can be implemented if it 'contributes to improving the production or distribution of goods or to promoting technical or economic progress'.

If it can be shown that efficiencies of the types listed in the first positive condition in Article 81(3) outweigh the allocative efficiencies resulting from conduct contrary to Article 81(1), and the three other conditions in Article

81(3) are fulfilled, Article 81(1) can be declared inapplicable because of the net effects of the agreement.[37]

The efficiencies relevant under Article 81(3) should be limited to productive efficiencies. If the agreement in question has a negative impact on static and dynamic competition, then it must be assessed whether the agreement makes it possible for the parties to realize productive efficiencies. To strike the correct balance between the negative effects caught by Article 81(1) and the positive effects named in Article 81(3), it is critical to understand what kind of productive efficiencies can be taken into account under Article 81(3) when assessing agreements that have an effect on dynamic competition. This can be illustrated by two examples.

An R&D joint venture may lead to productive efficiencies in the production of new knowledge. Instead of maintaining two parallel R&D projects in the separate R&D departments of two competing undertakings, the joint venture makes it possible to carry out the same project with half the staff. The R&D joint venture may also have positive effects on dynamic competition, but the effects on the processes of dynamic competition must be assessed under Article 81(1).

Another example is licensing agreements. A licensing agreement makes it possible for parties other than the right holder to use new and efficient technology in the production of goods, or to produce a new product. Making new knowledge available enhances productive efficiency. Further, licensing agreements can in themselves contribute to dynamic efficiency in the sense that licensing agreements are a means for right holders to earn an acceptable profit from the use of protected knowledge by others. The effects on dynamic competition are relevant under Article 81(1).

Efficiencies related to 'technical progress' pursuant to Article 81(3) should thus be interpreted as relating to productive efficiencies in the production of new knowledge and innovations. If an agreement results in productive efficiencies related to the production or distribution of the parties involved, the agreement may in theory be implemented even if it restricts dynamic competition, provided that the productive efficiency gains outweigh the dynamic efficiency loss caused by reduced dynamic competition, and provided the other conditions in Article 81(3) are fulfilled.

3.4 Article 82 EC

Article 82 EC prohibits undertakings with a dominant position on the relevant market from abusing their market position. Article 82 is directed

---

[37] See Cases 56 and 58/64, *Consten and Grundig v. Commission*, [1966] ECR 299, at 348.

towards unilateral conduct by dominant undertakings that has to be deemed abusive.

The exclusivity of an IPR may result in a dominant market position for the right holder. If an IPR makes it possible to produce a product superior to other products, and other suppliers do not have access to the knowledge protected by the IPR, the holder of the IPR can have a dominant position in the technology market and in the markets for products produced with the superior technology. But IPRs do not necessarily secure for the holder a *de facto* monopoly or dominant position in the technology market or in the product market. There may be alternative technologies or product substitutes that are viewed by the consumer as equally good. This must be decided based on a definition of the relevant market. In cases where IPRs put the right holder in a dominant market position, the question arises whether the holding, acquisition or exploitation of IPRs can constitute an abuse of a dominant position, and if so in what circumstances.

To have a dominant position is in itself not contrary to Article 82. That an undertaking succeeds in its R&D efforts and is granted a patent on a superior product or technology is thus not in breach of Article 82, even if a new and superior product is preferred by the consumers to such an extent that competing producers are forced out of the market or a new and superior technology makes it possible to produce at very low cost, resulting in prices with which other producers cannot compete.

Under Article 82, the Court of Justice has also distinguished between the existence and exercise of IPRs, and has made clear that the mere ownership of an IPR cannot be attacked under Article 82. In *Volvo v. Veng*, a case on refusal to license, the Court held:[38]

> [T]he right of the proprietor of a protected design to prevent third parties from manufacturing and selling or importing, without its consent, products incorporating the design constitutes the very subject-matter of his exclusive right. It follows that an obligation imposed upon the proprietor of a protected design to grant to third parties, even in return for a reasonable royalty, a licence for the supply of products incorporating the design would lead to the proprietor thereof being deprived of the substance of his exclusive right, and that a refusal to grant such a licence cannot in itself constitute an abuse of a dominant position.

The Court of Justice thus respects the 'very subject matter' of an IPR, and conduct based on this subject matter.[39] It is on the other hand clear that if a dominant undertaking uses an IPR to reduce competition this may constitute

---

38 Case 238/87, *Volvo v. Veng*, [1988] ECR 6211, para. 8.

39 See also Joined Cases 241–242/91 P, *RTE and ITP v. Commission* ('*Magill*'), [1995] ECR I-743, para. 49.

an abuse contrary to Article 82. An analysis of the impact of the conduct in question on the incentives to innovate will give a foundation for assessing whether the conduct is within the 'specific subject matter' of the IPR. Conduct not contributing to dynamic competition is outside the economic rationale of an IPR, and will be caught by Article 82, regardless of whether the conduct is perfectly legitimate from an IP-law point of view. Conduct that increases the economic incentives to innovate should not be classified as an abuse on the basis of its effects on allocative efficiency alone.

In *Magill*, the Court then stated that it is clear 'that the exercise of an exclusive right by the proprietor may, in exceptional circumstances, involve abusive conduct'.[40] The question then was under what exceptional circumstances conduct based on the exclusive right of an IPR may constitute an abuse contrary to Article 82.

It can be argued that the case law of the Court of Justice relating to refusal to license IPRs shows that whether there are exceptional circumstances must be decided on the basis of an analysis of the conduct on dynamic competition. The Court established in *Magill* and in *IMS Health*[41] that three conditions must be fulfilled for a refusal to license an IPR that covers indispensable input for competitors to enter a downstream market to be contrary to Article 82. First, the refusal to license must prevent the competitor offering a new product on the secondary market for which there is a potential consumer demand. Second, the refusal must not have an 'objective justification'. Third, the refusal must reserve to the owner of the IPR the market for the supply of a 'secondary' product in the Member State concerned by eliminating all competition on that market.

The first condition deals with the effects of a refusal to license on dynamic competition. The Court of Justice stated in *IMS Health*[42] that the first condition:

> relates to the consideration that, in the balancing of the interest in protection of the intellectual property right and the economic freedom of its owner against the interest in protection of free competition, the latter can prevail only where refusal to grant a licence prevents the development of the secondary market to the detriment of consumers.

The Court expressly built this statement on the opinion of Advocate General Tizzano. His interpretation of the case law of the Court of Justice on refusal to license IPRs led him to conclude that:[43]

---

40 *Ibid.*, at para. 50.

41 Case 418/01, *IMS Health*, [2004] ECR I-5039.

42 *Ibid.*, at para. 42.

43 Opinion of AG Tizzano, Case 418/01, *IMS Health*, [2004] ECR I-5039, at para. 61.

> for an unjustified refusal to be deemed abusive, it is not sufficient that the intangible asset forming the subject-matter of the intellectual property right be essential for operating on a market and that therefore, by virtue of that refusal, the owner of the copyright may eliminate all competition on the secondary market.

Whether a refusal to license constitutes an abuse must, according to Advocate General Tizzano, be decided by using a balancing test weighing the interest of the owner of an IPR against society's interest in protecting free competition: [44]

> Even where those circumstances obtain, in weighing the balance between the interest in protection of the intellectual property right and the economic freedom of its owner, on the one hand, and the interest in protection of free competition, on the other, the balance may in my view come down in favour of the latter interest only if the refusal to grant the licence prevents the development of the secondary market to the detriment of consumers. More specifically, I consider that the refusal to grant a licence may be deemed abusive only if the requesting undertaking does not wish to limit itself essentially to duplicating the goods or services already offered on the secondary market by the owner of the intellectual property right but intends to produce goods or services of a different nature which, although in competition with those of the owner of the right, answer specific consumer requirements not satisfied by existing goods or services.

Thus, a restriction of static competition in the market is in itself not sufficient for a refusal to license to constitute an abuse. It must in other words be accepted that conduct based on an IPR restricts static competition. A refusal to deal only constitutes an abuse if it prevents the development of a secondary market. If this is the case, the conduct of the dominant undertaking will have effects contrary to the purpose of the IPR to further innovations, and will represent a restriction of dynamic competition. The effects of a refusal to license on dynamic competition are thus decisive for the fulfilment of the first condition.

This does not mean that static competition is not relevant for the abuse analysis. The effects on static competition come into play in the third condition. If a refusal to supply restricts dynamic competition contrary to the first condition, and there is no objective justification for the refusal, the refusal in addition has to entail 'the elimination or substantial reduction of competition to the detriment of consumers in both the short and the long term' in a secondary market to constitute an abuse.[45] O'Donoghue and Padilla give the following explanation of the rationale behind the third criteria:[46]

---

44 *Ibid.*, at para. 62.

45 Opinion of AG Jacobs in Case C-7/97, *Oscar Bronner v. Mediaprint*, [1998] ECR I-7791, para. 51.

46 O'Donoghue, Robert and A. Jorge Padilla (2006), *The Law and Economics of Article 82*, Oxford: Hart Publishing, p. 443.

> If the downstream market is already competitive, or would become so in the near future through competitors' introducing their own products, no useful purpose would be served in imposing a duty to deal, even if the dominant firm's input is essential for competition from certain (presumably less efficient) undertakings. In economic terms, the only plausible justification for a duty to deal is that the welfare loss to consumers is very large due to the dominant firm's 'genuine stranglehold' over the market. Absent this condition, the usefulness of a duty to deal evaporates and the negative effects on *ex ante* investment decision making becomes even greater.

If competition on the secondary market is sufficient, even workable, the market mechanism sees to it that the consumer surplus is not reduced even if the undertaking claiming a licence cannot participate in competition in the secondary market. In such cases possible negative effects on dynamic competition will be outweighed by workable static competition.

The Court of Justice's analysis of refusals to license illustrates that unilateral conduct based on IPRs must be analysed on the basis of a balancing approach. The underlying rationale of this balancing approach may be explained by the common economic goals of competition law and IP law, but the concept of dynamic competition must be made operational so as to apply in the analysis of the different kinds of allegedly abusive conduct based on IPRs under Article 82. In its judgment in *IMS Health*, following up its judgment in *Magill*, the Court of Justice, in my opinion, develops a concept of dynamic competition related to the first condition. The second condition represents a balancing approach, in which the effects on dynamic competition are seen together with the effects on static competition. If unilateral conduct based on an IPR is to represent an abuse, the conduct must have effects on dynamic competition that contravenes the economic rationale behind the IPR in question. Further, static competition must also be restricted. If that is not the case, competition will put pressure on undertakings to innovate, and the conduct will in sum not have adverse effects on investments in R&D activity.

4 Concluding remarks

Competition has to take into consideration the dynamic aspects of IPRs. Today competition-law analysis is not sufficiently equipped with the analytical tools necessary to do this. Fragments of an economics-based theoretical framework and rudiments of a concept of dynamic competition can be found in the existing framework for applying Articles 81 and 82, but must be developed and refined. A method for analysing conduct based on IPRs under Articles 81 and 82 may be developed on the basis of an economic analysis of the goals of competition law and IP law, where it is established that both bodies of law share the same basic objectives. Competition promotes innovations, and it is on the basis of dynamic efficiency as a common objective that a concept of dynamic competition must be developed.

2 Is there a 'more economic approach' to intellectual property and competition law?

Josef Drexl

1 Introduction

European competition law has been undergoing a fundamental reform for several years. As to the standard of control, this development started with the adoption of the so-called Umbrella Regulation No. 2790/1999 on vertical agreements.[1] It continued with the adoption of the Guidelines on the application of Article 81(3) EC[2] and the new Merger Regulation[3] in 2004 and is now about to be continued in the current process of preparing guidelines on Article 82 EC.[4] The *leitmotiv* of this reform, generally known as the 'more economic approach',[5] has been described by former EC Competition Commissioner Mario Monti in the following words:[6] 'In making this revision, we have shifted from a legalistic based approach to an interpretation of the rules based on sound economic principles'.

1 Commission Regulation (EC) No. 2790/1999 of 22 December 1999 on the application of Article 81(3) of the Treaty to categories of vertical agreements and concerted practices, OJ 1999 No. L 338, p. 21.

2 Commission – Notice – Guidelines on the application of Article 81(3) of the Treaty, OJ 2004 No. C 101, p. 97.

3 Council Regulation (EC) No. 139/2004 of 20 January 2004 on the control of concentrations between undertakings (the EC Merger Regulation), OJ 2004 No. L 24, p. 1.

4 The process of drafting such guidelines officially commenced with the publication of the DG Competition discussion paper of December 2004 on the application of Article 82 of the Treaty to exclusionary abuses, http://ec.europa.eu/comm/competition/antitrust/others/discpaper2005.pdf, accessed 4 November 2007.

5 See, for example, Hildebrand, D. (2005), 'Der more economic approach in der Wettbewerbspolitik', *WuW*, 513; Schmidtchen, Dieter (2005), 'Der more economic approach in der Wettbewerbspolitik', Center for the Study of Law and Economics, Discussion Paper Series, 2005 No. 4 = http://www.uni-saarland.de/fak1/fr12/csle/, accessed 4 November 2007; Schmidtchen, Dieter (2004), 'Effizienz als Leitbild der Wettbewerbspolitik: Für einen more economic approach', Center for the Study of Law and Economics, Discussion Paper Series 2004 No. 11 = http://www.uni-saarland.de/fak1/fr12/csle/, accessed 4 November 2007.

6 Monti, Mario (2003), 'EU Competition Policy after May 2004', Speech at the Fordham Corporate Law Institute, New York, 24 October 2003, http://www.eurunion.org/news/speeches/2003/031024mm.htm, accessed 4 November 2007.

Intellectual property rights play a major role in assessing many competition law cases, for instance, when authorities and courts have to deal with licensing clauses, IP rights as part of the assets of merging firms or a refusal to license such a right. For competition law enforcement, intellectual property constitutes a sub-issue in the context of different fields of competition law enforcement (restrictive agreements, control of market dominance, mergers and even state aid). In the process of implementing the more economic approach so far, the Commission gave greatest attention to IP rights in adopting the Technology Transfer Block Exemption Regulation (TTBER) in 2004,[7] which adopts the overall approach of the Umbrella Regulation for licensing agreements. Today IP rights are considered in particular in the review of the application of Article 82 EC, triggered by the Commission's Discussion Paper on exclusionary practices in December 2005.[8] Apparently, the Commission follows the normative structure of European competition law also when implementing the more economic approach in IP-related cases. In the Discussion Paper on exclusionary practices, IPRs are only analysed in the context of broader groups of cases for which the Commission develops specific tests. Accordingly, refusal to license is seen as a sub-group of refusal-to-deal cases.[9]

In contrast to this practice, the following analysis will highlight intellectual property rights as a comprehensive topic of competition law enforcement and ask more fundamental questions about the economic approach to IP and competition law. While there is a price to be paid, namely a certain superficiality when it comes to the assessment of individual cases, it is hoped that the analysis will help to define a general framework for a more economic approach to intellectual property and competition law. Such a framework, of course, may then prove most helpful for drafting possible guidelines on Article 82 EC.

The chapter will be structured in three parts. First, it will describe the 'more economic approach' of the Commission in general terms and place it in context with other schools of competition policy (section 2 *infra*). Secondly, the chapter will turn to economics and intellectual property and discuss different arguments of economics on the relationship of competition law and IPRs (section 3 *infra*). The third and last part of the analysis will make suggestions on a framework for a more economic approach to the application of competition law to IP-related cases (section 4 *infra*).

---

7 Commission Regulation (EC) No. 772/2004 of 27 April 2004 on the application of Article 81(3) of the Treaty to categories of technology transfer agreements, OJ 2004 No. L 123, p. 11.

8 *Supra* note 4.

9 Discussion Paper, *supra* note 4, paras 237–40.

2 The 'more economic approach' in European competition policy

2.1 How it all developed

The adoption of the Umbrella Regulation on vertical agreements[10] in 1999 marks an important departure from the previous 'form-oriented' and 'legalistic' approach to defining the requirements of a block exemption under Article 81(3) EC.[11] Whereas the former block exemption regulation contained a list of explicitly exempted contract clauses, the Commission now freed the undertakings of this straitjacket and introduced the new market-share approach. Modern economics had taught the Commission that, outside the blacklist of hard-core restrictions, agreements would only harm competition if there were sufficient market dominance. The new approach meant neither to weaken nor to strengthen enforcement of Article 81 EC but to make it economically more consistent by better targeting those agreements that actually restrain competition and by not pursuing those that are pro-competitive. This new approach was later extended to other block exemption regulations, including the TTBER[12] and the Guidelines on the application of Article 81(3) EC.[13] These documents not only give information about the practice of the Commission but also advise the competition authorities and courts in the Member States within the framework of the decentralized application of Article 81(1) and (3) EC under Regulation 1/2003 on how to apply the law most appropriately.

Given the fact that the central concept of market dominance has always been part of the provisions of Article 82 EC and merger-control law, it may seem astonishing that the Commission decided to extend the more economic approach to these fields as well. As to merger control, the Commission was mostly reacting to three judgments of 2002 in which the Court of First Instance (CFI) annulled decisions by the Commission.[14] By replacing the previous market-dominance test by the so-called SIEC (significant impediment to effective competition) test,[15] the Commission hopes to have a better chance to successfully ban mergers in cases involving non-coordinated

---

10 *Supra* note 1.

11 See also Waelbroeck, Dennis (2006), 'Vertical Agreements: 4 years of Liberalisation by Regulation n. 2790/99 after 40 years of Legal (Block) Regulation', in Hanns Ullrich (ed.), *The Evolution of European Competition Law*, Cheltenham, UK and Northampton, MA, US: Edward Elgar, p. 85.

12 *Supra* note 7.

13 Guidelines on the application of Article 81(3) EC, *supra* note 2, para. 4.

14 Case T-342/99, *Airtours v. Commission*, [2002] ECR II-2585; Case T-5/02, *Tetra Laval v. Commission*, [2002] ECR II-4381; Case T-310/01, *Schneider Electric v. Commission*, [2002] ECR II-4071.

15 Article 2(3) of the EC Merger Regulation, *supra* note 3.

effects in oligopolistic markets.[16] By holding that the Commission had not sufficiently justified its decision, the CFI effectively pushed the Commission to improve its economic reasoning. As an additional consequence of this, the Commission created the new position of chief economist with a mandate to evaluate Commission decisions from the perspective of economics.

Concerning the application of Article 82 EC, extension of the 'more economic approach' is clearly dominated by the way of thinking developed in the framework of the reform of Article 81(3) EC. The objective of the reform consists in 'develop[ing] and explain[ing] theories of harm on the basis of a sound economic assessment for the most frequent types of abusive behaviour' so as to better capture 'behaviour that has actual or likely restrictive effects on the market, which harm consumers' and to refrain from 'intervening in the functioning of markets unless there is clear evidence that they are not functioning well'.[17]

2.2 *The 'more economic approach' as a market-oriented and effects-based approach*

However, the 'more economic approach' of modern EC competition law is only insufficiently described by the overall importance given to the concept of market dominance. Even more characteristically, the Commission advocates a 'market-oriented' and 'effects-based' approach, according to which the illegality of specific behaviour, outside the area of hard-core restrictions recognized in the framework of Article 81 EC, can only be assessed on the basis of the economic effects of that behaviour on the relevant market.

This concept was initially developed in the Guidelines on vertical restraints, which read as follows:[18] 'In applying the EC competition rules, the Commission will adopt an economic approach which is based on the effects on the market; vertical agreements have to be analysed in their legal and economic context'.

These ideas were then most extensively described by the Guidelines on the application of Article 81(3) EC. These Guidelines explicitly state that they are based on the 'economic approach' already introduced in the Guidelines on vertical restraints, horizontal cooperation agreements and technology transfer

---

16 See Recital 25 of the EC Merger Regulation, *supra* note 3.

17 Competition Commissioner Neelie Kroes, 'Preliminary Thoughts on Policy Review of Article 82', Speech at the Fordham Corporate Law Institute, New York, 23 September 2005, http://europa.eu/rapid/pressReleasesAction.do?reference=SPEECH/05/537&format=HTML&aged=0&language=EN&guiLanguage=en, accessed 1 August 2007.

18 Commission Notice – Guidelines on vertical restraints, OJ 2000 No. C 291, p. 1, para. 7.

agreements.[19] Whereas the Guidelines maintain the form-oriented approach to assessing restrictions by 'object' in the sense of Article 81(1) EC,[20] they develop a test for restrictions by 'effect' that requires a thorough market analysis already in the framework of the prohibition of Article 81(1) EC. The Guidelines state:[21]

> For an agreement to be restrictive by effect it must affect actual competition to such an extent that on the relevant market negative effects on prices, output, innovation or the variety and quality of goods and services can be expected with a reasonable degree of probability. . . . This test reflects the economic approach which the Commission is applying. The prohibition of Article 81(1) only applies where on the basis of a proper market analysis it can be concluded that the agreement has likely anti-competitive effects on the market.

In the current debate on Article 82 EC, the Commission, in its Discussion Paper of December 2005, proposes applying that approach to the control of exclusionary practices. The Discussion Paper reads as follows:[22] 'In applying Article 82, the Commission will adopt an approach which is based on the likely effects on the market'.

This market-oriented and effects-based approach is not undisputed. It requires competition law enforcers to analyse the economic effects in the individual case. A specific agreement may turn out restrictive 'by effect' in one case, but may be unproblematic in another. Lawyers are badly placed to assess the lawfulness of a given behaviour in a system that requires them to look at the likely effects of that behaviour on the market. They need to cooperate with economists who, for instance, will have to define the market in applying the requirements of the modern-style block exemption. The price to be paid for economic precision is a loss of legal certainty.[23] In addition, the Commission seems to require an *ex ante* evaluation of the 'likely' effects of such behaviour in the future. Such predictions are not only difficult to make. Above all they have to rely on economic theories of the working of markets and thereby depart from a facts-based approach. Authorities may well have a harder time convincing courts of the soundness and validity of such predictions. Those

---

19 Guidelines, *supra* note 2, para. 5.

20 *Ibid.*, paras 21–3.

21 *Ibid.*, para. 24; see also Commission Notice – Guidelines on the application of Article 81 to technology transfer agreements, OJ 2004 No. C 101, p. 2, at para. 15 (with a similar wording).

22 Discussion Paper, *supra* note 4, para. 4.

23 On this argument in the context of the TTBER, see Drexl, J. (2004), 'Die neue Gruppenfreistellungsverordnung über Technologietransfer-Vereinbarungen im Spannungsfeld von Ökonomisierung und Rechtssicherheit', *GRUR Int.*, 716.

merger cases that the Commission lost before the CFI in 2002 illustrate the problem. Whereas in merger-control law economic forecasts are unavoidable, the Commission in introducing its economic approach advocates an *ex ante* evaluation although authorities and courts, especially in the framework of Regulation 1/2003, usually make *ex post* decisions on behaviour falling within the scope of Articles 81 and 82 EC.

2.3 Does efficiency matter?

Most economists advocate efficiency as the ultimate goal of competition policy. In order to locate the 'more economic approach' in the context of different schools of competition policy, it is therefore crucial to know whether the Commission advocates an efficiency approach as well. The answer to that question is complex.

In general terms, when explaining the goals of competition law, the Commission refers explicitly to the concept of allocative efficiency, but only mentions it along with other objectives. Still, in the Guidelines on vertical restraints, the Commission formulates the goals of European competition law to be pursued in the framework of the economic approach, and these are identical to the efficiency approach of economists:[24] 'The protection of competition is the primary objective of EC competition policy, as this enhances consumer welfare and creates efficient allocation of resources'.

According to this formula, competition law aims at protecting competition, but only does so because such protection enhances efficiency and – as an expression of aggregate welfare and efficiency – overall consumer welfare. The Guidelines only add one additional objective of EC competition law, namely that of enhancing market integration.[25]

In the Guidelines on the application of Article 81(3) EC, the Commission repeats this formula from the Guidelines on vertical restraints.[26] But after having made this statement, the Commission turns to the assessment of the four requirements of Article 81(3) EC. The Commission identifies the first requirement of Article 81(3) EC, namely of a contribution 'to improving the production or distribution of goods or to promoting technical or social progress', as a clear-cut efficiency test that allows the balancing of pro and anti-competitive effects. However, a different view of the goals of EC competition law comes into play once the analysis turns to the other three requirements. This is true in particular with regard to the second requirement of

---

24 Guidelines on vertical restraints, *supra* note 18, para. 7.

25 *Ibid.*, para. 7. The goal of enhancing market integration in the EU is criticized in the light of the efficiency goal by Waelbroeck, *supra* note 11, at 99–105 (suggesting giving up territorial protection as a hard-core restraint in the Umbrella Regulation).

26 See Guidelines on the application of Article 81(3) EC, *supra* note 2, para. 33.

'allowing consumers a fair share of the benefit'. This additional requirement guarantees that agreements that cause overall harm to consumers may not be justified by efficiency gains.[27] In this sense, EC law does not apply an aggregate welfare standard but rather a 'consumer surplus standard'. With regard to the fourth requirement of 'not affording the undertakings the possibility of eliminating competition in respect of a substantial part of the products in question', the Commission explicitly recognizes that ultimately rivalry and the competitive process must be given priority over potentially pro-competitive efficiency gains.[28]

Indeed in the light of the normative structure of Article 81(3) EC, it may even be concluded that the law as it stands contradicts the Commission's reference to efficiency as the ultimate goal of EC competition law. Efficiency may only be pursued to the extent that efficient outcomes do not conflict with the final goal of protecting the competitive process and consumers' economic interests. Notwithstanding this critique, protection of consumer interests and of the competitive process in addition to enhancing market integration does not contradict an economic approach to EC competition law. Whether such normative goals will be reached or not in a given situation may be analysed from a market-oriented economics-based perspective. And this is actually what the Commission undertakes in its Guidelines on the application of Article 81(3) EC.

In its Discussion Paper on Article 82 EC, the Commission again repeats the 'efficiency formula' already used in the Guidelines on vertical restraints. However, it adds wording that hints at a concept that finds the goal of efficiency in harmony with that of protecting effective competition and consumer interests as well as that of market integration:[29]

> With regard to exclusionary practices[[30]] the objective of Article 82 is the protection of competition on the market as a means of enhancing consumer welfare and of ensuring an efficient allocation of resources. Effective competition brings benefits to consumers, such as low prices, high quality products, a wide selection of goods and services, and innovation. Competition and market integration serve these ends since the creation and preservation of an open single market promotes an efficient allocation of resources throughout the Community for the benefit of consumers.

---

27 Cf. Guidelines on the application of Article 81(3) EC, *supra* note 2, para. 85.

28 *Ibid.*, *supra* note 2, para. 105.

29 Discussion Paper, *supra* note 4, para. 4.

30 It has to be noted that this reference to exclusionary practices leaves open the possibility of recognizing diverging objectives of Article 82 with regard to exploitative and discriminatory practices that are not covered by the Discussion Paper; cf. Discussion Paper, *supra* note 4, para. 3.

In fact, if all these goals could be pursued in perfect harmony, the efficiency debate would be of a purely academic nature. As can be seen from the normative structure of Article 81(3) EC, however, conflicts may well arise. In the framework of merger control and the application of Article 82 EC, the Commission wants to resolve such conflicts between efficiency on the one hand and effective competition and consumer protection on the other hand under the heading of the so-called efficiency defence. A merger, for instance, may well result in the creation or strengthening of a dominant position, but may still be cleared if the requirements of the efficiency defence are met.[31]

However, in its Horizontal Merger Guidelines, the Commission defines a threshold for the defence that will hardly ever be met. Formulated as cumulative requirements, efficiencies may only be taken into account if they benefit consumers, are merger-specific and are verifiable.[32] In its more detailed reasoning, the Commission refers to criteria known from Article 81(3) EC, namely the 'consumer surplus standard' and the maintenance of effective competition. According to the Commission, '[t]he relevant benchmark in assessing efficiencies claims is that consumers will not be worse off as a result of the merger'.[33] Simultaneously, the Commission acknowledges that passing efficiency gains on to consumers will often depend on the existence of competitive pressure from remaining competitors or potential entrants.[34] Obviously, potential conflicts between an efficiency approach and the goals of effective competition and the protection of consumer interests will be resolved in favour of the latter, also in the field of merger law.

The Commission also refers to the concept of an efficiency defence in its Discussion Paper on Article 82 EC.[35] In this context, the Commission faithfully follows the example of Article 81(3) EC, suggesting a cumulative test based on four requirements: (1) efficiencies must be realized or likely to be realized as a result of the conduct concerned; (2) such conduct must be indispensable to realize these efficiencies; (3) these efficiencies must benefit consumers; and (4) competition in respect of a substantial part of the products

---

31 The EC Merger Control Regulation only mentions this possibility in its recital no. 29. According to this recital, in such a case the merger would not be considered to significantly impede effective competition.

32 Guidelines on the assessment of horizontal mergers under the Council Regulation on the control of concentrations between undertakings, OJ 2004 No. C 31, p. 5, paras 78–88.

33 *Ibid.*, para. 79.

34 *Ibid.*, para. 84. Here, the Commission advocates a balancing approach. The greater the possible negative effect on competition, the more claimed efficiencies must be substantial, likely to be realized and likely to be passed on to consumers.

35 In general terms, see Discussion Paper, *supra* note 4, paras 84–92.

concerned must not be eliminated. Again, protection of consumer interests and effective competition is given priority over a pure efficiency approach.

It has to be mentioned that the Discussion Paper specifies the general efficiency defence for certain types of exclusionary conduct. In particular, the Commission discusses an efficiency defence in the case of a 'refusal to start supplying an input', including an intellectual property right.[36] This defence will be discussed more intensively below.[37]

We may conclude that the 'more economic approach' of the Commission strongly relies on the concept of economic efficiency at least as an analytical tool for assessing the potential impact of a given conduct on a relevant market (the market-oriented approach). In this regard, the Commission advocates sophisticated economic reasoning that is characteristic of the Post-Chicago School in the United States. However the Commission does not accept efficiency as the ultimate and single goal of competition policy. It rather embraces the normative judgment of EC competition law made in the context of Article 81(3) EC in favour of a 'consumer surplus standard' and the protection of effective competition as goals that may not be overthrown by mere efficiency considerations and it extends this judgment to other fields of EC competition law. Thereby the 'more economic approach' maintains its distinctive European nature, although it moves EC competition law closer to US antitrust law by applying Post-Chicago School economic reasoning.

3 The economics of intellectual property rights and competition policy

Among economists, there is no agreement on the relationship between IPRs and competition policy. A traditional and normative approach would look at IPRs as 'exemptions' from competition, allowing competition-law application only if the right is used to restrain competition outside the scope of the exclusive right (the so-called inherency theory).[38] Such a theory, however, takes the IP right as granted without explaining its economic rationale. Economists who discuss IPRs with regard to competition policy usually hint at the function of IPRs to enhance 'dynamic' efficiency as opposed to mere 'allocative' efficiency. Today there are basically two different views that are advocated on how dynamic efficiency – or dynamic competition – can best be promoted by the comprehensive regulatory framework of intellectual property and competition

---

36 Discussion Paper, *supra* note 4, paras 66–8.

37 Section 4.5 *infra*.

38 On this theory see, for example, Rahnasto, Ilkka (2003), *Intellectual Property Rights, External Effects, and Anti-trust Law*, Oxford: Oxford University Press, pp. 42–9. Such a theory was explicitly set out in sections 17 and 18 of the German Act on Restraints of Competition regarding the control of licensing agreements before German law was harmonized with Article 81 EC in 2005.

law. According to the first view, competition law enforcers should largely refrain from interfering with the exclusivity of the property right even if the specific right creates market dominance. Such interference would generally harm the incentive structure of innovation. According to the second view, intellectual property and competition law share the common goal of enhancing dynamic competition. Dynamic efficiency will only be attained if competition law keeps markets open and maintains competitive pressure on the right-holder to compete with better products (the theory of complementarity).

3.1 Does the ECJ follow a normative or an economic approach?

In developing its more economic approach to intellectual property and competition law, the Commission has to respect the interpretation of EC competition law by the European Courts. In the current process of preparing guidelines on the application of Article 82 EC with regard to exclusionary practices, the Commission has to give due regard to the judgment of the ECJ in *IMS Health*,[39] by also taking into account the most recent *Microsoft* decision of the CFI.[40] In *IMS Health*, the ECJ clarified its earlier decision in *Magill*[41] in the sense that a refusal to grant a licence for a copyright that is indispensable for carrying on a particular business can only be considered abusive in the sense of Article 82 EC under the three cumulative conditions (the so-called cumulative theory) that (1) the refusal is preventing the emergence of a new product for which there is a potential consumer demand, (2) this refusal is unjustified and (3) it excludes any competition on a secondary market.[42] The Court is not very explicit on the economic rationale of this test. As to the first and very decisive requirement, the so-called new-product rule, the Court seemed to argue in the sense of a normative weighing of interests:[43]

> [The first condition, namely on the emergence of a new product,] relates to the consideration that, in the balancing of the interest in protection of the intellectual property right and the economic freedom of its owner against the interest in protection of free competition, the latter can prevail only where refusal to grant a licence prevents the development of the secondary market to the detriment of consumers.

This approach cannot be described as the expression of an inherency theory since the Court, under said conditions, is prepared to apply Article 82 EC with

39 Case C-418/01, *IMS Health*, [2004] ECR I-5039.

40 Case T-201/04, *Microsoft v. Commission*, [2007] ECR II-0000 (not yet officially reported).

41 Joined Cases C-241 and 242/91 P, *RTE and ITP v. Commission* (‘*Magill*’), [1995] ECR I-743.

42 *IMS Health*, *supra* note 39, at para. 38.

43 *Ibid.*, at para. 48.

the effect of controlling the use of a given right within its scope of exclusivity. Still, the Court relies on the recognition of the intellectual property right as a legal fact that may not be questioned by competition law as such. The basis for that concept was already laid down by the Court in the earlier *Volvo* decision, in which it was held that a refusal to license even by a dominant firm may not be considered an abuse of dominance 'as such' since the exclusivity of the reproduction right constitutes the very subject matter of the intellectual property right.[44] Later, in *Magill*, the Court clarified that intervention under Article 82 EC in a refusal-to-license case may only be justified under 'exceptional circumstances'.[45]

From an economic perspective, the ECJ seems to argue in the sense of an inherent conflict between IP law and competition law. The question of how to strike a balance between the exclusivity of the property right and the economic freedom of its holder on the one hand and the interest in protecting free competition on the other hand is answered by the Court in *IMS Health* by referring to the interest of consumers in having access to a new product that would otherwise not be offered by the right-holder in the secondary market.[46]

Some commentators argue that the Court thereby actually referred to the very goal of IPRs of enhancing dynamic efficiency.[47] In fact, IPRs are thought to exclude competitors from imitating the subject matter of protection, simultaneously inciting them to compete by offering better products (competition by substitution). It may well be true that the ECJ intended to allude to his concept when the decision was formulated. Still, the new-product rule is not consistent with any economic rationale.[48] Most importantly, the ECJ requires competitors to 'substitute' on the secondary product or service market and not on the primary market for the subject matter of the intellectual property right.

In *IMS Health*, the copyright in question consisted in a brick structure, dividing the German territory into 1860 areas ('bricks'). This structure was used by the right-holder to collect data on the sales of pharmaceuticals for its

---

44 Case 238/87, *Volvo v. Veng*, [1988] ECR 2611, para. 8; see also *IMS Health*, *supra* note 39, at para. 34.

45 Joined Cases C-241 and 242/91 P, *RTE and ITP v. Commission* ('*Magill*'), [1995] ECR I-743, para. 49; see also *IMS Health*, *supra* note 41, at para. 34.

46 *Ibid.*, at para. 49.

47 See for instance Derclaye, Estelle (2004), 'The IMS Health Decision: A Triple Victory', *World Competition*, **27**, 397, at 403; see also Eilmansberger, Thomas (2005), 'How to Distinguish Good From Bad Competition Under Article 82 EC: In Search of Clearer and More Coherent Standards for Anti-Competitive Abuses', *C.M.L. Rev.*, **42**, 129, at 159.

48 For an earlier critique, see Drexl, J. (2004), 'IMS Health and Trinko – Antitrust Placebo for Consumers Instead of Sound Economics in Refusal-to-Deal Cases', *IIC*, **35**, 788, at 799–801.

customers, the pharmaceutical companies. Whereas the copyright was meant to enhance creativity, namely the development of different creative structures, the ECJ ordered the referring court to decide whether the petitioner of the copyright licence intended to provide a better service (collecting marketing data by using the same structure) to the pharmaceutical companies.[49]

In *Magill*, the copyright protected the listings of television programmes for individual broadcasting companies in the Republic of Ireland and the United Kingdom. Thereby these companies were able to exclude competition in the market for printed TV guides and prevent the offer of comprehensive TV guides on that market. Those comprehensive TV guides were considered by the ECJ as a new product for which consumer demand existed.[50] However, this 'new product' was not meant to substitute the subject matter of the IP right by another copyrighted work. On the contrary, the petitioner (*Magill*) wanted to compete by imitating the very subject matter of protection and wanted to offer a new and better product only on the secondary product market. The 'innovation' intended by the petitioner of the licence in *Magill*, namely comprehensive TV guides as opposed to guides that only gave the schedule of a single TV station, was completely unrelated to the goals of copyright law and therefore could not be a requirement for a duty to license.

The same holds true for *IMS Health*: better services with regard to the collecting of marketing data do not seem related to a duty to license in a brick structure protected by copyright, a right that is only meant to enhance creativity, but not the efficiency of the provision of said services. Hence, competition law may have a good reason to intervene in cases in which the IP right is used to prevent the emergence of a new product in a secondary market. However, the economic rationale of the specific IP right as such should not prevent competition law enforcers from protecting competition in secondary markets in cases in which the petitioner does not intend to offer a new product.

It may be added that, in *Magill*, the Court concluded that the prevention of a new product has to be considered an abuse in the sense of Article 82 lit. b) EC.[51] Although not repeated in *IMS Health*, there are better arguments that the new product rule was initially formulated without clear consideration of the economics of the IP right. Since Article 82 lit. b) EC only gives an example of abusive behaviour, the ECJ's characterization of the new-product rule as a

---

49 *IMS Health*, *supra* note 39, at paras 49 *et seq.*

50 *Magill*, *supra* note 41, at para. 54.

51 *Ibid.*, para. 54. See also Eilmansberger, Thomas (2005), 'The Essential Facilities Doctrine Under Art. 82: What is the State of Affairs After IMS Health and Microsoft?', *K.C.L.J.*, **16**, 329, at 336 *et seq.* (discussing whether the prevention of a new product should be accepted as a case of abuse in its own right in the sense of Article 82(b) in *IMS Health*).

necessary (cumulative) element of the test to be applied in refusal-to-license cases needs to be questioned. In sum, the case law of the ECJ does not contribute anything to developing a consistent economic approach to intellectual property and competition law.

The situation is different in the field of applying Article 81 EC to licensing agreements. In the so-called *Maize Seeds* case of 1982, the ECJ relied on concepts of promoting and spreading innovation to draw the line between an open exclusive licence, held to be legal, and anti-competitive licensing.[52]

3.2 The concepts of dynamic efficiency and dynamic competition

For the development of a more economic and effects-based approach to intellectual property and competition law, it is vital to know whether the concept of dynamic efficiency can and should be relied upon.

Static neo-classical economics was able to explain and define the concept of allocative efficiency. Allocative efficiency is defined as the optimal economic use of existing resources. The Chicago School of Economics added to allocative efficiency the concept of productive efficiency, expressing economies of scale as an effect of more efficient use of existing resources by larger firms as compared to smaller ones. The third aspect of dynamic efficiency is today considered to be most important for the growth of economies. It relates to the optimal use of resources for enhancing innovation and the development of new – often as yet unknown – products.[53]

Efficiency, as the maximization of aggregate welfare,[54] has to take into account all three forms of efficiency. However, there is a fundamental difference between allocative efficiency in particular and dynamic efficiency. Whereas judgments on allocative efficiency can rely on available knowledge on existing resources, nobody knows about the results of investment in research and development and the possibility of marketing them. Therefore, it is impossible to apply the concept of dynamic efficiency in the practice of

---

52 Case 258/78, *Nungesser v. Commission* ('*Maize seeds*'), [1982] ECR 2015, paras 57 *et seq.*

53 For a recent description of the three forms of efficiencies, see Schwalbe, Ullrich and Daniel Zimmer (2006), *Kartellrecht und Ökonomie, Moderne ökonomische Ansätze in der europäischen und deutschen Zusammenschlusskontrolle*, Frankfurt am Main: Verlag Recht und Wirtschaft, pp. 5–12.

54 This chapter does not use the term 'consumer welfare', often used in the US, which might easily be confused with the European 'consumer surplus standard' as defined in the second requirement for an exemption by Article 81(3) EC. According to the 'consumer welfare standard', as advocated in particular by the Chicago School, efficiency is still enhanced if firms engaging in the relevant behaviour win more than consumers lose. Such a concept is in line with the Kaldor-Hicks criterion of efficiency but contradicts the concept of Article 81(3) EC.

competition policy in the way it might be done with regard to the efficient use of existing resources known to competition law enforcers.[55]

Assessment of competition problems in the light of the efficiency criterion always tends to be an *ex ante* assessment. This is so in particular when it comes to dynamic efficiency. We know that innovation should be promoted, but we are unable to make any judgment on the welfare effects of applying or not applying competition law to IP-related cases.

This is why a process-oriented concept of 'dynamic competition' should be preferred to the concept of dynamic efficiency. Competition law should aim at protecting the competitive process that enhances innovation. The emphasis of the analysis would have to be on the given market situation and factors that induce firms to be innovative. This approach avoids any judgment on the prospective welfare gains or losses of an intervention. Whereas the concept of dynamic efficiency argues in the sense of an impossible *ex ante* assessment of the effects of efficiency, the concept of dynamic competition can rely on the facts that characterize competition in the relevant markets. This approach enables competition law enforcers to apply an *ex post* assessment to the greatest extent possible.

3.3 The neo-Schumpeterian approach to intellectual property and competition law

In the framework of an economic efficiency assessment, it would regularly be necessary to balance a loss in allocative efficiency (price competition) with gains in dynamic efficiency (innovation).[56] This balancing approach appropriately describes the mechanism of the intellectual property right. The IPR excludes imitation and thereby price competition by a competitor who might well be better placed to produce the good or service in question. However, allowing imitation would negatively affect the incentive structure of the IP system. The question remains how such a balance should be struck given the fact that dynamic efficiency is impossible to measure.[57]

Many economists therefore favour a cautious approach when it comes to the application of competition law to intellectual property rights and, thereby, often refer to Schumpeter and his idea of 'creative destruction'.[58] In fact, Schumpeter has to be praised for describing capitalism as an 'evolutionary process' that is driven by 'new consumers' goods, the new methods of production or transportation, the new markets, the new forms of industrial organiza-

55 Cf. Schwalbe and Zimmer, *supra* note 53, pp. 10 *et seq.*

56 See Schwalbe and Zimmer, *supra* note 53, p. 12.

57 See section 3.2 *supra*.

58 Schumpeter, Joseph R. (1942; new edition 1976), *Capitalism, Socialism, and Democracy*, New York, NY: Harper & Brothers, pp. 81–6.

tion that capitalist enterprise creates'.[59] According to Schumpeter's concept of 'creative destruction', capitalism is not revolutionized from outside, as communists argue, but by innovation from within.[60] Based on this consideration, Schumpeter criticizes the assessment of oligopolistic structures at only a given point of time without taking into account the evolutionary process over time, and above all, the strong concern of competition policy about price competition.[61] What really drives competition, according to Schumpeter, is 'competition from the new commodity, the new technology, the new source of supply, the new type of organization'.[62] Thus, as early as 1942, Schumpeter gave an appropriate and modern description of dynamic competition. He also made the argument that potential competition by innovation in the future may prevent firms with monopoly power from abusing this power today.[63]

Whereas the preceding ideas are generally accepted, another argument Schumpeter makes in the context of his description of dynamic competition, and which is most often cited in defining the relationship between IPRs and competition, proves to be more critical. According to Schumpeter, firms will engage in strategies, including patent policies, that are restrictive in the short run but manage to serve the purpose of attracting the investment necessary for the innovative process.[64] Schumpeter did not conclude that dynamic competition makes competition law intervention dispensable; he only opposed a competition policy that indiscriminately bans all restrictive behaviour without taking into account the virtues of creative destruction. He admits that defining the appropriate policy is an extremely challenging task:[65]

> It is certainly as conceivable that an all-pervading cartel system might sabotage all progress as it is that it might realize, with smaller social and private costs, all that perfect competition is supposed to realize. This is why our argument does not amount to a case against state regulation. It does show that there is no general case for indiscriminate 'trust-busting' or for the prosecution of everything that qualifies as a restraint of trade. Rational as distinguished from vindictive regulation by public authorities turns out to be an extremely delicate problem which not every government agency, particularly when in full cry against big business, can be trusted to solve.

Despite this cautious and thoughtful approach, Schumpeter is nowadays taken by some economists and lawyers as an authority for the argument that

---

59 *Ibid.*, pp. 82 *et seq.*
60 *Ibid.*, p. 83.
61 *Ibid.*, p. 84.
62 *Ibid.*, pp. 84 *et seq.*
63 *Ibid.*, p. 85.
64 *Ibid.*, pp. 89 *et seq.*
65 *Ibid.*, p. 91.

monopoly power is necessary to enhance innovation and dynamic efficiency. Only monopolists will make the amount of profit needed for the investment in further innovation.[66]

This conclusion has remarkable effects on how one would have to view the relationship between intellectual property and competition law. Even in situations in which a given intellectual property confers monopoly power, the exclusivity ought to be protected against competition law intervention. Application of competition law would only negatively affect the incentive structure of the IP system. According to economists advocating this view, the concept of competition *in* the market is replaced by a 'Schumpeterian' concept of competition *for* the market.[67]

Proponents of this neo-Schumpeterian theory admit that refraining from intervention in the IP right has its costs, namely a loss in allocative efficiency and price competition. However, they recommend that competition law enforcers should refrain from interfering with the IP right because of potentially greater losses in dynamic efficiency. In this context, Ahlborn et al. state:[68]

> When considering whether forcing the disclosure of companies' trade secrets or compelling them to license valuable IP, policymakers must therefore balance the gains from stimulating short-term competition with the losses from the reduced investment in innovation. They should keep in mind, however, that while the allocative efficiencies that arise in the short term as a result of intervention are relatively easy to measure, the long-term costs of such actions are uncertain and difficult to quantify. Competition agencies and courts should avoid deciding in favour of short-term allocative efficiency if the only reason is their greater ability to visualize that side of the equation.

Recently Evans and Padilla, advocating a 'neo-Chicago approach', have brought more theoretical precision to this argument.[69] The two authors, based on economic theory, assess the likelihood and costs of different kinds of errors

---

66 See, for instance, Ahlborn, Christian, Vincenzo Denicolò, Damien Gérardin and A. Jorge Padilla (2006), 'DG Comp's Discussion Paper on Article 82: Implications of the Proposed Framework and Antitrust Rules for Dynamic Competitive Industries', http://ec.europa.eu/comm/competition/antitrust/others/057.pdf, accessed 1 August 2007, p. 15.

67 Ahlborn et al., *supra* note 66, p. 16.

68 *Ibid.*, p. 18. See also the reference made to Gérardin, Damien (2004), 'Limiting the Scope of Article 82 of the EC Treaty: What Can the EU Learn from the US Supreme Court's Judgment in Trinko in the Wake of Microsoft, IMS and Deutsche Telekom', *C.M.L. Rev.*, **41**, 1519, at 1540.

69 Evans, David S. and A. Jorge Padilla (2005), 'Designing Antitrust Rules for Assessing Unilateral Practices, A Neo-Chicago Approach', *U. Chi. L. Rev.*, **72**, 73.

policymakers may commit in combating unilateral restraints. They argue that the cost of condemning pro-competitive practices is higher than the costs of exonerating anti-competitive practices. It is clear from the outset that within a concept of dynamic competition that requires predictions about the consequences of any regulatory decision, but is unable to measure these consequences, the model developed by Evans and Padilla has to recommend that competition law enforcers refrain from any intervention in IP-related innovation markets.[70]

Hence, the neo-Schumpeterian concept can be brought down to the very simple conclusion: never interfere with intellectual property rights as you cannot measure the costs of such intervention!

3.4 The theory of complementarity advocated by the Commission

Obviously, the neo-Schumpeterian view conflicts with the judgment in *IMS Health*, in which the ECJ upheld the possibility of a duty to license under Article 82 EC.[71] This is all the more true when we turn to the Commission's policy advocated in the framework of applying Article 81 EC to technology transfer agreements.

In adjusting the more economic approach to the field of technology transfer agreements, and in conformity with the IP Guidelines of the US antitrust authorities,[72] the Commission refers to a concept of complementarity of the two fields of intellectual property law and competition law:[73]

> The fact that intellectual property laws grant exclusive rights . . . does [not] imply that there is an inherent conflict between intellectual property rights and the Community competition rules. Indeed, both bodies of law share the same basic objective of promoting consumer welfare and efficient allocation of resources. Innovation constitutes an essential and dynamic component of an open and

---

70 This model is actually applied to innovation markets by Ahlborn et al., *supra* note 66, p. 23; Ahlborn, Christian, David S. Evans and A. Jorge Padilla (2005), 'The Logic and Limits of the Exceptional Circumstances Test in *Magill* and *IMS Health*', *Fordham Int'l L.J.*, **28**, 1109.

71 Neo-Schumpeterians criticize the new-product rule of *IMS Health*; see Gérardin, *supra* note 68, at 1431 (hinting at the lack of economic rationale and the lack of clarity).

72 Antitrust Guidelines for the Licensing of Intellectual Property, Issued by the US Department of Justice and the Federal Trade Commission, 6 April 1995, note 1, subpara. 3, http://www.usdoj.gov/atr/public/guidelines/0558.htm, accessed 1 August 2006. See also *Atari Games Corp. v. Nintendo of America, Inc.*, 897 F.2d 1572, 1576 (Fed. Cir. 1990): '[T]he aims and objectives of patent and antitrust laws may seem, at first glance, wholly at odds. However, the two bodies of law are actually complementary, as both are aimed at encouraging innovation, industry and competition'.

73 TT Guidelines, *supra* note 21, para. 7.

> competitive market economy. Intellectual property rights promote dynamic competition by encouraging undertakings to invest by developing new or improved products and processes.[[74]] So does competition by putting pressure on undertakings to innovate. Therefore, both intellectual property rights and competition are necessary to promote innovation and ensure a competitive exploitation thereof.

The conflict between the neo-Schumpeterian view and the theory of complementarity is very straightforward: Whereas in the neo-Schumpeterian world, firms will only invest if they have monopoly profits at their disposal, the Commission conceives competitive pressure from other firms as an additional requirement along with the IP system to convince firms to invest in innovation. Without the intellectual property right competitors can compete by imitation and will not invest in better products. Without competitive pressure there are no guarantees that the right-holder will actually reinvest monopoly profits. In a competitive scenario, however, a competitor can hope to win monopoly profits in the future by investing in innovation. In a monopolistic situation, in contrast, the dominant firm can already make monopoly profits without having to reinvest its return in future innovation.[75] Because of such flaws in the neo-Schumpeterian monopoly theory, the concept of complementarity is now supported by many.[76]

The theory of complementarity, as can be seen from the above-cited passage, prefers the concept of dynamic competition to that of dynamic efficiency. The Commission's approach thereby is process-oriented. Intervention under competition law is not advocated for the sake of enhancing efficiency, but in order to safeguard the competitive pressure needed for the maintenance of the overall incentive structure for innovation.

The theory of complementarity argues in favour of an intervention whenever there is a restraint of dynamic competition. Dynamic competition can easily be explained by the effects of a given IP right on the relevant market.

---

74 On the incentive structure of the patent system, see Granstad, Ove (1999), *The Economics and Mangagement of Intellectual Property, Towards Intellectual Capitalism*, Cheltenham, UK and Northampton, MA, USA: Edward Elgar, pp. 83 *et seq*.

75 On this striking argument, see Schwalbe and Zimmer, *supra* note 53, p. 25.

76 Drexl, *supra* note 48, at 791–4; Drexl, J., B. Conde Gallego, S. Enchelmaier, M. Leistner and M.-O. Mackenrodt (2006), Comments of the Max Planck Institute for Intellectual Property, Competition and Tax Law on the DG Competition discussion paper of December 2005 on the application of Article 82 of the EC Treaty to exclusionary abuses, *IIC*, **37**, 558, para. 5; Ghidini, Gustavo (2006), *Intellectual Property and Competition Law – The Innovation Nexus*, Cheltenham, UK and Northampton, MA, USA: Edward Elgar, pp. 5–8; Heinemann, Andreas (2002), *Immaterialgüterschutz in der Wettbewerbsordnung*, Tübingen: Mohr-Siebeck, pp. 1 and 25–7.

The IP right, whether it is a patent, a trademark or a copyright, excludes competition by *imitation*, thereby potentially reducing the level of price competition. In an ideal world, exclusion of imitation incites competitors to compete by better products that may still be marketed in the same market without infringing on pre-existing IPRs (competition by *substitution*). Simultaneously, competition by substitution will pressure the right-holder to further invest in innovation. It is the goal of competition law to protect this competitive mechanism of the IP system against distortions. Policymakers will have to identify failures of that system and react appropriately within the legal framework of competition law.

4 Fundamental principles for a 'more economic approach' to intellectual property and competition law

The theory of complementarity, already advocated by the Commission in the field of technology transfer agreements, is most appropriate as a starting point for developing a 'more economic approach' to intellectual property and competition law. This theory meets the two core requirements for such an approach. First, it is in line with the general goals of European competition law by avoiding a solely efficiency-oriented analysis and protecting effective competition and the economic interests of consumers. Secondly, it allows an analysis of the effects of a given behaviour connected to an individual IP right in the relevant market and will thereby tend to protect competition most appropriately from an economics perspective.

4.1 The effect of the given IPR on the relevant market

Whether a specific type of behaviour – a licensing agreement, a refusal to license or a merger involving IPRs – will cause a distortion of competition depends on the preliminary question concerning the effects of the very intellectual property right on that market. To identify these effects, competition law enforcers have to be IP experts. Different types of intellectual property pursue different goals and may produce different effects on the market.

4.2 IPRs are not meant to cause monopoly power as such

It would be consistent with the Schumpeterian concept[77] to advocate an IP system whose goal is to grant the right-holder monopoly power. However, this is not the effect of existing IP laws, even in the patent-law field. IPRs do not confer market dominance as such.[78] Copyrighted works are, provided that they

[77] See section 3.3 *supra*.

[78] This was also explicitly confirmed by the ECJ in *Magill*; see *supra* note 41, para. 46. The US Supreme Court has recently repealed its case law according to which

attain a sufficient level of creativity, unique by nature. Still, copyrighted works usually compete in relevant markets. Movie fans cannot watch all the movies that are produced by Hollywood and other studios. They have to make a choice as to which movie they want most to see and for which they are willing to pay the required price. The same is true in the market for literature.[79] In the pharmaceutical industry, a patent for a revolutionary new substance may well confer monopoly power on the patent-holder. However, the legal exclusivity of a patent does not protect such monopoly power for the whole of the patent term. Since substitution is not excluded, the patent-holder will have to fear that a potential competitor may come up with a more innovative, but not infringing invention that will conquer the market. Hence, many IP rights allow competition *in* the market. In other situations, firms will compete *for* the market, while competition *in* the market may be excluded for some time. Even in the latter case, intervention is not required so long as competition by substitution is not excluded as such. The long-run perspective explains why a short-run restriction on price competition must not be considered anti-competitive.[80]

The fact that IPRs do not create monopolies as such, but only exclude competition by imitation, is most important in the field of Article 82 EC. A duty to license requires that the right-holder actually holds a dominant position. Only a few IPRs will meet this requirement. Whether this dominant position is the result of the IPR as such or whether additional factors external to the IP right have to be considered the source of such dominance is immaterial so far.

---

it was presumed that a patent confers market power; see *Illinois Tool Works Inc. et al. v. Independent Ink, Inc.* (Judgment of 1 March 2006), http://www.supremecourtus.gov/opinions/05pdf/04-1329.pdf, accessed 4 November 2007. On this case see also Jones, Clifford, chapter 10, in this volume; and Grimes, Warren, chapter 11, in this volume. See, in general, Landes, William M. and Richard A. Posner (2003), *The Economic Structure of Intellectual Property*, Cambridge, MA and London, UK: Belknap Press, p. 374.

[79] Cf. Landes and Posner, *supra* note 78, p. 377. The situation is different in the field of academic and scientific writing, where scholars and researchers depend on access to information. However, monopoly power in that field will typically not be conferred on the original author, but on the academic and scientific publishers; on this problem see Drexl, J. (2006), 'Droit d'auteur et information scientifique – Analyse concurrentielle, protection des bases de données et perspective allemande', in IRPI (ed.), *La propriété intellectuelle en question(s) – Regards croisés européens*, Paris: Litec, p. 73.

[80] Cf. Heinemann, *supra* note 76, pp. 25 *et seq.* (strongly relying on the distinction between the short-run and long-run perspective with regard to the theory of complementarity).

4.3 Protecting dynamic competition when substitution is not possible

According to the theory of complementarity, competition law will only have to intervene in those exceptional circumstances in which dynamic competition is distorted. Such distortion requires that the behaviour of the right-holder or the relevant IPR itself hampers or even excludes competition by substitution.

There are two very different situations in which competition by substitution might be hindered as a consequence of the IPR. In the first situation, it is the IPR itself that excludes substitution. Thereby the IPR counteracts the very goal of its existence, namely of enhancing further innovation. In the second situation, market circumstances external to the IPR preclude substitution.[81]

A situation of the first type was present in the *Magill* case. British and Irish law granted copyright protection for the listings of TV programmes, thereby enabling the TV stations to monopolize the underlying information.[82] The ECJ was right in holding that market dominance already existed in the upstream market for the information as a necessary input for marketable TV programmes in the downstream market. Here it was the copyright as such that excluded competition. Whereas copyright is only meant to protect creativity and not to control access to information, the copyright in *Magill* went beyond this line and allowed the right-holder to monopolize the downstream product market. Accordingly, the Community legislature quite rightly stated in the Computer Program Directive of 1991[83] that copyright protection for such programs does not extend to ideas and principles underlying a computer program, including those which underlie its interfaces,[84] and that decompilation of programs is deemed to be lawful without the authorization of the right-holder where it is indispensable to obtain the information necessary to achieve the interoperability of an independently created computer program with other programs.[85] Not having the power to harmonize domestic copyright law, the only option the ECJ had in *Magill* was to confirm a duty to license under Article 82 EC. Notwithstanding this correct conclusion, it is also clear that such distortions of competition caused by the internal design of the IP system would be much better addressed by a reform within the IP system.

---

81 On those two cases, see also Drexl, J. (2007), 'Abuse of Dominance in Licensing and Refusal to License: A "More Economic Approach" to Competition by Imitation and to Competition by Substitution', in Claus-Dieter Ehlermann and Isabel Antanasiu (eds), *European Competition Law Annual 2005*, Oxford: Hart Publishing, p. 647, at 656–60.

82 See *Magill*, *supra* note 41, para. 47.

83 Council Directive 91/250/EEC of 14 May 1991 on the legal protection of computer programs, OJ 1991 No. L 122, p. 42.

84 Article 1(2) of said Directive.

85 Article 6(1) of said Directive.

The situation was quite different in the *IMS Health* case. The problem was not essentially that the copyright for the brick structure unintentionally barred access to information.[86] Indeed, competitors had developed a different structure and offered their services to potential customers, the pharmaceutical companies. These companies, however, refused to switch because they had invested considerably in the development and implementation of the system. Use of IMS Health's brick structure had become a *de facto* industry standard that prevented pharmaceutical companies from using a different system of collecting marketing data.[87] Although the copyright prevented competitors from using freely the same structure, the reasons why competitors were in need of the licence were located outside the IP system. In other words, it was not the IPR as such that resulted in market dominance and finally in a restriction of dynamic competition, but external market failures. Substitution of the subject matter of protection is no viable business option for competitors in the service market, since customers in that market would not accept any other, maybe more creative brick structure. Similar situations may arise in all information technology markets where network effects force competitors to use the same standard. If the standard is IP-protected, competitors will not be able to compete by substitution.

In such situations in which markets do not accept substitution, it would make no sense to require that the right-holder intends not just to duplicate, but to offer a better product.[88] Imitation may be allowed provided that the pro-competitive effects, consisting in a higher level of price competition, are not outweighed by counter-incentives for the initial investment in innovation made by the right-holder.[89]

A duty to license may even more easily be justified in situations of follow-on innovation.[90] In such situations, the duty to license will restore the initial mechanism of the IP system to promote dynamic competition.

---

[86] See, however, Wielsch, D. (2005), 'Wettbewerbsrecht als Immaterialgüterrecht', *EuZW*, 391 *et seq.*, arguing that the copyright had a similar effect to that in *Magill*.

[87] This was most clearly stated by the Commission in its Decision of 3 July 2001, Case COMP D3/38.044 – *NDC Health/IMS Health: Interim Measures*, para. 89 = http://ec.europa.eu/comm/competition/antitrust/cases/decisions/38044/en.pdf, accessed 4 November 2007.

[88] See, in more detail, Drexl, *supra* note 81, at 654.

[89] See *ibid.*, at 662 *et seq.*; Drexl et al., *supra* note 76, para. 23.

[90] On follow-on innovation, see also Discussion Paper, *supra* note 4, para. 240, holding that a refusal to license in such cases could be considered abusive even if the licence is not sought to directly incorporate the technology in new goods and services.

4.4 Intellectual property is different from tangible property

It is often debated whether intellectual property should be dealt with differently under competition law as compared to 'real' property. The US IP Guidelines consider intellectual property as essentially comparable to any other form of property.[91] This statement is nowadays primarily understood to counter claims according to which intellectual property should be immunized against antitrust intervention. Indeed, from a perspective of constitutional rights, intellectual property does not deserve stronger protection than other property.

Apart from the constitutional dimension, however, competition law has to take into account the specific economics of IPRs. Dynamic competition is an argument with respect to intellectual property. The same is not necessarily true in the context of tangible property. If the owner of a ferry harbour excludes competitors' ships from using his harbour this may well lead to a monopolization in the downstream market of sea transport services. However, unlike the situation of a refusal to license, such exclusion will not have any impact on the level of innovation. Therefore, a test developed in the field of tangible property, like the essential facility doctrine, may well be inappropriate to capture the pro and anti-competitive effects a given right produces in a relevant market. This can clearly be seen in the case law on Article 82 EC. In *IMS Health*, the ECJ tries to apply the general concept of leveraging to a refusal, which is only possible after confirming that a hypothetical upstream market would be sufficient,[92] but the Court has to formulate the new-product rule as a specific requirement for refusal-to-license cases.[93] The Commission in its Discussion Paper on Article 82 EC wants to apply the general test in refusal-to-supply cases to a refusal to license as well. Nevertheless, the Commission has to admit that an 'additional' requirement is needed in such cases and thereby refers to the new-product rule of the ECJ.[94] Hereby the Commission implicitly admits that the general test is not appropriate to capture adequately distortions of dynamic competition in IP-related cases.

---

91 US IP Antitrust Guidelines, *supra* note 72, note 2.0. a).

92 Although such a hypothetical market can be imagined, the ECJ did not realize that the right-holder in *IMS Health* had gained a dominant position in the downstream service market because of the standardization that took place as a consequence of the protected brick structure in that downstream market and not as a result of leveraging market dominance from the hypothetical upstream licence market; see Drexl et al., *supra* note 76, at para. 11.

93 Whether the new-product rule will only be required for IP cases has so far been left undecided by the ECJ; cf. Case C-7/97, *Bronner*, [1998] ECR I-7791, paras 39–41.

94 Discussion Paper, *supra* note 4, paras 237–40.

A much better approach would consist in developing an IP-specific test for refusal-to-deal cases. Such a test, namely one that considers the refusal to license an essential IPR as an abuse in the sense of Article 82 EC, was suggested in another publication and need not be repeated here.[95] It suffices to stress that the different economics of IPRs requires the development of an IP-specific test that adequately mirrors the economics of IPRs in a manageable legal form.

4.5 IPRs do not serve the goal of guaranteeing profit for investment in innovation

In applying competition law to IP-related cases, policymakers have to be careful about not making arguments meant to defend the exclusivity of the IP right that clearly lie outside the scope of protection of the IP right.

Nowadays, it has almost become common to argue that firms making an investment in innovation must receive a reward for that investment.[96] Even Competition Commissioner Neelie Kroes has said:[97] 'I fully support the need for innovative products to enjoy strong intellectual property protection so that companies can recoup their R&D expenditure and be rewarded for their innovative efforts'. Such talk may well influence the practice of competition law. The Commission refers to this concept explicitly to justify its suggestion for an efficiency defence in refusal-to-license cases:[98] '[A] dominant firm should be allowed to exclude others for a certain period of time in order to ensure an adequate return on . . . investment [in innovation], even when this entails eliminating effective competition during this period'.

This recoupment argument – recouping investment in R&D by later monopoly profits – is neither part of the existing IP system nor can any economic reasoning justify such an exception to the protection of effective competition.

---

[95] See Drexl et al., *supra* note 76, paras 20–4. In a similar sense, see Conde Gallego, B. (2005), 'Die Anwendung des kartellrechtlichen Missbrauchsverbots auf "unerlässliche" Immaterialgüterrechte im Lichte der IMS Health- und Standard-Spundfass-Urteile', *GRUR Int.*, 16.

[96] See, for example, Ahlborn et al., *supra* note 66, p. 42.

[97] The citation can be found in a press release of the Commission of 15 June 2005 on its decision in *AstraZeneca*, in which the Commission for the first time applied Article 82 EC to a pharmaceutical patent; see 'Commission fines AstraZeneca 60 million for misusing patent system to delay market entry of competing generic drugs', IP/05/737 = http://europa.eu/rapid/pressReleasesAction.do?reference=IP/05/737&format=HTML&aged=0&language=EN&guiLanguage=en. See also Commission Decision of 15 June 2005, Case COMP/A.37.507/F3 – *AstraZenica*, http://ec.europa.eu/comm/competition/antitrust/cases/decisions/37507/prov_version.pdf, accessed 1 August 2007.

[98] Discussion Paper, *supra* note 4, para. 235.

First of all, the IP system only protects specific achievements, patentable inventions and copyrighted works for instance, and not investment in innovation as such.[99] Whether investment in the pharmaceutical industry leads to an invention for which a patent will be granted is all but certain. In addition, even a patent does not guarantee adequate profit. A drug may only be sold if it receives market approval from the authorities. In addition, drugs also must meet consumer needs. A new drug has to be 'useful' beyond the requirements of patentability in the sense that it effectively combats certain diseases affecting a considerable number of patients. Proponents of the 'recoupment' argument are aware of the fact that investment in innovation is basically risky. It is in fact this very risk – that not all investment in R&D will pay – to which proponents of the recoupment argument refer to justify an exception to competition.[100] Still, the argument does not take into account the fact that competition law would only be authorized to intervene in situations in which the mechanism of dynamic competition is seriously distorted, namely in situations in which the IP right as such leads to a restriction on competition or in which external market failures – cases of standardization and network effects – exclude competitive pressure by substitution. Whereas nobody can deny that firms have to cross-subsidize failed investment in R&D by profits made from successful investment, no argument can be made that such cross-subsidizing requires an exemption from competition law in such situations. The recoupment argument constitutes a partial victory for the neo-Schumpeterian school of thinking, which should not be adopted for European competition policy.

4.6 Distinguishing between different types of IPRs

The concept of dynamic competition, based on the idea that IPRs are thought to promote innovation, meets the logic of IPRs that are technology-oriented, hence of patent law in particular. Other IPRs, such as trademarks and copyrights, pursue different goals and apply slightly different legal mechanisms.

Trademark law is intended to increase market transparency by enabling consumers to distinguish products and services according to their source. Still, the trademark system indirectly creates incentives for the right-holder to invest in the quality of the product or service so as to raise the value of the trademark and the goodwill connected to it.

Copyright is hoped to enhance creativity, and not innovation. Whether innovation models might easily be applied to copyright still requires consideration.

---

[99] In Europe, only *sui generis* protection of databases provides for protection of 'substantial investment'; see Article 7(1) of Directive 96/9/EC of 11 March 1996 on the legal protection of databases, OJ 1996 No. L 77, p. 20.

[100] In this sense see also the Commission in its Discussion Paper, *supra* note 4, para. 235.

Whereas investors in innovation usually make their decisions based on economic considerations, the authors of copyrighted works are often driven by non-economic incentives. Whereas the degree of technological innovation can only be measured according to an invention's responsiveness to actual consumer needs, such responsiveness is obviously insufficient for the evaluation of a work's degree of creativity.

Most progressive forms of art, literature and music often have a hard time finding a market. Cultural policy argues in favour of cultural diversity, whereas consumer responsiveness would (and does) induce firms in the entertainment industry to favour the average consumer taste. Finally, continental European copyright systems, based on the *droit d'auteur* tradition, attribute the initial right to the creator of the work (so-called creator principle), but face problems when it comes to guaranteeing authors a just return for their production vis-à-vis large exploiters, whereas in the patent law field, firms investing in innovation will usually acquire the original patent. Competition policy should take those specific concerns of copyright law into account.[101] This seems most important in the context of the current debate on the future of collecting societies in Europe.[102]

5 Conclusion

European competition law is in need of a more economic approach to intellectual property and competition law. The case law of the European Court of Justice on refusal to license proves that a normative approach to striking a balance between the exclusivity of the IPR and competition law intervention cannot provide a test that adequately mirrors the goals and functions of the specific IPR in the context of the relevant market.

The more economic approach advocated so far by the Commission constitutes an appropriate basis for the application of EC competition law to intellectual property. In this sense, protection of effective dynamic competition in the relevant market should be preferred to an analysis based on the concept of

---

[101] On the relationship of the recently reformed German law on contractual protection of authors and performing artists (the so-called 'Urhebervertragsrecht') with European competition law, see Drexl, Josef (2005), 'Der Anspruch der Werkschöpfer und ausübenden Künstler auf angemessene Vergütung in der europäischen Wettbewerbsordnung', in Ansgar Ohly, Theo Bodewig, Thomas Dreier, Horst-Peter Götting, Maximilian Haedicke and Michael Lehmann (eds), *Perspektiven des Geistigen Eigentums und Wettbewerbsrechts, Festschrift für Gerhard Schricker*, München: C.H. Beck, p. 651.

[102] Cf. Drexl, Josef (2007), 'Competition in the Field of Collective Management: Preferring "creative competition" to Economic Efficiency in European Copyright Law', in Paul Torremans (ed.), Copyright Law: A Handbook on Contemporary Research, Cheltenham, UK and Northampton, MA, US: Edward Elgar, p. 255.

dynamic efficiency. This preference avoids the impossible predictions on the gains and losses regarding unknown future innovation that would be caused by competition law intervention. It rather relies on an analysis of the process of dynamic competition in existing relevant markets.

The Commission would be well advised to extend its concept of complementary goals of IP law and competition law from the field of technology transfer agreements to the area of abuse of dominance (Article 82 EC) and merger control. Simultaneously, the Commission should shield European competition law practice from neo-Schumpeterian ideas, which promote monopoly power based on IPRs as a requirement for future investment in innovation.

The more economic approach would require competition law enforcers to distinguish between the effects of a given right on competition by imitation and, in particular, on competition by substitution, the latter being the engine of innovation according to the theory of complementarity. Dynamic competition may be excluded as a consequence of internal regulatory failures of the IP system or external market failures, as in the situation of standardization and monopolization. In the context of Article 82 EC, the effects of a given IPR on the relevant market can only be captured appropriately by an IP-specific test.

The Commission should work to achieve a comprehensive competition policy for IPRs that includes control of licensing agreements under Article 81 EC, control of market dominance under Article 82 EC and merger control. For the moment, analytical progress is most needed and, because of the case law of the ECJ, most difficult to achieve, in the field of Article 82 EC. Since competition problems may also arise as a consequence of regulatory failures within the IP system, DG Competition should also become more involved in European IP legislation.[103] *Ex ante* competition-oriented IP legislation is a much more effective way to protect competition than *ex post* control under Article 82 EC.

---

[103] In the US, the Antitrust Modernization Commission recently critically reviewed potential anti-competitive effects of the patent system as such; see Antitrust Modernization Commission, Report and Recommendations, April 2007, http://www.amc.gov/report_recommendation/amc_final_report.pdf, accessed 4 November 2007; see, in particular, Resolutions 20 and 21 relating to standard setting and administration of the patent law system respectively.

3 The contestability of IP-protected markets

Andreas Heinemann

1 Introduction

IP protection and contestability? At first sight, this subject seems to be paradoxical: the very sense of an IPR is excluding others from the use of the protected knowledge. IPRs are granted in order to protect their owners from contestability. On the other hand, every IPR has a well-defined scope. It does not in itself confer market power or even dominance, but only gives exclusiveness over certain knowledge. Others keep the right to develop substitutes, to 'invent around' or to be active in neighbouring markets not covered by the exclusive right in question. Typically, it is in the interest of the IPR owner to make the most of her privilege. The fundamental problem consists in telling the difference between what is allowed and what is prohibited in this respect. Or to put it another way: how far does the scope of reward for an IPR go? This chapter will show that – under certain conditions – the owner of an IPR cannot make use of the whole spectrum of rights granted to her under IP legislation. The chapter will analyse which limits should be set to the freedom of an IPR holder. Even IP-protected markets have to stay open to a certain extent, not only in the long run, but also in the face of abusive short-term strategies. Restrictions on the freedom of the IPR holder are not only compatible with the model of dynamic competition and the promotion of innovation, but they are even required by these concepts. The simplistic view that the application of competition law to IPRs merely enhances static competition 'by imitation' to the prejudice of dynamic competition 'by innovation' is rejected. The argument is based on the theory of contestable markets and its focus on barriers to entry.

2 The theory of contestable markets

2.1 The notion of 'contestable markets'

The notion of 'contestable markets' was coined by Baumol, Panzar and Willig in their famous book published in 1982.[1] The central point regards the role of

[1] Baumol, William J., John C. Panzar and Robert D. Willig (1982), *Contestable Markets and the Theory of Industry Structure*, San Diego, CA: Harcourt Brace Jovanovich.

potential competition compared to actual competition: even a market with only one supplier, that is a monopoly, may be a competitive market if barriers to entry are low or non-existent.[2] If there are no legal obstacles to entering that market, if there is perfect information, access to the technology needed, no strategic behaviour by the incumbent and, above all, no sunk costs, the incumbent is threatened by the possibility of other firms entering that market. Under this menace he will not charge monopoly prices, but come close to a price level corresponding to a competitive market. The consequence for competition policy would be that market dominance cannot be measured by market shares, but should be based on the criterion of contestability. Potential competition, the authors argue, is equivalent to actual competition.[3]

The first objection to this approach is obvious: the conditions mentioned, such as perfect information and absence of sunk costs, correspond to those of the concept of perfect competition, which are not met in the real world. Therefore, only an attenuated version may be upheld: in order to determine the existence of a dominant position, the degree of contestability has to be taken into account. If the assumption is correct that in the real world transaction costs are rather high,[4] the perspective of potential competition is only one criterion among others to establish a dominant position. But even if the role of potential competition has to be qualified, it is the merit of the theory of contestable markets to have underlined and specified how important the openness of markets and the hypothetical reactions of (potential) competitors are for the establishment of market dominance.[5]

2.2 *Practical relevance for European competition policy*

The theory of contestable markets has been endorsed by European competition law in the form of the concept of potential competition and barriers to entry.

---

2 See generally von Weizsäcker, Carl Christian (1980), *Barriers to Entry*, Berlin: Springer; Jickeli, J. (1992), 'Marktzutrittsschranken im EG-Kartellrecht', *WuW*, 101 and 195; OECD (2006), 'Barriers to Entry', Competition Policy Roundtables, 6 March 2006, http://www.oecd.org/dataoecd/43/49/36344429.pdf, accessed 4 November 2007.

3 Another consequence would be the definitive farewell to the structure-conduct-performance approach; see Mestmäcker, Ernst-Joachim and Heike Schweitzer (2004), *Europäisches Wettbewerbsrecht*, Munich: C.H. Beck, 2nd ed., p. 612.

4 Richter, Rudolf and Eirik Furubotn (1996), *Neue Institutionenökonomik*, Tübingen: Mohr Siebeck, pp. 56 *et seq.*; Wallis, John J. and Douglas C. North (1988), 'Measuring the Transaction Sector in the American Economy, 1870–1970', in Stanley L. Engerman and Robert E. Gallman (eds), *Long-term Factors in American Economic Growth*, Chicago: The University of Chicago Press, pp. 95 *et seq.*

5 Mestmäcker and Schweitzer, *supra* note 3, p. 612, underline the importance of the contestable-markets theory for dynamic thinking in the competitive process.

These aspects play an important role in all fields of European competition law. But it is merger control where they have left the most prominent trace. When appraising the compatibility of a concentration with the Common Market, one of the things that has to be taken into account is the 'potential competition' from undertakings located inside or outside the European Community, in accordance with Article 2(1) lit. a) of the EC Merger Regulation. According to lit. b) of that Article, the 'legal or other barriers to entry' are part of the analysis. The European Commission has taken over to some extent the concept of contestable markets by pointing out in several guidelines the importance of entry barriers for assessing the effects of certain behaviour on competition.[6] These guidelines are not restricted to merger control but concern also the cartel interdiction (Article 81 EC) and the abuse of dominant positions (Article 82 EC). One example is market definition: in former times the relevant market was defined by focusing on substitutability from the perspective of the other market side (in most cases the demand side) using, for instance, the cross-price elasticity of demand embodied in the SSNIP test.[7] The concept of contestability has enriched the traditional concept by adding to it the supply-substitution test. According to this test, the suppliers who are able to switch their production to the products in question without meeting insurmountable obstacles are also part of the relevant market.[8]

However in its notice on the definition of relevant market the Commission draws a distinction between the supply-substitution test and potential competition: in defining markets potential competition is not taken into account because it is too remote.[9] This caveat reflects the practical need of competition law, which cannot rely on potential developments that are too far in the future. For this reason, the Commission's texts fix certain time limits: according to the guidelines on technology transfer agreements, entry barriers are low if market entry by potential competitors is expected within one or two years.[10]

---

6 See, for example, Notice on the definition of relevant market for the purposes of Community competition law, OJ 1997 No. C 372, p. 5, paras 20 *et seq*.; Guidelines on the assessment of horizontal mergers under the Council Regulation on the control of concentrations between undertakings, OJ 2004 No. C 31, p. 5, paras 68 *et seq*.; Commission Notice – Guidelines on the application of Article 81 of the EC Treaty to technology transfer agreements, OJ 2004 No. C 101, p. 2, para. 138.

7 SSNIP = Small but Significant and Non-transitory Increase in Price; see, for example, Guidelines on market analysis and the assessment of significant market power under the Community regulatory framework for electronic communications networks and services, OJ EC 2002 No. C 165, p. 6, paras 40 *et seq*.

8 See European Commission, Notice on the definition of relevant market, *supra* note 6, paras 20 *et seq*.

9 *Ibid*., para. 24.

10 Guidelines on the application of Article 81 of the EC Treaty to technology transfer agreements, *supra* note 6, para. 138.

According to the horizontal merger guidelines, market entry is only considered as timely if it occurs within two years.[11]

The concept of potential competition, supply substitution and barriers to entry used by the Commission is deeply indebted to the theory of contestable markets.[12] However, when assessing economic reality it is much more difficult to determine possible or potential developments. Therefore the European Commission gives priority to the effects of certain behaviour on actual competition by bringing up the concept of potential competition only as an additional argument.[13] This is due to the fact that in real life there are always higher or lower sunk costs which reduce the significance of potential competition.[14]

2.3 The theory of contestability applied to intellectual property

How does IP protection fit into the concept of contestable markets? IPRs are generally seen as barriers to entry.[15] In so far as they prevent a competitor from entering a certain market, this evaluation is understandable. On the other hand, IPRs are not in themselves a restraint of competition or a barrier; they constitute private rights for certain types of information which in the absence of special protection would not be produced sufficiently. Thus, IPRs are at the very basis of the competitive process since they transform knowledge into protected goods that can be evaluated and traded on markets through assignment and licensing.[16] Carl Christian von Weizsäcker has rightly stated that the

---

[11] Guidelines on the assessment of horizontal mergers, *supra* note 6, para. 74.

[12] In the guidelines on technology transfer agreements the Commission also refers in a prominent way to the concept of sunk costs, which is so pivotal in the contestable-markets theory; see the Guidelines on the application of Article 81 of the EC Treaty to technology transfer agreements, *supra* note 6, para. 138.

[13] See, for example, Notice – Guidelines on the application of Article 81(3) of the Treaty, OJ 2004 No. C 101, p. 97, para. 114 ('While sources of actual competition are usually the most important, as they are most easily verified, sources of potential competition must also be taken into account.').

[14] Expressly in this sense the Guidelines on the application of Article 81 of the EC Treaty to technology transfer agreements, *supra* note 6, para. 138 at the very end.

[15] See, for example, the list of barriers to entry in the European Commission's Guidelines on technology-transfer agreements, *supra* note 6, para. 138, or in its Guidelines on the assessment of horizontal mergers, *supra* note 6, para. 71.

[16] Ullrich, Hanns and Andreas Heinemann (2007), in Ulrich Immenga and Ernst-Joachim Mestmäcker (eds), *Wettbewerbsrecht, Vol. 1, Kommentar zum Europäischen Kartellrecht*, Munich: C.H. Beck, 4th ed., *GRUR B*, notes 22 *et seq*. See also the general inquiries on the relationship between IPRs and competition law, for example, Anderman, Steven D. (1998), *EC Competition Law and Intellectual Property Rights*, Oxford: Clarendon Press; Anderson, Robert D. and Nancy T. Gallini (eds) (1998), *Competition Policy and Intellectual Property Rights in the Knowledge-based Economy*, Calgary: University of Calgary Press; Carrier, M. (2002), 'Unraveling the Patent-Antitrust Paradox', *U. Pa. L. Rev.*, 150, 761; Ghidini, Gustavo (2006),

use of a patent against infringements is not a violation of free competition. Patent protection can only be qualified as a 'barrier to entry' if it is excessive, that is if the positive effect on innovation is smaller than the negative effect on imitation and diffusion of a certain technology.[17] This bars a simplistic view that puts the stress solely on the exclusive effects of IPRs.[18] The effect on competition can only be evaluated by taking into account the whole legal and economic context. For this purpose, a precise definition of all relevant markets is necessary. Recent case law of the ECJ has created some debate on market definition in the context of IPRs.

3 Market definition and dominance in the context of IPRs

The general rules on market definition apply to IP-protected markets, too.[19] Particular difficulties concern the existence of different vertical market levels and the bounds of the relevant product market.

3.1 Vertical market levels

3.1.1 Uncertainty in the case law on the vertical structure of IP-related markets In its 2001 *IMS Health* decision[20] the European Commission was

---

Intellectual Property and Competition Law – The Innovation Nexus, Cheltenham, UK, and Northampton, MA, US: Edward Elgar; Govaere, Inge (1996), *The Use and Abuse of Intellectual Property Rights in E.C. Law*, London: Sweet & Maxwell; Heinemann, Andreas (2002), *Immaterialgüterschutz in der Wettbewerbsordnung*, Tübingen: Mohr Siebeck; Tom, W. and J. Newberg (1997), 'Antitrust and Intellectual Property: From Separate Spheres to Unified Field', *Antitrust L.J.*, 66, 167.

17 von Weizsäcker, Carl Christian (2005), 'Marktzutrittsschranken', in Peter Oberender (ed.), *Effizienz und Wettbewerb*, Berlin: Duncker & Humblot, pp. 43, 46 *et seq*. See generally Bartl, Ulrich (2005), *Immaterialgüterrechtliche Marktzutrittsschranken im System des Art. 82 EG*, Baden-Baden: Nomos.

18 Another possibility would be to maintain the label 'barrier to entry' for IPRs but to remove the negative connotation of that label. In this sense, see OECD, *supra* note 2, p. 20 note 6 ('First, entry barriers, or the hope of creating them, provide greater incentives to create new products and services. Intellectual property rights, for example, are an effective incentive to innovate precisely because they help to deter and prevent entry.').

19 See, for example, Commission notice on the definition of relevant market, *supra* note 6.

20 European Commission of 3 July 2001, Case COMP D3/38.044 – *NDC Health/IMS Health:* Interim measures, OJ 2002 No. L 59, p. 18; later withdrawn, see European Commission of 13 August 2003, OJ 2003 No. L 268, p. 69, and the critique of this withdrawal by Heinemann, Andreas (2004), 'Interne und externe Begrenzungen des Immaterialgüterschutzes am Beispiel des *IMS Health*-Falls', in Reto M. Hilty and Alexander Peukert (eds), *Interessenausgleich im Urheberrecht*, Baden-Baden: Nomos, p. 207, at 217 *et seq*.

very reticent about accepting the existence of different vertical market levels in the context of IPRs. The Commission had tried to prove a leveraging abuse without defining two different markets between which market power had allegedly been transferred. The Commission contented itself with stating that the copyright-protected structure at issue consisting of 1860 bricks was indispensable for carrying on business in the market for regional sales data for pharmaceutical products. But it had not examined whether the copyright-protected database formed an independent upstream market.[21] This reasoning was astonishing in two regards. In the first place, it is generally recognized that a leveraging abuse can only occur where two different markets exist.[22] Secondly, it would have been easy to establish the existence of two markets. The facts of the *IMS Health* case are similar to those in the ground-breaking *Magill* decision, where the ECJ had established an abusive leveraging of a dominant position on the (copyright-protected) market for programme schedules onto the secondary market of weekly television guides. Later, in the 2004 ECJ preliminary ruling in the *IMS Health* case, the Advocate General and the court did not hesitate to establish two separate markets. The court went one step further by stating that 'it is sufficient that a potential market or even hypothetical market can be identified'.[23] It is sufficient – according to the ECJ – 'that two different stages of production may be identified and that they are interconnected, the upstream product is indispensable inasmuch as for supply of the downstream product'.[24] In this view, the existence of a separate upstream market is not even excluded by the fact that the corresponding product is not (yet) marketed separately.

3.1.2 Licensing markets and goods markets Thus markets are defined very narrowly in the vertical chain. This approach is sometimes criticized by pointing to its consequences: as IPRs can normally be licensed, there is always a

---

21 European Commission of 3 July 2001, *supra* note 20, paras 179 *et seq.*

22 See, for example, Casper, M. (2002), 'Die wettbewerbsrechtliche Begründung von Zwangslizenzen', *ZHR*, 166, 685, at 703. The European Commission is certainly right in stating that an abuse in the sense of Article 82 EC does not necessarily presuppose the existence of two separate markets (note 184 of the 2001 decision). For example, the limitation of production, markets or technical development (Article 82 lit. (b) EC) takes place in one market only. However, leveraging abuse is defined by the existence of two separate markets. Käller, Anja (2006), *Die Verweigerung einer immaterialgüterrechtlich geschützten Leistung und das Missbrauchsverbot des Art. 82 EG*, Baden-Baden: Nomos, pp. 284 *et seq.*, even requires a dominant position on a third market that is upstream in relation to the licensing market.

23 Case C-418/01, *IMS Health*, [2004] ECR I-5039, para. 44.

24 *Ibid.*, para. 45.

primary licensing market and a secondary goods market.[25] It is true that this result may be inadequate where the holder of the IPR would never be willing to license his right. For instance, in the case of a painter, who would perhaps sell his paintings but never use them in another way, it would be highly artificial to distinguish between a licensing market (for licences of the copyright on his paintings) and a goods market for the tangible paintings. However, this aspect can be taken into account by the notion of 'potential' or 'hypothetical' market: as far as personal works protected by copyright are concerned it may be inappropriate to assume a separate licensing market. But this is an exception. In purely economic terms, the IPR holder always has the choice of exploiting the protected knowledge herself or leaving the exploitation to others by licensing the right. Even if she prefers the first strategy, it is adequate to assume an independent (and in this case: potential) licensing market, because the decision to 'build or license' may change at any time.[26] For this reason, US law starts with the distinction of technology (= licensing) markets and goods markets. In the Antitrust Guidelines for the Licensing of Intellectual Property[27] the US antitrust authorities state that antitrust analysis generally has to start with the markets for final or intermediate goods using the intellectual property in question. In certain cases, the analysis of technology markets (or even innovation markets) may also be necessary.[28]

The distinction of licensing and of goods markets is a helpful analytical tool. The approach of the European (and US American) authorities should therefore be followed.[29] It is true that in IP-related cases this distinction will regularly lead to an upstream licensing market and a downstream goods market, that is to the phenomenon of dependent markets. Therefore, it is even more important to underline that there is no automatic abuse in these cases. It does not follow from the qualification of a certain market as 'dependent' that the dominant firm in the upstream market has to license its IPRs to those who

---

[25] Wirtz, M. and M. Holzhäuser (2004), 'Die kartellrechtliche Zwangslizenz', *WRP*, 683, at 689; for an opposing view; see also Lober, A. (2002), 'Die IMS-Health-Entscheidung der Europäischen Kommission: Copyright K.O.?', *GRUR Int.*, 7, at 9.

[26] Eilmansberger, T. (2003), 'Abschlusszwang und Essential Facility Doktrin nach Art. 82 EG', *EWS*, 12, at 21 *et seq.*

[27] US Department of Justice and Federal Trade Commission, 'Antitrust Guidelines for the Licensing of Intellectual Property', 6 April 1995, http://www.usdoj.gov/atr/public/guidelines/0558.htm, accessed 4 November 2007.

[28] US IP Antitrust Guidelines, *supra* note 27, note 3.2.

[29] In this sense Conde Gallego, B. (2006), 'Die Anwendung des kartellrechtlichen Missbrauchsverbots auf "unerlässliche" Immaterialgüterrechte im Lichte der *IMS Health- und Standard-Spundfass*-Urteile', *GRUR Int.*, 16, at 19 *et seq.*, with a comprehensive discussion of diverging positions.

want to become active in the dependent market. It all depends on the interpretation of what is an abuse in the sense of Article 82 EC.

3.2 Scope of the relevant product markets

Before tackling the concept of abuse, the relevant product markets have to be defined. The general rules apply: the relevant product market consists of all goods or services that are regarded as substitutable by the other market side.[30] On this basis, relevant markets may be wide or narrow; generalizations as to their normal scope are not possible, as everything depends on the preferences of the other market side. Objective factors, such as for example product qualities, are not relevant in themselves. Besides, one feature of vertically related markets may also become pertinent in the IP context: it is recognized that preferences in a downstream market may influence the definition of the upstream market. This is the case for example in distribution, where the preferences of consumers at the retail level are relevant for retailers when buying at the wholesale level.[31] The same is true of broadcasting rights. There are upstream markets for broadcasting rights, for instance for sport events, and there are downstream television markets for the transmission of these events. For the definition of the upstream markets, the preferences of the TV stations are decisive. Since these preferences are heavily influenced by the viewing preferences of the audience, viewers' preferences in the end are crucial for the definition of the relevant product markets for broadcasting rights.[32]

The *IMS Health* case is a good example illustrating that this influence may also exist in IP-related cases. As pointed out above, there is an upstream market for the copyright-protected brick structure and a downstream market for regional sales data on pharmaceutical products. As the pharmaceutical industry is only interested in sales data presented in the 1860 brick structure,[33] the relevant upstream market has to be defined narrowly: firms who want to become active in the service market for pharmaceutical sales data need the 1860 brick structure. Other structures are not valid substitutes in their view. Cross-price elasticity is thus approximately zero: an increase in price for the 1860 brick structure would not entail an increase in demand for other structures. Therefore

---

30 See section 2.2 *supra*.

31 See Möschel, Wernhard (2007), in Ulrich Immenga and Ernst-Joachim Mestmäcker (eds), *Wettbewerbsrecht, Vol. 2, Kommentar zum deutschen Kartellrecht*, Munich: C.H. Beck, 4th ed., § 19, para. 25 with references in note 75.

32 See Heinemann, A. (2006), 'Sportübertragungsrechte im europäischen Kartellrecht am Beispiel der Olympischen Spiele', *ZEuP*, 337, at 348.

33 This statement relies on the fact-finding of the European Commission, *supra* note 20; the ECJ left it to the national court to establish the indispensability of the 1860 brick structure; see Case C-418/01, *IMS Health*, [2004] ECR I-5039, para. 47.

IMS Health has a dominant position in this narrowly defined market for the 1860 brick structure. Other methods of collecting and presenting sales data are not part of that market.[34]

Not only may upstream markets be influenced by downstream markets, but this effect may work also vice versa. Markets for spare parts or accessories often have to be defined narrowly as, from the perspective of the other market side, only products designed for the same main product are interchangeable. Narrow market definitions may also occur in the context of cultural goods. Very detailed preferences of consumers could lead to atomistic definitions of relevant markets, for example for a certain novel, or at least for a certain author who for his readers is not interchangeable.[35] In the area of sport very narrow product markets have been defined, too.[36] These narrow market definitions are correct if – according to the concept of substitutability – the products in question are not interchangeable for the other market side. However, in order to avoid atomistic exaggerations, the preferences not of single consumers, but of a sufficiently aggregate group have to be taken into account.

3.3 Dominance

It is generally recognized that an IPR does not in itself confer a dominant position.[37] The general rules apply. A dominant position exists when an enterprise has 'the power to behave to an appreciable extent independently of its competitors, customers and ultimately of its consumers'.[38] Normally, competitors are able to develop substitutes that are part of the same market, thus preventing independent behaviour on the part of the IPR holder. It is also conceivable that the very existence of an IPR will be an incentive for competitors to develop superior products not covered by the incumbent's exclusive

---

[34] For an opposing view, see Drexl, J., B. Conde Gallego, S. Enchelmaier, M. Leistner and M.-O. Mackenrodt (2006), 'Comments of the Max Planck Institute for Intellectual Property, Competition and Tax Law on the DG Competition Discussion Paper of December 2005 on the Application of Art. 82 EC to Exclusionary Abuses', *IIC*, 558, paras 11–13 and 21, assuming a broad market definition.

[35] See in the US the decision of the District Court (S.D. New York 1994), *Vitale v. Marlborough Gallery*, 1994–1 Trade Cases para. 70654, in which a relevant product market for paintings by Jackson Pollock was assumed.

[36] For example, for certain soccer championships, see European Commission of 2 April 2003, *Newscorp/Telepiù*, OJ 2004 No. L 110, p. 73, paras 52 *et seq.*; of 23 July 2003, *UEFA Champions League*, OJ 2003 No. L 291, p. 25, paras 56 *et seq.*

[37] Joined Cases C-241/91 P and C-242/91 P, *RTE and ITP v. Commission* ('*Magill*'), [1995] ECR I-743, para. 46 ('So far as dominant position is concerned, it is to be remembered at the outset that mere ownership of an intellectual property right cannot confer such a position.').

[38] Case 27/76, *United Brands*, [1978] ECR 207, para. 65.

rights. As a consequence, IPRs may even strengthen the contestability of IP-related markets.[39]

On the other hand, there are IP-protected markets in which the owner of the exclusive right has a dominant position. According to general opinion, this is rather the exception. However the statistical data available on the relationship between IPRs and market dominance are scarce.[40] Much depends on the definition of the relevant product market. If markets for spare parts or accessories and certain cultural markets have to be defined narrowly (as suggested here), dominant positions may be the consequence.[41] Other examples are *essential facilities*. 'Essential' translated into the language of competition law means 'no substitutes available'. Therefore very often the owner of an essential facility has a dominant position; otherwise his facility would not be essential. Finally, dominant positions occur in surroundings characterized by network effects, meaning that the utility of a certain network increases with the number of other participants using the same network.[42] A result of this are natural monopolies. New customers have a clear incentive to join the larger network and not a competing one.

Even if the general estimation is correct that dominant positions are rather the exception in the IP context, the examples have shown that they nevertheless exist. In this context, it is extremely important to stress the fact that market definition and the establishment of dominance do not predetermine the legality or illegality of certain behaviour. It is not dominant positions that are prohibited, but their abuse. The most important task consists of clarifying under which conditions an abuse has to be assumed. It seems clear that to do so economic concepts have to be called upon. This chapter proposes to give a greater weight to the theory of contestable markets.

---

39 See Intellectual Property and Competition Review Committee (Australia), 'Review of Intellectual Property Legislation under the Competition Principles Agreement', http://www.ipaustralia.gov.au/pdfs/ipcr/finalreport.pdf, p. 25, accessed 4 November 2007.

40 But see OECD (1989), *Competition Policy and Intellectual Property Rights*, Paris: OECD, p. 16: According to one study, the licensor faced no alternative supplier in 27 per cent of the cases. In 34 per cent of cases two to five alternatives existed, in 10 per cent of cases five to ten alternatives, and in 29 per cent of cases ten or more substitutes were on the market.

41 But see Discussion Paper of December 2005 on the Application of Article 82 of the Treaty to Exclusionary Abuses, http://europa.eu.int/comm/competition/antitrust/others/discpaper2005.pdf, accessed 4 November 2007, paras 243 *et seq.* In spite of a narrow market definition, competition in the primary market may exclude dominance in the secondary market.

42 See Spindler, G. and K. Apel (2005), 'Urheber- versus Kartellrecht? – Auf dem Weg zur Zwangslizenz?', *JZ*, 133. In the horizontal merger guidelines the network effect is referred to as a barrier to entry: Guidelines on the assessment of horizontal mergers, *supra* note 6, para. 72.

4 Modes of contestability

4.1 Contestability of IPRs themselves

IPRs may be registered or unregistered rights; the former may be examined or unexamined. In any case, there must be the possibility of challenging their validity and their scope, in *inter partes* proceedings before the civil courts or in special proceedings before the competent IP authority. This may be called contestability in a procedural sense. It is not in the public interest that those IPRs be maintained or enforced that go beyond what is provided for in IP legislation. The public interest in challenging invalid IPRs is so strong that the corresponding remedies are not necessarily competition-law remedies but belong to general private or procedural law. The most important cases are IPRs obtained by fraud on the competent IP authority, or 'sham litigation', that is objectively baseless enforcement of invalid IPRs. If this behaviour constitutes at the same time a violation of competition law, competition-law remedies apply in addition to the general private-law remedies. Both Articles 81 and 82 EC are relevant in this context. As regards restrictive agreements, no-challenge clauses in licensing agreements violate the public interest in annihilating invalid IPRs. Therefore, according to Article 5(1) lit. c) of the Technology Transfer Block Exemption Regulation (TTBER),[43] no-challenge clauses do not benefit from the exemption. Thus, the possibility of challenging the validity of IPRs is also guaranteed by European competition law on licensing.[44]

As far as unilateral conduct is concerned, Article 82 EC applies. For example, the European Commission has fined *AstraZeneca* for a violation of Article 82 EC. According to the fact-finding of the Commission, the enterprise gave misleading information to several patent offices in order to gain extended patent protection for a certain drug.[45] Thus fraudulent acquisition of an IPR is

[43] Commission Regulation (EC) No. 772/2004 of 27 April 2004 on the application of Article 81(3) of the Treaty to categories of technology transfer agreements, OJ 2004 No. L 123, p. 11.

[44] This does not restrict the capacity of the licensor to terminate the licensing agreement if the licensee challenges the validity of the IPR. But see the limitations to the right to terminate the agreement in technology pools in the Guidelines on the application of Article 81 of the EC Treaty to technology transfer agreements, *supra* note 6, para. 229.

[45] More precisely: by filing an application for supplementary protection certificates (SPCs) for that product. See European Commission of 15 June 2005, *AstraZeneca/Commission* ('*Losec*'), Press Release IP/05/737, http://europa.eu/rapid/pressReleasesAction.do?reference=IP/05/737&format=HTML&aged=1&language=EN&guiLanguage=en, accessed 4 November 2007. See Fagerlund, N. and S. Rasmussen (2005), 'AstraZeneca: The First Abuse Case in the Pharmaceutical Sector',

subject to the administrative sanctions of European competition law. The leading cases for objectively baseless enforcement of invalid IPRs in US antitrust law are the *Handgards* cases.[46] In Europe, national jurisdictions deal with these cases on the basis of national private law. The general problem arises that liability may be based on wrongful filing of a civil suit, although filing a suit is among the civil rights under the rule of law.[47]

4.2 Contestability of IP-related markets

Of central interest in our context is not the procedural aspect of contestability, but the metes and bounds of IP-based market dominance. What are the legal consequences if an IPR (exceptionally) covers a relevant product market thus conferring a monopoly in the antitrust sense? Is the IPR holder subject to restrictions, and if so, to what extent? In order to answer these questions it is useful to distinguish three different constellations. The first one is vertically related markets. Does an IPR also attribute to its owner the control over up- and downstream markets without restriction? The second group of cases concerns neighbouring markets that do not stand in a vertical relationship to the main market in question. For example in the *Microsoft* case, the markets for server software or media players cannot be qualified as upstream or downstream markets in relation to the market for client PC operating systems.[48] May IPRs be used to conquer such neighbouring markets? And finally, as regards the IP-protected main market itself, does competition law provide for limits even at the heart of protection?

4.3 Vertically related markets

4.3.1 IPRs and secondary markets Frequently IPRs do not only cover a

---

Competition Policy Newsletter, (3), 54; Hirsbrunner, S. (2005), 'Neues aus Brüssel zum Verhältnis von Patent- und Kartellrecht: die AstraZeneca-Entscheidung der Europäischen Kommission', *EWS*, 488. An action for annulment before the CFI is pending (T-321/05).

46 *Handgards, Inc. v. Ethicon, Inc.*, 601 F.2d 986 (9th Cir. 1979); *Handgards, Inc., v. Ethicon, Inc.*, 743 F.2d 1282 (9th Cir. 1984). See US IP Antitrust Guidelines, *supra* note 27, at 32.

47 Recently, the German Federal Court of Justice (BGH) has confirmed the established practice of the courts according to which the baseless invocation of IPRs may trigger claims for damages even against a *bona fide* right holder, but only outside public court procedures; see BGH of 15 September 2005, [2005] NJW 3141, and Sack, Rolf (2006), *Unbegründete Schutzrechtsverwarnungen*, Cologne: Carl Heymanns.

48 From an economic perspective this should be true even if the proper functioning of the server software depends on smooth interaction with the client PC operating system.

certain primary market, but also many or all secondary markets.[49] A copyright on a book does not only protect against copying the book but also against translating, renting, turning the book into a movie, broadcasting, etc.[50] The same is true for patents: a patent on a certain chemical substance gives absolute protection covering all possible kinds of use if the patent was not confined to a certain application. The largest field is given to vertical relationships if the distinction of licensing and goods markets is accepted as suggested here.[51] Even the production or the marketing of a protected good is a downstream market in relation to the licensing market for the IP-protected subject matter.

Competition law accepts the choices made by IP law. When IP legislation attributes to the right holder certain downstream markets, it is not the task of competition law to correct the solution made by the legislature. This may be illustrated using the example of design protection. Some countries accord, subject to several conditions, design protection for spare parts, which is particularly important for the car industry. It is clear that the owner of the design right does not commit an abuse by refusing to license his right to independent spare-part manufacturers. It is the very sense of the design right to reserve the production of the spare parts in question to the owner of that right. Another question is, of course, whether the legislature would not be better advised to provide for exceptions in the design protection law concerning spare parts that are produced by independent spare-part manufacturers and sold for repair purposes.[52] But if the legislature decides in favour of full protection, a refusal to license the design right is legal, as long as there are no other kinds of abuse, for example a limiting-of-production abuse arising from the decision not to continue the production of the spare parts although many cars in need of these parts are still in circulation.[53]

---

49 Ullrich underlines the tendency of recent extensions of IP protection to cover all secondary markets as well; see Ullrich, Hanns (2007), in Ulrich Immenga and Ernst-Joachim Mestmäcker (eds), *Wettbewerbsrecht, Vol. 1, Kommentar zum Europäischen Kartellrecht*, Munich: C.H. Beck, 4th ed., *GRUR A*, para. 29.

50 Admittedly this statement is not correct in an IP sense: an IPR protects the immaterial good in relation to which the book, the movie etc. are derivatives on the same market level. However, in an economic sense (which is relevant for competition law analysis), a movie based on a novel belongs to a downstream market.

51 See section 3.1.2 *supra*.

52 The European Commission has proposed to liberalize spare-part markets for repair purposes; see Commission Proposal for a Directive of the European Parliament and of the Council amending Directive 98/71/EC on the legal protection of designs, COM(2004) 582 final; and Drexl, J., R.M. Hilty and A. Kur (2005), 'Design Protection for Spare Parts and the Commission's Proposal for a Repairs Clause', *IIC*, 36, 448; against such a reform see Straus, Joseph (2005), 'Design Protection for Spare Parts Gone in Europe?', *EIPR*, 27, 391.

53 Case 238/87, *Volvo*, [1988] ECR 6211, para. 9.

4.3.2 Case law of the ECJ It goes without saying that the owner of the IPR is free to decide whether he wants to license his right or not. As the ECJ constantly says, 'the refusals to grant a licence [. . .] cannot in itself constitute abuse of a dominant position'.[54] But this does not exclude the possibility of compulsory licensing in 'exceptional circumstances'.[55] In *Magill*, the ECJ listed three criteria for the existence of an abuse pursuant to Article 82 EC. First, by the refusal to license his copyright the copyright owner prevented the appearance of a new product (*in casu* a comprehensive weekly TV guide for Ireland), which constituted an abuse according to Article 82(b) EC; secondly, there was no justification for such refusal; and thirdly, the copyright owners 'reserved to themselves the secondary market of weekly television guides by excluding all competition on that market . . . since they denied access to the basic information which is the raw material indispensable for the compilation of such a guide'.[56] There has been an intense discussion about the exact meaning of these criteria. Does an abuse in the sense of Article 82 EC presuppose that all three conditions are simultaneously met? Or do they stand in an alternative relationship, that is, is it sufficient that there is an artificial restraint on production or the abusive conquest of a secondary market?[57] In *IMS Health* the ECJ seems to assume that the three criteria of the *Magill* decision have to be construed as cumulative.[58] However, this interpretation of the court decision is not beyond doubt. According to the court, 'it is sufficient that three cumulative conditions be satisfied',[59] which also allows the conclusion that the simultaneous presence of the three criteria is sufficient for an abuse in the sense of Article 82 EC but not necessary.[60]

---

54 Joined Cases C-241/91 P and C-242/91 P, *RTE and ITP v. Commission* ('*Magill*'), [1995] ECR I-743, para. 49.

55 *Ibid.*, para. 50.

56 *Ibid.*, paras 54–6.

57 See for example Conde Gallego, *supra* note 29, at 16; Conde Gallego, Beatriz and Dimitris Riziotis (2004), *IIC*, 35, 571; Drexl, J. (2004), 'IMS Health and Trinko – Antitrust Placebo for Consumers instead of Sound Economics in Refusal-to-Deal Cases', *IIC*, 35, 788; Eilmansberger, T. (2005), 'How to Distinguish Good From Bad Competition Under Article 82 EC', *C.M.L. Rev.*, 42, 129; Körber, T. (2004), 'Geistiges Eigentum, essential facilities und "Innovationsmissbrauch"', *RIW*, 881; Leistner, M. (2005), 'Intellectual Property and Competition Law: The European Development from Magill to IMS Health Compared to Recent German and US Case Law', *ZWeR*, 138; Merdzo, P. (2005), 'Der Fall "IMS Health" und das Spannungsverhältnis zwischen nationalen Immaterialgüterrechten und dem europäischen Wettbewerbsrecht', *ZEuS*, 135.

58 Case C-418/01, *IMS Health*, [2004] ECR I-5039, para. 38.

59 *Ibid.*

60 In this sense Anderman, S. (2004), 'Does the *Microsoft* Case Offer a New

4.3.3 Limits to the exercise of IPRs on downstream markets A cumulative interpretation of the *Magill* criteria would constitute a farewell to leveraging theory for the whole branch of IP. Leveraging in itself could no longer be considered as an abuse. Only in combination with the prevention of a new product could the behaviour fall under Article 82 EC. Thus there would be different rules for compulsory licences and 'ordinary' refusal-to-deal cases. Such unequal treatment for tangible and intellectual property is not appropriate.[61] The dominant enterprise could control all downstream markets if it only supplied them sufficiently. As this is normally the case (the facts of *Magill* being a very untypical exception), compulsory licences would only be possible if the 'prevention of a new product' included the situation of competitors offering products of better quality.[62] Apart from such exceptions, there would be virtually no competition-law limits on the capacity of an IPR owner to conquer downstream markets.

This does not seem compatible with the actual state of European competition law on leveraging, and touches directly on the subject of contestability. Beginning with *Commercial Solvents*, European law has always started from the assumption that the leveraging of dominant positions onto other markets may constitute an abuse if the success in the neighbouring market is not based on competition on the merits.[63] Of course, the concept of 'competition on the

---

Paradigm for the "Exceptional Circumstances" Test and Compulsory Copyright Licenses under EC Competition Law?', *Comp. L. Rev.*, 1(2), 1, at 13–14. In this sense also the *Microsoft* judgment of the CFI of 17 September 2007, Case T-201/04, *Microsoft v. Commission*, [2007] ECR II-0000, para. 332 ('It also follows from that case-law that the following circumstances, in particular, must be considered to be exceptional [. . .]') and para. 336 ('In the light of the foregoing factors, the Court considers that it is appropriate, first of all, to decide whether the circumstances identified in *Magill* and *IMS Health* [. . .] are also present in this case. Only if it finds that one or more of those circumstances are absent will the Court proceed to assess the particular circumstances invoked by the Commission').

61 In favour of similar rules for all forms of property see, for instance, Leistner, *supra* note 57, at 150 *et seq.*; Ritter, C. (2005), 'Refusal to Deal and "Essential Facilities": Does Intellectual Property Require Special Deference Compared to Tangible Property?', *World Competition*, 28, 281. Drexl, Conde Gallego, Enchelmaier, Leistner and Mackenrodt, *supra* note 34, at para. 14, underline the fact that no consistent economic reason for the additional condition (prevention of a new product) has been delivered so far.

62 In this sense, see Leistner, *supra* note 57, at 152 and 160.

63 This position has been made very clear in the ECJ's *Télémarketing* decision according to which an abuse may occur 'where, without any objective necessity an undertaking holding a dominant position on a particular market reserves to itself . . . an ancillary activity which might be carried out by another undertaking as part of its activities on a neighbouring but separate market, with the possibility of eliminating all competition from such undertaking'; Case 311/84, *Télémarketing*, [1985] ECR 3261,

merits' is a vague one. But it better fits Article 82 EC to specify the abuse by taking into account all circumstances of the single case than to leave *a priori* all downstream markets to the owner of an IPR, let alone to combine two completely different forms of abuse such as leveraging and the limitation of production in the sense of Article 82 lit. b) EC.

4.3.4 Scope of reward and the concept of contestability The solution proposed here consists of defining the 'scope of reward' of a certain IP right in order to identify neighbouring markets that are not necessarily reserved to the right holder.[64] A comparison with the world of tangible property may illustrate what is meant: it is generally recognized that the owner of a train station or a harbour has (perhaps) a monopoly over services related to the use of that station or of that harbour. But she has not got the right to leverage this strategic advantage onto the market for transport services. Independent railway or shipping companies must retain the right to use this infrastructure.[65] This is tantamount to saying that the scope of reward for building a station or a harbour does not include a privileged position in transport markets.

Nothing has been put forward so far that would exclude the application of this reasoning to IPRs. It is true that one of the classical patent theories is 'reward theory', according to which the grant of an exclusive right is the reward for having made an invention.[66] But even this theory has never claimed an absolute reward shielding IPRs from the application of the general laws. Therefore, it is crucial to determine how extensively the scope of reward of an

---

para. 27. See, generally, Nothhelfer, Wolfgang (2006), *Die leverage theory im europäischen Wettbewerbsrecht*, Baden-Baden: Nomos.

64 Eilmansberger, *supra* note 26, at 17 *et seq.*, asks in this context to what extent the results of a certain effort have to be attributed to its author. See also Eilmansberger, T. (2005), 'The Essential Facilities Doctrine under Art. 82: What is the State of Affairs after IMS Health and Microsoft?', *K.C.L.J.*, 16, 329, at 341–2. Jung, P. (2004), 'Die Zwangslizenz als Instrument der Wettbewerbspolitik', *ZWeR*, 379, at 395 *et seq.*, underlines the importance of determining markets not covered by the intended scope of IP protection. Also in this sense Ghidini, Gustavo and Emanuela Arezzo (2007), 'On the Intersection of IPRs and Competition Law With Regard to Information Technology Markets', in Claus-Dieter Ehlermann and Isabela Atanasiu (eds), *European Competition Law Annual 2005*, Oxford: Hart Publishing, p. 105.

65 Unfortunately, this group of cases has become famous under the label of 'essential facilities', thus allowing a discussion as to whether IPRs may be qualified as essential facilities. If the label 'leveraging' had been chosen, it would have been possible to address the very core of the problem, namely which limits exist to extending a dominant position over other markets.

66 The other theories are the incentive theory, the disclosure theory and the natural-law theory of intellectual property. See for example Beier, Friedrich-Karl (1979), 'Die Bedeutung des Patentsystems für den technischen, wirtschaftlichen und sozialen Fortschritt', *GRUR Int.*, 227.

IPR has to be drawn. To avoid any misunderstanding: the task does not consist of determining the scope of the IPR itself and of acts that must qualify as an infringement of that right.[67] The goal is rather to determine downstream markets which – from a competition law perspective – should not be monopolized by the owner of an IP right.

The theory of contestable markets could be helpful here. The central statement of this doctrine is: the lower barriers to entry are the more acceptable monopolies are. Applied to our context, this might mean that the first criterion that has to be used to assess a dominant IPR owner's behaviour is whether barriers to entry to the IP-protected main market are increased. Does the behaviour in downstream markets have the strategic goal of protecting the primary market against competition by substitution? If so it cannot be tolerated, because the very goal of IPRs is to exclude competition by imitation in order to promote competition by innovation, including substitution.[68]

4.3.5 Further conclusions for downstream markets If a dominant firm's behaviour in a downstream market does not have the goal of strengthening its position in the primary market, the following principles should apply: if the activity in the downstream market is protected by IPRs there is in principle no obligation for the proprietor to license his right and to open up the downstream market to competitors. As has been demonstrated above,[69] the scope of reward of an IPR normally also covers downstream markets. There may be downstream markets that are so remote from the legislative rationale that the extension of the IPR towards them by a dominant enterprise may be abusive.[70] In

---

67 This is the primary question of IP law rather than of competition law. If the result is negative (no violation of IP law), competition-law problems do not arise because everybody may use the knowledge in question. However the former 'scope of the patent' or 'inherency' doctrine (which grants antitrust immunity to behaviour that does not go beyond the scope of an IPR) should not be applied any longer; see Carrier, *supra* note 16, at 788 *et seq.*; Heinemann, *supra* note 16, at 328 *et seq.*

68 Very clear in this sense is the multi-layer approach of von Weizsäcker, C.C. (1981), 'Rechte und Verhältnisse in der modernen Wirtschaftslehre', *Kyklos*, 34, 345. The importance of maintaining competition by substitution will be underlined in the context of the *Microsoft* case, section 4.5 *infra*.

69 See section 4.3.1 *supra*.

70 An example is the *Magill* case. Would the TV stations be obliged to license their copyright-protected programme listings even if they had edited a comprehensive weekly TV guide themselves? In our opinion, the scope of reward of a copyright on programme listings does not extend to the downstream market of weekly TV guides. The discussion that could arise from this statement shows that the Irish copyright was clearly defined too broadly. In this sense see, for example, Doutrelepont, C. (1994), 'Mißbräuchliche Ausübung von Urheberrechten?', *GRUR Int.*, 302 (306), Cohen Jehoram, H. and K. Mortelmans (1997), 'Zur "Magill"-Entscheidung des Europäischen Gerichtshofs', *GRUR Int.*, 11, at 12 and 15.

the first place, however, it is the task of the IP legislature to attribute certain downstream markets to the proprietor of an IPR or not. It is not the task of competition law to overrule this decision. For example, if the legislature provides for patent protection for a chemical substance itself and not only for a certain application of this substance, competition law has to accept the fact that as a consequence the patentee will control all subordinate markets for the different uses that will be developed in the future. It is true that other inventors may obtain a patent for a new use of that substance. But this 'dependent' patent cannot be exploited without the consent of the first patentee. There is no general obligation under European competition law for the owner of the first patent to permit the use of his patent. It is primarily the task of IP legislation to solve these problems.[71]

Even if a leveraging reproach is unfounded in these cases, Article 82 EC remains applicable under different aspects. The owner of an IPR is subject to the prohibition of imposing unfair prices if he is in a dominant position (Article 82 lit. a) EC). Failure to work may constitute a limitation of production in the sense of Article 82 lit. b) EC (as in the *Magill* case).[72] Dissimilar conditions to equivalent transactions are prohibited (Article 82 lit. c) EC); this applies to IPRs, too.[73] The same is true of abusive bundling (Article 82 lit. d) EC).[74] The abuse forms in lit. b) and c) especially may give rise to compulsory licences, that is restrictions on the dominant enterprise in a downstream market.

4.3.6 In particular: collective creation of IPRs It is worthwhile pointing out another group of cases (not mentioned in the 'laundry list' of Article 82

71 For the problem of dependent patents such a solution has been found in Article 31 lit. l) TRIPs, which has to be transposed into national law by all WTO members. However, it seems shocking that the compulsory licence presupposes an important technical advance 'of considerable economic significance', which is rather cynical with regard to pharmaceutical products. Is the improvement of health care not important enough even if the benefits are not 'of considerable economic significance'? See Heinemann, *supra* note 16, at 183, note 282.

72 However Article 82 lit. b) EC must be handled carefully, especially in the copyright context. If an author does not desire the cinematographic adaptation of his book, competition law has to accept his decision. This cannot be qualified as a 'limitation of production' in the sense of Article 82 lit. b) EC. Many more examples could be found.

73 This was the essence of the German *Standard Tight-Head Drum* decision; see BGH, (2004) *GRUR*, 966 = (2005) *IIC*, 36, 741 (English translation); Buhrow, A. and J. Nordemann (2005), 'Grenzen ausschließlicher Rechte geistigen Eigentums durch Kartellrecht', *GRUR Int.*, 407 (414); Conde Gallego, B., *supra* note 29, at 16; Heinemann, Andreas (2005), 'Kartellrechtliche Zwangslizenzen im Patentrecht', *ZWeR*, 198.

74 Which will be at the centre of the next chapter on non-vertical neighbouring markets.

EC) that is particularly important to the topic of abuse in downstream markets. These are the cases where the IPR in question was not created by a single entity but by several enterprises together. These may be competitors, but it is also possible that the participants come from different vertical levels. Often, this kind of cooperation aims at creating common standards allowing interoperability and a general reduction in transaction costs. In other cases, IPRs have been developed independently, but block or complement each other. Here, the goal of cooperation is the pooling of IPRs in order to resolve blocking positions.

In the first place, such cooperation is subject to Article 81 EC. Rules have been adopted concerning patent or technology pools.[75] The pooled technologies must be complementary and essential in order to avoid hidden price fixing. Pools holding a strong position in the market should be open and non-discriminatory.[76] When a dominant position exists, licences should be non-exclusive.[77] It should be added that similar rules also apply to standard setting by non-governmental standards organizations. The adoption of a standard in such an organization requires that the IPR owner declare his willingness to grant a licence to anybody.[78] This means that cooperation between owners of IPRs may be useful. But there are considerable competitive risks that require measures favouring market access, that is contestability.

In our view, these principles have to be applied in the context of Article 82 EC, too. If a standard is the result of cooperation between different enterprises from a certain branch of trade but these do not proceed to adopt an official standard including a declaration of their willingness to license to anybody, an intolerable foreclosing of downstream markets is the result. Standards for a whole sector should be developed either alone (then the scope of reward normally extends to the downstream markets) or together, but then only on the basis of openness.

---

[75] Guidelines on the application of Article 81 of the EC Treaty to technology transfer agreements, *supra* note 6, paras 210 *et seq.*; see also Ullrich, Hanns, chapter 6, in this volume.

[76] TT Guidelines, *ibid.*, paras 223 *et seq.*

[77] *Ibid.*, para. 226 ('These requirements are necessary to ensure that the pool is open and does not lead to foreclosure and other anticompetitive effects on down stream markets.').

[78] European Commission (1992), *Intellectual Property Rights and Standardization*, COM(92) 445 final, notes 2.2.3–2.2.5, 4.3.1 *et seq.* See also the Guidelines on the applicability of Article 81 of the EC Treaty to horizontal cooperation agreements, OJ 2001 No. C 3, p. 2, paras 159 *et seq.*, in particular paras 174 *et seq.* ('To the extent that private organisations or groups of companies set a standard or their proprietary technology becomes a de facto standard, then competition will be eliminated if third parties are foreclosed from access to this standard.').

These rules may be illustrated by the *IMS Health* case. If *IMS Health* had developed the 1860 brick structure alone, then it would be fair to say that the enterprise should be rewarded with an unlimited use of its copyright in the downstream market for regional sales data on pharmaceutical products. The scope of reward for the copyright-protected structure would cover precisely the use of the structure for its primary purpose.[79] However, the facts of the case are different. The 1860 brick structure was developed not only by employees of *IMS Health*, but also by collaborators of undertakings of the pharmaceutical industry. The cooperation went so far that a German court recognized joint authorship by the employees of *IMS Health* and the pharmaceutical firms involved.[80] According to the position suggested here, the sector-wide elaboration of a standard may only be practised on the basis of openness. Otherwise the participating firms could cooperate in order to foreclose downstream markets. Therefore, the *IMS Health* case should be decided in favour of access-seeking competitors.[81] It may be added that cases of joint standard setting are frequent: the leading German case (*Standard Tight-Head Drum*) may also be assigned to this group of cases.[82]

4.4 Other neighbouring markets

4.4.1 Leveraging between conglomerate markets IPRs do not only extend to vertically related markets. They have effects on other product markets too. The *Microsoft* case is best suited to illustrating this connection. Let us assume that there are different product markets for PC (client) operating systems and for applications of, for instance, internet browsers, server software or media players.[83] Although the applications are dependent on an operating system, an operating system is not an upstream market for application software. Since applications need interoperability with an operating system in order to work,

---

79 However, as in the *Magill* case (see *supra* note 70), the question could be raised whether the extension of copyright protection to methods of structuring data is a wise decision by the legislature; see Leenen, Anne-Katrin (2005), *Urheberrecht und Geschäftsmethoden*, Baden-Baden: Nomos, who answers this question in the negative.

80 Regarding the procedural difficulties of this joint authorship see Heinemann, A., *supra* note 20, at 209 *et seq.*

81 The question of whether competitors propose a 'new product' is therefore not relevant in this case; see section 4.3.3 *supra*.

82 See *supra* note 73.

83 This assumption is not unanimously shared. In the US *Microsoft* case, the Court of Appeals criticized the establishment of an independent browser market; see *United States of America v. Microsoft Corporation*, 253 F.3d 34 (D.C. Cir. 2001) = http://www.esp.org/misc/legal/USCA-DC_00-5212.pdf, accessed 4 November 2007, at 62 *et seq.*

and since the Windows operating system is ubiquitous, it is possible to impede competing software products by withholding interoperability information. Consequently, the phenomenon of leveraging is not only possible in vertically related markets but also between markets in a complementary or simply a 'conglomerate' relationship.[84]

4.4.2 The European Commission's Microsoft *decision*[85] According to the findings of the European Commission, Microsoft abused its dominant position in the market for operating systems to conquer the market for work group server operating systems, where it is now also in a dominant position.[86] As the Commission states, Microsoft did not rely on the better quality of its server software, but took measures to establish 'privileged connections between its dominant client PC operating system and its work group server operating system'.[87] This means the server software of competing companies (the main competitor on this market being Sun Microsystems) was not fully compatible with the *Windows* client operating system, so a strong incentive existed for customers to instal the server software of Microsoft. It seems that the level of interoperability previously had been much higher.[88] The Commission judged the creation of compatibility problems as a leveraging abuse, namely the extension of the dominant position in the market for client PC operating systems to the market for server operating systems.[89] At the same time, this behaviour constitutes an abuse in the sense of Article 82(b) EC, that is the limiting of a technical development to the prejudice of consumers.[90]

---

84 In the context of merger control, markets without a vertical relationship to the main market in question would constitute conglomerate mergers.

85 See, for example, Bartosch, A. (2005), 'Der Zugang zu einer wesentlichen Einrichtung', *RIW*, 241; Leupold, H. and S. Pautke (2005), 'IMS Health vs. Microsoft', *EWS*, 108; Messina, M. (2005), 'Article 82 and the New Economy: Need for Modernisation?', *Comp. L. Rev.*, 2(2), 73; Stopper, M. (2005), 'Anmerkung zu EuG – Rs. T-201/04 – (Der Microsoft-Beschluss des EuG)', *ZWeR*, 87; Vinje, T. and N. Dodoo (2005), 'Microsoft v. EC: In the European Courts', *CRi*, 97. The following remarks are based on the analysis in Heinemann, Andreas (2005), 'Compulsory Licences and Product Integration in European Competition Law – Assessment of the European Commission's *Microsoft* Decision', *IIC*, 36, 63.

86 European Commission of 24 March 2004, Case COMP/C-3/37.792 – *Microsoft*, http://europa.eu.int/comm/competition/antitrust/cases/decisions/37792/en.pdf, accessed 4 November 2007.

87 *Ibid.*, para. 1064.

88 *Ibid.*, paras 578–88.

89 *Ibid.*, paras 533 and 546–791.

90 *Ibid.*, paras 693–701. The lock-in to the Windows server operating system prevents customers benefiting from innovations by competing server software.

The second part of the decision concerns the integration of the Windows Media Player into the Windows operating system.[91] The tying of Windows and the media player (the software necessary to present audio and video content on a computer) is found to be an abuse because the ubiquitous presence of Microsoft's Media Player 'creates disincentives for OEMs to ship third party streaming media players pre-installed on their PCs, and harms competition on the market for streaming media players'.[92]

The Commission ordered Microsoft to make interoperability information available to all interested undertakings, and to allow them the use of the information 'on reasonable and non-discriminatory terms'.[93] Moreover, the enterprise was obliged to offer a fully functioning Windows version not incorporating the media player. The Commission's decision was upheld by the CFI in all aspects relevant to our subject.[94]

4.4.3 The IP aspect The IP context of this case seems to be evident: software is protected by copyright. Moreover, the *Microsoft* case has invoked certain patent rights. However, the Commission did not specify the state of the existing IPRs,[95] but put forward 'exceptional circumstances' in the sense of the *Magill* decision that would allow a compulsory licence in any case. Therefore, even if the extent of IP protection is not clear, the *Microsoft* case has to be considered as an example of the IP antitrust problem. The principles developed in the context of vertically related markets apply: the establishment of an abuse should not depend solely on the prevention of a new product. Leveraging of market power from one market to another may constitute an abuse, if the behaviour in question is not covered by the 'scope of reward' of the respective IPRs. In the context of vertically related markets, it has been

---

91 See Grimes, W. (2002), 'The Antitrust Tying Law Schism: A Critique of *Microsoft III* and a Response to Hylton and Salinger', *Antitrust L.J.*, 70, 199, 222 *et seq.*, who – in the context of US antitrust law – points out the importance of having the same rules for tying and product integration. See also Warren, G. (2005), 'Counterproductive Incentives for Innovation? – Exclusionary Conduct in the Sale of an IP Product', *IIC*, 36, 214.

92 European Commission – *Microsoft, supra* note 86, para. 1066.

93 *Ibid.*, Article 5 (annexed to the end of the decision). The obligation of disclosure aims at creating compatibility of competing server and media player software.

94 CFI, Case T-201/04, *Microsoft v. Commission*, [2007] ECR II-0000 (not yet officially published).

95 European Commission – *Microsoft, supra* note 86, para. 190 ('More generally, it is possible that ordering Microsoft to disclose such specifications and allow their use for the purposes of implementation by third parties in their products would constitute an interference with Microsoft's intellectual property rights').

said that IPRs to a large extent also cover downstream markets.[96] In the context of conglomerate markets this principle does not apply. It is rather the exception that IP protection in a certain market is intended to cover all adjacent markets. In the *Microsoft* case for example, it does not seem plausible that IP protection for the operating system should also imply the right to conquer all neighbouring markets which are dependent on smooth interoperability with the operating system. It is not the goal of IP protection of an operating system to reserve to its owner all markets that for network reasons depend on full disclosure of interface information.[97] The market for server software, for example, was created by other enterprises. Why should their prospects be destroyed only because Microsoft decides to exploit a strategic position in the market for client PC operating systems to conquer the market for server software? The least one could say is that the scope of reward of Microsoft's IP rights for the client PC operating system does not rule out an ordinary Article 82 EC application, including the leveraging abuse, which is recognized in European law.[98]

4.4.4 Contestability of conglomerate markets The space for contestability should be much greater in markets that do not stand in a vertical relationship but are just neighbouring or – in the language of merger control – conglomerate markets. It should not be legal for a dominant enterprise to use an IPR in order to subjugate markets for which the IPR was not granted, and whose vulnerability is only due to the network effect or, more generally, to the need for interoperability. The example of conglomerate markets demonstrates how wrong a cumulative interpretation of the *Magill* criteria would be: the neighbouring markets should stay contestable even if the IP owner is active in them.

On the other hand, the discussion of the legal remedies in these cases is not very advanced. Certainly, once an abuse has been established, a 'making available' obligation will be necessary, that is the disclosure of the interface information needed for interoperability. At the same time, the European Commission obliged Microsoft to offer a Windows version without the media

---

96 See section 4.3.5 *supra*.

97 As regards access to IT interfaces see von Westernhagen, Alexandra (2006), *Zugang zu geistigem Eigentum nach europäischem Kartellrecht – Eine Darstellung der rechtlichen, technischen und wirtschaftlichen Grundlagen für die Offenlegung von Softwareschnittstellen anhand des Microsoft-Verfahrens*, Baden-Baden: Nomos.

98 Another example of IP-based behaviour beyond the scope of reward is the use of an IPR to also dominate the service markets for maintenance of IP-protected products. For the difficulties in assessing other secondary markets see Conde Gallego, B., *supra* note 29, at 23 *et seq*. For US antitrust law see the analysis of the case law by Carrier, *supra* note 16, at 774 *et seq*.

player. In our view this remedy is not adequate, because it hampers technological innovation. Instead contestability should be strengthened by removing or at least lowering barriers to entry. In the case of software, this could be done for example by a 'must carry' obligation (the dominant enterprise would have to distribute the competing products together with its own) or by other measures using the network effect to competitors' advantage.[99]

4.5 The contestability of the protected main market

The observations above have tried to clarify under which conditions neighbouring markets in a vertical or conglomerate relationship should stay contestable against the backdrop of IP protection in a primary market. Let us turn to these primary markets now. The starting point is the fact that the scope of reward for an IPR of course covers the market for which the right has been primarily conferred. Therefore, the owner of that right may reserve to himself this primary market if he does not employ abusive behaviour such as for example limiting production or discrimination.[100] But even in the primary market there are limits to IP-based behaviour. The very point of IP protection is the exclusion of imitation so as to spur competition by substitution.[101] If certain behaviour aims at preventing such substitutes, it cannot therefore be justified by IP arguments. Again, the best example is the *Microsoft* case. Both in the US case, which focused on the browser question, and in the European case, concentrating on the server software and media player problems, a constant pattern of reasoning ascertained by the authorities is the strategic pertinence of these adjacent markets for the primary market of the operating system. The goal for Microsoft was not only success in neighbouring markets, but the defence of the Windows monopoly itself. It was important for Microsoft to be successful in the browser market, because one day application programs could be written on the basis of a browser, thus undermining the overwhelming importance of the Windows operating system as it exists today. Further, whoever wants to threaten the dominant position of the Windows client PC operating system will have to establish interoperability with the server operating system. Once Microsoft dominates the latter area, it will be even more difficult for competitors to attack the Windows client PC operating system. The same argument can be made with reference to media player software.[102]

---

[99] See Heinemann, *supra* note 85, at pp. 80 *et seq*. However the CFI in Case T-201/04, *Microsoft v. Commission*, [2007] ECR II-0000 (not yet officially published) confirmed the code removal order of the European Commission.

[100] In our view, an exception also applies in cases in which the IPR in question is the result of industry-wide cooperation; see section 4.3.6 *supra*.

[101] Conde Gallego, *supra* note 29, at 17 and 27.

[102] European Commission – *Microsoft*, *supra* note 86, paras 769 and 974.

The answer of the authorities is to oblige Microsoft to make interoperability information available to all interested undertakings. The goal of this measure is not only to keep neighbouring markets open, but also to not rule out from the outset that one day the dominant position of the Windows operating system might be menaced by an alternative solution.

This example shows how important it is that the IP-protected primary market also stays contestable. One cannot justify monopolies by the possibility of competition by substitution in the long run, but at the same time allow a behaviour aiming precisely at nipping such substitutes in the bud.

5 Conclusion

The theory of contestable markets is well suited to justifying IP protection and – at the same time – determining the limits imposed by competition law. The concept says that even if an IPR (exceptionally) confers market power or a dominant position, the market is competitive if barriers to entry are low, and if therefore there is at least sufficient potential competition. By looking at different market constellations, the proposition is made here to determine the appropriate extent of antitrust intervention by means of the 'scope of reward' of IPRs. Whereas the scope of reward is rather large in relation to downstream markets, it is much more restricted in conglomerate markets. The interdiction of abuse of a dominant position therefore has to be applied flexibly. It has been shown that the combination of the leveraging test with a 'limiting of production' condition (as possibly suggested by the ECJ in its *IMS Health* decision) would not be consistent with economic thinking along these lines. It is true that the leveraging theory has recently come under fire.[103] In its *Trinko* decision, the US Supreme Court was rather reserved towards the 'monopoly leveraging' concept, stipulating that leveraging 'presupposes anticompetitive conduct'.[104] The Supreme Court denied an anti-competitive refusal-to-deal situation because a standing business relationship had not been terminated, but 'something brand new' had been aimed at.[105] We think that, under the

---

[103] See, for example, Motta, Massimo (2004), *Competition Policy – Theory and Practice*, Cambridge: Cambridge University Press, pp. 362 *et seq*. On the other hand, see Nothhelfer, *supra* note 63, who defends the legitimacy of the leveraging concept.

[104] *Verizon Communications Inc. v. Law Offices of Curtis V. Trinko*, 124 S.Ct. 872 (2004). This stands in contrast to the 1992 *Kodak* decision, where the Supreme Court stated: 'The Court has held many times that power gained through some natural and legal advantage such as a patent, copyright, or business acumen can give rise to liability if "a seller exploits his dominant position in one market to expand his empire into the next"', *Eastman Kodak Co. v. Image Technical Services, Inc.*, 504 US 451, 480, note 29 (1992).

[105] For an analysis of the *Trinko* decision see Drexl, *supra* note 57; Geradin, Damien (2004), 'Limiting the Scope of Article 82 of the EC Treaty: What Can the EU

contestability test, the criterion of the termination of an existing business relationship is irrelevant. The scope of reward should settle the question of when an IPR exceptionally has to be opened up in favour of competitors. Unfortunately, the European Commission in its discussion paper on Article 82 EC[106] does not proceed to a deeper analysis of the leveraging concept, although the discussion paper is supposed to transfer the *more economic approach* to Article 82 EC.[107]

Another merit of the theory of contestable markets is its focus on real market conditions. It does not look at abstract concepts, but places barriers to entry at its centre, meaning all financial and non-financial obstacles which might hamper the mechanism of competition. The more IPRs function as barriers to entry in a particular case, the weaker is potential competition and the stronger the need for competition law. On the other hand, its application must not reduce incentives for innovation.[108] However, innovative efforts may be increased if the incumbent is exposed to competition in neighbouring markets, and if – at least in the long run – the monopoly based on network effects is menaced by substitution. This shows that it would not be adequate to point only to the dangers of an excessive application of competition law. An under-application of competition law is just as dangerous.[109] The goal should be open markets tolerating market power as long as contestability is guaranteed.

Learn from the US Supreme Court's Judgment in Trinko in the Wake of Microsoft, IMS, and Deutsche Telekom?', *C.M.L. Rev.*, 41, 1519; Leistner, *supra* note 57, at 155 *et seq.*

[106] Discussion Paper on the application of Article 82, *supra* note 41. See also the numerous comments on this paper, available at http://ec.europa.eu/comm/competition/antitrust/others/article_82_contributions.html, accessed 4 November 2007.

[107] See the critique by Heinemann, A. (2006), 'Gefährdung von Rechten des geistigen Eigentums durch Kartellrecht? Der Fall "Microsoft" und die Rechtsprechung des EuGH', *GRUR*, 705, at 712 *et seq.*

[108] See Tom, W. (1998), 'Summary', in OECD, *Competition Policy and Intellectual Property Rights*, Paris: OECD, p. 455 ('The intellectual property regime, which provides incentive for innovation to occur in the first place, must take pains to ensure that intellectual property rights are not unnecessarily broad and too all-encompassing, for excessively broad IPRs can have a dampening effect on subsequent innovation. Competition policy, which seeks to maintain competition, including the competition that spurs further innovation, must take care that its policies do not dampen the incentive for the initial innovation.'). See also Eilmansberger, *supra* note 64, at 341 *et seq.*

[109] Ritter, *supra* note 61, at 298, with reference to opposing views in note 60.

4 Assessing the effects of intellectual property rights in network standards

Mark-Oliver Mackenrodt

1 Introduction

This chapter analyses the effects of intellectual property protection on innovation in network markets. Assessing the pro-competitive and anti-competitive effects of intellectual property rights (IPRs) can provide important information for legal policy in several situations. Most importantly, an assessment of the economic effects of intellectual property rights is warranted if the optimal design of an intellectual property right is to be determined. Further, one might consider resorting to a competitive-effects analysis in the application and construction of intellectual property law in order to incorporate economic learning into decision making.[1] Finally, the pro-competitive and anti-competitive effects of intellectual property protection are determinative in the application of antitrust law to business strategies that include the use of intellectual property rights.[2]

It is the main objective of intellectual property law to create incentives for innovation. However, while they increase dynamic competition, intellectual property rights also lead to a decrease in static competition. The concepts of static competition and dynamic competition are introduced in section 2 *infra*. Competitive pressure and incentives that are provided by intellectual property law both serve to induce innovation (see section 3 *infra*). The competitive pressure as well as the effects of intellectual property rights are determined by market mechanisms. In network industries, market mechanisms exhibit specific features as compared to conventional markets (see section 4 *infra*). In network markets, intellectual property rights exhibit strategic effects, because they can be used as an instrument to introduce incompatibility into a network market. The strategic use of intellectual property rights can make protection more costly (see section 5 *infra*).

---

[1] See US FTC (2003), 'To Promote Innovation: The Proper Balance of Competition and Patent Law and Policy', http://www.ftc.gov/os/2003/10/innovationrpt.pdf, accessed 4 November 2007, Recommendation 10 at p. 17.

[2] It is, however, preferable for economic effects to be taken into account earlier, in the design of intellectual property rights, in order to avoid later conflicts.

Finally, the innovation effects of intellectual property rights in network standards are assessed by analysing the interplay between intellectual property rights and network effects. The effects of intellectual property rights are determined in terms of their effect on static competition as well as on dynamic competition. Network markets exhibit features of both dynamic and static competition. The prevailing character of the competitive process in network markets depends on whether there is a standard race or a lock-in. Accordingly, the competitive effects of intellectual property rights are analysed in two different scenarios: first, the effects during a standard race are analysed (see section 6 *infra*). Second, the effects of intellectual property rights are assessed in network markets where a lock-in has occurred after the tipping of the market (see section 7 *infra*).

2 The concepts of dynamic competition and static competition

As intellectual property rights involve a trade-off between dynamic and static competition, the economic effects of intellectual property rights are to be assessed with respect to their impact on both static and dynamic competition.

Static competition in a neo-classical sense refers to competition with regard to the parameters of price and quantity.[3] In a merely static setting the competitors basically compete on cost advantages in production in order to achieve lower prices or to expand quantity. In static neo-classical price theory the competing products are deemed to be identical. Consumers derive the same utility from the products of competing manufacturers and choose the manufacturer only on the basis of prices. This assumption implies that competitors are free to imitate each other and that the features of the products are not protected by intellectual property rights.[4] Therefore static competition takes the form of competition by imitation.[5] If network products of competing manufacturers adhere to the same network standard, there is static intra-network competition with regard to the network standard.

Static competition leads to static efficiency, which is also referred to as

[3] An overview of neo-classical price theory can be found in Hovenkamp, Herbert (2005), *Federal Antitrust Policy*, St Paul, MN: Thompson West, § 1; Gellhorn, Ernest, William Kovacic and Steven Calkins (2004), *Antitrust Law and Economics*, St Paul, MN: West Group, chapter III.

[4] However, methods in the production of the product might be protected by patents. A superior method of production leads to a cost advantage. A patent might render this cost advantage more durable.

[5] Competition by substitution and competition by imitation as analytical tools are discussed by Drexl, Josef (2004), 'IMS-Health and Trinko – Antitrust Placebo for Consumers Instead of Sound Economics in Refusal-to-Deal Cases', *IIC*, **35**, 788, at 790.

allocative[6] or productive[7] efficiency. Productive efficiency means that a firm that is under competitive pressure tends to operate at lower costs. Allocative efficiency refers to the allocation of scarce resources in such a way that they will generate the highest utility. Allocative efficiency is achieved through the price mechanism, with prices reflecting consumer preferences.

By contrast, dynamic competition takes place through the introduction of superior products and through improvements in quality.[8] With dynamic competition the competing products differ in quality or in product features that provide consumers with different degrees of utility. The specific features of competing products will often be protected by intellectual property rights. As the competing products are alternative means to achieve the same purpose,[9] dynamic competition can also be referred to as competition by substitution. In network markets, competition between networks (inter-network competition) takes the form of dynamic competition.

Dynamic competition leads to dynamic efficiency. Dynamic efficiency refers to the rate of introduction of new products into a market.[10] The consumer benefit from dynamic competition consists in the higher utility that consumers attribute to the new products. The impact of dynamic competition on overall welfare[11] is often considered to be considerably higher than the consumer benefit from lower prices due to intense static competition.[12]

---

6 For a definition of allocative efficiency see for example Motta, Massimo (2004), *Competition Policy*, New York, NY: Cambridge University Press, at p. 40; Drexl, *supra* note 5, at 804.

7 For a definition of productive efficiency see for example Motta, *supra* note 6, at 46.

8 See for example Hovenkamp, *supra* note 3, § 5.2; Motta, *supra* note 6, at 39.

9 Of course, new products might also create a completely new demand without fully replacing older technologies. For example communication by e-mail did not completely replace communication by fixed telephone lines. As consumer preferences differ, a new product or a new product feature will often not completely render older products worthless or make them disappear from the market.

10 Motta, *supra* note 6, at 55. Tirole, Jean (1988), *Industrial Economics*, Cambridge, MA: MIT Press, chapter 10, points out that process innovation can be dealt with as a subgroup of product innovation.

11 For different concepts of welfare see for example Motta, *supra* note 6, at 18–21.

12 Tirole, *supra* note 10, chapter 10, and Peritz, Rudolph (2001), 'Dynamic Efficiency and US Antitrust Policy', in Antonio Cucinotta, Roberto Pardolesi and Roger van den Bergh (eds), *Post-Chicago Developments in Antitrust Law*, Cheltenham, UK and Northampton, MA, US: Edward Elgar, p. 108, at 116, stress the overall importance of innovations in an economy. With regard to patent policy, Hovenkamp, *supra* note 3, § 5.2, points out that with a well-devised patent policy the welfare gains from an innovation outweigh the welfare losses that result from a decrease in price competition.

Concepts of dynamic competition are highly complex.[13] In particular formal economic modelling proves difficult. An important line of theories dates back to the economist Joseph Schumpeter. Dynamic competition in Schumpeter's sense refers to markets in which quality and product improvements are the main factors in the competitive process, rather than price and quantity.[14] Conditions for Schumpeterian competition can best be found in high-technology markets. However, the competitive process can rarely be characterized as merely static or merely dynamic. Very often both elements will be present in a market depending on the length of a product cycle.

3 Incentives and competitive pressure as instruments to induce innovation

To evaluate the effects of intellectual property rights on innovation, it is important to note that there are two main mechanisms to induce innovation, the creation of incentives and the creation of competitive pressure.

Intellectual property rights seek to generate an incentive for innovation by influencing the competitive process. In particular, intellectual property rights reduce static competition in order to instigate dynamic competition (section 3.1 *infra*). An optimally designed IP system leaves room for competitive pressure to reinforce dynamic competition. At the same time, antitrust law seeks to keep up the competitive pressure in a market in order to induce both dynamic competition and static competition (section 3.2 *infra*). Conflicts between the two bodies of law may arise where – exceptionally – intellectual property rights lead to a distortion of dynamic competition or to a loss in static competition that does not correspond to a gain in dynamic competition.

However, the modern view regards the two bodies of law as not being in fundamental conflict, but rather as being complementary.[15] This view correctly

---

[13] A discussion of different concepts of dynamic competition is provided by Ellig, Jerry and Daniel Lin (2001), 'A Taxonomy of Dynamic Competition Theories', in Jerry Ellig (ed.), *Dynamic Competition and Public Policy*, New York, NY: Cambridge University Press, at pp. 16–44.

[14] See Schumpeter, Joseph (1950), *Capitalism, Socialism and Democracy*, reprint 1976, New York, N.Y.: Harper Perennial, at pp. 81, 87; Schumpeter uses the term 'creative destruction'.

[15] Heinemann, Andreas (2002), *Immaterialgueterschutz in der Wettbewerbsordnung*, Tübingen: Mohr Siebeck, at pp. 25, 26; Drexl, Josef, Beatriz Conde Gallego, Stefan Enchelmaier, Markus Feil and Mark-Oliver Mackenrodt (2004), 'Comments on the Draft Technology Transfer Block Exemption Regulation', *IIC*, **35**, 187, at 188; Drexl, *supra* note 5, at 798; Drexl, Josef, Beatriz Conde Gallego, Stefan Enchelmaier, Matthias Leistner and Mark-Oliver Mackenrodt (2006), 'Comments of the Max Planck Institute for Intellectual Property, Competition and Tax Law on the Directorate-General Competition Discussion Paper of December 2005 on the Application of Art. 82 of the EC Treaty to Exclusionary Abuses', *IIC*, **37**, 558, at 560 *et seq.*

emphasizes that antitrust and intellectual property law share the common economic goal of promoting innovation and dynamic efficiency. The European Technology Transfer (TT) Guidelines[16] as well as the US IP Antitrust Guidelines[17] are expressly based on the concept of complementarity. Therefore, an assessment of the effects of intellectual property rights has to consider the interplay of the intellectual property right with market mechanisms. Even though antitrust law and intellectual property are complementary, they differ in the means through which they seek to foster dynamic competition.

3.1 Incentives for innovation and intellectual property law

Intellectual property law relies on exclusion to promote dynamic efficiency. IPRs exclude static competition by imitation in order to provide an incentive for innovative activity and to stimulate dynamic competition by substitution.[18] Intellectual property rights create the prospect of appropriating the results of investment in research and development. However, this comes at the price of productive inefficiency. Accordingly, intellectual property protection involves a trade-off between a reduction in static competition and the intended promotion of dynamic competition. In many cases the gain in consumer welfare through the introduction of new products as a consequence of more intense dynamic competition will be considerably higher than the welfare loss caused by a decrease in static price competition.[19]

Because IPRs change the competitive pressure in the market, there is an interweaving between intellectual property rights on the one hand and market mechanisms and the competitive process on the other hand: IPRs do not through their own merits lead to innovation. They rather constitute an instrument within the competitive process of the market and turn innovations into economic goods.[20] It is the working of the competitive process that creates the prospect of appropriating supra-competitive gains in the market if an innova-

---

16 Commission Notice – Guidelines on the Application of Article 81 of the EC Treaty to Technology Transfer Agreements, OJ 2004 No. C 101, p. 2, at para. 7.

17 Antitrust Guidelines for the Licensing of Intellectual Property, Issued by the US Department of Justice and the Federal Trade Commission, 6 April 1995, http://www.usdoj.gov/atr/public/guidelines/0558.htm, accessed 4 November 2006, Section 1.0.

18 See for example Motta, *supra* note 6, at 57; Farrell, Joseph and Michael Katz (1998), 'The Effects of Antitrust and Intellectual Property Law on Compatibility and Innovation', *Antitrust Bull.*, **43**, 609, at 612.

19 Hovenkamp, *supra* note 3, at § 5.2.

20 For a deeper discussion see Ullrich, Hanns and Andreas Heinemann (2007), 'Die Anwendung der Wettbewerbsregeln auf die Verwertung von Schutzrechten und sonstigen Kenntnissen', in Ulrich Immenga and Ernst-Joachim Mestmäcker (eds), *Wettbewerbsrecht, EG/Teil 2*, 4th ed., Munich: C.H. Beck, p. 119, paras 21–3.

tion is protected by intellectual property rights. The return on the innovation is determined by the market, not by the intellectual property right itself. Intellectual property rights unfold their effects only in interaction with a market. By excluding static competition by imitation, intellectual property rights do not necessarily lead to an economic monopoly. Rather, the economic effect and the returns from an intellectual property right are determined by the particular market mechanisms. Accordingly, the European Court of Justice ruled in its *Magill* decision in 1995 that an intellectual property right does not in itself create a dominant position.[21] Quite similarly the US Supreme Court stated in its decision *Independent Ink* that patents do not create a presumption of market power.[22] In a market where it is difficult to invent around the patent, a patent will lead to considerable market power and yield high returns. By contrast, a patent will lead to lower returns and to only little market power if a technology can easily be replaced by an alternative technology. Accordingly, intellectual property rights do not award a fixed reward to innovators. Rather, the patent system assumes that the return that can be realized in a particular market reflects the value of the innovation to society.

As a question of legal policy other mechanisms such as trade secrecy or a reward system could serve to provide an incentive for innovation.

For example enterprises could simply keep their inventions secret in order to prevent imitation and to extract higher profits from the market.[23] However, secrecy would entail several welfare losses to society as compared to a patent system: patents allow for a more effective societal division of labour as they can be licensed by the most efficient innovator to the most efficient producer. An innovator will not in all cases have at his disposal the production facilities to exploit his patents effectively, but with an innovation only being protected by secrecy, innovators will be reluctant to pass on their knowledge to a more efficient producer. Further, patent protection requires the disclosure of an innovation in order to receive protection. Patent disclosure and licensing lead to wider diffusion of innovations in a society and allow for follow-on innovations by third parties. Unlike trade secrecy, which is theoretically infinite in duration, an innovation that is protected by a patent is up for free use once the patent term has expired.

---

21 Joined Cases C-241 and 242/91P, *RTE and ITP v. Commission* ('*Magill*'), [1995] ECR I-743, para. 47.

22 *Illinois Tools Works et al. v. Independent Ink*, 126 S.Ct. 1281 (2006); see also Drexl, *supra* note 5, at 798.

23 Landes, William M. and Richard Posner (2003), *The Economic Structure of Intellectual Property Law*, Cambridge, MA: Harvard University Press, at pp. 326 and 330.

As a further alternative to patent protection there could be a reward system in which inventors are directly compensated for their invention, which then is free for use by everybody.[24] Such a system would avoid the welfare loss that transpires from the exclusion of static competition. However, compensating the innovator directly would require an evaluation of the societal welfare effect of an innovation. Such an appraisal is burdened with considerable practical problems. It is up to the market, rather than an agency, to determine the value of a new product. A patent system, by granting exclusivity for a limited time, leaves it to the market to reward the innovator.

In sum, intellectual property rights are designed to influence the competitive process in order to promote dynamic competition. The optimal degree of intellectual property protection depends on the difficulty of inventing around the intellectual property right[25] or in other words on the particular market. To determine the optimal trade-off between dynamic and static competition it remains to be analysed how IPRs interact with the specific market mechanisms in network markets to achieve dynamic efficiency. It is important to point out that in some cases an intellectual property right might be used to hinder innovation or to manipulate the path of innovation.[26] If a particular intellectual property right provides an incentive for such a strategy, the resulting dynamic inefficiency has to be included in the trade-off.

3.2 The competitive pressure for innovation and antitrust law

Antitrust, by contrast, relies on competitive pressure to spur innovative activity.[27] The competitive pressure, in turn, depends on the particular market mechanisms involved.

A monopolist has only limited incentive to bring new or improved products to the market.[28] As long as his dominant market position is unchallenged he reaps supra-competitive profits. If the monopolist introduced a superior product into the market the profits from this product would cannibalize his monopoly rent.[29] As a rule, a monopoly is therefore dynamically inefficient. For example a monopolist for internet services via cable has little incentive to invest in fast internet services through telephone lines. Gains from users who

---

24 See for example Tirole, *supra* note 10, chapter 10.4.

25 Landes and Posner, *supra* note 23, at 300.

26 Menell, Peter (1998), 'An Epitaph for Traditional Copyright Protection of Network Features of Computer Software', *Antitrust Bull.*, **43**, 651, at 673.

27 See for example Heinemann, *supra* note 15, at 27; Hovenkamp, *supra* note 3, at § 5.2.

28 Tirole, *supra* note 10, at section 10.1.3; Motta, *supra* note 6, at 55 *et seq.*

29 Cabral, Luis (2000), *Introduction to Industrial Organization*, Cambridge, MA: MIT Press, at p. 294.

switch away from the cable service would only eat up the monopolist's profits from internet services via cable. By contrast, a company that does not own a cable network has a higher incentive to invest in internet services via telephone lines, as this investment would serve to conquer a new market.

However, the incentive for a monopolist to engage in innovative activity rises if he is under a competitive threat from firms that might enter the market through an innovation.[30] If a competitor succeeded in establishing an innovation in the market, the incumbent monopolist would lose his monopoly rent. Therefore, for fear of losing his monopoly rent, the incumbent monopolist has an incentive to be the first to make an innovation in order to keep competitors off the fences. As a rule, the outlook of gaining supra-competitive profits in a market attracts competitors to enter the market through an innovation. Nonetheless, if barriers to entry make the establishment of new innovations difficult, an incumbent monopolist has only a low incentive to innovate. The incentive of a market outsider to innovate is considerably higher than that of an incumbent with regards to drastic innovations.[31] A drastic innovation is one that renders the existing product obsolete. In network markets a drastic innovation is one that leads to the establishment of a new network standard.

In sum, antitrust law seeks not only to promote static competition but at the same time to induce innovations by keeping up the innovative pressure in a market. The competitive pressure depends on market mechanisms.

4 The specific market mechanisms in network markets

The term 'network effects' refers to a particular set of market mechanisms. In the presence of network effects market mechanisms exhibit specific economic features not found in conventional markets.[32] Market mechanisms determine both the competitive pressure in a market and the trade-off that is involved in IPRs. Accordingly, the particular market mechanisms in network markets are essential for assessing the effects of IPRs in network standards.

4.1 The rising demand curve in network markets

The microeconomic concept of network effects owes its name to the classical network industries such as telephone networks, in which network effects were

---

30 See for example Motta, *supra* note 6, at 60.

31 Cabral, *supra* note 29, at 298.

32 The economic theory of network effects is based on the writings of Katz, M. and C. Shapiro (1985), 'Network Externalities, Competition, and Compatibility', *Am. Econ. Rev.*, **75**, 424; Katz, M. and C. Shapiro (1994), 'Systems Competition and Network Effects', *J. Econ. Persp.*, **8**, 93; Economides, N. (1996), 'The Economics of Networks', *IJIO*, **14**, 673; Arthur, W.B. (1989), 'Competing Technologies, Increasing Returns, and Lock-in by Historical Events', *Econ. J.*, **99**, 116.

first analysed. Network effects occur if the value of a product to consumers increases with more consumers using this product or a complementary product.

Physical networks, such as for example telephone networks, exhibit direct network effects. The utility of a network product is higher if more users are connected in a network by using the same network standard. For example, a telephone network becomes more valuable if there are more users, because in a larger network a higher number of connections can be realized. Indirect network effects are generated in virtual networks, where the value of a network good rises if more customers use a product that is complementary to the network good. In such virtual networks users are not connected physically. Rather, the two complementary products are connected through their adherence to the same network standard. For example, a digital rights management system (DRM system) that is embodied in a certain player software can be interpreted as connecting the providers and the consumers of digital content. Between the consumers of digital content and the providers of digital content indirect network effects are generated. The more media content is accessible for consumers through a certain DRM-technology standard, the more consumers will use this technology. At the same time, if a certain DRM technology is used by more consumers, more content providers will offer their content as being accessible with this technology. Likewise, computer operating systems have been interpreted as virtual networks that generate indirect network effects: the more customers use a certain operating software, the more software applications are programmed for this operating system. In turn, more consumers will be attracted to an operating system if a high amount of application software is available for that standard.

As a consequence, the demand curve in network markets exhibits particular features as compared to conventional markets. In conventional markets, the demand curve is basically downward sloping because the willingness of consumers to pay decreases as the market gets saturated with a high quantity of a product. By contrast, in network markets the demand curve is initially upward sloping because the value of a network to consumers – and the willingness of consumers to pay – rises as the network grows. A network that is growing will attract even more consumers because higher network effects are generated.

4.2 Technology adoption in network markets

For assessing the effects of IPRs it is important to note that the adoption of a technology in network markets exhibits two specific features.

First, network markets are prone to tipping in favour of a single network technology once a critical mass of customers has been built up for a particular standard. If a network enterprise attracts an additional customer it wins twice over: not only does it gain an extra profit from the new customer, but at the same time the network technology standard grows in value as network effects rise. In turn the network will attract even more customers. At the same time, a network technology that loses a customer becomes less attractive to the remaining customers because the network effects decrease. Consequently, more consumers will be induced to switch to a network that offers greater network effects. At some point this effect adds up to a sudden change in market shares in favour of the winning network standard. Once a network technology has reached critical mass, the whole market tips in favour of a single standard and competing network technologies have to exit the market. Only a few competing networks can survive through product differentiation, but they will only conquer a minor share of the market. Consequently, in a market equilibrium under incompatibility a single network standard nearly dominates the whole market and reaps the major part of profits in the market. The market share and the profits of the second-largest network enterprise will be considerably smaller. Network markets are therefore characterized as winner-takes-most markets.

Second, once a network market has tipped in favour of a technology standard the market structure becomes durable. Consumers are locked in to the network standard and network effects constitute barriers to entry for new technologies.[33]

5 The strategic effects of intellectual property rights in network markets

In network markets, intellectual property rights exhibit particularly strong strategic effects because they can be used as a tactical instrument to create and enforce incompatibility or to introduce compatibility by opening or closing a network standard.[34]

Compatibility means that network goods that are based on the same standard need not be produced by the same firm. With direct network effects, compatibility means that users of a network good can connect to users of a similar network good that is produced by a competitor. For example, if two telephone networks are incompatible, telephone calls are only possible within each network and not between competing networks. With indirect network effects, compatibility means that a network good can be combined with a complementary network good that is produced by a competing firm. For example, an operating system that only supports application software that is produced by the same firm constitutes an incompatible virtual network. However, an operating system is more valuable to consumers if it is compatible with a wide variety of

---

33 See section 7.1.1 *infra*.

34 Farrell and Katz, *supra* note 18, at 612.

application software. Consumer welfare in terms of network effects is highest if there is compatibility between network goods. Compatibility through standardization leads to a maximization of network effects.

If a network standard is protected by intellectual property rights the right owner can deny competitors access to the network standard.[35] By creating incompatibility through intellectual property rights, firms can use their customer base as a strategic factor. Under compatibility, all competing networks that are based on this network standard equally benefit from the network effects and the overall network effects are highest. By contrast, with incompatibility, each single network profits only from those network effects that are created by its own customer base. With incompatibility the network market is prone to tip in favour of the single network enterprise that first attains a critical mass of customers, while competing networks will have to exit the market.

The strategic choice between compatibility and incompatibility depends on the firm's expectations about the success of its own market penetration: a network enterprise will choose incompatibility if it expects to be the first to conquer a critical mass of customers. With the market tipping in its favour, the network enterprise will reap the profits of the whole market while competitors have to exit the market. In this case the network enterprise has used network effects as a strategic instrument. By contrast, a network enterprise will choose compatibility if it fears that the market will tip in favour of a competitor because the competitor will reach a critical mass first or because competing networks are introducing compatibility between their networks in order to tip the market in their favour. In general, network enterprises will tend to have an open standard in the early stage of a network product in order to rapidly build up critical mass. Once critical mass has been achieved and customers are locked in to a network standard, a network enterprise has an incentive to enforce its intellectual property right in order to exclude competing producers of network goods from the network effects and in order to realize high profits from customers who are reluctant to switch away.

Using network effects as a strategic factor though introducing incompatibility takes a multitude of shapes.[36] For example, the decision to enforce or not

---

[35] It should be noted, however, that intellectual property rights are not the only means to introduce incompatibility into a network market. As an alternative, a network standard could be protected through secrecy.

[36] The particular strategic effects of intellectual property rights are only sketched out here. For an overview of the interplay of network effects and antitrust see for example Economides, *supra* note 32; Lemley, M. and D. McGowan (1998), 'Legal Implications of Network Economic Effects', *Cal. L. Rev.*, **86**, 479, at 537; Economides, N. and L. White (1994), 'Networks and Compatibility: Implications for Antitrust', *Am. Econ. Rev.*, **38**, 651.

to enforce an intellectual property right is informed by particular strategic considerations if network effects are present: as long as a network enterprise seeks to rapidly build up a critical customer base, a network enterprise has an incentive not to enforce its intellectual property rights.[37] By contrast, once a network market has tipped in favour of a right owner, she has an incentive to enforce her rights and to charge higher prices if consumers are now locked in to her particular network standard.

A network enterprise that participates in a standardization process has an incentive to conceal its IPRs in a proposed network standard. A multi-sided standardization process serves to end a standard war. Once the standardization organization has made a certain technology the market-wide standard, a right holder has an incentive to enforce her IPR because through the standardization the market has tipped in her favour. The market power conveyed by the IPR is considerably higher after the standardization then before the standardization. The difference between *ex ante* market power and *ex post* market power indicates that the power of the IPRs in network markets is due not merely to an innovative lead but also to the particular market mechanisms.

With indirect network effects, the owner of a virtual network has an incentive to have an open network standard in order to attract a critical mass of customers for the network product as well as for the complementary product. Once the virtual network standard has attracted a critical mass of customers in one of the product groups, he has an incentive to close the standard. With a closed standard, only the complementary products that have been produced by the owner himself profit from the network effects that have been built up. Such a strategy could be implemented through a tie[38] between two complementary products that is enforced through an intellectual property right in the interface. If there are high network effects for one of the products, customers who want to profit from these network effects will have to buy the complementary product by the same producer. For example if there are high network effects for a certain operating software, the standard owner can close the software interface for application software that is produced by competitors.

The strategic use of intellectual property rights influences static competition because the exclusion of competitors leads to higher prices. A greater

---

[37] See for example Blackburn, D. (2006), 'Network Externalities and Copyright Enforcement', Working Paper, Harvard University, http://www.davidjhblackburn.com/papers/externalities.pdf, accessed 4 November 2006; Takeyama, Lisa (1994), 'The Welfare Implications of Unauthorized Reproduction of Intellectual Property in the Presence of Demand Network Externalities', *J. Ind. Econ.*, **42**, 155.

[38] An economic model for tying in the presence of network effects is provided by Carlton, D. and M. Waldman (2002), 'The Strategic Use of Tying to Preserve and Create Market Power in Evolving Industries', *RAND J. Econ.*, **33**, 194.

reduction of static competition means that intellectual property protection is more costly. At the same time, strategic use of intellectual property rights influences dynamic competition. Enterprises are discouraged from engaging in research and development if their chances to succeed in a market are lower due to frequent anti-competitive behaviour.[39] With fewer competitors in the market there will be fewer sources of innovation.

However, it is a difficult task to anticipate all possible abuses when one is designing intellectual property rights. Business strategies that are implemented through IPRs may also have pro-competitive effects in network markets. Denying intellectual property protection from the outset just because some strategies are pernicious would amount to a per se interdiction of all strategies that are implemented through the use of intellectual property laws. Given the wide range of different competition strategies in network markets, it seems unfeasible to address the various strategies by a single, clear-cut policy decision within intellectual property law. Rather, the strategic use of IPRs in network markets will in most cases be addressed more appropriately by the application of the antitrust laws.[40] Antitrust law is more flexible and less formalistic than intellectual property law and can therefore better respond to changes in market behaviour. As a consequence of the strategic role of IPRs in network markets, conflicts between antitrust law and intellectual property law will be more frequent in network industries than in conventional markets. Nonetheless, the legislators should refrain from granting rights that clearly invite pernicious strategies. Therefore, the fact that intellectual property rights create a particularly high potential for conflicts should serve to caution against the creation of too strong intellectual property rights that later only have to be cut back by antitrust law.

6 Effects on innovation during a standard race

The effects of intellectual property rights on innovation in network markets are determined by the interplay between network effects and intellectual property rights. Intellectual property protection for network standards is desirable if this leads to an increase in dynamic competition and to only a small decrease in static competition. A positive trade-off between dynamic and static competition would be an argument for protecting network standards through intellectual property rights. By contrast, if the trade-off is more ambiguous weaker protection is warranted.

---

[39] Menell, *supra* note 26, at 674 points to the possible negative impact on dynamic competition.

[40] An overview of antitrust issues in network markets is provided by Economides and White, *supra* note 36.

During a standard race, the competitive process exhibits strong dynamic elements that are reinforced if intellectual property rights are present, so that even a dynamically inefficient standard race might occur (section 6.1 *infra*). At the same time static competition is of minor importance (section 6.2 *infra*).

A standard race means that the firms compete to be the first to establish their standard in the market. In network markets a standard race can occur if no prior network standard has been established in the market. Further, in some network markets even after the market has tipped the next innovator can easily make the market tip in favour of a superior network standard. In such a market, a new standard race occurs right after the tipping of the market. During a standard race there is by definition incompatibility between competing network standards. If compatibility were introduced the standard race would end and there would only be a single standard and static competition within the standard.

6.1 Strong dynamic competition as a standard race

During a standard race there is fierce dynamic competition between network enterprises to be the first to establish its own network standard in the market.

Even if no IPRs are involved, the incentive first to establish an innovative standard is higher in network markets than in conventional markets for two reasons. First, under incompatibility the market equilibrium in network markets is characterized by a single firm reaping the profits of nearly the whole market. Contrary to most conventional markets, network markets are winner-takes-most markets.[41] At the same time, firms who do not gain a critical mass will have to exit the market and will completely lose their sunk-cost investment. Consequently, the competitive pressure to engage in dynamic competition is higher in network markets than in conventional markets. In markets where there is a lock-in after the termination of the standard race, the competitive pressure is even higher because the resulting market position is more durable. Intellectual property protection for network standards reinforces the lock-in and creates an even higher incentive for innovation.

However, the high incentive to win the standard race in a network market can lead to dynamic inefficiency because it provides network companies with an incentive to over-invest: in a network market, only the first innovator has the prospect of recouping its investment in research and development while the second-placed innovator is likely to lose its entire investment. By contrast, in conventional markets the market shares of several companies that are not in first place are often large enough for several companies to recoup their investments and to be rewarded for their contribution to developing a new product.

---

[41] Kwoka, John and Lawrence White (2004), *The Antitrust Revolution*, 4th ed., Oxford: Oxford University Press, at p. 419.

Network companies, consequently, tend to engage in costly standard wars. In network markets even a slight and temporary competitive advantage might suffice to make the whole market tip and translate into a long-lasting advantage. Network companies will engage in substantial investments in order to overtake their competitors and are tempted to exaggerate their market prospects to capital markets and consumers because consumer expectations determine the value of the network.[42] In network markets, companies have a stronger incentive to engage in inefficient duplicative investments than in conventional markets. In the end, the overall sum of the investments made by all network companies might be higher than the value of the innovation to society. At the same time consumers who have chosen a network standard that had to exit the market get stranded with their sunk investment in network equipment.

Even absent network effects, patent protection by its own virtue may result in an inefficient patent race.[43] A patent provides the prospect of reward only to the first innovator who is actually awarded the patent.[44] An innovator who is in second place loses her investment in research and development. Consequently, once innovative efforts are close to delivering patentable results, firms have an incentive to boost their investment to an amount even higher than the expected return of the patent because they fear losing their sunk costs if they are only second at the patent office.

If IPRs are available for network standards the concerns about a dynamically inefficient standard race are aggravated through the interplay of network effects and IPRs. Intellectual property rights in standards further amplify the

---

42 Certain aspects of the dot-com crisis around the turn of the millennium have been explained by the specific market mechanisms in network markets. Expectations of the financial markets and of consumers were overblown and a large number of network companies failed. At the same time those network companies that were first placed in their segments were extraordinarily successful.

43 See for example Landes and Posner, *supra* note 23, at 301; for an economic model for patent races see for example Tirole, *supra* note 10, chapter 10.22.

44 It is reported that Elisha Grey (1835–1901) filed a patent application for a telephone on 14 February, 1867, only a few hours after Alexander Graham Bell. The US Patent Office awarded Bell the first patent for a telephone. Alexander Graham Bell founded the Bell Telephone Company, which was later named AT&T. AT&T enjoyed a lengthy monopoly in the US telephone market and was broken up by the US antitrust authorities in 1982, more than a hundred years after the award of the patent for telephones. The outstanding market position of AT&T even after the expiration of the patent can be explained by network effects in the telephone industry. For an analysis of the AT&T case see for example Noll, Roger and Bruce Owen (1994), 'The Anticompetitive Uses of Regulation: United States v AT&T (1982)', in John Kwoka and Lawrence White (eds), *The Antitrust Revolution*, 2nd ed., Oxford: Oxford University Press, at p. 328.

incentive to first establish a network standard in a market and then intensify dynamic competition. With intellectual property rights at hand, network enterprises can more easily enforce incompatibility after the tipping of the market and thereby make their market position more durable and more profitable. The prospect of windfall profits leads to inefficient patent races.[45] If the incentive provided by an intellectual property right is optimal in a market without network effects, the incentive is likely excessive if network effects are present.[46]

6.2 The low concern for static competition during a standard race

During a standard race, static competition is of minor importance. There is little strategic rationality in raising prices or restricting quantity at this stage of a network market. On the contrary, in order to rapidly establish an installed base of consumers, network companies will prefer to lower prices and expand output so as to reach a higher number of customers. Any advantage through supra-competitive prices will soon be lost once a network market has tipped in favour of a competing standard that gained its critical mass through a low-price strategy.[47]

Accordingly, intellectual property rights do little harm to static competition during a standard race. Further, a network enterprise has an incentive not to enforce an intellectual property right in a network standard while there is a standard race. Allowing copying leads to a quicker dissemination of the network standard and enlarges the enterprise's customer base.

6.3 Conclusion on competitive effects during a standard race

In sum, during a standard race the competitive pressure in network markets leads to intense dynamic competition. In this stage, an additional incentive to innovate through an intellectual property rights protection for network standards might be dispensable. Rather, intellectual property protection for network standards might aggravate concern over an inefficient standard race.

At the same time, during a standard race, there is little concern that intellectual property rights might lead to a decrease in static competition, as competitive pressure prevents supra-competitive prices and quantity restrictions.

---

45 Landes and Posner, *supra* note 23, at 300.

46 Farrell and Katz, *supra* note 18, at 638.

47 In the video standard war between VHS and Beta, the Beta standard was considered technologically superior in its implementation and was promoted by a high-price strategy. By contrast, VHS, by pursuing a low-price strategy, rapidly built up a critical mass of customers and permanently established its standard in the market while the Beta standard nearly disappeared.

7 Effects on innovation during a lock-in

A lock-in occurs if a standard race is terminated and network effects constitute a barrier to the establishment of a new technology in the market. A standard race is terminated through the market-wide establishment of a single network standard.

During a lock-in, the incentive for innovation as well as the competitive pressure depends on whether there is compatibility or incompatibility in the market. There is usually incompatibility in the market if a standard race ends with the tipping of the network market.[48] This means that only a single network firm is active within the standard. Incompatibility is very often enforced through IPRs in the standard. By contrast, it is more probable that competitors can unilaterally introduce compatibility into the market if a standard is not protected by IPRs.[49] Accordingly, in this section the competitive process under incompatibility is used as a reference scenario for assessing the effects of IPRs in network standards during a lock-in.

By contrast, compatibility prevails if the standard race is terminated through a multilateral standardization procedure. In this case, no participant in the standardization procedure is excluded from the network market by an intellectual property right in the standard.[50] Further, compatibility is the market equilibrium if a network company that introduces incompatibility has to fear that the market will tip in favour of its competitors who support compatibility. For example, there is compatibility between competing e-mail networks. An e-mail system that allowed its users to communicate only with other users of the same e-mail system would be less attractive and would probably have to exit the market.

During a lock-in, dynamic competition is weak because the establishment of a new innovation is more difficult than when network effects are absent. Intellectual property rights in the network standard aggravate this difficulty (section 7.1 *infra*). Static competition becomes more important. However, intellectual property rights in network standards result in a greater decrease in static competition than would occur in conventional markets (section 7.2 *infra*).

---

48 The strategic decision of a network company to introduce compatibility depends on its prospects of winning the standard race on its own and on the compatibility decisions of its competitors.

49 Farrell and Katz, *supra* note 18, at 613.

50 The participants in a standardization process usually sign agreements on the licensing of intellectual property rights that might exist in a prospective standard. As a consequence, such an IPR is not used to exclude participants from using the standard. The participants might however have to pay a reasonable licensing fee for using the standard.

7.1 Dynamic competition during a lock-in

During a lock-in, dynamic competition with regard to the network standard is weak (section 7.1.1 *infra*). With regard to innovations that do not change the network standard, IPRs in the standard lead to complete exclusion of dynamic competition (section 7.1.2 *infra*).

7.1.1 The weak competitive pressure to improve the network standard during a lock-in If a network technology is already established in the market, the competitive pressure for innovations in the standard is lower than in conventional markets because consumers are locked in to the incumbent technology.

If a consumer switches away from a large established network to a smaller network he gives up higher network effects and thereby incurs switching costs. Also, many network technologies require a considerable upfront investment in the technology, for example in a particular hardware. These investments are sunk costs, because a consumer who leaves a network does not recover prior investments. Sunk costs further raise the switching costs. The lock-in is aggravated by a collective action dilemma when it comes to switching to a superior technology: for the entirety of consumers it is socially desirable for a superior network technology to become established in the market. However, it is rational for an individual consumer who is averse to risk not to be the first to switch to the new network standard. An early switcher initially loses network effects and has to bear the risk that the new technology will fail to achieve a critical mass of customers. In this case the new network technology will have to exit the market, and an early switcher become stranded with his investments in that technology. Consequently, an individual consumer will be reluctant to switch away from an incumbent network until the new technology has achieved a critical mass and until the market is close to tipping.

As a result, network effects constitute a significant barrier to entry even for technologically superior market entrants. If consumers are locked in to a network standard that is inferior there is considerable dynamic inefficiency.[51] For an innovation to replace the incumbent network standard it is not sufficient for the innovation simply to provide a slightly higher degree of utility to consumers. Rather, the improvement must be large enough to make up for the loss in network effects that consumers face if they switch to the new technology. In consequence, a larger innovative leap is required for an innovation to constitute a competitive threat to the incumbent.[52] Small, but still socially desirable innovations might be excluded from reaching the market. In network

---

51 Menell, *supra* note 26, at 677; Farrell and Katz, *supra* note 18, at 639.

52 Farrell and Katz, *supra* note 18, at 639.

markets, the incumbent is under less competitive pressure to engage in innovative activity than in conventional markets. Schumpeter explicitly notes[53] that dynamic competition is only effective if there is an 'ever-present threat' to a monopolist that new products will be introduced and if there is competitive pressure that 'disciplines before it attacks'. Network effects, however, insulate an incumbent monopolist from dynamic competition.

An incumbent monopolist has little incentive to introduce a new and innovative network standard that replaces his own standard. The profits from the new standard would only cannibalize his monopoly profits. Market outsiders, however, have a higher incentive to improve a network standard because they have a prospect of winning the whole market. If a network standard is protected by IPRs the incumbent can exclude competitors from improving the existing standard. Also, IPRs help to enforce incompatibility. By contrast, with several network firms using the standard under compatibility, there would be a higher number of potential innovators. IPRs therefore aggravate the negative effects of the lock-in. On the other hand, IPRs might provide an additional incentive for overcoming the inertia in the market structure. However, this additional incentive comes at the price of an even stronger lock-in after the next tipping of the market. Just as during a standard race[54] the incentive provided by the market mechanisms might be sufficient.

7.1.2 Dynamic competition and follow-on innovations With regard to product features that do not constitute part of the network standard, dynamic competition is weak if the network standard is protected by IPRs that help to enforce incompatibility.

Such follow-on innovations within a standard do not lead to incompatibility, because they do not alter the features that form the standard. For example, transportation services in a railway network might be provided by a single transportation enterprise only. It is unlikely that competition for better railway transportation services will be created through a duplication of the railway networks. With compatibility, however, several transportation companies might compete for a higher quality of services within the same railway network. Quite similarly, there is compatibility through mandated interconnection between competing telecommunications networks. Recent years have shown that there is high potential for innovation in advanced telecommunications services that are based on the same network standard. If the standard of an operating system is open, several software application enterprises can compete to offer a wider variety of software applications to customers.

---

53 Schumpeter, *supra* note 14, at 85.
54 See section 6.1 *supra*.

However, follow-on innovations require access to the network standard. Under incompatibility, there is little competitive pressure for an incumbent to introduce follow-on innovations, because this enterprise is the only one in the market and network effects prevent potential innovators from entering the market. An incumbent has an incentive to introduce follow-on innovations if this allows him to attain higher returns from consumers. However, absent competitive pressure, a monopolist incumbent is less motivated to engage in research and development.[55] Also, follow-on innovations reach fewer customers if there is monopoly pricing within the standard.

With compatibility, by contrast, several companies have access to the network standard. Accordingly, there is higher competitive pressure to invest in follow-on innovations and there are multiple potential sources of innovations. Because network effects are the same for all companies within the standard, there is no distortion of consumer preferences with regard to follow-on innovations.[56] Follow-on innovations lead to product differentiation within a network standard. Product differentiation raises consumer welfare because it satisfies a wider range of consumer preferences.

In sum, if intellectual property protection for a network standard leads to incompatibility there is less dynamic competition for follow-on innovations, because the right holder can deter competitors from research and development.[57] The positive effects of sharing a standard have to be balanced against possible adverse effects on the incentive to establish an improved standard in the market:[58] intellectual property protection for the standard should rather be denied if there is little innovative potential in the network standard itself but a high innovative potential for follow-on innovations.

7.1.3 Conclusion on dynamic competition and intellectual property rights after the tipping of the market In sum, after the tipping of a network market there is little competitive pressure for an incumbent monopolist to innovate, as she is entrenched by entry barriers and as consumers are locked in to using the standard. IPRs in network standards aggravate the lock-in effects. At the same time, IPRs create the prospect of a more enduring monopoly. This might produce an additional incentive to overcome the inertia of the market structure. As regards follow-on innovations that require access to the standard, dynamic competition is more intense when there is compatibility in the market. The potential for innovations in the standard itself has to be carefully

---

55 Farrell and Katz, *supra* note 18, at 639.
56 *Ibid.*
57 Menell, note 26, at 674; Farrell and Katz, *supra* note 18, at 639 and 642.
58 Farrell and Katz, *supra* note 18, at 648.

weighed against the potential of follow-on innovations, which might be substantial.

7.2 Static competition during a lock-in

After a standard race is terminated, static competition becomes more important because there is only limited dynamic competition that might correct losses in static competition.

In terms of static competition, IPRs involve a higher trade-off in network markets than in conventional markets. If IPRs create incompatibility, there is a complete exclusion of static competition, which results in a monopoly (section 7.2.1 *infra*). Accordingly, IPRs in network standards lead to a broader scope of protection and to a higher reward than in conventional markets. At the same time, the reward is not necessarily due to the innovative quality of the network standard but to the network's particular market mechanisms. Accordingly, there is only a weak nexus between the loss in static efficiency and the innovative degree in the standard (section 7.2.2 *infra*).

7.2.1 The weak nexus between static loss and dynamic gain The higher loss in static efficiency in network markets results in higher returns on IPRs. However, the loss in static competition and the high returns do not necessarily represent the innovative value of a standard.

The effective scope of protection by an IPR is larger in network markets than in conventional markets because an IPR in a standard covers the whole market.[59] In conventional markets, intellectual property rights do not necessarily convey an economic monopoly because consumers can substitute away to a different technology that serves the same purpose. In network markets, by contrast, consumers have little alternative to an incumbent network standard because there is only a single enterprise once the market has tipped. At the same time, it is more difficult for market entrants to invent around an IPR that controls a market standard. Greater difficulty of inventing around an intellectual property right leads to greater protection.[60] Accordingly, an IPR in a network standard more likely awards a monopoly position that is uncontested by a near rival. As a consequence, the expected reward from an intellectual property right is higher in a network market than in a conventional market because the market position is more durable and because even a close winner in the standard race reaps the gains of the whole market.[61]

---

59 Farrell, Joseph (1995), 'Arguments for Weaker Intellectual Property Protection in Network Industries', *StandardView*, **3**(2), 46, at 47.

60 Landes and Posner, *supra* note 23, at 300.

61 Farrell, *supra* note 59, at 48.

Basically, intellectual property law leaves it to the market to determine the value of an innovation to society. The returns of a patent are considered as a proxy of the contribution of an innovation to societal welfare. In conventional markets, the difficulty of substituting a technology represents the innovative lead that a technology has over alternative technologies. The position of the leading enterprise is constrained by the second-placed firm that offers an alternative technology. The respective returns of the firms are supposed to reflect each company's contribution to technological progress.

In network markets however, the difficulty of substituting for an IPR in a network standard is not merely determined by the innovative achievement of the invention itself. Rather, the difficulty of inventing around a network standard is in addition due to the particular market mechanisms in the presence of network effects. Accordingly, there is only a weak nexus between the degree of innovation that is involved in a network standard and the high returns that are magnified by network effects. Even a technologically simple and arbitrary network standard might lead to a maximization of network effects and an intellectual property right in such a standard might cover the whole market and yield high returns.

The value of a network standard is determined by both its degree of innovation and the maximization of network effects that is achieved through a market-wide standardization. Intellectual property protection is more warranted if the particular standard involves a high degree of innovation as compared to alternative standards. In this case the resulting losses in static competition more closely correspond to an innovative achievement. By contrast, imitation should rather be allowed where the monopoly does not flow from the intellectual property right as such but from the particular market mechanisms at work.[62] If two network standards are quite close in their performance just before the tipping of a network market but one standard becomes dominant after the tipping, there is an indication that the dominance is due not merely to the technological lead but also to market mechanisms. A high reward is less justified if an innovation is obvious[63] or if a standard is only slightly different from alternative standards. In these cases the high reward and the static loss are more likely due to the market mechanisms than to the innovative achievement.

As a consequence, patent protection for network standards is preferable to copyright protection or trademark protection.[64] A copyright requires only a

62 Drexl, *supra* note 5, at 790.
63 Farrell, *supra* note 59, at 47.
64 Menell, *supra* note 26, at 677.

minimal threshold of originality.[65] Patent protection, by contrast, involves an examination of the novelty and non-obviousness of the standard by the patent office.

7.2.2 Conclusion on static competition and intellectual property rights In sum, IPRs lead to a greater reduction of static competition in network markets than in conventional markets. Unlike in conventional markets IPRs in network standards cover the whole market and convey monopoly power – even if a standard is only of little innovative value. Compatibility, by contrast, leads to high network effects and to static competition within the standard.

The high returns on an IPR in network markets are not necessarily a proxy for the value of an innovation to society. They are quite often due rather to the specific market mechanisms in network markets and to the fact that the existence of a single market-wide network standard maximizes network effects.

Intellectual property protection should be limited to cases where a network standard involves a significant innovative achievement. Imitation should rather be allowed where the value of a standard is due more to its standardization effect than to its innovative achievement.

8 Conclusion

The economic effects of IPRs are to be assessed in terms of their effect on both dynamic and static competition, as these rights involve a trade-off between dynamic and static competition. Dynamic competition is generated by both the competitive pressure in the market and the incentives that are provided by IPRs. In turn, the competitive pressure as well as the effect of IPRs hinge on the market mechanisms. As market mechanisms are specific in network markets, network effects influence the competitive pressure as well as the effects of IPRs. Intellectual property rights in a network standard are an important strategic instrument to enforce incompatibility. Incompatibility changes the character of the competitive process in network markets.

During a standard race, there is high competitive pressure to innovate. If in addition intellectual property rights in network standards are available, the incentive for innovation is further raised. However, too high an incentive to innovate might produce an inefficient standard race. The incentives for innovation that are provided by the market mechanisms might already be sufficient.

Harm to static competition through IPRs is negligible during this stage of a network market because distortions in static competition will rapidly be corrected. After the tipping of the network market, there is only weak competitive pressure to innovate because consumers are locked in to the established

65 Menell, *supra* note 26, at 678.

technology and because network effects constitute barriers to entry even for superior technologies. IPRs in network standards intensify the lock-in but might, at the same time, provide an additional incentive to overcome the inertia of network markets. If IPRs in the standard help to more easily enforce incompatibility, dynamic competition with regard to product features that do not form the standard is weakened. A complex weighing is mandated between the potential for innovation in the standard itself and the potential for such follow-on innovation.

As to static competition, IPRs lead to a higher trade-off during a lock-in. Unlike in conventional markets, intellectual property rights in network standards convey monopoly power and cover the whole market. Further, in network markets the market power conveyed by an IPR and the lack of contestability are only a weak proxy for the innovative height of the underlying innovation as both are due in large measure to specific market mechanisms. Intellectual property protection is therefore more costly and might be excessive.

In sum, intellectual property protection for network standards involves a more complex trade-off than in conventional markets. The balancing of the effects on innovation is rather tilted towards weaker protection.

PART 2

CONTRACTUAL ARRANGEMENTS

5 The new EC competition law framework for technology transfer and IP licensing

Steve Anderman

1 Introduction

EC competition policy and intellectual property rights (IPRs) are becoming widely recognized as complementary components of a modern industrial policy. Although each has other aims, both pursue the common aim of improving innovation and consumer welfare. Yet they do so by using rather different means. Intellectual property legislation such as patents, copyright and design rights laws offer IP right holders a period of exclusive rights to exploit their IPRs as a reward and incentive to innovation and R&D investment. Modern competition policy attempts to keep markets innovative by maintaining effective competition. The means used to pursue this aim include maintaining access to markets and preventing 'foreclosure' or illegitimate monopolization of markets.

At first sight there seems to be a potential clash in the methods used by the two systems of legal regulation to achieve their common aim. The concern to maintain access to markets appears to be almost completely opposed to the concept of exclusive rights to make, use and sell a product. Indeed, historically there was a period when the misunderstanding of the economic effects of IPRs led EC competition policy to attempt to place overly strict limits on the exercise of IP rights, particularly in the field of patent licensing.[1]

Today, however, EC competition policy treats the economic effects of IPRs more realistically. The Community Courts and the Commission take the view that the market power associated with an IPR-protected product must be established empirically. Equally importantly, EC competition law gives explicit recognition to the positive contribution that IPRs make to competition as well as innovation. In the first place, it is now openly accepted that the incentives to innovation created by IPRs produce new competitors in existing markets and indeed create new products, which open up entirely new markets. Secondly, it is now presumed that the licensing of IPRs is also generally pro-competitive as

[1] See discussion in Anderman, Steve and John Kallaugher (2006), *Technology Transfer and the New EC Competition Rules: Intellectual Property Licensing after Modernisation*, Oxford: Oxford University Press, chapter 2.

well as pro-innovative in its effects and helps to ensure that IPRs are more widely diffused throughout the Common Market. The EC competition authorities also acknowledge that too heavy a regulatory burden on the exercise of IPRs could discourage investment in IPRs in the EU.[2]

However, in extreme cases in which IPRs are used unjustifiably by their owners to exclude competitors from markets, EC competition policy reserves a right to intervene to limit the exercise of IPRs. It tends at that point to view intellectual property rights as any other form of private property rights subject to the prohibitions of competition law. This can apply to the unilateral exploitation of an IPR by its owner;[3] it can also apply to the agreement between the IP owner and a licensee to exploit the IPR in a particular territory or field of use.[4] On the other hand, it makes important concessions to the fact that IPRs have different qualities than other types of property rights, by developing, under Article 82, the test of 'exceptional circumstances'.[5] This test evidences respect for the pro-competitive features of IPRs and their contribution towards innovation and helps to reconcile competition law with IPRs in an innovation perspective. The 'exceptional circumstances' test represents an important acceptance by competition law that IPRs are not the same as all other forms of property rights, even while maintaining that the exercise of IPRs must be subject to the regulatory limits of competition policy. IPR specialists express reservations about whether competition law has drawn the line at the right position. In terms of the current need to establish an industrial policy that promotes innovation by both IPRs and competition policy, it is certainly necessary to subject the 'exceptional circumstances' test to continual review to ensure that it represents the best balance between EC competition policy and the exercise of IPRs.

Moreover, some of the general doctrines of competition law have the incidental effect of ensuring that the intervention of competition law in the exercise of IPRs is in fact kept to exceptional cases. For example, under Article 82, EC competition law accepts that the achievement of an economic monopoly by means of investment in R&D and intellectual property rights is a legitimate course of conduct for a firm, in a form of 'competition on the merits'. Furthermore, the special responsibilities of a dominant firm towards weakened

---

2 Commission Notice – Guidelines on the Application of Article 81 of the EC Treaty to Technology Transfer Agreements, OJ 2004 No. C 101, p. 2, para. 8.

3 See, for example, Case C-418/01, *IMS Health*, [2004] ECR I-5039.

4 See, for example, the Technology Transfer Block Exemption Regulation (TTBER): Commission Regulation (EC) No. 772/2004 on the Application of Article 81(3) of the Treaty to Categories of Technology Transfer Agreements, OJ 2004 No. L 123, p. 11.

5 See, for example, Case C-418/01, *IMS Health*, [2004] ECR I-5039, para. 36.

competition do not preclude an IPR owner from continuing to compete by preventing copying, even if the exercise of this right denies competitors access to primary markets.[6] Further, EC competition law acknowledges that the pricing of IPRs, even by dominant firms, must include a return that adequately reflects the reward/incentive function of IPRs.[7]

The relationship between EC competition policy and IP licensing can be viewed through a similar lens. To what extent do the general doctrines of competition law result in legal rules that give due recognition to its pro-competitive features and its contribution to innovation while protecting competition concerns? To what extent does competition policy provide special protection in this sphere analogous to the 'exceptional circumstances' test of Article 82? The answer cannot usefully be given without a close look at the details of the regulatory framework as it has evolved into its present form.

The current stage of EC competition policy towards IP licensing has evolved through three main stages in promoting its aims of innovation as well as competition. In the 1970s there was a strong concern to limit the scope for licensing because of the influence of the doctrines of the US Supreme Court about patent monopoly and the 'Nine No-Nos' of the US Department of Justice and Federal Trade Commission in respect of patent licensing as well as internal EC worries about market partitioning that were heightened by the *Grundig*[8] case. During this period little thought was given to the pro-competitive features of IPRs and IP licensing or the damaging economic effects of a restrictive competition policy upon investment in IPRs.

By the mid-1980s, both concerns of this earlier stage had been diminished by events. The EC officials were influenced by the change in approach within the USA. The doctrines of the Warren US Supreme Court, in the face of severe criticisms by the Chicago School, were replaced by a more economically realistic assessment of the market power of patent holders by the courts and the legislators. Moreover, the regime of 'the Nine No-Nos' was dismantled under the IP-friendlier policy of the DOJ/FTC. This change coincided with a new approach in the EC: the acceptance of vertical exclusive IP licences as pro-competitive in the *Nungesser* case in the ECJ[9] and the adoption of the Patent Licensing Block Exemption Regulation (2349/84) and the Know-how BER (556/89) by the European Commission. During this period, too, EC concerns about market partitioning were partially eased by the growth of the doctrine of exhaustion and the build up of established pathways of inter-state trade. The

6 Case 238/87, *Volvo v. Veng*, [1988] ECR 6211, para. 8.

7 *Ibid.*, Opinion by the Advocate General.

8 Joined Cases 56 and 58/64, *Grundig and Consten v. Commission*, [1966] ECR 299.

9 Case 258/78, *Nungesser v. Commission* ('*Maize Seeds*'), [1982] ECR 2015.

period culminated with the unified 1996 Technology Transfer Block Exemption Regulation (240/96), or TTBER. Shortly before that, the US Federal Trade Commission and the Antitrust Division of the Justice Department had in 1995 produced their Antitrust Guidelines for the Licensing of Intellectual Property, offering a rather different regulatory model.[10]

With the modernization of EC Competition law we have entered the third stage – a period of regulation consisting of the new TTBER (772/2004) and Guidelines with a more flexible and economic approach, a partial harmonization with the Vertical Agreements BER and a new paradigm for assessing the enforceability of licensing agreements. The modernization of competition policy within the Commission, necessary to adapt it to the realities of an enlarged Europe of 27 Member States, consists of a number of procedural reforms set out in Regulation 1/2003. These include the end of prior notification of agreements to the Commission, the end of the Commission's exclusive competence to determine the scope of Article 81(3) and the conferral of such competence upon national competition authorities and national courts. The reforms also ended the possibility of formal applications for individual exemption to the Commission and the assumption of non-validity for agreements that were not covered by a block exemption. These reforms were meant to usher in a greater reliance upon self-assessment by the parties to commercial agreements, either by finding that an agreement fit within a block exemption regulation or by legal advisers assessing the validity of the contents of the agreement in the light of Articles 81(1) and 81(3) and the Guidelines accompanying the new BERs, Community court cases and Commission decisions and notices.

This chapter examines the current regulatory framework of competition policy towards IP licensing, and the new methods of assessment of licensing agreements it requires, in the light of its role within an overall policy attempting to promote innovation. It seeks to determine to what extent the Commission has adopted a proportionate role for competition law in regulating IPRs in this field.

The test of an effective regulatory framework is to strike an appropriate balance between two types of innovation-promoting policies: competition law and intellectual property law. This necessitates a choice between allowing the process of technology licensing room to 'breathe', so that the parties can shape their own agreements according to their needs, and protecting the public inter-

---

10 See the comparison of the two regulatory regimes in Anderman, Steve (1998), *EC Competition Law and Intellectual Property Rights: The Regulation of Innovation*, Oxford: Oxford University Press; see also Korah, Valentine (1996), *Technology Transfer and the EC Competition Rules*, Oxford: Oxford University Press.

est in workably competitive markets. If the limits created by the regulation are too tight, the incentives to the parties to enter into licensing agreements will be significantly reduced and the benefits obtained from the process of technology transfer will be lost because firms will license to territories outside the EU and export in instead of locating manufacturing establishments in EU countries. Of course, if the restrictions are too loose, there will be greater risks of anti-competitive practices, which can choke innovative markets by barriers to entry. In view of the many economic benefits of the licensing process and the economic costs of overly restrictive regulation, however, the onus should lie upon the regulators to carefully calibrate their restrictions and adopt proportionate methods of regulation.

The chapter will concentrate on the new substantive competition rules regulating IP licensing agreements, but it will also make reference to the new procedure for assessing licensing agreements.

2 The new legal framework for IP licensing in the EU

The key element in regulating IP licensing agreements today is the Commission's Technology Transfer Block Exemption Regulation, TTBER (772/2004), and its accompanying Guidelines. The new Regulation offered the Commission an opportunity to re-evaluate its policy towards the process of licensing IP-protected technology as part of a wider EC industrial policy as well as part of the modernization process.

The process of technological intellectual property licensing is on balance a highly pro-competitive activity. One effect of the process is to raise the level of technology throughout the EU by creating incentives for its introduction and diffusion by IP right holders who have neither the means nor the inclination to exploit the product themselves in new territories. Because a licensing agreement invariably requires some degree of manufacture as well as sale, it results in a technological lift to the licensee that would not occur if the licensor merely manufactured elsewhere and exported the finished product into the EU for distribution. Technology licensing agreements also introduce new products to existing markets, adding to competition and in some cases actually creating new markets. By adding to competition and innovation, as empirical studies have shown, IP licensing also enhances competitiveness in world trade.

In the course of drafting an IP licensing agreement, the parties must inevitably place certain contractual obligations upon each other to achieve the object of their agreement. Many licensees will be reluctant to undertake the risks of investment in manufacture and sale of a new product without the protection of an exclusive licence that limits direct competition from the licensor and other licensees within the licensed territory. Most licensors will not give an exclusive licence without the *quid pro quo* of a minimum royalties clause. In addition most licensors will not license their IP without the reassurance of obligations undertaken by licensees designed to protect the integrity and value of the IP once it is licensed. For example, most licensors will insist on certain obligations of confidentiality in respect of know-how, limits on sublicensing, quality controls on materials used and limits on the use of the licensed IP once the licensing agreement has expired. They may also insist on obligations by the licensee to grant back licences for improvements as well as obligations not to exploit technologies that compete with the licensor and an obligation not to challenge the validity of the licensed IPR. Many of these may be viewed as commercially indispensable to induce licensors to license their technology in the first place, although some may take a form that raises competition concerns.

On occasion contractual restrictions can be used as a device to create competitive restraints. Some royalty arrangements can help to underpin a price-fixing scheme. Some technology transfer agreements can make use of exclusive territorial protection or output restrictions as a cover for market-sharing agreements. In a European perspective, exclusive licensing agreements can have a secondary effect of reinforcing the isolation of national markets from the single market by excessive territorial protection. Moreover, some IP licensing agreements have the potential to create conditions of dominant market power in the licensed market and foreclose competitors from that market. Even though IP licensing agreements rarely have this result, particularly when they are agreements between non-competitors, they have been the subject of detailed competition block exemption regulations since the early 1980s.

3 The main features of the new Technology Transfer Regulation

The European Commission has proclaimed that the new TTBER's assessment of IP licensing agreements takes 'due account of the dynamic aspects of technology licensing', making 'in particular . . . no presumption that intellectual property rights and licence agreements as such give rise to competition concerns'.[11] Within the safe haven itself, the new TTBER offers many advantages: it applies to a wider array of IPRs; it offers greater flexibility and longer periods of protection. It also reduces the list of non-exemptible 'hard-core restraints' that, if included in a licensing agreement, make it void in its entirety. The shorter blacklist, particularly for vertical licensing agreements, leaves a wider scope for exemptible clauses. There is also a short list of excluded restrictions that are unenforceable under the TTBER but can be severed from a licensing agreement without affecting its overall enforceability within the Regulation.

---

[11] TT Guidelines, para 9.

One problem with the introduction of market shares is that they have made the application of the 'safe haven' unpredictable *ex ante*, that is at the time when an IP licensing agreement is signed. The market shares of IP-protected products, often new and often based on extensive R&D, tend to be volatile. The Commission is willing to accept that the designation of the parties as competitors or non-competitors can be settled at the time the agreement is made and in the absence of the effects of the licence itself. Thus if the parties start off as non-competitors, the agreement remains an agreement between non-competitors, even if they later become competitors during the course of the agreement.[12]

However, the Commission has been unwilling to offer any such *ex ante* assurance in respect of market shares. If the market share increases during the course of the agreement beyond the market-share limits, the agreement will no longer benefit from the block exemption. At that point, the agreement is not invalid but it no longer enjoys the benefit of the 'safe haven'. The Commission offers the reassurance that above the market-share thresholds there is no presumption of illegality.[13] The procedure of the Commission has been reformed by Regulation 1/2003 so that there is no longer a need to submit a precautionary notification to the Commission to ensure provisional validity to a licensing agreement. Its validity stands or falls depending on its contents at the time it is challenged. Thus, if an agreement is caught by Article 81(1) and falls outside the block exemption, it is no longer automatically void under Article 81(2). Its legal status can be self-assessed by the parties using the contents and framework of analysis set out in the Guidelines to determine whether the agreement is exemptible under Article 81(3).

The parties will now be required to assess the legal status of the agreement by reference to the detailed Guidelines as well as the relevant court judgments and Commission decisions to ensure that the agreement will remain exemptible even if the market share of the licensed product grows beyond the limits of the safe haven. No longer can the TTBER be used as a self-contained list of commandments that if followed ensure exemptibility for a licensing agreement during the entire period of its duration. Instead, the parties must learn to navigate in the choppy waters outside the safe haven of the TTBER itself.

The Commission seems to be encouraged by the fact that this method of self-assessment is similar to that in use in the USA under the IP Licensing Guidelines of the Federal Trade Commission and the Antitrust Division of the US Justice Department. However, the introduction of this new method of self-assessment within the EC calls for a rather radical change in legal practice in

---

[12] Article 4(3) TTBER.

[13] TT Guidelines, paras 24 and 131.

a sensitive area of commercial life. This move may be inevitable in a decentralized and modernized world of competition policy, but the abrupt change in legal practice will result in a new and more demanding methodology for assessing the competition-law assessment of licensing activity.[14]

The new regulatory framework can perhaps best be described under four main headings: (1) the new wider scope and duration for IP licensing; (2) the new distinction between 'horizontal' and 'vertical' licensing agreements; (3) the new market-shares thresholds; and (4) the new method of assessing individual restrictions in licensing agreements.

4 The contents of the new Technology Transfer Regulation and the Guidelines

4.1 The scope and duration of the Regulation

The Regulation extends to a wide range of IPR licensing agreements and assignments: pure and mixed patent[15] and know-how agreements have been expanded to include software copyright licensing agreements and design rights licensing agreements. All these IPRs are viewed as the 'core' technology to be licensed.[16]

The Regulation also allows a wider variety of non-core IPRs to be included in the licensing package along with the core 'technology'[17] as long as they are 'ancillary' provisions,[18] that is their licensing (i) must not constitute the primary object of the agreement and (ii) must be directly related to the manufacture or provision of the contract products. This formula, clearer than its predecessor, tests whether the non-core IPR is included essentially to enable the licensee to better exploit the core licensed technology. If it appears that licensing the 'ancillary' IPR, say a trademark, is the real purpose of the agreement, it will not be exempted under the TTBER.

The Regulation offers a both wider and more clearly defined scope for IP licensing than its predecessor. Moreover, although the Regulation itself does not extend to copyright licensing other than software licensing, the Guidelines state that the principles set out in the Regulation and Guidelines will apply to traditional forms of copyright by analogy.[19] The Guidelines are less positive

---

14 See, for example, Anderman and Kallaugher, *supra* note 1; Korah, *supra* note 10.

15 'Patents' are broadly defined to include utility models, designs, topographies of semiconductor products and plant breeders' certificates; Article 1(1)(h) TTBER.

16 Article 1(1)(b) TTBER.

17 TT Guidelines, para. 53.

18 No. 9 of the Recitals and Article 1(1)(b) of the TTBER.

19 TT Guidelines, para. 51.

about pure trademark licensing; they state that the Regulation is not intended to extend to pure trademark licensing, even by analogy.[20] Consequently, the types of IPR that can be licensed and either fall within the safe haven or can be self-certified as acceptable under Article 81, if not extending to all IP licensing, are nevertheless more inclusive than under previous regulatory regimes.

The application of the block exemption, however, requires that the licensing agreement must be concluded for the purpose of *producing* contract products,[21] meaning products incorporating or produced with the licensed technology.[22] Licences contained in agreements that are primarily for *reselling* or *distribution* purposes are excluded and parties to such agreements will have to look to the Vertical Agreements BER for exemption. In respect of sublicensing, agreements by licensees to *sublicense* the licensed technology are covered but pure *sublicensing* agreements are not exempted by the TTBER, although the principles of the Regulation will apply by analogy to such agreements.[23] Finally, since the Regulation only deals 'with agreements where the licensor permits the licensee to exploit the contract products', it 'should not deal with licensing agreements for the purpose of *sub-contracting research and development*'. Recital 5 indicates that the exemption could apply to exploitation by the licensee in the form of manufacturing and selling 'possibly after further research and development by the licensee'.[24]

The exemption conferred by the Regulation has a potentially longer duration than its predecessor; it can last 'as long as the intellectual property right in the licensed technology has not expired, lapsed or been declared invalid or, in the case of know-how, for as long as the know-how remains secret'.[25] If the know-how becomes publicly known as a result of action by the licensee, the exemption will continue to apply for the duration of the agreement. The block exemption will apply separately to each licensed property right covered by the agreement but will continue in effect until the date of expiry, invalidity or the coming into the public domain of the last intellectual property right that constitutes 'technology' as defined by Article 1 of the TTBER. The Regulation itself expires in 2014 so contracts cannot be expected to remain block-exempted after that date. On the other hand, licensing agreements that are self-certified as exempted can last longer than 10 years, the limit imposed by the 1996 TTBER on know-how, if the know-how remains secret or the patent remains valid.

20 TT Guidelines, para. 53.
21 Article 2 TTBER.
22 TT Guidelines, para. 41.
23 TT Guidelines, para. 42.
24 TT Guidelines, para. 44.
25 Article 2(2) TTBER.

4.2 The distinction between 'licensing agreements between competitors' and 'licensing agreements between non-competitors'

The 1996 version of the TTBER persisted with the view that most IP licensing agreements should be treated as potentially 'horizontal' agreements between competitors, in part because the licensee often evolves into a competitor as the result of the experience with manufacturing the new technology. Yet the overwhelming evidence is that at the time a licensing agreement is signed, most are actually 'vertical', or agreements between non-competitors. The economic realism of the new Regulation has resulted in a division of licensing agreements into two categories – agreements between non-competitors or agreements between competitors – and in a recognition that the regulatory concerns are considerably greater in the case of agreements between competitors. This has resulted in a re-evaluation of prohibited restraints in the case of licensing agreements between non-competitors and the creation of a deservedly more benign regulatory regime. This reform is far-reaching because it applies not only within the confines of the safe haven but also up to a point at which the parties' market shares may be as high as 40–50 per cent as long as they fall below dominance.

Moreover, the Regulation gives an expansive definition of 'agreements between non-competitors'. It applies not only to the paradigmatic vertical case of an agreement between an inventor and a manufacturer but also to an agreement between two manufacturers as long as they are not competitors in respect of the licensed product. In 'product markets' competitors are defined as 'actual' competitors, that is competing undertakings who in the absence of the technology transfer agreement would have been active in the relevant product and geographic markets in which the contract products are sold without infringing each other's intellectual property rights.[26] The one complication is that in product markets, 'competitors' also includes a narrow category of 'potential' competitors, who realistically are in a position to undertake the necessary investments and accept the switching costs of entering the same market should the price of the product be raised.[27] In 'technology markets', the definition of competitor is limited to 'actual' competitors.[28]

A further feature of the Regulation that is helpful to IP licensing is that it defines the parties as 'competitors' or 'non-competitors' at the time the contract is made and will not allow the natural competition that may develop as a result of the licensing agreement as the manufacturing expertise of the licensee matures to affect the designation of the contract. Thus if the parties

---

26 Article 1(j)(ii) TTBER; Guidelines, *supra* note 2, paras 24 and 31.

27 Article 1(j)(ii) TTBER.

28 Article 1(j)(i) TTBER.

are non-competitors at the time the agreement is made, they will not be re-designated for the purposes of the exemption during the term of the agreement unless the agreement is materially amended.[29] The distinction between agreements between competitors and agreements between non-competitors is particularly noticeable in two regulatory contexts: the market-share limits of the Regulation (Article 3) and the types of hard-core restrictions in licensing agreements (Article 4).

4.3 The market-share thresholds

The Regulation may have been helpful to IP licensing in these respects, but it has created complications for IP licensing by introducing a system of market-share thresholds to harmonize it with the regulatory methods of the Vertical Agreements Regulation. By establishing a new legal regime in IP licensing that places such limits on the 'safe haven' of the block exemption,[30] the TTBER radically alters the nature of the overall legal framework for IP licensing. Under the guise of giving greater recognition to the economic realities of IP licensing, the TTBER creates legal uncertainty for the parties in volatile new technology markets. For licensing agreements between non-competitors, or 'vertical' licensing agreements, the block exemption will not apply when the licensed product exceeds 30 per cent of the relevant market[31] because such agreements normally pose a lower risk to competition.[32] For the parties to agreements between competitors, or 'horizontal' licensing agreements, the exemption will not apply if the licensed product exceeds a 20 per cent market share.[33] In defining the market for the licensed *product*, both actual and potential competition are relevant.[34] If the agreement is to license *technology* only actual competition will be considered.[35]

The fact that market-share thresholds may have been accepted in vertical-distribution agreements does not necessarily mean that they are an appropriate regulatory device to apply to technology-transfer agreements. There are important differences between distribution and licensing agreements. IP licensing agreements often entail the higher economic risks of manufacture. Moreover, their products are more volatile. Furthermore, technology markets are difficult to define. An innovative product can break through to a market,

---

29 Article 4(3) TTBER; TT Guidelines, *supra* note 2, para. 31; see also paras 32–3.
30 TT Guidelines, paras 26–33.
31 Article 3(2) TTBER.
32 TT Guidelines, paras 68 *et seq.*
33 Article 3(1) TTBER; Guidelines, paras 66, 67, 69 and 131.
34 Article 1(j)(ii) TTBER; Guidelines, paras 28, 29 and 67.
35 Article 1(j)(i) TTBER; Guidelines, paras 30 and 66.

replacing other products, or it can flop. High market shares can occur suddenly and unexpectedly. If success meets with automatic disqualification from the block exemption because of market-share limits, there will be a disincentive to license in the first place.

If the product that is the subject of a technology transfer agreement exceeds the market-share ceiling at any time during the course of the contract, it will lose the benefit of the block exemption. As mentioned, the Regulation makes no concession to the volatility of relationships during the term of the licensing agreement as it did in respect of status of the parties as competitors or non-competitors, whereby parties defined at the outset as non-competitors will not be redesignated as competitors for the duration of the agreement unless the agreement is materially amended.[36]

If an agreement should lose its exemption under the TTBER, it will not be automatically prohibited by Article 81(1); nor will any notification be required to the Commission. Indeed, the agreement may still be individually exempted by an analysis of Article 81(3) as it applies to the agreement using the Guidelines and the case law of the Community courts and the Commission. However, to lawyers accustomed to the old-style block exemption regulation, the greater legal security of the safe haven of the block exemption will be replaced by the seemingly more precarious legal situation of self-assessment.

4.4 The hard-core restrictions

The new Regulation places considerable emphasis upon a narrow blacklist of prohibited 'hard-core' restrictions whose presence in a licensing agreement make it unexemptible under the Regulation but also almost always unenforceable under Article 81 generally. The hard-core restrictions have been drafted on the supposition that they are 'almost always anti-competitive'.[37] They correspond quite closely to the US concept of per se anti-competitive restrictions. They rarely if ever enjoy the benefits of a balancing rule-of-reason analysis under Article 81(3). The hard-core restrictions have been defined differently depending upon whether the licensing agreement that contains them is between competing undertakings or between non-competing undertakings.

4.4.1 Restrictions on licensing agreements between competitors For cases in which the licensee competes with the licensor at the time the agreement is concluded, the Regulation contains four main hard-core restrictions. The first three are basic anti-cartel competition rules, bans on price fixing,[38] reciprocal

---

36 Article 3(1) TTBER; TT Guidelines, para. 31.
37 TT Guidelines, para. 74.
38 Article 4(1)(a) TTBER; TT Guidelines, paras 79–80 and 156.

output limitations[39] and market allocation clauses.[40] The fourth is a prohibition on licensors restricting the licensee's ability to carry out R&D and exploit its own technology.[41]

Perhaps in partial recognition of this fact, the Regulation provides that if the agreement between competitors takes the form of a non-reciprocal licensing agreement, the licensor is allowed under an exception to Article 4(1)(c) TTBER to offer an exclusive licence, that is a licence to produce and sell the contract products without the licensor himself producing goods in that territory or selling the contract goods from that territory. In such a case, the licensee will merely be doing what the licensor was entitled to do and hence that restriction, on its own, cannot be viewed as anti-competitive. Indeed, it may even be argued that Article 81(1) does not apply to a simple exclusive licence between licensor and licensee as long as the agreement involves no third parties such as other licensees.[42]

A second analogous exception consists of field-of-use provisions. A field-of-use restriction limits the exploitation of the licensed technology by the licensee to one or more particular fields of use, leaving untouched the licensor's ability to exploit the licensed technology in another field. A good example is offered by a maize seed variety that is licensed for animal food only with the licensor retaining exclusive rights to exploit the seed variety for human foodstuffs. Field-of-use restrictions may be 'exclusive' or 'sole' and are treated for competition purposes as analogous to exclusive or sole territorial licences. Again, as long as the field-of-use obligation is limited to the licensing agreement, it is little more than a sub-division of the licensor's own powers and may not even be caught by Article 81(1).

4.4.2 Restrictions on agreements between non-competitors For agreements between non-competitors (Article 4(2) TTBER), the hard-core restrictions are more varied in their concerns. They include price fixing and they extend to territorial restrictions and to restrictions of active and passive sales to end users by a licensee who is part of a selective distribution system.

The territorial restriction prohibition is contained in Article 4(2)(b), which states that an agreement may not be exempted if it has as its object '(i) the restriction of the territory into which, or of the customers to whom, the licensee may sell the contract products . . .'. It then provides a limited list of

39 Article 4(1)(b) TTBER; TT Guidelines, paras 82–3 and 175.

40 Article 4(1)(c) TTBER; TT Guidelines, para. 84.

41 The one exception is where the restriction is indispensable to prevent the disclosure of the licensed technology; Article 4(1)(d) TTBER.

42 Cf. Article 4(2) of Regulation 17/62, discussed in Anderman, *supra* note 10, at pp. 52–3.

exceptions consisting of permitted territorial restrictions, including obligations on licensees not to sell *actively* into the exclusive territory of another licensee, not to sell at all into the exclusive territory of the licensor, to manufacture or provide contract products only for its own use and so on.

The Commission has acknowledged the indispensability of protection against *passive* sales for licensees, arguing that 'it is likely that licensees would not enter into the licence agreement without protection for a certain period of time against passive (and active) sales into their territory by other licensees'.[43]

This statement recognizes the strategic importance of protection from passive sales as an incentive in the technology-transfer agreement, and the Regulation provides that licensors can provide every licensee with protection for two years from the sale of the licensed product in its territory against passive sales by other licensees manufacturing the same licensed product in other territories. The theory is that the two years should be sufficient for each licensee to familiarize itself with the production process so as to achieve the efficiencies that will allow it to catch up and compete on equal terms with other licensees.[44]

5 Excluded restrictions

The Commission has also created a short list of *prima facie* excluded restrictive conditions in Article 5 TTBER, which, unlike hard-core restrictions, are only void in themselves; they will not affect the remainder of the agreement. The Commission has in effect introduced a severability rule for such clauses. Whilst they cannot be exempted as part of the block exemption, they can be exempted individually if they meet the four conditions of Article 81(3). There are three main excluded restrictions: (a) any direct or indirect obligation by the licensee to assign or to grant an exclusive licence in respect of its own several improvements to the licensed technology; (b) any direct or indirect obligation on the licensee not to challenge the validity of the IPRs held by the licensor; and (c) in a vertical licensing relationship, any direct or indirect obligation limiting the licensee's ability to exploit its own technology or limiting the ability of any of the parties to the agreement to carry out research and development unless indispensable to prevent the disclosure of the licensed know-how to third parties.

---

[43] Draft Commission Regulation on the application of Article 81(3) of the Treaty to categories of technology transfer agreements, OJ 2003 No. C 235, p. 11, para. 93.

[44] See discussion in Guidelines, paras 107–16.

6 The new methods of assessing individual restraints in licensing agreements

The Regulation introduces new methods of assessing the typical restraints found in IP licensing agreements from a competition point of view. Gone is the form-based stricture of lengthy white lists and grey lists that served both as a reassuring aid to drafting and as a legal straitjacket. The parties no longer have to draft their agreements following a strict menu of white, grey and blacklisted clauses and can give their licensing agreements a form that more closely corresponds to their commercial needs. Instead, the parties are faced with a short list of hard-core restrictions that will render the agreement unenforceable and 'excluded restrictions' that are severable and viewed as non-exemptible within the 'safe haven'.

While the new Regulation is emphatic about what is *not* allowed in an enforceable licensing agreement, it is less forthcoming about what *is* allowed. It proceeds upon the assumption that what is not prohibited is allowed. Traditional lawyers will continue to analyse the TTBER and Guidelines legalistically, teasing answers from the occasional provisos, exceptions and implicit negatives that can be read into the Articles of the Regulation, in particular the hard-core restrictions. However, it is not enough to assess licensing agreements simply by avoiding the proscriptions of the hard-core restrictions and excluded restrictions. The parties are led by the logic of the new legal framework to perform an analysis of the objects and the competitive *effects* of the provisions of their licensing agreement with the aid of Guidelines and court and Commission decisions. They must ultimately rely on their own interpretation of the lawfulness of the contents of their licensing agreements, for the new regulatory framework places a premium upon self-assessment by the parties and their legal advisers rather than a quick-look procedure by the Commission.

To analyse a licensing agreement for the purposes of self-certification, the parties must be able to understand how its terms will be treated differently by competition law depending not only on their form and their purpose but also on their *effects*. An analysis of effects will vary depending upon *inter alia* whether the agreement is between competitors or non-competitors and the degree of market power of the parties to the licensing agreement on the relevant product market as well as entry barriers to that market.[45] This legal analysis places a premium on two separate steps.

First, it is necessary to clarify whether or not a term of the agreement is caught by Article 81(1) in the first place. The key issue raised at this stage of the analysis is whether the agreement as a whole or the term itself will have

45 TT Guidelines, para. 132.

the effect of extinguishing competition that might have thrived had the agreement not occurred or the clause not been inserted. The Commission's Guidelines on the Application of Article 81(3)[46] suggest that the following two questions should be asked:

(1) Does the agreement restrict actual or potential competition that would have existed without the *agreement*? If so, the agreement may be caught by Article 81(1). In making this assessment it is necessary to take into account competition between the parties and competition from third parties. For instance, when two undertakings established in different Member States undertake not to sell products in each other's home markets, (potential) competition that existed prior to the agreement is restricted. Similarly, when a supplier imposes obligations on his distributors not to sell competing products and these obligations foreclose third party access to the market, actual or potential competition that would have existed in the absence of the agreement is restricted. In assessing whether the parties to an agreement are actual or potential competitors the economic and legal context must be taken into account. For instance, if due to the financial risks involved and the technical capabilities of the parties it is unlikely on the basis of objective factors that each party would be able to carry out on its own the activities covered by the agreement, the parties are deemed to be non-competitors in respect of that activity.

(2) Does the agreement restrict actual or potential competition that would have existed in the absence of the contractual *restraint(s)*? If so, the agreement may be caught by Article 81(1). For instance, when a supplier restricts its distributors from competing with each other, (potential) competition that could otherwise have existed between the distributors is restricted. Such restrictions include resale price maintenance and territorial or customer sales restrictions between distributors.

Secondly, it is essential to understand which types of clauses are exemptible and why. An exemptible clause is one that may be caught by Article 81(1) but in certain circumstances can be exempted under Article 81(3). In analysing exemptible clauses, it is also necessary to understand how the line is drawn between exemptibility and non-unenforceability depending on both the form of the clause and its *effect*. Under the new regulatory framework certain clauses, such as output restrictions, non-compete and tying clauses that were previously blacklisted, are now viewed as having pro-competitive effects in certain circumstances and hence being potentially exemptible. The analysis of clauses and agreements under Article 81(3) will depend upon the application of the four conditions in Article 81(3). However,

46 TT Guidelines, *supra* note 2, para. 18.

in the context of IP licensing agreements, the Articles of the Regulation, the Guidelines and previous case law give considerable guidance on the legal effect of the typical clauses of licensing agreements.

In applying this two-step analysis of Article 81 to specific licensing restraints in the new legal environment it is useful to look separately at territorial and non-territorial restraints.

6.1 Territorial restraints under the new framework

The degree of territorial exclusivity that the licensor can offer the licensee lies at the heart of the commercial exchange in a technology licensing agreement. The licensee is prepared to take on the risks of investing capital in manufacturing premises and plants and a distribution system rather than the costs of an elaborate in-house R&D programme. However, unless there is some protection from competition from the licensor and other licensees in its home territory it will have little incentive to take on such risks. The licensee's need for time to tool up, to acquaint itself with the technology and to establish itself as a manufacturer with a distribution system before being subjected to competition from the licensor or other prior licensees is often so great that without such contractual protection many licensees would be deterred from making the investment.

If there were no competition policy constraints, the licensing agreement would be used to confer several levels of protection. The first level of protection would be protection against the licensor itself. This would include an obligation not to grant a licence to manufacture to another licensee in the licensed territory and not to sell directly into the licensed territory. The second level of protection also includes protection against the direct sales from other licensees. These direct-sales restrictions could be limited to 'active' sales in the sense that the other licensees would be prohibited in their licensing agreement from advertising and establishing selling facilities in the territory, or could extend to 'passive' sales restrictions, which would prohibit a licensee from responding to orders received from within the territory of another licensee.

Licensees would of course prefer to have as much territorial protection as possible, but there are limits to what can be secured simply by using the IP licensing contract. It would be unlawful for a licensor to require licensees to bind their buyers not to export. Moreover, the doctrine of exhaustion keeps open the paths of parallel trading between buyers and sellers in two different licensed territories. Hence the most that can be done lawfully in the licensing agreement is to place limits on the capacity of licensees (or the licensor) to directly sell to other licensees or in the licensor's territory.

To the extent that the licensor can offer these protections to the licensee, it will be able to offer an inducement to investment by the licensee that will go a long way towards minimizing the financial risks of manufacturing and introducing new products into a market. However, despite the obvious economic benefits of encouraging technology transfer, and the indispensability of territorial protection, EC competition law has proved to be cautious in following the logic of incentives, preferring to give priority to its concerns to keep open the flow of inter-state, intra-technology trade between exclusive territories. The courts and the Commission have acknowledged the importance of territorial exclusivity as an incentive to technology transfer and indeed the general pro-competitive nature of licensing agreements. However, in their decisions on territorial restraints in licensing agreements, they have been reluctant to encourage 'bottom-up' integration by the spread of IP-protected technology manufacture throughout the Common Market, preferring to rely on top-down negative integration by using competition law to limit restrictions on sales between licensees.

6.1.2 Exemptible exclusive territoriality For historical reasons related to the integration dimension of EC competition law, the Commission has never fully recognized the indispensability of exclusive territorial restrictions under Article 81(1) and the logic of applying the ancillary restraints doctrine to territorial exclusivity in licensing agreements. The Draft Regulation stated:[47]

> Where the licensee is facing substantial sunk investments, agreements granting an exclusive licence are likely to fulfil the conditions of Article 81(3) except where there are no real alternatives to the licensor's technology on the market or where most of the available technologies have been licensed to the same licensee.

Within the safe haven and presumably under Article 81(3) more generally, in the case of vertical IP licensing agreements, the scope for territorial exclusivity in the block exemption is quite wide. The Regulation and Guidelines distinguish between two types of territorial protections: restrictions on production within a given territory (exclusive or sole licences) and restrictions on the sale of products incorporating the licensed technology into a given territory and to a given customer group (sales restrictions).

6.1.3 Exclusive and sole licences Under the block exemption, the first form of territorial protection that a licensor can offer a licensee is protection from competition from *manufacture* of the licensed goods within the licensed territory by either the licensor or other licensees.

If the licensor gives the licensee an exclusive licence, it provides that the licensee is the only one who is permitted to manufacture using the licensed

47 *Supra* note 43, para. 157.

technology within a given territory. It consists of an obligation by the licensor thus not to produce itself or license others to produce within a given territory. A sole licence, in contrast, is limited to an obligation by the licensor not to license other licensees to produce within a given territory. It presupposes a reservation of such a right by the licensor.

The Guidelines offer three rules for exclusive and sole licensing. First, an exclusive licence (or sole licence) between non-competitors – if caught by Article 81(1) – is likely to fulfil the conditions of Article 81(3) *up to the level of dominance*. There are probably two reasons for this. First, as the Guidelines themselves point out:[48]

> [t]he right to grant an exclusive licence is generally necessary in order to induce the licensee to invest in the licensed technology and to bring the products to market in a timely manner. This is particularly the case where the licensee must make large investments in further developing the licensed technology. To intervene against the exclusivity once the licensee has made a commercial success of the licensed technology would deprive the licensee of the fruits of his success and would be detrimental to competition, the dissemination of technology and innovation.

In addition, all the licensor is doing is sharing its exclusive rights under the patent or other IPR. The alternative to the exclusive licence realistically would be no new product on the market. The exemption would appear applicable both within and outside the safe haven as long as the technology licensed did not achieve a dominant position in the relevant market.

For similar reasons, an exclusive licence offered by a licensor in a non-reciprocal agreement between competitors (in essence a vertical agreement) is block-exempted up to the market-share threshold of 20 per cent, and above the market-share threshold the likely anti-competitive effects of such exclusive licensing must be analysed.

The third category, consisting of reciprocal exclusive licensing between competitors, is generally viewed as a hard-core restriction falling under Article 4(1)(c). Reciprocal sole licensing between competitors is block-exempted up to the market-share threshold of 20 per cent. Above the threshold, in cases in which the parties have a significant degree of market power, the Guidelines state that 'such agreements may facilitate collusion by ensuring that the parties are the only sources of output in the market based on the licensed technologies'.[49]

6.1.4 Sales restrictions The second type of territorial protection offered by the licensor as an inducement to agree to a licence are *sales restrictions*, that

---

[48] Guidelines, *supra* note 2, para. 165.
[49] TT Guidelines, para. 163.

is obligations not to sell in a particular licensed territory. The Regulation again distinguishes between licensing agreements between competitors and licensing agreements between non-competitors.

In the case of agreements between *non-competitors* sales restrictions between the licensor and a licensee are block-exempted up to the market-share threshold of 30 per cent. Even above the market-share threshold, restrictions on all sales by licensees to territories or customer groups reserved for the licensor may fall outside Article 81(1) if the licensor or licensee would not have licensed without such a condition. 'A technology owner cannot normally be expected to create direct competition with himself on the basis of his own technology'.[50] Again, this would appear to be the case for restrictions on the sales above the market-share limits up to the level of dominance.

The Guidelines add that '[a]bove the market share threshold restrictions on active sales between licensees' territories and customer groups limit intra-technology competition and are likely to be caught by Article 81(1) when the individual licensee has a significant degree of market power'.[51] Such restrictions, however, may fulfil the conditions of Article 81(3) if they are necessary to prevent free riding and to induce the licensee to make the investment necessary for efficient exploitation of the licensed technology inside his territory and to promote sales of the licensed product. In other words, even above the market-share limits and below dominance, restrictions on *active* sales are exempted for the period of the validity of the licensing agreement.

Restrictions on *passive* sales by licensees, in contrast, are permissible for two years from the date on which the licensee benefiting from the restrictions first put the product incorporating the licensed technology on the market inside his exclusive territory. Passive-sales restrictions exceeding this two-year period will be viewed as hard-core restrictions falling within Article 4(2)(b).

In the case of *non-reciprocal agreements between competitors*, restrictions on active and passive sales by the licensee or the licensor into the exclusive territory or to the exclusive customer group of the other are also block-exempted. Even above the market-share threshold of 20 per cent, if such restrictions are indispensable for the dissemination of valuable technologies, they may be exempted under Article 81(3). The Guidelines take a very conservative view of the possibilities of exempting such vertical restrictions. If the *licensor* has a relatively weak market position in the territory where he himself exploits the technology, and if restrictions on active sales are indispensable to induce the licensor to grant the licence, protection against the risk of facing

50 TT Guidelines, para. 172.
51 TT Guidelines, para. 174.

active competition from licensees in his main area of activity may be exemptible.

Similarly, passive-sales restrictions could be viewed as indispensable within the meaning of Article 81(3) for the period of time required for the protected *licensee* to penetrate a new market and establish a market presence in the allocated territory or vis-à-vis the allocated customer group. This protection against active sales only partially allows the licensee to overcome the asymmetry it faces from other licensees already established on the market.

In a *reciprocal agreement between competitors*, restrictions on active and passive sales to customers and territories allocated to a licensee are hard-core restrictions.[52] Such restrictions are thought by the competition authorities to have a high potential for market sharing since they prevent both parties from selling actively and passively into territories and to customer groups which they actually served or could realistically have served in the absence of the agreement. But this is further evidence of a broad-brush approach adopted by the Commission to horizontal licensing agreements.

6.1.5 Quantity limitations and output restrictions Output limitations imposed on the licensee in agreements between *non-competitors* are often pro-competitive because they promote technology transfer.[53]

> As a supplier of technology the licensor should normally be free to determine the output produced with the licensed technology by the licensee. If the licensor were not free to determine the output of the licensee, a number of licence agreements might not come into existence in the first place, which would have a negative impact on the dissemination of new technology. This is particularly likely to be the case where the licensor is also a producer, since in that case the output of the licensees may find their way back into the licensor's main area of operation and thus have a direct impact on these activities.

The Commission has indicated that output restrictions in licence agreements between non-competitors are block-exempted up to the market-share threshold of 30 per cent, provided that the licensor is not obliged to limit the output of *other licensees* or the total output of *all licensees*. If he is thus obliged, it is considered that the agreement is implementing a concerted practice limiting output at the level of the licensees.

The main anti-competitive risk flowing from output restrictions on licensees in agreements between non-competitors, according to the Commission, is reduced intra-technology competition *between licensees*. The

---

52 Article 4(1)(c) TTBER.

53 TT Guidelines, para. 178.

significance of such anti-competitive effects depends on the market position of the licensor and the licensees and the extent to which the licensee, due to the output limitation, is prevented from satisfying demand for the products incorporating the licensed technology.

In some cases, output limitations may also be used to facilitate the partitioning of markets and to extend territorial protection beyond what is allowed under the TTBER and the present guidelines, for example when quantities are adjusted over time to cover only local demand or when sales restrictions on licensees require them not to sell into a territory or customer group reserved for the licensor.

Reciprocal output restrictions in licence agreements between *competitors* constitute a hard-core restriction covered by Article 4(1)(b) of the TTBER, but output restrictions imposed on the licensee in a non-reciprocal agreement or on one of the licensees in a reciprocal agreement are block-exempted up to the market-share threshold of 20 per cent.

6.1.6 Field-of-use restrictions Field-of-use restrictions may be viewed as simply a partial allocation of the IP protection conferred upon the right holder and hence the competition effects are little different from those caused by unilateral action. Even when combined with territorial exclusivity, field-of-use restrictions can be pro-competitive in effect by encouraging the licensor to license his technology for applications that fall outside his main field of exploitation. The Guidelines point out (in paragraph 185) that in 'agreements between non-competitors the licensor is normally also entitled to grant sole or exclusive licences to different licensees limited to one or more fields of use. Such restrictions limit intra-technology competition between licensees in the same way as exclusive licensing and are analysed in the same way'.[54] The Guidelines require that a distinction be made between *field-of-use* restrictions, in which the licence is limited to one or more technical fields of application or one or more product markets, and *customer restrictions*, which are hard-core restrictions under Articles 4(1)(c) and 4(2)(b) of the TTBER. Field-of-use agreements between actual or potential competitors are block-exempted up to the market-share threshold of 20 per cent.

6.2 Non-territorial restraints under the new legal framework

Under the new legal framework it is also necessary to analyse non-territorial restraints differently depending on whether they occur in vertical or in horizontal licensing agreements. It is helpful to categorize non-territorial restraints into two main types: non-restrictive and exemptible. The first type consists of

---

[54] TT Guidelines, para. 185; cf. also discussion of exclusive and sole licences, *supra* section 6.1.3.

certain non-territorial restraints that are normally not restrictive of competition. The main criterion used by the Community, courts and Commission for finding a contractual restraint to be non-restrictive under Article 81(1) is the 'ancillary restraints' test, that is those provisions that are absolutely indispensable to IPR licensing agreements because without them the value of the IPRs could be lost.

The second type of provision commonly found in licensing agreements is one that although caught by Article 81(1) is nevertheless exemptible under Article 81(3). This requires a different calculus, a use of the Guidelines and the relevant case-law to make an assessment of the applicability of the four conditions of Article 81(3) to the particular clause. Insofar as a specific non-territorial restraint is block-exempted, it offers a promising case for exemption in agreements made in respect of licensed products exceeding market-share thresholds. It is also important to be able to distinguish when such a provision crosses the line between exemptible and non-exemptible because it overlaps with a hard-core restriction.

6.2.1 Non-territorial restraints not restrictive of competition With the removal of a white list of exemptible restrictions, which was offered in previous regulations, it is useful to revive the distinction between non-restrictive and exemptible clauses in licensing agreements. The white lists in previous regulations tended to combine contractual restraints not caught by Article 81(1) with those that were so caught but nevertheless exempted in a single white list of clauses. For parties engaged in self-certification it is wise to make such distinctions clearer. The Guidelines offer assistance in this endeavour by setting out a list of examples of obligations in licence agreements that are 'generally not restrictive of competition within the meaning of Article 81(1)'.[55] These include:

(a) confidentiality obligations,
(b) obligations on licensees not to sub-license,
(c) obligations not to use the licensed technology after the expiry of the agreement, provided that the licensed technology remains valid and in force,
(d) obligations to assist the licensor in enforcing the licensed IPRs,
(e) obligations to pay minimum royalties or to produce a minimum quantity of products incorporating the licensed technology, and
(f) obligations to use the licensor's trade mark or indicate the name of the licensor on the product.

---

55 TT Guidelines, para. 155.

These clauses offer examples of what the courts and the Commission have labelled 'ancillary restrictions', or those restrictions that are indispensable to effectuating the main purpose of the licensing agreement. Each one has been viewed in the context of its role as an indispensable restraint to allow the licensing agreement to be made in the first place.

Other clauses are less obviously non-restrictive of competition under Article 81(1) and require exemption. In such cases the vertical/horizontal distinction becomes crucial. For example, a non-competition clause, that is an obligation on the licensee not to use third-party technologies that compete with the licensed technology, may have certain pro-competitive functions. It can reassure the licensor to an exclusive licence that the licensed property will be commercially exploited and offer protection should the exclusive licensee be attracted to competing technology.

The TTBER therefore exempts non-compete obligations both in the case of agreements between competitors and in the case of agreements between non-competitors up to the market-share thresholds of 20 and 30 per cent, respectively. However, they must not directly or indirectly limit the licensee's ability to exploit its own technology or limit the ability of any of the parties to the agreement to carry out research and development, unless such a restriction is indispensable to prevent the disclosure of the licensed know-how to third parties.[56]

A second area of micro-regulation attempting to establish a balance in the TTBER occurs when the licensor requires grantbacks of improvements. The licensing of patents and/ or know-how, either separately or together, almost inevitably leads to improvements being discovered by licensees. Some improvements can themselves be patentable. Most consist of know-how that can be protected through contract. Some improvements are 'severable'; that is they are products or processes capable of being exploited independently of the original intellectual property right. They are defined in the Guidelines[57] as improvements that can be worked without use of the original licensed product. Other improvements are 'non-severable'; they are capable of being used only in conjunction with the protected product or process in the original licence.

Typically, licensors are reluctant to license without a right of disclosure and use of the licensee's improvements. Disclosure is needed in order to monitor the licensee's development and use of the improvements. The right of use allows the licensor to improve the original product or process for its own use and for the use of other licensees. A number of licensors would prefer such rights to be exclusive or even assigned back, reasoning that the improvements

56 See Articles 5(2) and 4(1)(d) TTBER.
57 TT Guidelines, para. 98(a).

are derived from the original invention. They would view a contractual commitment to granting back improvements as part of the *quid pro quo* for granting the licence in the first place. Some recognize that there is more of an incentive for the licensee to develop and communicate improvements if the licensee can share in the fruits of its severable improvements by licensing them to third parties, but the concern about creating extra competitors often leads to a reluctance to cede too much freedom to licensees.

From the viewpoint of EC competition policy, the issue of the stimulus to innovation provided by improvements is too important to be left to freedom of contract. Excessive unilateral control over improvements by strong licensors and/or licensees in the form of restraints in licensing contracts must be curtailed in the interest of promoting the development and diffusion of technology. The restraints in licensing agreements must not be drawn so widely that they stifle the incentives of licensees to improve the technology and disclose the results of their improvements more widely. Yet the rules should not be so unfriendly to licensors that they create a chilling effect on licensing.

The balance struck in the new TTBER depends upon whether or not the improvement by the licensee is severable or non-severable, that is whether or not the licensee can work the technology without using the licensed product or process. In the case of severable improvements, the licensor is barred from including a provision requiring the licensee to *assign* any or all of its severable improvements to the licensor.[58] The TTBER also provides that the licensor can only require the licensee to license back *on a non-exclusive basis* any severable improvements made by the licensee to the licensed product or process or any new applications.[59] On the other hand, the licensor can require exclusive licences of non-severable improvements. Moreover, the TTBER places no reciprocal obligation upon licensors to license their improvements to the licensee or indeed to cross-license the improvements of other licensees back to the licensee. The Commission offers an explanation in the Guidelines to the effect that it helps innovation when the licensor is given the freedom to require non-reciprocal non-exclusive grantbacks. Yet it places licensees in a difficult position, because on the one hand it allows passive sales from other licensees after two years, thus opening up competition between licensees, yet it places the licensor in a position to favour some licensees and disfavour others.

6.2.2 Quality controls and licensing A third complex area of regulation is that of quality controls and licensing. The concern of the licensor to ensure

58 Article 5(1)(b) TTBER; Guidelines, paras 109–11.
59 Article 5(1)(a) TTBER; Guidelines, paras 109–11.

that the licensee preserves quality standards lies at the heart of the licensing decision, particularly when the licensor's trade mark is associated with the licensed product. In general the insistence on minimum *quality* specifications by itself, as long as they are agreed upon in advance and based on objectively verifiable criteria, has not been viewed as restrictive of competition under Article 81(1). Moreover, the licensor can reserve a right to monitor quality standards by carrying out related checks. These provisions are recognized by the Court of Justice and the Commission as indispensable to an appropriate exploitation of the invention.[60] In the previous Technology Transfer Regulation the Commission whitelisted an obligation on the licensee (Article 2(1)(5)):

> to observe minimum quality specifications, including *technical specifications*, for the licensed product or to procure goods or services from the licensor or from an undertaking designated by the licensor, in so far as these quality specifications, products or services are necessary for:
> (a) a technically proper exploitation of the licensed technology; or
> (b) ensuring that the product of the licensee conforms to the minimum quality specifications that are applicable to the licensor and other licensees.

In other words, it deals with tie-ins justified by quality specifications as a special exemptible category, applying the restrictions in respect of technical exploitation and conformity with standards for the licensor and even allowing a tie-in where necessary for such purposes.

On the other hand, quality specifications can also mask a tie-in. In the context of technology licensing, tying occurs when the licensor makes the licensing of one technology (the tying product) conditional upon the licensee taking a licence for another technology or purchasing a product (the tied product) from the licensor or someone designated by him.

The TT Guidelines recognize that tying can actually be pro-competitive in two types of situations: when the tied product is necessary for a technically satisfactory exploitation of the licensed technology; or when it is necessary to ensure that production under the licence conforms to quality standards desired by the licensor. The Guidelines explain:[61]

---

60 See, for example, European Commission of 13 October 1988, Case IV/31.498 – *Delta Chemie /DDD*, OJ 1988 No. L 309, p. 34; quality standards applied to manufacturing and marketing were held not to be caught by Article 81(1) because they were 'inspired by the legitimate desire of the licensor to ensure the strict conformity of the products'.

61 TT Guidelines, para. 194.

> In such cases tying is normally either not restrictive of competition or covered by Article 81(3). Where the licensees use the licensor's trademark or brand name or where it is otherwise obvious to consumers that there is a link between the product incorporating the licensed technology and the licensor, the licensor has a legitimate interest in ensuring that the quality of the products is such that it does not undermine the value of his technology or his reputation as an economic operator.

The Guidelines also point out that:

> [t]ying is also likely to be pro-competitive where the tied product allows the licensee to exploit the licensed technology significantly more efficiently [than other available alternatives]. For instance, where the licensor licenses a particular process technology the parties can also agree that the licensee buys a catalyst from the licensor which is developed for use with the licensed technology and which allows the technology to be exploited more efficiently than in the case of other catalysts.[62]

In such cases, where 'the restriction is caught by Article 81(1), the conditions of Article 81(3) are likely to be fulfilled *even above* the market share thresholds'.[63]

In cases in which the licensor does not occupy a dominant position and the relationship is predominantly vertical there is no need to prohibit tie-ins. The case law of the Commission reinforces that view particularly in respect of know-how. In *Jus Rol* for example, an obligation placed upon the licensee to buy a pre-mix from the licensor was regarded as essential to ensure the proper proportions in the preparation of the mix as well as the correct results in the final product.[64] The tie-in was justified as necessary to ensure consistency of quality in the licensed product. In *Delta Chemie*[65] and *Moosehead/ Whitbread*[66] the Commission acknowledged that the tie-ins were justified by the need to ensure consistency of manufacture and marketing in situations where the trade mark figured prominently in the agreement.

Under the TTBER, tying is block-exempted in the case of agreements between competitors up to the market-share threshold of 20 per cent and in the case of agreements between non-competitors up to the market-share threshold of 30 per cent. The market-share thresholds apply to any relevant technology or product market affected by the licence agreement, including the market for

---

62 TT Guidelines, para. 195.

63 *Ibid.*, emphasis added.

64 European Commission of 22 December 1987, Case IV/31.208, *Rich Products/Jus Rol*, OJ 1987 No. L 52, p. 51.

65 European Commission of 13 October 1988, Case IV/31.498, *Delta Chemie/DDD*, OJ 1988 No. L 309, p. 34.

66 European Commission of 23 March 1990, Case IV/32.736, *Moosehead/ Whitbread*, OJ 1990 No. L 100, p. 32.

the tied product. Above the market-share threshold it is necessary to balance the anti-competitive and pro-competitive effects of tying. The Guidelines explain: [67]

> The main restrictive effect of tying is foreclosure of competing suppliers of the tied product . . . In the absence of market power in the tying product the licensor cannot use his technology for the anticompetitive purpose of foreclosing suppliers of the tied product. Furthermore, as in the case of non-compete obligations, the tie must cover a certain proportion of the market for the tied product for appreciable foreclosure effects to occur.

So there has been a major loosening of the regulatory framework in respect of tying.

6.2.3 Royalties From a competition point of view, it is now accepted by the Commission and the courts that, for the most part, Article 81(1) should have little application to bargains struck over royalty payments as long as they have been freely negotiated between the parties.

The Guidelines[68] state in respect of royalties that the:

> parties to a licence agreement are normally free to determine the royalty payable by the licensee and its mode of payment without being caught by Article 81(1). This principle applies both to agreements between competitors and agreements between non-competitors. Royalty obligations may for instance take the form of lump sum payments, a percentage of the selling price or a fixed amount for each product incorporating the licensed technology. In cases where the licensed technology relates to an input which is incorporated into a final product it is as a general rule not restrictive of competition that royalties are calculated on the basis of the price of the final product, provided that it incorporates the licensed technology. In the case of software licensing royalties based on the number of users and royalties calculated on a per machine basis are generally compatible with Article 81(1).

However the parties are not left entirely free of regulation of royalty arrangements in licensing agreements under Article 81. There are competition concerns with bargains that in some way go beyond the pure exchange of royalty for the licensed product in terms of (a) duration and (b) the base for calculating royalties; in both cases, the concern is that the licensor might exceed its entitlement under the scope of the IPR grant.

6.2.4 Duration The freedom to spread royalty payments for the use of the technology over a period extending beyond the duration of the licensed IPRs

---

67 TT Guidelines, para. 193.
68 TT Guidelines, para. 156.

as well as after the licensed know-how has entered the public domain is now accepted within the safe haven and broadly within Article 81(3), even though it is outside the TTBER.

The Guidelines[69] point out that:

> [n]otwithstanding the fact that the block exemption only applies as long as the technology is valid and in force, the parties can normally agree to extend royalty obligations beyond the period of validity of the licensed intellectual property rights without falling foul of Article 81(1). Once these rights expire, third parties can legally exploit the technology in question and compete with the parties to the agreement. Such actual and potential competition will normally suffice to ensure that the obligation in question does not have appreciable anti-competitive effects.

If an agreement provides that there is a right for either party to terminate the agreement, then there is greater assurance that the period for calculating the royalties is part of the original bargain struck in respect of the original intellectual property package.

Even assuming a right to terminate, however, there is still a residual concern for royalties on expired patents, which could reduce the parties' freedom of contract in respect of the method of paying royalties. In the case of licensed patents, under the new technology transfer block exemption, the agreement may contain an obligation on the licensee to continue paying the royalties over a period going beyond the duration of the licensed patents, essentially as a device to facilitate payment under the original bargain that is struck between licensor and licensee.[70]

6.2.5 The base for calculating royalties Connected with the regulation of the duration of royalty payments are the restrictions imposed by Article 81(1) on the base for calculating royalties in terms of the products used as the basis of calculation. In the original Patent Licensing Regulation, any clause charging royalties on unpatented products, products not produced by a patented process or products produced by no longer secret know-how was blacklisted. In the know-how block exemption, clauses that charged royalties on goods not produced using the licensed technology or using it after it had been made public by the licensor in violation of the agreement were similarly proscribed.[71] Finally, when a royalty

---

69 TT Guidelines, para. 159.

70 In contrast, in the case of know-how, the parties are given the freedom to determine the nature of the obligation to continue paying royalties until the end of the agreement even if the know-how becomes publicly known; Article 2(1)(7)(a) TTBER.

71 Case 193/83, *Windsurfing International v. Commission*, [1986] ECR 611; see also European Commission of 15 December 1986, Case IV/31.302, *Boussois/Interpane*, OJ 1987 No. L 50, p. 30.

rate is set that takes the form of a restriction on a party's ability to determine prices, it will be viewed as a hard-core restriction whether the agreement is between competitors or one between non-competitors.[72]

6.2.6 No-challenge clauses No-challenge clauses are obligations undertaken by the licensee not to challenge the validity of the licensor's IPRs after becoming more closely acquainted with the protected product or process as a result of the licence. The desire of a licensor to insert a no-challenge clause in an IP licence is often so strong that without such contractual protection many might be reluctant to license their IP at all. The risk of a licensee using its intimate knowledge of the patent process acquired as a result of a patent licence to devalue the investment in the R&D for opportunistic reasons could deter a decision to license at all or at the very least restrict it to partners over which there were extra-contractual controls.

For many years, however, this factor was viewed as completely overshadowed by the issue of public policy that the rules of competition law should not indirectly encourage the weakening of the integrity of the patenting process.[73] Thus in a number of cases, the Commission found that the presence of a no-challenge clause was a restriction of competition because it prevented the licensee from removing 'an obstacle to his freedom of action'.[74] In *Davidson Rubber*,[75] the Commission insisted upon the licensor removing the no-challenge clause as the price of granting the exemption. It deemed the fact that the licensee was in the best position to detect a weakness in the validity of the IPR a reason not to allow the licensor to restrain him. On the other hand, the right to challenge can be opportunistically misused by licensees seeking to avoid their contractual obligation to pay royalties or to have greater opportunity to use rival technology. In *Bayer and Henneke v. Sullhofer*,[76] the ECJ held on an Article 177 reference that, before a no-challenge clause could be found to be contrary to Article 85(1), it must be looked at in its legal and economic context, and that is a task for the national court.

In the current version of the TTBER, no-challenge clauses are not blacklisted but they are excluded restrictions under Article 5. On the other hand, the licensor may reserve a right in the licence to the effect that if the licensee chal-

---

72 Article 4(1)(a) and (2)(a) TTBER.

73 See, for example, European Commission of 10 January 1979, COMP IV/29.290, *Vaessen/Moris*, OJ 1979 No. L 19, p. 32, paras 34 *et seq.*

74 *Ibid.*

75 European Commission of 9 June 1972, Case IV/17.448, *Davidson Rubber*, OJ 1972 No. L 143, p. 31.

76 Case 65/86, *Bayer and Henneke v. Sullhofer*, [1988] ECR 611.

lenges the validity of the licensor's IPRs held in the Common Market, the licensor is entitled to terminate the technology transfer agreement.

Moreover, the Guidelines have acknowledged that no-challenge clauses may be an indispensable restraint in a patent or other IP dispute settlement agreement as long as the IP is not obviously invalid.[77]

7 Assessment of the new regulatory framework: the benefits of wider scope and flexibility

There is little doubt that the wider scope of the block exemption, extending to software agreements and designs, and the abandonment of the strait-jacket of limited categories of restraints have created greater flexibility for the parties to IP licensing agreements to draft agreements relating to their commercial needs. The use of Guidelines not only helps to create a framework of analysis for new clauses in licensing agreements; it also creates a basis for expanding the Article 81 analysis to new types of IPRs. For example, the licensing of *sui generis* databases, merchandise licences, agreements for the use of non-software copyright and related rights such as phonographic producers', performing artists', broadcasters' and satellite rights as well as rental rights in principle can be analysed by analogy to the principles in the Guidelines even if they may not fit the label of technology transfer.

There is also little doubt that there are benefits derived from the greater economic realism of the new Regulation and Guidelines. The distinction between licensing agreements between competitors and those between non-competitors allows a far more liberal regulatory regime for 'vertical' licensing agreements, which are after all the majority of IP licensing arrangements. The reduced blacklist for vertical agreements means that a number of previously non-exempted restrictions can be given a more balanced treatment. Certain restraints such as field-of-use provisions, output restrictions, customer restrictions between non-competitors, non-compete clauses and tie-ins can offer efficiencies and are now capable of exemption in the appropriate circumstances.

The retention of a regulatory regime of hard-core restraints that includes clauses that are not almost always anti-competitive may be questioned. In particular, the outright ban on exclusive territories and customer restrictions in licensing agreements between competitors may be overbroad, particularly when the competitor retains the right to exploit its own technology. A greater concern for innovation would recognize that cooperation between competitors is sometimes the only way forward and that competition policy should apply a more nuanced regulatory rule. Nevertheless, this stage of reform has concentrated on ensuring that genuine vertical IP licensing agreements should be

[77] TT Guidelines, *supra* note 2, para. 209.

treated more leniently, and that is an extremely important gain in the regulatory framework.

The introduction of market-shares limits has had its critics. Many have argued that Article 82, the withdrawal procedures and the prohibition of hard-core restrictions are adequate safeguards against misuse of market power. Moreover, the market shares are set at rather low levels for technology-transfer agreements. Many have complained about the uncertainties created above the market-share limits. Finally, it is certainly true that market shares are only an approximation of market power and indeed at times a rather arbitrary indicator of market power.

In principle, however, the greater the degree of actual market power enjoyed by the licensed product, the greater will be the competition concern. In the US Guidelines, the point is made that the concerns with market share are directed to the potential of licensed products with high market shares to create anti-competitive foreclosure and raise competitors' costs.

In any event, it is important to see how the nature of the safe haven has changed. In previous regulations, the safe haven of the block exemption was prescriptive. It conferred an exemption on the parties without the agreement being notified to the Commission or litigated in the courts. After modernization, the effect of the TTBER, along with the other block exemption regulations, is more declaratory in the sense that it states that certain types of licensing agreements are clearly exemptible, and this serves to warn Member State courts and competition authorities to stay within certain parameters in their interpretation of the application of Article 81(3) to IP licensing agreements. Now the analytical framework provided by the Guidelines can at times become even more important than the TTBER, because of the unpredictability of market shares. The radical nature of the change in the legal framework from legally certain BERs to Guidelines and BERs limited by market-share maxima will certainly require greater economic literacy on the part of IP licensing legal specialists. However, equally important will be the need for Continental lawyers specializing in competition law to accept the shift from legal certainty to an analytical framework provided by guidelines and case law.

6 Patent pools – policy and problems

Hanns Ullrich

1 Introduction

Contractual arrangements between two or more holders of a certain stock of patents for the joint exploitation of their exclusive rights vis-à-vis third parties are commonly referred to as patent pools. These may take various forms in accordance with the purpose of the pooling. Generally a distinction is made between arrangements involving centralization of the exploitation, on the one hand, by transfer of control to a joint venture or even an independent enterprise acting as an agent or on its own behalf and, on the other, by way of bundling individually held patents for licensing by one of the partners.[1] While these differences are not totally irrelevant to an antitrust analysis, given that the form chosen may reflect the competitive strategy the pooling arrangement is to serve,[2] its economically and analytically characteristic feature is that the exploitation of industrial property rights[3] relating to the technology of two or more enterprises is made the subject of an agreement on the building of a joint

1 Recent legal literature on the organization of pools is scarce; antitrust literature tends to use a narrow definition by requiring central control over exploitation by either transfer of property or exclusive licensing to a central unit, and thus foregoes one of the essential criteria of antitrust legality, which is free parallel licensing by the partners; see Stumpf, Herbert and M. Groß (2005), *Der Lizenzvertrag*, Frankfurt am Main: Recht und Wirtschaft, 8th ed., notes 543 *et seq.*; Schulte, Hans-Jürgen (1971), *Lizenzaustauschverträge und Patentgemeinschaften im amerikanischen und im deutschen Recht*, Frankfurt am Main: Athenäum, pp. 94 *et seq.*; for practical examples see *infra* note 9. For an economic typology see Bekkers, Rudi, Erik Iversen and Knut Blind, 'Patent Pools and Non-assertion Agreements: Coordination Mechanisms for Multi-party IPR Holders in Standardization', Paper for the EASST 2006 Conference, Lausanne, 23–6 August http://www2.unil.ch/easst2006/Papers/B/Bekkers%20Iversen%20Blind.pdf, accessed 4 November 2007, section 2.5.

2 See section 2.1.1 *infra*. Note that pooling involves a policy decision on who is to determine and pay the costs of the patenting strategy for the pooled patents (where to apply, how to process applications, where and how long to maintain, where and how to enforce the patents etc.).

3 Typically patents and patent applications, but also utility models; possibly also copyright in software; hardly any other forms of know-how (not suited to independent control or to mass exploitation) or of design (although conceivable in certain industries, pooling of designs would raise competition law problems of its own).

patent package and on the central administration of its licensing to third parties.[4] Joint third-party licensing distinguishes patent pools from cross-licensing agreements, whereby parties mutually grant each other licences on their exclusive rights for individual use in accordance with the agreed terms. Cross-licensing frequently goes together with pooling, typically when the patentees themselves do business in downstream product or service markets. But cross-licensing among partners in a pool is not of its essence. Both types of arrangement raise their own problems of analysis and assessment under competition law; where they co-exist, additional issues may arise.[5]

Patent pooling is a recurrent phenomenon. Originally pools were established in assembly industries or for system technologies, where they may serve to combine the working of independent inventions.[6] Some of these pools have been challenged in the USA, and successfully so mainly when they involved restrictions going beyond mere pooling (that is, as is required to make inventions function together as elements of complex technologies).[7] In the EU,

---

4 A broad definition is also given by the TT Guidelines (Commission Notice – Guidelines on the application of Article 81 of the Treaty to technology transfer agreements, OJ 2004 No. C 101, p. 2), paras 41 and 210. Note that independent 'collecting' of patents for assembly into a package and autonomous exploitation does not constitute a pooling case under the antitrust laws (but may raise issues of market dominance and its abuse).

5 See section 2.1.1 *infra.* Note that, as a general matter, under European law cross-licensing agreements are governed by the TTBER (Commission Regulation 772/2004 of 27 April 2004 on the application of Article 81(3) of the Treaty to categories of technology transfer agreements, OJ 2004 No. L 123, p. 11), and that they are so governed by analogy to the TTBER even if they are concluded between more than two parties (TT Guidelines, *supra* n. 4, para. 40). By contrast, US antitrust enforcement agencies tend to apply similar criteria to both types of arrangements; see the US IP Antitrust Guidelines (Antitrust Guidelines for the Licensing of Intellectual Property, Issued by the US Department of Justice and the Federal Trade Commission, 6 April 1995, note 1, section 3, http://www.usdoj.gov/atr/public/guidelines/0558.htm, accessed 4 November 2007), section 5.5; Department of Justice (DoJ) & Federal Trade Commission (FTC) (2007), Antitrust Enforcement and Intellectual Property Rights: Promoting Innovation and Competition, Washington, DC, http://www.ftc.gov/reports/innovation/P040101PromotingInnovationandCompetitionrpt0704.pdf, accessed 4 November 2007, pp. 59 *et seq.*

6 See Merges, Robert (2001), 'Institutions for Intellectual Property Transactions: The Case of Patent Pools', in Rochelle C. Dreyfuss, Diane L. Zimmerman and Harry First (eds), *Expanding the Boundaries of Intellectual Property*, Oxford: Oxford University Press, p. 123, at 135 *et seq.*; for a detailed presentation of pre-World War II pools see Neumeyer, Friedrich (1932), *Patentgemeinschaften und deren Aufbau bei amerikanischen Industrieverbänden*, Marburg, Elwert'sche Verlagsbuchhandlung, *passim*; see also Kronstein, Heinrich (1967) *Das Recht der internationalen Kartelle*, Berlin: Schweitzer, pp. 32 *et seq.*, 187 et *seq.*

7 See Andewelt, Roger B. (1985), 'Analysis of Patent Pools under the Antitrust

patent pools attracted little enforcement attention[8] until two currents converged: a clarification of US enforcement policy vis-à-vis non-restrictive or pro-competitive pooling that accompanied cooperative research and standardization in the information industry,[9] and the internationalization of research collaboration and of joint standard-setting in precisely these industries and in telecommunications, in which large European enterprises were involved or even played a major role.[10] Just as assembly industries or system technologies presuppose the combination of a large variety of patents of different component manufacturers, modern information and telecommunication technologies require the interoperability of all elements, a matter that is solved through innovation-driven, that is, patent-based standardization.[11] Frequently enough, pools thus are both the result and the companion of more or less strategic, tight or loose innovation alliances, and sometimes they have even been supported by public money, at least in their early stages.[12] While

Law', *Antitrust L.J.*, **53**, 611, 633 *et seq.*; Pietzke, Rudolf (1983), *Patentschutz, Wettbewerbsbeschränkungen und Konzentration im Recht der Vereinigten Staaten von Amerika*, Cologne: Carl Heymanns, pp. 83 *et seq.*; Schulte, *supra* note 1, at 107 *et seq.*, 129 *et seq.*

[8] European Commission, 11th Report on Competition Policy 1981, No. 93 (*Concast/Mannesmann*); *ibid.*, no. 94 (*IGR-Stereo TV*); see also, as regards the latter pool, 14th Report on Competition Policy 1984, no. 92.

[9] See US IP Antitrust Guidelines, *supra* note 5, and their implementation by a number of Business Review Letters of the DoJ, namely of 26 June 1997 (*MPEG LA/MPEG 2* – compression technology standard); of 16 December 1999 (*Philips, Sony, Pioneer* – DVD-ROM, DVD-Video formats); of 10 June 1999 (*Hitachi, Matsushita, Mitsubishi* – DVD-ROM, DVD-Video formats); of 12 June 2002 (*3G Patent Platform* – 3G Standards).

[10] See Bekkers *et al.*, *supra* note 1, at section 4, giving a full account of the technological, economic and organizational development; see also *ibid.*, at section 2.5, with Table 2, listing recent standard-based patent pools. As regards cooperative standard-setting see Lemley, Mark A. (2002), 'Intellectual Property Rights and Standard-Setting Organisations', *Cal. L. Rev.*, **90**, 1889; Blind, Knut *et al.* (2002), 'Study on the Interaction between Standardization and Intellectual Property Rights', http://www.isi.fhg.de/publ/downloads/isi02b56/interaction.pdf, accessed 4 November 2007, pp. 59 *et seq.*, 83 *et seq.*; Ullrich, H. (2007), 'Patente, Wettbewerb und technische Normung', *GRUR*, 817, all with references.

[11] See Blind, Knut (2004), *The Economics of Standards*, Cheltenham, UK and Northampton, MA, US: Edward Elgar, pp. 94 *et seq.*, 186 *et seq.*; Ullrich, *supra* note 10, at 819 *et seq.*, both with references; see also the DoJ Business Review Letters, *supra* note 9.

[12] See, as regards the GSM standard and UMTS technology, Bekkers *et al.*, *supra* note 1, at section 4.2 (public procurement as well as public subsidies); as regards Community research funding and its contractual mechanisms, including consortium agreements, see Godt, Christine (2006), 'Forschungs-, Wissenschafts- und Technologiepolitik', in Manfred A. Dauses (ed.), *Handbuch des EU-Wirtschaftsrechts* (loose-leaf), Munich: C.H. Beck, notes 26 *et seq.*

the latter aspect is generally neglected by antitrust law,[13] the former may lead to the concurrent application of different sets of competition rules.[14] However, due to the general benevolence vis-à-vis both cooperative R&D and pooling (as well as standardization[15]), no real conflicts have emerged yet.

Indeed, when reassessing its approach to technology transfer agreements in more economics-based terms in 2001, the European Commission sought to make its enforcement policy regarding 'technology pools' match the new reality and the US American example. With this in view and in order to escape the narrow limits set for Commission regulations exempting categories of restrictive agreements from the prohibition rule of Article 81(1) EC, the Commission developed 'Guidelines'[16] that set forth its framework of analysis and criteria of evaluation for pooling arrangements. While these Guidelines may also indirectly bind national competition authorities, but not all the courts, they will nevertheless provide guidance to all interested parties and institutions. They may, therefore, serve as a frame of reference for a critical analysis of the current enforcement policy under the EU competition rules. As a cursory glance at the assessment of pooling agreements under the antitrust laws by the US administrative authorities will show, this enforcement policy is not EU-specific, in fact was not even 'invented here', but simply illustrates the practice of the major jurisdictions.

---

13 Criticized by Monopolkommission, *Wettbewerbspolitik vor neuen Herausforderungen*, Hauptgutachten VIII 1988/1989, Baden-Baden: Nomos, no. 1082; Ullrich, Hanns (1988), *Kooperative Forschung und Kartellrecht*, Heidelberg: Verlag Recht und Wirtschaft, pp. 166 *et seq.*

14 Articles 1(1)(b) and 2(8), (9) and (11) of Commission Regulation 2659/2000 of 29 November 2000 on the application of Article 81(3) of the Treaty to categories of research and development agreements, OJ 2006 No. L 304, p. 7, exempt the joint exploitation of the results of prior collaborative R&D. In view of Articles 3(4), 4 and 5 the question may arise whether Regulation 2059/2000 privileges joint R&D-based pools over other pools.

15 See Commission Notice – Guidelines on the application of Article 81 EC Treaty to horizontal cooperation agreements, OJ 2001 No. C 3, p. 2, paras 159 *et seq.*; Ullrich, *supra* note 10, at 823 *et seq.*

16 Article 1(1) lit b), Council Regulation 19/65, OJ 1965 No. L 36, p. 533, authorizes the Commission only to grant 'block exemptions' for categories of bilateral agreements, a limitation that, in the past, has hampered dealing fully with pools (see Article 5(1), Commission Regulation 240/96 of 31 January 1996 on the application of Article 81(3) of the Treaty to categories of technology transfer agreements, OJ 1996 No. L 31, p. 2). The problem of whether to implement the new approach via a group exemption regulation or via guidelines is discussed in European Commission, Evaluation Report on Block Exemption Regulation 240/96 for Technology Transfer Agreements, Brussels, December 2001, paras 132 *et seq.* In the end, the guidelines approach has been chosen; see TT Guidelines, *supra* note 4, paras 210 *et seq.*

2 Competition law issues

2.1 Clear criteria for complex contracts?

2.1.1 Multi-layer structure In an ideal world of independent innovation, enterprises would develop by themselves all the technology they needed for their production and their products, would patent their inventive elements to protect themselves against imitation and would license the patents to third parties in different markets, as a matter of mutually profitable technology transfer. This would have its little complications at the intersection of technologies and products – after all, even the ideal world would know a division of work and labour – but these complications would be overcome by autonomous adaptation and by standardization. In the real world, however, technologies largely are common knowledge. Many people work with them, contribute to their creation and improvement, specialize in some of them and try to control their intersections, and all seek patent protection of their achievements as a matter not only of competitive rivalry, but of obtaining power over markets. As a result, instead of well rounded-up domains of proprietary knowledge, the field becomes scattered with pieces of it. Thus, the owners may come to block each other, either entirely or as regards optimizing their technologies. Ideally, again, they would trade for rights to use the complementary technologies, and thus enter into licence exchanges, in particular into cross-licensing. But there may be too many complementary technologies dispersed among too many enterprises, so that both licensing-in and licensing-out between holders of complementary technologies and, more importantly, licensing out the technology (or its individually held parts) to users becomes difficult and costly. Pooling arrangements between some or most, possibly even all the holders of complementary technologies are one way to overcome the fragmentation of complex technology, in particular of system technologies.[17] Patents help identify the fragments and their owners, and they allow the owners to pool these fragments on commercial terms while retaining some – broad or narrow – control, just as they generally enable trade in technology markets.[18]

---

[17] Cf. Merges, *supra* note 6, at 124 *et seq.*, 133 *et seq.*, stressing, however, more the fragmentation of property than its cause, the – natural – fragmentation of technologies in an innovative system that is based on both competition and specialization (or division of labour). The fragments are, indeed, usually brought under a bundle of patents held by the 'owner' of the technology.

[18] See Ullrich, Hanns (2001), 'Intellectual Property, Access to Innovation, and Antitrust: Harmony, Disharmony, and International Harmonization', in Dreyfuss *et al.*, *supra* note 6, p. 365, at 371 *et seq.*; *ibid.* (1996), 'Lizenzkartellrecht auf dem Weg zur

This transactional explanation of patent pooling and of its efficiency-enhancing effects on the use of technologies is by no means new.[19] However it makes it clear that, unlike licensing transactions in general, pools serve less the transfer than the assembly of technologies. It also explains why they tend to have a multi-layered structure. Both aspects are mirrored by the Commission's Guidelines. These distinguish patent pooling from licensing transactions on the ground that the latter concern the right to – practically and effectively – use the licensed technology in production whereas the former merely constitute agreements on the licensing of technology (as a package) to third parties.[20] This distinction points to the two dimensions of any pool, which are, on the one hand, the internal relationship between the partners of the pool and, on the other, the pool's relationships with third parties, the potential licensees. However, it reveals very little of their complexity and interdependence.

Indeed, as regards the internal relations between the pool partners, another distinction has to be made between pools whose members act only in the technology market[21] and pools whose members, either all or in part, are also present in product markets. While the former typically aim merely at package-building in view of third-party licensing and, therefore, will only exceptionally include a licence exchange between the members of the pool,[22] the latter will frequently depend on an exchange, which has been agreed upon earlier or, sometimes, concomitantly. Although in such cases the pool agreement may only be the offspring or the implementation of a cross-licensing arrangement, the Guidelines do not deal with the latter in the context of technology pools, but discuss them separately.[23]

Mitte', *GRUR Int.*, 554, at 564 *et seq*.; Merges, *supra* note 6, at 155 *et seq*., qualifies the pooled patents as 'bargaining chips', the exclusivity of which tends to be transformed into a mere liability regime. Albeit correct, this feature characterizes cross-licensing systems better than patent pools, which essentially are about third-party licensing on the basis of (joint) control over the exclusivity.

19 See Schulte, *supra* note 1, at 101 *et seq*., 100 *et seq*.; Kronstein, *supra* note 6, at 183 *et seq*.; Andewelt, *supra* note 7, at 612 *et seq*. and 633 *et seq*. (quoting from *Standard Oil v. US*, 283 US 163, 171 *et seq*. (1931)).

20 TT Guidelines, *supra* note 4, para. 41.

21 These may be research institutions, but also firms specializing in technology development (for example, in the biotechnology industry) or firms that have withdrawn from product markets.

22 For example, for research and development purposes.

23 The TT Guidelines, *supra* note 4, paras 78, 204 and 207, deal with cross-licences as reciprocal licences, which, in principle, qualify for treatment under the TTBER. The draft of the TT Guidelines as published on the home page of the Commission on 25 September 2003 (para. 211) treated cross-licensing entered into to dissolve blocking situations as a less restrictive minus by comparison to pool-building.

This silence raises the question of how the agreement on pooling and the internal licence exchange interrelate, and of how to take account of a given interrelationship. On the one hand, licence exchanges are treated like any other technology transfer agreements. They may thus benefit from the group exemption under the TTBER[24] depending on their market share and on whether or not they contain hardcore restrictions, both criteria depending in turn on whether they are horizontal or vertical in nature. To the extent that a vertical relationship can be assumed (as the Guidelines invite one to do when they define the horizontal or vertical nature of an agreement by reference to patent-law positions rather than by reference to actually existing rivalry between the holders of such positions),[25] even pool-related cross-licensing agreements will find themselves in a 'safe harbour'. Even if, exceptionally, this were not the case, they would still enjoy the favourable treatment that the Guidelines promise agreements providing for the transfer of technology.[26] All in all, it would seem that cross-licensing in support of pool-building has been sufficiently facilitated, unless the limits set to reciprocal agreements by Article 4(1) TTBER apply. It is presumably only in these cases that the question may arise whether the benefit of pooling may justify rather restrictive cross-licensing between pool members.

On the other hand, the conceptual distinction between the pooling agreement and the exchange of licences between pool members, which possibly supports the former, disregards the impact the latter may have on the pool's relationship with third parties. It may indeed affect the nature of the competitive relations

---

24 Even if multilateral; see *supra* note 5.

25 See the TT Guidelines, *supra* note 4, paras 29, 30, 32 and 204; Article 1(l)(j) TTBER. Note that while the Guidelines recognize a horizontal relationship in cases where an enterprise would enter a market within a foreseeable time, they apparently do consider blocking patents to be absolute obstacles. Irrespective of their legal strength or weakness (which the Guidelines take into account), blocking patents may, however, be overcome by R&D efforts as a matter of normal dynamic competition, except, of course, in the case of standardization. Even if they cannot be so overcome, the point remains that the Guidelines misconceive technological competition, which precisely is (among other things) about creating blocking situations for rivals. Agreements resolving such situations may produce efficiencies and, therefore, may benefit from Article 81(3) EC on this account, if they also meet the other criteria of Article 81(3). Exempting them a priori by a fictitious redefinition of the nature of the agreement is a political rather than a legal approach, and an unwarranted one under Article 2 Regulation 1/2003.

26 See TT Guidelines, *supra* note 4, paras 8, 9, 37, 130 and 131 (extending *de facto* the group exemption). Note that cross-licensing of complementary technologies, when it does not contain additional restrictions, does not even come under Article 81(1); such agreements that do contain additional restrictions may still benefit from Article 81(3); see the TT Guidelines, paras 204 and 207.

between members and non-members, since the former's technological basis is broadened. It may also strengthen the pool members' competitive advantage, if additional knowledge, in particular know-how, is exchanged, or if it gives them, as it most likely does, some lead time. The Guidelines also note this problem of an uneven playing field for pool members and outsiders, but do so only with regard to licence royalties.[27] However, since the overall bargain struck in a licence exchange may be quite different from that made in third-party transactions, discriminatory royalties may be justified and non-discriminatory royalties may not mirror the realities of the overall arrangement. In short, the analytical separation of a licence exchange between pool members from the pooling agreement may miss synergetic effects between the two, be they positive or negative, or both.

2.1.2 The pooling agreement In fact, one may even wonder whether defining a pooling agreement solely in terms of building a package of patents that is sufficiently complete and comprehensive to be effectively licensed to third parties provides a broad enough basis for an evaluation under competition law. After all, pooling involves a selection of which patents to pool and a decision on which royalties to charge, which members will make not only with a view to what the market may need and yield. Rather, they will act according to what they think their own competitive position on the market will or should be. Whenever one or more members are themselves present in product markets, pool-building is a tactical exercise serving their strategic interests in these markets, not a business in itself. In that sense, cross-licensing and pooling are complementary exercises, the former determining the latter. The Commission's Guidelines, however, are less concerned with what pool members retain for themselves as a matter of positioning themselves in the markets than with what the parties put in the pool, and how this (and the pool's licensing practice) affects technology and possibly downstream markets. Thus, the focus is mainly on pools formed by technology suppliers acting on upstream markets alone.

The Guidelines then assess the pooling agreement as such with regard to its potential for anti-competitive effects, which essentially would arise, first, from price fixing between pool members when setting the royalty rates for the licensing of their inputs; second, from collective bundling, that is, when the package includes patents that may and should be made available independently; third, from reduced incentives for innovation efforts by members; and finally, from hindering market penetration by alternative technologies.[28]

---

27 TT Guidelines, *supra* note 4, para. 226 (concerning powerful pools).

28 TT Guidelines, *supra* note 4, paras 213 and 219. The Guidelines emphasize

Against this negative potential the Guidelines set essentially two positive promises that pooling agreements may make, namely, on the one hand, a reduction of transaction costs for both the patent owners as licensors and for third parties as licensees as a result of the central administration of the licence grant[29] and, on the other, a reduction of overall licence fees, since pooling tends to limit the accumulation of royalties as would occur in case of individual licensing-out.[30] These (and other[31]) benefits are likely to arise if the risks of anti-competitive effects can be excluded or at least contained.

To guarantee such optimization the Guidelines rely on a double distinction between, on the one hand, the pooling of complementary rather than substitute patents, meaning patents that are competitively interchangeable with respect to the configuration of a product or the working of a process of manufacture, and, on the other, essential and non-essential patents. Substitute patents are non-essential by nature; complementary patents are essential if there is no substitute for them; if there is one, they are not essential.[32]

According to these distinctions, pools are held to be merely pro-competitive and, therefore, per se valid under Article 81(1) EC, if they only contain

---

the negative effects on alternative innovation resulting from pools supporting a technical standard; they do not, however, make clear whether a lessening of innovative competition between pool members results more from a licence exchange between them than from the pooling agreement as such.

[29] TT Guidelines, *supra* note 4, paras 214 and 217. The Guidelines focus more on the transaction cost savings of the licensee, but they also benefit the licensor, since third parties' willingness to license-in is enhanced. Such transaction cost savings relate to the cost of selecting technologies, searching for licensors and negotiating one rather than a larger number of transactions as well as to the costs associated with implementing and maintaining the licensing relationship.

[30] TT Guidelines, *supra* note 4, paras 214 and 217. Note that royalty-setting for 'essential' patents (see the following text) may become rather difficult and extreme; it also invites hold-up tactics.

[31] Other efficiency arguments are frequently forwarded, such as a clearing function of the pool or a reduction of litigation risks and costs; see Bekkers *et al.*, *supra* note 1, at 31; Andewelt, *supra* note 7, at 614 *et seq*. However, patent clearing may be achieved by less restrictive arrangements (see section 2.3.1 *infra*) and avoidance of patent litigation is an ambiguous argument when patent validity is doubtful (see TT Guidelines, paras 229 and 233, and section 2.3 *infra*). Also, it really relates to cross-licensing more than to pooling, and it holds true only for litigation among patent owners. Third parties will find a pool to be a deterrent from otherwise promising litigation, since invalidation or non-infringement of one patent will not shake the licence agreement (see also TT Guidelines, para. 229).

[32] TT Guidelines, *supra* note 4, paras 215, 216 and 218 (stating that when technologies are in part complementary, in part substitutes, they will be treated like fully complementary technologies, because licensees will tend to take to make an overall deal even if the licence were negotiated independently from the pool.

essential technologies.[33] They do not involve horizontal price fixing, rather they cap cumulative royalties; they do not result in undue bundling, nor will they limit innovative competition. They simply bring the necessary elements of a technology together for easy licensing. Therefore, according to the Guidelines, the pooling agreement is immune to challenge even if pool members are market-dominating enterprises.[34] By contrast, if the pooling agreement includes to a 'significant extent' substitute technologies as well, it is considered to restrict inter-technology competition and to amount to collective bundling; if it is to a large extent composed of substitute technologies, it becomes a case of price fixing. On all these accounts, Article 81(1) applies and justification under Article 81(3) is held to be unlikely, since the transaction cost savings will concern part of the pool at best, and the inclusion of substitute technologies will hardly be a matter of indispensability. In this regard, it will not help if parties remain free to license independently, since this is unlikely to occur.[35]

In between the merely pro-competitive and the fundamentally anti-competitive pooling agreements are those that may qualify for justification under Article 81(3) EC, namely pools relating (also) to non-essential complementary technology or a non-significant part of substitute technologies. These types of pools, which may either be established in that form or be a result of a transformation of the nature of technologies due to the emergence of alternatives,[36] tend to foreclose competition by third-party technologies as the transaction cost advantage of the pool tends not only to attract licensees, but also makes them adhere to the pooled technology.[37] Therefore the Guidelines introduce some countervailing criteria that should help to justify pooling of these technologies, such as the requirement that their inclusion must (really) be pro-competitive, that licensors should remain free to individually license their technologies, that in cases of multi-purpose technologies these should also be made available independently with respect to fields of use that are not within

---

33 TT Guidelines, *supra* note 4, para. 220, although making a reservation regarding the conditions for the licence grant, which is not particularly clear. Since pool partners are presumed not to be competitors (see *supra* note 25), the reservation cannot mean the internal agreement between pool members regarding the terms of third-party licensing. The relationship between the pool and third parties is dealt with separately anyway (see section 2.1.3 *infra*).

34 TT Guidelines, *supra* note 4, para. 220.

35 TT Guidelines, *supra* note 4, para. 219; what a 'significant' part of substitute technologies means is not clear. DoJ and FTC, Antitrust Enforcement, *supra* note 5, at 77 *et seq*., suggest a more lenient approach than the Business Review Letters did, and would inquire whether the inclusion of some substitutes is efficient.

36 TT Guidelines, *supra* note 4, para. 222.

37 TT Guidelines, *supra* note 4, para. 221.

the pool's legitimate scope and that, wherever possible, pooled technologies should also be made in smaller packages rather than only as a bulk package.[38] Clearly, these countervailing criteria are more likely to minimize the anti-competitive effects of pooling in theory than to actually outweigh them in practice. The Guidelines do not specify the circumstances under which the criteria of Article 81(3) will be met *in concreto*, such as a sufficient participation of consumers in the efficiency gains, indispensability of pooling by reference to its objectives or non-elimination of substantial competition. Rather, they escape dealing with these crucial criteria by adding a few general, in part contradictory, in part redundant considerations to the effect that 'the stronger the market position of a pool the greater the risk of anti-competitive effects', that pools holding a strong position on the market 'should be open and non-discriminatory' and that pools 'should not unduly foreclose third party technology or limit the creation of alternative pools'.[39]

In accordance with this block-exemption-like approach – small pools of complementary patents need not worry, big pools of complex technologies may have a problem – the Guidelines outlaw some hardcore restrictions, such as non-competition agreements or the shielding of possibly invalid patents by raising the risks of validity challenges.[40]

2.1.3 The pool and third parties The rules on third-party licensing by the pool constitute the third layer of analysis. Again, conceptually it may be an isolated exercise; in reality, it is tightly intertwined with the other layers. For one thing, by limiting the exclusivity of pools that need to pass the test of Article 81(3),[41] the Guidelines seek to assure potential licensees of at least some freedom of choice to enhance competition in technology as well as – indirectly – in downstream markets. In addition, the principle that the pool's licensing relationships with third parties are not different from the bilateral relationship between a licensor acting individually and its licensee and that,

---

[38] *Supra* note 36. As the TT Guidelines note at para. 222, lit. d), breaking down the pooled technology into smaller packages requires separate determination of attributable royalties and, in case of long-term pools, a right to terminate in part the licence by which a pool member contributes to the pool. The more general point is that the licensing relation between the pool and its members should be flexible rather than firmly exclusive.

[39] TT Guidelines, *supra* note 4, para. 224. It is not quite clear whether the 'open and non-discriminatory' nature of a pool refers to membership in the pool or to third-party licensing, since the latter is dealt with in paras 225 *et seq*., and since industry-wide pools are not excluded (cf. TT Guidelines, para. 231).

[40] TT Guidelines, *supra* note 4, paras 227 and 229; see also *supra* note 31.

[41] See section 2.1.2 *supra*, text following note 37.

therefore, Regulation 772/2004 may fully apply,[42] is not without problems, nor does it carry as far as it seems at first glance. The problem arises from the fact that the determination of the competitive nature of the licensing relationship as horizontal or vertical may not be made simply by reference to the position of the pool, but must take account of the position of its members. If it were otherwise, pool partners might be able to achieve more protection from licensee competition by acting through a pool than they could when acting alone, because, as such, the pool is active only on the technology market, where frequently its licensees are not present. Consequently whenever a licensee is a competitor of a member of the pool,[43] third-party licensing by the pool must be considered to be horizontal in nature at least with regard to Articles 4 and 5(2) TTBER. Still, the application of the TTBER to the pool's licensing transaction with third parties tends to put pool members in a better position than they would have been acting individually, because it is based on the assumption that the pool's transactions are of a bilateral character. While technically speaking this is true and a logical result of the centralization of the administration of the patent package, it in fact produces a parallelism of the pool members' position as licensors, a matter that may not be totally irrelevant when they are really competitors.[44]

Finally, in practice, the application of the TTBER to third-party licensing, whether directly or 'by analogy', may not carry very far, because many of the modern patent pools relate to innovative technological standards and, as such, mostly hold a dominant position in the relevant technology markets.[45] If such

---

[42] TT Guidelines, *supra* note 4, paras 212, 223; see also Commission Press release IP/03/1152 of 7 August 2003 – 'Commission Clears Philips/Sony CD Licensing Program', http://europa.eu/rapid/pressReleasesAction.do?reference=IP/03/1152&format=HTML&aged=0&language=EN&guiLanguage=en, accessed 4 November 2007. Note that the Guidelines would largely apply the principles of TTBER 'by analogy' even beyond the market share thresholds of Article 3 TTBER. Indeed, in dealing with specific restrictions in licence agreements, they hardly ever differentiate according to market-power thresholds, but use a general Article 81(1) and (3) reasoning; see Ullrich, Hanns (2007), 'The Interaction between Competition Law and Intellectual Property Law – An Overview', in Claus D. Ehlermann and Isabel Atanasiu (eds), *European Competition Law Annual 2005: The Interaction between Competition Law and Intellectual Property Law*, Oxford: Hart Publishing, p. XXVII, at section 2.2; see also recital 12 of the TTBER and *supra* note 26.

[43] Typically, this will be the case when the pool is 'vertically integrated' in that members act not only in the technology market, but also in downstream product markets. Note that licence exchanges between pool members, by broadening their technological capacity, might result in additional horizontal relationships.

[44] As to the determination of competitive relations between pool members, see *supra* note 25.

[45] See Ullrich, *supra* note 10, at 823 *et seq.* with references.

is the case, then third-party licensing becomes subject to particular limitations, which are derived from Article 82 EC. Thus instead of enjoying freedom as regards fixing the level of royalties first among members and then vis-à-vis third parties, 'royalties and other licensing terms should be fair and non-discriminatory' both with respect to the various licensees and by reference to pool members as licensees.[46] In addition, in order to avoid foreclosure on downstream markets, licences must be non-exclusive.[47] Also, grant-back obligations, which the pool is allowed to impose on third parties as a matter of maintaining its technological (and market) position, must be non-exclusive and limited to technologies that are essential or important in using the pooled technology.[48]

2.2 Problems and perspectives

2.2.1 Testing the tests Looking only at pools as package-building for a necessarily centralized administration of otherwise dispersed patents for third-party licensing, the Guidelines seem to provide a fairly consistent, internationally accepted[49] framework of evaluation under general competition-law aspects. However, as one examines it further, one cannot but realize that it is more of a theoretical framework that has been conceived in a welfare-economics analysis, but whose criteria rest on rather soft assumptions. To begin with, the Guidelines consistently refer to technology pools without distinguishing between the various intellectual property rights a pool might cover or offer for central licence grants.[50] However information and telecommunication technologies, which are the object of most modern pools, typically encompass a considerable amount of copyrighted software for which the essentiality criterion does not fit. Both legally and factually, its substitution is essentially a

---

46 TT Guidelines on Technology Transfer Agreements, *supra* note 4, paras 225 and 226; see also section 2.1.2 *supra*, following note 27.

47 TT Guidelines, *supra* note 4, para. 226.

48 TT Guidelines, *supra* note 4, para. 228. In this respect, the Guidelines do not really depart much from Article 5(1)(a) and (b) TTBER, since pool licences rarely involve know-how. The meaning of 'important' improvements is not clear. Presumably it simply means non-essential complementary patents.

49 See DoJ and FTC, Antitrust Enforcement, *supra* note 5, at 66, restating a US practice, which actually, in respect of pools, served as a model for the Commission's Guidelines on Technology Transfer Agreements.

50 See the TT Guidelines, *supra* n. 4, para. 216 with note 69. The different terminology at para. 221 ('complementary patents') indicates that the Guidelines have been conceived of in view of patent pools and, in fact, the focus of the administrative decisions taken under US or EU competition law is on the pooling of patents.

matter of cost, albeit possibly of economically unreasonable cost.[51] Therefore even if presumably copyright is not usually at the core of technology pools, the essentiality test would have to be relaxed in regard of copyright pools so as to become a test of economic reasonableness. This, indeed, is what US practice suggests in any case,[52] and what some authors plead for in Europe as well.[53]

The fact of the matter is that the essentiality test is inherently ambiguous. It has its origin in technological standardization, where it serves to limit the inclusion of patented technology in standards, and it does so quite well where standards are set descriptively.[54] It is not as suitable for performance standards, but apparently is also used for pools relating to such standards, or else essentiality could not change over time.[55] In such cases, the availability of alternative technologies is really only a matter of costs. Outside a standardization context, even the reference point for determining essentiality becomes elusive, because, by definition, whichever way parties define their technology,[56] unless it has a monopoly (and is thus a *de facto* standard), alternative technologies will be available, and the more there are, the more the essentiality criterion will lose its competitive meaning. Indeed, if any technology could be made 'essential' with regard to a given pooling project, the question arises of which purpose the pool really is to serve, since the transaction cost argument will no longer hold. As transaction costs for licensing in a patent decrease, the transaction costs for choosing the right pool will rise.[57] This does

---

[51] Unlike patents, copyright neither protects the technical teaching as such nor excludes independent (re)invention/creation, but it may nevertheless serve as a default protection where software patents are unavailable; for the point made here, see also Ullrich, Hanns (2005), 'Patent Pools: Approaching a Patent Law Problem Via Competition Policy', in Claus D. Ehlermann and Isabel Atanasiu (eds), *European Competition Law Annual 2005: The Interaction between Competition Law and Intellectual Property Law*, Oxford: Hart Publishing, pp. 305, at 311 *et seq.*, with references regarding the differences between software protection by patents and by copyright.

[52] See DoJ and FTC, Antitrust Enforcement, *supra* note 5, at 77 with references.

[53] See Plompen, Peter (2007), 'The New Technology Transfer Guidelines (TTG) as Applied to Patent Pools and Patent Pool Licensing: Some Observations Regarding the Concept of "Essential Technologies"', in Claus D. Ehlermann and Isabel Atanasiu (eds), *European Competition Law Annual 2005: The Interaction between Competition Law and Intellectual Property Law*, Oxford: Hart Publishing, pp. 295, at 298 *et seq.*

[54] They may then be defined along the claims of a patent; see Plompen, *supra* note 53, at 298 *et seq.*

[55] TT Guidelines, *supra* n. 4, para. 222.

[56] The problem is discussed in DoJ and FTC, Antitrust Enforcement, *supra* note 5, at 74 *et seq.*

[57] For an earlier presentation of the argument see Ullrich, *supra* note 51, at 313 *et seq.*

not mean that pools for other than standardized technology are always a problem under competition law. But it does mean that outside standardization it is not essentiality that determines the pro-competitive nature of a pool, but rather it is the reverse: the question of whether the pool is pro-competitive determines what may be considered essential. This test, by the way, would also be better for standard-related pools, as it may help avoid over-standardization through inclusion of (mostly 'ancillary') technologies in the standard that otherwise are substitutable, because fully equivalent.

2.2.2 Powerful pools There may be more room for a detailed critique. The concept of complementarity is vague as well. Strictly speaking, it is met only when patents are legally interdependent,[58] which really would be a case of essentiality 'by definition'.[59] But this is only the starting point of a *continuum* towards simple usefulness of certain forms of assembling complex technologies. Reliance on non-exclusivity of the pool as a way to limit its competitive impact[60] is warranted only where the partners of the pool and a third party may really be expected to be willing to negotiate licences individually and effectively, a hope that is as little likely to materialize as the pool is successful, as there are more than two or three pool partners[61] and as the number of potential licensees is large.[62] Also grant-backs will contribute to its success, their non-exclusivity being as little suited to slow it down as is the non-exclusivity of the pool itself.[63]

A more general criticism, however, would be two-pronged. One point is that the criteria are borrowed from US antitrust law, where an unstructured general principle of competition law allows implementing rules developed in accordance with current doctrinal thinking,[64] and to be tested in court on a

---

58 That is, in the case of improvements falling within the scope of the claims of a principle patent, a case that in many patent systems is subject to some rule of mandatory licensing.

59 Term used by Plompen, *supra* n. 53, but with reference to standards.

60 This is not to imply that requiring non-exclusivity is always meaningless; on the contrary, see references *supra* note 8, and DoJ and FTC, Antitrust Enforcement, *supra* note 5, at 73 *et seq.* (the *Summit-VISX* decision by the FTC).

61 See DoJ and FTC, Antitrust Enforcement, *supra* note 5, at 79 with note 146.

62 Note that potential licensees having sufficient bargaining power are already consulted by pool members during the standardization process so as to make the patent-based standard acceptable; see Plompen, *supra* note 53, at 301.

63 The main purpose of grant-back clauses in third-party licences is to link technological improvements to the pool and to prevent hold-ups by third-party patents; see also DoJ and FTC, Antitrust Enforcement, *supra* note 5, at 80 *et seq.*

64 Most frequently quoted are Merges, *supra* note 6; Shapiro, Carl (2001), 'Navigating the Patent Thicket: Cross Licenses, Patent Pools, and Standard Setting',

case-by-case basis, if there are plaintiffs to challenge them. In the EU, Article 81(3) EC sets forth a four-step test, for which the Guidelines may provide some guidance, but which still must be met *in concreto*.[65] In this regard, beyond describing pro- and anti-competitive effects of pools, the Guidelines do little if anything to specify the criteria of indispensability and of non-elimination of competition in respect of substantial parts of the market. In particular, they do not even touch upon the question of whether less restrictive alternatives than pools may be available to achieve sufficient transaction cost savings, such as clearing arrangements.[66] Also they deal with market-dominating pools within the framework of Article 81 as if they were exceptional cases whose problems could be solved by setting, on the basis of Article 81, some marginal constraints on their organization and conduct.[67]

The other general point of criticism is, indeed, that the Guidelines essentially were conceived in view of standard-related, or, as they more realistically say, standard-supporting pools,[68] as most modern pools are established as part of a standardization strategy of industry, but that they are not very explicit as to how the standardization nexus impacts (or should impact) on the competitive assessment. It is true that the Guidelines relate only to Article 81 EC, and that there are quite a few pools associated with less important *de facto* standardization efforts. These, however, are in any case only of marginal concern for modern, more economics-based competition law enforcement.[69] The point really is that the Commission has not only a rather standardization-friendly enforcement policy,[70] but that standardization, by its very nature, aims at

---

http://haas.berkeley.edu/~shapiro/thicket.pdf, accessed 4 November 2007; Carlson, Steven C. (1999), 'Patent Pools and the Antitrust Dilemma', *Yale J. Reg.*, **16**, 359; Lerner, J. and J. Tirole (2004), 'Efficient Patent Pools', *Am. Econ. Rev.*, **94**, 691; Barton, John H. (2001), 'Antitrust Treatment of Oligopolies with Mutually Blocking Patent Portfolios', *Antitrust L.J.*, **69**, 851; and, of course, Andewelt, *supra* note 7.

65 The US IP Antitrust Guidelines, *supra* note 5, section 4.2, also uses a 'least-restrictive-alternative' test; see also DoJ and FTC, Antitrust Enforcement, *supra* note 5, at 73, but neither in the US nor in the EU will the test be used to ask whether there is an alternative to pooling, let alone whether the pool is oversized (or undersized) in terms of members or objectives as long as the patents meet the criteria of essentiality and complementarity.

66 See section 2.3.1 *infra*.

67 TT Guidelines, *supra* note 4, paras 220, 224, 226 and 230.

68 TT Guidelines, *supra* note 4, paras 211 and 225.

69 See Communication from the Commission – Notice – Guidelines on the application of Article 81(3) of the Treaty, OJ 2004 No. C 101, p. 97, paras 24 *et seq.*; Guidelines on horizontal cooperation agreements, *supra* note 15, paras 19 and 168.

70 Guidelines on horizontal cooperation, *supra* note 69, paras 159 *et seq.*; Ullrich, *supra* note 10, at 823 *et seq.*

market dominance by the standardized technology,[71] and that it is precisely in those industries where (interoperability) standardization is most important that crucial standardized technology is 'supported' by a few major pools.[72] Therefore, some clarification regarding 'big' standard-supporting pools would have been helpful. For instance, how does the principle that 'the stronger the market position of the pool the greater the risk of anti-competitive effects'[73] apply to a standard-supporting pool that extends beyond essential to simply complementary technology?[74] Why should openness of a standard-supporting pool mean only openness of its licensing policy rather than also open access to the pool,[75] given that the Commission favours participation of all interested parties in the creation of the standard and of the pool,[76] and what might be the (limiting) conditions? Should not pools that support publicly recognized or *de facto* industry-wide standards be mandatorily required to separately grant specific field-of-use licences and to make smaller packages of the pooled technology available,[77] and may they ever encompass other than essential technology, given that substantial competition is eliminated? What does the obligation of market-dominating enterprises to set 'royalties and other licensing terms' at a 'fair' level mean, given that, under the rules of at least the publicly recognized standardization organizations, any inclusion of intellectual property in standards requires the willingness to grant licences at 'reasonable and non-discriminatory' (RAND) conditions, if not at 'fair, reasonable

71 See Ullrich, *supra* note 10, at 819 *et seq.*; there are exceptions, but they are more limited than is indicated by the TT Guidelines, *supra* note 4, para. 211 with note 68; see Choumelowa (2003), 'Competition Law Analysis of Patent Licensing Arrangements – The Particular Case of 3 G 3P', *Comp. Pol'y Newsletter*, (1), 41; Bekkers *et al.*, *supra* note 1, at section 4.2.

72 See references *supra* note 9, at 10; also Pena Castellot, M.A. (2003), 'Commission settles allegations of abuse and clears patent pools in the CD market', *Comp. Pol'y Newsletter*, (3), 53 (relating only to third-party licensing).

73 TT Guidelines, *supra* note 4, para. 224.

74 Remember, pools relating only to essential patents are per se lawful, irrespective of market power; see *supra* note 34.

75 TT Guidelines, *supra* note 4, paras 224 and 226.

76 TT Guidelines, *supra* note 4, para. 230; and see section 2.3.2 *infra*.

77 TT Guidelines, *supra* note 4, para. 222, lit. c) and d); see also Commission Press release IP/03/1152 – 'Commission Clears Philips/Sony CD Licensing Program', *supra* note 42, and Commission Press release IP/06/139 of 9 February 2006 – 'Commission Closes Investigation Following Changes to Philips CD-Recordable Disc Patent Licensing', http://www.europa.eu/rapid/pressReleasesAction.do?reference=IP/06/139&format=HTML&aged=1&language=EN&guiLanguage=en, accessed 4 November 2007. Both press releases refer to considerable reductions of the royalty rates, but do not explain them.

and non-discriminatory' (FRAND) conditions.[78] Are the Guidelines using the term 'fair' with a particular meaning?[79] Are standard-supporting pools that dominate the market not held to a duty to license rather than only to a non-discrimination rule, as the Guidelines seem to imply?[80] What about the 'other licensing terms', given that the 'sub-exemption' rule of Article 4 TTBER, if applicable at all,[81] does not apply to licence grants by market-dominating licensors? Would Article 82 EC impose still other constraints, at least in cases of hyper-market-dominance, which pools may acquire that support mandatory or quasi-mandatory standards?

2.3 Beyond competition law

2.3.1 Pools for patents and patents for pools Both the technical[82] and the normative problems of correctly assessing technology pools again raise the questions of which problems they are intended to solve and whether, as institutions, they really present the best solution. This question reaches beyond competition law, but it may hold some answers for a competition-law problem, namely the determination of the least restrictive way to achieve the legitimate objective of creating technological synergies by bringing dispersed patents together.

---

78 See Ullrich, *supra* n. 10, at 826 *et seq.* with references.

79 If fair means fair to consumers, rather than reasonable as a patent reward, particular problems arise, because any essential patent in the pool arguably is as valuable as the entire package. So what would the relative share of pool members be and how can they agree on what is fair to the consumer? See also section 2.3.1 *infra*, note 82.

80 See German Federal Supreme Court (Bundesgerichtshof, BGH) of 13 July 2004 – *Standard-Spundfass II*, WuW DE-R 1329 = *Standard Tight-Head Drum*, (2005) *IIC*, **36**, 741 (English translation), with comments by Matthias Leistner.

81 See section 2.1.3 *supra*.

82 As regards, in particular, determination of essentiality, competition authorities must rely on the advice of technical experts, and require firms to consult independent experts; see TT Guidelines, *supra* note 4, para. 232. Nevertheless, parties seem to tend to exaggerate essentiality; see, for example, Pena Castellot, *supra* note 72, at 58.: In the Philips/Sony Pool, of 44 patents claimed as essential, only four were essential, one per partner. Melamed, Douglas and D. Lerch (2006), 'Uncertain Patents, Antitrust, and Patent Pools', in Claus-Dieter Ehlermann and Isabel Atanasiu (eds), *European Competition Law Annual 2005: The Interaction between Competition Law and Intellectual Property Law*, Oxford: Hart Publishing, pp. 275, at 288 *et seq.*, suggest taking the example of uncertainty about essentiality as an argument for expanding the admissibility of pools to patents that subsequently turn out to be non-essential. The thrust of this argument, however, seems to be directed at preventing ambushes by (partner) licensors rather than at enhancing the pro-competitive effects of pools.

Although an old argument,[83] the main reason for reversing the traditional antitrust hostility towards pools was the increasing coverage of technological fields, such as those of the information and telecommunication industries, by a multitude of 'overlapping' patents belonging to diverse enterprises.[84] Pools were reinvented and 're-justified' as a means to overcome the 'anti-commons' problem of such overcrowding. The steady expansion of patent protection into new fields, in particular software-related technology and biotechnology, as well as the no less steady increase in patenting activity of industry,[85] provides sufficient factual evidence for this argument. Whether this factual background is solid enough to support pool-building as a general means to cut through the resulting 'patent thicket'[86] is a matter of a policy judgment on the soundness of these patent-law developments. Certainly, however, their factual support of pool-building becomes shaky when the pooled patents are shaky.[87] Certainly also, much of the ominous patent thicket is not simply out there, but self-made. The increase of patenting activity is due to – rather sophisticated and complex – patenting strategies of firms, including tactics of blocking, defensive, cumulative patenting and patenting in view of cooperation and standardization.[88] The pool is as much made to get patents together as patents are taken to get pools together. The transaction-costs rationale may become overshadowed by a strategic purpose.

---

83 See Kronstein, *supra* note 6, 40 *et seq.*, 172 *et seq.*

84 See Merges, *supra* note 6; Shapiro, *supra* note 64.

85 Both problems as well as that of the solidity of patents granted have become a matter of general concern; see Wissenschaftlicher Beirat beim Bundesministerium für Wirtschaft und Technologie, 'Patentschutz und Innovation', Opinion of 24 March 2007, http://www.bmwi.de/BMWi/Redaktion/PDF/G/gutachten-des-wissenschaftlichen-beirats-patentschutz-und-innovation,property=pdf,bereich=bmwi,sprache=de,rwb=true.pdf, accessed 4 November 2007; Ullrich, Hanns (2007), 'National, European and Community Patent Protection: Time for Reconsideration', in Ansgar Ohly and Dietmar Klippel (eds), *Geistiges Eigentum und Gemeinfreiheit*, Tübingen: Mohr Siebeck, p. 61; Ghidini, Gustavo (2006), *Intellectual Property and Competition Law*, Cheltenham, UK and Northampton, MA, US: Edward Elgar, pp. 13 *et seq.*; all with references.

86 Shapiro, *supra* note 64, who coined the term 'patent thicket', expressly (but wrongly) excludes this issue from his analysis, as he is more interested in providing a practical solution to an existing problem.

87 See DoJ and FTC, Antitrust Enforcement, *supra* note 5, at 78; TT Guidelines, *supra* note 4, para. 229.

88 See generally Granstrand, Ove (1999), *The Economics and Management of Intellectual Property*, Cheltenham, UK and Northampton, MA, US: Edward Elgar, 176 *et seq.*, 209 *et seq.*; with regard to standardization, see Blind, *supra* note 11, at 125 *et seq.*; Simcoe, Timothy S. (2005), 'Explaining the Increase in Intellectual Property Disclosure', http://www.rotman.utoronto.ca/timothy.simcoe/papers/SSO_IPR_Disclosures.pdf, accessed 4 November 2007; Bekkers *et al.*, *supra* note 1, at section 4.

In standardization, that purpose is to create pools that allow the use of the network effects of standards for rapid diffusion of new technologies and acquisition of market power.[89]

Whatever weight may be given to such overarching strategies, where they exist, the problem is that the transaction-costs argument does not generally carry as far as it seems at first glance. It does not do so, in fact, because, while there are large pools covering a considerable stock of (essential) patents,[90] there are even more that have only a few members and a few patents, sometimes concerning the core of a technology, sometimes holding only elements of a systems technology that other pools 'co-own'. The argument does not carry far in law either. On the one hand, it is too broad, in that it applies to all patents relevant to a technology, be they essential,[91] complementary or only (particularly) advantageous. On the other hand, it does not explain why pooling is required rather than a less binding arrangement. Many of the transaction costs are, indeed, search costs,[92] with other transaction costs becoming minimal once the searching process is successful and results in a limited number of essential patents. Consequently, clearing arrangements may be a less restrictive alternative to fully fledged pools. While pools may also fulfil clearing functions,[93] looser, but no less efficient clearing institutions exist or have been proposed.[94] They also have less effect on the essential function of patents

---

89 See for an overview Ullrich, *supra* note 10, at 819 *et seq.* with references.

90 See *supra* note 82 and, for a situation of dispersed essential patents with a large number of 'lonely' patent holders and a few pools (which are unable to solve the transaction cost problem), Bekkers *et al.*, *supra* note 1, at section 4.2 (Table 6) regarding UMTS.

91 Note that the essentiality requirement is intended to address the restriction/royalty price-fixing problem (see section 2.1.2 *supra*), and thus only reflects a trade-off between admitting pools for the sake of saving transaction costs and limiting them in the interest of competition.

92 Many of the search costs relate to finding relevant patents, screening and assessing them. A well-run patent department in a firm should be aware of them anyway, and some of them should even be well-known from joint R&D. But the reality apparently is different, one of the problems being that, on the one hand, there are too many patents 'out there' (see *supra* note 85), and, on the other, that one 'blocking' patent (or a small number of them, 'blocking' being a matter of technical context) may frustrate a firm's line of innovation by raising its costs beyond profitability.

93 This is stressed by Bekkers *et al.*, *supra* note 1, at section 3.1. By contrast, and different from licence exchange, pools mostly do not provide for know-how transfer beyond the patented teaching; contra: US Patent and Trademark Office (2000), White Paper 'Patent Pools: A Solution to the Problem of Access in Biotechnology Patents?', Washington, DC, www.uspto.gov/web/offices/pac/dapp/opla/patpoolcover.html, accessed 4 November 2007, section V.

94 See Van Overwalle, Geertrui (ed.) (2006), *Gene Patents and Clearing Models* (Proceedings of the Workshop, Leuven, 8 June 2006) (forthcoming); van Zimmeren,

as property rights and, while they may be set up by private institutions, they may also be established by patent offices as a matter of improving the operation of the patent system.[95]

2.3.2 Democratic pooling? Approaching the problems underlying patent pools more from the side of the patent system is justified not only because this is where the problems originate, but also because pools tend to overtask competition law the larger and the more important they are. Thus the Commission suggests an 'institutional framework' for pools,[96] which in part restates the obvious, in part demonstrates helplessness, in part is unrealistic and at any rate is beyond the remit of the Commission. It is indeed obvious that the pool must avoid the exchange of 'sensitive information',[97] since collusion is what they are most suspected of. Prescribing that the pool's expert should have expertise and be independent or otherwise is not to be trusted[98] really indicates helplessness vis-à-vis the information advantage of pool members. Inviting pools to adhere to democratic rules of procedure of standardization and pool-building, in that the procedure should be open to all interested parties and in that committees should be composed of representatives of all interests,[99] is unrealistic for most of the smaller, yet ambitious pools, and it misses the reality of large pools, which support standards of publicly recognized standardization organizations. These seek to follow democratic procedures anyway, although without reaching democratic results,[100] and this not

E., B. Verbeure, G. Matthijs and G. Van Overvall (2006), 'A Clearing House for Diagnostic Testing: The Solution to Ensure Access to and Use of Patented Genetic Invention?', *Bull. WHO*, **84** (5), 352. The clearing-house concept seems to find most sympathy in the field of biotechnology; see Graft, G. and D. Zilberman (2001), 'Towards an Intellectual Property Clearinghouse for Agricultural Biotechnology', *IP Strategy Today*, (3) = http://www.cnr.berkeley.edu/csrd/technology/ipcmech/IPCM-background.html, accessed 4 November 2007, but standardization organizations could play a more active role as well (as yet, their databases are limited to essential patents notified by industry on a voluntary basis within a standardization project), and so could patent offices (instead of delegating this task to private pools; see, for the US PTO, *supra* note 93).

95 See for both arguments Ullrich, *supra* note 51, at 321 *et seq*.

96 TT Guidelines, *supra* note 4, paras 230 *et seq*.

97 TT Guidelines, *supra* note 4, para. 234; see also DoJ and FTC, Antitrust Enforcement, *supra* note 5, at 81 *et seq*. But why should 'clean room' arrangements provide a privilege for the pool? The question is not whether the doors and windows were shut or half-open, but what the parties did inside and outside (!) the pool.

98 TT Guidelines, *supra* note 4, para. 233 (the summary in the text is a true presentation of the contents of the Guidelines).

99 TT Guidelines, *supra* note 4, para. 231.

100 See Ullrich, *supra* note 10, at 824, with references to the literature pointing to the sociological reasons underlying democratic deficits of large associations.

only because the crucial parameters of the pool's business are cleared beforehand between the more important players as a matter of making the process more efficient.[101] Finally, as regards the modes of organization of institutions of self-regulation, such as pools, the general point is that competition authorities are neither experts nor competent in these matters, but must stick to the principle that they have to assess the economic objective and impact of the pool's activities, not the form in which these activities are cast or generated. Their task is not to evaluate the democratic or other organizational merits of a pool, let alone to come to any inferences on that ground,[102] but to assess clearly the pro- or anti-competitive nature of its activities.

3 Conclusion

There is a more far-reaching problem underlying the European TT Guidelines' recommendation regarding the institutional framework for pools. Some pooling in one form or another is a necessary part of patent-based systems innovation. Most of such modern technological systems innovation, such as in information technology, telecommunications and also, albeit for different reasons, biotechnology, is global in nature or spreads naturally beyond state boundaries. Therefore, keeping domestic enforcement practice of competition law in harmony with the policy of other jurisdictions is reasonable as a matter of avoiding, for legitimate pools, additional transaction costs resulting from compliance with different legal orders, and possibly also as a matter of allowing both domestically and extra-territorially rooted pools to operate on a par. However, the 'common approach' that has actually been chosen clearly shows the limits of the modern, economics-based assessment of restrictive agreements. Its narrow analytical framework invites, possibly obliges, authorities to look at each competitive practice in isolation rather than to put it in its transactional context. In the case of pools, neither a preceding joint research effort nor the standardization project that a pool may support is taken into consideration. Each step is examined separately as to its potential for microeconomic efficiency gains and its likely pro- or anti-competitive effects, with a view to containing the latter and to recognizing the former. The overall firm strategy, however, the effort of a – small or large – group of enterprises to jointly control in various constellations the development of markets, and in particular the innovation process, and the negative effects for

---

[101] See Plompen, *supra* note 53, at 301. Plompen's candid statement simply points to a practical necessity and reality (as is shown by the protracted proceedings typical of major standardization projects; see Bekkers *et al.*, *supra* note 1, at section 4).

[102] Possibly resulting in tolerating some pools in view of their 'democratic' appearance, and not others.

the system of free competition resulting therefrom, remain out of sight, or are even neglected deliberately.[103]

Moreover, to the extent that patent pools represent a sort of escape device intended to compensate for failures in the patent system, a harmonizing, in fact an imitative rather than an imaginative treatment under the rules of competition, neglects, possibly even negates, the differences that exist between national patent systems and the potential they might hold for solving at least part of the pooling problem.[104] At the same time, suggesting, as a matter of precaution, an 'institutional framework' for such pools bespeaks the gap that exists between the narrowly focused thinking of present-day competition law and the broader approach needed to deal with the theoretical and practical complexity of the systemic context. Within this context 'democratically' controlled institutions of (self-)regulation may play a useful role as 'complements' in the overall operation of patent protection.

---

[103] The relationship between collaborative research and development, standardization and industrial policy is well known; see Godt, *supra* note 12; Ullrich, *supra* note 10, at 824 *et seq*.

[104] See reference *supra* n. 95.

7 The competitive effects of patent field-of-use licences*

Mark R. Patterson

1 Introduction

A common patent licensing technique is the field-of-use licence, under which the patentee grants the right to use the patented invention, but only in a specified way. In both the EU and the United States, the competition agencies view field-of-use licensing as generally pro-competitive, because the ability to provide different licensing terms for different users can encourage broader licensing of inventions.[1] For example, the US Supreme Court has upheld a field-of-use licensing arrangement under which several patentees licensed third parties to manufacture audio amplifiers using their patented technologies, but only for home use.[2] This arrangement allowed the patentees to reserve the right to manufacture for commercial use, which was apparently more profitable, while still allowing the technologies to be used broadly for home applications. If licensing had required the patentees to share the commercial business as well, they might not have licensed the technologies for home use at all.

However field-of-use licensing need not always be pro-competitive. The anti-competitive concerns can be especially great when the patentee imposes restrictions on the ultimate purchasers of the patented products rather than on

* This Chapter was written before the recent US Supreme Court decision in *Quanta Computer, Inc. v. LG Electronics, Inc.* (June 2008).

1 See, for example, Commission Notice: Guidelines on the application of Article 81 of the EC Treaty to technology transfer agreements (hereinafter TT Guidelines), OJ 2004 No. C 101, p. 2, para. 182 ('Field of use restrictions may have pro-competitive effects by encouraging the licensor to license his technology for applications that fall outside his main area of focus.'); Delrahim, Makan (Deputy Assistant Attorney General, Antitrust Division, US Department of Justice), 'The Long and Winding Road: Convergence in the Application of Antitrust to Intellectual Property', Remarks presented at The George Mason Law Review Symposium, 6 October 2004, http://www.usdoj.gov/atr/public/speeches/205712.htm, accessed 4 November 2007 (discussing the use of field-of-use licences to practise price discrimination among licensees and observing that 'allowing the firm that developed the [innovation] to price discriminate may increase social welfare by promoting the efficient commercialization of the asset').

2 *General Talking Pictures Corp. v. Western Electric Co.*, 305 U.S. 124 (1938).

manufacturing licensees.[3] In recent United States cases, patentees have used field-of-use licensing to prevent purchasers from repairing those products and to enforce distribution restraints.[4] It is not clear that in these contexts the use restrictions facilitate broader licensing. Instead, the restrictions may allow the patentee to price-discriminate or to control more fully activities in related markets, neither of which is necessarily pro-competitive.

The effects of these recent field-of-use licensing arrangements in the US have not been carefully examined, because the courts have accorded them very deferential treatment. The Federal Circuit Court of Appeals has established a test that depends in theory on whether the restraint is 'within the scope of the patent claims',[5] a criterion that could have been used to assess the relationship of use restrictions to the patentee's inventive contribution. Subsequent decisions, however, have turned simply on the Federal Circuit's view that any contractual condition on a licence makes the exhaustion doctrine inapplicable,[6] and on the court's unwillingness to evaluate the effects of any licence restrictions that are not per se antitrust violations. As a result, lower courts in the US have given patentees *carte blanche* to define by contract the permissible uses of their inventions.

In Europe, patentees may not have the same freedom, but the law is currently unclear. The use restrictions in the recent US cases have been contained in agreements with downstream purchasers that use, but do not themselves produce, goods embodying the patented technology. Although the EC's Technology Transfer Block Exemption Regulation (TTBER) explicitly addresses use licensing,[7] the TTBER applies only to agreements that transfer technology for the production of products, not to agreements regarding the final sale of the products.[8] Instead, use-licensing arrangements like those at issue here presumably would be governed by the same rules that apply to unpatented products, and how those rules would be applied in this context is

---

3 See section 3.3 *infra.*

4 See, respectively, *Arizona Cartridge Remanufacturers Association, Inc. v. Lexmark International, Inc.*, 290 F. Supp. 2d 1034 (N.D. Cal. 2003), *aff'd*, 421 F.3d 981 (9th Cir. 2005), and *Pioneer Hi-Bred International, Inc. v. Ottawa Plant Food, Inc.*, 283 F. Supp. 2d 1018 (D. Iowa 2003). Both cases are discussed further below.

5 *Mallinckrodt, Inc. v. Medipart, Inc.*, 976 F.2d 700, 708 (Fed. Cir. 1992).

6 Under the exhaustion doctrine, or first-sale doctrine, a patentee's rights in its invention are exhausted upon the first sale of the invention. The applications of this doctrine in the US and EC are discussed more fully in the text accompanying notes 14–18 and 49–54 *infra.*

7 See Article 4(c)(i), (ii) Commission Regulation 772/2004 on the application of Article 81(3) of the Treaty to categories of technology transfer agreements, OJ 2004 No. L 123, p. 11.

8 See *infra* text accompanying notes 32–4.

unclear. Recent patent cases in the UK and Germany have taken a substantive approach that would not allow contract to trump patent law,[9] but the EC courts, notably the Court of First Instance in *GlaxoSmithKline*,[10] have become more accepting of the use of contract by patentees to maximize their returns.

In the next section, this chapter outlines the legal background for field-of-use licensing in the US and Europe. The subsequent section then describes several recent cases from the lower US courts and shortcomings in the analyses of those courts,[11] comparing them to the law in Europe. In short, the unbridled field-of-use licensing in the US allows patentees to define by contract the nature of patent infringement, without regard to previous limitations on infringement. The final section describes alternative means that patentees could use to achieve the pro-competitive purposes served by field-of-use licensing.

2 The legal framework for use licensing in the United States and Europe

2.1 The United States

2.1.1 The Supreme Court In the United States, the Supreme Court has said that a patentee 'may grant a license "on any condition the performance of which is reasonably within the reward which the patentee by the grant of the patent is entitled to secure"'. This statement, from *General Talking Pictures Corp. v. Western Electric Co.*,[12] a 1938 case that is still the Court's leading case on use licensing, appears to contemplate review of the economic justification for a licence restriction, by focusing on whether the restriction provides the patentee with rewards beyond those to which the patent entitles it. The case involved a restriction in an agreement that permitted a licensee to manufacture goods using the patented technology for a limited market. Because manufacturing licensees can be viewed as standing in the shoes of the patentee, use

---

9 See *infra* text accompanying notes 99–106.

10 Case T-168/01, *GlaxoSmithKline Services v. Commission*, [2006] ECR II-2969. This case is discussed in sections 2.2.3 and 3.2.2 *infra*.

11 Previous articles criticizing the Federal Circuit's approach are Kobak, Jr., J.B. (1993), 'Contracting Around Exhaustion: Some Thoughts About the CAFC's *Mallinckrodt* Decision', *J. Pat. & Trademark Off. Soc'y*, **75**, 550; Stern, R.H. (1993), 'The Unobserved Demise of the Exhaustion Doctrine in US Patent Law', *EIPR*, **15**, 460, at 462; Stern, R.H. (1994), 'Post-Sale Patent Restrictions After *Mallinckrodt* – An Idea in Search of Definition', *Alb. L.J. Sci. & Tech.*, **5,** 1, at 8; Carstensen, P.C. (2006), 'Post-Sale Restraints via Patent Licensing: A "Seedcentric" Perspective', *Fordham Intel. Prop., Media & Enter. L.J.*, **16**, 1053.

12 305 US 124 (1938). See also *supra* text accompanying note 2.

restrictions on them can reasonably be treated as economically equivalent to individual decisions by the patentee itself.[13]

But the Supreme Court has not upheld the use of patent infringement suits to enforce licence restrictions on the ultimate users of patented products.[14] Although it has never said that such restrictions could not be enforced through patent law, it has described the exhaustion principle in a way that suggests that conclusion, saying that when a patentee 'sells a machine or instrument whose sole value is in its use, he receives the consideration for its use and he parts with the right to restrict that use'.[15] The Court has indicated that any restrictions on the ultimate users of patented products would be part of contract law, not patent law: 'The extent to which the use of the patented machine may validly be restricted to specific supplies or otherwise by special contract between the owner of a patent and the purchaser or licensee is a question outside the patent law and with it we are not here concerned'.[16] As a result, such contracts appear, under the Supreme Court's cases, to receive no exemption from antitrust law. But those cases are now decades old, and different legal rules have been adopted in subsequent lower-court decisions.

2.1.2 The Federal Circuit The Federal Circuit Court of Appeals, which is the primary appeals court for patent issues in the United States, has replaced the Supreme Court's substantive approach with a formal one. The source of the formal approach is *Mallinckrodt, Inc. v. Medipart, Inc.*,[17] where the

---

[13] The Court has suggested this analogy: The owner of a patented article can, of course, charge such price as he may choose, and the owner of a patent may assign it or sell the right to manufacture and sell the article patented upon the condition that the assignee shall charge a certain amount for such article. *Bement v. National Harrow Co.*, 186 US 70, 93 (1902).

[14] In *General Talking Pictures*, the Court did allow an infringement suit against a downstream purchaser, but the Court's focus was on the licence restrictions imposed on the manufacturing licensee. The Court emphasized that the licensee had manufactured the products outside the scope of its licence, which was limited to a particular field of use. *Ibid.*, at 126. The purchaser was liable for infringement, the Court made clear, not because *it* had used the products outside the scope of a licence, but because, knowing that the manufacturing licensee had exceeded the scope of *its* licence, the purchaser was 'in no better position than if it had manufactured the amplifiers itself without a license'. *Ibid.*, at 127. See generally Stern, *supra* note 11, at 462.

[15] *Adams v. Burke*, 84 US 453, 456 (1873).

[16] *Motion Picture Patents Co. v. Universal Film Mfg. Co.*, 243 US 502, 509 (1917) (citing *Keeler v. Standard Folding Bed*, 157 US 659 (1895)); see also *Keeler v. Standard Folding Bed*, 157 US 659, 666 (1895) ('It is, however, obvious that such a question would arise as a question of contract, and not as one under the inherent meaning and effect of the patent laws.').

[17] 976 F.2d 700 (Fed. Cir. 1992).

Federal Circuit reviewed the validity of a restriction that took the form of a 'single use only' restriction on the patented product, which was a 'nebulizer' for the delivery of radioactive or medicinal substances in aerosol form to the lungs of medical patients. The alleged infringer accepted the used products from hospitals, sterilized them with high doses of radiation, repackaged them with new (unpatented) components, and resold them to the hospitals.

The first step in the Federal Circuit's analysis was to determine that the exhaustion doctrine was inapplicable. Here the court relied on the purported 'condition' on the sale of the product created by the 'single use only' notice. Although the court explicitly did not decide whether the notice was sufficient to create a contract, it rejected the District Court's reliance on the exhaustion doctrine as applicable only to unconditional sales. As the Federal Circuit described its approach in a later case, '[t]his exhaustion doctrine . . . does not apply to an expressly conditional sale or license'.[18]

With the patentee's patent rights not exhausted, the next step was to determine whether the restriction was permissible as a matter of patent law. Here the Federal Circuit set out a test that appeared to be consistent with the Supreme Court's: 'The appropriate criterion is whether Mallinckrodt's restriction is reasonably within the patent grant, or whether the patentee has ventured beyond the patent grant and into behavior having an anticompetitive effect not justifiable under the rule of reason'.[19] The first part of this test is consistent with the Supreme Court's approach if asking whether a restriction 'is reasonably within the patent grant' is the same as asking whether it 'is reasonably within the reward which the patentee by the grant of the patent is entitled to secure'. The second part of the test then, by making the restriction subject to antitrust law, would effectively treat it as any other contractual restriction, as the Supreme Court directed.

But as applied, the Federal Circuit's approach to determining whether the restriction is 'within the patent grant' has resulted in a very broad scope for field-of-use restrictions. Whereas the Supreme Court appeared to focus on the economic effects of a restriction, the Federal Circuit in *Mallinckrodt* stated what appeared to be a more technical test, asking whether the restriction 'relates to subject matter within the scope of the patent claims'.[20] It has not explained, however, what is required for a restriction to 'relate' to patent claims. At its broadest, as the requirement has in fact been interpreted, it could simply mean that the defendant's activity, if entirely unauthorized, would constitute infringement. That interpretation would effectively remove any limitations on field-of-use licensing.

18 *B. Braun Medical Inc. v. Abbott Labs.*, 124 F.3d 1419, 1426 (Fed. Cir. 1997).

19 976 F.2d 700, 708.

20 *Ibid.*

The Federal Circuit has provided little further analysis of these issues in subsequent cases,[21] leaving development of the law to lower courts. In its most recent opinion on these issues, however, the Federal Circuit appears, in passing and perhaps in *dictum*, to have eliminated all doubt about the status of field-of-use licences:[22]

> Under the patent laws, a patentee has the right to exclude others from making, using, or selling a patented invention. 35 USC § 154(a)(1). Conduct falling within the scope of protection includes, *inter alia*, limited use licensing and charging of royalties. Field of use licensing restrictions, i.e., permitting the use of inventions in one field and excluding it in others, are also within the scope of the patent grant.

In making these statements, the court cited not only *Mallinckrodt* but also *General Talking Pictures*, which as described above was a more narrow decision involving entirely different circumstances. Moreover, the Supreme Court's cases have made a number of statements that appear inconsistent with this categorical statement by the Federal Circuit.[23]

2.1.3 The IP Guidelines Although these court decisions establish current US law, the federal antitrust agencies have expressed their own views on field-of-use licenses. In the agencies' Antitrust Guidelines for the Licensing of Intellectual Property,[24] they state that field-of-use licences 'may serve procompetitive ends by allowing the licensor to exploit its property as efficiently and effectively as possible'.[25] They follow this statement, interestingly, with an example that illustrates use licensing with restrictions on ultimate purchasers.[26] However the example restrictions truly limit the *field* of use (to hospitals or group medical practices); they do not limit the manner in which the purchasers may use the intellectual property within that field, as the 'single use only' restriction in *Mallinckrodt* did. That is, the restrictions approved in the example are akin to those in *General Talking Pictures*, in that

21 In addition to the *Scruggs* cases quoted in the text, the Federal Circuit considered a use licence in *B. Braun Medical Inc. v. Abbott Laboratories*, 124 F.3d 1419 (Fed. Cir. 1997), but neither *Scruggs* nor *Braun* provided significant additional analysis. See *infra* text accompanying notes 64–5.

22 *Monsanto Co. v. Scruggs*, 459 F.3d 1328, 1338 (Fed. Cir. 2006) (citing *Mallinckrodt*, 976 F.2d 700, 703; *Brulotte v. Thys Co.*, 379 US 29 (1964) [royalties]; *General Talking Pictures Corp. v. Western Electric Co.*, 305 US 124 (1938)).

23 See *supra* text accompanying notes 14–16 and *infra* text accompanying notes 94–5, 111–12.

24 US Department of Justice and Federal Trade Commission, Antitrust Guidelines for the Licensing of Intellectual Property (6 April 1995).

25 *Ibid.*, § 2.3.

26 *Ibid.*, Example 1.

they serve to partition the market among purchasers, rather than to those in *Mallinckrodt*, which partition the market within individual purchasers.

2.2 *The European Community*

2.2.1 The Technology Transfer Block Exemption In the European Union, unlike the US, field-of-use licensing is addressed by regulation. Use licensing can be exempt from Article 81(1) EC under the EC's Technology Transfer Block Exemption Regulation (TTBER).[27] The TTBER generally exempts licensing restrictions between firms whose market shares do not exceed specified thresholds,[28] unless the restrictions fall into 'hardcore' or 'excluded' categories, which field-of-use licensing generally does not.[29] Above the market-share thresholds, the TTBER does not apply, but the TTBER's accompanying Guidelines[30] indicate that even then the Commission does not view use restrictions as troublesome when they are non-reciprocal ones between non-competitors: 'Field of use restrictions in agreements between non-competitors whereby the licensor reserves one or more product markets or technical fields of use for himself are generally either non-restrictive of competition or efficiency enhancing'.[31]

For most of the licensing arrangements in the recent US cases, though, the TTBER would probably not be applicable at all. Consider *Mallinckrodt*, for example, which involved a licence to a user of the patented product, not to a producer of it. The TTBER applies only to 'technology transfer agreements entered into between two undertakings permitting the *production* of contract products',[32] so the licence in *Mallinckrodt* would not qualify as a technology

---

27 See *supra* note 7.

28 If the parties are non-competitors, the block exemption applies so long as the share of neither party exceeds 30 per cent; see Article 3(2) of the TTBER. If they are competitors, the block exemption applies so long as the parties' combined share does not exceed 20 per cent; Article 3(1) TTBER.

29 Article 4(1)(c)(i) and (ii) TTBER specifically excludes non-reciprocal use licensing between competitors from the hardcore category, and use licensing does not fall into any of the hardcore categories for licences between non-competitors.

30 Commission Notice – Guidelines on the application of Article 81 of the EC Treaty to technology transfer agreements, OJ 2004 No. C 101, p. 2, para. 182 (hereinafter TT Guidelines).

31 TT Guidelines, para. 184.

32 Article 2 TTBER (emphasis added); see also TTBER Guidelines, para. 41 ('It follows from Article 2 that for licence agreements to be covered by the TTBER they must concern "the production of contract products", i.e. products incorporating or produced with the licensed technology. In other words, to be covered by the TTBER the licence must permit the licensee to exploit the licensed technology for production of goods or services (see recital 7 of the TTBER)').

transfer agreement under the TTBER. Agreements that do not involve production using the patented technology would be exempted, if at all, under the Vertical Agreement Regulation, as is discussed below.[33]

Perhaps it could be argued that because the purchaser in *Mallinckrodt* arranged for the reconditioning of the nebulizer, the 'licence' of the nebulizer permitted the 'production' of the product. But the 'licence' in *Mallinckrodt* actually forbade the reconditioning, so it seems difficult to view the *Mallinckrodt* licence, or the other similar ones discussed below, as permitting production of the patented product.[34] The sale in *Mallinckrodt* permitted the reconditioning, in the sense that it made the product available, but the licence agreement itself did not permit reconditioning. The result is that although field-of-use licences like the one in *Mallinckrodt* have been treated by the US courts no differently from the licence in *General Talking Pictures*, the former would not be exempt under the TTBER while the latter could be, since it did involve the production of patented products.

This conclusion is only reinforced by the definition of a field-of-use licence provided in the TT Guidelines. That definition is critical because if a particular restriction were not in fact a field-of-use licence, but some other sort of restriction, it could fall within a 'hardcore' or 'excluded' category of the TTBER. The Guidelines state that 'the field of use must be defined objectively by reference to identified and meaningful technical characteristics of the licensed product'.[35] This approach appears to contrast with the Federal Circuit's approach in the US, where that court appears to view *any* restriction on use as a field-of-use restriction, regardless of whether it is related to the patented technology.

This difference might play out particularly in restrictions that could be viewed as customer or territorial restrictions, as the Guidelines discuss.[36] Reciprocal customer and territorial restrictions between competitors are 'hardcore' restrictions under the TTBER, and thus would not be exempt, regardless of market share.[37] Perhaps a use restriction like that in *Mallinckrodt* could be viewed as a customer restriction, since it prevented transfers of the nebulizer to the defendant for reconditioning. But the restriction was not really focused on customer groups,[38] and in any event the licence was not reciprocal, so a

[33] See *infra* this section and section 2.2.2.

[34] The *Monsanto* cases discussed below differ in this respect, however. See *infra* section 4.2.3.

[35] TT Guidelines, para. 180.

[36] *Ibid.*

[37] See Article 4(1)(c) TTBER.

[38] In para. 180, the Guidelines state that '[t]he fact that a technical field of use restriction may correspond to certain groups of customers within a product market does not imply that the restraint is to be classified as a customer restriction'.

hardcore characterization seems unlikely for those use restrictions to which the TTBER would apply.

2.2.2 The Vertical Agreements Block Exemption If a use restriction does not involve 'the production of contract products', the applicable block exemption, if any, would be the Vertical Agreements Regulation.[39] But application of the Vertical Agreements Regulation is also problematic. This Regulation applies to agreements between undertakings[40] where each operates 'at a different level of the production or distribution chain'.[41] Most of the purchasers in the US cases have used the finished product in their own operations, rather than distributing it to downstream purchasers. These purchasers would probably not be viewed as operating in the distribution chain at all.

That conclusion seems correct even if the purchaser transferred the product to another firm for reconditioning. In this respect, it is possible to draw by analogy on the motor vehicle block exemption, where the regulation states that '"independent repairer" means a provider of repair and maintenance services for motor vehicles not operating within the distribution system set up by the supplier',[42] suggesting that independent aftermarket reconditioners of patented products would not be viewed by the Commission as within the distribution chain. In that case, no block exemption would apply.

If the Vertical Agreements Regulation were applicable, it appears that it could exempt use restrictions on much the same basis as would the TTBER,

39 Commission Regulation 2790/1999 of 22 December 1999 on the application of Article 81(3) of the Treaty to categories of vertical agreements and concerted practices, OJ 1999 No. L 336, p. 21; see also Commission Notice – Guidelines on Vertical Restraints, OJ 2000 No. C 291, p. 1 (2000) (hereinafter Vertical Restraints Guidelines).

40 In addition to the issues discussed in the text, the applicability of the vertical agreement block exemption (and of the TTBER) might be prevented because in some cases the use restrictions could apply to end-users that are individuals, in which case the restrictions might not even be subject to Article 81, which applies only to agreements between 'undertakings'. See Article 81 EC Treaty; Article 2(1) Vertical Agreement Regulation; Vertical Restraint Guidelines, para. 24. That would not in fact be an issue in a case such as *Mallinckrodt*, where the end-users were hospitals, but in the *Lexmark* case, discussed below, some of the users were individuals who were purchasing toner cartridges for their laser printers. However, most of the end-users to which use restrictions have applied have in fact been 'undertakings' rather than individual consumers, because they typically use the patented products in other economic activities. See Louri, V. (2002), '"Undertaking" as a Jurisdictional Element for the Application of EC Competition Rules', *Leg. Iss. Econ. Integr.*, **29**(2), 143.

41 Article 2(1) Vertical Agreements Regulation.

42 Article 1(m) Commission Regulation 1400/2002 of 31 July 2002 on the application of Article 81(3) of the Treaty to categories of vertical agreements and concerted practices in the motor vehicle sector, OJ 2002 No. L 203, p. 30.

assuming the market-share criteria were satisfied.[43] As with the TTBER, use restrictions are not hardcore restrictions under the Vertical Agreement Regulation, although here again also they might in certain circumstances be viewed as customer restrictions, which could be hardcore restrictions. The analysis of this issue would presumably be much the same as that presented above for the TTBER.

A more significant issue, perhaps, is that in a case like *Mallinckrodt*, which involves the reconditioning and resale of a product that is purportedly subject to the licence restrictions at issue, the patentee and the reconditioners might be viewed as competing undertakings, which would make the Vertical Agreements Regulation inapplicable.[44] The regulation defines 'competing undertakings' as 'actual or potential suppliers in the same product market', where the 'product market includes goods or services which are regarded by the buyer as interchangeable with or substitutable for the contract goods or services'.[45] Whether a reconditioned product should be viewed as competing with the original product is not entirely clear in this context. The parties are, of course, not competing until the original product is sold, because there is no opportunity to recondition the original product until then, so the reconditioner is not a competing undertaking at the time of entry into the licence agreement.

Given the intellectual property aspects of this issue, it may be appropriate to apply the TTBER's definition of 'competing undertakings' as 'undertakings which, in the absence of the technology transfer agreement, are both active on the relevant . . . market[s] on which the contract products are sold without infringing each others' intellectual property rights'.[46] Even if the TTBER is not technically applicable, it may be appropriate to apply the criteria from this definition, which asks whether it is the technology transfer agreement itself that enables the competition, and whether the activity at issue infringes the patentee's rights. The reconditioners are in these cases not parties to the licence agreements, so it seems that their activities do not depend on those agreements. That is, so long as the products are sold, the reconditioners' activities would be possible, regardless of any agreement with the end-users.

The next question under the TTBER's approach to determining competitor status is whether the reconditioning and resale infringe the patentee's rights. That is a question of substantive patent law, turning on the contours of the repair doctrine, not a question that is answered by either the Vertical

---

[43] The exemption applies where the market share of the supplier (or the buyer in the case of exclusive-supply agreements) is no more than 30 per cent; Article 3 Vertical Agreements Regulation.

[44] *Ibid.*, Article 2(4).

[45] *Ibid.*, Article 1(a).

[46] Article 1(j)(ii) TTBER.

Agreement Regulation or by the TTBER. Thus it is not clear that the criteria used in the block exemption regulations are well-suited to evaluating field-of-use licensing. For the Vertical Agreement Regulation as for the TTBER, this is not surprising. These licences are not being used for the usual purpose for which vertical intra-brand restraints are adopted, which is to prevent free-riding *within* the distribution system.[47] Instead, they are being used to implement more complete control of the patented product, at least in part to effect price discrimination.

Given this divergence from the focus of the Vertical Agreements Regulation, it may be appropriate to consider the statement in the Vertical Restraints Guidelines that 'where the nature of the product does not require selective distribution, such a distribution system does not generally bring about sufficient efficiency enhancing effects to counterbalance a significant reduction in intra-brand competition'.[48] The efficiency-enhancing effects here would simply be greater returns on the patented product. Although that concern is not addressed directly by the Vertical Agreements Regulation, it has been the focus of recent EC cases.

2.2.3 The Community courts The EC courts, if not the Commission, have recently become more forgiving of licensing restrictions, at least in the pharmaceutical area. Traditionally, the European Court of Justice vigorously defended exhaustion principles, at least where territorial restrictions, and thus the free movement of goods, were at issue.[49] But in the September 2006 *GlaxoSmithKline* judgment,[50] the Court of First Instance upheld GlaxoSmithKline's use of contractual price differentials to discourage parallel trade. The court held that the Commission did not give sufficient consideration to the efficiency gains, in the form of innovation, that could be made possible by the national partitioning of markets.[51] Although the court did not make entirely clear what consideration was required, it imposed on the Commission the burdens of evaluating the prospective innovation benefits and of balancing those benefits against the harms to competition of the territorial partitioning.[52]

---

47 The *Ottawa Plant Foods* case discussed at section 3.2.2 (under *US cases*) *infra* may be an exception. On the free-riding argument generally, see section 4.1 *infra*.

48 Vertical Restraints Guidelines, para. 186.

49 See, for example, Joined Cases C-267/95 and C-268/95, *Merck*, [1996] ECR I-6285.

50 Case T-168/01, *GlaxoSmithKline Services v. Commission*, [2006] ECR II-2969.

51 *Ibid.*, at paras 294–303.

52 *Ibid.*, at paras 241, 301 and 304.

Whether this approach will be applied more widely remains to be seen. *GlaxoSmithKline* is not entirely an aberration. In the ECJ's decisions on rental rights for video recordings, the court has permitted copyright owners to prohibit the rentals in one country of video recordings purchased in another. The court emphasized the importance of a derogation from the exhaustion principle to the extent that it is necessary to ensure that the video recording owners were able to recover 'remuneration . . . which secures for them a satisfactory share of the rental market'.[53] Although the decisions were focused on Articles 28 and 30, and involved copyrights rather than patents, they still suggest that the court may respond to arguments that intellectual property owners must be allowed to impose limitations to protect their revenues.

On the other hand, both *GlaxoSmithKline* and the video recording cases emphasized conditions in the particular markets at issue in the cases, so they might not indicate that the EC courts would accept such arguments in general.[54] But the narrow focus in those cases might be related to the fact that both sets of cases involved territorial restrictions, which are viewed particularly harshly in the EC. A patentee arguing for discrimination among uses, rather than territories, might be received more favourably. All this leaves the likely treatment of these use-licensing arrangements under Article 81 uncertain: the exhaustion doctrine applies, territorially at least, if not so strongly for uses, yet even territorially there may be derogations from the doctrine to protect patentees' profits.

It is worth considering also how use-licensing restrictions might be analysed under the *Magill* and *IMS Health* line of cases under Article 82.[55] Although those cases involved unilateral refusals to license rather than licence restrictions, most of the US use-licensing cases have involved suits against unlicensed defendants who received the patented products from the licensees, so one could view the issue as relating to the patentee's refusal to license the

---

53 Case C-61/97, *Foreningen af danske Videogramdistributører v. Laserdisken*, [1998] ECR I-5171, para. 15; Case 158/86, *Warner Brothers Inc. v. Christiansen*, [1988] ECR I-2605.

54 The same was true of Advocate General Jacobs in another recent *GlaxoSmithKline* case; Opinion of AG Jacobs, Case C-53/03, *Syfait v. GlaxoSmithKline*, [2005] ECR I-4609, paras 93 and 100. Advocate General Jacobs indicated that geographic market partitioning might be necessary to enable the patentee to generate the revenue that provides the incentive for its research. However, he limited his opinion to the peculiar parallel trade circumstances in the pharmaceutical industry. The ECJ itself decided that it did not have jurisdiction to hear the case, which had been referred to it by the Hellenic Competition Commission.

55 See Joined Cases C-241/91 P and C-242/91 P, *RTE and ITP v. Commission* ('*Magill*'), [1995] ECR I-743; Case C-418/01, *IMS Health*, [2004] ECR I-5039; see also Case C-7/97, *Bronner*, [1998] ECR I-7791.

defendants. For example, in *Mallinckrodt*, it would be Medipart, the reconditioner, to which Mallinckrodt refused to grant a licence. The implications of the *Magill* and *IMS Health* cases are very well explained in the chapter on unilateral refusals to license,[56] and the discussion here will focus only on the use-licensing context.

The key requirement of the *Magill* line of cases in the context of use licensing is that for a licence to be required it must be that the 'refusal [to license] prevented the appearance of a new product for which there was a potential consumer demand'.[57] As the Commission in its recent Discussion Paper on Article 82 points out, this requirement will be satisfied only where the potential licensee 'does not intend to limit itself essentially to duplicating the goods or services already offered on this market by the owner of the IPR, but intends to produce new goods or services not offered by the owner of the right and for which there is a potential consumer demand'.[58] In cases involving the reconditioning of patented products, one could argue that because the patentee is already providing the product (in its unreconditioned form), the potential licensee's provision of the reconditioned product is not in a new market, and therefore no licence would be required.

On the other hand, reconditioning might itself be a new market, in that the reconditioned product might be viewed by consumers as distinguishable from the new one. Reconditioned products generally sell for less than new ones, even where they are reconditioned by the original manufacturers, which suggests that consumers do not find the new and reconditioned products entirely interchangeable. As will be seen below, though, in some of the recent cases, the existence of a separate market is not so clear, or the patentee can be viewed as providing its own product in that market.[59]

2.2.4 National law Because patent law is central to these cases, some of the issues would likely be decided by national courts in Europe, rather than under EC law. For example, even if a determination were made that a contractual restriction was valid under competition law, it would still be possible that the restriction would not be enforceable under national patent law. That is, a patentee might be able to bring a breach-of-contract action for a violation of

---

[56] Conde Gallego, Beatriz, chapter 9, in this volume.

[57] Joined Cases C-241/91 P and C-242/91 P, *RTE and ITP v. Commission* ('*Magill*'), [1995] ECR I-743, para. 54; see also Case C-7/97, *Bronner*, [1998] ECR I-7791, para. 40.

[58] DG Competition Discussion Paper of December 2005 on the application of Article 82 of the Treaty to exclusionary abuses, para. 239, http://ec.europa.eu/comm/competition/antitrust/art82/discpaper2005.pdf, accessed 4 November 2007.

[59] See *infra* text accompanying note 144.

the restriction, but not be permitted to pursue it through an action for patent infringement. This is exactly the approach suggested by the US Supreme Court for certain use restrictions.[60]

A survey of national laws on these issues is beyond the scope of this chapter. In any event, a search has failed to identify any European cases exactly on point. Indeed, most commentary on the exhaustion issue focuses only on the question of international territorial exhaustion.[61] Nevertheless, the sections below discuss several European cases that touch on related issues in the repair-reconstruction doctrine.[62]

3 Field-of-use licensing: contract and patent analyses

As Richard Stern has said, at least under a broad interpretation '*Mallinckrodt* would permit patentees to accomplish many things that previously were infeasible'.[63] This prediction has been borne out as United States cases subsequent to *Mallinckrodt* have, with little analysis, narrowed even further the scrutiny that will be applied to field-of-use licences. A later Federal Circuit case, *B. Braun Medical Inc. v. Abbott Laboratories*,[64] recast the question of whether the use restriction is within the scope of the patent claims into the question of whether 'the patentee has "impermissibly broadened the 'physical or temporal scope' of the patent grant with anticompetitive effect"',[65] *Braun* offered as examples of such impermissible broadening tying and an enforcement of the patent beyond its term, and suggested that limitations on use licensing would be limited to those practices.

However, a patent's scope is defined by more than the 'physical' products its claims cover and the 'temporal' period of its coverage. It is also defined by the classes of conduct that the patent can be used to prohibit. It may be possible for a patentee to impermissibly broaden the scope of acts that constitute infringement, not just the scope of the patent. As will be seen below, in several

---

60 See *supra* text accompanying notes 14–16 and *infra* text accompanying notes 111 *et seq.*

61 See, for example, Conde Gallego, Beatriz (2003), 'The Principle of Exhaustion of Rights and Its Implications for Competition Law', *IIC*, **34**, 473; Ullrich, Hanns (1999), 'International Exhaustion of Intellectual Property Rights: Lessons from European Economic Integration', in Marianne Dony and Aline De Walsche (eds), *Mélanges en Hommage à Michel Waelbroeck*, Brussels: Bruylant, pp. 250–4.

62 See *infra* text accompanying notes 99–106.

63 Stern, *supra* note 11, at 8.

64 124 F.3d 1419 (Fed. Cir. 1997).

65 *Ibid.*, at 1426, quoting *Windsurfing International, Inc. v. AMF, Inc.*, 782 F.2d 995, 1001 *et seq.* (Fed. Cir. 1986) (quoting *Blonder-Tongue Laboratories, Inc. v. University of Illinois Foundation*, 402 US 313, 343 (1971)), and citing Mallinckrodt, 976 F.2d, 700 and 704.

of the cases at issue here, there would be no infringement in the absence of the use restrictions, even if there were no licence. It is only by adoption of the use restrictions that patentees are able to transform permissible conduct into infringement.[66] A buyer's violation of a use restriction is a breach of contract, and, because in the view of the Federal Circuit the contract is also a licence that defines the buyer's rights under the patent, the breach of contract becomes patent infringement.[67] Thus, the patentee's use restrictions define the scope of infringement.

The paragraphs below argue that this broadening of the scope of infringement can be prevented by requiring, first, an independent infringement inquiry. That is, the court should conduct, at the threshold, without regard to whether the alleged infringer has consented to a field-of-use licence, an initial inquiry into whether the patent at issue is infringed. If the conduct at issue would not be infringement in the absence of the licence, as would be the case for permissible repair, a breach of a contract should not constitute patent infringement.

---

66 The general approach of the analysis here is similar to that in Kobak, Jr., *supra* note 11, in that it focuses on the use of contract to escape substantive limitations of patent law. The scope of this phenomenon has in recent years increased dramatically beyond that in the immediate post-*Mallinckrodt* period in which Kobak was writing. The use of state contract law to extend patent protection could be viewed as a preemption issue, as it has in the software context. See Note by Mauk, J.E. (2001), 'The Slippery Slope of Secrecy: Why Patent Law Preempts Reverse-Engineering Clauses in Shrink-Wrap Licenses', *Wm and Mary L. Rev.*, **43,** 819. But a proper application of the limits of patent law would eliminate the pre-emption problem by eliminating the extension of protection. Cf. Lemley, M.A. (1999), 'Beyond Preemption: The Law and Policy of Intellectual Property Licensing', *Cal. L. Rev.*, **87**, 111, at 138–44.

67 *Mallinckrodt, Inc. v. Medipart, Inc.*, 976 F.2d 700, 707 note 6 (Fed. Cir. 1992) ('[T]he remedy for breach of a binding license provision is not exclusively in contract, for a license is simply a promise not to sue for what would otherwise be patent infringement.' Citations omitted.). Interestingly, European Community trade mark law takes a different approach. Both the trade mark regulation and the trade mark directive identify specific licence provisions whose contravention will subject a licensee to trade mark enforcement. Those provisions are limited to those 'with regard to its duration, the form covered by the registration in which the trade mark may be used, the scope of the goods or services for which the licence is granted, the territory in which the trade mark may be affixed, or the quality of the goods manufactured or of the services provided by the licensee'. See Article 22(2) Council Regulation (EC) No. 40/94 of 20 December 1993 on the Community trade mark, [1994] OJ 1994 L 11, p. 1; Article 8(2) First Council Directive 89/104/EEC of 21 December 1988 to approximate the laws of the Member States relating to trade marks, [1989] OJ 1989 No. L 40, p. 1. This enumeration of the licence violations whose violation will constitute infringement serves a similar purpose to the initial infringement inquiry advocated in the text. In each case, the effect is to limit the intellectual property owner's freedom to define unilaterally the scope of infringement.

This issue echoes two similar issues in the US copyright area. First, several cases have considered contractual clauses in copyright licences that eliminate the fair-use right to reverse engineer the copyrighted software.[68] For example, the Federal Circuit in *Bowers v. Baystate Technologies, Inc.*[69] concluded that 'private parties are free to contractually forego the limited ability to reverse engineer a software product under the exemptions of the Copyright Act'.[70] *Bowers* affirmed only the contract claim, though, without considering copyright infringement, and even suggested, although somewhat obscurely, that the contract might not change the limits of copyright law.[71] But a contractual prohibition on reverse engineering has also apparently been found, though also somewhat obscurely, to make reverse engineering copyright infringement.[72] The use of contract to redefine copyright law is similar to the applications of contract to patent law described above. The copyright context is arguably less troubling, though, in that the applicability of the fair-use defence is not entirely clear in the cases that have allowed its elimination.[73]

Second, courts and commentators alike have expressed concern about the effect of the Digital Millennium Copyright Act (DMCA) on copyright fair use.[74] The DMCA creates a cause of action against one who circumvents a technological protection measure for a copyrighted work.[75] There is an exception for

---

68 Most courts considering the issue have held that reverse engineering is a fair use; see, for example, *Atari Games Corp. v. Nintendo of America, Inc.*, 975 F.2d 832 (Fed. Cir. 1992); *Sega Enterprises Ltd. v. Accolade, Inc.*, 977 F.2d 1510 (9th Cir. 1992). The contractual elimination of this fair-use right has generally been decried by commentators; see, for example, Madison, M.J. (1998), 'Legal-Ware: Contract and Copyright in the Digital Age', *Fordham L. Rev.*, **67**, 1025; Lemley, Mark A. (1995), 'Intellectual Property and Shrinkwrap Licenses', *S. Cal. L. Rev.*, **68**, 1239; Rice, D.A. (1992), 'Public Goods, Private Contract and Public Policy: Federal Preemption of Software License Prohibitions Against Reverse Engineering', *U. Pitt. L. Rev.*, **53,** 543.

69 320 F.3d 1317 (Fed. Cir. 2003).

70 *Ibid.*, at 1325–6.

71 *Ibid.*, at 1326 ('[A] party bound by such a contract may elect to efficiently breach the agreement in order to ascertain ideas in a computer program unprotected by copyright law.').

72 *Davidson & Associates v. Jung*, 422 F.3d 630 (8th Cir. 2005).

73 The courts that have concluded that reverse engineering is a fair use have generally focused on its use to make interoperable products, but interoperability was not the central issue in either *Bowers* or *Davidson*. Cf. *Alcatel USA, Inc. v. DGI Technologies, Inc.*, 166 F.3d 772 (5th Cir. 1999) (holding that a contractual tying restriction that prevented achievement of interoperability was copyright misuse).

74 See, for example, Lipton, J.D. (2005), 'Solving the Digital Piracy Puzzle: Disaggregating Fair Use from the DMCA's Anti-Device Provisions', *Harv. J. L. & Tech.*, **19,** 111; Burk, D.L. (2003), 'Anticircumvention Misuse', *UCLA L. Rev.*, **50**, 1095.

75 17 USC § 1201.

circumvention for the purpose of reverse engineering to achieve interoperability,[76] but reverse engineering is only one form of fair use permitted by the Copyright Act, and the DMCA has no general fair-use exception. Hence, one who circumvents a technological measure protecting a copyrighted work may be liable under the DMCA, even if the use to which the copyrighted work would be put is a fair use, and thus permissible under the Copyright Act. This problem has arisen in a number of contexts,[77] and is presumably not the result Congress intended when it passed the DMCA. Nevertheless, one could argue that at least the result is one created by statute. The amendments of patent law effected by use licensing have, in contrast, been created by the courts with very little analysis.

3.1 Contract analysis

Before discussing the patent issues further, it is important to emphasize that in these cases the courts' conclusions that there are valid contracts are also questionable. As described above, the 'single use only' restriction in *Mallinckrodt* was embodied in a notice on the patented product. There was no clear act of consent to the restriction by the purchasers. This is typical of the other recent US cases. For example, in *Pioneer Hi-Bred International, Inc. v. Ottawa Plant Food, Inc.*,[78] the basis of the contract was again a notice on the product sold, in that case bags of corn seed. And the same was true in *Monsanto Co. v. McFarling*[79] and *Monsanto Co. v. Scruggs*,[80] where cotton and soybean seeds were at issue.

The key problem in the courts' contract analyses in these cases is that, generally speaking, notice of the terms that a seller would like to impose is not sufficient to establish a contract on the basis of those terms. This point was recognized by the Federal Circuit in *Hewlett-Packard Co. v. Repeat-O-Type Stencil Manufacturing Corp.*:[81]

> The question is not whether the patentee at the time of sale intended to limit a purchaser's right to modify the product. . . . Each case turns on its own particular facts, but a seller's intent, unless embodied in an enforceable contract, does not create a limitation on the right of a purchaser to use, sell, or modify a patented prod-

---

76 17 USC § 1201(f).

77 See Electronic Frontier Foundation, *Unintended Consequences: Seven Years under the DMCA* (April 2006), http://www.eff.org/IP/DMCA/DMCA_unintended_v4.pdf, accessed 4 November 2007.

78 283 F. Supp. 2d 1018 (D. Iowa 2003). The author served as an expert witness for the defendant in this case.

79 363 F.3d 1336 (Fed. Cir. 2004).

80 342 F. Supp. 2d 568 (N.D. Miss. 2004), *aff'd*, 459 F.3d 1328 (Fed. Cir. 2006).

81 123 F.3d 1445 (Fed. Cir. 1997).

uct as long as a reconstruction of the patented combination is avoided. A noncontractual intention is simply the seller's hope or wish, rather than an enforceable restriction.[82]

In *Repeat-O-Type*, however, the patentee had simply included a package insert that, in the court's word, 'suggest[ed]' the patentee's desired restriction. Therefore, although the court's refusal to enforce the restriction appeared to turn on the lack of any assent to it by the purchaser, it could also have been a product of a more equivocal notice than those at issue here.

In any event, in *Mallinckrodt*, where the 'single use only' notice was clear (and thus perhaps more than a 'suggestion'), the Federal Circuit took an entirely different approach. It said there that 'a license notice may become a term of sale, even if not part of the original transaction, if not objected to within a reasonable time'.[83] In this respect, *Mallinckrodt* relied on § 2-207 of the Uniform Commercial Code, adopted in most US states. Section 2-207 is designed to address the 'battle of the forms' created in sales of goods when contracting parties exchange documents with different terms. Under this Section, as *Mallinckrodt* says, a restriction 'may become a term of sale' without explicit assent under certain circumstances.

But the circumstances in which this 'may' happen do not include those in these cases. Although this issue cannot be discussed in detail here, two obstacles to applying § 2-207 can be noted. First, for § 2-207 to apply, the relevant communication must be a 'definite and seasonable expression of acceptance or a written confirmation which is sent within a reasonable time',[84] and the product notices in the recent cases do not appear to qualify. Second, even if the notices met this requirement and were sufficient to be, in the language of § 2-207, 'construed as proposals for addition to the contract', such proposals do not become part of the contract if 'they materially alter it', which restrictions limiting the purchaser to a single use or eliminating the right of resale certainly seem to do.[85]

---

82 *Ibid.*, at 1453.

83 976 F.2d at 708 note 7 (citing (UCC § 2-207(2)(c)).

84 The distinction is important, because receipt of a written statement expressing contract terms puts the purchaser on notice of contractual implications in a way that a simple notice on a product does not. The transactions at issue might actually involve acceptance by conduct, which is governed by a different subsection, § 2-207(3). That subsection provides that 'the terms of the particular contract consist of those terms on which the writings of the parties agree, together with any supplementary terms incorporated under any other provisions of [the UCC]'. The use restrictions in these cases would thus not become part of the contract under this subsection.

85 UCC § 2-207(2)(b). In addition, if the sales are to non-merchants, such as individual consumers, the additional terms do not become part of the contract in any

These issues were discussed more carefully in an analogous case, *Step-Saver Data Systems, Inc. v. Wyse Technology*,[86] which involved copyright rather than patent law. The additional terms in *Step-Saver* were printed on the box of the software that was the subject of the transaction. The copyright owner, TSL, argued that the additional terms, denials of warranties, were binding upon the purchaser, Step-Saver. In addition to holding that the denials of the warranties would materially alter the contract, and thus would not be binding on Step-Saver without its assent, the court drew the critical distinction between notice and assent that eluded the *Mallinckrodt* and *Ottawa* courts.[87]

The contrast between the careful analysis in *Step-Saver*, which goes on over 10 pages of the printed opinion, and the one- or two-sentence perfunctory conclusions of the patent cases is striking, and hard to explain. Perhaps it derives from the fact that in the patent cases, the use restrictions that are at issue seem more like issues of patent law than contract law, in contrast to the warranty disclaimers in *Step-Saver*. Contract law is essential to these cases, though, and the courts should not be imposing 'licence' conditions on purchasers without carefully determining whether there is in fact a licence.

It is true that courts have upheld various instances of 'shrink-wrap' and 'click-wrap' licences, although largely in the copyright context. But the courts that have done so have generally relied both on a requirement that the licensee acknowledge that it is aware of the licence term (typically by responding to a computer program inquiry) and on its having a clear chance to decline the term (sometimes by returning the product). In *Mallinckrodt*, *Ottawa*, and *Scruggs*, the conditions were simply printed on the products or packaging, and it is not clear that the patentees gave purchasers an option to return the product if they did not accept the condition.

The only one of the recent US cases that might arguably meet those conditions is *Arizona Cartridge Remanufacturers Association, Inc. v. Lexmark International, Inc.*,[88] where the condition was a prohibition on refilling a laser-printer toner cartridge. The condition was printed on the toner cartridge package, so the only acknowledgment of the condition would have come through opening the package. But the notice on the package offered purchasers the option of returning the package to the seller, the option that courts have relied

---

case. Most of the US cases have involved sales to merchants, but one, *Arizona Cartridge Remanufacturers Association, Inc. v. Lexmark International, Inc.*, 290 F. Supp. 2d 1034 (N.D. Cal. 2003), 421 F.3d 981 (9th Cir. 2005), involved sales to individual consumers. In *Lexmark*, the use restriction prohibited the refilling of laser-printer toner cartridges, and the restriction was printed on the cartridge packaging.

86 939 F.2d 91 (3d Cir. 1991).

87 See *ibid.*, at 104.

88 290 F. Supp. 2d 1034 (N.D. Cal. 2003), *aff'd*, 421 F.3d 981 (9th Cir. 2005).

upon in finding contractual consent in shrink-wrap cases.[89] In addition, the package notice also explained that Lexmark offered buyers the option of paying a higher price for a cartridge that they were permitted to refill.[90] The other cases lacked even these limited indications of the consent of buyers.

3.2 Infringement analysis

Even if the buyers of these patented products had entered into valid licence contracts with the patentees, it is not clear that those contracts should be enforceable. *Mallinckrodt* left open the possibility that a field-of-use licence might go beyond the scope of the patent claims, but the courts considering these issues generally have not given that possibility serious consideration. Indeed, the Federal Circuit in *Scruggs* apparently held that all field-of-use licences are within the scope of patents.[91] Furthermore the lower courts have generally relied on the mere existence of the patents and on the court's views that the purchasers have assented to the restrictions. A dramatic example is *Lexmark*, where the court failed to examine, or even refer to, the patents at issue.

Serious consideration of the validity of use restrictions requires a more careful focus on patent law. More specifically, as suggested above, it is the scope of infringement that is at issue in these cases. In the United States, patent law authorizes a patentee to sue any party that 'without authority makes, uses, offers to sell, or sells any patented invention, within the United States, or imports into the United States any patented invention'.[92] European law is similar.[93] Because these cases involve 'use' licensing, one would expect that it would be the scope of the prohibition on unauthorized 'use' of the invention that would be at issue.

In fact, though, the particular conduct challenged in most of these cases is better characterized as 'making' the invention, rather than 'using' it. That was the case in *Mallinckrodt*, for example, where the alleged infringer, Medipart, did not itself use the patented products but only reconditioned them for hospitals. Similarly, in *Lexmark* the parties to the litigation were remanufacturers of the patented toner cartridges, not the ultimate users of the cartridges. And in *Ottawa Plant Foods*, as discussed below, the defendant was simply a reseller

---

89 See 421 F.3d 981, 983 *et seq.*

90 *Ibid.*

91 See *supra* text accompanying note 22.

92 35 USC § 271(a).

93 For example, section 60(1) of the UK Patents Act 1977 provides that 'a person infringes a patent for an invention if . . . where the invention is a product, he makes, disposes of, offers to dispose of, uses or imports the product or keeps it whether for disposal or otherwise'.

of the patented product; it neither used nor made the product. Thus, despite the fact that the licence restrictions at issue in these cases were termed 'field of use' restrictions, the forms of infringing conduct in these cases were the 'making' and the 'selling', not the 'using' of the patented product.

Of course, we might say in normal language that making and selling a product are uses of it. But the fact that the statute distinguishes among these various activities suggests that we should be cautious about treating them as one. By doing so, as will be seen below, the courts have permitted patentees to transform permissible making and selling into impermissible using.

3.2.1 Making and repair When a patentee alleges that another is liable for infringing its patent by making the invention, an essential question should be whether the 'making' of the invention is permissible under patent law. If so, there can be no infringement regardless of whether there is a violation of a use restriction. So the first question in these cases should be whether there would be an infringing act independent of the licensing restriction. If not, the violation of a use restriction might be a breach of contract, but even a breach of the contract would not be infringement.

In the United States, in *Lexmark* and in *Mallinckrodt*, the allegedly infringing acts involved arguable 'makings' of the invention. By refilling toner cartridges or sterilizing and repackaging nebulizers, the alleged infringers in those cases arguably 'made' new toner cartridges or nebulizers. But these 'makings' of the inventions might have been permissible because they were repairs of the patented inventions. In *Aro Manufacturing*,[94] the Supreme Court held that purchasers of patented products have the right to repair those products:[95]

> [A]lthough there is no right to 'rebuild' a patented combination, the entity 'exists' notwithstanding the fact that destruction or impairment of one of its elements renders it inoperable; and that, accordingly, replacement of that worn-out essential part is permissible restoration of the machine to the original use for which it was bought.

That is, the Supreme Court has defined infringement to exclude repair, placing it outside the boundary of infringing activity.

In *Mallinckrodt*, however, the Federal Circuit said that a patentee can eliminate the right of repair by contract. To reach this conclusion, *Mallinckrodt*

---

[94] *Aro Manufacturing Co., Inc. v. Convertible Top Replacement Co., Inc.*, 365 U.S. 336 (1961).

[95] *Ibid.*, at 342, citing *Wilson v. Simpson*, 50 U.S. 109, 123 (1850). The focus in both *Aro* and in *Wilson v. Simpson* was on inventions that were combinations of components.

relied on the Supreme Court's holding in *Aro* that application of the repair doctrine requires that the initial sale of the product be authorized.[96] But because Mallinckrodt's initial sale of the nebulizers to the hospitals *was* authorized, and the only conduct that was arguably unauthorized was the reconditioning, whose validity turns precisely on the repair doctrine, this is impermissible bootstrapping. When this holding of *Mallinckrodt* is combined with the Federal Circuit's view that conduct by the licensee that is outside the scope of the licence is patent infringement,[97] the Federal Circuit can be seen to have redefined the scope of infringement for 'making' the patented product. Under *Mallinckrodt*, repair is only a permitted activity if the patentee chooses not to forbid it.

No doubt the Federal Circuit does not view itself as rewriting Section 271 of the Patent Act. Instead, it presumably views the right of repair as something akin to an implied licence. Under that view, repairing a patented product is always infringement, statutorily, but it is sometimes licensed by the patentee. The problem is that there is no support in the Supreme Court's decisions for the implied-licence interpretation. The Court in *Aro* was quite explicit: 'The [patent] monopolist cannot prevent those to whom he sells from . . . reconditioning articles worn by use, unless they in fact make a new article'.[98] Although the Federal Circuit would presumably take the view that because the licence is conditional there is no 'sale', the Supreme Court's decisions provide no support for this view in the repair context.

In the European Union, the significance of the repair–reconstruction distinction is generally a matter of patent law, rather than competition law, and is therefore primarily governed by national law in Europe. The law in recent cases in at least two European countries appears to reflect an approach like that of the US Supreme Court, rather than that of the Federal Circuit. For example, the issue was explored in the 2004 *Flügelradzähler* decision of the German Federal Supreme Court.[99] The court in that case said that the issue requires a

---

96 972 F.2d 700, 709, quoting *Aro Mfg. Co. v. Convertible Top Replacement Co.*, 377 U.S. 476, 480 (1964).

97 *Mallinckrodt, Inc. v. Medipart, Inc.*, 976 F.2d 700, 707 note 6 (Fed. Cir. 1992) ('[T]he remedy for breach of a binding license provision is not exclusively in contract, for a license is simply a promise not to sue for what would otherwise be patent infringement.' Citations omitted.).

98 365 US 336, 343 (quoting *United States v. Aluminum Co. of America*, 148 F.2d 416, 425 (2d Cir. 1945)).

99 See Decision of the German Federal Supreme Court (BGH), 4 May 2004, Case No. X ZR 48/03 – '*Flügelradzähler*', (2004) GRUR 758 = '*Impeller Flow Meter*', (2005) *IIC*, **36**, 963 (English translation). The discussion in the text draws on Hölder, N. (2005), 'Contributory Patent Infringement and Exhaustion in Case of Replacement Parts – Comment on a Recent Supreme Court Decision in Germany', *IIC*, **6**, 889.

balancing of the patentee's interest in the exploitation of its invention and the purchaser's interest in the unhindered use of it. More specifically, it said that a replacement of parts is permissible if they are parts 'which are usually expected to have to be replaced during the life of the device'.[100] On the other hand, the replacement is impermissible if 'the technical effects of the invention are reflected exactly in the replaced parts'.[101]

These principles are not self-explanatory. Indeed, Niels Hölder has said, with regard to another of the same decision's formulations, that 'it cannot be deduced from the decision . . . what the [German] Supreme Court exactly means by "representing essential elements of the inventive concept" and what importance it attaches thereto'.[102] Hölder argues, relying on the court's tests, for a fact-specific inquiry that would turn both on the replacement part's 'closeness to the invention' and on the frequency with which it must be replaced.[103] Although there remains this uncertainty with regard to the repair–reconstruction boundary,[104] the basic approach here is similar to that of the *Aro* case in the US.

More importantly for present purposes, the *Flügelradzähler* approach is based on economic effect, not on contract. Although the court concluded that the defendant had exceeded the bounds of the repair doctrine, so that there was no question of any contractual elimination of the repair right, the opinion does not suggest the possibility of such a contractual approach.[105]

Moreover, a recent decision by the House of Lords in the UK, *United Wire Ltd v. Screen Repair Services (Scotland) Ltd*, addresses the contract issue directly:[106]

> Repair is one of the concepts (like modifying or adapting) which shares a boundary with 'making' but does not trespass upon its territory. I therefore agree with the Court of Appeal that in an action for infringement by making, the notion of an implied licence to repair is superfluous and possibly even confusing. It distracts attention from the question raised by section 60(1)(a), which is whether the defendant has made the patented product. As a matter of ordinary language, the notions

100 Hölder, *supra* note 99, at 894.
101 *Ibid.*
102 *Ibid.*, at 898.
103 *Ibid.*, at 897.
104 See *infra* text accompanying notes 138–42.
105 The court's only comment regarding the intent of the patent holder suggests that it would be its patent rights, not contract, that allow it to enforce that intent: 'It is for the patent holder to decide whether to issue such consent; it is this power that constitutes the essential content of his exclusive right'. See Decision of the Federal Supreme Court (BGH), *supra* note 99, (2005) *IIC*, **36,** 963, at 968.
106 *United Wire Ltd v. Screen Repair Servs. (Scotland) Ltd*, 4 All E.R. 353 (H.L. 2000).

> of making and repair may well overlap. But for the purposes of the statute, they are mutually exclusive. The owner's right to repair is not an independent right conferred upon him by licence, express or implied. It is a residual right, forming part of the right to do whatever does not amount to making the product.

This decision makes clear that at least in the UK the Federal Circuit's approach of allowing the contractual elimination of the repair right is not accepted. On the contrary, because repair is conduct outside the scope of patent infringement, no consent is needed by purchasers for repair, and if they agreed to cede that right by contract, any breach of the resulting contract would not be patent infringement. A combination of this fundamental approach to the right of repair with a definition of the repair–reconstruction boundary through an effects-based analysis like that in the *Flügelradzähler* decision provides a much sounder approach to the problem than the contractual approach of *Mallinckrodt*, especially in light of the casual approach to finding a contract that has prevailed in the US.

3.2.2 Selling and reselling In the United States, in *Ottawa Plant Foods*,[107] the allegedly infringing act was a resale of the patented product. The patentee Pioneer had actually, subsequent to the events at issue in the case, imposed an explicit prohibition on resale. The restriction at issue in the case, however, stated that purchasers' uses of the patented product, seed corn, were limited 'only to produce forage or grain for feeding or processing'.[108] Pioneer argued that under this restriction resales were impermissible, contending that, since a purchaser that resold the corn was not using it to produce forage or grain, the resale was outside the scope of the licence and was therefore infringement.

But the reselling of a patented product had not been viewed, prior to *Ottawa*, as 'selling' the product for infringement purposes. On the contrary, the Supreme Court, although less explicit on this issue than courts of other jurisdictions, has on several occasions made clear that there is no infringement liability for resales of patented goods; that is the essence of the first-sale doctrine. By defining a resale as a 'use', and allowing the patentee to eliminate the right to that use with a 'field-of-use' licence, *Ottawa* redefined the boundaries of infringement for 'selling' in a way analogous to *Mallinckrodt*'s redefinition of 'making'.

If the law as stated in *Ottawa Plant Foods* is correct, a patentee can eliminate the first-sale doctrine by contract. No other court has gone this far, but Federal Circuit *dictum* in another recent case indicates that the court agrees

---

[107] *Pioneer Hi-Bred International, Inc. v. Ottawa Plant Food, Inc.*, 283 F. Supp. 2d 1018 (D. Iowa 2003).

[108] *Ibid.*, at 1024 *et seq.*

with this general approach. In *Anton/Bauer, Inc. v. PAG, Ltd*,[109] the court said that '[t]he [Supreme] Court's statements in [*United States v. Univis Lens Co.*] demonstrate how closely related the exhaustion doctrine is to the grant of an implied licence. Indeed, they suggest that an implied licence stems from the exhaustion of a patent right'.[110]

If the court means to suggest here that the exhaustion doctrine is *merely* an implied licence that can be eliminated by the patentee,[111] there is no support for that claim in *Univis* or in any other Supreme Court decision. The Supreme Court has made clear its view that some efforts to enforce restrictions imposed by a patentee would be merely contractual, and could not support infringement suits. Indeed, it made that point in a case that, like *Ottawa*, involved a purchaser's sales of the patented goods outside the territory assigned to the original seller:[112]

> Whether a patentee may protect himself and his assignees by special contracts brought home to the purchasers is not a question before us, and upon which we express no opinion. It is, however, obvious that such a question would arise as a question of contract, and not as one under the inherent meaning and effect of the patent laws.

The Court indicated in *Univis*, the case cited by the Federal Circuit in *Anton/Bauer*, that such contracts 'derive . . . no support from the patent and must stand on the same footing under the Sherman Act as like stipulations with respect to unpatented commodities'.[113] This seems a clear statement that the Supreme Court's view is that a patentee cannot change the rules of exhaustion by contract, just as a patentee cannot deny the right of repair by contract. Nevertheless, the court in *Ottawa*, like the Federal Circuit, made clear its reliance on the contractual restriction to make the exhaustion doctrine inap-

---

109 329 F.3d 1343 (Fed. Cir. 2003).

110 *Ibid.*, at 1350.

111 Alternatively, the statement might just reflect unintentional conflation of the implied licence and exhaustion doctrines. For an excellent discussion of the two doctrines that illustrates how the Federal Circuit sometimes fails to maintain a distinction between them, see Pichler, Rufus J., William I. Schwartz and Stephen M. Obenski, 'Recent Developments in the Law of Patent Exhaustion and Implied Licenses', Presentation at the 7th Annual Advanced Patent Law Institute, San Jose, California, 30 November–1 December 2006, http://www.conferences.utcle.org/law/cle/conferences/archive/PJ06/18_Pichler_PJ06_ses18_pap.pdf, accessed 26 January 2007.

112 *Keeler v. Standard Folding Bed Co.*, 157 US 659, 666 (1895).

113 *United States v. Univis Lens Co.*, 316 US 241, 251 (1942) (citing *Ethyl Gasoline Corp. v. United States*, 309 US 436 (1940)). Although *Univis* involved resale price maintenance, the Court's reasoning in that case is consistent with that in its cases addressing territorial restrictions.

plicable, expanding the scope of infringement to encompass resales of patented products.[114]

In the European Union, the exhaustion principle has traditionally been strongly defended in the resale context, but the recent *GlaxoSmithKline* decision raises some questions about current law. As described above,[115] that case allowed the patentee to use differential pricing to discourage parallel imports. GlaxoSmithKline's approach did not, however, directly restrict resales, but instead charged different prices in the initial sale depending on where the patented pharmaceuticals would be resold. More importantly, the Court of First Instance focused carefully on the economic effects of the restrictions and insisted that the Commission evaluate those effects more carefully.

It is exactly that sort of searching examination of economic effect that the US courts' approach avoids. Although such an examination would no doubt be more difficult than the US courts' combination of an undemanding approach to finding contractual use restrictions together with an unwillingness to evaluate the enforceability of the restrictions, the more thorough examination would better balance the legitimate interests of both competition and patent law. A recognition of the important purposes served by the exhaustion doctrine need not mean that patentees are denied the ability to ensure adequate returns on their invention, as *GlaxoSmithKline* demonstrates.

However, *GlaxoSmithKline* leaves open an important question raised by the US cases. *GlaxoSmithKline* was a competition-law judgment, not a patent-law one. Even if it were ultimately decided that GlaxoSmithKline's contractual restrictions were valid, that would not necessarily mean that they could be enforced through patent law. That is, the result of a determination of the restrictions' validity could be that GlaxoSmithKline could continue to maintain its price differentials, and could enforce them through breach-of-contract actions, but it need not be the case that it could sue those who act outside the restrictions for patent infringement. That would presumably be a question of national law, and it would be particularly problematic to allow infringement suits against downstream purchasers that are not parties to the contracts with the patentee, as has been allowed in the US cases.

3.3 Restrictions on downstream purchasers

As described above, both the US Supreme Court and the TTBER have distinguished between use restrictions sought to be enforced against manufacturing

---

114 283 F. Supp. 2d at 1033 ('Ottawa has failed to generate a genuine issue of material fact that the sale of *Pioneer*® brand seed corn was *not always* conditional, so that, in the face of undisputed evidence that the sales *were* conditional, the "patent exhaustion" defense is simply inapplicable as a matter of law', emphasis added).

115 See section 2.2.3 *supra*.

licensees and those sought to be enforced on the ultimate purchasers of patented products. There are a variety of reasons to draw this distinction.[116] Most fundamentally, as described above, several of these cases have involved patent-infringement suits against parties that had not themselves entered into the licence contract in which the use restriction was included. As a result, those parties would not necessarily know of the restrictions at issue, and the cost of obtaining that information could be significant, raising the cost of product distribution.[117]

This has not troubled the US courts because of the view, derived from the Federal Circuit, that when a use restriction is violated, there is no valid licence of the patent rights. In that case, the infringement suit against the downstream purchaser is equivalent to one against the purchaser of an illegally manufactured product, and knowledge of infringement is not central to patent law. But even some of the courts that have been willing to enforce shrink-wrap licences as contracts have been unwilling to allow the contract to create infringement suits against non-parties. For example, in *ProCD, Inc. v. Zeidenberg*,[118] one of the most prominent shrink-wrap cases, Judge Easterbrook seemed to suggest that if the defendant there had passed the software on to another, downstream user, no infringement suit could have been brought against that downstream user:[119]

> A copyright is a right against the world. Contracts, by contrast, generally affect only their parties; strangers may do as they please, so contracts do not create 'exclusive rights.' Someone who found a copy of [the copyrighted, shrink-wrap-licensed software] on the street would not be affected by the shrinkwrap license – though the federal copyright laws of their own force would limit the finder's ability to copy or transmit the application program.

Of course, the parties in the present cases may not have been equivalent to someone finding an invention on the street. They might have been on notice of the patentee's efforts to impose restrictions on the use of the inventions. That in fact was the theory on which the Supreme Court in *General Talking*

---

116 The discussion here focuses on concerns at the level of legal doctrine. These sorts of restrictions also present more fundamental, economy-wide concerns. See Carstensen, Peter C. (2006), 'The New Feudalism: Post Sale Patent Licensing and the Destruction of the Dynamic Economy' (draft manuscript).

117 See Kobak, Jr., J.B. (2005), 'Exhaustion of Intellectual Property Rights and International Trade', *Global Econ. J.*, **5**, 1, at 1 ('In theory the [exhaustion] doctrine enables the IP owner to receive fair reward for surrendering its right to withhold a product from the market but thereafter permits free disposition and movement of chattels, preventing IP rights from unduly disrupting distribution systems.').

118 86 F.3d 1447 (7th Cir. 1996).

119 *Ibid*., at 1454.

Pictures allowed imposition of liability on a downstream purchaser.[120] But in that case the violation of the terms of the licence was by the manufacturing licensee, not the downstream purchaser, and it is not clear that the Court would have allowed a restriction that applied only to that downstream purchaser.[121]

The problem posed here is emphasized by the fact that the first buyers in several of these cases did not violate the licence terms. For example, the stores in which the toner cartridges in *Lexmark* were sold did not refill the cartridges, nor did the grain sellers in *McFarling* and *Scruggs* replant seeds. Consequently, in those cases there were valid sales in compliance with the licence terms, which would be expected to bring the exhaustion doctrine into play. By allowing infringement suits against downstream purchasers who were the first to fail to comply with the licence terms, the courts have basically allowed patent rights to be revived after a first sale that should have exhausted those rights.

Beyond the TTBER, it is not clear how these issues might be addressed in European law. *GlaxoSmithKline*'s requirement of an evaluation of the importance of contractual restrictions to protect patentees' returns on their inventions calls for an assessment of the strength of those arguments in particular circumstances. It is not clear that the argument could be convincingly made that it is necessary to impose restrictions on cases involving downstream purchasers, or that the benefits of doing so would outweigh the harms. Moreover, in *GlaxoSmithKline*, the court emphasized that parallel imports in the pharmaceutical industry do not necessarily benefit consumers, as contemplated by Article 81(3), because it may be the importers, rather than consumers, that pocket the differences in price.[122] One could infer from these comments that to the extent that a restriction injures the ultimate consumers of a patented product, as some of the use licensing here can be seen to do, the restriction should be scrutinized more carefully.[123]

---

120 *General Talking Pictures Corp. v. Western Electric Co.*, 305 US 124, 126 (1938).

121 Indeed, Justice Black would not have allowed liability on the purchaser even under the facts in the case. See *ibid.*, at 132 *et seq.* (Black, J., dissenting).

122 Case T-168/01, *GlaxoSmithKline Services v. Commission*, [2006] ECR II-2969, paras 121 *et seq.*

123 Article 73 of the European Patent Convention states that a European application may be licensed 'in whole or in part', but it does not make clear what remedies are available to a patentee if the licence terms are violated. Interestingly, the not-adopted 1989 proposal for a Community Patent appears to explicitly provide that a patentee in such circumstances could bring an infringement suit only against the licensee, not against downstream purchasers. According to Article 42(2) of the Agreement relating to Community patents, OJ 1989 No. L 401, p. 1, '[t]he rights conferred by the Community patent may be invoked against a licensee who contravenes any restriction in his licence . . .'.

This focus on the different positions occupied by intermediaries and by ultimate purchasers could also carry over into the informational issue discussed above. The imposition of restrictions on downstream purchasers not only injures those purchasers directly, by limiting the uses to which they can put the inventions, but also injures them indirectly, by imposing on them the cost of ascertaining the applicability of use restrictions when they themselves may not have been parties to the contract at issue. This reinforces the possibility that the more explicit focus on the ultimate consumers in Europe may counsel against enforcing restrictions on downstream purchasers, at least where they are unaware of the terms of the restriction.

4 The benefits of use licensing

The examples of field-of-use licensing illustrated above appear to be directed at two goals. First is the basic purpose of intellectual property protection itself, which is the prevention of free-riding on the creator's inventive efforts. Second is price discrimination. Several of the field-of-use licences in these cases did not so much discriminate among different uses of the inventions as discriminate based on the number of uses the purchasers could make of the patented products. The nature of the limitation was quite explicit in the 'single use only' restriction of *Mallinckrodt*, but it was also the effect of the no-refilling restriction of *Lexmark*, and the restriction in *Ottawa Plant Foods* allowed *Pioneer* to maintain geographical territories in which it charged different prices.

The following discussion questions the application of field-of-use licences for these two goals. Although the goals may be valid ones, it is not clear that use licensing serves them, or that it does so in the least restrictive way. In fact, patentees have available to them solutions that address each of these problems more specifically.

4.1 Free-riding

4.1.1 'Free-riding' in downstream markets A patentee might argue that any competitor in a secondary market that involves the patented product is, by definition, free-riding on that product. This is in fact the argument made by Lexmark with respect to the refilling of its toner cartridges. This argument may appear to receive some support from the statement in the US antitrust agencies' Antitrust Guidelines for the Licensing of Intellectual Property that '[t]he Agencies will not require the owner of intellectual property to create competition in its own technology'.[124]

---

124 US Department of Justice and Federal Trade Commission, 'Antitrust Guide-

However, competition in a secondary market is not necessarily competition in the technology of the patentee. The question, then, is whether the patentee should be entitled to restrict competition in downstream markets regardless of whether the particular nature of that competition relates to the patented technology.[125] In this respect, *Mallinckrodt*'s test for the validity of a use restriction, asking whether the restriction 'relates to subject matter within the scope of the patent claims', could be read to limit the patentee's power to the restriction of competition that is related to the patentee's technology, as distinguished from the patentee's product in general. Any use restrictions that go beyond that limit should be impermissible.

This view is provided direct support by the US Supreme Court's decision in *Eastman Kodak Co. v. Image Technical Services, Inc.*[126] In that case, Kodak denied independent service providers of its equipment access to parts, some of which were patented, for that equipment. Kodak argued that the servicers were free-riding on its investments in equipment – but Kodak did not argue that the service providers were *directly* free-riding on its equipment investments, because the owners of the equipment had purchased it from Kodak. Kodak did not argue that the service providers were directly free-riding in the parts market, either, because they sought to buy the parts from Kodak. Instead, Kodak's argument was that the service providers were *indirectly* free-riding because, as the Court described the argument, 'they have failed to enter the equipment and parts markets'.[127] The Court rejected that argument, stating that '[t]his understanding of free-riding has no support in our case law'.[128] Kodak would have had a valid free-riding argument if the independent servicers were free-riding on Kodak's investments in the *services* market, but simply competing in the secondary market did not constitute free-riding on the primary market.

A similar approach is reflected under the EC's Motor Vehicle Block Exemption. That exemption treats as a hardcore restriction a refusal by an automobile manufacturer to provide either spare parts or technical information to independent operators that provide aftermarket repair or maintenance for the vehicles.[129] Thus it views 'the market for repair and maintenance services' as

---

lines for the Licensing of Intellectual Property', 6 April 1995, http://www.usdoj.gov/atr/public/guidelines/0558.htm, accessed 4 November 2007, Section 3.1.

[125] For a broader discussion of this general issue, see Patterson, M.R. (2000), 'When is Property Intellectual? The Leveraging Problem', *S. Cal. L. Rev.*, **73**, 1133. Cf. *supra* text accompanying notes 55–8 (on *IMS Health*).

[126] 504 U.S. 451 (1992).

[127] *Ibid.*, at 485.

[128] *Ibid.*

[129] Article 4(1)(i)–(k) and (2) Commission Regulation 1400/2002 of 31 July 2002 on the application of Article 81(3) of the Treaty to categories of vertical agreements and concerted practices in the motor vehicle sector, OJ 2002 No. L 203, p. 30.

one that is independent economically of the market for automobiles, and although the aftermarket is dependent on parts and information from the primary market, the use of those parts and that information is not impermissible free-riding.

In fact, the aftermarket activities against which the patentees claim protection in these cases often are unrelated to the patentees' inventive activities.[130] That is most clear in *Ottawa*, where the patent at issue was for corn seeds, yet the defendants' activities were as resellers of those seeds. Thus, the patentee was using its patent on seeds to restrain competition in seed distribution, an area in which so far as the case shows it had produced no innovation. The inventions in *Lexmark* were also unrelated to the activity of the defendant in that case. Although Lexmark had a variety of patents on various aspects of toner cartridge technology, none of them was on an invention related to the refilling, or even the filling, of the cartridges. Hence, it does not appear that the refillers could be viewed as free-riding on Lexmark's inventions; instead, the refillers had created a secondary market in which Lexmark's inventions played no role.[131]

4.1.2 Patents related to the use at issue As I have argued elsewhere,[132] though, the situation would be different if the patentee's inventive activity related to the secondary market. In *Kodak*, for example, if the independent service organizations were using Kodak inventions that made servicing of the machines easier, one could reasonably argue that Kodak would be entitled to prevent such use. It is for this reason that it is important to examine the actual claims of the patents at issue in these cases, a task in which the courts seldom engage.

If a patentee believes that the use to which a purchaser will put the patentee's invention will infringe upon the patentee's rights, the patentee is always free to seek a patent on that use. So, for example, if Lexmark believed that it had created an innovation that entitled it to exclude others from refilling its toner cartridges – such as an improved filling system – it could have described that innovation and sought patent protection for it. It could have done so, for example, by claiming either the system itself or the process of refilling that it made possible. Likewise in *Ottawa*, if Pioneer had created some innovation in the distribution system from which it sought to exclude the defendant, it could have sought patent protection for the new system. This is in fact the approach that one would expect a patentee to take to address free-riding on its inventive

---

130 A significant exception is found in the *Monsanto* cases, discussed at section 4.2.3 *infra*.

131 *Lexmark*, however, did play a role in that after-market. See *infra* text accompanying note 144.

132 See Patterson, *supra* note 125.

effort. If the patentee has not produced any innovation related to the uses it seeks to prohibit, it should not be permitted to restrict those uses.

It is true that patent law allows the patentee to exclude others from 'using' its invention, whether or not the patentee seeks protection on a particular feature of the invention. As described above, however, the 'uses' that patentees sought to prevent in the recent cases were not really uses but instances of repairing and reselling the invention. That is, they restrict 'uses' that patent law has previously determined the patentee may not restrict. To bring those uses back within the scope of patent law, the patentee should be required to demonstrate its specific entitlement to them, through a process patent.

Mallinckrodt illustrates how far from meeting this requirement these cases can be. The inventions in *Mallinckrodt* included aerosol nebulizers,[133] a manifold for transmitting the aerosol to a patient,[134] and the combination of nebulizer, manifold and shielding box.[135] The District Court in *Mallinckrodt* pointed out that the defendant, Medipart, did not even disassemble the nebulizer-manifold combinations that it received from hospitals, but simply sent them to be radiation-sterilized and then packaged them with new unpatented components before returning them to the hospitals.[136] The court also made clear that the radiation sterilization, the only 'use' to which Medipart put the patented inventions, was not the subject of any of the patents at issue: 'Neither the specifications nor the claims of any of the patents in suit state that the nebulizer and/or manifold are for single use only or must be disposed of. Nor do they claim that either the manifold or the nebulizer are clean or disinfected.'[137] Thus, *Mallinckrodt* had received no patent protection related to the 'use' to which Medipart put the Mallinckrodt inventions.

In this respect, *Mallinckrodt* can be contrasted with another Federal Circuit case, *Jazz Photo Corp. v. International Trade Commission*.[138] The Fuji patents at issue in *Jazz Photo* related to single-use cameras that Jazz Photo had refurbished by putting new film in the used camera casings, or 'lens-fitted film packages' (LFFPs). The court concluded, perhaps questionably, that a multi-step process for replacement of the film was permissible repair rather than impermissible reconstruction.[139] Putting aside possible shortcomings in the

---

133 US Patent Nos. 4,456,179; 4,251,033; 4,116,387.

134 US Patent No. 4,529,003.

135 US Patent No. 4,782,828.

136 *Mallinckrodt, Inc. v. Medipart, Inc.*, 15 U.S.P.Q. 2d (BNA) 1113, 1990 US Dist. LEXIS 1974, at *2–*4 (N.D. Ill. 1990), *rev'd*, 976 F.2d 700 (Fed. Cir. 1992).

137 *Ibid.*, at *2.

138 264 F.3d 1094 (Fed. Cir. 2001).

139 The court's conclusion seems questionable because the amount of work performed in the refurbishment was considerable, both quantitatively and qualitatively:

basic repair conclusion, though, one of the patents at issue included claims directed specifically at the loading of film into the cameras,[140] and the District Court had specifically found these claims infringed, a conclusion reversed by the Federal Circuit on the ground that 'defense of repair is applicable to process claims, as well as to apparatus claims, when the patented process was used in the United States and the patent right has been exhausted for the articles produced thereby'.[141]

However, this seems to misstate the repair–reconstruction rule. The courts have generally indicated that if the act of repair involves the use of a patented replacement part, the repair would not be permissible. For example, in *Aro*, the Supreme Court characterized the question as 'whether the replacement of an *unpatented* part, in a patented combination, that has worn out, been broken or otherwise spent, is permissible "repair" or infringing "reconstruction"'.[142] In the same way that the replacement of a patented replacement part, unless obtained from the patentee, oversteps the repair doctrine, it seems that use of a patented repair process would also be impermissible.[143] This would not prevent repair of the products in general, but would prevent only use of that particular process for repair. In the same way that new uses of unpatented products are patentable, so there should be no obstacle to patenting a new method of repairing a patented product.

> We conclude that for used cameras whose first sale was in the United States with the patentee's authorization, and for which the respondents permitted verification of their representations that their activities were limited to the steps of (1) removing the cardboard cover, (2) cutting open the plastic casing, (3) inserting new film and a container to receive the film, (4) replacing the winding wheel for certain cameras, (5) replacing the battery for flash cameras, (6) resetting the counter, (7) resealing the outer case, and (8) adding a new cardboard cover, the totality of these procedures does not satisfy the standards required by precedent for prohibited reconstruction; precedent requires, as we shall discuss, that the described activities be deemed to be permissible repair.

Ibid., at 1098 *et seq*. It was not clear whether all the respondents had used this process. For those that had not, or for which the process used was unclear, the appeals court let stand the ITC's reconstruction decision.

140 See *ibid.*, at 1108 *et seq.* (citing US Patent No. 4,972,649).

141 *Ibid.*, at 1108 (citation omitted).

142 *Aro Mfg. Co. v. Convertible Top Replacement Co.*, 365 US 336, 342 (1961) (emphasis added).

143 It may be true that many repair processes would not be patentable, because they would be obvious. But in *Jazz Photo* the administrative law judge, the Commission and the court all concluded that the infringers' burden of showing invalidity had not been met. Given that conclusion – that is, that the film-loading method was new and non-obvious – it is not clear that repairers such as *Jazz Photo* should be able to use the process without permission from the patentee.

Whether the law in Europe would support this approach is not entirely clear. Under Article 82 and the *Magill* line of cases, it would be critical whether the patentee itself was active in the aftermarket.[144] In a case such as *Lexmark*, where the patentee itself provided cartridge refilling services, it seems that the *Magill* cases would not require the patentee to grant a licence to the aftermarket reconditioner. But the reconditioner needs no licence if repair is permissible under patent law. Thus, the legality of aftermarket activities in Europe is more likely to turn on whether patentees will be permitted, as they have been in the US, to deny by contract the right to perform acts that would otherwise be non-infringing. As described above, it appears that at least some national patent cases would not permit such contractual alteration of patent law.[145] Furthermore, the Motor Vehicle Block Exemption Regulation suggests that the Commission would seek to maintain effective competition in the aftermarket.[146] In addition, it seems likely that the *GlaxoSmithKline* approach of focusing on the need for a contractual restraint to ensure the patentee's returns would be less compelling where the patentee was seeking returns only indirectly related to its invention.

4.2 *Price discrimination and financing*

The price discrimination that results from the use licensing in these cases may serve either of two purposes. First, it may increase the patentee's profits, as price discrimination generally does. Whether this is a valid goal is not entirely clear, especially where the price discrimination is accomplished through arrangements affecting distinct markets related to that for the patented product. Second, the price discrimination may, either with or without increasing the patentee's profits, serve to provide a means to allow buyers to pay for the patented products over the life of the product. In this context, although the advantages of such a contractual arrangement are clear, it is not evident that the arrangement need be enforceable through patent law.

4.2.1 *Price discrimination in related markets*

The permissible scope of price discrimination in patented products is not entirely clear. In the US, it is generally accepted that 'there is no antitrust prohibition against a patent owner's using price discrimination to maximize his income from the patent'.[147] But this statement could be interpreted too broadly. Tying arrangements are often used to price-discriminate, yet use of

---

144 See *supra* text accompanying notes 55–9.
145 See *supra* text accompanying notes 99–106.
146 See *supra* text accompanying note 129.
147 *USM Corp. v. SPS Technologies*, 694 F.2d 505, 512 (7th Cir.).

them is impermissible if the patentee has market power. The Supreme Court has condemned the use of other patent-infringement suits that facilitated price discrimination even where no unpatented products were involved, where the exhaustion doctrine was implicated. For example, it has not allowed patentees to enforce territorial restrictions after the first sale of the product.[148]

One can perhaps conclude that there is no prohibition on price discrimination accomplished directly, by charging different prices to different purchasers, but that a price-discrimination goal will not save an otherwise impermissible restriction. If that is the rule, then the use restrictions at issue here seem unlikely to be saved by their enablement of price discrimination by patentees. Because they enable price discrimination by effectively redefining the limits of infringement, as described above, they go far beyond the direct forms of price discrimination that the Supreme Court has approved.

Moreover, the effect of these restrictions is to use the patent to restrain competition in a second market, much as with tying restrictions. This is most evident in *Ottawa*, where the restriction restrained competition in the downstream dealer market, where the defendant resold the seed, but in *Mallinckrodt* and *Lexmark* as well, the restrictions restrained competition, or potential competition, in downstream markets for reconditioning services. Although there was no formal tie in these cases, the similar effect of the use restrictions at issue suggests that the mere fact that they allow price discrimination would not be sufficient to justify them.

4.2.2 Price discrimination through contract Nevertheless, considering as an example the reconditioning cases, the alleged infringers, by repairing the patented products, prevented the patentees from making additional sales of the products. This prevention of additional sales made it more difficult for the patentees to price-discriminate based on intensity of use. As a result, the overall financial return of the patentees was decreased, and it is possible that lower returns could lessen patentees' incentives for invention.

It is hard to see why this should be viewed as problematic in itself,

---

148 Several early Supreme Court cases concerned purchases of patented goods within the territory of one licensee and resales of those goods in the territory of another licensee. The goal of the geographic allocation of territories was presumably price discrimination (although it could have been the prevention of free-riding), yet the Supreme Court repeatedly rejected infringement suits in this context. See, for example, *Adams v. Burke*, 84 US 453 (1873); *Keeler v. Standard Folding Bed*, 157 US 659 (1895). The Supreme Court has permitted patentees to impose pricing restrictions on manufacturing licensees, where necessary to protect patentees' profits, *United States v. General Electric Co.*, 272 US 476 (1926), but it has condemned resale price maintenance for patented goods in other contexts. See, for example, *Straus v. Victor Talking Machine Co.*, 243 US 490 (1917).

however. A patent does not entitle the patentee to profits, or even to a particular pricing technique, but only to exclusion of its competitors, and that exclusion is limited by the other rules of patent and competition law. In any event, it is not clear for most of these inventions that the patentee would be unable to price them profitably, even if reuse of the products were not possible. Patentees sell many reusable products without the sorts of licence restrictions at issue in these cases, and, except in exceptional cases,[149] there is no indication that it would be impossible to price the products at issue in the cases discussed here in such a way as to make their sales profitable.

Moreover, even if a single sale would be difficult, there is no obstacle to a patentee's use of a long-term financing arrangement or some other sort of contractual solution. That is, through contract a patentee could achieve exactly the same effect as that of the use restrictions involved in the cases discussed above, but it would not be able to enforce them through patent law. The absence of patent protection would mean that patentees would be limited to contract remedies for violations of the contracts, but there is no reason to think that those remedies would be insufficient to protect the patentees' legitimate interests in these areas (again, except in the exceptional cases discussed below).

The boundaries on the patentees' contractual interests would be policed by the limits placed on contractual restraints by competition law, but that is entirely appropriate. The restrictions discussed above generally involve restrictions on downstream markets, and it is competition law, not patent law, that has developed a body of doctrine to police market relationships. Also competition law, unlike patent law, can weigh the benefits to patentees of contractual restrictions against the costs to consumers.[150]

This approach is more consistent with the one of the US antitrust agencies as described in the Antitrust Guidelines for the Licensing of Intellectual Property than is the *Mallinckrodt* approach. The Guidelines state that the agencies will generally apply the rule of reason, rather than the per se rule, to licensing arrangements. The *Mallinckrodt* approach, in contrast, results in per se legality for restrictions that courts determine are within the patent grant, and the recent *Scruggs* case goes further by explicitly adopting a rule of per se legality for field-of-use licensing.[151] As a result, the current approach serves to circumvent the competitive analysis called for by the Guidelines rather than to provide a considered alternative.

Confining the patentee's remedies to those of contract law also receives

---

149 See section 4.2.3 *infra*.

150 As noted above, though, Niels Hölder has argued that patent law's repair doctrine can serve this purpose as well. See *supra* text accompanying notes 99–103.

151 See *supra* text accompanying note 22.

some indirect conceptual support from the scope of the TTBER. As discussed above, most of the field-of-use restrictions discussed here would not be treated as technology transfers under the TTBER. In that sense, they are not really uses of the patentee's technology at all. Instead, they involve restrictions that under pre-*Mallinckrodt* interpretations of the exhaustion doctrine would not be viewed as implicating patent rights at all. As both the TTBER and US Supreme Court doctrine recognize, the domain of these restrictions should be limited to contract law.

4.2.3 Exceptional cases requiring patent protection The seeds and replanting restrictions at issue in *Monsanto Co. v. McFarling*[152] and *Monsanto Co. v. Scruggs*[153] might be an exception. Each of those cases imposed restrictions on the ability of farmers to save second-generation seed harvested from planting the first-generation patented seed. The patentee's concern here seems valid, in that seeds do not just reproduce themselves once, but can multiply. Thus, in theory the sale of one seed could enable the purchaser to produce an unlimited number of additional seeds. This does indeed pose a unique problem for the patentee, and one that is not easily solved by contract. But the very uniqueness of the problem suggests that it should not be addressed by a general rule allowing patentees to define the scope of infringement by contract. Instead, it seems that if these inventions pose particular incentive problems, the law should address that specific issue and tailor a solution addressed to those particular problems.

This is exactly what the District Court in *Scruggs* did in its initial decision on a preliminary injunction, providing an analysis analogous to that in *GlaxoSmithKline*:[154]

> In this case, the single use restriction does fall within the patent grant. Given the fact that the gene technology at issue is passed on to subsequent generations of seed, Monsanto's restriction to the production of a single commercial crop is logically intended to protect its patent monopoly and to thereby permit it to capture revenue in the form of future sales of technology. Without the prohibition against the saving of seed for replanting or resale, Monsanto's patent would soon be rendered useless by virtue of the potential for exponential multiplication of the seed containing its patented technology. Given the risk of Monsanto's thus losing control of its technology, the limited license of its technology was the only reasonable alternative available to it if it hoped to garner a reasonable return on its sizeable investment while making the technology available for commercial use at a reasonable price to consumers.

152 363 F.3d 1336 (Fed. Cir. 2004).
153 459 F.3d 1328 (Fed. Cir. 2006).
154 342 F. Supp. 2d 568, 753.

The problem in this context is that it is difficult to evaluate claims that a particular licensing approach is essential to 'garner a reasonable return' on the patentee's inventive activity. Although such a claim is plausible in the *Monsanto* cases, Monsanto in fact uses a different licensing technique that allows seed saving in countries other than the United States.[155] It is possible, of course, that it can do so precisely because of the returns it receives by not allowing seed saving in the US, but the information that would allow evaluation of that possibility is, if it exists at all, in the possession of Monsanto.

Hence the placement of the burdens of production and persuasion in such cases is critical. The CFI in *GlaxoSmithKline* addressed this issue, but left the relevant questions unanswered. It concluded that GlaxoSmithKline had produced sufficient evidence to require the Commission to conduct a more full evaluation, but it explained neither what the criteria were for determining the sufficiency of the evidence nor what the specific nature of the required evaluation by the Commission was. Thus, although *GlaxoSmithKline* appears to set the inquiry on the proper path, only future cases will show where that path leads.

5 Conclusion

There is widespread concern, at least in the US, that IP protection has been extended too far.[156] This concern has focused primarily on contractual and statutory limitations to the use of copyrighted materials[157] and on the quality of patent examination, which may lead to the issuing of too many questionable patents. The field-of-use licensing cases from the US discussed in this chapter present in a sense a combination of these problems. Like contractual extensions of copyright, the licensing practices discussed here allow intellectual property owners to extend their protection into areas not intended by the legislature. Further, although the patents on which these extensions of protection are based might not be fundamentally flawed, use licensing can extend protection into areas that are unrelated to the patentee's inventive contribution.

Whether Europe could follow the US in allowing effectively unlimited breadth for use licensing is not clear. There appear as yet to be no cases exactly on point, and the issues presented involve both competition law, where EC law would generally apply, and patent law, where national law would be applicable. Although the EC courts allow some scope for patentees to maximize their returns through licensing restrictions, it is not clear how far this freedom

155 Reply Brief of Appellants 21–2, *Monsanto Co. v. Scruggs*, Nos. 04-1532, 05-1120, 05-1121 (Fed. Cir. filed 26 September 2005).

156 See, for example, First, Harry (2007), 'Controlling the Intellectual Property Grab: Protect Innovation, Not Innovators', *Rutgers L.J.*, 38, 365.

157 See *supra* text accompanying notes 68–77.

would extend to use licensing,[158] and national patent law in at least the UK and Germany appears to place limits on patentees' freedom to alter patent rules through contract.[159]

Consequently, in Europe these cases may receive closer scrutiny than they have in the United States. Careful examination of the transaction that is claimed to have ceded the purchaser's rights is necessary, to determine if a contract has been formed. Also, and more fundamentally, it is critical to determine whether, even if there is a contract, the challenged conduct falls within the statutory definitions of patent infringement. If not, the patentee may have a breach-of-contract action, but no contract can transform permitted conduct into patent infringement. More careful scrutiny in both areas can restore appropriate limits to patent protection.

158 See *supra* section 2.2.3.
159 See *supra* text accompanying notes 99–106.

8 Patent and know-how licences under the Japanese Antimonopoly Act

Junko Shibata

1 Introduction

When granting a licence, the licensor imposes various collateral conditions on the licensee, or vice versa. In such a case, depending on the details of the licence and the position of the licensor and licensee in the market, the act of licensing may constitute an unreasonable restriction of trade, a private monopolization or an unfair trade practice, all of which violate the Japanese Antimonopoly Act (AMA).[1]

2 Section 21 AMA on intellectual property

For a long time, there has been a debate in Japan on the relationship between competition law and IP law. Section 21 of the Japanese AMA provides for an exemption from the AMA, namely: 'The provisions of this act shall not apply to such acts recognizable as the exercise of rights under the Copyright Act, the Patent Act, the Utility Model Act, the Design Act, or the Trademark Act'. The discussion has been focused on how to understand this provision.

It is now generally acknowledged that the protection of the IP right should not consequently lead to a monopoly in the relevant market as defined under competition law. The 1999 Guidelines for Patent and Know-how Licensing Agreements (1999 Guidelines)[2] provide the Japan Fair Trade Commission's (JFTC) views regarding the relationship between restrictions in patent licensing agreements and Section 21 of the AMA. According to the 1999 Guidelines, acts that are recognized as an exercise of rights under the Patent or other Acts are not subject to the application of the AMA. This statement might be understood to mean that certain licensing restrictions are an exercise of IP rights and therefore are categorically exempted from the AMA. A critical position would argue that the assessment of such clauses in the light of the AMA should not be combined with the problem of whether or not the proper

---

[1] Available at http://www.jftc.go.jp/e-page/legislation/index.html, accessed 4 November 2007.

[2] Available at http://www.jftc.go.jp/e-page/legislation/index.html#ama, accessed 4 November 2007.

exercise of the IP rights is recognized. However, on the other hand, the Guidelines note that those acts can also often restrict the business activities of other firms. Therefore, even if acts are possibly considered to be the exercise of rights under the Patent Act or another relevant Act, if these acts are contrary to the purpose of the IP system, namely to encourage innovation with competition, the acts are not deemed as the exercise of IP rights. Examples of this can be found in the Guidelines; for instance, if an act is conducted as a part of a series of acts that constitute an unreasonable restraint of competition or private monopolization, the act is considered to be contrary to the purpose of the IP system. Furthermore, even if an act on its face seems to be an exercise of rights under the IP laws, if, after evaluating its purpose and particular circumstances and the extent of its impact on competition in a market, this act is considered to run counter to the purpose of the IP system, it is possible that the AMA will also apply to this act, since it would no longer be deemed an 'act recognizable as the exercise of rights' under the IP laws.

Judging from this statement of the Guidelines, ultimately, it is first necessary to evaluate such acts in the light of the provisions of Section 21 of the AMA. In principle, the exercise of a patent right cannot be treated differently under the AMA, and all licensing restrictions are generally subject to the AMA.[3]

3 The 1999 Guidelines

The 1999 Guidelines are applied to patent and know-how licensing agreements, including those between three or more parties, reciprocal licensing agreements, such as cross-licensing agreements, patent pools and multiple licensing agreements. Other IP rights, such as copyrights and trademarks, can be covered, according to the Guidelines, to some extent, depending on the nature of such other IP rights. Here, a case-by-case approach will be adopted.

The European Commission has revised the Technology Transfer Block Exemption Regulation (TTBER),[4] simplifying the structure of the block exemption by removing in particular the whitelisted clauses, whereas Japan's 1999 Guidelines still contained a list of such clauses.

---

[3] The exercise of an IP right will be subject to the AMA if it impedes or restricts competition in the sense of the AMA. Concerning this point, see Chaen, S. (2002), 'Intellectual Property Rights and Antimonopoly Act (1)', *Keizaihou-Kouza*, (2), 167.

[4] Commission Regulation (EC) No. 772/2004 of 27 April 2004 on the application of Article 81(3) of the Treaty to categories of technology transfer agreements, OJ 2004 No. L 123, p. 11. See, generally, Anderman, Steve, chapter 5, in this volume; Drexl, J. (2004), 'Die neue Gruppenfreistellungsverordnung über Technologietransfer-Vereinbarungen im Spannungsfeld von Ökonomisierung und Rechtssicherheit', *GRUR Int.*, 716.

The European TTBER establishes a framework that distinguishes between agreements between competitors and non-competitors. Japanese antitrust authorities in general tend to distinguish between horizontal and vertical restraints and then adopt different standards for each under the AMA, but the 1999 Guidelines do not make any special distinction between restrictive agreements between competitors and those between non-competitors.

4 Section 3 AMA on restrictive behaviour

Section 3 of the AMA, containing the Japanese ban of unreasonable restraint of trade, prohibits any agreement or concerted action that is employed in a manner that mutually restricts business activities, if it causes substantial restriction of competition in the market. For instance, in a licensing agreement for patents, mutual restrictions regarding such factors as the sales price, manufacturing volume, sales volume, sales outlets, sales territories of the patented products, the field of research and development, the technology used and the parties to whom the licence may be granted, in practice, are imposed between competitors, and these restrictions substantially restrict competition in a market for particular products or particular technologies. Irrespective of whether a licensing agreement takes the form of cross-licensing, multiple licensing or a patent pool, such restrictions are regarded as an unreasonable restraint of trade and will be illegal under the AMA. On the other hand, the 1999 Guidelines still acknowledge that cross-licences, multiple licences and patent pools encourage competition in general.[5]

In addition, the 1999 Guidelines do not provide for the application of market-share thresholds or a safe harbour and establish no clear exemptions regarding licensing agreements between competitors. It is assumed that a licensing agreement between competitors has the potential to restrict competition by facilitating coordination between them. In the decisions regarding agreements in unreasonable restraint of trade in which the JFTC has intervened, especially the market share of the parties has been taken into account, and in most of the cases a 50 per cent share has been held to be problematic.[6] In the agreements under consideration, for instance, restrictions on sales volume, sales prices or customers have been mutually imposed.

As regards the hard-core restrictions, such as restrictions on sales prices, partitioning of the sales territory and restrictions of active or passive sales to end-users, there should be no substantial difference between the Japanese

---

[5] Concerning patent pools, see 'Guidelines on Standardization and Patent Pool Arrangements', 2005, http://www.jftc.go.jp/e-page/legislation/index.html#ama, accessed 4 November 2007.

[6] See Negishi, Akira and Masayuki Funada (2006), *Dokusenkinshi hou kaisetsu (Japanese Antitrust Law)*, 3rd ed., Tokyo: Yuhikaku, p. 157.

1999 Guidelines and the TTBER. The European TTBER indicates that hardcore restrictions as such are considered to be almost always anti-competitive based on the nature of the restriction.

5 Section 19 AMA on unfair trade practices

The Japanese AMA provides for the control of unfair trade practices as one further important category of restraint of trade. Section 19 of the AMA condemns restraints when they undoubtedly constitute 'unfair trade practices'. Section 2(9) of the AMA defines 'unfair trade practice' as 'any act . . . which tends to impede fair competition and which is designated by the JFTC'. According to the Designation of Unfair Trade Practices by the JFTC,[7] unfair trade practices cover acts such as refusal to deal, discriminatory pricing, unjustified low-price sales, deceptive customer inducement, customer inducement by unjustified benefits, tie-in sales, exclusive dealing, resale price restriction, selling on restrictive terms and abuse of dominant bargaining position.

Whether or not these trade practices are to be considered illegal under the AMA depends on their effect on competition in the market and the nature of each practice.

5.1 Some controversial restrictions in licence agreements and the concept of unfair trade practices

Price restrictions in licence agreements between non-competitors fall within the black category of unfair trade practices and violate the AMA, as is the case for every sector. There is no debate in respect of the illegality of price restriction.

Apart from price restriction, however, the other restraints concerning unfair trade practices are dealt with differently under the AMA. Restrictions that will not, in principle, fall within the category of unfair trade practices are the following: granting licences separately to manufacture, restrictions on use and sales, restrictions on duration, territorial restrictions and restrictions on the field of technology. Those kinds of licensing activities can generally be regarded as exploitation activities within the scope of the Patent Act, and are considered to be an exercise of rights provided for under the Patent Act. Moreover, since such acts are seen to have a negligible effect on competition in the market, they are not deemed to cause problems under the AMA. In addition, requiring a licensee to maintain a minimum production volume of the patented products or a minimum number of times of use of the patented

---

7 Designation of Unfair Trade Practices of 18 June 1982, Fair Trade Commission Notification No. 15 of 1982, http://www.jftc.go.jp/e-page/legislation/ama/unfairtradepractices.pdf, accessed 4 November 2007.

process will not, in principle, fall within the category of unfair trade practices, if it secures a minimum royalty income.

Those restrictions are treated as belonging to the white category of acts that are legal in principle. This viewpoint of the Guidelines is on a par with the assumption in the European TTBER that antitrust agencies will intervene only where restraints prevent competition that would have taken place in the absence of the licence.

On the other hand, it has been a subject of controversy whether restrictions on territory, restrictions on the field of technology and restrictions on minimum production volume should be recognized as the exercise of a patent and accordingly as not falling within any category of illegal behaviour in the first place.[8] It should not be forgotten that those restrictions in licence agreements could eliminate competition and divide a market between licensor and licensees or among the licensees. Therefore these restrictions should be assessed in accordance with the general Antimonopoly standards as well. There is no reasonable ground for categorically exempting these restraints simply because they are based on IP licensing.

Regarding these restrictions, the TTBER notes that exclusive licence to produce on the basis of the licensed technology in a particular territory is generally exempted, considering the purpose of a licence agreement to give the licensee an incentive to invest in and develop the licensed technology. In addition, exclusive licensing between non-competitors is likely to fulfil the conditions of Article 81(3) EC, and the Commission will therefore only exceptionally intervene against exclusive licensing in such agreements. As regards restrictions on the field of technology and output restrictions in the case of agreements between non-competitors, when the market share of neither party exceeds 30 per cent on the affected relevant technology and product market, the exemption does not apply to the agreement.

The safe-harbour concept of the TTBER does not figure under the Japanese 1999 Guidelines. However, in a similar provision, the Japanese 1991 Guidelines Concerning Distribution Systems and Business Practices set the level for 'influential market position' at 10 per cent of the relevant market. While this forms one of the standards for enforcing or regulating unfair trade practices, it would be wrong to conclude that the 1991 Guidelines necessarily limit market share to 10 per cent as a precondition for applying the AMA.

Thirdly, according to the TTBER, non-competitors may not agree on restrictions on the territory into which the licensee may sell, or on the

---

8 For details, see Takigawa, T. (2003), 'Antitrust Intervention in Intellectual Property Licensing and Unilateral Refusal to License: A Comparative Analysis of Japanese and U.S. Policies', *Antitrust Bull.*, 885.

customers to whom she may sell. But several exemptions are made. Restrictions on active selling can produce pro-competitive effects, while restrictions on passive selling are not only caught by Article 81(1) EC, but will not be exempted under Article 81(3) EC. The 1999 Guidelines do not address restrictions of sales territory and therefore the standards of the Japanese 1991 Guidelines concerning Distributions System and Business Practices will be applied in practice. The 1991 Guidelines also distinguish between active and passive selling in view of the nature of restrictions of territory, but some of the exemptions of the TTBER are not acknowledged in Japan. Those are restrictions on passive sales by the licensee into an exclusive territory or to a customer group allocated to another licensee, which are exempted for two years, and restrictions on the licensee not to sell to unauthorized distributors. These exemptions are handled in line with selective distribution systems and are actually not related to the IP right itself. The assumption that selective distribution is exempted is not included in the Japanese AMA.

Since customer restrictions may have an adverse effect on competition in a market by restricting the freedom of the licensee to select sales outlets, this can fall within the category of unfair trade practices and be in violation of the AMA.

The European TTBER lists four types of restrictions that may not be block-exempted, namely exclusive grant back, assignment back, non-challenge clauses and obligations regarding R&D activities that promote innovation. As in the case of the European TTBER, the 1999 Guidelines hold that these restrictions or obligations are likely to fall within the category of unfair trade practices (black or blackish grey[9]). An exclusive grant-back is the most typical licensing condition that reduces the incentives of the licensee to innovate, while non-exclusive grant-back may be covered by the block exemption and will not, in principle, fall within the category of unfair trade practices in the 1999 Guidelines.

5.2 Know-how licensing agreements

As with the TTBER, the 1999 Guidelines are applied to know-how licensing agreements as well. In this regard there is a decision by the JFTC,[10] in which a Japanese company and a Taiwanese chemical company had concluded a know-how licensing agreement for 10 years. These companies are the most important companies in their respective national market for chemical products, and the Japanese company granted a know-how licence related to the chemical

---

9 Restrictions 'highly likely to fall within the category of unfair trade practices and be in violation' of the AMA are regarded as 'blackish grey'.

10 JFTC of 13 October 1995, Case – *Asahidenka-kougyou*, *Shinketsushu*, **42**, 163.

products. According to the agreement in question, the Taiwanese company was allowed to manufacture the product after termination of the agreement but it is not permitted to export the products (based on the know-how) to Japan. Under the terms of the 1999 Guidelines, the restriction on employing the know-how after the termination of the know-how licensing agreement can be legal, provided that such restriction is indispensable to prevent the disclosure of licensed know-how to third parties. However, in this case, the JFTC recognized that know-how had in fact been disclosed and, consequently, the reasonable necessity to protect the know-how no longer existed.

5.3 Non-assertion provisions

Non-assertion provisions (NAPs) prohibit the licensee from asserting own IPRs. In the case of patents, such a licensing agreement may prevent a licensee from exercising all or a part of his current or future patent rights against the licensor or any other person designated by the licensor. If such a prohibition is likely to have an adverse effect on competition in a market, it will fall within the category of unfair trade practices. This would be the case, for example, if the restriction increased the licensor's influence in the relevant product or technology field, or impeded the licensee's incentive to engage in research and development, thereby hampering the development of new technologies.

In July 2004, the JFTC issued a recommendation to Microsoft on its violation of the AMA.[11] The JFTC found that Microsoft was 'dealing on restrictive terms'. Microsoft, in licensing its Windows operating system, 'has concluded agreements with manufacturers of personal computers, containing certain provisions that licensee covenants not to sue, bring, prosecute, assist or participate in any judicial, administrative or other proceedings of any kind against Microsoft, its subsidiaries, or other licensees for infringement of the licensee's patents'. In this recommendation, the following factors were taken into account. First, since Microsoft started licensing Windows 95 in 1995, the market share of Windows has dramatically increased. In 2003, Microsoft's market share reached around 95 per cent and Microsoft obtained a dominant position in both the worldwide market and the Japanese market of PC operating systems. Since 1998, Microsoft has been strengthening the anti-virus function of Windows, and also some PC manufacturers that were granted the licence for Windows have developed technologies with an anti-virus function. Secondly, Microsoft holds a dominant position and end users prefer Microsoft strongly. Therefore it is an important business strategy for PC manufacturers to get a licence for every new version of Windows and to ship PCs with Windows

---

[11] See http://www.jftc.go.jp/e-page/pressreleases/2004/july/040713.pdf, accessed 4 November 2007.

installed. Thirdly, even though any technologies that had been developed and were to be developed by PC manufacturers were incorporated into the coming Windows version, non-assertion provisions would restrain such PC manufacturers from asserting the infringement of their technology against Microsoft and its licensees. In particular, PC manufacturers that own patents in the field of technology of anti-virus functions, although such PC manufacturers' patents are likely to be infringed by Windows, are restrained from enforcing such patents against Microsoft and most other PC manufacturers. Finally, this situation may cause these PC manufacturers to lose their incentive to invest and develop technology related to anti-virus functions, resulting in a tendency to impede fair competition in this field of technology in Japan.

The recommendation proposed that Microsoft should terminate its unlawful behaviour. Microsoft has not accepted this recommendation and a hearing procedure by the JFTC has begun.

This recommendation given to Microsoft is well founded. The holder of an IP right is not allowed to infringe other IP rights, even when they come from improvement innovation. A patent itself simply prohibits others from exploiting it and accordingly licensing does not give rise to any special additional function of the patent. From the aspect of promoting R&D activities and the effective use of technology as well, the NAP can have an anti-competitive effect, since the agreement reduces the incentives of one party to innovate and adversely affects an essential part of the competitive process.

5.4 Refusal to license

Finally, the problem of refusals to license deserves special consideration. Intellectual property, in line with all other property, grants its owner the right to exclude others from using it. Generally, the owner of IP rights can decide whether or not to grant a licence.

Accordingly, refusal to license should in principle fall outside the scope of the AMA. Nevertheless, if refusal to license cannot be in violation of competition law, simply because licences are based on IP rights, it will also deprive the potential licensee of an incentive to make the relevant investment. Thus the function of IP law would be reduced to protecting the IP right as an aim in itself. More importantly, imposing reasonable licensing fees would not reduce the incentive for innovation. The AMA does not have any provision that specifically regulates abuse based on excessive pricing, and there is still a discussion on how best to deal with high pricing, including licensing fees, in the AMA.[12]

[12] Hienuki, T. (2002), 'Intellectual Property Rights and Market Power', *Keizaihou-kouza*, (1), 310.

According to the 1999 Guidelines, refusal to license is not categorically classified, but there is nevertheless one statement on the problem. According to this statement, refusal to license in the case of patent pools, cross-licensing and concentration of patents can hardly constitute a proper exercise of a patent right, and if the business activities of the other undertaking or newcomer are excluded by this refusal, a violation of the AMA could be recognized, as long as the conditions of Section 3, which prohibits private monopolization, that is, the equivalent of Section 2 of the US Sherman Act, are fulfilled. According to the definition in the AMA, a private monopolization is recognized when an undertaking, individually or by combination or conspiracy with another undertaking, excludes or controls the business activities of the other undertaking, thereby causing a substantial restraint of competition in a market for particular products or particular technologies. In one decision, the so-called *Patent Pool in Pachinko Makers* case,[13] the JFTC found the concerted refusal to license in the form of a patent pool to be a violation of Section 3 of the AMA. The patent pool members had cooperated to refuse to grant a licence to non-member manufacturers with a view to excluding the entry of competitors. The JFTC held that such actions go beyond the scope of the exercise of the patent. Additionally, the market share of the members of this patent pool is significantly high, namely 90 per cent. The essential patents were pooled in order to produce pachinko machines.[14]

Meanwhile, however, the question is how to apply the AMA to individual unilateral refusals to license. How to deal with this type of refusal under the current antimonopoly legal regime has yet to be settled. The JFTC has never applied the AMA to individual unilateral refusals to license, and the Guidelines have not made it clear which section may be applied to such a case.

Yet, on the basis of the 1999 Guidelines, Section 3 of the AMA on private monopolization could apply to unilateral refusals to license, as in the case of coordinated refusal to license. The application of Section 3 will be taken into account in the case of individual unilateral refusal, provided that all conditions concerning private monopolization are fulfilled.

In addition, the JFTC has never applied the so-called essential-facilities doctrine in its enforcement of the AMA based on the current legal system. Although the JFTC advocated a new provision directly relating to essential facilities, similar to Section 19(4)(4) of the German Act Against Restraints of Competition, it was not successful due to strong opposition from Japanese

---

13 JFTC of 6 August 1997, Case – *Patent Pool of Pachinko Makers*, *Shinketsushu*, **44**, 238.

14 Pachinko is a gaming device used for amusement and prizes and is similar to a pinball machine. The machines are widespread in Japan in establishments called 'pachinko parlours', which also often feature a small number of slot machines.

industry. The JFTC was of the opinion that *de facto* standards, technical information, networks or infrastructure in the telecommunications, energy or air sector could be regarded as essential facilities, and that the JFTC was supposed to specify what has to be considered as an essential facility.

Apart from Section 3 of the AMA, more importantly, the unjustly unilateral refusal to license is likely to fall under the prohibition of unfair trade practices of Section 19 of the AMA.[15] In a case where a dominant party or a party in an influential market position refuses to deal and consequently the other party has difficulty finding an equivalent substitute, this refusal, in principle, is deemed an unjust unilateral refusal. This is also the case when the patent holder in a dominant or influential position refuses to grant a licence. In such a case, the question that follows is whether its refusal is justified, and provided that the patent holder holds a dominant position at least, it will be significantly hard to justify its refusal to license.

Furthermore, this will be the case if the dominant position of the owner of *de facto* standard technology derives from not only its technical superiority but also its network efficiency. In such a case, the IP laws should not ensure the incentive for innovation in such a way that the owner of *de facto* standard technology could receive the benefits brought about by that *de facto* standard. Thus, the refusal to license could be regarded as an unfair trade practice within the current AMA under certain circumstances.

In addition, individual unilateral refusal to license could be banned under the provision on abuse of a dominant bargaining position over another party as one case of unfair trade practices.[16] If the licensee is dependent on the licensing so as to carry out her business activities, dominant bargaining power will exist. The dominant bargaining power could be defined as relative power, which is not the same as dominant market power but would be rather similar to the concept applied by Section 20(2) of the German Act Against Restraints of Competition. Still, the question that remains is how the conditions of the abuse in a case of unilateral refusal to license could be defined within the scope of the provision concerning abuse of a dominant bargaining position.

6 Conclusion

It can be recognized that between IP laws and competition laws there is tension but no fundamental contradiction. Both sets of laws seek to promote economic growth in order ultimately to enhance consumer welfare. The IP laws do this by creating an exclusive right, which is meant to work as an incentive to innovation. As already stated, IP laws are not intended to create

---

15 See Section 2 of the Designation of Unfair Trade Practices, *supra* note 7.

16 See Section 14 of the Designation of Unfair Trade Practices, *supra* note 7.

monopolies in the market. Granting an exclusive right over a particular technology will not lead to a monopoly so long as alternative technologies exist.

The question of which legal regime should be applied when judging the legality or otherwise of the exercise of an intellectual property right goes to the heart of the nature of the right itself. From the viewpoint of patent law, the Patent Act itself is meant to strike an adequate balance between protection of the innovation and exploitation of the innovation. The patent system as a whole should be designed not only to ensure direct protection of the patent right, but also to promote incentives for improving the invention, or further innovations, including follow-up inventions. For instance, even if the exercise of the IP right substantially restricts competition in the market and is thus prohibited under competition law, there is no fundamental contradiction with the principles on which the patent system is based. The exercise of an IP right should not be permitted if it is not in line with the ultimate purpose of IP laws, namely to promote economic growth, a goal they have in common with competition laws. In the so-called pro-patent age, competition policy should be appropriately applied to the exercise of patent rights, considering the ultimate purpose that patent rights are designed to serve. Companies under competitive pressure will have more incentive to innovate and thereby gain a larger market share. What we need now is a competition or IP policy to promote innovation incentives with competition.

The owner of the IP right is not required to create competition in the use and exploitation of its own technology. Nevertheless, especially in the pro-patent age, it is no longer appropriate that the patent holder should always have the exclusive right to decide whether to grant a licence or not. The legality of the refusal to license should be examined under general competition principles.

As explained, in interpreting the provisions of the AMA, the 1999 Guidelines based their approach on whether or not the licensing restrictions under assessment are thought to fall within the exercise of an IP right. On the assumption that IP laws and competition laws serve a common purpose, the 1999 Guidelines are compatible with general competition principles. The new Guidelines are expected to be published soon. They might be brought in line with the TTBER and could be compared with the TTBER and so we can expect a further harmonization of antitrust principles.[17]

---

[17] This chapter does not cover the new Guidelines for the Use of Intellectual Property under the Antimonopoly Act, published in September 2007. In the new Guidelines, the categorical classification has been diminished and a more flexible and economic approach has been adopted.

PART 3

UNILATERAL RESTRAINTS

9 Unilateral refusal to license *indispensable* intellectual property rights – US and EU approaches

Beatriz Conde Gallego

1 Introduction

The question of whether, and if so, under which conditions the owner of an intellectual property right (hereafter 'IPR') can be compelled as a matter of competition law to grant a licence to a third party (which in most cases will be a competitor) touches the interface problem at its very heart. As a matter of principle, nobody would contest that the owner of an IPR may lawfully exclude third parties from making, using or selling the IP-protected product or service. Moreover, it is also undisputed that the right of exclusion inherent to IPRs includes the right to refuse to grant a licence and that this right may be limited only in certain (exceptional) circumstances.[1] Consensus disappears, however, when it comes to determining these circumstances. Not only does a gulf exist between the approaches followed on both sides of the Atlantic.[2]

---

[1] See for European law Case 238/87, *Volvo*, [1988] ECR 6211, para. 8; Joined Cases C-241/91P and C-242/91P, *RTE and ITP v. Commission* ('*Magill*'), [1995] ECR I-743, para. 49; Case C-418/01, *IMS Health*, [2004] ECR I-5039, para. 34. For the US see *Hartford-Empire Co. v. United States*, 323 U.S. 386, 432 (1945) (holding that the patent owner 'has no obligation either to use [the patent] or to grant its use to others'); *Stewart v. Abend*, 495 US 207, at 228 (1990) (stating that 'a copyright owner has the capacity arbitrarily to refuse to license one who seeks to exploit the work'); *In re Independent Service Organizations Antitrust Litigation (CSU v. Xerox)*, 203 F.3d 1322, at 1327 (Fed. Cir. 2000), at 1327 and 1329, *cert. denied*, 121 S.Ct. 1077 (2001) (confirming that the patentee's right to refuse to sell or license its intellectual property right is limited only in certain circumstances). For German law see German Federal Supreme Court (Bundesgerichtshof), judgment of 13 July 2004, Case K ZR 40/02, *Standard-Spundfass*, (2004) *GRUR*, 966 = *Standard Tight-Head Drum*, (2005) *IIC*, **36**, 741, at 746 (English translation).

[2] In contrast to the application of the competition rules to licensing agreements, where a clear approximation between the US IP Antitrust Guidelines (Antitrust Guidelines for the Licensing of Intellectual Property, Issued by the US Department of Justice and the Federal Trade Commission, 6 April 1995, http://www.usdoj.gov/atr/public/guidelines/0558.htm, accessed 4 November 2007) and the European TTBER (Commission Regulation (EC) No. 772/2004 on the Application of Article 81(3) of the

Even within one and the same jurisdiction views on how to approach the relationship between IPRs and competition law in this specific area diverge.

The following analysis critically reviews the current approaches to refusal to license in US antitrust law and in European competition law and the principles underlining them. In a first step, the legal background in the United States (section 2 *infra*) and in the European Union (section 3 *infra*) will be presented. The analysis will show that notwithstanding the formal recognition that IPRs and competition law pursue the common goal of promoting innovation, that is dynamic competition,[3] the last consequences of this assertion are not actually drawn. Therefore an alternative approach, which builds on an understanding of IPRs and competition law as complementary and thus makes the impossibility to compete in the market by offering substitutive products (that is, the impossibility to compete by substitution) the relevant criterion for ordering a duty to license, will be proposed (section 4 *infra*). Finally, some concluding remarks will be made (section 5 *infra*).

2 The US approach towards refusal to license

The US law on refusal to license is informed by two different sets of cases. On the one hand, the Courts of Appeals of three different circuits have had the opportunity to deal with refusal-to-license cases under Section 2 of the Sherman Act in the course of the last 12 years; all of them have presumed the legality of a unilateral refusal to license in nearly absolute terms (section 2.1 *infra*). On the other hand, the *Trinko* decision of the US Supreme Court,[4] although dealing more generally with the refusal of a local monopolist to give access to its telecommunication network, also contains relevant principles for refusal-to-license situations (section 2.2 *infra*).[5]

Treaty to Categories of Technology Transfer Agreements, OJ 2004 No. L 123, p. 11) can be observed. For a comparative analysis see Feil, M. (2005), 'The New Block Exemption Regulation on Technology Transfer Agreements in the Light of the US Antitrust Regime on the Licensing of Intellectual Property', *IIC*, **36**, 31.

3 See US IP Antitrust Guidelines, *supra* note 2, section 1.0, and the European TT Guidelines (Commission Notice – Guidelines on the application of Article 81 of the Treaty to technology transfer agreements, OJ 2004 No. C 101, p. 2), para. 7.

4 *Verizon Communications Inc. v. Law Offices of Curtis V. Trinko, LLP*, 540 U.S. 398 (2004).

5 On the relevance of the *Trinko* judgment for refusal-to-license cases see Drexl, J. (2004), '*IMS Health* and *Trinko* – Antitrust Placebo for Consumers Instead of Sound Economics in Refusal-to-Deal Cases', *IIC*, **35**, 788; Fox, Eleanor M. (2007), 'Monopolization, Abuse of Dominance, and Refusal to License Intellectual Property to Competitors – Do Antitrust Duties Help or Hurt Competition and Innovation? How Do We Know?', in Claus-Dieter Ehlermann and Isabela Atanasiu (eds), *European Competition Law Annual 2005: The Relationship between Competition Law and Intellectual Property Law*, Oxford: Hart Publishing, p. 633.

2.1 Case law in the Circuit Courts: per se legality if the refusal to license remains within the scope of the IPR

The first of the cases considered involved the refusal of Data General, a computer manufacturer, to license copyrighted diagnostic software to independent service organizations that competed with Data General in the maintenance and repair of Data General's computers.[6] After recognizing that (unlawful) exclusionary conduct can include a monopolist's unilateral refusal to license a copyright, the First Circuit stated that the 'author's desire to exclude others from use of its copyrighted work is a presumptively valid business justification for any immediate harm to consumers'.[7] While the court did formulate such a presumption as a rebuttable one, it nevertheless acknowledged that 'cases in which antitrust liability is unlikely to frustrate the objectives of the Copyright Act are certainly rare'.[8] In particular, the court admitted that the presumption could be rebutted by evidence that the monopolist had acquired the IP protection in an unlawful manner. In the specific case, however, the court concluded that there was no evidence to rebut the presumption since the service market had never been a competitive one, the copyrights of Data General were valid and the diagnostic software was innovative.[9]

Some years later, when confronted with similar facts, the Ninth Circuit endorsed the rebuttable presumption established in *Data General*.[10] It however modified it in the sense that it applied the presumption to both patents[11] and copyrights. Furthermore, the court considered that the presumption of legality could be rebutted by evidence of anti-competitive intent on the part of the IP holder in refusing to license.[12] Thus, the court held the facts that only 65 of more than a thousand parts were covered by patents and that Kodak

---

6 *Data General Corp. v. Grumman Systems Support Corp.*, 36 F.3d 1147 (1st Cir. 1994).

7 *Ibid.*, at 1187. Note that an identical line of reasoning has also been put forward by Microsoft to justify its refusal to disclose the information requested by Sun Microsystems in the *Microsoft Europe* case; see European Commission of 24 March 2004, Case COMP/C-3/37.792 – *Microsoft*, http://europa.eu.int/comm/competition/antitrust/cases/decisions/37792/en.pdf, accessed 4 November 2007, para. 709. This argument has been rejected by the European CFI, see Case T-201/04, *Microsoft v. Commission*, [2007] (not yet reported), para. 690 (existence of an IPR is no justification in itself of a refusal to provide interoperability information).

8 *Ibid.*, at 1187, note 64.

9 *Ibid.*, at 1188.

10 *Image Technical Services, Inc. v. Eastman Kodak Co.*, 125 F.3d 1195, at 1218 (9th Cir. 1997), *cert. denied*, 118 S.Ct. 1560 (1998).

11 The *Data General* court relied on earlier precedents to affirm an exception of patents to the antitrust laws; see *supra* note 6, at 1186.

12 *Supra* note 10, at 1218.

had not invoked its IPRs in almost 10 years of litigation to be (enough) evidence of the pretextual nature of the invocation of the IPRs.[13]

In contrast to the approach followed by the First and Ninth Circuits, which even though in very narrow terms have admitted the possibility of refuting the presumption of legality of a refusal to license, the Federal Circuit has – at least with regard to patents – established a per se rule of legality.[14] Again, the Federal Circuit had to decide on a complaint by an independent service organization that the refusal of Xerox, one of the leading manufacturers of copiers and printers, to sell and license its protected replacement parts and software maintenance had the effect of driving that organization out of the service market. As to Xerox's refusal to license its copyrights, the Federal Circuit just followed the *Data General* doctrine explained above.[15] Concerning the refusal by Xerox to license its patents, however, the court held that 'absent exceptional circumstances, a patent may confer the right to exclude competition altogether in more than one antitrust market'. Concretely, the Federal Circuit considered these exceptional circumstances to be present where the patent was obtained through fraud, where a lawsuit to enforce the patent was a sham, or where the patent holder used her right to refuse to sell or license patented parts to gain a monopoly in a market beyond the scope of the patent.[16]

Despite some dissimilarities in the approaches taken by the three Courts of Appeals, they all, however, agree on granting absolute (or nearly absolute) antitrust immunity to conduct – the refusal to license – within the scope of the IPR. Hence, the scope of the right becomes the decisive criterion to draw the borderline between legitimate and unjustified restraints of competition. By following this approach, the courts stick to the (already outdated) inherency doctrine. Whereas this theory may well have informed the relationship between IPR and competition law in the past,[17] modern thinking has moved

---

13 The *Kodak* decision has been much criticized as to the extent the subjective intent of the right holder may open the door to evidence of the defendant's intent to injure competition. For a narrow reading of the *Kodak* decision limiting the evidence of the right holder's intent to those situations in which the invocation of the IPRs is a *post hoc* justification for conduct that has nothing to do with the protection of intellectual property, see Hovenkamp, Herbert, Mark D. Janis and Mark A. Lemley (2005), 'Unilateral Refusals to License in the US', in François Lévêque and Howard Shelanski (eds), *Antitrust, Patents and Copyright*, Cheltenham, UK and Northampton, MA, US: Edward Elgar, p. 12, at 31.

14 *In re Independent Service Organizations Antitrust Litigation (CSU v. Xerox)*, 203 F.3d 1322, at 1327 (Fed. Cir. 2000).

15 *Ibid.*, at 1329.

16 *Ibid.*, at 1327.

17 For an historical overview of how views on the relationship between IPRs and competition law have evolved see Federal Trade Commission (2003), 'To Promote

away from assessing the interface problem in formalistic terms along the scope of the right.[18] Indeed, a theory that gives primacy of one area of law over the other reflects an understanding of IPRs and antitrust as in conflict with each other. Clear-cut solutions of the form of a per se rule of legality (or even a strong presumption of legality), however, are difficult to reconcile with a view of IPRs and competition law as complementary instruments in promoting innovation.

Although US courts do not expound much on the grounds that justify such a broad exception from the antitrust rules, underlying their cautious approach towards an antitrust duty to license is certainly the fear of the negative effects that such an obligation would have on the incentives to invest and innovate arising from the IP system.[19] The need to preserve companies' long-term economic incentives was also one of the crucial arguments in the *Trinko* judgment of the US Supreme Court for rejecting (in very broad terms) a monopolist's duty to deal under Section 2 of the Sherman Act.

2.1 The Trinko *decision of the US Supreme Court: protecting firms' incentives to invest and innovate*

As pointed out before, the *Trinko* case did not expressly concern a refusal to license, but the more general question of whether a monopolist violates

---

Innovation: The Proper Balance of Competition and Patent Law and Policy', available at http://www.ftc.gov/os/2003/10/innovationrpt.pdf, accessed 4 November 2007; Heinemann, Andreas (1999), 'Intellectual Property Rights and Competition Policy – The Approach of the WTO Working Group on Trade and Competition', in Roger Zäch (ed.), *Towards WTO Competition Rules*, Berne: Staempfli Publishers, p. 299, at 302. In European law, the ECJ has developed the concept of the 'specific subject-matter' of the IPR. Although this concept may at first sight correspond to the inherency doctrine, neither the ECJ nor the Commission has used it to shield conduct covered by the IPR from the application of the competition rules; supporting this view see Anderman, Steve D. (1998), *EC Competition Law and Intellectual Property Rights – The Regulation of Innovation*, Oxford: Oxford University Press, p. 13.

[18] This is for example the approach now followed by the US DOJ and the FTC when assessing anti-competitive clauses in licensing agreements in the US IP Antitrust Guidelines, see *supra* note 2. Likewise, § 17 of the German Act on Restrains of Competition, which only applied to those licensing clauses outside the scope of the IPR and thus immunized restrictions on the licensee concerning, for example, scope, field of use or territory, has recently (after the seventh amendment of the Act of July 2005) been removed. Among the critical voices in the German literature on the inherency doctrine see Heinemann, Andreas (2002), *Immaterialgüterschutz in der Wettbewerbsordnung – Eine grundlagenorientierte Untersuchung zum Kartellrecht des geistigen Eigentums*, Tübingen: Mohr Siebeck, at p. 145 (with further references).

[19] See *Data General Corp. v. Grumman Systems Support Corp.*, 36 F.3d 1147, at 1186 (1st Cir. 1994), and *Image Technical Services, Inc. v. Eastman Kodak Co.*, 125 F.3d 1195, at 1218 (9th Cir. 1997).

Section 2 of the Sherman Act when refusing to deal with competitors.[20] While the Supreme Court did not deny an application of Section 2 of the Sherman Act to refusal-to-deal cases, it restricted it to those termination situations with a clear element of short-term profit sacrifice.[21] In limiting the scope of application of Section 2 of the Sherman Act, the Supreme Court relied on three main arguments: (1) maximizing firms' freedom to act and to use their property as they choose is pro-competitive since it induces firms to invest and innovate; (2) courts are in principle ill-suited to determining the terms of dealing (or of granting access); and (3) compelling negotiation may facilitate collusion.[22]

As to the first of these arguments, the Supreme Court noted that 'the mere possession of monopoly power, and the concomitant charging of monopoly prices, is not only not unlawful, [but] it is an important element of the free-market system'. In the Court's view, 'the opportunity to charge monopoly prices – at least for a short period – is what attracts business acumen in the first place and induces risk taking that produces innovation and economic growth'. Therefore, 'to safeguard the incentive to innovate, the possession of monopoly power will not be found unlawful unless it is accompanied by an element of anticompetitive *conduct*',[23] which the Court considered not to be present in this case.

Irrespective of whether this argument fits with the facts of the case,[24] it is clear that the Supreme Court endorses a quite one-sided view of the relationship between economic power and innovation.[25] Thus the Supreme Court presumes that innovation is higher in monopolistic markets. However, while it is generally accepted that a certain degree of market power and the possibility

---

[20] More specifically, the Supreme Court had to decide on the relationship between the antitrust rules and the 1996 Telecommunications Act.

[21] Concretely, the Supreme Court considered the *Aspen Skiing* case, a case in which the defendant had terminated a voluntary course of dealing and where the Court could thus infer an anti-competitive intent to be 'at or near the outer boundary of § 2 liability'; *Verizon Communications Inc. v. Law Offices of Curtis V. Trinko, LLP*, 540 U.S. 398, at 409 (2004).

[22] *Ibid*., at 407.

[23] *Ibid*., at 407.

[24] Verizon was the result of a merger between – among others – NYNEX and Bell Atlantic. In turn, these two companies resulted from the break-up of AT&T in 1981. While the break-up of AT&T contributed to introducing competition in the long-distance telecommunication markets, the local telecommunication markets continued to be controlled by the respective local incumbents (NYNEX and Bell Atlantic, among others). Hence, Verizon had had the possibility to charge monopoly prices for (at least) a period of over 20 years. Whether this may be considered a 'short period of time' is, however, more than doubtful.

[25] For a critical analysis of the *Trinko* decision in view of its static Chicago School approach see Drexl, Josef (2004), *supra* note 5, at 795.

to recoup investments spur innovation, it is also well known that a monopoly is dynamically inefficient.[26] Without any competitive constraints, the monopolist has no incentive to invest in innovation. One may reasonably wonder what market forces can constrain a company that, after the *Trinko* decision, is allowed to build an infrastructure or a facility to the exclusion of competitors. Admittedly, competitors will be obliged to invest in the construction of an alternative infrastructure. However, whether this alternative is always the most socially beneficial may be doubted.[27] The reliance of the Supreme Court on the 'benefits' of a monopoly, moreover, not only implies a departure from the more sophisticated and close-to-reality economic theory of the Post-Chicago School applied in former antitrust decisions,[28] but also contrasts with empirical research showing that, generally, competition and open markets provide better incentives for innovation.[29]

If transposed to the context of IPRs, the *Trinko* judgment just confirms the 'immunity' of IPRs from the application of antitrust law. Indeed, if there is no duty to deal in cases not involving IPRs, there would be no obligation to share IPRs with competitors, since exclusivity is the primary characteristic of these rights.[30] Moreover, it is difficult to imagine how antitrust law could control the exercise of an IPR by a monopolist if the monopoly power derived from such rights is generally held to trigger innovation.[31]

3 The European approach towards refusal to license

By contrast with the United States, in the European Union, both the Commission and the European courts may well impose a duty to license that interferes with the scope of the IPR if the exceptional circumstances required are present. From a comparative perspective, such an – at first sight 'IP-unfriendly' – outcome

---

26 See Motta, Massimo (2004), *Competition Policy – Theory and Practice*, Cambridge: Cambridge University Press, pp. 55–8.

27 Thus, Economides, N. (2005), 'Vertical Leverage and the Sacrifice Principle: Why the Supreme Court Got Trinko Wrong', *N.Y.U. Ann. Surv. Am. L.*, **61**, 379, at 403, makes the point that increasing social benefits from markets does not necessarily imply that investment should be maximized. Concretely, he points out that the purpose of the 1996 Telecommunications Act was to create competition without having to duplicate local networks.

28 Drexl, *supra* note 5, at 796.

29 For an overview of different studies see Lowe, Philip and Lucas Peeperkorn (2007), 'Intellectual Property: How Special is its Competition Case?', in Claus-Dieter Ehlermann and Isabela Atanasiu (eds), *European Competition Law Annual 2005: The Relationship between Competition Law and Intellectual Property Law*, Oxford: Hart Publishing, p. 91, at 95.

30 See Fox, *supra* note 5, at 637.

31 Drexl, *supra* note 5, at 796.

may appear startling, the more so as considerations of long-term incentives as well as the contractual freedom of the right holder also play a major role when determining the exceptional circumstances that justify the application of Article 82 EC. Moreover, while the Commission has to respect the interpretation of Article 82 EC by the Community courts, it has nevertheless been willing to affirm the existence of such exceptional circumstances more readily. In the following sections the current jurisprudence of the ECJ will be first examined (section 3.1 *infra*). Thereafter, the Commission's approach will be analysed. In so doing, the focus will be on the Commission's Discussion Paper on the application of Article 82 EC to exclusionary abuses (section 3.2 *infra*).[32]

3.1 The ECJ's approach towards refusal to license

The Community courts have dealt with the question as to when a refusal to license on the part of a dominant right holder constitutes an abuse in the sense of Article 82 EC in several cases, starting in 1988.[33] This chapter will just concentrate on the most recent judicial authority, namely the *IMS Health* judgment.[34] After all, the *IMS Health* judgment has to be seen as the attempt of the ECJ to answer not only the particular questions posed by the referring national court, but the many other questions raised by its previous rulings.

The *IMS Health* case concerned the refusal of the world leader in data collection on pharmaceutical sales and prescriptions to license its copyrighted '1860-brick structure', which was used for processing regional sales data and had developed into a *de facto* industry standard for the provision of sales data services in Germany. After reiterating the principle that a refusal to license

---

32 DG Competition Discussion Paper of December 2005 on the application of Article 82 of the Treaty to exclusionary abuses, http://ec.europa.eu/comm/competition/antitrust/others/discpaper2005.pdf, accessed 4 November 2007.

33 See the references *supra* note 1. For a short overview of the case law of the ECJ on refusal to license see Whish, Richard (2003), *Competition Law*, London: LexisNexis, pp. 758–62. A comprehensive analysis of the Community courts' jurisprudence up to 1998 may be found in Anderman, *supra* note 17, pp. 195–220. See also Derclaye, Estelle (2003), 'Abuses of Dominant Position and Intellectual Property Rights: A Suggestion to Reconcile the Community Courts Case Law', *World Competition*, **26**, 685; Leistner, Matthias (2005), 'Intellectual Property and Competition Law: The European Development from Magill to IMS Health compared to recent German and US Case Law', *ZWeR*, 138, at 141.

34 Case C-418/01, *IMS Health*, [2004] ECR I-5039. This analysis is not able to take into account the most recent judgment of the CFI in the *Microsoft* case, see Case T-201/04, *Microsoft v. Commission*, [2007] ECR II-0000 (not yet reported). However, this judgment does not put in question the fundamental results of this analysis, but rather confirms them.

cannot in itself constitute an abuse of a dominant position,[35] the ECJ went on to clarify the circumstances under which the refusal may nonetheless violate Article 82 EC. Accordingly, in the first place, access to the IP-protected product or service must be indispensable to carry on a particular business. If this is the case, three cumulative[36] conditions must be satisfied: (1) the refusal must prevent the emergence of a new product for which there is a potential consumer demand; (2) it must be unjustified; and (3) it must exclude any competition on a secondary market.[37]

The definitive answer given by the Court is certainly welcomed as far as legal certainty is concerned. Yet one may still have serious doubts whether the approach followed may solve the (competition) problems posed by *indispensable* IP-protected products or services in a convincing manner.

It has been pointed out that by requiring that the refusal to license 'prevents the development of a secondary market to the detriment of consumers',[38] the ECJ does away with the leveraging of market power between two distinct markets as an independent form of abuse in cases involving IPRs.[39] Given that dominant firms have an economic interest in supplying (neighbouring) markets with their own products and that therefore situations where there is enough room for a new product to be offered will certainly be rare, the interpretation made by the ECJ limits extremely the possibility to impose a compulsory licence while giving dominant right holders a free hand to control dependent markets.[40] Furthermore, it is also doubtful whether this interpretation is in line

35 *Ibid*., para. 34.

36 Therewith, the ECJ has put an end to one of the most debated questions after the *Magill* judgment, namely whether the new-product condition and the requirement that competition be excluded in a secondary market had to be read cumulatively or rather alternatively. As examples of this debate see Derclaye, *supra* note 33, at 693; Fine, Frank (2002), 'NDC/IMS: A Logical Application of Essential Facilities Doctrine', *ECLR*, **23**, 457, at 460; Heinemann, Andreas (2003), 'Immaterialgüterrecht und Kartellrecht: Konflikt oder Koexistenz?', in Carl Baudenbacher (ed.), *Neueste Entwicklungen im europäischen und internationalen Immaterialgüterrecht*, Basel: Helbing & Lichtenhahn, pp. 208 and 216; Temple Lang, John (2002), 'Compulsory Licensing of Intellectual Property in European Community Antitrust Law', paper presented for the Department of Justice/Federal Trade Commission Hearings, Washington, DC, http://www.ftc.gov./opp/intellect/020522langdoc.pdf, accessed 4 November 2007, p. 21.

37 Case C-418/01, *IMS Health*, [2004] ECR I-5039, para. 38.

38 *Ibid*., para. 48.

39 See Heinemann, A. (2005), 'Compulsory Licences and Product Integration in European Competition Law – Assessment of the European Commission's *Microsoft* Decision', *IIC*, **36**, 62, at 72; Leistner, *supra* note 33, at 151.

40 Heinemann, *supra* note 39, at 73.

with the goal of Article 82 EC of maintaining an effective competition structure.[41] The case law of the Community courts and the decisional practice of the Commission show that damage to the competitive process may occur where a dominant undertaking uses its market power in a given market to prevent entrance to or to exclude competitors from a separate, but related market.[42] Whereas exclusionary practices of this type can directly harm consumers, neither the Commission nor the European courts have considered this as being decisive in order to affirm an abuse under Article 82 EC. This approach reflects the understanding that the openness of markets and fair access to them guarantee at best the functioning of competition in the long run.[43] Thus, there is in principle no reason to tolerate unjustified exclusionary conduct by the dominant IP holder where this conduct results in the prevention of the development of a secondary market, even if it is not directly to the detriment of consumers.

This criticism is based on the assumption that by refusing to grant the licence the right holder is extending her market power on one market to another (related) market. Yet the characterization of the *IMS Health* case as a leveraging case is far from obvious (see section 3.1.1 *infra*). Also, if the conclusion is reached that there is only one market, the new-product requirement appears more understandable (even if not entirely accurate) (see section 3.1.2 *infra*).

3.1.1 IMS Health*: a leveraging case?* One of the most discussed issues prior to the *IMS Health* judgment was whether two markets are required in order to qualify a refusal to license as abusive, and the criteria according to which these two markets are to be determined.[44]

---

41 In this sense Conde Gallego, B. and D. Riziotis (2004), 'Comments on the IMS Health judgment', *IIC*, **35**, 571, at 571.

42 See, for example, Joined Cases 6 and 7/73, *Istituto Chemioterapico and Commercial Solvents v. Commission*, [1974] ECR 223; Case 311/84, *Télémarketing*, [1985] ECR 3261. See also European Commission of 30 October 1994, Case IV/34.503 – *Sea Containers v. Stena Sealink – Interim measures*, OJ 1994 No. L 15, p. 8, and European Commission of 12 March 2002, Case COMP/37.859 – *De Poste-La Poste*, OJ 2002 No. L 61, p. 32.

43 See Fox, Eleanor M. (2003), 'We Protect Competition, You Protect Competitors', *World Competition*, **26**, 149.

44 See Casper, M. (2002), 'Die wettbewerbsrechtliche Begründung von Zwangslizenzen', *ZHR*, 685, at 698; Heinemann, *supra* note 36, at 214; Fine, *supra* note 36, at 458; Lober, A. (2002), 'Die IMS-Health-Entscheidung der Europäischen Kommission: Copyright K.O.?', *GRUR Int.*, 7, at 11; Temple Lang, *supra* note 36, at 11.

As to the first of these questions, the ECJ, following the analysis made previously by Advocate General Tizziano,[45] held that in view of its earlier case law the application of Article 82 EC to refusals to deal or to license requires the existence of two separate markets: a primary (upstream) market, constituted by the protected product or service, and a secondary (downstream) market, where these goods or services are used as an input for the production of other goods or services.[46] Then, the ECJ went on to explain that the upstream market may be a hypothetical one – that is, there is no need for the relevant products or services to be independently marketed – and affirmed the existence of such a separate upstream market where (1) a product or service is indispensable to carry on an economic activity and (2) there is an actual demand for it.[47]

Albeit closely related, the explicit recognition that an (upstream) market may be a hypothetical one and the concrete definition of that market should not, however, be confounded.[48] Thus, if one concludes – with the Court – that the application of Article 82 EC presupposes the existence of two separate markets, abstaining from requiring that the relevant products or services be marketed separately is just cogent; any other answer would have left the decision about the existence of separate markets up to the dominant firm and provided it with an incentive to integrate vertically as well as to avoid granting licences.[49] In order to define that market, however, this criterion provides little guidance. Rather, one has to look at the two other criteria, namely the indispensability of the products or services and the actual demand for them.

Only a few months after the *IMS Health* judgment, the German Federal Supreme Court (BGH) made a similar market definition in its *Standard Tight-Head Drum* (*Standard-Spundfass*) decision.[50] As in the *IMS Health* case, the right holder was refusing to license a patent that had also become an industry standard.[51] When deciding whether the patent holder had a dominant position

---

45 Opinion of AG Tizziano, Case C-418/01, *IMS Health*, [2004] ECR I-5039, para. 55.

46 Case C-418/01, *IMS Health*, [2004] ECR I-5039, para. 42.

47 *Ibid.*, paras 44 *et seq.*

48 See, however, Fine, *supra* note 36, at 458; Geradin, Damien (2004), 'Limiting the Scope of Article 82 EC: What can the EU Learn From the US Supreme Court's Judgment in *Trinko* in the Wake of *Microsoft*, *IMS*, and *Deutsche Telekom*?', *C.M.L. Rev.*, **41**, 1519, at 1530.

49 See Conde Gallego and Riziotis, *supra* note 41, at 572; Wirtz, M.M. and M. Holzhäuser (2004), 'Die kartellrechtliche Zwangslizenz', *WRP*, 683, at 689. On the economic background of this argument see Drexl, *supra* note 5, at 798.

50 (2005) *IIC*, **36**, 741 (English translation), see also *supra* note 1.

51 Despite some differences – the *Standard Tight-Head Drum* case involved not a copyright, but a patent and the right holder had already granted some licences – the

in the sense of sections 19 and 20 of the German Act Against Restraints of Competition,[52] the BGH concluded that 'if an industry standard stipulates a product design that is protected by an IPR, then the grant of licences for the disputed IPR represents a market of its own on which the right holder, being the only supplier, holds a dominant position'.[53] The BGH emphasized further that this marked definition resulted not from the patent holder being able to exclude third parties from the use of the technical specifications covered by the patent, but rather from the fact that these specifications were not substitutable by any different technical design.[54]

This definition of an upstream market has been criticized as being somewhat artificial.[55] Indeed, accepting the market definition proposed by the ECJ would mean that there are always two markets as soon as the IPR is indispensable and there is somebody asking for a licence. Hence, while heavily contested as regards its outcome, the Commission's decision found much more support as to the conclusion that the '1860-brick structure' and the regional data services did not constitute separate markets.[56]

The delimitation between a primary market and a secondary (related) market is not always easy. In the legal literature, therefore, different criteria have been proposed to facilitate this task. Thus, it has been suggested to look at the scope of the IPR in the first place. Accordingly, the primary market would encompass all products that have been primarily developed on the basis

---

two cases are well suited to comparison. Remarkably, in the *Standard Tight-Head Drum* case the technical specifications covered by the patent had been adopted by the German Association of the Chemical Industry, to which the leading chemical companies belong, as the industry standard. For more detail see Leistner, *supra* note 33, at 158.

52 Likewise, the application of Article 82 EC presupposes the holding of a dominant position in a relevant market. The Commission had established that *IMS Health* was in a quasi-monopoly situation in the market for regional data sale services (European Commission of 3 July 2001, Case COMP D3/38.044 – *NDC Health/IMS Health: Interim Measures*, OJ 2002 No. L 59, p. 18, para. 58). The ECJ assumed a dominant position on the part of *IMS Health* and dealt with the issue of market definition when finding the abuse.

53 (2005) *IIC*, **36**, 741, at 744.

54 *Ibid.*, at 745.

55 See with regard to the *IMS Health* judgment Geradin, *supra* note 48, at 1530; Höppner, T. (2004), 'Die Pflicht interne Produktionsmittel zu vermarkten – zugleich Anmerkung zum EuGH-Urteil IMS', *EuZW*, 748; Leupold, H. and S. Pautke (2005), 'IMS Health v. Microsoft – Befindet sich die Kommission bei kartellrechtlichen Zwangslizenzen (erneut) auf Konfrontationskurs mit dem EuGH', *EWS*, 108; Wielsch, D. (2005), 'Wettbewerbsrecht als Immaterialgüterrecht', *EuZW*, 391, at 393; Wirtz and Holzhäuser, *supra* note 49, at 689.

56 See Jung, P. (2004), 'Die Zwangslizenz als Instrument der Wettbewerbspolitik', *ZWeR*, 397; Lober, *supra* note 44, at 12. On different grounds Fine, *supra* note 36, at 460.

of the IPR; other products for which the IPR is merely an ancillary component would belong to a separate market.[57] Furthermore, the existence of only one (primary) market could also be assumed if the product offered by the company requesting the licence widely resembles the IP-protected product.[58] In this context, a distinction is made as to whether the licence is needed in order to produce a compatible product – in which case this product would belong to a separate market – or to produce the IP-protected product itself.[59]

If applied to the *IMS Health* case, these criteria lead to the conclusion that there is only one market for the IPR and the product embodying the right: the undertaking requesting the licence intended to supply the same customers (the pharmaceutical companies) with a product that only slightly differed from the one offered by *IMS Health*; moreover, the copyrighted database was developed with the aim of collecting and structuring sales data for the regional sales reports.[60] This conclusion is even clearer in the *Standard Tight-Head Drum* case, where the technical specifications covered by the patent and the chemical drum definitely constituted a unity.

So far, the cases considered are different from the *Magill*[61] and *Bronner*[62] cases, which the ECJ cited as precedents. In *Magill*, the copyright arose incidentally out of broadcasting television programmes; access to the programme information was needed in order to become active in the related market for TV viewers' magazines. In *Bronner*, the refusal involved the dominant firm's own method of reaching consumers, a clearly complementary market to the market for daily newspapers.[63]

---

57 See Casper, *supra* note 44, at 699; Eilmansberger, T. (2005), 'How to Distinguish Good From Bad Competition Under Article 82 EC: In Search of Clearer and More Coherent Standards for Anti-Competitive Abuses', *C.M.L. Rev.*, **42**, 129, at 160; Marquardt, P.D. and M. Leddy (2003), 'The Essential Facilities Doctrine and Intellectual Property Rights: A Response to Pitofsky, Patterson, and Hooks', *Antitrust L.J.*, **70**, 847, at 873; Temple Lang, *supra* note 36, at 13; Wirtz and Holzhäuser, *supra* note 49, at 689.

58 See Lober, *supra* note 44, at 11.

59 See Heinemann, *supra* note 18, at 521.

60 Even AG Tizziano repeatedly states that the undertaking seeking the licence pretends access to the *same market* where the dominant undertaking, and IP right holder, is *exploiting its right*; *supra* note 45, at paras 30, 46 and 60. Supporting the view that there is only one market see Ghidini, Gustavo (2006), *Intellectual Property and Competition Law – The Innovation Nexus*, Cheltenham, UK and Northampton, MA, US: Edward Elgar, p. 107 (at note 28).

61 *Magill*, *supra* note 1.

62 Case C-7/97, *Bronner*, [1998] ECR I-7791.

63 On this group of refusal-to-deal cases see Glazer, K.L. and A.B. Lipsky (1995), 'Unilateral Refusals to Deal Under Section 2 of the Sherman Act', *Antitrust L.J.*, **63**, 749, at 766.

In fact, the market definition conducted by the ECJ and the BGH seems to blur the lines between these two different sets of cases. Even in those situations that have been traditionally considered as one-market situations it will be possible to distinguish an (upstream) licensing market and a (downstream) product or service market. The consequences of this reach farther than may be assumed at first glance. Namely, with this market definition the ECJ has opened the door to capture (abusive) exclusionary behaviour by the IP holder in the primary market where the IP-protected product is being exploited, provided that the additional new-product requirement is fulfilled.

3.1.2 The new-product requirement Against this backdrop, the cumulative approach followed by the ECJ also appears more comprehensible.[64] Thus, in the absence of an unambiguous leveraging element, the ECJ had to tie the application of Article 82 EC to an additional abusive element if the *Volvo* principle, according to which a refusal to license as such does not constitute an abuse of a dominant position, was to be followed. In view of the judicial precedents (*Magill*) the new-product requirement was self-evident.

Moreover, demanding that the undertaking requesting the licence 'does not limit itself essentially to duplicating the goods or services already offered . . . by the [right holder], but intends to produce new goods or services'[65] seems perfectly in line with the rationale underlying the IP system.[66] Hence, since IP protection is designed to promote innovation, that is, to promote the development of new products and services by *inter alia* forcing the right holder's competitors to offer substitute products, the exercise of an IPR to the opposite effect, namely to prevent the development of a new product or service, must be held illegal under competition law. Conversely, as long as the requesting undertakings are merely 'me too' competitors, there is in principle no reason to limit the exclusivity enjoyed by the IP right holder.

---

64 Still, the criticism remains that in 'pure' leveraging situations, this approach is excessively restrictive. In the Discussion Paper on exclusionary abuses, however, the Commission seems not to apply the 'new product' requirement to those kinds of abuses where it identifies a leveraging of market power from one market to another; see *supra* note 32, para. 241 (with regard to the refusal to supply information needed for interoperability) and 246 (with regard to aftermarkets).

65 Case C-418/01, *IMS Health*, [2004] ECR I-5039, para. 49.

66 On this apparent harmony see Drexl, J. (2007), 'Abuse of Dominance in Licensing and Refusal to License: A "More Economic Approach" to Competition by Imitation and Competition by Substitution', in Claus-Dieter Ehlermann and Isabela Atanasiu (eds), *European Competition Law Annual 2005: The Relationship between Competition Law and Intellectual Property Law*, Oxford: Hart Publishing, p. 647, at 653.

Even if one accepts this view, this does not necessarily mean that by applying this criterion all problematic – and both from the competition law as well as from the IP perspective *exceptional* – situations are answered satisfactorily. Thus, apart from the difficulty in tracing the line between the product already offered by the IP owner and a possible new one, the new-product criterion implies that by obtaining the licence the requesting undertaking will be able to offer a new product.[67] While in those situations in which this is the case a compulsory licence may restore competition,[68] there are, however, other situations in which the ability of competitors to compete by substitution, that is, by offering alternative products or services, is of little relevance. The cases considered here are examples thereof.

Once an IP-protected subject matter turns out to be the standard on the market – be it an official standard agreed on by a standard-setting body or a producer organization or be it because of the existence of lock-in and network effects – the right holder becomes protected from having to face competition from other (even superior) technologies. Not only does the access to the product market depend on having access to the IPR, competition on that market will moreover depend on the ability of undertakings to offer the standardized product. In a situation like that, requiring the licence-requesting undertaking to intend to offer a new product will make no sense. The same is true with regard to the very much debated issue of the grant of IP (design) protection for spare parts.[69] Here too, given the fact that so-called must-match spare parts are purchased in order to replace another part, thereby preserving or restoring the original appearance of the complex product, undertakings may only compete by offering those spare parts that would fulfil this task, that is, by offering those spare parts that are identical to the original. However, whereas in the spare-parts case the total blocking of competition is an automatic and inevitable consequence of IP protection being granted and should therefore be addressed within intellectual property law,[70] it is

---

[67] See Drexl, *supra* note 66, at 654.

[68] The *Magill* case, on which the ECJ very much relied, was such a case: by getting access to the copyrighted programme information, *Magill* would have been able to put on the market a comprehensive weekly television guide which up until then was not offered by the IP right holders and which competed with the daily TV programmes and the non-comprehensive TV magazines offered by them.

[69] For a very profound analysis of this topic see Kur, Annette, chapter 13, in this volume. See also Drexl, J., R.M. Hilty and A. Kur (2005), 'Design Protection for Spare Parts and the Commission's Proposal for a Repairs Clause', *IIC*, **36**, 448.

[70] In this sense the Commission has proposed to introduce a repair clause in the Design Directive; see Proposal of 14 September 2004 for a Directive of the European Parliament and of the Council amending Directive 98/71/EC on the legal protection of designs, COM/2004/0582 final = http://eur-lex.europa.eu/LexUriServ/site/en/com/2004/com2004_0582en01.pdf, accessed 4 November 2007.

for competition law to give an adequate answer to those other situations in which competition by substitution is not possible as a result of external market conditions.

To this end, the new-product criterion definitely does not help further. Before making a proposal as to the way these (exceptional) situations could be addressed under Article 82 EC, the European Commission's standpoint in refusal-to-license cases will be examined next.

3.2 The Commission's approach towards refusal to license

As pointed out above, the Commission has been more willing to affirm a duty to license under Article 82 EC. Concretely, it ordered IMS Health to grant a licence on its copyrighted structure.[71] Also, it held that Microsoft had infringed Article 82 EC by refusing to supply Sun Microsystems with the interoperability information they needed to offer compatible products, even on the assumption that such information is protected by IPRs.[72] Without attempting to examine these two decisions in detail, the line of reasoning applied by the Commission in order to reach such an outcome is worth considering (section 3.2.1 *infra*). Moreover, whereas previous to the *IMS Health* judgment the conditions for applying Article 82 EC to refusals to license remained to a large extent uncertain, the scope for interpretation has now been significantly reduced. Nevertheless, and even if the Commission has to be cautious in departing from previous case law, in its Discussion Paper on the application of Article 82 EC to exclusionary abuses[73] it has introduced a small but significant deviation so as to accommodate the excessively restrictive new-product condition to a broader set of situations (section 3.2.2 *infra*).

3.2.1 The Commission's approach before the IMS Health *judgment* As already mentioned, the Commission did not construe the *IMS Health* case as a leveraging case. It considered the German market for regional sales data services to be the (only) relevant market where IMS Health had a near-monopoly position.[74] It also did not deem it necessary to prove that the refusal to license in this particular case prevented the appearance of a new product.

---

[71] European Commission of 3 July 2001, Case COMP D3/38.044 – *NDC Health/IMS Health: Interim Measures*, OJ 2003 No. L 59, p. 18, para. 49 (suspended by both the President of the CFI, Case T-184/01R, *IMS Health v. Commission*, [2001] ECR II-3193 and the President of the ECJ, Case C-481/01P(R), *IMS Health v. Commission*, [2002] ECR I-3401).

[72] European Commission of 24 March 2004, Case COMP/C-3/37.792 – *Microsoft*, *supra* note 7.

[73] See *supra* note 32.

[74] *Supra* note 71, at para. 56.

The Commission did refer to the *Magill* judgment; it nevertheless saw the prevention of a new product as just one possible exceptional circumstance.[75] In finding an abuse, the Commission rather focused on the fact that the customer industry had become dependent on the copyrighted structure and that therefore it was not possible for competing undertakings to offer substitute products.[76] Under these conditions, which the Commission held to be very specific and exceptional, the exclusive use of the protected structure was a means of monopolizing the market for regional data services. Irrespective of whether the Commission's interpretation of the earlier jurisprudence was correct – which it turned out not to be – it is clear that it deemed the ability of undertakings to compete by substitution the decisive criterion to intervene under Article 82 EC Treaty in refusal-to-license cases.

In contrast with the *IMS Health* case, in *Microsoft* the Commission considered that by refusing to supply interoperability information, *Microsoft* had leveraged its market power on the market for client PC operating systems to the market for work group server operating systems.[77] Furthermore, in line with its understanding of the case law, the Commission did not explicitly discuss the new-product criterion.[78] However, it considered as given that to the extent that the lack of interoperability hindered competitors from bringing their more innovative features to the market, the refusal to supply limited technical development in the sense of Article 82(b) EC.[79] More significantly,

---

75 *Ibid.*, para. 67.

76 *Ibid.*, para. 211. In this respect, the Commission rejected *IMS Health's* argument that for determining the indispensability of the brick structure the subjective or evolving attitudes of customers were of no relevance. In the Commission's view (*ibid.*, at para. 129), 'to give the views of the customers no weight in these proceedings would have been to consider the question of whether the structure was indispensable only from the perspective of the possibilities of creating any new brick structure, without regard to whether or not it was at all possible to use that structure to compete on the relevant market'.

77 *Supra* note 72, at paras 533 and 546.

78 At the time the *Microsoft* decision was issued, the ECJ had not yet ruled on the *IMS Health* case, although the opinion of AG Tizziano had already hinted at the necessity of this criterion.

79 *Supra* note 72, para. 693. Despite this, many authors doubted that the *Microsoft* decision would be upheld by the CFI if the cumulative IMS test is applied; see Heinemann, *supra* note 39, at 74; Körber, T. (2004), 'Geistiges Eigentum, essential facilities und "Innovationsmissbrauch"', *RIW*, 881, at 889; Leistner, M., *supra* note 33, at 161; Thyri, P. (2005), 'Immaterialgüterrechte und Zugang zur wesentlichen Einrichtung – Der Fall Microsoft im Licht von IMS-Health', *WuW*, 388, at 396. Affirming the compatibility of both rulings Leupold and Pautke, *supra* note 55, at 114. As to the recent decision of the CFI, confirming a violation of Article 82 EC, see *supra* note 7.

however, when considering the objective justification put forward by Microsoft, the Commission applied a new balancing test, which weighs the possible negative impact of a duty to supply or license on the dominant right holder's incentives to innovate against the positive impact of such a duty on the level of innovation of the whole industry.[80] The Commission has now to a large extent transferred this reasoning to its assessment of refusals to license in the Discussion Paper on exclusionary abuses.

3.2.2 Refusal to license in the Commission's Discussion Paper on exclusionary abuses Unsurprisingly, in the Discussion Paper the Commission closely follows the *IMS Health* ruling. Accordingly, for a refusal to license to be abusive the Commission considers that the following conditions have to be met:[81]

(1) the behaviour of the right holder amounts to a refusal to license;
(2) the right holder holds a dominant position on a relevant market;
(3) the IPR is indispensable to carry on an economic activity in the downstream market;[82]
(4) the refusal to license has a likely market-distorting foreclosure effect in the downstream market;
(5) the refusal to license is not objectively justified *and* the imposition of a duty to grant a licence has no negative effects on long-run incentives to innovate; and
(6) the refusal to license prevents the emergence of a new product for which there is a potential consumer demand *or* the licence is indispensable as a basis for follow-on innovation.

---

80 *Supra* note 72, para. 783. Referring to this and making an economic comparison between the new-product requirement and the incentives-balancing test see Lévêque, F. (2005), 'Innovation, Leveraging and Essential Facilities: Interoperability Licensing in the EU Microsoft Case', *World Competition*, **28**, 71, at 75. Much more critical towards this balancing test is Forrester, Ian S. (2007), 'Regulating Intellectual Property Via Competition? Or Regulating Competition Via Intellectual Property? – Competition and Intellectual Property: Ten Years On, the Debate Still Flourishes', in Claus-Dieter Ehlermann and Isabela Atanasiu (eds), *European Competition Law Annual 2005: The Relationship between Competition Law and Intellectual Property Law*, Oxford: Hart Publishing, p. 59, at 87.

81 *Supra* note 32, paras 225–40.

82 Note, however, that the Commission merely refers to a 'distinct market' and to a 'leveraging of market power from one market to another' when assessing refusals to supply information needed for interoperability (paras 226 and 241). From this follows *a contrario* that, although the Commission follows the market definition made by the ECJ (paras 226 *et seq.*), it does not consider 'classical' refusal-to-license cases as leveraging cases.

However, in contrast with the excessively normative approach of the ECJ,[83] the Commission does present an economic justification for adopting such an approach. Hence, it rightly points out that competition policy towards refusals to supply or license has to take into account both the effect of having more short-run competition and the possible long-run effects on investment incentives.[84] In balancing the gains in (static) allocative efficiency against the losses that a duty to license would have in the incentives to innovate, and therefore in dynamic efficiency, the Commission clearly places the emphasis on the latter. Consequently, the Commission develops a defence in favour of the right holder in the sense that effective competition may be excluded for a limited period of time in order to allow the IP owner to ensure an adequate return on her investments.[85] As a result, the attainment of allocative efficiency will in principle be a goal of competition law enforcement only as long as the effects on the incentives to innovate of the dominant right holder are (at least) neutral. With regard to IPRs, the Commission presumes this to be the case when the investments behind innovations leading to intellectual property rights were not particularly significant.[86]

The Commission's analysis, however, will not terminate here. Rather, the effects of a duty to license on the dominant right holder's incentives to innovate will be weighed up against the positive impact that such an obligation may have for follow-on innovation. Indeed, the Commission introduces this 'new' concept at two different stages of the analysis. Firstly, it will assess the possible positive effects on incentives to make follow-on investments in innovation when considering the objective justifications and efficiencies alleged by the right holder.[87] Secondly, while sticking to the new-product condition, the Commission goes beyond a strict reading of it. Thus, it states that even in cases in which the licence is not sought to directly incorporate the technology

---

83 See Drexl, *supra* note 5, at 799, and Drexl, *supra* note 66, at 649 (criticizing the ECJ).

84 *Supra* note 32, para. 213.

85 *Ibid.*, para. 235.

86 *Ibid.*, para. 236. See, however, Drexl, J., B. Conde Gallego, S. Enchelmaier, M. Leistner and M.-O. Mackenrodt (2006), Comments on the DG Competition Discussion Paper on the application of Article 82 of the EC Treaty to exclusionary abuses, *IIC*, **37**, 558, at 571 (criticizing the idea of linking the degree of protection afforded to innovators with the size of the investment); see also Ahlborn, Christian, Vincenzo Denicolò, Damien Geradin and A. Jorge Padilla (2006), 'DG Comp's Discussion Paper on Article 82 EC: Implications of the Proposed Framework and Antitrust Rules for Dynamically Competitive Industries', http://ec.europa.eu/comm/competition/antitrust/others/article_82_contributions.html, accessed 4 November 2007, p. 52.

87 *Supra* note 32, para. 236.

in a clearly identifiable product, the refusal to license may be abusive if it is indispensable as a basis for follow-on innovation by competitors.[88]

From a systematic point of view and given the fact that the new criterion would also encompass situations in which the licence-requesting undertaking intends to introduce a new product or service, the Commission should reconsider whether the very much contended new-product criterion should be entirely abandoned. Moreover, according to the Discussion Paper, whether the refusal to grant a licence hinders follow-on innovation on the part of competing undertakings will only be examined after the five other conditions are fulfilled.[89] This would, however, mean that in a situation in which the dominant IP owner could show that the investments behind the protected innovation have been 'particularly significant' and could thus argue that her incentives to innovate were negatively affected by a duty to license, the positive impact that such a duty would have on the ability of competitors to further innovate would be disregarded from the outset. This outcome runs contrary to an understanding of competition law as a means of guaranteeing that the exercise of the IPRs does not hinder competition by substitution and of promoting dynamic efficiency. Consequently, the Commission should also consider departing from the proposed approach of requiring an additional condition in refusal-to-license cases. Instead, it should assess altogether the effects of an obligation to license on dynamic competition, with regard to both the right holder's and the competitor's incentives to innovate.

Apart from these methodological inconsistencies, the Commission ably manages to exhaust the tight scope for manoeuvre left after the *IMS Health* judgment. Furthermore, by focusing on the impact of a refusal to license on the innovation level of competitors, the Commission recognizes that there may be situations in which the exclusionary effect of IPRs may have a negative impact on their ability to compete by substitution. Nonetheless, the approach proposed by the Commission still fails to give answer to a large and significant group of refusal-to-license situations. Hence, although the Commission mentions that in those cases in which a technology has become the standard access to the IPRs is likely to be indispensable,[90] it does not explain how these constellations will fit with the tests proposed.[91] As pointed out above, the new-product requirement does not make any sense; but the hindering-of-follow-on-innovation rule as well is ill-suited to cope with this kind of IP-related competition problem.

88 *Ibid.*, para. 240.
89 *Ibid.*, paras 237 and 239.
90 *Ibid.* at para. 230.
91 See Drexl *et al.*, *supra* note 86, at 570.

4 Alternative approach to refusal to license: impossibility to compete by substitution as the central criterion for a duty to license

To be sure, the necessity to develop an alternative approach to adequately apprehend this kind of situation may not be that obvious. Actually, at the centre of the concerns are situations in which access to the protected subject matter would just enable the requesting undertakings to become active in a market by offering the same (or largely the same) products that the right holder is already offering (or would be able to do). In contrast with a situation in which the refusal to license hampers the sequential technical progress – behaviour clearly in conflict with the goals of the IP system – affirming a duty to license in these situations will imply that somebody is drawing on somebody else's innovative efforts without the goal of promoting innovation being (at least apparently[92]) attained. Yet the search for corrective mechanisms, that is, a duty to license, may still be justified, both from the perspective of competition law as well as from the point of view of the IP system.

As repeatedly pointed out, by allowing the right holder to exclusively exploit the protected subject matter, that is, to exclude competition by imitation, the IP system encourages her to invest in the creation of innovative products and compels competing undertakings to develop new and improved products. By doing so, the IP system furthers competition by substitution and contributes to dynamic efficiency. For its part, competition law aims at protecting competition in the market and ensures that undertakings feel pressure to innovate. Moreover, the incentives to innovate arising from IPRs are only effective if it is guaranteed that competitors may come up with new products that can substitute for the product protected by the IPRs. The complementary theory builds on these premises.

From this, it follows that IPRs are in principle shaped in such a manner as not to exclude competition by substitution.[93] On the other hand, it also follows from this that those situations in which IP protection does not reach the goal of promoting competition by substitution are neither catered to nor covered by the economic rationale behind the IP system.[94] If these cases are looked at

---

92 Still, the argument could be made that in the middle and long run the licensees would become potential innovators of the licensed product; see Conde Gallego and Riziotis, *supra* note 41, at 573.

93 On how competition considerations are taken into account in the drafting of IP legislation see Kur, A. (1996), 'Gedanken zum Systemkonformität einer Sonderregelung für Must-match-Ersatzteile im künftigen europäischen Geschmacksmusterrecht', *GRUR Int.*, 876, at 879.

94 In the words of the BGH in the *Standard Tight-Head Drum* case, (2005) *IIC*, **36**, 741, at 746 (see also *supra* note 1):

> [For] the case at hand, it is sufficient to recognize that the requirements for objective

from a competition-law perspective, an intervention is justified given that the losses of allocative efficiency resulting from excluding imitation would not be outweighed by the gains in dynamic efficiency.[95]

Once it is clear that the possibility of ordering a compulsory licence in order to enable imitation should not be excluded from the outset, the question still remains as to the legal standard that should be applied. According to the considerations above, the impossibility of competing by substitution should be the central criterion. Concretely, the assessment of refusals to license could be approached in the following manner:[96]

(1) In the first place, market dominance should be established in a relevant market. Excluding those cases in which the scope of protection has been drawn too broadly, market dominance will normally exist in the relevant product market. Moreover, the absence of substitutes may have different reasons. Thus, market dominance may arise from the technical superiority of the protected product. Market dominance may, however, also be due to external market circumstances such as *de iure* or *de facto* standardization.

(2) In a second step, it should be determined whether the basic mechanism of competition by substitution does work. Article 82 EC should only be applied if competition by substitution is excluded. In legal terms, this requirement is to be phrased as an indispensability test. Concretely, the question to be asked is not only whether there are actual substitutes for the IPR, but also – as the Commission aptly points out[97] – whether it is possible to 'invent around' the IPR. At this point, it becomes clear that most of the cases in which the right holder would have a dominant position would fall outside the application of Article 82 EC. Thus, the fact that no actual substitutes exist when the licence is requested does by no means mean that such substitutes cannot be developed. This is indeed

---

justification [. . .] may not be too low if the market-dominating position of a patent proprietor is derived not (solely) from the creative achievement underlying the invention, but is based at least in part on the fact that access to a downstream product market is dependent on adherence to a patent's specifications due to the existence of a standard or a standard-like set of conditions [. . .]. In this case, *the standard makes it difficult or impossible for the patent-based solution to fulfil the spirit and purpose of patent protection by proving itself in competition with different technical solutions. . . .* (Emphasis added)

95 Drexl, *supra* note 5, at 804.

96 At this point, the author will follow the proposal of the Max Planck Institute for Intellectual Property. The author played an active part in the working group that elaborated this proposal. See Drexl *et al.*, *supra* note 86, at 568.

97 *Supra* note 32, para 230.

what makes the difference between a *successful* and an *indispensable* IPR.[98] Whether an IPR has become indispensable will depend on the facts. In many cases, to determine this will require a thorough market analysis as well as – in particular with regard to *de facto* standards[99] – difficult predictions.[100]

(3) If the preceding analysis comes to the conclusion that there is no possibility of competing on the market absent the licence, in a third step the pro- and anti-competitive effects of a duty to license should be assessed in the light of the concept of dynamic competition. To this end, a further distinction has to be made. Thus competition by substitution may be re-established by granting the licence. Actually, these are the kinds of situations that the Commission attempts to apprehend under the concept of 'follow-on' innovation. In other situations, however, the licence will only make possible competition by imitation. In both cases, the effects of the licence on the overall incentive structure of the IP system have to be carefully considered.

In general terms, a duty to license would be justified whenever it would enable substitution by a different and more innovative product. Though the right holder has an interest in recouping the investments made, there is no (cogent) reason why this interest should prevail to preclude an application of Article 82 EC, which is aimed at re-establishing competition by substitution, as the main goal of the IP system. Moreover, the interest of the right holder in recouping her investments could (and should) be sufficiently accounted for when fixing the amount of the royalties.[101]

In the cases in which the licence merely facilitates imitation, the balancing exercise is more complex. Indeed, if the right holder can foresee that she may have to permit others to imitate her invention or work, she will be reluctant to make the initial investment to create it. While the counter-incentives of a duty to license in future innovative efforts are surely a strong argument to not order

---

98 It is therefore quite misleading when the Commission's Discussion Paper (*ibid.*, para 238) states that the protection afforded by the exclusive right 'would be eroded if the holder of a *successful* IPR would be required to grant a licence to competitors from the moment the IPR or the product incorporating the IPR becomes dominant in the market' (emphasis added).

99 On the relationship between network effects and IPRs see in much more detail Mackenrodt, Mark-Oliver, chapter 4, in this volume.

100 For an overview of different situations in which an IPR may be indispensable see Conde Gallego, B. (2006), 'Die Anwendung des kartellrechtlichen Missbrauchsverbots auf "unerlässliche" Immaterialgüterrechte im Lichte der IMS Health- und Standard-Spundfass-Urteile', *GRUR Int.*, 16, at 21.

101 In this sense see also Ghidini, *supra* note 60, pp. 108 et seq.

it, focusing just on them would be too one-sided. Hence, in a situation in which competition by substitution is not possible, the exclusion of competition by imitation harms consumers. Not only are consumers deprived of price competition; without having to face significant competitive constraints, it is also likely that in the middle or long run the dominant right holder would reduce investments in product quality and innovation. Furthermore, whereas it is true that a duty to license will reduce the benefits earned by the right holder, it is not so clear that the overall incentives to innovate will be reduced. Firstly, if, because of the given market conditions that exclude competition by substitution, the right holder gets the whole market, the exclusivity afforded by the IPR clearly over-compensates. In many cases also, the right holder would already have made the initial investment before realizing that she would have to share her invention with others. Secondly and more importantly, restricting the exclusivity of the IPRs in situations where competition by substitution is not possible should be understood as an attempt to correct an 'anomalous' situation that is not covered by the rationale of the IPRs and should therefore leave the overall incentives arising from the IP system untouched.

6 Conclusion

Despite many years of discussion, the debate on how to approach unilateral refusals to license on the part of dominant undertakings still flourishes. In fact, recent cases show that it has won new vigour. The approaches taken to date, however, remain unconvincing. Neither does the formalistic criterion of the scope of the right reflect the complementarity between intellectual property and competition law, nor does an approach that exclusively focuses on the right holder's freedom to act as the only means to maintain incentives to innovate provide an adequate answer in all cases. Indeed, the argument that a duty to license undermines the incentives to innovate arising from the IPRs is often made too readily and without taking into consideration the specific market situation in which the IPR produces its effects. In line with the 'effect-based' approach now endorsed by the European Commission, this chapter has proposed looking at the concrete effects of an IPR in a given market and considering ordering a compulsory licence whenever competition in that market depends on having access to the IPR.

10 Patent power and market power: rethinking the relationship between intellectual property rights and market power in antitrust analysis

Clifford A. Jones

1 Introduction – Spilled ink: the Supreme Court, patent tying, and presumptions of market power

On 1 March 2006, the Supreme Court of the United States decided in *Illinois Tool Works, Inc. v. Independent Ink, Inc.*[1] that it would abandon its longstanding rule that market power is presumed in cases where a patented product is tied to the purchase of unpatented products in a tying arrangement giving rise to claims under the Sherman and Clayton Antitrust Acts. Speaking for a unanimous Supreme Court, Justice Stevens stated: [2]

> Congress, the antitrust enforcement agencies, and most economists have all reached the conclusion that a patent does not necessarily confer market power upon the patentee. Today, we reach the same conclusion, and therefore hold that, in all cases involving a tying arrangement, the plaintiff must prove that the defendant has market power in the tying product.

In so ruling, the Supreme Court both brought an end to an arguably unhealthy intertwining of patent law and antitrust law that had existed since the early twentieth century and simultaneously brought about a new convergence of antitrust tying law and the law of patent abuse. Whether this results in an improvement in antitrust tying law is open to question,[3] but indisputably there is a new or restored alignment with regard to the role of market power in both antitrust tying and the law of patent abuse.

In *Illinois Tool Works*, the antitrust claim of the plaintiff Independent Ink arose from its manufacture of less expensive although apparently equal-quality ink for use in the defendant's patented industrial piezoelectric print heads

[1] 547 US 28, 126 S.Ct. 1281 (2006).

[2] 547 US 28, 126 S.Ct. 1281, at 1293 (2006). Justice Alito did not participate in the decision.

[3] See also Grimes, Warren, chapter 11, in this volume.

used to print labels and barcodes on cartons and packaging. Defendant Trident's (Illinois Tool Works) patented printheads held 85 percent of the market and its unpatented ink, which Trident required licensees to use, sold for $325 per bottle. In contrast, Independent Ink sold its 'chemically indistinguishable' replacement ink for $125 to $189 per bottle, some 60 to 70 percent less. Purchasers of the printheads were forbidden to refill the ink containers that attached to the printheads with ink made by anyone but Trident.

Independent Ink's claim for tying under Section 1 of the Sherman Act[4] (not Section 3 of the Clayton Act[5]) was dismissed by the District Court on summary judgment for failure to prove that Trident had market power in the relevant market,[6] but reinstated by the Court of Appeals on the grounds that existing jurisprudence presumed the existence of market power from the possession of a patent in the tying product.[7] The claims were remanded by the Supreme Court with instructions to permit Independent Ink to introduce actual evidence of market power rather than relying on a presumption of market power based on the use of a patented item as a tying product.

The Supreme Court reached its decision to abandon the presumption of market power based on several factors, although perhaps the primary reason

---

4 15 USC § 1 (2000). This provision prohibits 'contracts, combinations, and conspiracies' in restraint of trade. A violation is felony.

5 15 USC § 14 (2000). For no reason apparent from the case, no parallel claim was brought under the Section 3 of the Clayton Act. This section provides that '[i]t shall be unlawful for any person engaged in commerce, in the course of such commerce, to lease or make a sale or contract for sale of goods, wares, merchandise, machinery, supplies, or other commodities, whether patented or unpatented, for use, consumption, or resale within the United States or any Territory thereof or the District of Columbia or any insular possession or other place under the jurisdiction of the United States, or fix a price charged therefore, or discount from, or rebate upon, such price, on the condition, agreement, or understanding that the lessee or purchaser thereof shall not use or deal in the goods, wares, merchandise, machinery, supplies, or other commodities of a competitor or competitors of the lessor or seller, where the effect of such lease, sale, or contract for sale or such condition, agreement, or understanding may be to substantially lessen competition or tend to create a monopoly in any line of commerce'. This reaches tying agreements because a requirement to buy the tied product is an agreement not to 'use or deal in' the goods of a competitor of the seller. A violation of this provision is not a crime, unlike violations of Section 1 of the Sherman Act.

6 *Independent Ink, Inc. v. Trident, Inc.*, 210 F. Supp. 2d 1155, at 1177 (C.D. Cal. 2002).

7 *Independent Ink, Inc. v. Illinois Tool Works, Inc.*, 396 F.3d 1342, at 1351 (Fed. Cir. 2005): 'We conclude that the Supreme Court has held that there is a presumption of market power in patent tying cases, and we are obliged to follow the Supreme Court's direction in this respect. The time may have come to abandon the doctrine, but it is up to the Congress or the Supreme Court to make this judgment.'

was the Court's determination that the presumption had been imported from cases involving the doctrine of patent abuse, and because Congress had acted in 1988 to require a showing of market power in such cases, the Court felt that the underpinnings of the doctrine should be re-examined in light of that statutory revision. In addition, the Court recognized that most recent economic and legal research indicated that as an empirical matter, most patents did not convey significant market power in a relevant antitrust market and did not have significant economic value. Finally, the court gave weight to the fact that antitrust law had become more receptive to possible pro-competitive benefits of tying agreements in general, and in particular, that the enforcement policy of the Department of Justice now took the view that intellectual property in general did not raise a presumption of market power. Accordingly, the Court determined that the burden of proof should rest on a plaintiff to show actual market power in a tying antitrust case rather than presuming the existence of such power from the use of a patented product as a tying product.

As is typical of most decisions of the US Supreme Court, *Illinois Tool Works* does not address the broader issues raised by tensions between antitrust law and intellectual property rights but confines its attention to the issues essential to resolve the specific dispute between the parties. The Court did not express any opinions on the sufficiency of the claims or supporting evidence advanced by Independent Ink, but left those issues for the district court to address on remand.[8] While the judgment itself is narrow, indeed basically procedural rather than substantive, it provides an appropriate occasion to discuss some of the underlying issues in a broader context.

2 A brief history of the road to *Illinois Tool Works*

2.1 *The tying offence in antitrust law*

A tying arrangement is 'an agreement by a party to sell one product [the tying product] but only on the condition that the buyer also purchases a different (or tied) product, or at least agrees that he will not purchase that product from any other supplier'.[9] Although tying has been said, as in *Northern Pacific*,[10] to be

---

8 Independent Ink argued, persuasively, that the record contained ample evidence of actual market power, which would have justified affirming the Court of Appeals for the Federal Circuit, but the Court declined to reach that issue and left it for the lower court.

9 *Eastman Kodak Co. v. Image Technical Servs., Inc.*, 504 US 451, 462 (1992) (citation omitted).

10 The classic statement of per se rules is found in *Northern Pac. R. Co. v. U.S.*, 356 US 1, at 5 (1958): 'There are certain agreements or practices which because of their pernicious effect on competition and lack of any redeeming virtue are conclusively

per se a violation of Section 1 of the Sherman Act, this is no longer taken literally. Rather, as Sullivan and Grimes note, tying arrangements are in practice examined under a 'structured rule of reason' analysis.[11]

Tying claims under Section 1 of the Sherman Act generally involve proof of four elements, of which market power is normally one; this is the key aspect that takes it out of traditional per se analysis: (1) two separate products or services are involved; (2) the sale or agreement to sell one product or service is conditioned on the purchase of another; (3) the seller has sufficient economic power in the market for this tying product to enable it to restrain trade in the market for the tied product; and (4) a not insubstantial amount of interstate commerce in the tied product is affected.[12]

Northern Pacific notwithstanding, later cases made it clear that, outside the patent context, tying was only unlawful if the defendant had 'market power' in the market for the tying product. As described in *Fortner II*,[13] this requirement of 'market power' necessitated an inquiry into 'whether the seller has the power, within the market for the tying product, to raise prices or to require purchasers to accept burdensome terms that could not be exacted in a completely competitive market'. In *Jefferson Parish*,[14] involving a requirement that patients of a hospital use a particular anesthesiology service firm, the Court stated:[15]

> [T]he essential characteristic of an invalid tying arrangement lies in the seller's exploitation of its control over the tying product to force the buyer into the purchase of a tied product that the buyer either did not want at all, or might have preferred to purchase elsewhere on different terms. When such 'forcing' is present, competition on the merits in the market for the tied item is restrained and the Sherman Act is violated.

---

presumed to be unreasonable and therefore illegal without elaborate inquiry as to the precise harm they have caused or the business excuse for their use'. At that time, the Court considered tying to be one of them, finding that Northern Pacific's tie of land leases to use of its shipping was illegal because Northern Pacific's landholdings gave it 'sufficient economic power to impose an appreciable restraint on free competition in the tied product' (*ibid.*, at 11).

[11] Sullivan, Lawrence A. and Warren S. Grimes (2000), *The Law of Antitrust: An Integrated Handbook*, St. Paul, MN: West, § 7.1, p. 383.

[12] ABA Section of Antitrust Law (2002), *Antitrust Law Developments*, 5th ed., Chicago: ABA, Vol. 1, pp. 175, 179 with note 997.

[13] *United States Steel Corp. v. Fortner Enterprises, Inc.*, 429 U.S. 610, at 620, 97 S.Ct. 861, 51 L.Ed.2d 80 (1977) ('*Fortner II*').

[14] *Jefferson Parish Hospital District No. 2 v. Hyde*, 466 U.S. 2, at 16, 104 S.Ct. 1551, 80 L.Ed.2d 2 (1984).

[15] *Ibid.*, 466 U.S. 2, at 12.

The Court in *Jefferson Parish* found that a 30 percent market share was insufficient in that case to show market power, and lower courts subsequently have been reluctant to condemn tying arrangements where the defendant's market share is under 30 percent.[16] The market-power requirement was reaffirmed by the Court in *Kodak*,[17] where it held that tying 'violates § 1 of the Sherman Act if the seller has "appreciable economic power" in the tying product market and if the arrangement affects a substantial volume of commerce in the tied market'.

In *Illinois Tool Works*, the first, second, and fourth elements of a tying arrangement were clearly present. The arrangement was clearly a classic tying arrangement, as found by the Court of Appeals: 'We thus have an explicit tying agreement conditioning the sale of a patented product (the printhead covered by the '226 patent (and possibly other patents as well)) on the sale of an unpatented one (the ink)'.[18] Independent Ink's *prima facie* case thus turned on a showing of market power, which was provided by the presumption previously recognized by the Supreme Court as stemming from the patented product in its decisions in *International Salt*[19] and *Loew's*,[20] as noted in section 3 *infra*.

The case was presented by Independent Ink purely as a claim that this arrangement violated Section 1 of the Sherman Act; there was no parallel claim of violation of Section 3 of the Clayton Act.[21] Nonetheless, the Clayton Act of 1914 arguably has an important place in the development of tying doctrine involving patented products because of its relationship to the judgment of the Supreme Court in *Henry v. A.B. Dick Co.*[22]

2.2 *Patents and tying: the patent misuse doctrine*

The first case to come to the Supreme Court involving tying and patents, *Henry v. A.B. Dick Co.*, although not an antitrust case, was remarkably similar to *Illinois Tool Works* in that it involved the licence of a patented mimeograph

---

16 See Hovenkamp, Herbert (1999), *Federal Antitrust Policy: The Law of Competition and Its Practice*, 2nd ed., St. Paul, Minn.: Thompson West, § 10.3, at p. 397 with note 19 (collecting cases).

17 *Eastman Kodak Co. v. Image Technical Services*, 504 U.S. 451, at 462, 112 S.Ct. 2072, 119 L.Ed.2d 265 (1992).

18 396 F.3d 1342, at 1345 (Fed. Cir. 2005).

19 *International Salt Co. v. United States*, 332 U.S. 392 (1947).

20 *United States v. Loew's, Inc.*, 371 U.S. 38 (1962).

21 396 F.3d 1342, at 1346, note 4. See also ABA Section of Antitrust Law, *supra* note 12, p. 179 with note 997 (noting that courts apply similar standards in tying cases under the Sherman and Clayton Acts). However, the Clayton Act only applies to ties in goods or merchandise, not to ties in services.

22 224 US 1 (1912).

machine for use 'only with the stencil paper, ink and other Supplies' made by the plaintiff.[23] The defendant in that case was found subject to contributory patent infringement liability for selling third-party ink for use in the mimeograph machine, even though the dissenting justices argued that such tying violated antitrust policy.[24] In 1914, partly in response to this decision, Congress enacted Section 3 of the Clayton Act.[25] Section 3 makes it unlawful 'to lease or make a sale or contract for sale of goods . . ., whether patented or unpatented' on the condition that the purchaser shall not use the goods of a competitor where the condition may substantially lessen competition or tend to create a monopoly.[26]

Congress intended Section 3 to overrule the *A.B. Dick* decision and to prohibit sales of patented products conditioned on the sale of other separate goods.[27] The Supreme Court promptly applied this congressional policy only three years later in *Motion Picture Patents Co. v. Universal Film Management Co.*[28] There the Court considered whether a company could license a patented film projection machine on the condition that it be used solely with the company's films. The Court expressly overruled *A.B. Dick* and refused to enforce this requirements tie in light of the 'persuasive expression of public policy' in Section 3 of the Clayton Act.[29]

The ruling of non-infringement in *Motion Picture Patents* ultimately led to the formulation of the patent-misuse defence, in which a court declines to enforce the patent when it has been used or is attempted to be used to extend the patent monopoly (distinct from an *antitrust* monopoly) beyond its proper scope. It is generally considered that the seminal case laying down the patent-misuse (or abuse) doctrine is *Morton Salt Co. v. G.S. Suppiger Co.*,[30] in which the Court ruled, not that Morton Salt violated the Clayton Act by selling its salt injection machines on condition that only its salt be used in the machines, but that a court of equity should not enforce Morton Salt's patent monopoly when the patent was used as the effective means of restraining competition in the

---

23 224 US 1, at 11 (1912).

24 *Ibid.*, at 29–36.

25 See Statement of US Senator Walsh (1978), in Earl W. Kintner (ed.), *The Legislative History of The Federal Antitrust Laws and Related Statutes*, New York, NY: C. Boardman, Vol. 3, pp. 2129 *et seq.* (introducing legislation in order to prevent the imposition of tying arrangements like the one upheld in *Henry v. A.B. Dick Co.*, 224 U.S. 1, 35 (1912)).

26 15 USC § 14.

27 Kramer, V.H. (1985), 'The Supreme Court and Tying Arrangements: Antitrust as History', *Minn. L. Rev.*, **69**, 1013, at 1023.

28 243 US 502 (1917).

29 *Ibid.*, at 516–18.

30 314 U.S. 488 (1942).

sale of an unpatented article.[31] The Court held that a court in equity should not protect a patent from infringement until the actions restraining competition with the patentee's sale of an unpatented product had been abandoned and 'the consequences of the misuse of the patent have been dissipated'.[32] The Court stated:[33]

> The grant to the inventor of the special privilege of a patent monopoly carries out a public policy adopted by the Constitution and laws of the United States, 'to promote the Progress of Science and useful Arts, by securing for limited Times to . . . Inventors the exclusive Right . . .' to their 'new and useful' inventions. But the public policy which includes inventions within the granted monopoly excludes from it all that is not embraced in the invention. It equally forbids the use of the patent to secure an exclusive right or limited monopoly not granted by the Patent Office and which it is contrary to public policy to grant.

Patent misuse 'is an affirmative defense to an accusation of patent infringement, the successful assertion of which requires that the alleged infringer show that the patentee has impermissibly broadened the "physical or temporal scope" of the patent grant with anticompetitive effect'.[34] The concept of patent misuse thus arose to restrain practices that did not in themselves violate any law, but that drew anti-competitive strength from the patent right, and thus were deemed to be contrary to public policy. The policy purpose was to prevent a patentee from using the patent to obtain market benefit beyond that which inheres in the statutory patent right.[35] Two types of conduct that comprise patent misuse are charging royalties after the expiry of the patent, and using a patented product having market power to require the purchase of unpatented goods or supplies.[36] The patent-misuse defence has never been fully codified, although it was limited in the 1952 Patent Act, 35 USCA § 271(d).

The market power requirement stems from the 1988 Patent Misuse Reform Act in which Congress adopted a new version of the statute narrowing the patent-misuse defence. The current version of the statute, 35 USCA § 271(d), reads:

---

31 *Ibid.*, at 490.

32 *Ibid.*, at 493.

33 *Ibid.*, at 492 (citation omitted).

34 *Virginia Panel Corp. v. MAC Panel Co.*, 133 F.3d 860, at 868 (Fed. Cir. 1997) (citations omitted).

35 *Mallinckrodt, Inc. v. Medipart, Inc.*, 976 F.2d 700, at 704 (Fed. Cir. 1992).

36 *Braun Medical, Inc. v. Abbott Laboratories*, 124 F.3d 1419, at 1426 (Fed. Cir. 1997).

> No patent owner otherwise entitled to relief for infringement or contributory infringement of a patent shall be denied relief or deemed guilty of misuse or illegal extension of the patent right by reason of his having done one or more of the following: (1) derived revenue from acts which if performed by another without his consent would constitute contributory infringement of the patent; (2) licensed or authorized another to perform acts which if performed without his consent would constitute contributory infringement of the patent; (3) sought to enforce his patent rights against infringement or contributory infringement; (4) refused to license or use any rights to the patent; or *(5) conditioned the license of any rights to the patent or the sale of the patented product on the acquisition of a license to rights in another patent or purchase of a separate product, unless, in view of the circumstances, the patent owner has market power in the relevant market for the patent or patented product on which the license or sale is conditioned.*[37]

It was this provision, Section 271(d)(5), on which the Supreme Court relied in part in *Illinois Tool Works* in concluding that since Congress had required a showing of market power in the tying product market for purposes of establishing patent misuse, market power should not be presumed for purposes of antitrust tying violations. Until the Patent Misuse Reform Act, market power had not been required to establish patent misuse, and the amended statute had arguably created a divergence in the market-power requirements for patent misuse and tying violations involving patented products.[38] The Court noted that '[w]hile the 1988 amendment does not expressly refer to the antitrust laws, it certainly invites a reappraisal of the *per se* rule announced in *International Salt*'.[39]

2.3 *Unnatural unions?* International Salt *and* Loew's

As noted above, the early cases involving patented products and tying were patent infringement actions in which the anti-competitive consequences thought to derive from such requirements ties were assessed by reference to the public policy in favour of competition found in the antitrust laws, but there was no actual determination that such ties violated any particular antitrust law. Rather, it was simply ruled that the patent could not be enforced. This changed in the *International Salt*[40] case under Section 1 of the Sherman Act where the

---

37 Emphasis added.

38 One could also argue that it was the Court's decisions in *Fortner II* and *Jefferson Parish* that had created the divergence in antitrust tying law, and Congress was intending to resolve it. In either case, the judgment in *Illinois Tool Works* removed any remaining differences by treating all tying arrangements as requiring a showing of market power rather than allowing the presumption to arise from the use of a patented product.

39 126 S.Ct. 1281, at 1290 *et seq.* (2006).

40 *International Salt Co. v. United States*, 332 U.S. 392 (1947).

defendant held patents over 'machines for utilization of salt products'.[41] The machines were leased on the condition that the lessee purchase from the defendant 'all unpatented salt and salt tablets consumed in the leased machines'.[42] The Supreme Court held that this arrangement violated the Sherman Act, holding that 'the patents confer no right to restrain use of, or trade in, unpatented salt'.[43] The Court found that by tying the lease of machines to the purchase of salt, and 'contracting to close this market for salt against competition, [the defendant] engaged in a restraint of trade for which its patents afford no immunity from the antitrust laws'.[44]

The Court made no inquiry of the defendant's market power, finding that 'the admitted facts left no genuine issue. . . . [T]he tendency of the [patent tying] arrangement to accomplishment of monopoly seems obvious'.[45] Justice O'Connor, in her concurring opinion in *Jefferson Parish*, identified *International Salt* as the source of the Court's presumption-of-market-power rule in antitrust cases and suggested that the doctrine was borrowed from the patent-misuse cases.[46] In fact, the Court in *Illinois Tool Works* seemed to give more than usual deference to the position of the Justice Department in its Intellectual Property Guidelines, perhaps because it represented a change in position from that of the Justice Department in *International Salt*, in which the presumption was expressly sought by the Justice Department.[47]

In *United States v. Loew's, Inc.*,[48] relying on *International Salt*, the Court made clear that, where the tying product is patented or copyrighted, market power may be presumed rather than proven. *Loew's* involved the tying of less popular films to popular copyrighted films by movie distributors in their

---

41 *Ibid.*, at 394.

42 *Ibid.* As noted, *infra*, the direction of the borrowing suggested by Justice O'Connor was in fact incorrect.

43 *Ibid.*, at 395 *et seq.*

44 *Ibid.*, at 396.

45 *Ibid.*

46 *Jefferson Parish Hospital District No. 2 v. Hyde*, 466 U.S. 2, 37 *et seq.*, with note 7 (O'Connor, J., concurring). The Court in *Illinois Tool Works* (547 U.S. 28, at pp. 38–9) agreed: 'The presumption that a patent confers market power migrated from patent law to antitrust law in *International Salt Co. v. United States*, 332 U.S. 392, 68 S.Ct. 12, 92 L.Ed. 20 (1947)'. Earlier cases under the Clayton Act, such as *International Business Machines Corp. v. United States*, 298 U.S. 131 (1936), found tying violations but did not involve a presumption of market power.

47 *Ibid.* The US IP Antitrust Guidelines state that the federal antitrust enforcement agencies 'will not presume that a patent, copyright, or trade secret necessarily confers market power upon its owner', even in tying cases, see Department of Justice and the Federal Trade Commission (1995), *Antitrust Guidelines for the Licensing of Intellectual Property*, sections 2.2 and 5.3.

48 371 U.S. 38, 83 S.Ct. 97, 9 L.Ed.2d 11 (1962).

licences to television stations. The Court stated that in tying cases not involving intellectual property the 'standard of illegality is that the seller must have sufficient economic power with respect to the tying product to appreciably restrain free competition in the market for the tied product'.[49] However, '[t]he requisite economic power is presumed when the tying product is patented or copyrighted'.[50]

The *Loew's* Court confirmed that patent tying was a distinct doctrine when it noted the defendants' argument 'that their behavior is not to be judged by the principle of the patent cases . . ., but by the general principles which govern the validity of tying arrangements of non-patented products'.[51] The *Loew's* Court also stated that it need not inquire into whether the distributors had market power. '[T]he mere presence of competing substitutes for the tying product . . . is insufficient to destroy the legal, and indeed the economic, distinctiveness of the copyrighted product'. The subsequent Supreme Court cases that have required proof of market power in tying cases not involving intellectual property have consistently reaffirmed the holdings of *International Salt* and *Loew's* that no proof of market power was necessary in patent or copyright tying cases. The *Fortner II* Court in 1977 expressly restated the presumption of market power in cases of patent tying, stating that 'the statutory grant of a patent monopoly in [*International Salt*] . . . represented tying products . . . sufficiently unique to give rise to a presumption of economic power'.[52] Likewise, the *Jefferson Parish* Court in 1984 stated that 'if the Government has granted the seller a patent or similar monopoly over a product, it is fair to presume that the inability to buy the product elsewhere gives the seller market power'.[53]

From the time of the decisions of the Supreme Court in *Motion Pictures Patents Co.* (1917) and *United Shoe Machinery Corp. v. United States*[54] (1922) (decided under the Clayton Act), there existed a convergent or at least consistent rule in patent law and antitrust law that use of patented products in tying unpatented products resulted in denial of patent protection (for example, non-infringement or patent misuse) and liability under the antitrust laws. The presumption of market power in antitrust cases existed since at least *International Salt* (1947). This consistency (or 'intertwining') began to unravel in 1988 when Congress added the requirement of a showing of market power to the law of patent misuse. Antitrust liability under the presumption

49 *Ibid.*, at 45.
50 *Ibid.*
51 *Ibid.*, at 48.
52 429 U.S. 610, at 619 (1977).
53 466 U.S. 2, at 16 (1984).
54 258 U.S. 451 (1922) (tying shoe manufacturing machines to supplies).

persisted until the Court's 2006 reexamination of the presumption in *Illinois Tool Works*.

2.4 *Rethinking the convergence: the Patent Reform Act of 1988 and* Illinois Tool Works

The Court in *Illinois Tool Works* quickly dismissed its prior antitrust case law and completed the 'untwining' of patent-misuse and antitrust jurisprudence that the Court itself had carried out in *International Salt*. Relying heavily on the 1988 patent statute amendment, the Court noted that:[55]

> After considering the congressional judgment reflected in the 1988 amendment, we conclude that tying arrangements involving patented products should be evaluated under the standards applied in cases like *Fortner II* and *Jefferson Parish* rather than under the *per se* rule applied in *Morton Salt* [sic] and *Loew's*. While some such arrangements are still unlawful, such as those that are the product of a true monopoly or a marketwide conspiracy, see, for example, *United States v. Paramount Pictures, Inc.*, 334 U.S. 131, 145–146 (1948), that conclusion must be supported by proof of power in the relevant market rather than by a mere presumption thereof.

In addition to the congressional amendment, the Court at various times referred to the altered position of the enforcement agencies (DOJ and FTC), the consensus of academic opinion on the insupportability of the presumption, and the Court's own shift in its views of the reprehensibility of tying arrangements in general over nearly the last 30 years since *Fortner II*. Not mentioned, but doubtless underlying the shift in a broader sense, is the Court's watershed judgment in *G.T.E. Sylvania* concerning vertical restrictions, in which the Court famously noted:[56]

> Accordingly, we conclude that the *per se* rule in *Schwinn* must be overruled. In so holding we do not foreclose the possibility that particular applications of vertical restrictions might justify *per se* prohibition under *Northern Pac. R. Co.* But we do make clear that *departure from the rule-of-reason standard must be based upon demonstrable economic effect* rather than – as in *Schwinn* – upon formalistic line drawing. . . . When anticompetitive effects are shown to result from particular vertical restrictions they can be adequately policed *under the rule of reason, the standard traditionally applied for the majority of anticompetitive practices* challenged under § 1 of the [Sherman] Act.

One way to view the Court's ruling in *Illinois Tool Works* is that the Court is stripping away a remaining vestige of antitrust formalism left hanging on

---

55 126 S.Ct. 1281, at 1291 (2006).

56 *Continental T.V., Inc. v. G.T.E. Sylvania, Inc.*, 433 U.S. 36, at 58 (1977) (emphasis added).

since *Sylvania*, and this was simply a matter of tidying up leftover chores. One could draw on the references in *Sylvania* to the property-based reasoning in *Schwinn* (which *Sylvania* overruled) and consider that it was inevitable that the patent power-market power presumption would fall given the Court's new emphasis on 'demonstrable economic effect'. Under this view, it seems obvious that a presumption of market power from patents (for example, a 'formalistic line-drawing' rather than a 'demonstrable economic effect') would be doomed in light of the voluminous antitrust literature and jurisprudence indicating that there was no necessary correlation between the scope of a patent monopoly and the definition of a product market (and therefore market power) in the antitrust sense. Moreover, since economic studies had indicated that a relatively small proportion of patents generate much economic value, it seemed obvious that relatively few could generate true market power.[57] The economic argument that tying generally (without regard to patent tying) often produces economic efficiencies also mitigates against the notion that use of patented products as tying products should be presumed unlawful. Therefore, from a purely factual standpoint (since the majority of patents did not convey market power), it could be (and frequently was) argued that the patent power-market power presumption was therefore insupportable. Hence, the Court in *Illinois Tool Works* abandoned the presumption of market power it had itself created and in the view of many correctly held that market power had to be demonstrated in order to make out a *prima facie* tying violation under Section 1 of the Sherman Act.

3 Beyond convergence, or rethinking the rethinking: reflections on IP and market power, antitrust and innovation

Put in historical perspective, *Illinois Tool Works* arguably represents the latest IP upswing in the vicissitudes of the tension between antitrust and intellectual property.[58] In the early twentieth century, patents were seemingly transcendent, as exemplified in the *A.B. Dick* case discussed previously,[59] in which the

---

57 Independent Ink argued with considerable support that patents involved in litigation because they are used to impose ties, as opposed to the universe of patents, do in fact confer market power, and therefore the presumption should be retained although considered rebuttable. However, the Court did not accept this view. An 'involved in litigation' test in practice would have amounted to retaining the per se rule, since the issue would not arise unless the patent were involved in litigation.

58 For example, *SCM Corp. v. Xerox Corp.*, 645 F.2d 1195, 1203 (2d Cir. 1981): 'The conflict between the antitrust and patent laws arises in the methods they embrace that were designed to achieve reciprocal goals. While the antitrust laws proscribe unreasonable restraints of competition, the patent laws reward the inventor with a temporary monopoly that insulates him from competitive exploitation of his patented art.'

59 See section 2.2 *supra*.

Supreme Court not only permitted the tying of unpatented ink to patented mimeograph machines but recognized contributory infringement liability for those who sold the ink! Following the passage of the Clayton Act, this example of patent supremacy was overruled as noted in *Motion Picture Patents Co. v. Universal Film Mfg. Co.*,[60] only to see what is perhaps the subsequent historical high-water mark of patent protection in the 1926 *General Electric* case,[61] in which the Supreme Court permitted patentees to fix the product price charged by competing licensees who sold the patented good in competition with the patentee.

Then, in the 1930s, the Court began to see patent and other IP rights as inherently anti-competitive, rendering decisions that found patent misuse[62] or presumed market power even in cases where there almost certainly was none, and giving rise to the market power presumption now eliminated by the Supreme Court in *Illinois Tool Works*.[63] Following the *Sylvania* case, and the emphasis of the Court on demonstrable economic effect, the per se rules have been trimmed back, including the treatment of tying in *Fortner II* and *Jefferson Parish*, and the once-famous 'Nine no-nos' of patent licensing[64] are now largely judged under the rule of reason.[65] This IP up-swing in the cycle followed the general rise of Chicago School economics. As Hovenkamp notes:[66]

---

60 243 U.S. 502 (1917). See also at note 28 *supra*.

61 *United States v. General Electric Co.*, 272 U.S. 476 (1926).

62 This doctrine arguably began in *Carbice Corp. of Am. v. American Patents Dev. Corp.*, 283 US 27, at 29 (1931), in which the Court refused to enforce an action for contributory infringement against one who sold dry ice to licensees of the patentee's patented ice box, when its licence required licensees to purchase their ice exclusively from the patentee. The Court considered this an attempt to 'extend its monopoly' to cover unpatented supplies.

63 See also *International Salt Co. v. United States*, 332 U.S. 392 (1947); *Mercoid Corp. v. Mid-Continent Inv. Co.*, 320 U.S. 661, at 669 (1944) (finding patent misuse when the patentee bundled the different elements in a combination patent); *Morton Salt Co. v. G.S. Suppiger Co.*, 314 U.S. 488 (1942); *B.B. Chem. Co. v. Ellis*, 314 US 495, at 498 (1942) (patentee who tied shoe insole material to its patented insole machine could not bring infringement action); *Leitch Mfg. Co. v. Barber Co.*, 302 U.S. 458, at 463 (1938) (condemning tying even when the tied element was an essential part of the patented process); *International Business Mach. Corp. (IBM) v. United States*, 298 U.S. 131 (1936) (tying of IBM's computing machines to its paper punch cards); *United States v. Paramount Pictures*, 334 U.S. 131, at 156–9 (1948) (condemning block-booking of feature films as enlarging 'the monopoly of the copyright'); and *United States v. Loew's*, 371 U.S. 38 (1962) (block-booking of television shows) (overruled in *Illinois Tool Works*).

64 See Jones, Clifford A. (1982), 'Antitrust and Patent Licensing Problems: Are the Nine "No-Nos" the Nine "Maybes"?', *Okla. Bar J.*, **53**, 1568.

65 See US IP Antitrust Guidelines, *supra* note 47.

66 Hovenkamp, Herbert J. (2005), 'United States Antitrust Policy in an Age of

> That era was quite properly brought to a close, mainly as a result of Chicago School writings that exploded the leverage theory of patents, and more general writings that began to treat patent rights as simply a species of property, with the attendant power to exclude, rather than as a species of monopoly. One result is that antitrust tribunals today are quite properly far more tolerant of IP rights today than they were from the 1930s through the 1960s, and antitrust claims in IP markets have become more difficult to prove. Now the question is whether [we] are in danger of going too far.

Hovenkamp suggests that statutory amendments in the US such as the Patent Misuse Reform Act of 1988, the Digital Millennium Copyright Act and the Sonny Bono Copyright Extension Act have generally expanded IP rights at the expense of antitrust and other rules.[67] He also suggests that such amendments are the product of interest-group lobbying rather than balanced assessments of appropriate antitrust and intellectual property policies.[68] While not suggesting that the purpose of antitrust is to regulate political markets and counselling that antitrust should not return to the market power presumptions of the past, Hovenkamp posits the following question of great interest:[69]

> How should antitrust respond to a regime in which the intellectual property laws very likely grant more than the optimal amount of protection and where the ongoing amendment process reflects significant capture by special interests? The harmful results include, at the least, costly impediments to innovation, the high licensing and transaction costs of negotiating through the thicket of IP rights, leading to underuse of innovations. On top of all of this is higher consumer prices.[70]

This question has prompted me to offer the following observations concerning certain approaches that might help to maintain or restore balance[71]

IP Expansion', Berkeley Center for Law and Technology, Law & Technology Scholarship, Paper 2, http://repositories.cdlib.org/bclt/lts/2, accessed 4 November 2007, p. 21.

[67] *Ibid.*, at 14.

[68] *Ibid.*, at 6–14.

[69] *Ibid.*, at 21.

[70] Citations omitted.

[71] To a certain type of mind, regrettably including the author's, the balance idea calls to mind certain parallels in the internationally famous generational pop-culture movie saga, George Lucas's Star Wars®, which at last count has reached six installments. Not having subtitled this essay 'Everything I Need to Know I Learned in Star Wars', I will spare the reader the details. For those who have been on the wrong planet since the original 1977 episode (is it only a coincidence Star Wars was released the same year as *Sylvania* and *Fortner II*?), suffice it to say, the saga tells the story, *inter alia*, of the struggle between the 'evil' Sith and the 'good' Jedi for control of freedom throughout the galaxy. It is a cycle of damnation and redemption, in which we follow the prophecy of Anakin Skywalker as the 'Chosen One', the one who will bring balance to 'the Force', but who instead betrays his Jedi ideals and training to turn to the

between antitrust and intellectual property rights where they seem to be in tension if not in conflict. As Drexl has noted, 'IP laws and competition law share the same economic rationale. They are both crucial for the establishment of competitive and innovative market conditions. These complementarities justify the application of competition law analysis with the objective of defining the limits of IP protection.'[72] It is clear that IP-antitrust conflicts cannot be resolved by simplistic rules applied in the past and ranging from 'the patent always wins' to 'antitrust always wins'. To this extent, *Illinois Tool Works* may be helpful in its result if not in its precise reasoning.

In reflecting on the decisional rationales advanced by the Court in *Illinois Tool Works*, it is submitted that they are unconvincing, and the Court may have got it wrong on some of its reasoning. In fact, the Court uses the historical intertwining of patent misuse and antitrust tying doctrines as a lever to attack the legal and policy underpinnings of the patent power equals market power presumption. I submit that the approach followed by the Court lacks legitimacy since it seizes upon one aspect of congressional policy (the Patent Misuse Reform Act of 1988) in the patent field and uses it to justify changing the law in the antitrust field. While on its face it seems logical to assert that since market power is now required for patent misuse, and if the market power presumption in antitrust was borrowed from the patent-misuse cases, therefore market power should be required to be demonstrated in antitrust cases, this suffers from the same conflation of antitrust and patent law principles that the Court criticizes. If it was an error to import patent-misuse doctrines into antitrust analysis in the first place, it must equally be an error to alter settled (or at least venerable) antitrust doctrine based on a congressional change to patent-misuse law. The Court's rationale fails to justify this approach.

A more careful reading of the history of the Sherman Act and the Clayton Act would not merely rely on Justice O'Connor's concurring opinion in *Jefferson Parish*, as the Court's opinion seemingly does in *Illinois Tool Works*, but would ask how the rule against tying unpatented supplies to

---

Dark Side of the Force as Darth Vader, all but destroying the Jedi, only to be redeemed in the next generation by his son Luke, who turns his father away from the Dark Side, destroys the evil Sith Lord Darth Sidious, and makes possible the return of the Jedi. If one assigns antitrust the role of the Jedi and IP the role of the Sith, it is possible to conceptualize the present situation as one where the IP 'Sith' are ascendant and it remains for scholars to find a way to turn back the cycle, restore balance, and enable the return of the antitrust 'Jedi'.

72 Drexl, Josef (2005), 'The Critical Role of Competition Law in Preserving Public Goods in Conflict with Intellectual Property Rights', in Maskus, Keith E. and Jerome H. Reichman (eds), *International Public Goods and Transfer of Technology Under a Globalized Intellectual Property Regime*, Cambridge: Cambridge University Press, p. 709, at 724.

patented goods came to be part of the patent-misuse cases. The answer, as is demonstrated above,[73] is that in the antitrust field, the Clayton Act overruled the Supreme Court's pro-patent ruling in *A.B. Dick*, resulting in the overruling of that decision by the Supreme Court in *Motion Picture Patents*. When the Supreme Court *subsequently* developed the doctrine of patent misuse, it applied the anti-tying rationale of the Clayton Act. Hence Justice O'Connor in *Jefferson Parish* and the Court in *Illinois Tool Works* have it just backwards: the market-power presumption was not borrowed from patent misuse; patent misuse borrowed antitrust policy as expressed in the Clayton Act, against tying patented goods to unpatented supplies. Thus, when the Court justifies reexamining the patent power-market power presumption by reference to the 1988 statute, the Court's stated basis for changing the antitrust law is unsatisfactory.[74]

The true rationale for the Court's decision must be that it now considers the presumption rule to be in error. Indeed, the Court places great weight on academic commentary supporting the notion that most patents do not in fact confer market power. While one must acknowledge the force of the factual argument that relatively few patents confer market power in the antitrust sense, and therefore there should be no presumption of market power, the Court's uncritical acceptance of this position is troublesome for reasons not discussed in the Court's judgment.

It should be recalled that the basic tension between patent law (or IP law more generally) and antitrust law derives from the fact that '[o]n the one hand, the IP laws create a right to exclude. On the other, antitrust regularly condemns practices because they exclude firms from markets.'[75] The classic justification for the right to exclude is of course the incentive given the inventor to invent under the constitutional power 'To promote the Progress of Science and useful Arts, by securing for limited Times to Authors and Inventors the exclusive Right to their respective Writings and Discoveries'.[76] With this in mind, one has to consider the factual argument that most patents have little value and convey little or no market power in a different light: if this is the case, does the patent system in fact achieve its purpose? In other words, should patents receive any substantial deference if the system is not efficient or effective?

---

73 See section 2.2 *supra*.

74 The Court's reference to US IP Antitrust Guidelines as expressions of enforcement policy is also unconvincing. Enforcement policy has nothing to do with the correct interpretation of the law. This is a purely makeweight argument.

75 Hovenkamp, *supra* note 66, at 1.

76 Article I § 8 of the US Constitution.

While the notion that the patent system creates incentives for invention and promotes the 'Progress of Science and useful Arts' seems intuitively correct, one might well say the same about the notion that expanding the patent monopoly to unpatented goods adversely affects competition. Yet, the Court now after *Illinois Tool Works* demands proof of market power, although no patentee is required to prove in court that her patent in fact is useful or valuable in order to recover damages or an injunction for patent infringement. The empirical data do seem to support the view that a large percentage of patents produce little or no economic value. One study found that 'at any given time, over about 95 percent of patents are unlicensed and over about 97 percent are generating no royalties'.[77] Another estimate was that 'eighty percent to ninety percent of patents never create any monetary return for the patent holder'.[78] Critics of the presumption of market power concluded from this research that patents do not produce market power in most cases; one might just as strongly conclude that (1) patents are an ineffective or inefficient method of promoting innovation, and (2) too many patents are being issued. What are the implications of these conclusions?

The truth is, we know very little about the relationship between patent rules and innovation amounting to much more than intuition. If we applied the same rigour of economic and legal analysis to patent law that the Court routinely applies in antitrust cases, the chances are the patent rules would fail even more often than do intuitional notions about antitrust and competition. Hovenkamp identifies the 'deep uncertainty about the optimal amount and scope of IP protection' as a significant source of the conflict or tension between antitrust and IP law.[79] Courts have consistently been unable to identify anything approaching a normative measure of the scope of appropriate patent exploitation.[80] We do not know the answers to such important questions as 'What is

---

77 Vermont, S. (2002), 'The Economics of Patent Litigation', in B. Berman (ed.), *From Ideas to Assets: Investing Wisely in Intellectual Property*, p. 327, at 332.

78 Feldman, R. (2003), 'The Insufficiency of Antitrust Analysis for Patent Misuse', *Hastings L.J.*, **55**, 399, at 437. See also Rapp, Richard T. and Lauren J. Stiroh (2002), 'Standard Setting and Market Power', Joint Hearings of the United States Department of Justice and the Federal Trade Commission, 18 April 2002, http://www.ftc.gov/opp/intellect/020418rappstiroh.pdf, accessed 4 November 2007, p. 1: 'Empirical research by Scherer, Pakes, Schankerman, Lanjouw and others has established and confirmed a useful generalization: that the distribution of patent values is skewed; most patents (and patented inventions) are worth very little and only a few have considerable value'.

79 Hovenkamp, *supra*, note 66, at 3.

80 See Kaplow, L. (1984), 'The Patent-Antitrust Intersection: A Reappraisal', *Harv. L. Rev.*, **97**, 1813, at 1848: 'In framing each of these tests, the Court seems to assume that there exists some transcendent notion of what constitutes "normal" or

the optimal length of time for patent or copyright protection? What is the appropriate scope of patent claims? When is a new collection of technologies or methods patentable? and – perhaps most fundamentally of all – what is the proper balance between the protection of new ideas and the public licence innovators must have to build on the innovations of their predecessors?'[81] Indeed, we do not even know that patents are necessary to promote technological innovation at all.[82]

While the reasoning of the Supreme Court in *Illinois Tool Works* is flawed in several respects, given the apparent fact that most patents do not confer market power, it does seem inappropriate to recognize a presumption of market power stemming from the use of patents in tying arrangements, so long as the law continues to recognize the illegality of tying arrangements where market power is shown in fact to exist. On the other hand, the abandonment of the presumption ought not to be taken as a sign that tying arrangements involving patents are per se legal. Moreover, if patent and IP rights are to be treated with no more suspicion than other forms of property in an antitrust context, then it necessarily follows that the existence of such rights is entitled to no more deference than other types of property.[83] Accordingly, courts should not hesitate, where market power is present and anti-competitive effects are demonstrated, to apply remedies without regard to the IP character of the property involved. Compulsory licensing or other disclosure remedies[84] should not be withheld merely because IP rights are involved. The other side of the coin

"proper" patent exploitation. Moreover, patent-antitrust doctrine is noted for its indeterminacy and its frequent shifts in direction. These circumstances suggest that, in reality, courts lack any such uniform conception of the appropriate scope of a patent.'

[81] Hovenkamp, *supra* note 66, at 4.

[82] See Boldrin, Michele K. and David K. Levine (2003), 'Perfectly Competitive Innovation', http://www.dklevine.com/papers/pci23.pdf, accessed 4 November 2007.

[83] Hovenkamp, *supra* note 66, at 27: 'One corollary of the principle that an IP right is simply property is that no special deference is due to the IP laws when courts fashion remedies for proven antitrust violations. For example, ordering compulsory licensing for a proven antitrust violation is no different than fining a firm or ordering divestiture of a plant. While we do not want to deter innovation, we do want to deter antitrust violations either [*sic*]. While the Patent Act provides that a refusal to license is not patent misuse, that provision has the same status as the common law rule that the owner of real property has no duty to share it. That does not mean, however, that property rights cannot be forfeited for proven violations.' (Citations omitted.)

[84] Cf. the EC Commission ordering Microsoft under Article 82 EC to disclose software interface information as a remedy for abuse of dominant position. See European Commission of 24 March 2004, Case COMP/C-3/37.792 – *Microsoft*, C(2004)900 final = http://ec.europa.eu/comm/competition/antitrust/cases/decisions/37792/en.pdf, accessed 4 November 2007; confirmed by the CFI in Case T-201/04, *Microsoft v. Commission*, [2007] ECR II-0000.

of no presumptions of market power from patents is no presumption of immunity from full application of antitrust principles.[85] Only by truly eliminating all aspects of a double standard for IP rights will balance be brought to the intersections of IP and antitrust. Hence the rethinking of patent power and market power must not stop with the elimination of the vestiges of antitrust formalism. It should include elimination of patent and IP formalism as well.

[85] Recently, the Supreme Court may have begun to apply more rigour to the analysis of patentability, and address directly whether too many patents are being issued. In *KSR International Co. v. Teleflex, Inc.*, 550 U.S. 000 (not yet reported), 127 S.Ct. 1727; 167 L. Ed. 2d 705 (2007), decided 30 April 2007, the Court ruled that the Court of Appeals for the Federal Circuit had too narrowly applied the legal test for when an invention was obvious and therefore non-patentable. This may signal that courts will more carefully scrutinize patents that should not have been granted.

11 Making antitrust and intellectual property policy in the United States: requirements tie-ins and loyalty discounts

Warren S. Grimes

1 Introduction

Competition law and intellectual property (IP) law are at times complementary, at other times rivalrous. Finding the right policy balance is at once a formidable but vital task. At stake is achieving the right flow of IP incentives, a balance that encourages innovation without unduly undermining competition and the very innovation that IP is designed to promote.

This chapter examines how antitrust policy that bears on intellectual property is established and enforced in the United States. It begins by describing the overarching debate concerning the proper reach and interpretation of intellectual property rights. It then describes US agencies and courts that play a major role in establishing competition policy. Finally, it examines two substantive areas, requirements tie-ins and loyalty discounts on strongly branded products, to gain greater perspective on whether the mechanisms for establishing IP-related competition law policy are working well. Because of the strong public-choice bias that favors creation and extension of IP rights, the broader public interest in competition and constraining overly broad IP protection is often under-represented. The interaction between IP and competition law works best when the two US antitrust enforcement agencies, the Antitrust Division of the Department of Justice (DoJ) and the Federal Trade Commission (FTC), are vigorous advocates for competition.

2 The debate concerning the reach of IP rights

The antitrust and intellectual property debate has divided expert opinion in the United States. On one side of the issue are scholars, judges and policy makers who believe that more IP rewards are necessary to maximize beneficial innovation. These commentators generally embrace the view that IP rights are a form of property that entitles the owner to full exploitation of its value.[1]

[1] See Easterbrook, F. (1990), 'Intellectual Property is Still Property', *Harv. J. L. & Pub. Pol'y*, **24**, 108, at 112; Hylton, K.N. and M. Salinger (2001), 'Tying Law &

Higher rewards for IP rights, they argue, will enhance innovation, the primary purpose of IP rights. Conversely, they insist that antitrust enforcement limiting IP rights (such as the proscription on certain tying conduct) will reduce incentives for innovation.

On the other side of the issue are commentators who reject a rigid analogy between IP rights and traditional property.[2] These scholars stress important distinctions between traditional property (such as a plot of land that can be effectively used only by a limited number of people) and the subject matter of an IP right (an invention, a song, or a software program that can be used or enjoyed by an unlimited number of people). These critics point out that no property right can be fully exploited by its owner. Society puts a variety of limitations on a property owner, such as the zoning restrictions limiting the use of land or extensive safety and environmental regulation limiting the use of a motor vehicle. Finally, these critics point to the heavy costs of IP protection that reaches beyond what is necessary to promote innovation.

The underlying premise for the creation of IP rights is that they promote innovation that would not occur in their absence. But IP also generates substantial costs. Lemley has summarized the costs that any IP system imposes on society.[3] Each of these costs becomes an unwarranted burden to the extent that the IP system provides more of an incentive than is needed to encourage an appropriate level of innovation. The costs are: (1) direct harm to competition from the granting of exclusive rights that create static inefficiencies in the form of deadweight and wealth-transfer losses (these deadweight and wealth-transfer losses are reflected in reduced output of the IP-protected product and higher prices paid by consumers); (2) interference with creative efforts of those who do not hold IP rights (harm to dynamic efficiency); (3) rent-seeking behavior generated when IP holders expend resources to protect or extend their IP rights; (4) administrative costs, including the costs of granting IP rights and the publicly supported court costs involved in enforcing IP rights or limiting abusive exercise of IP rights; and (5) non-productive overinvestment in research and development when would-be creators vainly spend resources in pursuit of an IP reward.

Although it is impossible to determine where to set an IP reward to optimize innovation, there are increasing indications in the United States that IP

Policy: A Decision-Theoretic Approach', *Antitrust L.J.*, **61**, 469 (arguing for full exploitation of IP rights in property-law terms). For a more complete list of theorists taking this position, see Lemley, M. (2005), 'Property, Intellectual Property, and Free Riding', *Tex. L. Rev.*, **83**, 1031, at 1035, note 8.

[2] Lemley, *supra* note 1 (at 1035, note 8 with a list of other theorists who criticize the property law analogy); First, H. (2007), 'Controlling the Intellectual Property Grab: Protect Innovation, Not Innovators', *Rutgers L.J.*, **38**, 365.

[3] *Ibid.*, at 1058–64.

rewards are excessive. Holders, or would-be holders, of IP rights have substantial financial incentives to gain, hold, and extend those rights. This creates what is known as a public-choice problem.[4] The strong financial incentives of promoters of IP rights may not be matched by advocates of the public interest in competition and limited exclusivity. Copyright holders were, for example, forceful advocates for the extension of US copyrights for an additional 20 years.[5] These same incentives may lead to excessive applications for IP rights. First has written of an 'IP grab', pointing to examples of frivolous IP grants that will hinder rather than enhance innovation.[6] One such example is the 'one-click' internet sale. Amazon, the patentee, sued to enforce this patent against a rival on-line book seller. The proliferation of these and similar patents may create roadblocks to innovative firms trying to keep up to date with competitive trends.

3 The institutional players that set US antitrust & IP policy

In the United States, the most prominent non-legislative players that determine antitrust policy at its intersection with IP rights are two federal enforcement agencies, the Antitrust Division of the Department of Justice (DoJ) and the Federal Trade Commission (FTC), and two judicial tribunals, the US Supreme Court and the US Court of Appeals for the Federal Circuit.

3.1 The Antitrust Division of the Department of Justice

The DoJ's Antitrust Division is probably the most influential player in setting antitrust policy. It – along with its sister agency, the FTC – establishes guidelines for intellectual property licensing and a number of other central antitrust topics. Agency guidelines are widely cited by attorneys. Although purporting to state only agency policy, in cases involving the intersection of IP and competition law, judges nonetheless are influenced by, and often follow, the guidelines.

The Supreme Court is often guided in its antitrust opinions by the views expressed by the DoJ. Even in private suits not involving the government, the DoJ is frequently invited to file an *amicus* brief stating its views. Thus, in *Illinois Tool Works, Inc. v. Independent Ink, Inc.*,[7] a private suit in which the Court overturned the presumption of market power that had attached to

---

4 For a description of public choice theory, see Farber, D.A. and P.P. Frickey (1987), 'The Jurisprudence of Public Choice', *Tex. L Rev.*, **65**, 873.

5 In 1998, copyright protection was extended an additional 20 years. PL 105–298, 112 Stat. 2827, amending 17 USC § 302.

6 First, *supra* note 2.

7 547 U.S. 28, (2006). The author served as a consultant for Independent Ink during the Supreme Court litigation.

patented tying products, the DoJ's *amicus* brief urged the result that the Court reached. At several points in its opinion, the Court signals its reliance on agency views, including the IP Guidelines governing licensing.[8]

The Antitrust Division does not always convince the Court of the merits of its position (the Division's *amicus* brief in the 1992 *Kodak* case was not heeded).[9] The Division's position nonetheless carries great weight and may sway justices who are uncertain of their position on antitrust issues. For many years, the Antitrust Division championed competition over IP rights. This was certainly the case during the populist era of United States antitrust law. But beginning with the Presidency of Ronald Reagan in 1980, the Division has tended to take the side of IP rights advocates, treating IPRs as a form of property that entitles the owner to fully exploit any uncaptured consumer demand for the patented product. This view is reflected, for example, in the Department's *amicus* brief filed in *Illinois Tool Works*, which takes the position that more IP rewards mean more innovation and that a market power presumption would slow innovation.[10] Thus, in disparaging prior Supreme Court holdings that were hostile to extending a patentee's economic control to unpatented products, the government's brief argues that this 'limited view of the rights conferred by a patent is anachronistic under current law'.[11] Following up on this argument, the brief later states:[12] 'Reducing the patentee's options for efficient exploitation of its patent rights may, in turn, adversely impact incentives to innovate. Moreover, it may deprive consumers of the benefits of efficiency-enhancing practices.'

The Justice Department's *amicus* brief is, however, most remarkable for what it does not say. There is no mention of the substantial literature documenting the anti-competitive effects of the requirements tie, nor is there recognition that such requirements ties have been consistently condemned by the Supreme Court (see section 4 *infra*). There is no mention of the reality that,

8 547 U.S. 28, at 42 *et seq.*

9 *Eastman Kodak Co. v. Image Technical Services, Inc.*, 504 U.S. 451 (1992), Brief for the United States as *Amicus Curiae* Supporting Petitioner, 1991 U.S. S.Ct. Briefs LEXIS 429.

10 The *amicus* brief for the United States, http://www.usdoj.gov/atr/cases/f210500/210544.pdf, accessed 4 November 2007, includes this language (at p. 28):

> Perceived rewards from the efficient exploitation of intellectual property can induce intellectual property owners to invest in research and development, bringing new products to consumers. But conversely, a market power presumption that undermines perceived rewards may constitute a drag on innovation . . . (footnote omitted)

11 *Ibid.*, at 22.

12 *Ibid.*, at 29.

while most patents are of little or no value, litigants very seldom litigate over worthless patents. And while there is ample discussion of the costs to IP holders forced to defend their tying practices, there is no mention of the very substantial harm to competition, to innovation, and to the public treasury that will flow if IP rewards are excessive.

This 'the more the better' view of IP rights was voiced in a 2006 speech by the Deputy Assistant Attorney General of the Antitrust Division.[13] The speech was clothed in the rhetoric of IP as a property right and emphasizes the virtues of fuller exploitation of IP, including the right to exclude and to refuse to deal. Enforcement efforts involving IP-related practices such as licensing were said to be at the bottom of the Division's list of enforcement priorities. The theme of encouraging innovation by removing obstacles to full exploitation of property rights is not new for the Division, but the timing of the speech is noteworthy. At a time when even many patent-holding firms are decrying the excesses of the proliferation of meritless or fraudulently obtained patents, the Division continues to be an advocate not for competition and freedom of action for innovative non-IP holders, but for fuller exploitation of IP rights. As critics of this approach have stressed, one of the costs of excessive IP protection is reduced innovation as the proliferation of IP rights creates a choke hold on the creativity of those who do not hold these rights. Independent Ink, the relatively small but proficient ink producer that sued Illinois Tool Works, was an innovator in its own right as it responded to buyers looking for a more competitively priced alternative to Trident's over-priced ink.

3.2 The Federal Trade Commission

The FTC, like its sister agency, has the opportunity to shape antitrust policy through enforcement choices, through formulation of guidelines, and through speeches by prominent officials. The FTC has, more often than not, adopted a course parallel to that of the Antitrust Division. The FTC joined the Division in issuing the IP Licensing Guidelines in 1995 and also joined in the *Illinois Tool Works amicus* brief filed in 2005. In recent years, when compared with the Antitrust Division, the FTC has been a somewhat more aggressive advocate of competition that may restrain excesses in the IP system. Examples of this more aggressive stance include (1) the FTC's 2003 report documenting the need to balance competition and patent protection;[14] and (2) FTC enforce-

---

[13] Masoudi, Gerald F. (2006), 'Intellectual Property and Competition: Four Principles for Encouraging Innovation', http://www.usdoj.gov/atr/public/speeches/215645.pdf, accessed 4 November 2007.

[14] Federal Trade Commission (2003), 'To Promote Innovation: The Proper Balance of Competition and Patent Law and Policy (2003)', http://www.ftc.gov/os/2003/10/innovation.pdf, accessed 4 November 2007. Although the DoJ participated

ment actions challenging agreements between pharmaceutical patent-holding firms and generic producers.[15]

The FTC's enforcement action against Schering-Plough Corp. generated an adverse court of appeals decision,[16] prompting the agency to seek Supreme Court review. In an unusual action, the Justice Department filed an *amicus* brief with the Court opposing review.[17] The DoJ's influence with the Court was demonstrated when the Court denied the FTC's petition for *certiorari*.[18] The Department's brief follows the recent pattern of reluctance to advocate competition in IP-related disputes.[19]

3.3 The Supreme Court

As the nation's highest court, the Supreme Court establishes the final and binding interpretation of the broad language of the Sherman Act, an act with general language that leaves the Court with discretion that some have compared with the discretion accorded in common-law interpretation. Because the Court has jurisdiction over all questions that come before the federal judiciary, the nine justices tend to be generalists. Their interest on expertise in antitrust law or intellectual property law is uneven. The presence or absence of a particular justice with interest in these subjects can have a major impact on other members of the Court and the development of the law. During his time on the Court, Justice Lewis Powell, for example, had a substantial impact on antitrust jurisprudence, generally steering antitrust law toward a more 'Chicago' or minimalist role in challenging anti-competitive practices.[20] The current Court has several members who have interest or experience in antitrust. Justice Stephen Breyer is an established teacher and scholar

---

in the hearings that gave rise to the report, it has not followed through on an announced intent to produce its own report.

15 For a listing of cases, see FTC Report, 'Overview of FTC Antitrust Actions in Health Care Services and Products', http://www.ftc.gov/bc/0608hcupdate.pdf, accessed 4 November 2007.

16 *Schering-Plough Corp. v. FTC*, 402 F.3d 1056 (11th Cir. 2005).

17 DoJ *Amicus* Brief (2006), http://www.usdoj.gov/atr/cases/f216300/216358.pdf, accessed 4 November 2007.

18 *FTC v. Schering-Plough, Inc.*, 74 USLW 3722 (26 June 2006).

19 Because there was uncertainty about the validity of *Schering-Plough's* patent claims, and because the settlement between *Schering-Plough* and its generic rival ended any litigation on this point, First, *supra* note 2, has expressed disappointment that the DoJ's brief does not acknowledge 'the importance of limiting the ability of holders of patent rights to extract profits beyond the very uncertain scope of their rights'.

20 For a discussion of Justice Powell's role in antitrust cases, see Sullivan, E.T. and R.B. Thompson (2004), 'The Supreme Court and Private Law: The Vanishing Importance of Securities and Antitrust', *Emory L.J.*, **53,** 1571.

in the antitrust and intellectual property areas. Justice John Paul Stevens and Justice Antonin Scalia have strong and often opposing views about the role of antitrust. None of these justices appears to have the same impact in guiding today's Court that Justice Powell exercised during his time on the Court.

The Court's antitrust jurisprudence, as in other areas, is influenced by the tradition of filing concurring and dissenting opinions. These separate opinions have the advantage of allowing individual justices to espouse a particular economic or regulatory philosophy toward antitrust and intellectual property issues. When there is a consensus on the Court, this can sometimes produce meaningful and well-reasoned opinions that are based on coherent economic analysis. But unanimity may also be purchased at the cost of leaving little or no guidance about the *stare decisis* effect of the decision. Yet again, when consensus is not present, the Court may issue very fragmented opinions that also fail to provide meaningful guidance for lower courts or counseling lawyers. Newly appointed Chief Justice John Roberts appears, at least in the short term, to be guiding the Court toward fewer fragmented opinions and more unanimous results. Justice Roberts has publicly expressed the view that unanimous opinions create more stability and clarity in the law.[21] *Illinois Tool Works*, although a unanimous result (as was a second antitrust opinion announced a few days earlier)[22] provides little clarity beyond the proposition that the existence of a tie based on a patent does not establish, per se, the existence of market power.

The *Illinois Tool Works* opinion illustrates some of the disadvantages of constrained unanimity. The opinion is in some respects narrowly crafted, in other respects very sweeping in its reach. For example, at one point the opinion offers two examples of when tying conduct may be harmful (monopoly power and industry-wide conspiracy).[23] The Court's examples may have been limited to these two opinions because the justices could not find consensus on other examples. In eliminating the market power presumption, the Court switches from a fine to a broad brush, rejecting Independent Ink's arguments that requirements ties are quite a different animal than ties involving the simultaneous sale of products. Here, the broader approach may have been a route to consensus among the justices. Had the Court focused on the ill effects of requirements ties, consensus might have been more difficult.

---

21 During a speech at Georgetown University Law Center on 21 May 2006, Chief Justice Roberts indicated that 'unanimity, or near unanimity, promotes clarity and guidance for the lawyers and for the lower courts trying to figure out what the Supreme Court meant'. The Chief Justice's 21 May 2006 speech is reported at http://explore.georgetown.edu/news/?ID=15620, accessed 4 November 2007.

22 *Texaco Inc. v. Dagher*, 547 U.S. 1 (2006).

23 *Illinois Tool Works, Inc. v. Independent Ink, Inc.*, 547 U.S. 28, at 42 *et seq.*

The Court shifts, without apparent rhyme or reason, between economic policy arguments and legal reasoning employing principles of *stare decisis*. The result is quite unsatisfactory in terms of providing a coherent policy platform for counselors or trial courts confronting tying issues. The Court appears to have carefully picked a course of pragmatic consensus, weaving its way through a minefield of different views. The result was a clear holding nullifying the market-power presumption, but offering counselors little guidance on broader economic policy issues or on how patented-product tying cases should be tried in the wake of its holding.

3.4 The United States Court of Appeals for the Federal Circuit

The Federal Circuit is one of the few speciality courts in the federal judicial system. Intellectual property issues – for example claims of patent infringement or challenges to the validity of a patent – will be reviewed by this court, as will most issues of copyright law. The court's jurisdiction allows it to decide antitrust claims when they are ancillary to IP issues that are properly before it. Procedural issues may determine whether the Federal Circuit, or one of the courts of appeal of general jurisdiction, will first decide an important antitrust issue. However, because a high percentage of IP issues will be litigated in this court, the Federal Circuit is likely to have a key role in defining antitrust law's applicability to IP abuses.

Judges on the Federal Circuit develop a depth of understanding of IP issues and, when confronted with conflicts between IP and antitrust law, may be predisposed to favor IP protection. Not surprisingly, an antitrust issue may be decided one way by the Federal Circuit and quite differently by other federal circuits. For example, similar antitrust law and IP law issues were before the Federal Circuit in *In re Independent Service Organizations Antitrust Litigation*[24] and the Ninth Circuit Court of Appeals in *Image Technical Services, Inc. v. Eastman Kodak Co.*[25] The Ninth Circuit affirmed a district court judgment that found violations of the Sherman Act for tying conduct involving Kodak's patented micrographic equipment and parts. On analogous facts involving patented products of the *Xerox Corporation*, the Federal Circuit affirmed dismissal of similar antitrust claims.

Economic issues are open to analysis in antitrust cases and policy arguments about them are a routine part of an antitrust opinion. Attorneys who argue antitrust cases, and judges who decide them, are accustomed to dealing with economists and economic policy discussions. The intellectual property laws are more detailed than the antitrust laws. Courts deciding IP issues must

---

24 203 F.3d 1322 (Fed. Cir. 2000).

25 125 F.3d 1195 (9th Cir. 1997).

engage in more statutory interpretation and will address policy issues (such as the standards for determining novelty of an invention), but generally in a narrower context than would occur in an antitrust case. This difference in approach may influence the Federal Circuit and make that court less open to economic policy arguments.[26]

Of course, whatever bias or difference in approach may influence the decisions of the Federal Circuit, that court, as every other federal court of appeals, is obliged to follow the interpretations of the United States Supreme Court. In *Illinois Tool Works*,[27] the Federal Circuit's decision applying the market power presumption to a patented tying product was overturned by the Supreme Court.

4 Patents, requirements ties, efficiency and innovation

A tie-in occurs when a purchaser of a tying product is forced to purchase a second product (the tied product). Tying should be distinguished from the bundled sale of two or more products. The forcing element is lacking in bundled sales, which are, accordingly, generally pro-competitive or benign. Tying conduct can be condemned under Section 2 of the Sherman Act as an abuse of monopoly power or, when the forcing power is present, as a restraint of trade in violation of Section 1 of the Sherman Act or Section 3 of the Clayton Act.[28]

Ties involving the deferred purchase of the tied product are a suspect category because they raise information problems. Some purchasers of the tying product may not focus on the cost of subsequent purchases of the tied product. Moreover, even a savvy and well-informed purchaser may have difficulty projecting future use of the tying product and future competitive conditions in the tied-product market. These issues were explored in 1982 by Craswell,[29] and have been developed by Kaplow and others.[30] In the Supreme Court's 1992 opinion in *Eastman Kodak Co. v. Image Technical Services, Inc.*, the Court described life-cycle pricing difficulties that could make it impossible for the purchaser of the tying product to accurately project future needs and costs.[31]

---

26 Sullivan, L.A. (1995), 'Post-Chicago Economics: Economists, Lawyers, Judges, and Enforcement Officials in a Less Determinate Theoretical World', *Antitrust L.J.*, **63**, 669.

27 547 U.S. 28 (2006).

28 For a more in-depth discussion of tie-ins, see Sullivan, L.A. and W.S. Grimes (2006), *The Law of Antitrust: An Integrated Handbook*, 2nd ed., St. Paul, MN: Thomson West, at § 8.3.

29 Craswell, R. (1982), 'Tying Requirements in Competitive Markets: The Consumer Protection Issues', *Boston U. L. Rev.*, **62,** 661, at 671–9.

30 Kaplow, L. (1985), 'Extension of Monopoly Power Through Leverage', *Col. L Rev.*, **85**, 515; Sullivan and Grimes, *supra* note 28, at § 8.3c.

31 504 U.S. 451, 473 (1992).

4.1 Requirements ties

The case law suggests that most deferred-purchase ties are requirements ties.[32] Nalebuff points to two salient characteristics of the requirements tie that distinguish it from other tie-ins.[33] The first is that the tying and tied products stand in a complementary relationship. A computer printer is of no use without the ink needed to perform the printing function. A salt injection machine cannot be used without the proper form of salt. The second and related characteristic of requirements ties is that the value of the tying product depends on the intensity of its use. An intensive user of a computer printer is likely to value it more highly than a less intensive user. The same will be true for an intensive user of a salt injection machine. Requirements ties can also be described as metering ties because the sale of the tied product is a way of metering the use of the tying product.

A final salient characteristic of most requirements ties is that the seller charges a supra-competitive price for the tied product. Without this inflated price, the tie may foreclose rival sellers of the tied product and it may deprive consumers of choice, but it will be difficult to measure injury to consumers.

Most US Supreme Court decisions that have condemned tying arrangements have involved a requirements tie.[34] The United States Congress was focused on a requirements tie when it enacted Section 3 of the Clayton Act in 1914.[35] In the European Union, the term 'requirements tie' or 'metering tie' has not been used, but a 1979 decision of the Commission condemned such a

---

[32] There are occasional deferred-purchase ties that would not be requirements ties – for example, the sale of a cemetery's graveyard plot with a stipulation that the gravestone or stone-carving services later be purchased from the cemetery; see *Baxley-DeLamar Monuments, Inc. v. American Cemetery Association*, 938 F.2d 846 (8th Cir. 1991).

[33] *Illinois Tool Works, Amicus* Brief of Professor Barry Nalebuff, 2005 West Law 2427646, p. 5.

[34] *International Salt Co. v. United States*, 332 U.S. 392 (1947); *IBM Corp. v. United States*, 298 U.S. 131 (1936); *United Shoe Machinery Corp. v. United States*, 258 U.S. 451 (1922); *Motion Picture Patents Co. v. Universal Film Manufacturing Co.*, 243 U.S. 502 (1917). Although the plaintiff in the *Kodak* case alleged a tie between replacement parts and service, the case can fairly be included in the category of requirements ties because a purchaser of *Kodak's* micrographic equipment is likely to require spare parts in proportion to usage of the equipment. *Eastman Kodak Co. v. Image Technical Services, Inc.*, 504 U.S. 451 (1992).

[35] 15 USC § 14. Enactment of Section 3 was a response to congressional dissatisfaction with the outcome of *Henry v. A.B. Dick Co.*, 224 U.S. 1 (1912) (holding that a requirements tie with a patented tying product did not violate the Sherman Act). Kramer, V.H. (1985), 'The Supreme Court and Tying Arrangements: Antitrust as History', *Minn. L. Rev.* **69**, 1013, at 1023.

tie under ex-Article 85 EEC Treaty (now Article 81 EC).[36] A tying seller required users of its process patent for manufacturing sausage to purchase sausage casings only from the seller. The Commission declared this arrangement 'an unlawful extension by contractual means of the monopoly given by the patent'. The Commission did not suggest a concern that the patentee would gain a monopoly in the casings market but did conclude that the patentee would increase its return through use of the metered tie.

Sellers impose requirements ties to make money. The extra money that a seller garners could be the result of pro-competitive efficiencies or of anticompetitive gains. A number of possible explanations for tie-ins have been proposed.[37] To understand the competitive effects of requirements ties, both static or allocational efficiencies and dynamic efficiencies must be considered. Assuming no change in the products or services being marketed, efficient allocation is achieved if consumers receive the maximum allocation of these desired items. In contrast, dynamic efficiency is advanced when new or innovative products and services are developed and marketed to consumers.

4.2 Static or allocational analysis of requirements ties

Theorists have identified various theories that could explain how imposition of a requirements tie provides the seller with increased revenue. The most descriptive of these explanations is the implementation of metered price discrimination. Other possible theories include: (1) preserving the seller's reputation for quality; (2) efficiencies in distribution; (3) efficiencies in risk allocation; and (4) the leveraging of market power from the tying to the tied market. Aside from metered price discrimination, none of the other explanations is credible for most Supreme Court cases involving requirements ties. The discussion below addresses first the alternate explanations for imposing a requirements tie, then returns to metered price discrimination.

4.2.1 Alternate explanations of requirements ties A *reputation for quality* argument was advanced by Trident, the tying seller in *Illinois Tool Works*.[38] That case involved the tied sale of Trident's patented pizzo-electric printhead with the ink used in the printhead. Trident argued that the tied sale of its ink insured that customers would not purchase inferior inks that could cause the printhead to malfunction. But Trident's own test showed that Independent

---

36 European Commission Decision of 10 January 1979, Case IV/C-29.290 – *Vaessen/Morris*, OJ 1979 No. L 19, p. 32.

37 Sullivan and Grimes, *supra* note 28, at §§ 8.3b and 8.3c.

38 *Illinois Tool Works Inc. v. Independent Ink, Inc.*, Reply Brief for Petitioner *Illinois Tool Works, Inc.*, 2005 West Law 2902587, p. 12.

Ink's product was chemically indistinguishable from its own.[39] Moreover, major users of the printhead would be well-informed and unwilling to tolerate a product that caused substantial breakdowns or significant quality problems. Buyers should, in any event, be permitted freedom of choice to opt for varying levels of quality with corresponding adjustments in price. The Supreme Court has in the past been skeptical of quality-assurance claims, pointing out that the seller, without the anti-competitive consequences of a tie, can issue bulletins or provide information that will allow users to make an informed decision about which aftermarket product to purchase.[40]

Efficiencies in distribution are most likely to occur when the tying and tied product are purchased simultaneously. There are no substantial efficiencies evident when the purchaser makes future purchases of the tied product at an unknown frequency. If there were substantial efficiencies in a long-term supply relationship, one would expect that buyers would freely choose to enter into that relationship, without being forced to do so by the tying seller.

Risk-allocation efficiencies have also been cited as a justification for requirements tying. A purchaser of the tying product might be uncertain of the quality and utility of the product and prefer to pay a low up-front price while paying a higher per-use fee through metered sale of the tied product. Here again, however, if buyers really preferred to shift risk in this manner, they would freely choose a metered pricing arrangement without being forced into it by the manufacturer. A manufacturer might offer two differing plans to allow this freedom of choice. The first plan might be an offer to sell at a relatively high price, but with no metered use of the product. The second plan might be a lease for a relatively low price, but contingent on metering, preferably implemented without forced purchase of the tied product from the manufacturer. This plan should be free of antitrust concerns as long as the user is offered meaningful risk-allocation choices (a non-competitive offer to sell free of the metering would not obviate the antitrust risk).

Leveraging power from the tying-product market to the tied-product market also might explain the seller's gain from a requirements tie. Older Supreme Court decisions involving requirements ties rested to some extent on this theory. Leverage theory has been attacked by Bowman and others,[41] who

---

39 *Illinois Tool Works Inc. v. Independent Ink, Inc.*, Brief for Respondent *Independent Ink, Inc.*, 2005 West Law 2427645, pp. 5 *et seq.*

40 *Standard Oil Co. of California v. United States*, 337 U.S. 293, at 305–6 (1949) ('specification of the type and quality of the product to be used in connection with the tying device is protection enough').

41 Bowman, Jr., W.S. (1957), 'Tying Arrangements and the Leverage Problem', *Yale L.J.*, **67**, 19; Hovenkamp, Herbert (2005), *Federal Antitrust Policy: The Law of Competition and its Practice*, 3rd ed., St. Paul, MN: Thompson West, at § 7.9 (criticizing 'troublesome leverage theory').

argue that the tying seller possessing monopoly power can shift profits back and forth between the tying and tied products, but cannot increase the total return on the sale of the monopoly tying product and the tied product. This conclusion, however, will not hold if use of the tie makes entry into the tied-product market more difficult.[42] Moreover, even if there is no threat of monopolization in the tied-product market, a requirements tie can have adverse competitive effects when (1) buyers cannot discern at the time of purchase of the tying product what their total costs for subsequent purchases of the tied product will be; and (2) the market for the tied product is oligopolistic, so that the tying seller will reap higher returns through a tie that exploits the market's oligopolistic tendencies, perhaps by making discounted sales less likely.[43] In *Illinois Tool Works*, it seems unlikely that Trident's tie will somehow give that firm monopoly power in ink markets. But the tie will adversely affect the competitive pricing and choices for buyers in the tied-product market.[44]

4.2.2 How metered pricing might produce more efficient allocation of the tying product As seems evident from this analysis, the primary impetus for a seller to impose a requirements tie is likely to be a desire to engage in metered, discriminatory pricing. There is some discussion, however, whether the effects of metered pricing are pro- or anti-competitive. Perfect price discrimination could result in higher output and, in this sense, be pro-competitive. For example, if a seller can determine the reservation price for every purchaser of its product (the highest price that the purchaser is willing to pay), it could set a range of prices that would increase the number of purchasers above the level that would purchase if only a single uniform price were set. A uniform price on a printhead might be set at the seller's cost (C) plus a reasonable profit (RP). At this price (C + RP), the number of purchases would be X. If the same seller could discriminate perfectly, it could set its price higher than C + RP for those who valued the product highly, but somewhat lower than C + RP for those who placed a lower value on the product. The result would be additional sales of the product (X + Y) and a fuller exploitation of the market power that the printhead

---

42 See Nalebuff, B. (2004), 'Bundling as an Entry Deterrent Device', *Q. J. Econ.*, **119**, 159; Carlton, D.W. and M. Waldman (2002), 'The Strategic Use of Tying to Preserve and Create Market Power in Evolving Industries', *RAND J. Econ.*, **33**, 194; Whinston, M.D. (1990), 'Tying, Foreclosure, and Exclusion', *Am. Econ. Rev.*, **80**, 837.

43 It is possible, for example, that the price-guarantee tying arrangement in *International Salt* was an effort to lock in oligopolistic prices in the salt market. See the discussion of this case in Sullivan and Grimes, *supra* note 28, at § 8.3c.2.

44 See the discussion of allocative effects in the tied-product market, section 4.2.3 *infra*.

seller possesses. The seller could increase both sales and revenue and achieve optimal allocative efficiency.

4.2.3 Wealth-transfer loss as the primary injury from requirements ties
There are a number of problems with this model of perfect price discrimination. To begin with, one of the harms from monopoly power is the wealth-transfer losses to buyers who pay the supra-competitive price for a product. Most, perhaps all, of the seller's increased revenue from a requirements tie will be in the form of a wealth-transfer loss to buyers. In theory, the seller may also gain revenue from allocation gains that occur when low-intensity users are enticed to purchase more of the tying product. But this gain will occur only if the seller lowers the price of the tying product, something that the case law suggests may not occur at all.[45] Even if the tying seller does reduce the price of the tying product, the increased revenue received from additional sales of the tying product will be minimal because the seller has reduced its mark-up on the tying product. Finally, the increase in the price of the tied product may result in intensive users purchasing fewer tying products, so that there may be a net loss in sales of the tying product. Thus, revenue gains will flow primarily from sales of the tied product at supra-competitive prices, producing a substantial wealth-transfer loss to intensive buyers who would have purchased these products regardless of the tie.

Although some scholars reject wealth-transfer loss as a concern of antitrust,[46] many others believe that wealth-transfer loss, which in most cases will be substantially larger than any deadweight loss, is a primary, perhaps the paramount, concern of antitrust.[47] Measures of damages in antitrust cases are often based on loss to consumers from supra-competitive surcharges, an indication that, whatever the theoretical argument, antitrust law as practiced does provide a remedy for wealth-transfer losses. Thus, to condemn metered tying based on overpayments made by purchasers of the tied product is well within mainstream US antitrust interpretation. This result is likely to appeal to the consumer base that supports competition laws, and is sound economic policy.

---

[45] In *Eastman Kodak Co. v. Image Technical Services, Inc.*, 504 U.S. 451, 472 *et seq.* (1992), Kodak claimed that it did not reduce the price charged for parts or equipment when it imposed the tie involving Kodak service.

[46] Bork, Robert (1993), *Antitrust Paradox: A Policy at War With Itself*, New York: Basic Books at pp. 110–12; Rule, C. (1987), 'Merger Enforcement Policy: Protecting the Consumer, *Antitrust L.J.*, **56**, 739 *et seq.*

[47] Lande, R.H. (1982), 'Wealth Transfers as the Original and Primary Concern of Antitrust: The Efficiency Interpretation Challenged', *Hastings L.J.*, **34**, 67; Lande, R.H. (1988), 'The Rise and (Coming) Fall of Efficiency as the Ruler of Antitrust', *Antitrust Bull.*, **33**, 429, at 455–63.

4.2.4 Allocation effects in the tying-product market Even if one rejects prevention of power-based wealth transfer as a goal of antitrust, the conclusion that metered price discrimination will result in more efficient allocation (and therefore be pro-competitive) is still highly problematic. In order for the tie-in to produce more efficient allocation, there must be substantial transparency in the market so that buyers understand the costs of the bundled offer and sellers understand the reservation prices of buyers. If this transparency exists, it is possible that the tying seller can set the price of the tying and tied products at levels that will produce increased sales of the tying product. However, prescient buyers will look not just at the price of the tying product, but also at the cost of the tied product. If combined cost is too high, an intensive user with adequate information may purchase fewer tying products, undermining an efficient allocation. Thus, increased sales to low-intensity users may be offset by decreased sales to high-intensity users.

If there are information inadequacies for the tying seller and for a substantial segment of purchasers, the risk of inefficient allocation grows substantially. Buyers attracted to a low price on the tying product and not adequately cognizant of the future costs for the tied product may overbuy the tying product (a misallocation) and end up using it inefficiently – less often than they would use it if the tied product were sold at a competitive price. Consider the user of a Trident printhead that has a choice between employing the printhead more widely, or relying on a less attractive technology (for example, pre-printed bar code labels that are pasted on cartons). As the price for the ink for a Trident printhead gets higher, the incentive for the purchaser to make use of Trident's efficient technology is reduced, perhaps forcing this purchaser to continue use of a less preferred alternative.[48]

There is yet another reason to doubt that pro-competitive price discrimination will be achieved through a requirements tie's metered pricing. As the Supreme Court cases demonstrate, many requirements ties are not enforced against power buyers.[49] If powerful buyers are excepted from metered pricing, the buyers who value the tying product most will likely pay the lowest, not the highest, price. The brunt of discriminatory pricing ends up falling on smaller and less powerful firms, creating a competitive disadvantage for them in competing against firms possessing buyer power.[50]

---

48 For a similar allocation analysis, see *Illinois Tool Works Inc. v. Independent Ink*, *Amicus* Brief of Professor F. M. Scherer, 2005 West Law 2427642, pp. 12–17.

49 Exceptions for power buyers were made in *Eastman Kodak v. Image Technical Services*, 504 US 451, at 475 (1992); *IBM Corp. v. United States*, 298 U.S. 131, at 134 (1936). In *Northern Pacific Railway Co. v. United States*, 356 U.S. 1 (1958), the railroad did not impose the tie against 390 of its large customers. Cummings, F.J. and W. Ruhter (1979), 'The Northern Pacific Case', *J. L. & Econ.*, **22**, 329, at 344–5.

50 Sullivan and Grimes, *supra* note 28, § 8.3b2, at pp. 433 *et seq.*

4.2.5 Allocative effects in the tied-product market A requirements tie will result in the purchaser paying more for the tied or metering product. Even if this pricing is done in a fully transparent and open manner, its effect on allocation of tied products may be negative. The seller may sell more of the tying product and therefore also sell more of the tied product on which it garners a supra-competitive return. However, as noted above, the supra-competitive price for the tied product will create an incentive for buyers to use the tying product less intensively, and therefore purchase fewer tied items than would occur under competitive conditions. If buyers are prescient, they will understand that the high cost for the tied product is an overall charge for the tying product, and purchase fewer of them as well.

Additional distortions in allocation are likely because of the information problems associated with deferred-purchase ties (see section 4.3 *infra*). Even if a prescient buyer is able to fully and accurately anticipate future needs, price changes, and other market shifts, the buyer may have limited choice if other sellers of the tying product are engaging in comparable tying conduct.

Finally, before metered price discrimination can be adjudged pro-competitive, the evasion costs must be considered. Buyers forced to pay supra-competitive prices for the tied product will not passively accept this result. As a result of tying or exclusive dealing practices, automobile owners in the United States are forced to pay supra-competitive prices for parts that may be available only from the manufacturer of the vehicle, or a source approved by the manufacturer.[51] Consumers seeking a way around these high prices have indirectly given rise to a booming automobile theft market. Thieves steal a vehicle, strip its parts in a 'chop shop', then sell the parts at a price that vastly exceeds the street value of the car itself. Society bears these very substantial costs through higher law enforcement burdens, higher automobile insurance rates, and uninsured losses borne by theft victims.

In the *Illinois Tool Works* case, efforts to avoid the tie were unlikely to produce the array and extent of external costs that occur with automobile parts. However, buyers are likely to expend resources seeking alternative sources of ink. Whatever efficiencies might flow from the metered pricing scheme may be offset by Trident's own costs in attempting to enforce its tie and in customers' costs incurred in seeking a way to avoid supra-competitive tied-product prices.

Although requirements ties may in some cases be the most efficient way of implementing metered pricing, they are laden with anti-competitive risks that

---

[51] This example is provided by Scherer, Frederic M. (1996), *Industry Structure, Strategy, and Public Policy*, New York, NY: Harper Collins, at pp. 308–11. On the spare-parts discussion in the EU, see Kur, Annette, chapter 13, in this volume.

could be entirely avoided if the metered pricing could be implemented without a tie. For example, if the manufacturer of a printhead could incorporate a usage meter, something that sophisticated computer technology could easily accomplish, the manufacturer could implement a metered usage charge without the use of any tying and with no anti-competitive effects on the tied-product market. Buyers would retain a full range of choice to purchase the most competitive aftermarket product. Such direct metering charges may be unpopular with buyers, but that is hardly an argument for why the same metering should be allowed through the use of a tying mechanism that has very substantial additional anti-competitive consequences.

4.3 Dynamic efficiency analysis: will a requirements tie increase innovation?

Proponents of maximum exploitation of IP rights argue that the increased revenues achieved through tying a patented product to an unpatented product provide a desirable increased incentive for innovation. There is little doubt that increased return from a requirements tie creates a higher reward for an owner of a patent on the tying product. But the effect of the increased return achieved through a requirements tie, in contrast to the direct patent reward, (1) is arbitrary because it has no direct correlation to the value of the underlying patented tying product; and (2) may actually decrease overall innovation because of the constricting impact on the tied-product market.

The direct nature of the basic IP reward can be simply illustrated. If an inventor discovers a novel way to manufacture a solar-powered cigarette lighter, the inventor may receive a patent that grants exclusive rights to market this invention. If consumers deem this invention a valuable addition to their portfolio of goods at the price at which it is offered, they will purchase it and reward the patentee. The price and quantity of sales (and therefore the value of the patent reward) will correlate directly with the value that purchasers place on this new invention.

Contrast this with the additional reward that a requirements tie might provide the patentee if, for example, the lighter uses disposable wicks that must be replaced after a number of uses. The patentee's ability to enforce this requirements tie will depend on a variety of factors that have no correlation to the value of the underlying invention. For example, if similar wicks are already widely available in the market from a number of producers, the patentee will likely have difficulty imposing a tie that sets a premium price on the wick. Instead, the patentee will probably have to set the price for its wicks at or near the market price for similar wicks. On the other hand, if it happens that wicks of the necessary type are not available at all, or are available only at high oligopolistic prices, the patentee can easily impose a premium price on the wick that earns a much higher return. The point is that the amount of this return will depend on extrinsic factors (for example, the state of competition in the wick market) that have no correlation with the underlying value of the cigarette lighter.

There is an additional wrinkle to this story. If requirements ties are lawful, the inventor has an incentive to design the patented lighter in a way that functions with a special wick that only the patentee can readily provide. The additional cost incurred in designing the lighter with a difficult-to-replicate wick would not improve the technology, but instead would be a rent-seeking cost incurred by the patentee in an effort to enhance returns. Encouraging such rent-seeking design changes is decidedly not a legitimate purpose of IP laws, but it is an inevitable result of a competition policy tolerant of requirements ties.

This leads to the second reality about requirements ties and the likelihood that they will increase innovation. Because the patentee employing a requirements tie has an incentive to build and maintain sales of wicks, it will do everything possible to obstruct entry in that market, especially if the would-be entrant offers new or improved technology not offered by the patentee. As long as requirements ties are lawful, the patentee will have an incentive to restrain competition and entry in the tied product market. If requirements ties are unlawful, the patentee is more likely to welcome improvements in wicks that could increase the utility and value of its patented lighter.

These concerns give greater weight to the policy goals underlying Congress's 1914 enactment of Section 3 of the Clayton Act, designed to prohibit anti-competitive requirements ties whether the tying product is 'patented or unpatented'.[52] The case for anti-competitive effects of requirements ties is a strong one, reflected in venerable decisions of the Supreme Court, and consistent with correlating IP rewards with the value of the patented product. The Justice Department and the Federal Trade Commission had an opportunity to steer the law in a positive direction when *Illinois Tool Works* came before the Supreme Court in 2005. That opportunity was lost when the government's *amicus* brief focused on the market-power presumption to the exclusion of weighty policy concerns about the use of requirements ties.

5 Loyalty discounts on strongly branded goods

A holder of a strong brand may employ a loyalty discount to gain strategic advantage over its rivals. Trademark law allows a seller to build strong loyalty in the brand name, but, once that brand loyalty has been attained, nothing in trademark law either authorizes or forbids use of a strong brand to implement

---

52 15 USC § 14.

a loyalty or inventory-forcing discount. In the United States, such discounts have been challenged under the Sherman Act with varying results and modes of analysis.

5.1 Competitive analysis of a loyalty discount encompassing a strongly and weakly branded product

A loyalty discount is a reduction in price contingent on the buyer purchasing a minimum percentage of the buyer's needs from the seller. A buyer agreeing to purchase 80 percent of its needs for a particular product from the seller might, for example, be offered a 5 percent discount on the purchases. The Eighth Circuit found this sort of loyalty discount unobjectionable in *Concord Boat Corp. v. Brunswick Corp.*, where the court indicated that such discounts should be a Sherman Act violation only if they met the requirements for predatory pricing (below-cost pricing and a reasonable probability of recoupment).[53] In the Third Circuit's 2003 *en banc* decision in *Le Page's, Inc. v. 3 M Corp.*,[54] the Third Circuit held that the 3 M Corporation's loyalty discount involving Scotch brand tape and other products violated the Sherman Act. The *en banc* Third Circuit declined to require a showing of predatory pricing, focusing instead on whether 3 M's loyalty discount operated to prevent an equally efficient rival from matching its terms.

Loyalty discounts may be used in a variety of circumstances. An anti-competitive result is probable when a seller offers a loyalty discount on a strong brand (sold at a high margin) and a weak brand (sold at a low margin), and seeks to use the loyalty discount to disadvantage rival sellers of weak brands. Under such circumstances, application of a predatory pricing standard would tolerate conduct that is unambiguously anti-competitive.

Suppose that Acme Corporation has 80 percent of the market for widgets *and* a strong premium brand that accounts for almost all of these sales. Acme, however, also sells a weak or private-label brand in direct competition with one or more rival manufacturers of weak brands. Acme offers a 20 percent discount on a retailer's purchase of both premium brand and its private-label widgets if the retailer purchases 90 percent of its requirements for widgets from Acme.

This offer should be attractive to retailers. The seller of a strong brand enjoys vertical market power that allows a large factory mark-up. Borrowing from Robert Steiner's insights, a supplier's vertical market power is a product of a strong consumer demand for a particular product or brand.[55] This vertical

---

[53] 207 F.3d 1029 (8th Cir. 2001).

[54] 324 F.3d 141 (3d Cir. 2003) (*en banc*), *cert. denied*, 540 US 807 (2003).

[55] Steiner, R.L. (2004), 'The Evolution and Applications of Dual-Stage Thinking', *Antitrust Bull.*, **49**(4), 877, at 890–2.

power usually exists alongside the traditional horizontal market power, but not in every case. When vertical power exists, a consumer will switch stores in order to obtain the strong brand at the desired price.

Vertical market power is measured by a ratio of retailer and producer margins.[56] Typically, as the retailer's margin goes up, the producer's margin goes down, and vice versa. As Steiner concedes, this two-stage vertical market power measure is an oversimplification of real markets that can have multiple players involved in distribution. However, measuring the margins of both producers and retailers offers a much more principled, accurate, and instructive model than the current single-stage analysis, which looks only at horizontal market power.[57]

In the widget example, the retailer is pressured to carry the premium widget brand because customers will look for this brand in the store and may shop elsewhere if they do not find it. But the retailer has a strong incentive to also carry the weak brand because of the higher retail mark-up on such brands. Acme's loyalty discount will be attractive because the retailer can simply switch its purchasing from a rival's weak brand to Acme's weak brand and still enjoy an equivalent high retail mark-up. The retailer also receives a discount on purchases that it already makes for the premium brand of widgets (the bulk of its widget purchases).

Why would Acme offer this bundled discount package rather than simply discounting the price of its weak brand of widgets? Part of the answer is that by including a discount on premium brand widgets, Acme is offering a package that its rivals cannot match. The combined horizontal and vertical market power of premium brand widgets cannot be matched by Acme rivals that lack a strong brand of their own.

From Acme's point of view, there is another advantage to this loyalty discount. Large retailers may prefer not to become dependent on a single supplier for an important product. Such buyers would have a strategic preference to support at least one rival of Acme so that the buyer has choices in future purchases of widgets. This strategic preference for choice means that the buyer will continue doing business with Acme's rival, even if Acme has

---

[56] *Ibid.*

[57] As Steiner also acknowledges, there are industry structures in which the margins of retailers and manufacturers are positively related – in which total market power in the category may be very low, to the benefit of consumers, or very high, to their detriment. For example, Steiner has written about a case in which collusion between a manufacturer of a strong brand and its retailers resulted in high margins for both the manufacturer and the retailers. Steiner, R.L. (2004), 'Exclusive Dealing + Resale Price Maintenance: A Powerful Anti-competitive Combination', *Sw. U. L. Rev.*, **33**, 447.

matched the rival's price. In competing for the weak brand business, Acme will likely lose a price-matching game unless it can come up with an offer that the rival cannot match. If Acme prices its weak brand widgets below cost, it could win a price-matching game, but subject itself to predatory pricing claims. To avoid this risk, Acme employs a loyalty discount that includes a rebate on high-volume purchases of premium brand widgets. Lacking a strong brand of its own, the rival cannot match the offer because its weak brand has a lower sales volume and sells at a much lower margin.

The conclusions drawn from this example would appear to apply to the loyalty discount at issue in the *3 M* case. The purpose of 3 M's inventory-forcing discount was apparently to increase its sales of private-label tape, not to increase sales of its dominant Scotch brand. 3 M apparently also hoped to increase sales of other (probably weakly branded) products that were included in the bundle of goods subject to the loyalty discount.

One can find parallel cases, such as *SmithKline Corp. v. Eli Lilly & Co.*,[58] that fit the facts of the Acme example. *SmithKline* involved at least one strong brand or unique product that the purchaser needed in its inventory. The seller appeared to use this 'must-buy' item to anchor its loyalty discount and force purchasers to also purchase one or more weaker brands. The buyers were not retailers but hospitals. This may alter a dual-stage analysis, but the fundamental anti-competitive effect – that equally efficient rival sellers lacking equivalent strong brands cannot match the offer – remains the same.

5.2 Efficiencies as a defence for loyalty discounts

In its *amicus* brief filed with the Supreme Court, the DoJ suggested that efficiencies could explain and justify some loyalty discounts.[59] As in other Sherman Act bundling or foreclosure cases, a defendant should be allowed to introduce evidence of efficiencies that might tip the balance in its favor. Because price discounts allow a seller to increase sales, there is a possibility that scale efficiencies will be enhanced. Scale efficiencies, however, do not appear to have played a significant role in any of the litigated cases.

Some commentators have pushed the argument that bundling conduct, such as might be fostered by a loyalty discount, is a pro-competitive way to finance research and development when the tying product is patented.[60] This argu-

---

58 575 F.2d 1056 (3d Cir. 1978).

59 *Le Page's, Inc. v. 3 M Corp.*, Amicus Brief for the United States in the Supreme Court of the United States, usdoj/gov/atr/cases/f203900/203900.pdf, accessed 4 November 2007, p. 12.

60 Klein, B. and J. Wiley (2004), 'Competitive Price Discrimination as an Antitrust Justification for Intellectual Property Refusals to Deal', *Antitrust L.J.*, **70**, 599 (arguing that licensing restrictions and tie-ins involving intellectual property should be treated leniently because of the innovation gains that they bring).

ment, if accepted, would result in a troubling and potentially far-reaching erosion of the Sherman Act. Many tying products will involve a patent in at least a peripheral way. Many of these patents may have little or no market value. Even if the tying product is directly covered by a valuable patent, the additional gain from tying will depend on many external variables (for example, the state of competition in the tied-product market) that have nothing to do with the underlying value of the patented product.

Of course, any profit stemming from an exercise of market power, even if no patent is involved, could theoretically be used to finance R&D. If this line of logic were accepted, it would follow that all exercises of monopoly power could be justified as an incentive for, and a subsidy to, innovation.

5.3 What rules should govern loyalty discounts?

To summarize, in a loyalty-discount contest between a seller of both a strong brand and a weak brand and a rival seller of a weak brand, the rival will have a twofold handicap: (1) the rival lacking a strong brand is in all likelihood selling a small volume of goods to a given retailer, so that any loyalty discount must be larger in relative terms to match a loyalty discount offered by the seller of the strong brand; and (2) the rival is, even before a discounting war begins, likely to be selling its product at a substantially lower margin than the strong brand's seller.

The two-stage Steiner analysis demonstrates that a loyalty discount is suspect when employed by a manufacturer with a strong brand. At least for this fact pattern, a rule that loyalty discounts be condemned only when predatory pricing is demonstrated is bad antitrust policy. It has little to do with market realities. A seller possessing both horizontal and vertical market power will be selling a strong brand at a price nowhere near marginal cost (or average variable cost), a widely accepted threshold for predatory pricing. Such a seller can employ a loyalty discount to raise rivals' costs or drive them from the market while still maintaining as much as possible of the high margin that the combined market power allows.

In the context of cases such as *3 M* and *SmithKline*, where the defendant's conduct is of the inventory-forcing nature, there is no reason why the rules governing this conduct should be different than those governing tying or exclusive dealing. The loyalty discount just becomes the tool for enforcing tying or exclusive dealing. Courts should examine whether the defendant has market power (horizontal and vertical) and whether that market power is being abused through forcing behavior. Because the 'forcing' is in the form of a discounted price, the plaintiff cannot win by simply showing that the discount makes it more difficult for a rival to compete. The plaintiff must show that the discount is designed so that it could not be matched by an equally efficient rival.

In its *amicus* brief in the *3 M* case, the Justice Department urged the Court not to accept *certiorari* to review loyalty discounts.[61] The government's brief recognized that loyalty discounts could be anti-competitive if they allow a firm with a strong brand to raise the costs of equally efficient rivals. But the brief also suggested, without supporting examples or analysis, that loyalty discounts could be pro-competitive or benign in their impact. The Antitrust Division failed to avail itself of a prime opportunity to support a competition-friendly policy in a class of loyalty-discount cases that appear unambiguously anti-competitive.

6 Conclusion

The DoJ filed an *amicus* brief in both the *Illinois Tool Works* and *3 M* cases. In each of these cases, the Antitrust Division failed to seize a ready opportunity to establish sound competition-law restraints on pernicious behavior related to patented or trademarked products. These failures demonstrate the need for revitalized leadership in the Antitrust Division to address pressing issues involving the intersection of antitrust and IP rights and to accept the Division's traditional role as a counterweight to the public-choice bias that favors continued expansion of IP rights.

---

61 *Supra* note 59.

PART 4

MERGER CONTROL

12 New technologies and mergers

Josef Bejček

1 General remarks

1.1 Intellectual property rights and innovations

'Some of us often suppose that the best things in life are free. Most of us get along by developing the ideas of others. That is how the world progresses.'[1] Too strong protection of individual achievements may slow down the general advance. On the other hand, too weak protection can prevent anybody from inventing anything. From the point of view of a consumer, intellectual property rights (IPRs) are a kind of 'trade-off' between long-term gains and short-term gains. Consumers would be better off in the short term if the results of someone else's creative efforts could be freely copied, for this would lower the price of products involving IPRs. But from a long-term perspective, the consumers would become losers because they would be giving up the incentives that IPRs afford the creators.[2]

The main concern of this dilemma is illustrated by some lines from J.M. Clark's book *Competition as a Dynamic Process* from the year 1961 written in verse. He stated:

> We all agree that innovation
> Will benefit both world and nation
> The question we must answer later
> Is, will it help the innovator?

The analysis of the reality is unfortunately not too poetic. It is, of course, very cheap to criticize someone else's attempt to write in verse. Nevertheless, although it is sometimes argued that the pressure to rhyme makes the poet express his best ideas, it is obviously not the case in Clark's poetic attempt, for the question 'will it help the innovator' has to be answered in advance – before the innovation is made. It is not possible to state that otherwise there will be

---

1 See Chafee, Z., Jr. (1940), 'Unfair Competition', *Harv. L. Rev.*, **53**, 1289, at 1317 *et seq.*

2 See 'Competition Policy and Intellectual Property Rights' (2001), *OECD J. Comp. L. & Pol'y*, **2**(3), 123.

no innovation at all, but it is probably useful to have *ex ante* incentives to innovate, not only *ex post* incentives to transfer new technologies and products. Nevertheless, even without IPRs, *ex ante* investments would be undertaken.

It is broadly acknowledged and considered necessary that society has to encourage creative activities that support and keep in operation our information-based, high-technology economies. The appropriate means is reducing competition by a reduced protection of market power. A certain degree of monopolization among property rights owners is considered an acceptable price for supporting innovations. This is a substantial difference compared to the situation 30 years ago, when a total immunity of IPRs from antitrust law was practised.[3]

The economic issues involved in patent and copyright are well-known. There is an obvious conflict of interests here that needs to be harmonized. On the one hand, there is an interest in keeping the market in operation and protecting competition for that reason. On the other hand, there is an interest in supporting (or at least not disadvantaging) inventors, which results in securing a kind of monopoly for the owners of IPRs. This cannot, however, lead to misuse of monopoly power. The main goal is therefore to harmonize the 'protecting (without over-protecting) incentives to innovate'[4] and the protection of competition at the same time.

At first glance, an indisputable connection exists between the *ex ante* incentive to invent and to innovate (for example in terms of patent protection) and the *ex ante* protection of competition: market power (acquired, for instance, via IPRs) must not be abused. Intellectual property is neither a reserve, immune to competition law, nor automatically a sign of a monopolistic position that must be destroyed.

The partial goals and means of IPRs and of antitrust law are different despite their 'convergence' at the level of a common goal, namely to enhance general welfare by promoting dynamic competition. Therefore the requirements on legal certainty cannot be the same for both. IPRs have to be an *ex ante* guarantee of the incentive to innovate. Antitrust law, including merger control, is principally (except for rare situations of hard-core cartels) not able to offer the same level of legal certainty; instead, the result of its use depends on a complex decision-making process that takes into account so many issues

---

[3] Cf. Leary, Thomas B. (2004), 'The Economic Roots of Antitrust', Chinese Academy of Social Sciences (Beijing), Presentation of 1 July 2004, http://www.ftc.gov/speeches/leary/040916econrootsofantitrust.pdf, accessed 4 November 2007, p. 3.

[4] Pitofsky, Robert (2001), 'Antitrust and Intellectual Property: Unresolved Issues at the Heart of the New Economy', Presentation of 2 March 2001, http://www.ftc.gov/speeches/pitofsky/ipf301.htm, accessed 4 November 2007, p. 3.

that only some of them (including intellectual property rights) can be envisaged by the law and, moreover, generally speaking, only those that are subject to the 'rule of reason' assessment.

1.2 Mergers and intellectual property

As to mergers – as the narrower focus of this chapter – one can hardly assert that their legal regulation could convey any anti-protective issues with regard to the owner of IPRs (such as the ban on misuse of market power). Quite the contrary, sometimes a merger can bring about more profit for the owner of the IPR in question if these are legally used by one of the merging firms due to the more extensive use of the innovative product after the merger (the product is marketed on a broader scale and the holder of IPRs can obtain higher fees).

But the merger can lead to a dominant position in the relevant market that can be abused, or to a substantial lessening of competition. Thus, market dominance can be abused in many ways; post-merger market power based on the ownership of an IPR can be used in an anti-competitive way regardless of the fact that the inventor's protection works well. In that case, the ownership of an intellectual property right is only a special tool of general abuse of market power, and no specific protection of innovations takes place.

We can perhaps say that excessive protection against concentrations of undertakings may lead to a slowing down of general welfare – to the detriment of consumers, after all (due to losing the economic advantages of concentration in favour of preserving the perhaps dubious normative and theoretical principles of a structural approach to competition policy). On the other hand, insufficient protection against concentrations may lead to monopolization, thus slowing down general welfare to the detriment of consumers as well. In general (and regardless of whether a normal or high-tech industry is concerned), there is a choice to be made between two evils; either to prohibit a merger despite its potential to enhance efficiency, or to approve it despite the possibility of endangering competition in the future. It is a traditional conflict of aims: what will prevail – efficiency or competition? Implementing the same standards can improve efficiency and consumer welfare, but it can also cause similar consequences as a merger, namely the lessening or exclusion of competition.[5]

Antitrust law, from a purely economic point of view, is very cautious in this respect. Internal investments in capacity driven by the efforts to achieve better efficiency usually lead to an expansion of the firm and an increase of its

---

5 See Heinemann, Andreas (2003), 'Antitrust Law and the Internet', in Josef Drexl (ed.) (2003), *The Future of Transnational Antitrust*, Berne etc.: Staempfli & Kluwer Law International, p. 131.

market share. Efficiency considerations are also supposed to be behind the majority of mergers, which represent the external means of expansion.[6] Unlike mergers above a certain size threshold, antitrust law does not care about internal growth at all, irrespective of any turnover thresholds. Merger law has a pre-emptive function as an 'outer wall of defence'[7] against the threat of improperly exercised market power. The final decision on the acceptance of external growth is left to the antitrust authority and is generally based on a rule-of-reason analysis in a multi-criteria assessment.

As stated earlier,[8] the complexity of economic effects precludes a precise calculation of positive and negative factors. In spite of the need for legal practice to have precise rules, no general rules are appropriate for every single case. It is obvious that formal legal certainty may not prevail over the difficult decision of whether the proper post-merger balance will be achieved, for example, between the incentives to innovate and the threat of market power arising from intellectual property rights; between long-term and short-term efficiencies of the merger; between keeping the home market competitive and the chance to create a 'national champion' able to compete globally as a 'trade-off' for a competitive national market.

Going back to the uncertainty and controversy concerning the assessment criteria for mergers, we can refer to research results[9] showing that local competition matters in global industries and that local competition provides an exceptional stimulus to productivity growth that is extremely valuable to

---

[6] Nevertheless, 'there does not exist clear evidence that mergers, as a general rule, create efficiency gains. However, at least some mergers do create efficiencies' (see European Commission, Directorate General for Economic and Financial Affairs (2001), *European Economy*, (5), 70. The representative study of Dennis C. Mueller from the year 2003, including nearly 15,000 mergers all over the world, asserts that almost 60 per cent of mergers led to a great increase of profit (ca. 80 per cent), but within five years to a lowering of turnover as well. In the last 15 years 55.8 per cent of mergers are to be assessed as welfare-lowering mergers; up to 30 per cent of great mergers are not the consequence of globalization – they result rather from the syndrome of 'hubris' and of 'empire-building policy'; see Schmidt, Ingo (2005), *Wettbewerbspolitik und Kartellrecht*, 8th ed., Stuttgart: Lucius & Lucius, p. 107.

[7] See Leary, Thomas B. (2000), 'Freedom as the Core Value of Antitrust in the New Millennium', Speech given at the ABA, Washington, DC, 6 April 2000, http://www.ftc.gov/speeches/leary/learyantitrustspeech.htm, accessed 4 November 2007, p. 4.

[8] See, for example, Heinemann, Andreas, 'Intellectual Property Rights and Competition Policy – The Approach of the WTO Working Group on Trade and Competition', in Roger Zäch (ed.) (1999), *Towards WTO Competition Rules*, Berne etc.: Staempfli & Kluwer Law International, p. 299.

[9] See Porter, M.E. (2001), 'Competition and Antitrust: Toward a Productivity-based Approach to Evaluating Mergers and Joint Ventures', *Antitrust Bull.*, **46**, 919.

firms. The two major contributions of local competition are: (1) incentives and informational benefits (companies that compete at home are better prepared to compete with foreign rivals abroad); and (2) positive externalities (such as specialized labour pools, knowledge spillovers, specialized supplier information, and so on).[10]

This research may mitigate to some extent the liberal approach of antitrust authorities to approving mergers and to lowering the level of rivalry in home industries, as it shows the danger in arguments about the creation of 'national champions' in an industry in the home country in order to gain the scale to compete internationally ('global players'). According to this research, unless a firm is forced to compete at home, it will usually quickly lose its competitiveness abroad. Local competition matters for productivity and productivity growth, even in industries whose geographic scope is global. I presume that approvals of mergers based on short-term efficiencies and lessening or destroying rivalry are therefore at least disputable.

2 New technologies and antitrust law

The general intersection between antitrust law and intellectual property law mentioned above is not new at all. What is new is the scope and extent of the challenges connected with the rapid technological developments and with the substantially increasing impact of technology developments on the whole economy.[11] The enforcement in this area is not free from controversy. One pertinent question is whether the antitrust laws, which were originally designed to apply to traditional manufacturing and distribution industries, should be applied at all to competition in fast moving industries where products are quickly outmoded and market shares may be unstable.[12]

It is important not to allow economic growth, and the very existence of a workable market, to be endangered by the abuse of private market power. On the other hand, it is not less important to promote innovation and inventors by the means of the guaranteed exclusivity position of owners of intellectual property rights. 'It leaves open the question whether antitrust principles, developed primarily in the context of smokestack industries, should apply

10 *Ibid.*, at 929 *et seq.*

11 See Pitofsky, Robert (1999), 'Antitrust Analysis in High-Tech Industries: A 19th Century Discipline Addresses 21st Century Problems', Speech given at the ABA, Scottsdale, 25 February 1999, http://www.ftc.gov/speeches/pitofsky/hitch.shtm, accessed 4 November 2007; Baer, William J. (1998), 'Antitrust Enforcement and High Technology Markets', Speech given at the ABA, San Francisco, 12 November 1998, http://www.ftc.gov/speeches/other/ipat6.shtm, accessed 4 November 2007.

12 See Baer, *supra* note 11, at 1.

comparably and with equal force to new problems that emerge in connection with high-tech industries.'[13]

The fast moving high-tech industries open the way for new competitors who are able to override the other market participants and to dominate the market. Antitrust law enforcement in this sector, it would then seem, is less important except for price-fixing and other per se violations, because 'any [attempt] to create or exercise market power would quickly be corrected by market forces. . . . This caricature of high-tech markets' may be 'accurate in some cases and inaccurate in others'.[14]

There are undoubtedly some particularities of IPRs that justify a special and sensitive approach to the owners of those rights. On the other hand, there are some cases where the full enforcement of antitrust law is legitimate, regardless of whether IPRs or 'normal', tangible property rights are involved or not. There is some scepticism about whether high-tech industries require special rules and instead only some special facts should be taken into consideration; the predictions of future conduct may be inherently more difficult. What is required is a 'discriminating application of familiar principles to the special facts of a high-tech environment'.[15]

Today, after contrasting approaches in the past, 'enforcement of the antitrust laws no longer begins with the assumption that restrictive use of intellectual property is necessarily anticompetitive'.[16] Currently, enforcement is based on the presumption of balancing both antitrust and intellectual property rights and of incorporating the protection of IPRs into competition rules.[17] As Baer states:[18]

> [Antitrust law] starts with three basic assumptions about intellectual property: first, intellectual property is comparable to other forms of property, so that ownership [is connected with] the same rights and responsibilities[. S]econd, the existence of intellectual property does not automatically mean that the owner has market power[. A]nd third, the licensing of intellectual property may often be necessary in order for the

---

[13] Pitofsky, *supra* note 11.

[14] See Baer, *supra* note 11, at 2.

[15] For example, Leary, Thomas B. (1999), 'Antitrust Law as a Balancing Act', The 10th Annual Seattle Computer Law Conference, 17 December 1999, http://www.ftc.gov/speeches/leary/leary991217.shtm, accessed 4 November 2007, pp. 1 and 8.

[16] See Baer, *supra* note 11, at 4.

[17] See Heinemann, Andreas (2002), *Immaterialgüterschutz in der Wettbewerbsordnung*, Tübingen: Mohr Siebeck; Federal Trade Commission (2003), 'To Promote Innovation: A Proper Balance of Competition and Patent Law and Policy', 2 October 2003, http://www.ftc.gov/os/2003/10/innovationrpt.pdf.

[18] See Baer, *supra* note 11, at note 13 (referring to the US Antitrust IP Guidelines).

owner efficiently to combine complementary factors of production, and thus may be pro-competitive.

The ownership of intellectual property and the economic and social need for protection thereof was at one time an indispensable part of the complex criteria used in the assessment of mergers, especially when the merging firms were active in some of the many high-tech markets.

3 Some important features of new technologies affecting merger assessment

Concentration is usually and generally considered to potentially endanger competition because it lowers the number of competitors and permanently changes the market structure, thus jeopardizing the basic functions of free markets. As mergers may, however, bring important efficiencies, resulting, for instance, in a substantial drop of prices, a faster pace of innovation, a higher output, and consequently benefits for consumers, different points of view have to be harmonized in the process of pre-merger assessment.

High-tech markets are extremely innovative, and innovative markets are very dynamic and unstable. New technologies combined with the legal protection of intellectual property create a strong competitive advantage that can be used to override other competitors. New generations of products that undermine existing market power appear more frequently in high-tech industries than in mature industries. Market structure (network size) has in many cases lost its original impact on the competitiveness in the market – dominant firms are displaced rapidly through technical innovation and better marketing by newcomers who may in turn appear 'dominant'.[19] Existing market power of competitors in high-tech markets may be supposed to be transitory; many problems concerning competition might be 'self-corrected' through the rapid and seemingly perpetual introduction of new products.[20] Some argue that future market developments are hardly to be foreseen except in theoretical speculations,[21] and that the most desirable strategy as to new-economy mergers is forbearance, for there is no reason to believe that network effects only lead to 'snowballing' ('success breeds success'). In the mobile phone sector, for example, smaller, later entrants have gained significant market shares across Europe.[22] The recommendation based on this observation is not to block mergers, which would maintain a fragmented industry and impose

---

19 See Veljanovski, C. (2001), 'E.C. Antitrust in the New Economy: Is the European Commission's View of the Network Economy Right?', *ECLR*, **22**, 117.

20 See Pitofsky, *supra* note 11.

21 Veljanovski, *supra* note 19, at 118.

22 *Ibid*., at 116.

heavy costs in terms of higher prices to consumers, less innovation and lower productivity.[23] The connection between mergers and the capability and acceleration of innovation has to be assessed very carefully. Schumpeter's ideas (that large firms are the 'engine' of long-run progress; that their funds enable them to invent and to develop innovations and carry out demanding research; that innovations increase with the size of the firm and with market concentration) do not seem to have been proven empirically. The impact of the size of the firm and concentration (and therefore consequently of mergers) on innovation seems to be (if any) negligible.[24]

There is very often an extraordinary need for cooperation among competitors in the markets with new technologies, induced by the necessity of sharing the risk of innovations, combining complementary technologies and permitting economies of scale and scope. Some even argue that successful innovation requires cooperation among firms, and as a result some have suggested that antitrust must abandon its entrenched scepticism of cooperative arrangements and allow more freedom in high-technology markets.[25] This economic temptation to cooperate may lead, among other things, to agreements distorting or excluding competition or to the effort to avoid the principal ban of such agreements – competitors may withdraw their cooperative operations and transactions from the market simply by merging. Cooperation may then be performed 'under one hat', which is a 'double-edged' strategy that may mitigate or exclude the incentive to innovate. Some commentators even assert that increased concentration leads to diminished innovation.[26] Incentives to innovate might be harmed and reduced by a merger due to the unifying of two or more originally self-standing research departments under a single management; it might lead to a reduction in the number of research trajectories and to the lowering of spillovers to other firms. Those small firms dependent on such spillovers can even (because of a lack of cooperation with merging firms) be forced out of the market and competition for the final product might be thus weakened.[27] One may even doubt whether mergers do not sometimes create situations in which other firms are discouraged from innovations, for there is less rent to be made because of the great market share and research potential of the merged firms. The situation may be exacerbated when the merging entities possess important intellectual property rights and when the smaller

---

23 *Ibid.*, at 117.

24 See European Commission, *supra* note 6, at 20 and 70.

25 See Pitofsky, *supra* note 11, at 2.

26 See Azcuenaga, Mary L. (1997) 'Antitrust and Intellectual Property', Remarks before the ALI, Boston, 24 April 1997, http://www.ftc.gov/speeches/azcuenaga/aliaba97.htm, accessed 4 November 2007, p. 7.

27 See European Commission, *supra* note 6, at 20.

competitors are not able to produce compatible or supplementary products to those produced by the merging entities. The danger of spending money for research and development in vain can be substantiated in such cases.

Many questions connected with the new technologies raise concerns about the proper use or even appropriability of classical normative antitrust tools. For example, defining relevant markets is difficult enough under any circumstances. But it can become far more difficult in high-tech industries, where many products are not yet in existence.[28] Any merger assessment will necessarily be more difficult the more ambiguous and uncertain the definition of the relevant markets is. The definition of the relevant market by competition authorities might sometimes be rather arbitrary, for the importance of innovation – as one of the basic facts about the markets that need to be considered[29] – is expressed explicitly, although not detailed enough in practical terms. As to the possible new entry into a market dominated by new technologies, it is almost impossible to assess whether such an entry is likely, timely and of sufficient scope and magnitude.[30]

Barriers to entry, connected in some areas (such as biotechnology and the pharmaceutical industry) with high sunk costs caused by the enormous expense of research and development, force the competitors to share these costs either in a cooperative way or in a structural way (in the form of a merger). A merger would then lead both to the raising of capital that can be used for further technological development, results of which may be passed on to the consumers, and – on the other hand – to necessitating very high resources that may deter potential competitors and lead in turn to the strengthening of the market power of the merging firms. Difficulties in obtaining access to important technologies may create a barrier to entry; this can be due to the protection of their patent (technical barriers to entry). The combination of technical barriers with strategic barriers to entry (because of the established position of the incumbent firms on the market) is especially likely if well-known, leading high-tech firms are involved. These undertakings usually have a reputation, trade marks, and consumer loyalty at their disposal, but also, as a rule, high-level advertising and public relations. It is quite obvious that large firms are better capable of implementing innovations;[31] moreover, a successful innovation may help the large firm, while an unsuccessful innovation, it is

---

28 See Pitofsky, *supra* note 11, at 2.

29 See Final Draft of Commission Notice on the appraisal of horizontal mergers of 11 December 2002; similarly in the subsequently issued Guidelines on the assessment of horizontal mergers, OJ 2004 No. C 31, p. 5, paras 10, 15 and 20(b).

30 *Ibid.*, para. 18.

31 See Mische, Harald (2002), *Nicht-wettbewerbliche Faktoren in der europäischen Fusionskontrolle*, Baden-Baden: Nomos, p. 66.

supposed, will not jeopardize it substantially, as it would a small or middle-sized firm. There is a tension between entry conditions and efficiencies. As stated:[32]

> [i]t is not consistent to argue that barriers to entry are low while simultaneously arguing that the merger of two networks will result in substantial efficiencies. If there are considerable efficiencies to be achieved from rationalizing two networks this inevitably means that entry is not very easy either pre-merger or post-merger.

Mergers may be assessed as an impediment to innovations (for instance by increasing prices above marginal costs to the detriment of consumers, involving 'deadweight loss', or by reducing the merging firms' incentives to innovate, relaxing the efforts to minimize production costs, resulting in 'x-inefficiency'),[33] but they may be seen as an 'engine' thereof, too. Neither of these approaches has yet been empirically verified, and each one might be true in an individual case. Generally speaking, barriers to entry caused by a merger argue against clearance.

Tension between extremely high front-end investments and modest marginal costs of additional copies may lead firms to make use of leveraging effects on related markets (network efficiencies) and to recoup the profits from these markets by merging with the firms incumbent on those markets (internalization of network efficiencies). Network effects affect the 'first-mover advantage'. Supposing that the innovation of the first mover becomes a legally protected (patented) standard, the danger of the dominant market position of the first mover among other competitors (on the horizontal level) is obvious. There may be a 'first mover' incentive to merge with firms active in up-stream or down-stream markets (on the vertical level) with an eye to gain the profit stimulated in the related market by the innovation in the primary market (for instance when the producer of patented DVD player devices merges with producers of DVDs).

To put it in different words: leveraging is a kind of internalization and appropriation of positive externalities gained by the incumbent firms on the

---

32 Sanderson, M. and M. Trebilcock (2005), 'Merger Review in Regulated Industries', *Can. Bus. L.J.*, **42**, 166.

33 See Luescher, C. (2004), 'Efficiency Considerations in European Merger Control – Just Another Battle Ground for the European Commission, Economists and Competition Lawyers?', *ECLR*, **25**, 78. Nevertheless, a traditional price approach insisting on lower prices only and not taking into account the improvement of quality of (even more expensive) products and services may distort the substance of efficiency. Especially mergers in high-tech industries may bring about great efficiency gains despite higher prices of innovative products or services; see European Commission, *supra* note 6, at 27.

related market thanks to the innovation achieved in the primary market.[34] The merger can then serve as a leveraging tool and an extension of the dominant position from one relevant market to another.[35]

The effect of consumer 'lock-in' plays an important role in network industries as well. There are two aspects of it.[36] The first is the need to duplicate sunk investments in order to switch networks. The cost of adopting an incompatible technology imposes switching costs on consumers who switch to another network (for example from a Super 8 film camera to a Hi-8 video camera, and now again to a DVD video camera). The second aspect is that the holder of a technology has an incentive not to develop its own network but to exploit its locked-in, installed base. Promises by a firm to expand its network by charging low prices or providing lots of inexpensive software in the future are not necessarily credible.

Switching costs connected with the change from one network to another can effectively protect against the redistribution of new market shares in the market except for cases in which the new technology would bring about higher savings for the consumer than the switching costs.[37] It depends on the kind of technology – whereas for example the switching costs in the internet and mobile telephone markets are negligible, switching costs from the market for analogue video recorders or video players to the market for digital equipment are substantial and nearly prohibitive. Switching costs associated with shifting

---

34 For a precise analysis of this problem, see Rahnasto, Ilkka (2001), 'How to Leverage Intellectual Property Rights', doctorial thesis, University of Helsinki, pp. 111 *et seq.*

35 One of the recent important merger cases (European Commission of 21 January 2004, Case COMP/M.3304 – *GE/Amersham*, http://ec.europa.eu/comm/competition/mergers/cases/decisions/m3304_en.pdf) showed, among others, that leveraging analysis 'becomes redundant when there is no or limited complementarity between the products assessed'. The Commission rejected the allegations that a combination of GE's diagnostic imaging equipment and Amersham's diagnostic pharmaceutical business would result in the creation or strengthening of a dominant position through leveraging in the form of commercial, 'forced', or technical bundling; see Völcker, S.B. (2005), 'Developments in EC Competition Law in 2004: An Overview', *C.M.L. Rev.*, **42**, 1691, at 1734.

36 According to Church, Jeffrey and Roger Ware, 'Network Industries, Intellectual Property Rights and Competition Policy', in Anderson, Robert D. and Nancy T. Gallini (eds), (1998), *Competition Policy and Intellectual Property Rights in the Knowledge-Based Economy*, Calgary: University of Calgary Press, p. 227.

37 Nevertheless, Lofaro, A. and D. Ridyard, D. (2003), 'Switching Costs and Merger Assessment – Don't Move the Goalposts', ECLR, **23**, 268, assert that switching costs are too often cited as a reason for prohibiting mergers at lower levels of concentrations than would normally be justified, and that the switching costs need to be evaluated carefully against the circumstances of each case.

demand to potential substitutes create a barrier to entry and are to be considered when defining the relevant product market.[38]

Some new technologies call for a certain volume of products in order to be marketed effectively. This so-called critical mass of transactions may be high, and it may be decisive for the success of the new technology or product (for instance, a large subscriber base allowing for economies of scale). It may lead either to an aggressive pricing policy (in order to attain a dominant position) or to merging, with the same goal but without cutting the prices to beat competitors (instead: joining them on a higher price level), or to both. It is not exceptional for the production costs to drop even if the output increases (the so-called experience curve). Lowering the prices is then no predatory action, but rather efficiency passed on to consumers. Some argue that the orthodox idea that monopoly is a narcotic and that the reward of monopoly is to enjoy the 'quiet life' hardly describes many of the aggressive, dynamic, innovative high-technology firms in today's economy.[39] It is not out of the question that a low initial price will be regarded by the antitrust authority as predatory pricing regardless of the impossibility of attracting new customers in any other way. More customers lead to lower unit prices, which attract further subscribers, allowing a further lowering of the prices.[40] Achieving the critical mass is economically indispensable and therefore the usual recommendation[41] is not to prohibit the behaviour of firms leading to this goal, even if it were to strengthen a dominant market position. There is probably hardly any reasonable basis to generally reject mergers aiming at achieving the 'critical-mass level of production' externally (instead of by internal growth), even if it led to the same negative, potentially anti-competitive effect. Otherwise a special kind of conflict of goals would be generated, namely between the theoretical and normative conditions of workable competition on the one hand and consumer welfare on the other hand.

---

[38] See Commission Notice of 9 December 1997 on the definition of the relevant market for the purposes of Community competition law, OJ 1997 No. C 372, p. 5.

[39] See Pitofsky, *supra* note 11, at 3.

[40] See Veljanovski, *supra* note 19, at 119. This is pertinently characterized as a 'chicken and egg' problem.

[41] See Wissenschaftlicher Beirat beim Bundesministerium für Wirtschaft und Technologie (2001), 'Wettbewerbspolitik für den Cyberspace, Gutachten vom 6. Juli 2001', http://www.bmwi.de/BMWi/Redaktion/PDF/__Archiv/Cyber.pdf,property=pdf,bereich=bmwi,sprache=de,rwb=true.pdf, accessed 4 November 2007, p. 32. See also Sullivan, Lawrence A. and Warren S. Grimes (2006), *The Law of Antitrust: An Integrated Handbook*, 2nd ed., St. Paul, MN: Thompson/West, pp. 148 *et seq.*: 'Neither conclusive empirical evidence nor a convincing theoretical case that protecting a monopolist from competitive discipline will produce more innovation or ensure its more rapid marketing'.

Network efficiencies are not exclusively but very often connected with new technologies. There are frequently good short-term economic grounds to allow firms that are active in network markets to grow externally. For example, building one mobile phone network on one territory might be cheaper than building two or three networks, and, theoretically, a substantial part of the saved investment costs may be passed onto the consumer as a lower price for telecommunication services. Great market power might endanger competition in a long-term prospect. A network – once it achieves dominance through network efficiencies – can preclude competition for extended periods. Then it is easy for the monopolist to exclude would-be challengers. A network monopolist may have the ability to monopolize successive generations of a product, or complementary products or services, for example, in such a way that the monopolist allows only the manufacturing of products connected with the existing network. One result may be that over time, the best products or services may not win out.[42] Indeed, one can assert that there might be some purely economic short-term reasons for enabling the merger to operate in order to achieve maximized network efficiencies; on the other hand, there are very good reasons, concerning long-term efficiencies and social welfare based on the existence of competition, for doing just the opposite and for not clearing such a merger. External long-term efficiency and social welfare depending on competition should not be given up for 'internal' efficiency of the respective undertakings. The positive multiplying effect of a network can be preserved without having to jeopardize or distort competition by a merger when, for example, telecommunication firms are forced to interconnect their networks in order to enable access to any client of one firm to the network of the other. 'While compatibility would increase the size of the network and the social benefits from the network externality, it is likely to decrease the profits of the respective (incumbent) firm. . . . Compatibility equalizes the installed base of the entrant and of the present (incumbent) firm'[43] and changes the nature of the competition between the firms. 'Compatibility eliminates the installed-base advantage, and thus the monopoly, of the incumbent'.[44] Therefore a recommendation for the merger policy might be not to block the merger, supposing that some merger efficiencies are likely to occur, but to impose the introduction of compatibility or interoperability, if possible in technical terms. Network externalities connected with strong intellectual property protection potentially consolidate the sustained market dominance. The substance of a network results in a limited number of competing systems and

---

42 See Wissenschaftlicher Beirat, *supra* note 41, at 4.
43 Church and Ware, *supra* note 36, at 237.
44 *Ibid.*, at 240 *et seq.*

in standardization – that is, consequently, in monopolization.[45] The merger is only one possible way of lowering the number of competing systems, without necessarily being successful in setting the standard.

Technological follow-up relations between different products and services in high-tech industries may lead to many attempts to leverage one firm's position in one relevant market to the other upstream – or downstream – market in order to enhance the possibility of strategic network effects.[46] This is possible either in a cooperative way (cartel agreements, leveraging joint-ventures, strategic alliances) or in the form of a vertical merger or a partial acquisition. As a result, a 'gatekeeper effect', which enables a firm to gain control of portals or other gateways, may occur.[47] Thus Microsoft tried to acquire minority stakes in cable companies in many countries for the purpose of influencing these companies' decision to adopt Microsoft's software package for television set-top boxes for cable and television. The European Commission was concerned about the risk of Microsoft's dominating the market for next-generation television set-top boxes for cable TV, thereby foreclosing competition.

4 Merger-related ways of abusing intellectual property rights

Despite some specific features mentioned above, there is generally no reason to assess the behaviour of competing firms or their structural changes independently of the complex criteria of competition law. New technologies, even if covered by intellectual property protection, do not create a kind of 'competitive reserve', and 'none of the specific "high-tech" differences justifies a complete or even a substantial exemption'.[48] To understand the specific features thereof and their impact on workable competition is only a prerequisite for involving these aspects in the general assessment of the individual case. The existence of IPRs is only one of many numerous criteria to be taken into account when finding out whether there is any creating or strengthening of the possibility of restricting workable competition.[49] These rights may not be allowed to harm or to exclude competition behind the curtain of declared 'innovation antitrust immunity'.

4.1 Anti-competitive acquisitions

A main role of IPRs is to motivate innovators and to give them a guarantee that they will recoup a substantial part of profits if they contribute to economic

---

45 *Ibid.*, at 229.

46 *Ibid.*, at 239 *et seq.*

47 See Anderman, S. (2002) 'EC Competition Law and Intellectual Property Rights in the New Economy', *Antitrust Bull.*, **47**, Summer/Fall, 299.

48 See Pitofsky, *supra* note 11, at 3.

49 See Heinemann, *supra* note 5, at 616.

welfare. They do not incorporate any 'higher values' preventing IPRs from becoming anti-competitive after all. Acquisitions of patents can be used to acquire or maintain monopoly power. The typical scheme is that 'the merging firms are either the only two, or two of only a few firms capable of innovating in high-tech markets. In such situations, the acquisition would lead to almost certain anti-competitive effects'.[50] The acquisition of an equivalent patent covering the only known economic alternative to the monopolist's product or process is a kind of exclusionary conduct.

Such an acquisition forecloses potential competition by rivals who might otherwise have access to the patent. Even the acquisition of one out of several equivalent patents might have exclusionary effects. 'In industries where the main focus of competition is the development of new technologies rather than price competition, that competitive rivalry must be protected. If too much of the ability to innovate in a relevant market is concentrated in one entity, and substitutes are lacking, competition may suffer.'[51]

4.2 Patent pools

Sometimes merging may be functionally 'substituted' by multiple patents. If, for example, two firms have competing patents, each of them can be practised independently of the other and licensees may choose among them with respect to their own priorities. Supposing the two patents are equivalent and neither of them is superior to the other, 'one patentee licensing the other (or the patentees engaging in reciprocal licensing) with a price condition would probably be a masquerade for naked horizontal price fixing'.[52] Also, horizontal price fixing has in some respects the same consequences for consumers as the merger of the respective firms, namely the same price (higher than the competitive price, as a rule). Patent pooling might therefore be regarded as a quasi-merger among the patentees.

Of course, not every patent pool is fated to be anti-competitive. No concerns arise in cases where the patent pools are not a veil for a disguised cartel or for the hidden goal to foreclose markets. Patent pools may serve, similar to other types of purely financial pro-competitive cooperation, as a tool for developing, introducing and marketing new products or services depending on related patents, without the combining of which the new product would not be developed. Patent pools do not automatically equal blocking patents. Some new products or services may be developed only in such a way that

---

50 Baer, *supra* note 11, at 4.

51 *Ibid.*

52 See Areeda, Phillip and Louis Kaplow (1997), *Antitrust Analysis (Problems, Text, Cases)*, 5th ed., New York, NY: Aspen Law & Business, p. 433.

some different patent solutions have to be combined. Competing firms may set up the patent pool as a separate entity that contains the relevant patents needed to manufacture a product or a category of products,[53] or they may try to merge. Generally, combining substitutable intellectual property (and the related protective rights) in a merger will likely result in an anti-competitive foreclosure of the market, while combining complementary intellectual property will probably be considered pro-competitive, enabling the very development and production of the new product.

5 Assessing mergers with regard to innovations and dynamic efficiency

It has been convincingly argued[54] that there is little probability that most asserted goals of a merger could not have been achieved without the merger (that is, by different cooperative activities). Only a minority of asserted merger goals are merger-specific. According to modern economic theory, 'virtually anything that can be done with a merger can *in principle* be done instead with some kind of contract, perhaps a very complex (or restrictive) one'.[55] A realistic assessment of the theoretical substitutability of a merger by other means nevertheless leads one to ask what would really happen absent the merger. Might we perhaps adapt and extend this presumption to the new technologies and intellectual property rights connected with them: hardly any of the specific features of new technologies are merger-specific; instead, the new technology and the rights involved are subject to general merger assessment. Opinions about the general immunity of intellectual property rights to the complex competition analysis seem to have been seriously weakened theoretically (if not uprooted), and (what is much more important) they are not shared by antitrust authorities or courts all over the world.

Both merger-specific efficiencies and merger-specific inefficiencies to be expected and envisaged in a post-merger situation should be considered regardless of whether tangible property or intellectual property is concerned. As stated, maybe a little bit speculatively and in a double-edged way, 'direct competition between the parties pre-merger can be an important obstacle to achieving synergies without a merger, and thus tends to make efficiencies more merger-specific than they otherwise would be'.[56]

Innovations are in many industries the most important competitive factor. Therefore, the legal regulation of IPRs is placed at the very interface with

---

53 See Lind, R.C. and P. Muysert (2003), 'Innovation and Competition Policy: Challenges for the New Millennium', *ECLR*, **24**, 91.

54 See Farrell, J. and C. Shapiro (2000–1), 'Scale Economies and Synergies in Horizontal Merger Analysis', *Antitrust L.J.*, **68**, 685.

55 *Ibid.*, at 691.

56 *Ibid.*, at 710.

antitrust enforcement. Some kind of monopolization is inevitable for the protection of innovators (that is, of innovations). Mergers are hardly supposed to be principally a prerequisite for protecting innovations; they may more likely be a way to abuse a dominant position achieved by the joint possession of IPRs. Intellectual property rights of merging parties have to be included in the general analysis of whether the rationale behind the merger is probably pro-competitive[57] or not.

The question is how to assess or even measure different efficiencies (allocative, productive and dynamic ones) and the probability of achieving a higher standard of consumer welfare, and how to compare them with the actual or potential danger to competition.[58]

The development in many innovation markets is hard to predict. Nevertheless, it is necessary to have an idea about possible future developments in order to achieve a possible balance between actual profits and dynamic efficiency and to assess the impact of a merger on competition and, consequently, on consumer welfare in the future. As the relevant markets for some products might not yet have been developed in some industries (such as a pharmaceutical product that cannot be marketed before attaining state approval after a long testing period), a theoretical concept of the innovation market (that is, the market of innovations in the respective area) has been developed. The main reason might be that no dominant position, and thus danger of its abuse, can occur in a non-existing market, and therefore no market-dominance test can be used. Nevertheless, despite the fact that neither the European Commission nor US antitrust agencies have adopted an

---

57 See Kolasky, W.J. (2002), 'What is Competition?', Presentation at a seminar on convergence, The Hague, 28 February 2002, http://www.usdoj.gov/atr/public/speeches/200440.htm, accessed 4 November 2007, p. 3, arguing that most mergers have no adverse effect on competition and that the main task of competition authorities is to screen out the few bad mergers from the many good ones. There are, of course, substantially stricter general approaches to mergers. Thus, for example, Porter, *supra* note 9, at 943, asserts that mergers should be treated with special caution compared to other corporate growth strategies for five reasons: (1) The question is not whether there is a risk to competition but how much; (2) Society should be biased in favour of independent company activity over mergers, for things like introducing a new product or building a new factory are far more likely to boost productivity; (3) The empirical evidence is striking that mergers have a low success rate; (4) Smaller, focused acquisitions are more likely to improve productivity than mergers among leaders; (5) It is important not to assume that a merger will be efficient and profitable because companies propose it. Every merger needs to be weighed against the productivity growth standard.

58 See Leary, *supra* note 7, asserting that 'economic analysis is not an ultimate value, but a methodology that mediates between conflicting claims of freedom that are the core value of antitrust'.

innovation market concept,[59] the hypothetical development in the product markets that do not yet exist is taken into account as a regular part of the assessment of the technological and innovative potential of merging firms. Nor is this concept of 'future markets'[60] free from the obvious danger of a subjective and arbitrary evaluation of prognostic 'decisions' about future development in the market.

Despite the explicit theoretical rejection of the concept of 'innovation market', it may still implicitly and tacitly be applied. Thus, in *Monsanto/Pharmacia & Upjohn*[61] the Commission approved the merger of two companies with heavy investments in pharmaceutical products. The main reason was to enable the merged subject to make further demanding financial investments in already advanced long-term R&D projects, to allow the firms 'increasing R&D costs across a broader range of products and to spread the risk involved in every new research project over a larger capital base'. In that way the arguments of the merging parties were supported that they were facing strong competition from many multinational companies and that the proposed economies of scale would enable them to face this competition after the merger. Reasonable prediction of the future changes in the 'innovation market' may thus indeed be taken into account. Sustaining future competition (or a reasonable probability thereof) from third parties after the merger facilitates the clearance of a merger even when the merger will lower the number of research trajectories.[62]

Like other assets to be considered in merger assessment, intellectual property and its exercise might be subject principally to three methods (appraisal tests), which have been given special names, namely:

- the market dominance test (MD);
- the test of substantial lessening of (or substantial impediment to) effective competition (SLC, SIEC);

---

[59] See Ullrich, Hanns (1999), 'Antitrust Laws Relating to High Technology Industries – A Case for or Against International Rules?', in Zäch, *supra* note 8, p. 281; see also Landman, L.B. (1998), 'Protecting the Future: Competition to Innovate and Future Markets', *Antitrust Report*, June, p. 1, asserting that, despite the wording of the 1995 US IP Antitrust Guidelines on protecting competition in innovation markets, the agencies do not in fact define innovation markets but only future product markets. In other words, 'the agencies protect competition in markets for products which do not yet exist. The agencies do not protect competition in markets in which the "product" is innovation itself'.

[60] Derivable from Article 1(1)(b) Regulation 139/2004.

[61] Case COMP/ M. 1835, as referred to by Reimann, C. (2004), 'Essential Function vs. Essential Facility: Defining the Amount of R&D protection in High-tech Industries after *IMS* and *Microsoft*', *Comp. L. Rev.*, **1** (2), 49, 57 *et seq.*

[62] Case *Pfizer/Warner Lambert*, as referred to by Reimann, *ibid.*, at 58.

- the test of productivity growth standard.

While studying this issue, one cannot help getting the overwhelming impression that only different words or a different accentuation of the same complex assessment of mergers are being used.[63]

The *market dominance test* is a basis for assessing the future merger by inquiring whether the merger will probably cause or strengthen the dominant market position of the merging parties. This test is practised in many European countries, and it was and is used in the EC Merger Regulations 4064/1989 and 139/2004. However, Article 2(2) and (3) of ECMR 139/2004 states explicitly that the creation or strengthening of a dominant position is only an example (one possibility) of how effective competition in the common market or in a substantial part of it might be significantly impeded.[64] In other words, a possible significant impediment of effective competition as a consequence of concentration is not the only criterion of (in)compatibility of the concentration with the Common Market. It is groundless to assert (only on the basis of the ECMR wording) that a dominance paradigm in assessing mergers is continuing. It is not settled that there is a meaningful difference between 'significant impeding' and 'substantial lessening' of competition. Both terms allow a different interpretation but also a totally identical interpretation.

In the case of *Schneider Electric SA v. Commission*,[65] the Court of First Instance confirmed that Article 2(3) ECMR 4064/89 involves both the dominance test and the test of impediment to effective competition. With regard to the change of the wording of Article 2(2) in the new ECMR 139/2004, the controversy over whether the dominance concept contains one or two tests and whether just one part (creation or strengthening of a dominant position) or both (such a dominant position *and* a significant impediment to effective competition) must be satisfied to declare a merger incompatible with the Common Market does not look so critical. There have been cases decided by the European Commission in which a merger was not approved even despite

---

63 See Alfter, M. (2003), 'Untersagungskriterien in der Fusionskontrolle – SLC-Test versus Marktbeherrschende Stellung – Eine Frage der Semantik?', *WuW*, 20.

64 Article 2(2) ECMR: 'A concentration which would not significantly impede effective competition in the common market or in a substantial part of it, *in particular* [emphasis added] as a result of the creation or strengthening of a dominant position, shall be declared compatible with the common market'. Article 2(3) ECMR: 'A concentration which would significantly impede effective competition in the common market or in a substantial part of it, *in particular* [emphasis added] as a result of the creation or strengthening of a dominant position, shall be declared incompatible with the common market'.

65 Case T-310/01, *Schneider Electric v. Commission*, [2002] ECR II-4071; see comments by Luescher, *supra* note 33, at 78 *et seq.*

the fact that the parties to the merger had not achieved and would not achieve a dominant position.[66]

Different accents (neglecting the formal dominant position and considering the real impact on competition) are applied under the *SLC test*. Some concerns might be connected with the fact that strong innovative firms usually very rapidly achieve a dominant position even in the high-tech industries, and that the market-dominance test is therefore less useful. The standard of substantial lessening of competition is often said to provide a more adequate focus than that of dominance, because often markets will have a dominant firm in any case, and so 'for many mergers in the new economy the relevant question is whether a merger will strengthen or weaken competition in the process of determining the dominant firm'.[67] The SLC test is usually considered to be more flexible and less (legally) rigid than the dominance test, to be closer to the spirit of the economically based analysis undertaken in merger control[68] and to be a 'tougher' test for a merger's proponents than a dominance-based test.[69] The SLC test is supposed to 'address both unilateral and coordinated effects. By contrast, critics of the MD test suggest the MD test unduly limits the regulator's ability to tackle unilateral effects where a merger does not lead to single firm dominance'.[70]

It is obvious that flexible application and reasonable decision-making can in practice achieve results comparable with the SLC test, even if basically the theoretical concept named 'test of dominant position' were preserved.

The *test of productivity growth standard* has been proposed in order to stress the importance of the rate of innovations (dynamic efficiency) among the goals of antitrust policy.[71] According to this point of view, the traditional hierarchy of these goals is allegedly (without referring to the reason for this sequence) as follows: (1) limiting price-cost margins or firms' profitability as the most important outcome for consumers (allocative efficiency) resulting in limiting market power as the major focus of attention of antitrust authorities;

---

66 See European Commission of 19 March 2001, Case COMP/M.2353 – *RWE/Hidroélectrica del Cantábrico*, http://ec.europa.eu/comm/competition/mergers/cases/decisions/m2353_en.pdf., accessed 4 November 2007.

67 See Lind and Muysert, *supra* note 53, at 92.

68 Green Paper of 11 December 2001 on the Review of Council Regulation (EEC) No. 4046/89, COM(2001) 746/6 final = http://ec.europa.eu/comm/competition/mergers/review/green_paper/en.pdf, accessed 4 November 2007, p. 40.

69 See Goddard, G. and E. Curry (2003), 'New Zealand's New Merger Test: A Comparison of Dominance and Substantial Lessening of Competition Test', *ECLR*, **24**, 300.

70 See Dubow, B., D. Elliot and E. Morrison (2004), 'Unilateral Effects and Merger Simulation Models', *ECLR*, **25**, 114.

71 See Porter, *supra* note 9, at 919 *et seq*. and 933 *et seq*.

(2) cost or technical efficiency (static efficiency); (3) innovativeness (the rate of dynamic improvement, dynamic efficiency).

Porter suggests reversing the traditional hierarchy of goals and switching from 'profitability standard' to 'productivity growth standard', and explicates: 'because of its direct effect on productivity growth, the most important goal for society is a healthy process of dynamic improvement, which requires innovations in products, processes, or ways of managing'.[72] According to him, a faster rate of innovation overwhelms static economies of scale, particularly in an age in which a knowledge-based economy is the rule. Technical (static) efficiency should be the second most important goal, considering the value of the product or service. Instead of seeing higher prices as inherently undesirable for consumers, 'higher prices should be a danger sign in antitrust analysis only if they are not justified by rising customer value'.[73] Short-term consumer welfare measured by price is evaluated as a dubious goal. The static focus of antitrust and the rapid change in technology-intensive industries have undermined antitrust's legitimacy. Since innovation is the basic drive of productivity growth, promoting and protecting it should be central.[74]

The question of how to apply this 'productivity standard' in practice and what tools are to be developed in order to predict the future health of competition and future productivity growth is essential. A five-forces analysis proposed by Porter[75] suggests examining five factors, which I have somewhat condensed here:

- rivalry among existing competitors;
- threat of substitute products or services;
- threat of new entrants;
- bargaining power of suppliers;
- bargaining power of buyers.

Porter's criticism that current merger analysis is hamstrung by an unclear and questionable central goal (limiting short-term price–cost margins), that the Herschman-Herfindahl Index, on which the process is built, is a questionable measure of competition, that the merger evaluation is compromised by its reliance on short-term price and quantity analysis, and that the result is a 'false precision' and says little about what will occur in the long run[76] may be true. Nevertheless, special tools are undoubtedly needed, not only in the relevant

---

72 *Ibid.*, at 934.
73 *Ibid.*
74 *Ibid.*, at 936.
75 See *ibid.*, at 938 *et seq.*
76 *Ibid.*, at 949.

legal texts (in order to minimize arbitrariness and legal uncertainty and raise the transparency and predictability of merger assessment), but to enable practical proceedings of merger appraisal executed by the antitrust authorities, too. The methodological hindrance that is never to be completely surmounted is the next development, the assessment of which often lies in the space between value-conditioned preconceptions and some level of probability.[77]

6 Conclusion

The growing importance of innovation is indisputable. Drastic and rapid innovations admittedly may often disrupt the market (creating new winner-take-all races) and sometimes, and to some extent, act as a substitute for antitrust regulation (overturning the dominant firms as a self-corrective force).

Because of many specific features of innovation markets (some of them commented on in sections 3 and 4), however, the self-correcting force may be weakened or even excluded in practice. Dynamic efficiency considerations in assessing mergers (regardless of whether in an MD, SLC, SIEC, productivity-based or similar approach) are now and will in the future be more than ever an indispensable part of merger appraisal. The assessment of IPRs and antitrust (as double-edged tools to achieve a compromise between the values of innovation incentives and the protection of competition) is supposed to be more dynamic-efficiency oriented.[78]

In the EU, the former Commission Notice on the appraisal of horizontal mergers did not seem to share this conviction of the dynamic-efficiency solution.[79] The recommendations and general evaluations involved there are subject to interpretation, which may be very diverse.

The requirements that the consumers profit directly, and that this profit be

---

[77] Porter, *ibid.*, at 949, speaks of a *good* analysis that considers what could happen, although maybe only a *God's* analysis could be reliable.

[78] These considerations are no exception. Numerous cases have shown, for example, concessions of intellectual property protection in favour of sustainable long-term competition, as a main drive of productivity, in terms of Porter's theory (Porter, *supra* note 9, at 958), claiming that 'we should not be debating the size of the company, the market definition, nor what the "correct" Hirschman-Herfindahl Index should be. We should be debating the merger or joint venture's impact on productivity growth and on the health of competition, using tools that capture the richness of competition and match with the reality faced by firms'. See, for example, overviews and methodological recommendations in this sense as pointed out by Delrahim, Makan (2004), 'Forcing Firms to Share The Sandbox: Compulsory Licensing of Intellectual Property Rights and Antitrust', Presentation, London, 10 May 2004, http://www.usdoj.gov/atr/public/speeches/203627.htm, accessed 4 November 2007; Statement of the Federal Trade Commission's Bureau of Competition on Negotiating Mergers Remedies, http://www.ftc.gov/bc/bestpractices/bestpractices030401.shtm, accessed 4 November 2007.

[79] See Commission Notice of 11 December 2002 on the appraisal of horizontal

probable and timely, raise at least concern over whether the Commission will not tend to stick to short-term efficiencies rather than turning to long-term ones supporting the productivity-growth approach recommended by Porter. According to Paragraph 91 of the Guidelines, trade-offs between efficiency gains and anti-competitive effects across markets are not envisaged (for only direct benefit is considered).[80]

The new Guidelines on the assessment of horizontal mergers of February 2004 are a bit less peremptory in this respect. The overall competitive appraisal of the merger is envisaged, and the relevant benchmark in assessing efficiency claims is that the consumer will not be worse off as a result of the merger. Efficiencies should be substantial and timely and should *in principle* benefit consumers in those relevant markets where it is otherwise likely that competition concerns will occur.[81] Some trade-offs across the markets are therefore not excluded as an exception.

Basing the decision of whether to approve mergers on sound economics supported by strong empirical evidence[82] is a generally acceptable position. Nevertheless, in a particular case of innovation-related merger it may be quite inappropriate to rely on traditional empirical evidence.

On the other hand, the division of the burden of proof introduced by the Notice (and repeated by the Guidelines on horizontal mergers in paragraph 87)

---

mergers, http://ec.europa.eu/comm/competition/mergers/review/final_draft_en.pdf, accessed 4 November 2007. Some references to innovation are included, for example, in paragraph 13 (general importance of innovation as an element for considering the possible anti-competitive effects of merger), paragraph 18 (in cases where innovation is the main competitive force, the Commission will examine how the merger will affect the competitive pressure to innovate), paragraph 21 (access to leading technologies as a possible element of market power), paragraph 70 (on how the merger will affect the competitive pressure to innovate in the market; against mergers between competitors that previously provided the most important innovations and now block this pressure), paragraph 81 (barriers to entry consisting, for example, in the possession of innovation, R&D, intellectual property rights, access to important technologies), paragraph 83 (assessment of the likely evolution of market has to involve the impact of possible future innovations), paragraph 87 (the development of technical and economic progress as an efficiency, provided that it is to the consumer's advantage and does not form an obstacle to competition), paragraphs 90–94 (this efficiency-including development of new products or new services has to benefit the consumers directly and to be merger-specific, substantial, timely and verifiable, realistic and attainable and not merely theoretical, further verifiable and likely to materialize).

[80] See Luescher, *supra* note 33, at 86.

[81] See Guidelines of 5 February 2004 on the assessment of horizontal mergers under the Council Regulation on the control of concentrations between undertakings, OJ 2004 No. C 31, p. 5.

[82] See Kolasky, *supra* note 57, at 4.

that has been criticized as being discriminatory[83] does not raise any concern. Paragraph 95 of the former Notice and paragraph 87 of the Guidelines require the merging parties to prove efficiencies counteracting any adverse effects on competition that might otherwise result from the merger and therefore benefit consumers.[84] The burden of proving the creation or strengthening of a dominant position by the merger rests on the Commission. This division is the only possible and reasonable solution. Each of the parties to the proceeding (that is, the antitrust authority and the merging parties) is entitled to prove the facts and justified assumptions which it is best able to express. The opposite situation (the authority proving the efficiencies and the merging parties asserting the creation or strengthening of a dominant position) would be absurd. Moreover, each party to the proceeding has the right to challenge the evidence and allegations of the opposite party.

On this issue there is no contradiction[85] of the competition concept laid down in the ECMR according to which market dominance may be linked to the ability to raise prices above the competitive level in the absence of efficiency. Which party is supposed to supply the respective information is only a technical question, and it is the Commission that has to compare and assess different evidence and make a decision. What might be a problem is the possibility of imposing a heavier burden on the parties to prove efficiencies than on the Commission to assert the creation or strengthening of a dominant position. But the decision is subject to general judicial review. Generally, the need for flexibility in competition policy and for a very complex analysis in dynamic competitive markets is indisputable. As has been stated earlier, 'there are few shortcuts or rules of thumb that can be counted upon to produce the correct policy response in all or even most cases'.[86] A reasonable method of policy-making, particularly in dynamic competitive markets, seems to entail an inevitable compromise with the strict requirement of legal certainty, which can only be achieved in more or less general terms. In addition, some non-economic values usually play a part in any decision-making,[87] and 'antitrust

[83] Luescher, *supra* note 33, at 86.

[84] It is to be added that the Guidelines do not insist on direct benefit for consumers.

[85] Unlike Luescher, *supra* note 33, at 86.

[86] See Lind and Muysert, *supra* note 53, at 92.

[87] See Brunell, R.M. (2001), 'Appropriability in Antitrust: How Much is Enough?', *Antitrust L.J.*, **69**, 1, at 42, stating that 'empirical investigation is certainly worthwhile. But the limitation of dynamic efficiency analysis should be recognized, and the analysis should not obscure the "non-economic" values that are inherent in antitrust policymaking. . . . An informed guess about dynamic efficiency considerations is likely to be a function of the bias or ideological conviction of the observer.

enforcement along economic lines . . . incorporates large doses of hunch, faith, and intuition'.[88] The prediction of future developments and assessment of future potential anti-competitive effects and future potential efficiencies, which always contain an element of uncertainty and subjectivity,[89] call for a rule-of-reason approach in assessing mergers, particularly in high-tech industries.

The suspicion that the Commission Notice on appraisal of horizontal mergers favours short-term productive efficiency over long-term innovative efficiency has already been expressed.[90] A more traditional approach, oriented less toward productivity growth and long-term aims, seemed to dominate in the past. The Guidelines – as a result of comments to the Notice – seem to have opened a way to a more flexible and complex assessment of mergers.

The position of the Chicago School prevails in the US today, according to which the only goal of antitrust law is economic efficiency leading to the enhancement of consumer welfare; it is already a stable tendency in US antitrust decision-making practice. Some argue that antitrust law is the same as microeconomics[91] and that it has become a branch of economics.[92]

The support of economic efficiency and of the concept of consumer welfare is considered as a supreme principle of antitrust law.[93] There is no terminological unity on this issue. It is sometimes stated[94] that the goal of consumer surplus (which is the excess of value that consumers experience over what they pay) is being pursued in the US, although courts, officials and lawyers frequently describe this policy as the pursuit of efficiency.

The rivals of the Chicago School, who aimed at the recognition of further aims of antitrust law beyond economic efficiency (such as to prevent transfer of wealth from consumers to producers, to prevent accumulation of economic

---

Moreover, the determination of "what matters" will itself be highly controversial and cannot be settled apolitically. As many others have shown, the retreat to an efficiency-only standard is futile in its attempt to use objective or "scientific" means to resolve (or mask) controversial normative disputes'.

[88] Pitofsky, R. (1979), 'The Political Content of Antitrust', *U. Pa. L. Rev.*, **127**, 1051, at 1065, quoted by Brunell, *ibid.*

[89] See Leary, *supra* note 7, at 6.

[90] See Luescher, *supra* note 33, at 86.

[91] See Fox, E.M. and L.A. Sullivan (1987), 'Antitrust-Retrospective and Prospective: Where Are We Coming from? Where Are We Going?', *N.Y.U. L. Rev.*, **62**, 936, 945.

[92] Easterbrook, F.H. (1987), 'Allocating Antitrust Decisionmaking Tasks', *Geo. L.J*, **76**, 305.

[93] See Schlossberg, Robert S. (ed.) (2004), *Mergers and Acquisitions*, 2nd ed., Chicago: ABA, p. 379.

[94] See Gifford, D.J. and R.T. Kudrle (2005), 'Rhetoric and Reality in the Merger Standard of the United States, Canada, and the European Union', *Antitrust L.J.*, **72**, 423, 424.

power, to protect the freedom of decision-making of smaller firms, etc.) were suppressed in the discussion, and in particular decision practice does not support them.[95]

The goals of European competition law are set up and interpreted in a much more flexible way in fundamental legal documents of the EU and in the decision practice of the Commission and of the courts. The creation and functioning of a single market has a central role among them;[96] nevertheless, the support of consumer welfare and enhancing of economic efficiency are counted among them as well.[97]

Maintenance of competition and of free markets, keeping the producers under permanent pressure from competition in order to motivate them to improve quality, to innovate and to set reasonable prices – these elements were always considered to be the prerequisites of efficiency. Put in different terms, the goal of European competition law is to preserve free competition as a *tool* needed for achieving the aim of consumer welfare.

From this point of view the vilification of this motivation seems to be overhasty and not well supported.[98] According to some American specialists, the EU pursues its competition policy based on support for commercial rivalry rather than on support for consumer surplus[99] and enforces distributive values as well that may (and sometimes even do) prevail over the maximization of immediate consumer welfare. This policy of protection of competition is considered to protect the incumbent participants in the market against newcomers and is said to be able to result in the protection of competitors.

Letting firms grow 'externally', or by mergers, up to the near-monopoly stage with the reasoning (or belief) that consumers will be economically best

---

95 See Mayer, C. (2005), *Ziele und Grenzen des Kartellverbots im Recht der EG und der USA*, Baden-Baden: Nomos, pp. 35 *et seq*.

96 See, for example, Monti, M. (2002), 'Article 81 and Public Policy', *C.M.L. Rev.*, **39**, 1057, 1063; Whish, Richard (2003), *Competition Law*, 5th ed., London and Edinburgh: Butterworths, p. 21; Ehlermann, C.D. (1992) 'The Contribution of the EC Competition Policy to the Single Market', *C.M.L. Rev.*, **29**, 257.

97 See XXIInd Report on Competition Policy, 1992, p. 18, point 3. This Report, at p. 12, declares explicitly that one of the main goals of the European Competition Policy is to support consumer interests and to ensure that consumers participate in the welfare created by the European economy.

98 A representative analysis of the economic assessment of mergers (see European Commission, *supra* note 6, at 54) even asserts that the *majority* of economists is of the view that competition policy should not pursue exclusively the interests of consumers and that it is about the maximization of the *total* surplus, that is, the aggregate sum of contributions both to consumers and to producers. From this point of view the profit transfer from consumers to producers because of rising prices does not seem to be so dramatic.

99 See Gifford and Kudrle, *supra* note 94.

served by one provider may be justified from a short-term point of view. The lack of competitive pressure in the long term and the threat of future inefficiencies, however, can hardly be countervailed by any state regulation. In addition, state regulation is usually very expensive (it is at least more expensive than preserving the competitive market) and consequently may be economically detrimental to consumers (being paid for by taxpayers). Regulation then only imperfectly and expensively substitutes the cheap and efficient impact of existing competitive pressure.

An article under the headline 'Innovation is King (in Antitrust Agencies)' appeared in the *Business Week* on 15 May 2000. There, it is said that '[t]raditionally regulators concentrated on whether companies artificially hiked prices or reduced output. Now, they are increasingly likely to look first at whether corporate behaviour aids or impedes innovation'.[100] Mergers in high-technology industries (with their short-lived technologies and products) have previously been considered less dangerous for competition than would similar mergers in industries that have entered a stable phase.[101] The question remains whether antitrust authorities and judges will keep going in this direction.[102]

---

[100] See Gilbert, R.J. and W.K. Tom (2001), 'Is Innovation King at the Antitrust Agencies? The Intellectual Property Guidelines Five Years Later', *Antitrust L.J*, **69**, 43, at 69. They assert further that 'economic theory does not prove that more competition is better for R&D and statistical studies do not support that conclusion either. At the same time, neither economic theory nor statistical studies support a conclusion that highly concentrated markets promote R&D and there is considerable anecdotal evidence to the contrary.'

[101] See Jacquemin, Alexis (1994), *Goals and Means of European Antitrust Policy After 1992*, Malmö: Lund University Press, p. 47, referring to previous conclusions by Ordover and Baumol from 1988.

[102] Thus Anderman, *supra* note 47, at 308, criticizes the arbitrary definition of the relevant market in EC competition law. He argues that the findings of dominance are sometimes suspect and the definitions of abuse ignore the full entitlement of intellectual property rights holders to obtain what the market will bear. The *circulus vitiosus* (on the one hand, the markets have to exist in order to make full use of what the holders of IPR offer, but on the other hand, the market is often defined arbitrarily) is continuing.

PART 5

THE EFFECT OF IP LAWS AS SUCH ON COMPETITION

13 Limiting IP protection for competition policy reasons – a case study based on the EU spare-parts-design discussion

Annette Kur

1 Introduction

In September 2004, the European Commission launched its proposal for a repairs clause to be inserted in the Directive 98/71/EC on the protection of industrial designs.[1] The purpose of the proposed provision is to enable the independent making and distribution of 'must-match' component parts of complex products for repair purposes, in spite of the protection of such parts by an industrial design right, under the condition that consumers are correctly informed about the commercial origin of the part.

The proposal for a new Article 14 is worded as follows:

> 1. Protection as a design shall not exist for a design which constitutes a component part of a complex product used within the meaning of Article 12(1) of this Directive, for the purpose of the repair of that complex product so as to restore its original appearance.
> 2. Member States shall ensure that consumers are duly informed about the origin of spare parts so that they can make an informed choice between competing spare parts.

[1] Proposal of 14 September 2004 for a Directive of the European Parliament and of the Council amending Directive 98/71/EC on the legal protection of designs, COM(2004) 582 final = http://eur-lex.europa.eu/LexUriServ/site/en/com/2004/com2004_0582en01.pdf, accessed 4 November 2007. For a positive evaluation of the proposal see Drexl, J., R.M. Hilty and A. Kur (2005), 'Design Protection for Spare Parts and the Commission's Proposal for a Repairs Clause', *IIC*, **36,** 448. For a different opinion – in particular criticizing the Commission's interpretation of the EPEC study (*infra* note 12), see Straus, J. (2005), 'Design Protection for Spare Parts Gone in Europe? Proposed Changes to the EC Directive: The Commission's Mandate and its Doubtful Execution', *EIPR*, **27**, 391 (legal opinion delivered on behalf of the European Automobile Manufacturers Association (ACEA)). The Commission proposal was accepted by the European Parliament on 12 December 2007, with the addition that EU Member States presently granting full design protection for spare parts can continue to do so for a transition period of 5 years. Acceptance of the proposal by the Council remains unlikely, however (see *infra* note 4).

As implementation of the proposal would mean that vehicle manufacturers would lose the exclusionary position in the aftermarket for spares presently enjoyed in a number of member countries,[2] the automobile industry has organized resistance,[3] and receives political support not least in those Member States where it represents a key sector of the domestic economy.[4] Although it therefore appears doubtful at present whether, and if so, in which form the repairs clause will ever be adopted, the issue deserves further analysis under several aspects. First, it allows for an exemplary case study of a situation in which the adverse effects on competition resulting from the very existence of an intellectual property right cannot be solved with the help of doctrines currently applied in European competition law. Second, from a global perspective, it needs to be considered whether the curtailing of protection ensuing from the introduction of limitations that are motivated by competition aspects is compatible with rules of international law, in particular with the three-step test anchored in the design as well as the copyright, patent and trade mark provisions of TRIPS.

As not all readers of this *Handbook* may be familiar with current design legislation in the EU or with the historical background of the spare-parts debate, the following presentation will first give an overview of the relevant provisions, followed by a brief account of the legal situation concerning protection of spare parts in various EU member countries.

2 The background

2.1 The legal regime of design protection in the EU

2.1.1 The general framework The national rules of industrial design protection in the EU have been harmonized on the basis of Directive

---

2 Already a repairs clause of the kind proposed is operating in 10 EU Member States – Ireland, the UK, Belgium, the Netherlands, Luxembourg, Spain, Italy, Hungary, Latvia and Poland. Greek law also contains a repairs clause; however, it is only operative after five years of full protection and against payment of a remuneration. In Germany, the market for spare parts is *de facto* free, in spite of full design protection being theoretically available; see on this point section 2.2 *infra*.

3 Because of its neutral formulation, the proposal applies to all types of complex products. However, for practical reasons and under the present economic conditions, it is primarily of relevance for the car industry. Therefore, the following contribution focuses on the automotive sector only.

4 According to present information, the following EU member countries have announced their opposition to the proposal: Czech Republic, Finland, France, Germany, Slovakia and Sweden.

89/71/EC,[5] and a unitary regime has been established at the Community level by the Community Design Regulation (CDR).[6] Just as with trade marks, the registration of Community designs is administered by OHIM (Office for Harmonisation in the Internal Market – Trade Marks and Industrial Designs) in Alicante. The requirements, scope and duration of protection for (registered) industrial designs are regulated congruously in the CDR and the Design Directive. In addition, informal protection for Unregistered Community Designs (UCDs) is granted pursuant to Article 11 CDR for a period of three years after first publication of a (protectable)[7] design in the EU.

The requirements for protection are novelty and individual character (Articles 3 Design Directive and 4 CDR). In the large majority of member countries as well as at the OHIM, no substantive examination is undertaken in the registration process. Even without examination, the mere act of registration confers upon designs a legal presumption of validity that can only be rebutted by way of cancellation proceedings or by filing a counterclaim in an infringement suit. The duration of protection for registered designs is five years, with the possibility of subsequent prolongations up to a maximum of 25 years.

2.1.2 Specific requirements for component parts In the Directive as well as the CDR, component parts of complex products are expressly mentioned as items eligible for design protection (Articles 1(b) Design Directive and 3(b) CDR). However, protection can only be acquired by those parts or features of parts that remain visible during normal use, after the part has been incorporated in the entire product, provided that those visible parts or features fulfil in themselves the requirements of novelty and individual character (Articles 3(2) Design Directive and 4(2) CDR). Thus, in practice, all parts 'under the hood' of a car, like the motor, brakes, clutch and so on remain excluded from design protection.

Excluded from protection are further the 'must-fit' features of component parts, that is:

> features of appearance of a product which must necessarily be reproduced in their exact form and dimensions in order to permit the product in which the design is

5 Directive 98/71/EC of the European Parliament and of the Council of 13 October 1998 on the legal protection of designs, OJ 1998 No. L 289, p. 28.

6 Council Regulation (EC) No. 6/2002 of 12 December 2001 on Community designs, OJ 2002 No. L 3, p. 1.

7 That is, in order to be granted informal protection, UCDs must meet the same substantive requirements as registered Community designs, meaning they must be new and have individual character (see immediately *infra*).

incorporated or to which it is applied to be mechanically connected to or placed in, around or against another product so that either product may perform its function. (Articles 7(2) Design Directive and 8(2) CDR)

It is understood that the exclusion clause only concerns the interface between the various elements of which a complex product consists. Consequently, 'must-match' features, meaning those that are not mechanically indispensable for the interconnection – yet the reproduction of which is necessary in order to restore the original appearance – of the product as a matter of principle remain eligible for protection. Whereas that protection is uncontested as long as the rights are exercised on the primary market, the Commission's proposal would lead to a reduction of the exclusionary effects on the aftermarket to (little more than) zero.[8]

When it became apparent in the 1990s that it would be extremely difficult to reach an agreement on the issue,[9] further efforts to find a harmonized solu-

---

8 The repairs clause would still leave room for enforcement of design rights on the aftermarket, for example, when the person using the design on the aftermarket does not duly inform consumers about the true commercial origin of the part. It is interesting to note in this context that according to an amendment proposed by the Committee on Monetary and Economic Affairs in its opinion submitted to the European Parliament, the application of the repairs clause would be made directly dependent on due information being given to consumers about the commercial origin of the part, for example, by affixing a trade mark or other badge of origin.

9 The issue was extensively and controversially covered in the literature. See Beier, F.-K. (1994), 'Der Musterschutz von Ersatzteilen in den Vorschlägen für ein Europäisches Musterrecht', *GRUR Int.*, 716 and (1994) *IIC*, **25**, 840; Dreier, Thomas (2001), 'Primär- und Folgemärkte', in Gerhard Schricker, Thomas Dreier and Annette Kur (eds), *Geistiges Eigentum im Dienst der Innovation*, Baden-Baden: Nomos, p. 51, at 53, 69 and 75; Eichmann, H. (1996), 'Das europäische Geschmacksmusterrecht auf Abwegen?', *GRUR Int.*, 859; by the same author (1997), 'Kein Geschmacksmusterschutz für must-match Teile', *GRUR Int.*, 595; Gerster, Marc (1998), *Wettbewerbsbeschränkungen auf dem Markt für Kraftfahrzeugersatzteile*, Frankfurt am Main: Peter Lang, at pp. 178 *et seq.*; Gimeno, Luis (1997), 'Spare Parts in Spain and from a European Perspective', *EIPR*, **19,** 537; Govaere, Inge (1996), *The Use and Abuse of Intellectual Property Rights in E.C. Law*, London: Sweet & Maxwell, pp. 195 *et seq.*; Heinemann, Andreas (2002), *Immaterialgüterschutz in der Wettbewerbsordnung*, Tübingen: Mohr, pp. 530 *et seq.*; Horton, A. (1994), 'European Design Law and the Spare Parts Dilemma: The Proposed Regulation and Directive', *EIPR*, **16**, 51; Kroher, J. (1993), 'EG-Geschmacksmusterschutz für Kraftfahrzeug-Ersatzteile', *GRUR Int.*, 457; by the same author (1994), 'Kein Designschutz für Ersatzteile?', *GRUR*, 158; Kur, A. (1993), 'EG-Geschmacksmusterschutz und Kraftfahrzeug-Ersatzteile – eine Erwiderung', *GRUR Int.* 71; by the same author (1996), 'Gedanken zur Systemkonformität einer Sonderregelung für must-match-Ersatzteile im künftigen europäischen Geschmacksmusterrecht', *GRUR Int.*, 876; Lützenrath, Notker (1996), *Designschutz im Europäischen Binnenmarkt*, Hamburg:

tion for the spare-parts problem were postponed to a later date, and a 'transitional provision' (the so-called freeze-plus rule) was inserted in Article 14 of the Design Directive, according to which Member States are obliged:[10]

> to maintain in force their existing legal provisions relating to the use of the design of a component part used for the purpose of the repair of a complex product so as to restore its original appearance and shall introduce changes to those provisions only if the purpose is to liberalise the market for such parts.

Another 'transitional provision' was introduced in Article 110 of the CDR, to the effect that protection for parts registered as Community designs does not extend to the use of that part for repair purposes.

Finally, in Article 19 of the Design Directive, an obligation was anchored for the Commission to:

> submit [within three years after the date of implementation] an analysis of the consequences of the provisions of this Directive for Community industry, in particular the industrial sectors which are most affected, . . . for consumers, for competition and for the functioning of the internal market. At the latest one year later the Commission shall propose . . . changes to this Directive needed to complete the internal market in respect of component parts of complex products. . . .

As the Commission's consultations with the industry sectors affected, accompanied by extensive fact finding, did not lead to a result,[11] a study was undertaken.[12] On the basis of these materials, the Commission then elaborated its

---

LIT; Pilla, Marcus (2000), *Der Schutz von Ersatzteilen zwischen Geschmacksmuster- und Kartellrecht*, Berlin: Wissenschaftlicher Verlag Berlin; Riehle, G. (1993), 'EG-Geschmacksmusterschutz und Kraftfahrzeug-Ersatzteile', *GRUR Int.*, 49; by the same author (1996), 'Das künftige Musterrecht und die "Ersatzteilfrage"', *EWS*, attachment 1(7), 1; by the same author (1997), 'Kapituliert Europa vor der Ersatzteilfrage? "Free for all" und das künftige europäische Musterrecht', *EWS*, 361; by the same author (1999), 'Das europäische Musterrecht und die "Ersatzteilfrage" – Brüssel locuta causa *non* finita', *EWS*, 7; Schovsbo, Jens (1998), 'As If Made for Each Other – Intellectual Property Rights and Protection of Compatible Products', *IIC*, **29**, 510; Speyart, H.M.H. (1997), 'The Grand Design', *EIPR*, **19**, 603. The large majority of these authors have argued in favour of the repairs clause in its present or a modified form.

[10] On the debates preceding the freeze-plus clause see Kur, Annette (1999), 'Freeze Plus Melts the Ice – Observations on the European Design Directive', *IIC*, **30,** 620.

[11] See Extended Impact Assessment of the Proposal for a Directive of the European Parliament and of the Council amending Directive 98/71/EC on the Legal Protection of Designs, Commission Staff Working Document of 14 September 2004, SEC(2004) 1097 = http://ec.europa.eu/internal_market/indprop/docs/design/sec-2004-1097_en.pdf, accessed 4 November 2007, section 3.1 at p. 16.

[12] European Policy Evaluation Consortium (EPEC), 'Impact Assessment of

own Extended Impact Assessment[13] leading to the Commission Proposal of September 2004 on amending the Design Directive.

2.2 *The legal situation in selected Member States*

The design protection for spare parts and its consequences for the repairs sector became an issue for judicial and legislative debates even before the idea of harmonizing industrial design law in the EU was cast in its present form. The need arose when the car manufacturers commenced to explore, and to make massive use of, the potential of IP protection as a leverage tool for the exclusion of third parties from the aftermarket.[14] For some time, the legal situation proved to be particularly favourable for this purpose in the United Kingdom, where, due to the wording of the 1956 Copyright Act, three-dimensional reproductions of items depicted in a drawing were held to infringe the copyright existing therein irrespective of their artistic character.[15] The ensuing possibility for car manufacturers to prohibit any unauthorized manufacturing of virtually any part of which a car consists, including items whose measurements were exclusively determined by technical constraints, was halted by the decision of the House of Lords in the *British Leyland* case,[16] which held that to enforce the copyright in the drawing of an exhaust pipe against an independent manufacturer of such parts would amount to violation of the principle of non-derogation from a grant: once a car is sold, the manufacturer must accept that it is up to the owner alone to decide whether and by whom a repair is undertaken.[17] Legal consequences were further drawn in the 1988 Copyright,

---

Possible Options to Liberalise the Aftermarket in Spare Parts', Final Report to DG Internal Market, 18 November 2003, http://oami.europa.eu/en/office/pdf/spare.pdf, accessed 4 November 2007. See also the previous study undertaken for the Commission by Bradley, Keith (1992), *Design Protection and the European Car Component Industry*, London School of Economics/Business Performance Group.

[13] See note 11 *supra*.

[14] According to Riehle (1993), *supra* note 9, at 54, this move was motivated inter alia by the fact that to an increasing extent, the 'classical' forms of leveraging, like tying agreements and refusals to deliver, did not stand up to scrutiny under national and European competition law.

[15] This had been expressly confirmed by the House of Lords in the decision *Dorling v. Honnor Marine Ltd.*, [1964] W.L.R. 195; [1964] 1 All E.R. 241. An account of the legal situation in the UK prior to the *British Leyland decision* (see note 16 *infra*) is given by Moser, R. (1986), 'Zum Schutz technischer Konstruktionszeichnungen in Großbritannien', *GRUR Int.*, 779.

[16] *British Leyland Motor Corp. Ltd. v. Armstrong Patents Co., Ltd.* [1986] 1 All E.R. 855 (27 February 1986).

[17] Car companies, in particular the Ford company, had by that time begun to found their claims – instead of or in addition to copyright – on design rights. In an inquiry into these practices, the Monopolies and Mergers Commission came to the conclusion that the use of copyright *and* design right would lead to detrimental results

Designs and Patents Act (CDPA), where it was stipulated, first, that copyright in a (technical) drawing was not violated by a reproduction in three-dimensional form, and second, that so-called must-fit and must-match parts of complex products were to be excluded from industrial design protection.[18]

A different course was taken in France,[19] where the automotive industry was ultimately successful in claiming the entire market in 'must-match' spare parts for themselves. Their at times quite massive intervention against independent manufacturers as well as against retailers on the basis of both copyright and industrial design rights met with approval from the courts,[20] and has resulted in a complete clearance from the French market of those parts of any unauthorized competing business.[21]

The same route was followed in Italy for a while.[22] However, unlike in France, the car industry met with determined resistance, which was facilitated by the fact that their counterparts in the spare-parts sector – typically small and medium-sized industry who alone cannot withstand economic pressure for long – were comparatively well and efficiently organized. Their efforts triggered a lively discussion in the legal literature as well as a number of court decisions, most of which confirmed the eligibility in principle of parts for design protection, whereas the fulfilment of the actual protection requirements was often denied.[23] Finally, the issue was settled through a decision by the Italian Supreme Court.[24] In essence, the Court found that parts could not be protected at all if they did not display an independent aesthetic value, that is a

---

in the aftermarket for spare parts, and should lead to legislative consequences; *Ford Motor Company Limited*, Cmnd 9437 of February 1985, 3.11.

18 Section 213(3)(b)(i) and (ii) CDPA 1988. In the course of implementation of the Design Directive, the regulations have been changed from a total exclusion of protection to a repairs clause, that is an exclusion only with regard to the aftermarket (section 7A(5) of the Registered Designs Regulation 2001).

19 On the situation in France see in particular Riehle (1993), *supra* note 9, at 55 *et seq.*

20 Riehle (1993), *supra* note 9, at 55 *et seq.*, emphasizing that frequently criminal sanctions were used in order to deter those engaged in independent trade, leading to a recommendation by the French association of wholesalers (FEDA) not to trade in spare parts any longer.

21 Riehle (1993), *supra* note 9, with reference to Bonal (1989), *Le second marché des pièces de carosserie automobiles*, pp. 26 and 32 (Study commissioned by Consorzio Italiano delle componentistica di ricambio dei autoveicoli (CICRA)).

22 On the Italian situation see in particular Pilla, *supra* note 9; Riehle (1996), *supra* note 9.

23 For details see Pilla, *supra* note 9, at 109 *et seq.*; Riehle, *ibid.*

24 Corte di Cassazione, 24 July 1996, (1996) *Dir. Ind.*, 893. See Pilla, *supra* note 9, at 121 *et seq.*; in the same vein, Corte di Cassazione, 3 January 2001, (2002) *GRUR Int.*, 942 – '*Kfz-Außenspiegel*' (German translation). The landmark decision of 1996 has been criticized by Eichmann (1997), *supra* note 9, at 595.

value going beyond the features determining the appearance of the car as a whole.[25]

A middle path between general denial and effusive protection was followed in Germany. In a decision by the Federal Supreme Court dating from 1986, it was clarified that parts of a complex product were in principle eligible for protection, if they met the general protection requirements.[26] However – for reasons of political prudence or in view of the relatively high threshold for design protection requirements applying under German law prior to implementation of the Design Directive – the car companies in Germany never undertook the same massive attempts as in other EU countries to enforce design rights on the aftermarket. During the debates concerning the transposition of Design Directive 98/71/EC into German law, the representatives of vehicle manufacturers in Germany even issued an official statement that they did not intend to jeopardize competition at the retail level for spare parts, and would not try to enforce their rights in order to enlarge their market share at the cost of others.[27] For the German lawmakers, that declaration has furnished one important motive to reject proposals to introduce a repairs clause in the course of implementation of the Design Directive.[28] However, with the declaration lacking any binding force, its reliability for the future appears all but secure.[29]

---

25 Also in Italy, the situation had given rise to an investigation by the competition authority (Autorità Garante), leading to the conclusion that to extend the protection for parts to the aftermarket would have detrimental results and should be excluded by law; see expert report of the Autorità garante della concorrenza e del mercato, 'Normativa brevetti per modelli e disegni ornamentali per le parti staccate della carrozzeria delle automobili', 23 August 1994, (1995) *Riv. Dir. Ind.*, II 86 *et seq.*; summarized in English in (1995) *EIPR*, D-71. In the meantime, a repairs clause such as that proposed by the Commission has been inserted into Italian law; for details see Guizzardi, Silvia (2005), 'Reparaturklauseln und Eintragungsfähigkeit von Ersatzteilen in Italien – Probleme und Perspektiven', *GRUR Int.*, 299.

26 German Federal Supreme Court (BGH), (1987) *GRUR*, 518 – 'Kotflügel'.

27 '[D]ass sie den Wettbewerb im Einzelhandel nicht beeinträchtigen und den freien Werkstätten und dem freien Teilehandel durch Inanspruchnahme von Schutzrechten Marktanteile nicht streitig machen werden und somit das auskömmliche Nebeneinander der Marktteilnehmer nicht beeinträchtigt wird', quoted by the German Parliament's Legal Committee, *BT-Drucks*, 15/2191 of 10 December 2003.

28 In order to comply with Article 14 of the Design Directive, the provisions of the old design law remain in application with regard to the use of spare parts for repair purposes; see section 67(1) German Design Act.

29 Doubts in that regard are further triggered by the fact that the rejection of the repairs clause was also motivated by emphasizing the danger that without full design protection, parts might be imported, to an increasing extent, from non-EU countries (in the same vein see also Straus, *supra* note 1, at 403). In order to erect an efficient barrier against such imports, original manufacturers would obviously need to acquire, and seek

3 The ECJ's position

3.1 The Volvo v. Veng *and* CICRA v. Renault *decisions*

The legal situation in Italy as well as in the United Kingdom formed the background for the ECJ's landmark rulings in *Volvo v. Veng*[30] and *CICRA v. Renault*.[31] In the UK – prior to the legislation of 1988 that banned the design protection of must-match parts – Volvo had opposed the importation by Veng of parts manufactured abroad without authorization, while Veng had tried in vain to obtain a licence for its business. The second case, referred to the ECJ by the Milan appeal court, concerned a claim by CICRA, the spare part industry's national association, and by one of its members against Renault, seeking a declaration of invalidity of industrial designs for a number of body panel parts, plus a declaration that the independent manufacturing and selling of such parts did not violate national rules of unfair competition.

It is well known that the ECJ in the two decisions did not rule that the enforcement of design rights as such, or the refusal to grant a licence, amounted to an abuse of a dominant position in the meaning of ex-Article 86 EC Treaty (Article 82 EC). Instead, it was confirmed that the authority of the proprietor of an industrial design right to prevent the marketing of the same design constitutes the substance of the right, meaning that to prevent the application of existing national legislation to that effect would be 'tantamount to challenging the very existence of that right'.[32] Accordingly, to prohibit the exercise of the right on the basis of ex-Article 86 was only declared legitimate in presence of 'certain abusive conduct', such as 'an arbitrary refusal to deliver spare parts to independent repairers, the fixing of prices at an unfair level or the decision no longer to produce spare parts for a particular model even though many cars of that model remain in circulation'.[33]

While the ECJ's decisions in both cases are strikingly brief, the arguments brought forward by the parties opposing the exercise of the design right are more thoroughly considered in the two statements of opinion by Advocate General Mischo. In particular, he rejects the view articulated by the Italian

---

to enforce, rights in all parts that are in principle eligible for protection. It remains an open question how that strategy could be reconciled with the declaration of self-restraint that was quoted above.

30 Case C-238/87, *Volvo v. Veng*, [1988] ECR 6211.

31 Case C53/87, *CICRA v. Renault*, [1988] ECR 6039.

32 Case C-53/87, *CICRA v. Renault*, [1988] ECR 6071, para. 11; see also Case C-238/87, *Volvo v. Veng* [1988] ECR 6235, para. 8: 'An obligation imposed on the proprietor of a protected design right to grant to third parties . . . a licence . . . would lead to the proprietor thereof being deprived of the substance of his exclusive right . . .'.

33 Case C 53/87, *CICRA v. Renault*, [1988] ECR 6073, para. 16; likewise: Case C-238/87, *Volvo v. Veng*, (1988) ECR 6235, para. 9.

court that by protecting separately the appearance of a product as a whole and its individual parts, the creator would be over-compensated for his creative efforts. As the Advocate General puts it, he does 'not see in what way a national legislature would be exceeding the limits of the protection of industrial and commercial property if it allowed a car manufacturer to apportion [the] return or amortization between the price of the vehicle as a whole, . . . and the price of the spare parts',[34] 'provided', however, as he then explains in the *Volvo* opinion, 'that the apportionment is equitable'[35] – something that remains for the national courts and authorities to decide. He further concludes that:[36]

> if it were to be found that the monopoly enjoyed by motor vehicle manufacturers regarding spare parts produced by them . . . prompts them to abuse their dominant position *or if the temptation to engage in such abuse were considered too strong*, it would *of course* be open to the national legislatures or . . . the Community legislature . . . to regulate the exclusive rights in question by the means considered most appropriate.

3.2 *No way beyond?*

The *Volvo* and *CICRA* decisions are regularly invoked by those who argue that the Commission's proposal for a repairs clause clashes with general principles of intellectual property rights.[37] According to those arguments, national as well as Community law may not go further than imposing remedies, on a case-by-case basis, against a possible abuse of the exclusive position, in those instances that have been identified by the Court. However, the decisions hardly provide a solid basis for such contentions. On the contrary, a realistic evaluation of the practical implications of the Court's views demonstrates that there is more than sufficient reason for the Commission to take legislative action in the manner proposed. *Inter alia*, the following considerations account for this: as pointed out in the above-cited statement by Advocate General Mischo, the 'double reward' to be collected by the right holder by virtue of his exclusive position is not abusive if, but only as long as, the apportionment between the two markets of the return remains 'equitable'. The crucial question is, therefore, how that will be determined in practice. It needs to be recalled in this context that the ECJ held in the early decisions *Parke*

---

[34] Opinion of AG Mischo, Case C-53/87, *CICRA v. Renault*, [1988] ECR 6060, para. 31.

[35] Opinion of AG Mischo, Case C-238/87, *Volvo v. Veng*, [1988] ECR, 6229, para. 33.

[36] *Ibid.*, para. 34 (emphasis added).

[37] Most recently by Straus, *supra* note 1, at 394 *et seq.*; see also Beier, *supra* note 9, at 850. The argument is rejected by Drexl *et al.*, *supra* note 1.

Davis[38] and *Sirena*[39] that an above-average price of products covered by an IP right is not sufficient as such to establish abuse.[40] Indeed, there is hardly an objective scale against which the appropriateness of prices, and in particular the adequate reward for value added by inventive and creative efforts, could be measured. The lack of such a scale is not a serious problem either, because and as long as it is ultimately left to the market to decide how much more a customer is willing to pay for an IP-protected product in comparison with other, substitutable goods. However, the pertinent problem here is exactly that in a situation characterized by the complete absence of competition, the usual scheme does not work; the market cannot fulfil its crucial role of arbiter. Therefore, unlike the normal situation with regard to pricing of IP-protected commodities, courts and authorities cannot simply submit that the price is fair in the absence of particular circumstances indicating the opposite; instead, they need to undertake a proactive and comprehensive evaluation of the price-building factors, *inter alia* concerning the objective value added to the product by the design.[41] If the task is taken seriously, it will in all probability prove impossible to tackle without full disclosure of data by the car manufacturers, concerning *inter alia* the total amount, and the apportionment, of the design reward collected on the two relevant stages of the market. It is plain to see that such a consequence would neither befit the interests of the (national or European) authorities who might be burdened with a large number of complex investigations,[42] nor would it offer an appealing perspective for the car manufacturers themselves.

Against this backdrop – and unless the reference by the ECJ to a possible abuse by the setting of unjustified prices for spare parts is tacitly discarded as being meaningless in practice – the legal solution proposed by the Commission appears as a preferable, realistic way to deal with the matter. It is true that the repairs clause does curtail the possibility of collecting a double reward, and thereby encroaches on the right to oppose conduct by third parties, which, according to the ECJ, forms part of the very substance of the design

---

38 Case C-24/67, *Parke Davis*, [1968] ECR 55, at 72.

39 Case C-40/70, *Sirena*, [1971] ECR 68, para. 17.

40 See Opinion of AG Mischo, Case C-238/87, *Volvo v. Veng* [1988] ECR 6229, para. 32, where reference is made to *Parke Davis*.

41 On the basis of figures provided by the European Automobile Manufacturers' Association (ACEA), the Commission has calculated that design efforts concerning the outer appearance ('the skin') of a car account for 0.7 per cent of all R&D expenses; see Extended Impact Assessment, *supra* note 11, section 4.1.4 at p. 31, with reference to the ACEA's website. No figures are available as to the proportion in which those expenses are retrieved in the primary and in the secondary market.

42 On this point see in particular Riehle (1996), *supra* note 9, at 11 *et seq*, with references in note 111; Kur (1996), *supra* note 9, at 887.

right. On the other hand, the right holders' freedom to recoup investments in the design of the entire car as well as its individual parts remains intact – it only needs to be concentrated at one single stage, instead of being apportioned to separate market stages. From an economic point of view – and submitting that the car manufacturers' rent-seeking in the aftermarket does not lead to an unjustified monopoly reward, but amounts, in sum, to an equitable total return on investment – the effect of the repairs clause, namely that gains owed to exclusivity must be collected in their entirety in the primary market, appears as a technicality rather than a reduction of possible gains in their substance.[43]

The appropriateness of the Commission's approach is further confirmed by the fact that no need exists to make specific investments in spare part design in the aftermarket that could only be recovered through an exclusive position. Unlike in the typical situation underlying the grant and exercise of exclusive IP rights, here there is no risk of market failure. With regard to production and distribution of parts in the secondary market, potential competitors normally do not have cost advantages over the original manufacturer.[44] The right owner is therefore not exposed to hazardous competition. What is lost is solely the chance to achieve overly high profit margins. Referring to the words of Advocate General Mischo: from that point of view, the repairs clause is neither more nor less than a straightforward and consequent way to rule out any 'temptation to engage in abuse' with regard to pricing, and therefore is 'of course' legitimate for the lawmaker to embark upon.

---

43 The argument is also employed the other way round, namely that if the original manufacturers are forced to make all their gains on the primary market, prices for new cars will rise proportionally, and it will no longer be possible to undertake cross-subsidizing in the aftermarket in the sense that by demanding higher prices for parts for which there is a high turnover, the prices for parts that are more rarely needed can be kept lower. The point of that argument is that in the end, consumers will not be able to profit from a liberalization of the spare parts market. That sort of reasoning is, however, rightfully countered in the Commission's Extended Impact Assessment, *supra* note 11, section 3.3 at p. 18, by stating that first, 'the possibility to pass on higher costs on the primary market will be limited by competition in that market' and that, secondly, 'it is not for design protection to legally sustain cross-subsidising', whilst it is emphasized that as a matter of principle, vehicle manufacturers remain perfectly free to use such strategies as a marketing instrument.

44 As is emphasized in the Extended Impact Assessment, *supra* note 11, section 4.1.2. at p. 21, it is rather so that independent manufacturers have higher market entry costs in the aftermarket than vehicle manufacturers and/or OEM suppliers, sustaining the view that even without design protection, the market share to be acquired by them will remain relatively small, albeit not insignificant; see also EPEC study, *supra* note 12, at 15. On comparative cost advantages see also Drexl *et al.*, *supra* note 1, at 455.

3.3 New developments – and a change of paradigm?

The ECJ's jurisprudence has developed considerably since the *Volvo* and *CICRA* decisions. In *Magill*[45] and *IMS Health*,[46] more general criteria have been elaborated to address the interface between IP and competition law. Contrary to what was held in the earlier decisions, it is now generally acknowledged that under certain circumstances, even a mere refusal to license can amount to abuse within the meaning of Article 82 EC.

Whether those changes would have any bearing on the issue of spare parts protection, however, remains open to doubt. As was made clear in particular in the *IMS Health* decision, abuse will only be found if, in addition to a complete elimination of competition in a relevant downstream market, the refusal to license prevents, without objective justification, the offer of a new product for which there is substantial consumer demand.[47] A person who intends to manufacture a specific type of car bodywork panel, for example can hardly claim to be offering a new product, as long as the car manufacturer himself is able and willing to supply the part in question.[48]

Indeed, it appears that the ECJ's criteria were deliberately formulated so as to avoid conflicting with previous rulings. In addition, it appears to have been the intention that a markedly cautious approach towards possible interferences with IP law should be observed. However, as understandable as this attitude

---

[45] Joined Cases C-241/92 and C-242/92, *RTE and ITP v. Commission* ('*Magill*') [1995] ECR I-153.

[46] Case C-418/01, *IMS Health*, [2004] ECR I-5039.

[47] Comments on *IMS Health* have mostly taken a critical stand towards the requirement of cumulative criteria; see Conde Gallego, B. and D. Riziotis (2004), 'Comment on the IMS Health decision', *IIC*, **35**, 571; Drexl, J. (2004), 'IMS Health and Trinko – Antitrust Placebo for Consumers Instead of Sound Economics in Refusal-to-Deal Cases', *IIC*, **35,** 798; Geradin, D. (2004) 'Limiting the Scope of Article 82: What Can the EU Learn from the U.S. Supreme Court's Judgment in *Trinko* in the Wake of *Microsoft*, *IMS*, and *Deutsche Telekom*?', *C.M.L. Rev.*, **41,** 1519, at 1531 *et seq*. and 1538 *et seq*.; Heinemann, A. (2005) 'Compulsory Licences and Product Integration in European Competition Law – Assessment of the European Commission's *Microsoft* Decision', *IIC*, **36,** 63 *et seq*. and 71 *et seq*. Supporting the decision: Derclaye, E. (2004), 'The IMS Health Decision: A Triple Victory', *World Competition*, **27**, 397, at 402. The necessity of a new product being offered is also confirmed in principle in DG Competition's Discussion Paper of December 2005 on the application of Article 82 EC to exclusionary clauses, http://ec.europa.eu/comm/competition/antitrust/art82/discpaper2005.pdf, accessed 4 November 2007 (cited: DG Competition's Discussion Paper 2005), paras 239 *et seq*.

[48] This result may however be questioned in view of the fact that the vehicle manufacturers deliver the product only to their own authorized dealers and not to those rendering independent repair services. From this perspective, the enabling of independent repairs might figure as a 'new product'.

may be, the present rules to be extracted from case law, in particular from the *IMS Health* decision, fail to address the crucial points in this matter.

As is elaborated in more detail in another contribution to this volume,[49] the efforts by the ECJ to distinguish between two separate markets, while not completely irrelevant or incorrect, are not always helpful either, all the more so as the contours of the ECJ's market definition remain somewhat diffuse and imprecise. Moreover, the additional criterion of a 'new product' is an indication of an inherent weakness in the approach chosen rather than a relevant tool for resolution of critical cases. It is therefore recommended instead to pay attention to the specifics of IP protection and its relationship to competition aspects, with the common goal of both legal fields being to enhance not only allocative, but in particular dynamic competition. This means that first, it has to be tested whether an IPR confers dominance in the relevant market; second, it needs to be asked whether the good covered by the right is 'indispensable' in the sense that competition by substitution is excluded for structural or market-specific reasons, and third, the pro- and anti-competitive effects of a duty to license must be assessed in the light of the concept of dynamic competition. Although on the basis of that approach, a licence would be justified primarily if it enabled substitution by a different, potentially more innovative product, even a licence to imitate may be an appropriate remedy, if imitation is the only way an alternative can be offered to consumers, and provided that the denial of exclusivity will not have detrimental effects on investments in innovation in the relevant market.[50]

If the *Volvo* and *CICRA* decisions[51] were re-evaluated in the light of that new approach, their outcome would in all probability be different. There is no doubt that in the aftermarket, spare parts matching the original product are indispensable within the meaning set out above. Furthermore, on the basis of the general criteria applied to the assessment, original manufacturers hold a

49 Conde Gallego, Beatriz, chapter 9, this volume; by the same author (2006), 'Missbrauch von Immaterialgüterrechten und Kartellrecht', *GRUR Int.*, 16; see also Drexl, J., B. Conde Gallego, S. Enchelmaier, M. Leistner and M.-O. Mackenrodt (2006), Comments of the Max Planck Institute for Intellectual Property, Competition and Tax Law on the DG Competition Discussion Paper on the application of Article 82 of the EC Treaty to exclusionary abuses, *IIC*, **37**, 558.

50 See Drexl *et al.*, *supra* note 49, at para. 18. On the concept of innovation and its relevance for the assessment of compatibility of restrictive (licensing) practices with competition law principles see Ullrich, Hanns (2004), 'Expansionist Intellectual Property Protection and Reductionist Competition Rules: A TRIPS Perspective', *J.I.E.L.*, **7**, 401. The author warns that a strongly innovation-oriented approach might lead to a competition policy that is biased towards right holders' interests, which, in a global perspective, might run counter to the interests of developing countries.

51 *Supra* notes 30 and 31.

dominant position on that market.[52] For the ensuing analysis in the light of dynamic competition, it has to be noted, first, that only imitation, meaning offering a part with an identical shape, will be able to provide consumers with a substitutable alternative. Second, the fact that in the aftermarket for spare parts, there is neither room for innovation nor a need for the original creator to make specific investments in design efforts that could only be retrieved by the grant of an exclusive right furnishes another motive for the finding that the refusal to license amounts to abuse.[53]

It is important to emphasize at this stage, however, that even in the case of the new paradigm being accepted by the ECJ, an express legal regulation of the issue within design legislation proper would not become unnecessary or superfluous.[54] A general, fundamental division of tasks must be observed between the legislature promulgating intellectual law provisions, on the one hand, and competition authorities acting on the basis of competition law, on the other. Competition rules are charged with addressing conflicts arising out of the individual circumstances in a specific situation; they are not an appropriate instrument to solve structural problems ensuing from the very existence of an intellectual property right. If a serious problem of the latter type arises, it is therefore primarily a task for the legislature, and not for competition authorities, to react.[55] Whereas the distinction between these two categories of

---

52 See the analysis proposed in DG Competition Discussion Paper, *supra* note 47, paras 249 and 251 *et seq*. One crucial aspect in deciding whether the holder of an exclusive right on the primary market has to be considered as dominant in the aftermarket is the question of whether consumers have sufficient price information to carry out accurate life-cycle calculations (*ibid.*, para. 256). Such information is lacking, or seriously deficient, in this case, as the development of prices over the life cycle of a car, as well as the question as to how often a demand for replacement will occur due to a crash or other damage, cannot possibly be foreseen at the time when the car is bought. On this point see also Drexl *et al.*, *supra* note 1, at 450.

53 See Drexl *et al.*, *supra* note 49, at para. 24, where the question is left unanswered, but it is recommended 'that the Commission apply the same analytical framework of refusal to license to cases in which the right holder excludes competition in aftermarkets'.

54 On this point see already Drexl *et al.*, *supra* note 1, at 453.

55 This is not to say that courts and competition authorities are under a general ban to act against conduct where the distortion of competition is actually rooted in a failure of the legislature to correct inherent imbalances of intellectual property law rather than in the individual circumstances of the case as such (that is, in situations like those in *Magill*; *supra* note 45). However, apart from the fact that it is definitely preferable from a systemic point of view for those cases to be regulated within IP law, it must also be considered that in a democratic society with a clear division of tasks between legislative, executive and judicial institutions, courts and authorities must be cautious not to override too easily deliberate decisions that have been made by the legislature; see also the following text.

conflict may pose difficulties in some instances, it is very obvious in this particular case that for the spare parts issue, the individual circumstances of specific cases do not play a role; the negative consequences for competition are due neither to the specific quality of the design, such as its high degree of originality, nor to the individual behaviour of the right holder. Instead, the total blocking of competition in the aftermarket is an automatic and inevitable result simply of the design right being granted. In such a situation, the legislature is called upon to take action; it would fail to meet its obligations if an attempt were made to escape that task by referring the problem to competition law.

3.4 Future scenarios

3.4.1 Could a repairs clause be based on competition rules, irrespective of the outcome of the present legislative process? While legislative action therefore clearly remains the preferable option, the question persists regarding a possible role for the competition rules in the likely case that the Commission's proposal does not find the necessary majority in the Council. What are the chances for those promoting a more liberalized regime for the spare parts market to gain at least a partial victory on the basis of primary Community competition law?[56]

It must be emphasized, first, that even from a strictly conservative approach, there exists an undeniable demand for the ECJ to elaborate more thoroughly on the question of how the fixing of prices at an unfair level will be assessed in the absence of competition – in particular, how and by whom it will be demonstrated that the apportionment of the design reward between the primary and the secondary market leads to such a result that, in sum, it can still be considered fair and equitable. As was pointed out above, the remarks made to that effect in the *Volvo* and *CICRA* decisions are hardly satisfactory; they do not provide reliable guidelines for a workable solution.[57] Apart from that, however, a general re-evaluation of the previous jurisprudence could only be expected if the ECJ accepts and adopts the critical arguments brought forward with regard to the deficiencies in the *IMS Health* type of reasoning as related above.

---

[56] Being entitled to a compulsory licence on the basis of Article 82 is of course more restrictive and economically less attractive for independent and OEM manufacturers than the repairs clause.

[57] In Case C-238/87, *Volvo v. Veng*, [1988] ECR 6211, the claim was originally grounded *inter alia* on abusive pricing by Volvo, but the contention was expressly withdrawn in the course of the proceedings.

This further invites the question of whether in that case – that is, with the ECJ endorsing a new approach based on considerations of dynamic competition – a refusal to license the manufacturing and/or marketing of must-match parts would regularly have to be regarded as abusive, irrespective of the provisions applying under design legislation proper. In other words: would the competition aspects be ponderous enough even to override a deliberate decision by the lawmakers that full and unrestricted design protection should be granted on the aftermarket?

There is no easy answer to this. On the one hand, the rules safeguarding freedom of competition form part of primary Community law and therefore rank high as constituent elements of the Internal Market. On the other hand, the freedom of legislature in the Member States and at the Community level to take sovereign decisions legitimized by the parliamentary process must also be duly respected. Indeed, as a matter of principle, the latter aspect should generally be given preference in a democratic society. It therefore appears consistent to accept the fact that explicit legislation will generally prevail vis-à-vis the principle of free competition, at least within a certain margin of freedom to be reserved for political discretion. If, after weighing all the arguments, the legislature rejects the idea of inserting a clause allowing the reproduction of protected parts,[58] as a deliberate political move to further the interests of the national or regional car industry,[59] this would in principle exclude subsequent

---

58 For the sake of clarification, it must be pointed out here that an express rejection of the repairs clause by the Community legislature with the consequences set out above would only occur in the case that it is decided, after (new) legislative procedures, that all members must accept full design protection for spare parts on the aftermarket. At least at present, it is extremely unlikely that such a solution would ever be adopted. If the Commission proposal fails and no compromise solution can be found, the present situation under the 'freeze plus' rule (see section 2.1.2 *supra*) will therefore persist. In that scenario, the remarks made above with regard to the prevalence of legislative decisions only relate to the legal situation in those Member States where the legislature has definitely confirmed that even in view of the detrimental impact on competition it wants to give preference to the vehicle manufacturers' interests.

59 It may be necessary to consult the legislative history in order to obtain more information on that point. For instance in Germany, it must be taken into account that an important motive for not introducing a repairs clause has been the declaration of the car manufacturers that they would not try to enforce their rights in a way that would increase their market share at the expense of others (see section 2.2 *supra*, with reference to the legislative documents). It would therefore not clash with the principle of paying due respect to legislative decisions in general if abuse were to be found in a situation where, contrary to the above-cited contention, vehicle manufacturers in Germany commenced making massive use of design rights in order to clear the aftermarket of all unauthorized business, as has happened previously in other countries, such as in France (see section 2.2 *supra*).

claims of abuse against the car manufacturers in case of refusal to license. It is another question whether the legislative decision as such might be challenged on other grounds.[60]

3.4.2 Could protection be maintained on other grounds if the repairs clause were accepted? As another scenario for possible decisions to be taken by the ECJ, the following situation remains to be considered. Assuming that the Commission's proposal is accepted and implemented in its present or a slightly altered form, the aim of liberalization throughout the EU would still be distorted if other legal grounds were readily available to right owners that would result in a prohibition on making and selling car body parts. One such possibility could be offered by trade mark law; the other option is copyright.

With the discussions about a repairs clause pending, it has indeed become more frequent than before for car manufacturers to apply for trade mark registration of the car as a whole as well as of its body panel parts.[61] Trade marks, by contrast to industrial designs, are subject to substantive examination in all EU member countries as well as at the Community level. Protection will therefore be denied *ab initio* if the part lacks a distinctive character, that is, if it does not, in itself, convey a message about its commercial origin to the average consumer.[62] However, for those (few) parts that pass the test, the path might be open for the right holder to enjoin others from making and marketing the identical product.[63] Making use of that prohibitive option would raise two

---

[60] Riehle claims that to grant full protection to car manufacturers in the aftermarket is tantamount to offering hidden subsidies; see Riehle (1996), *supra* note 9, at 17.

[61] See, for example, T-128/01, *DaimlerChrysler v. OHIM*, [2003] ECR II-701 (concerning the form of a vehicle grille).

[62] This has been constantly held by the ECJ, in particular in cases concerning the distinctive character of three-dimensional trade marks; see for example Joined Cases C-53 to 55/01, *Linde*, [2003] ECR 2003 I-3161; Case C-218/01, *Henkel v. Deutsches Patent- und Markenamt*, [2004] ECR I-1725; Joined Cases C-456 and 457/01, *Henkel v. OHIM*, [2005] ECR I-5089.

[63] Another way of using trade-mark rights is to claim that irrespective of the admissibility of commercializing the part as such, it must in any case not be offered with reference made to the original holder's trade mark. Although that argumentation runs counter to the ECJ's ruling in Case C-228/03, *Gillette*, [2005] ECR I-2337 (see also decision by the Frankfurt appeal court, note 66 *infra*), anecdotal evidence holds that the strategy is successful in practice, in particular regarding preliminary measures like seizure of goods etc., as the authorities usually dealing with such measures (bailiffs, first instance courts etc.) frequently consider the use of the trade marks on, or in connection with, a non-original product as *prima facie* evidence for an infringement, instead of embarking on an assessment of the more complicated question of whether the use of the trade mark is admissible on the basis of the limitations set out in Article 6(1)(c) of the Trade Mark Directive.

questions that ultimately have to be decided by the ECJ, namely, first, whether reproduction and selling of the part (accompanied by an indication of its true commercial origin) constitute use in a trade-mark sense, meaning use 'as a mark',[64] and second, even if use 'as a mark' is confirmed, whether the conduct of competitors is nevertheless admissible on the basis of the limitation provisions in European trade mark law, which allow, *inter alia*, the use of a sign to indicate the intended purpose of a product to serve as a spare part.[65] Without going into detail here – and with all necessary caution as regards attempts to anticipate ECJ jurisprudence – it can be submitted that the Court would take a rather critical stand towards the use of trade-mark law as a means to block the spare parts market. It therefore appears safe to assume that the ECJ would at least give a positive answer to the second question,[66] if not denying the first one already.

Copyright, on the other hand, poses a more serious problem. In particular in a country such as France, virtually all body parts qualifying for industrial design protection would at the same time be eligible for copyright protection. Therefore, even in the case of a repairs clause being inserted into the Design Directive, the French right holders would still be in a position to maintain their exclusive rights, unless it is found that its enforcement clashes with prevalent principles of primary Community law.[67]

The decision on this point would again depend primarily on the ECJ's willingness to modify the criteria established in the *IMS Health* decision. If the dynamic competition test is accepted as the approach to be followed for the assessment of abuse, it would most likely have to follow that copyright also has to cede in favour of a competition-friendly solution.[68] In the opposite case,

---

64 See C-63/97, *BMW*, [1999] ECR I-905; Case C-206/01, *Arsenal Football Club*, [2002] ECR I-10273; Case C-408/01, *Adidas-Salomon*, [2003] ECR I-12537; Case C-48/05, *Adam Opel AG*, [2007] ECR I-1017.

65 See Articles 6(1)(c) Trade Mark Directive and 12(1)(c) Community Trade Mark Regulation. See also the decision by the Italian Corte di Cassazione, 10 January 2001, (2000) Dir. Ind., (4), 327 – *Fiat v. ISAM*.

66 This would be in line with Case C-228/03, *Gillette*, [2005] ECR I-2337, where the ECJ placed much emphasis on the interests of consumers to be informed about competing (compatible) products that are available in the market. In the same vein, the Oberlandesgericht (Court of Appeal) Frankfurt am Main has rejected claims by the holder of an automobile trade mark to enjoin a dealer in matching, non-original parts to use the mark in order to indicate the purpose of the articles; decision of 20 October 2005, 6 U 178/04.

67 A similar situation might exist even now in Belgium, as Belgian copyright as a matter of principle follows the same approach as French copyright, whereas a repairs clause has been inserted into the unitary design legislation in the Benelux countries.

68 This result would appear all the more appropriate because in this situation, the specific interests of the personal creator that need to be given particular consideration

however, that is if the ECJ remains unwilling to apply the competition provisions in the absence of a new product being offered, the prospects remain obscure. It is of course apparent that in the situation submitted here, that is after an amendment of the Design Directive introducing a repairs clause, the enforcement of copyright protection that is available in one particular country would be liable to create impediments for the free movement of goods, thus triggering the question of whether that effect is justifiable under Article 30 EC.[69] On the basis of the reasoning employed in the *Volvo* and *CICRA* decisions,[70] the answer to that question would most likely have to be in the affirmative: as was pointed out above, the ECJ has held that to deny the application of (national) legal rules ensuring exclusivity on the secondary market would affect the very substance of the right.

Nevertheless, in the light of (submitted) EU legislation in the field of industrial designs,[71] the issue would have to be reconsidered regardless of the ECJ's willingness to adopt a new approach towards the criteria applying under competition law. The question to be posed here is whether and under which circumstances national copyright protection can take precedence over the decision by the European lawmakers to liberalize the markets in spare parts, and thereby preserve impediments to the free movement of goods that were intended to be removed by the legal action taken at the Community level. For an answer to that question, the ECJ would have to consider not only *Volvo* and *CICRA*, but also its ruling in *Dior v. Evora*.[72] This case concerned a conflict between, on one side, the proprietor of rights to *Dior* perfume trade marks as well as of copyright in the shapes of the bottles and labels, and, on the opposite side, a drug-store chain selling those articles and displaying them in advertisements. There was no doubt that both the trade-mark rights and the copyright in the products themselves had been exhausted by the right holder's consent to putting them on the market in the EU. It was further decided that

---

in copyright (see Drexl *et al.*, *supra* note 49, at para. 8) can hardly be said to play a role; see also the following footnote and the text above.

69 In addition to the argumentation on the basis of Article 30, it could also be considered whether an attempt to raise claims based on national copyright law so as to counteract the decision by the EU legislature to allow the manufacture and distribution of such parts for repair purposes would not have to be considered as abuse, thus giving rise to the application of Article 82 EC, if there are no additional, specifically copyright-related reasons, for such claims, for instance the pertinent interests of personal authors to oppose the use.

70 *Supra* notes 30 and 31.

71 The cautious approach taken by the ECJ in *Volvo* and *CICRA* was, among other reasons, due to the fact that at the pertinent time there had been no harmonization at all of the relevant sector; see Case C-53/87, *CICRA*, [1988] ECR 6060, para. 10.

72 Case C-337/95, *Dior v. Evora*, [1997] ECR I-6013.

under trade-mark law, the right to oppose the use made of the signs in the advertising measures was in principle also exhausted.[73] The situation in copyright was slightly different, however, with the display of the products and packages in the advertisements strictly speaking amounting to a violation of the reproduction right, which is not subject to exhaustion. Nevertheless, the ECJ ruled that copyright could not be invoked either, arguing that there were no additional reasons for copyright to go further than trade-mark law in creating impediments for the free movement – and commercialization – of goods.

A similar argumentation would also be appropriate in the case of spare parts. There is no pertinent reason why copyright should be able to set aside a solution applying within design law throughout the EU. In particular, no such reason appears to derive from the specific goal safeguarded by copyright, namely to protect the personal interests of creators – at least as long as it cannot be demonstrated that the commercial benefits flowing from the aftermarket accrue directly to the (natural) person authoring the design in question. As in the *Dior v. Evora* decision, the fact that, strictly speaking, the specific subject matter of copyright will be tainted by granting preference to free movement of goods is no valid argument as such, but has to be weighed against the factors mentioned in Article 30, 2nd sentence EC, in particular the extent to which the enforcement of the IP right would lead to an artificial partitioning of markets. In addition, the balancing of interests to be undertaken in the framework of Article 30 must also take into account that the core objectives of the IPR remain intact as long as the proprietor is still in a position to retrieve his full design reward on the primary market, and that competitors on the aftermarket have no cost advantages vis-à-vis the proprietor, thereby excluding a risk of market failure concerning the creative efforts invested in the design.[74]

4 A dangerous precedent?

Amongst the misgivings voiced with regard to the repairs clause were warnings that this would be just the first step in an uncontrollable process of overall erosion of IPRs.[75] The argument holds that once enhancement of competition on a relevant market is accepted as a justification for setting aside the exclusivity of a design right, the same consideration might be employed in order to impose, for instance on patent holders, a general obligation to license.

---

[73] Unless the marketing measures were such that serious detriment to the trade mark's reputation might result, which would only occur in rare and exceptional cases.

[74] See at note 44 *supra* for a more detailed explanation of that line of reasoning.

[75] See already Opinion of AG Mischo, Case C-53/87, *CICRA*, [1988] ECR 6060, para. 34; Eichmann (1996), *supra* note 9, at 871; Beier, *supra* note 9, at 863; the argument is rejected by Kur (1996), *supra* note 9, at 886.

However, these fears fail to take account of the fact that the repairs clause concerns a situation when competition in a relevant market is not only restricted, as in the usual case of intellectual property protection, but when no substitutable products are available at all. Furthermore, the situation in the spare parts case is specific also insofar as the total blocking of competition ensues automatically and regularly from the mere fact that a certain part receives design protection, irrespective of the individual merits of the design.[76] By contrast, elimination of competition by virtue of a patent (or copyright, for that matter) will typically only occur under specific circumstances in individual cases, for instance when a certain technology has developed into a *de facto* standard. It would then be sufficient to react individually, as the case may be, on the basis of the competition provisions.[77] Lastly, even when an invention covered by a patent is without technical alternatives at a certain point in time, it will nonetheless typically engender an incentive for others to 'work around' it, that is, to invent other and better solutions. It is exactly that sort of incentive that is lacking with regard to the situation in the aftermarket for spare parts.

The strong misgivings voiced in parts of the intellectual property community are difficult to reconcile with the fact that the general principles on which the repairs clause is founded are by no means new or revolutionary. In particular, the rule that the reward earned for the value added by achievements covered by an IPR must be determined by the market, in competition with other, substitutable products, stands unquestioned even in traditional doctrinal writing.[78] Also, the supplement to this principle, namely that the restriction of competition resulting from the exclusive position granted by an intellectual property right is (only) justified because – and if – it serves to stimulate innovation or the creation of new products, is all but a novel, groundbreaking revelation.[79]

It is true, however, that those rules are regularly employed only with a view to furnishing a justification for the existence of exclusive rights as such. It is seldom realized that there are two sides to the coin, namely that in the absence

---

76 See also section 3.3 *supra* (at the end).

77 See section 3.3 *supra* on the division of tasks between legislature and executive/judicative institutions.

78 See, for example, Beier, F.-K. (1992), 'Gewerblicher Rechtsschutz, Soziale Marktwirtschaft und Europäischer Binnenmarkt', *GRUR*, 228, at 231. For a thorough elaboration of the argument see Ullrich, H. (1995), 'TRIPS: Adequate Protection, Inadequate Trade, Adequate Competition Policy', *Pacific Rim L. & Pol'y J.*, **4**(1), 152, at 194.

79 See von Weizsäcker, Carl Christian (1981), 'Rechte und Verhältnisse in der modernen Wirtschaftslehre', *Kyklos*, **34**, 345; Heinemann, *supra* note 9, at 14 *et seq.*

of the conditions mentioned above, it follows that the right must be limited accordingly in its scope and contents. Rather than embracing such possibly adverse consequences, the traditional attitude in IP law reflects what can be called a strictly proprietary logic:[80] once a right has been granted, it is assumed that full protection should be the general rule, whereas limitations are only accepted in exceptional cases, and must be anchored in considerations of general policy and welfare other than freedom of competition.[81] Contrary to that, the approach suggested here entails a change of perspectives, in the sense that free competition ought to be the general rule, whereas the capacity of an intellectual property right to achieve its objectives, including the aim of promoting dynamic competition, must be established with regard not only to its existence as such, but also concerning the concrete extension of the protection it confers.[82]

Again, this is not to be confused with a general erosion of IPRs in the sense that exclusivity would fall under a general verdict of 'uncompetitiveness'. The remedies at the legislative and executive level would become operative only under specific circumstances, and these would compel a thorough analysis before action is taken. Nevertheless, it is expected that the stronger accent placed on competition aspects will make a difference at least in certain cases. This concerns for instance situations when competition in a relevant market is absent due to the establishment of industry standards, thereby also foreclosing potential incentives to innovate.[83] Other examples might be found in the use of computer programs enabling the operation of exchange parts (the '*Lexmark*' situation[84]), or as a tool for diagnosis of technical malfunctions as

---

80 The notion (in German: 'Eigentumslogik') was introduced by Dreier, *supra* note 9, at 70.

81 For a typical reasoning on the basis of proprietary logic see Beier, *supra* note 9, in particular at 858 *et seq.*

82 The difference is highlighted by the following consideration: only from the point of view of proprietary logic does it make sense to argue that the Commission did not have sufficient ground for their proposal simply because the EPEC study, *supra* note 12, remained inconclusive with regard to the financial benefits ensuing for consumers; in this vein see Straus, *supra* note 1, at 399 *et seq.* From the different perspective endorsed here, it would be clear that even in case of doubt, the general rule – that is, that the relevant market should be open for competition – should regularly prevail over a full monopoly.

83 For an example, see decision by the German Supreme Court (BGH), 13 July 2004 (2005), Case KZR 40/02, *Standard-Spundfass*, (2004) *GRUR*, 966 = *Standard Tight-Head Drum*, (2005) *IIC*, **36**, 741 (English translation), analysed in more detail in the contribution by Conde Gallego, *supra* note 49, starting at note 51.

84 In *Lexmark International, Inc. v. Static Control Components, Inc.*, 387 F.3d 522 (6th Cir. 2004), it was not necessary to apply competition law, as protection was denied as such, or the acts undertaken by Static Control would at least have been found

a necessary step preceding the actual repair work.[85] In the latter cases, once the general (rather low) threshold for copyright protection has been passed, current copyright legislation would only allow for decompilation, but not for actual reproduction, of such programs. As a matter of principle, that will not be sufficient in order to gain access to the relevant market of exchange parts or repair services. The questions of whether and which remedies would apply in such cases, and whether the critical mass of problems automatically and uniformly engendered by the grant of (in this case) copyright is such that a general legal regulation should be introduced into copyright legislation proper, remain to be considered on the basis of a more thorough investigation than can be offered here.[86]

5 What about TRIPS?

Finally, the Commission's proposal has come under attack because it is suspected of violating obligations under international IP law. Misgivings in that regard had already been voiced in the 1990s, after the Commission had launched a compromise proposal according to which the use of spare part design for repair purposes was to be admissible following a three-year period of full protection. This was criticized as clashing with Article 26(3) TRIPS, where the minimum duration of industrial design protection is fixed at 10 years.[87]

The arguments against the present proposal are now based on Article 26(2), the provision incorporating the so-called three-step test.[88] The proviso stipulates that:

> [m]embers may provide limited exceptions to the protection of industrial designs, provided that such exceptions do not unreasonably conflict with the normal exploitation of protected industrial designs and do not unreasonably prejudice the legitimate interests of the owner of the protected design, taking account of the legitimate interests of third parties.

---

admissible under the 'fair use' exemption. With a flexible provision of the 'fair use' type lacking in the EU, however, the situation might pose more serious problems.

[85] The aspect is considered at least to a certain extent in Article 4(2) of Commission Regulation (EC) No. 772/2004 on the Application of Article 81(3) of the Treaty to Categories of Technology Transfer Agreements, OJ 2004 No. L 123, p. 11.

[86] See the more detailed analysis of Conde Gallego, *supra* note 49.

[87] The argument was however not correct, because the proposal did not entail a complete lapse of the design right, but only blocked its enforcement on the aftermarket. See Kur, A. (1995), 'TRIPS und der Designschutz', *GRUR Int.*, 192, at 193; by the same author (1996), 'TRIPS and Design Rights', in Friedrich-Karl Beier and Gerhard Schricker (eds), *From GATT to TRIPS*, Köln: Heymanns, p. 157.

[88] The compatibility of the proposed repairs clause is assessed, with a positive result, in the Commission's Extended Impact Assessment, *supra* note 11, section 7.2 at p. 47.

The legal impact of the three-step test has been explored by WTO Panels, in decisions concerning the corresponding regulations in copyright, patent and trade-mark law.[89] In spite of the fact that Article 26(2) has never been addressed directly, and that the wording of the provisions concerning other types of IPRs is slightly different, the panel decisions do allow for certain general conclusions to be drawn for the general lines of interpretation.[90] First, all panels have emphasized that the notion of 'limited exception' relates to the extent to which legal rights were curtailed by the limitation in question. Second, to assess the criterion of 'normal exploitation', the panels agree that the term 'normal' has an empirical as well as a normative connotation and that the two must be combined. Third, concerning the legitimate interests of the proprietor in relation to the interests of third parties, the panels have endorsed a normative evaluation that would however also take into account the proprietor's economic interests.

Transposing the criteria developed in the WTO Panel decisions to the Commission proposal, it has been contended that the repairs clause 'obviously violates *all* and *each* of the three criteria in Art. 26 (2) TRIPS'.[91] The exception would not be 'limited', as the proprietors of design rights were to be deprived of the substance of their exclusive right as regards its exploitation in the aftermarket; further, by negating the possibility of restricting or controlling competition in the aftermarket, normal exploitation of the right would be jeopardized; and lastly, as the absence of exclusivity on the aftermarket is liable to

---

[89] *Canada – Patent Protection of Pharmaceutical Products*, Panel Report of 17 March 2000, WT/DS114/R, http://www.wto.org/english/tratop_e/dispu_e/cases_e/ds114_e.htm, accessed 4 November 2007; *United States – Section 110(5) of the US Copyright Act*, WT/DS160/R, Panel Report of 15 June 2000, http://www.wto.org/english/tratop_e/dispu_e/cases_e/ds160_e.htm, accessed 4 November 2007; *European Communities – Protection of Trademarks and Geographical Indications for Agricultural Products and Foodstuff*, WT/DS174/R, Panel Report of 15 March 2005, http://www.wto.org/english/tratop_e/dispu_e/cases_e/ds174_e.htm, accessed 4 November 2007.

[90] For the following see in particular Senftleben, M. (2006), 'Towards a Horizontal Standard for Limiting Intellectual Property Rights? – WTO Panel Reports Shed Light on the Three-Step Test in Copyright Law and Related Tests in Patent and Trademark Law', *IIC*, **37,** 407; Dreier, Thomas (2005), 'Interpreting International IP Law', in Annette Kur, Stefan Luginbühl and Eskil Waage (eds), '. . . *und sie bewegt sich doch' – Patent Law on the Move: Festschrift für Gert Kolle and Dieter Stauder*, Köln: Heymanns, p. 45.

[91] Straus, *supra* note 1, at 397, emphasis in the original. Without mentioning the arguments in favour of TRIPS compatibility set out in the Extended Impact Assessment, *supra* note 11, section 7.2 at p. 47, the Commission is criticized for not addressing 'the implications which an *abolition* of design protection in component parts of complex products would have in view of international agreements entered into by the Member States and the Union itself' (*ibid.*, at 403, emphasis in the original).

cause substantial financial losses for which there is no compensation, the legitimate interests of the proprietor are said to be encroached upon. Regarding the legitimate interests of third parties, it is argued that they can (and should only) be taken into account by way of competition control, in particular by control of abusive pricing.

Before these arguments are considered in more detail, it may be of interest to point out that from an international perspective full design protection for spare parts is not the general rule.[92] For instance, a repairs clause was recently introduced, after thorough deliberations,[93] into Australian design legislation. In the USA, spare parts likewise do not receive protection.[94] This is due, first, to the rather strict criteria – novelty, ornamentality, and non-obviousness – applying with regard to protection of design patents;[95] it further results from the doctrine developed in (patent) jurisprudence that once a product is sold, acts undertaken for the purpose of repair are to be considered as lawful, as long as they do not amount to reconstruction.[96] Although different in its legal construction, this reasoning is similar in its effects to that underlying the proposed repairs clause; its compatibility with TRIPS would therefore have to be evaluated equally, should the issue ever be raised before a WTO Panel.

---

[92] Japan is one of the relatively few industrialized countries outside the EU where spare parts can be, and frequently are, protected as industrial designs (subsequent to substantive examination of the protection requirements), and where protection is also enforced in practice.

[93] Bureau of Industry Economics, 'The Economics of Intellectual Property Rights for Designs', Occasional Paper 27, May 1995, Canberra: Australian Government Publishing Service.

[94] On the situation in the USA see Fitzpatrick, J.F. (1989), 'Industrial Design Protection and Competition in Automobile Replacement Parts – Back to Monopoly Profits?', *U. Balt. L. Rev.*, **19**, 233.

[95] Even if the design is registered in the first place, the chances are rather high that it will not withstand scrutiny by the court when infringement claims are raised; see Fitzpatrick, *supra* note 94, at 242, with reference to complaints filed (and later withdrawn) by Volvo and Chrysler.

[96] The principle and relevant case law are comprehensively cited and discussed in *Jazz Photo v. ITC*, 264 F. 3d 1094 (Fed. Cir. 2001). The argumentation is somewhat similar to that of the House of Lords in the *British Leyland v. Armstrong* case (*supra* note 16). Also here, it is considered as decisive that 'the purchaser of a patented article has the rights of any owner of private property, including the right . . . to repair it'; *Jazz Photo v. FTC*, 264 F. 3d 1094, at [7] and [8], with reference to *Mitchell v. Howley*, 83 U.S. (16 Wall.) 544, at 548 = 21 L.Ed. 322 (1872). While the doctrine appears to apply primarily with regard to products that have been patented in their entirety, it has also been held to permit the replacement of patented parts that were needed for repair purposes; see *Dana Corp. v. American Precision Co.*, 827 F.2d 755, 3 USPQ 2d 1852 (Fed. Cir. 1987) (rebuilding of worn truck clutches).

Apart from that, it must also be considered that no obligation exists under TRIPS to protect the design of component parts in addition to the complex product in which they are assembled.[97] The wording of Article 25(1) leaves it to the WTO members to define the notion of what may constitute the object of industrial design protection, with the option implied to restrict that notion to articles marketed for their own sake, that is independently of the purpose to repair another product. In addition, Article 25(1) 3rd sentence, stipulates that '[m]embers may provide that . . . protection shall not extend to designs dictated *essentially* by technical *and functional* features' (emphasis added).

This wording is clearly, and deliberately, wider than that chosen in Article 7(1) of the European Design Directive, which only excludes 'features . . . solely dictated by technical . . . function'. Whereas this Directive in its present form therefore accepts in principle the protectability of so-called must-match features of component parts, nothing in TRIPS would hinder the adoption of a solution that totally excludes such parts from protection.[98] Should a WTO Panel therefore share the opinion that the repairs clause is in violation of TRIPS, a natural consequence for the EU lawmakers might be to exclude protection altogether. What might look at first glance like a victory for the car industry and the governments supporting it could then turn out to entail rather adverse consequences. From a general point of view as well, the result would be regrettable, because it would send a message that in order to safeguard competition aspects that they consider as important, WTO members have no choice but to adopt radical, far-reaching solutions like denying protection *in toto*, rather than being able to implement legal remedies in the form of limitations that are tailor-made to those specific situations where regulation is deemed necessary.

Nevertheless, the issues raised with regard to compatibility of the repairs clause with the three-step test in Article 26(2) TRIPS are of genuine interest and merit thorough consideration. In essence, the question posed here is whether TRIPS obliges WTO members to follow a purely 'proprietary logic',[99] or whether it allows the grant and extent of IP protection to be put in a structural context with competition-related considerations. This question is of relevance not only for the actual case considered here, but it is also of general interest for measures being taken by courts and authorities on the basis of competition law, if exclusivity is impaired thereby. Also with regard to those measures, it may become topical to assess whether in the light of the three-step test they may be applied on the basis of a dynamic competition

97 See Kur (1995), *supra* note 87, at 157 and 159.
98 Kur (1996), *supra* note 87, at p. 159.
99 See *supra* note 80 and accompanying text.

approach, that is not solely in situations where the individual conduct at stake would traditionally be labelled as 'abusive'. It is important to note here that the gist of this question is clearly different from what was brought to the fore in previous WTO Panel decisions, where the existence of competition on the relevant markets for the protected commodities was never put in doubt as such.

It is true that competition aspects are not very prominently addressed in TRIPS.[100] Apart from Article 40, dealing with anti-competitive practices in contractual licences, competition is only addressed under the heading of 'Principles' in Article 8(2) and, indirectly, in the 'Objectives' under Article 7.[101] According to Article 7, the:

> protection and enforcement of intellectual property rights should contribute to the promotion of technological innovation and to the transfer and dissemination of technology, to the mutual advantage of producers and users of technological knowledge, and in a manner conducive to social and economic welfare, and to a balance of rights and obligations.

For the situation at stake here, the question results whether, *e contrario*, IP protection ought to be denied where, for objective reasons, the grant of an exclusive position cannot possibly serve as an incentive for others to innovate.[102] Furthermore, as the aim of a regulation like the repairs clause is to counteract the potentially detrimental effects of a true and lasting monopoly, it may also find support in the concepts of social and economic welfare, as well as a balance of rights and obligations, that are expressly mentioned in Article 7.

In Article 8(2), it is stipulated that '[a]ppropriate measures . . . may be needed in order to prevent the abuse of intellectual property rights by right holders'.

Taken as such, the clause recalls Advocate General Mischo's words, that Member States are 'of course' entitled to enact legislation aimed at ruling out

---

[100] On the relationship between TRIPS and competition law aspects see in particular Ullrich, *supra* notes 50 and 78; Ricolfi, M. (2006), 'Is there an Antitrust Antidote against IP Overprotection within TRIPS?', *Marquette Intell. Prop. L. Rev.*, **10,** Special Issue, 305; Heinemann, *supra* note 9, at 581 *et seq.*

[101] In addition, Article 31 TRIPS, the provision on compulsory (patent) licences, may also be listed among the provisions dealing with competition law; Heinemann, *supra* note 9, at 588.

[102] Likewise, the question can be posed whether, by referring to the 'transfer and dissemination of technology', Article 7 makes way for imposing competition-related measures to ensure competition in downstream technology markets; see Ricolfi, *supra* note 100, at 324.

any temptation to engage in abuse of the monopolistic situation in the after-market for component parts.[103] This impression must be qualified, however, as Article 8(2) also contains the words 'provided that (the measures) are consistent with this Agreement'. There is an obvious risk that this phrase could be interpreted in such a restrictive manner as to deprive Article 8 of all substance.[104]

To a certain extent, however, these concerns have been soothed by the Doha process.[105] The importance of the general principles in the TRIPS Agreement is emphasized in the Doha Declaration on TRIPS and Public Health of November 2001,[106] stating that the commitment of Member States to TRIPS is not compromised by policies that are aimed at implementing the goals set out in Article 8, such as, in this particular case, protection of public health. It is further stipulated in Paragraph 5(a) of the same declaration that 'in applying the customary rules of interpretation of public international law, *each provision* of the TRIPS Agreement shall be read in the light of the object and purpose of the Agreement as expressed, in particular, in its objectives and principles' (emphasis added).

The wording sends a clear signal that the 'Principles' must be taken seriously.[107] Indeed, as was also demonstrated by the Doha process, they may even have a potential to compel changes in law and practice with regard to certain provisions anchored in Part II of the Agreement, in situations when it becomes clear that the unrestricted enforcement of those rules would clash with the spirit and wording of Article 8 (and Article 7).[108]

---

[103] See section 3.1 *supra*, at the end.

[104] Heinemann, *supra* note 9, at 587 *et seq*; Gervais, Daniel (2003), *The TRIPS Agreement – Drafting History and Analysis*, 2nd ed., London: Sweet & Maxwell, para. 2.84.

[105] See UNCTAD and ICTSD, *Resource Book on TRIPS and Development*, Cambridge: Cambridge University Press, pp. 119 and 131. Gervais, *supra* note 104, doubts that the Doha Declaration has lifted the legal status of the provisions to a higher level, but also contends that 'the impact of the Doha Declaration could convince a panel to take a longer look at how these provisions should be interpreted in the context of the Agreement as a whole'.

[106] Para. 4 of Declaration concerning the TRIPS Agreement and Public Health, WT/MIN(01)/DEC/2, 20 November 2001, http://www.wto.org/english/thewto_e/minist_e/min01_e/mindecl_trips_e.htm, accessed 4 November 2007.

[107] See also Ricolfi, *supra* note 100, at 326 *et seq.*

[108] On the basis of the Doha Declaration, it was possible to agree on a waiver concerning the enforcement of Article 31(f) TRIPS concerning the availability of compulsory licences for export of pharmaceuticals into the territory of WTO members without proper manufacturing capabilities, which later became the first substantive amendment of the TRIPS Agreement (new Article 31a TRIPS).

Of course, in the situation considered here, there is no question about changing any of the provisions in the design section of TRIPS. This is about no more – nor less! – than the correct way to interpret the three-step test in Article 26(2).[109] More specifically, it addresses the question of whether, in the light of the Objectives and Principles of the Agreement, Members may take into account, for legislative (or other) measures impairing the exclusive position conferred by an intellectual property right, the fact that the very existence of the right completely eliminates competition on the relevant market without thereby engendering an at least theoretical incentive to innovate.

To answer that question in the negative hardly appears as a tenable position. Doing so would be denying the fact that intellectual property protection does not exist for its own sake, as a sort of *l'art pour l'art*, but that it is part of a complex structural framework, with certain fundamental principles governing the interface between competition and protection interests. As was pointed out above, it has become clear, not least in the Doha process, that such ignorance would not be in accordance with the weight placed by the WTO membership at large on the Principles and Objectives on which the Agreement is founded.

Having come to that conclusion, the analysis of the individual requirements in the three-step test proceeds as follows.[110]

(1) *Limited exception*: As was pointed out above, all WTO Panels have held that it is decisive for this criterion that the exception be small in its scope. Whether or not this applies to the repairs clause depends on the point of departure that is taken for the measurement. If the car industry's particular interest in design protection for car body panels is considered as decisive, the effects entailed by the repairs clause cannot be qualified as small. The result is different, however, if the general objectives underlying the grant of exclusive design rights are held to form the correct basis for the assessment. Considering that the very purpose of industrial design is to attract customers by means of a specific product appearance, it determines that the operation of the repairs clause is indeed limited to specific, atypical situations – namely to those that are characterized by the fact that contrary to the general legal objectives, customers are no longer free to choose a design of their preference. In the light of what was said before about the necessity to view intellectual property not as an isolated asset, but within a structural and functional perspective, only the latter approach appears to befit the aims of the three-step test properly.

---

109 This is thus about the 'longer look' at the principles and objectives of TRIPS that panels must take when interpreting the three-step test; see Gervais, *supra* note 104.

110 See also the evaluation of the three-step test in the Commission's Extended Impact Assessment, *supra* note 88.

(2) *Normal exploitation*: Even on the basis of an entirely empirical understanding of the term 'normal',[111] it is hardly possible to argue that exploitation of monopoly rights in the aftermarket regularly forms part of the exclusive position granted to design right holders in general, or to car manufacturers in particular. As was pointed out above, it is rather the case that such rights are denied in the law and practice of a large number of WTO members. Furthermore, for the normative evaluation, which according to the WTO Panels must be combined with the empirical approach, there is no doubt that exploitation of the design right in the absence of actual and potential competition in the relevant market cannot be considered as the 'normal' case intended to be covered by the operation of the protection regime.

(3) *Legitimate interests*: For a normative assessment of the proprietors' interests, it is important to decide whether competition aspects can be considered in general as *motif juste* for measures limiting the scope of exclusivity in specific cases. According to the reasoning explained above, this question must be answered in the affirmative. In addition, the evaluation must also take into account the economic consequences of the proposal.[112] If, in this context, the car industry claims that it usually derives a substantial portion of its profits from the aftermarket, the question must be posed in return whether those profits can still be considered as equitable and fair, or whether they rather constitute a basically unjustified monopoly premium.[113] Furthermore, it needs to be recalled that the core aspects of right holders' legitimate interests, namely to be protected against market failure and to collect a fair and appropriate reward for the value added to the design product, are sufficiently safeguarded already in a situation when the sales price on the primary market is calculated with a view to allowing for a full return on investment in the design of the car including its body panel parts. At the same time, there is no doubt that recoupment of the full design reward in the primary market, instead of its apportionment to two separate stages, entails beneficial effects for market transparency as well as for the interests of third parties. To contend that WTO members, with regard to the latter, are bound in principle to an application of (traditional) competition rules only seems a somewhat phoney exercise in view of the fact that many WTO members do not have the necessary legal and institutional infrastructure to undertake an efficient control of competition, and that even in

---

[111] On the need to combine an empirical and a normative assessment with a view to this issue see Senftleben, *supra* note 90.

[112] See Senftleben, *supra* note 90.

[113] It is of interest to recall in this context that according to the Commission's calculations based on the vehicle manufacturers' own contentions, design investments in the outer appearance of a car account for not more that 0.7 per cent of all R&D investments; see *supra* note 41.

more developed systems, a detailed, comprehensive and regular control of price-setting in a large number of mass markets with monopolistic structure amounts to a 'mission impossible', so that the reference made to competition law is meaningless for all practical purposes.

The scrutiny of the proposed repairs clause under Article 26(2) TRIPS therefore does not reveal serious flaws flowing from the obligation to abide by international norms.[114] The same holds true, *mutatis mutandis*, with regard to individual measures taken by courts and competition authorities when competition is severely disturbed by the very existence of an intellectual property right, under the conditions set out above.

6 Concluding remarks

Apart from its actual economic and political context, the issue of spare parts protection in design legislation is of greater interest insofar as it is able to demonstrate, in an exemplary manner, how IP protection and competition interests, although usually complementary in the sense that both are instrumental in pursuit of the aim of dynamic competition, may collide at times, thereby creating a need for remedies to be implemented either within IP legislation proper or by way of individual measures taken by competition authorities and the courts. The considerations underlying such legislative remedies or individual measures are – or should be – basically the same. Nevertheless, a clear distinction exists between the tasks to be assumed by the legislature and the competition authorities, respectively: whereas competition rules are charged with addressing conflicts arising out of the individual circumstances in a specific situation, it is for the legislature to react when, in a foreseeable, critical mass of relevant cases, problems are certain to ensue from the very existence, and the exercise within its regular legal boundaries, of an intellec-

---

[114] It is suggested by Straus, *supra* note 1, at 397, that this author in her former writings has endorsed the compatibility of a repairs clause with international obligations only under the condition that fair remuneration be paid. This amounts to an over-interpretation of the article cited ((1996) *GRUR Int.*, 876), which was written at a time when the Commission's proposal did in fact foresee a remuneration right, so that it was of no need or interest to discuss the compatibility with international law of other solutions, such as the presently proposed 'pure' repairs clause. Furthermore, although it is true that this author formerly did support a solution implicating a right to remuneration – and personally would still welcome a compromise solution based on that concept – she has been persuaded by the repeated assertions made from all sides that such a clause would not function in practice (see already the express reservations made in that regard in Kur (1996), *supra* note 9, at 886 *et seq.*). Therefore, if for practical reasons a choice must be made between all or nothing, that is, a full monopoly or a repairs clause without remuneration, this author's opinion is, and always has been, that competition should prevail.

tual property right, without the circumstances of the individual case playing a decisive role.

This does not mean that courts and competition authorities are generally banned from acting against conduct where the distortion of competition is actually rooted in a failure of the legislature to correct inherent imbalances of intellectual property law rather than in the individual circumstances of the case as such. However, apart from the fact that it is definitely preferable from a systemic point of view for those cases to be regulated within intellectual property law proper, it also needs to be considered that courts and authorities must be careful not to override too easily deliberate decisions that have been made by the legislature. Indeed, it is a general postulate deriving from the fundamental division of institutional tasks within a democratic society that, within a certain margin of political discretion, policy choices deliberately adopted by the lawmakers must be respected even in view of a potential distortion of competition. On the other hand, this also means that the freedom for the legislature to make policy choices *in favour* of free competition is considerably larger than is generally conceded to courts and competition authorities.

Apart from that, the sovereignty of individual states or regional entities to formulate rules aimed at reconciling the extent of exclusive protection[115] with the principles forming the common structural framework of competition and intellectual property law remains in principle unimpeded by international norms.[116] In particular, such legislation or measures do not give rise to fundamental objections in view of the obligations resulting from the three-step tests embedded in the design as well as the patent, copyright, and trade mark provisions of the TRIPS Agreement.

---

[115] It goes without saying that this does not furnish an excuse to deviate from the express minimum requirements set out in Part II of the TRIPS Agreement. For an in-depth discussion of examples where this may or may not be the case see Ricolfi, *supra* note 100, at 342 *et seq.*

[116] At least in the meaning and to the extent explained above. For a sceptical view on WTO members' freedom to regulate their own competition law policies in view of an increasing tendency in the economically strong nations to place more emphasis on innovation instead of competition aspects see Ullrich, *supra* note 50.

14 One, none, or a hundred thousand: how many layers of protection for software innovations?

Gustavo Ghidini and Emanuela Arezzo[*]

1 Introduction

In 2002, the European Commission embarked on the arduous project of drafting a Proposal for a Directive (hereinafter PD) on the patentability of computer-implemented inventions (so-called CIIs).[1]

The PD was officially aimed at harmonizing different trends that had emerged in national patent systems and creating a uniform regime following, more or less, the blueprint drawn up by the European Patent Office (EPO) case law.[2] Such discrepancies within (software) patentability trends in Europe were considered a further obstacle towards the creation of a uniform patent policy in the EU and, consequently, discouraging the recourse to patent, especially by small and medium-sized enterprises (SMEs).[3]

Quite rightly, the European Commission thought that uniformity in the law would enhance legal certainty and thus confidence in patents as a valuable instrument to foster progress in such a prominent sector of the European economy.

At the same time, however, the PD reflected a 'defensive' concern: the massive number of software patents (especially those concerning business

* This chapter reflects opinions and ideas mutually shared by the authors. However, sections 2, 4 and 5 can be ascribed to Emanuela Arezzo, while the remaining paragraphs are attributed to Gustavo Ghidini.

1 See the first Commission Proposal of 20 February 2002 for a Directive on the patentability of computer-related inventions presented by the European Commission, COM(2002) 92 final = http://eur-lex.europa.eu/LexUriServ/site/en/com/2002/com2002_0092en01.pdf, accessed 4 November 2007.

2 See section 2.2 *infra*.

3 An example of diverging trends has been registered, for example, with regard to (software) business methods whose patentability has been denied in Great Britain, even when a 'technical contribution' is found (see *Merrill Lynch Appn.*, [1989] RPC 561 (Court of Appeal)), but welcomed by the German Federal Supreme Court (BGH), judgment of 13 December 1999, *Logic Verification*, (2002) *IIC*, **33**, 231 (English translation), with a comment by J. Betten).

methods) granted in the US and the seemingly huge numbers of European patents granted to American patent applicants in Europe had stimulated a restrictive approach towards the patentability of software 'as such' and business methods – an approach that in particular permeated the amendments proposed by the European Parliament.[4]

The same defensive concern probably motivated, aside from its (official and unofficial) goals, the Commission's decision to preserve copyright protection for computer programs, in accordance with Directive 250/91.[5] Indeed, the rationale for that decision, which ostensibly carries no contradictions,[6] surely lay in a desire to maintain an alternative means of protection for European firms – mostly SMEs – accustomed to protecting software with a much cheaper and easier-to-obtain tool.[7]

As is well known the defensive concerns expressed above eventually prevailed and, almost at the end of a tortuous and complex legislative process, in July 2005 the European Parliament rejected at the second reading the Council's Common Position, which led to the definitive closing of the procedure.[8]

---

4 Article 4(a) ('exclusion from patentability') of both the amended versions released by the European Parliament (P5_TA-PROV(2003)0402, http://www.minut.ee/files/mauri/euro/pocii.pdf, accessed 4 November 2007) as well as the political agreement on the Council's Common Position of 24 May 2005 (European Council political agreement on a common position, No. 9713/04, http://www.ffii.de/~jmaebe/swpat/st09713.en04.pdf, accessed 4 November 2007) explained that 'inventions involving computer programs, whether expressed as source code, as object code or in any other form, which implement business, mathematical or other methods and do not produce any technical effects beyond the normal physical interactions between a program and the computer, network or other programmable apparatus in which it is run shall not be patentable'. For an in-depth analysis of the PD see Ghidini, G., E. Arezzo, C. De Rasis and P. Errico (2005), 'Il software fra brevetto e diritto d'autore. Primi appunti sulla proposta di direttiva comunitaria sulle "invenzioni attuate per mezzo di elaboratori elettronici"', *Riv. Dir. Ind.*, **49**, 46; Panagiotidou, E. (2003), 'The Patentability of Computer Programs, according to the Commission's New Proposal for a Directive and to EPO Boards of Appeal Decisions', *C.T.L.R.*, (5), 126; Booton, D. and P. Mole (2002), 'The Action Freezes? The Draft Directive on the Patentability of Computer-implemented Inventions', *IPQ*, (4), 289.

5 Council Directive 91/250/EEC of 14 May 1991 on the Legal Protection of Computer Programs, OJ 1991 No. L 122, p. 42.

6 This is because under the commonly accepted fiction patents are to protect the technical features of computer programs while copyright is meant to cover just the written 'form of expression' of the same subject matter.

7 Copyright protection arises when the author completes her creation: indeed, many European states do not require fixation as an additional element, as the US traditionally does.

8 See European Parliament legislative resolution of 6 July 2005 on the Council

The dismissal of the PD has been applauded throughout Europe as a victory over evil, especially by the European supporters of the open-source movement, who had feared that the adoption of the Directive would put an end to open-source licensing practices. The legislative process has attracted a great deal of attention, and since the very beginning of the drafting process the European Commission has been accused of serving foreign interests.[9]

However, as noted by Commissioner Benita Ferrero-Waldner,[10] the PD failure does not amount to an elimination *tout court* of the patentability of CIIs. To the contrary, it simply means that there will not be any harmonization at the European level. Everything will stay the way it was before, which means that computer-implemented inventions will still be granted protection by national patent offices and by the EPO, whose prominent role in such a central area of patent policy has become even stronger.[11]

So what is the future of the European software industry going to look like? Should we try to convince the EPO to step back, erase 20 years of case law and just leave the floor to copyright protection? Are patents truly bad for our economy? Is copyright really the best alternative?

This chapter will try to answer at least some of these questions, hoping that the answers that it will provide might be of (at least some) guidance on how to deal with the problem at hand.

---

common position with a view to the adoption of a directive of the European Parliament and the Council on computer-implemented inventions, OJ 2005 No. C 157 E, p. 265 = http://eur-lex.europa.eu/LexUriServ/site/en/oj/2006/ce157/ce15720060706en02650265.pdf, accessed 4 November 2007.

[9] Jörg Tauss, Member of the German Parliament, claimed that the first proposal drafted by the European Commission was 'literally identical to a draft . . . whose author is believed to be a lawyer from the Business Software Alliance (BSA)', http://www.swpat.ffii.org/papers/eubsa-swpat0202/tauss020312/tauss020312.en.pdf, accessed 4 November 2007. For more details see Hoeren, T. (2003), 'European Union Commission and Recent Trends in European Information Law', *Rutgers Comp. & Tech. L.J.*, **29**, 1, at 4.

[10] Before the European Parliament, 6 July 2005, http://www.europarl.europa.eu/sides/getDoc.do?pubRef=-//EP//TEXT+CRE+20050706+ITEM-007+DOC+XML+V0//EN&language=EN, accessed 4 November 2007.

[11] In the rather confusing Community patent scenario the EPO has occupied a leading role in shaping patent policy in core areas of the European economy (especially biotechnological inventions and CIIs). It has been observed that while the EPO had had CIIs on the agenda of the next EPC revision conference for a long time, it politely waited for European bodies to take the lead. Now that Community authorities have stepped down, the EPO's role will be stronger than ever. See Ullrich, H. (2008), 'National, European and Community Patent Protection: Time for Reconsideration', in Ansgar Ohly and Diethelm Klippel, *Geistiges Eigentum und Gemeinfreiheit*, Tübingen: Mohr-Siebeck, p. 61.

2 The current legislative scenario in the aftermath of the dismissal of the CII Proposal Directive

2.1 Copyright protection for software

As is well known, although it does not define what a computer program is,[12] the Copyright Directive grants protection to programs in whatever form they are expressed – source or object code – and regardless of the medium they are embodied in (hence: also software incorporated in hardware); further, protection is also extended to design materials involved in the preparation of programs, provided that their nature is such that a computer program can result from them at a later stage.[13]

Copyright protection for software, however, like copyright protection in general, is explicitly restricted to its *expressions* – meaning the written forms of the program – and it is not meant to cover ideas and principles underlying software, which *should* remain in the public domain. Hence software algorithms and abstract ideas *should* be deemed, as a matter of principle, free for competitors to take.[14]

Authorship of the program will be held by the person or group of persons who has created it,[15] and the protection, in clear contradiction with the innovative pace characterizing the software industry, lasts for the life of the author plus 50 years after his or her death.[16]

The sole criterion to afford protection is the originality of the work, meaning that every computer program that is the fruit of the individual intellectual work of the author can enjoy copyright protection.[17] The Directive has deliberately endorsed a very low originality threshold (requiring that the program

---

12 The EU legislature deliberately suggested omitting the definition of a computer program within the final text of the Directive so as to avoid the risk that any classification therein could become obsolete 'as future technology changes the nature of programs as they are known today'. See Article 1(1) of the Proposal for a Council Directive on the Legal Protection of Computer Programs, COM(88) 816 final – SYN 183, submitted by the Commission on 5 January 1989, 89/C 91/05. The full text of the proposal is reported by Vinje, Thomas (1983), 'The Legislative History of the EC Directive', in Michael Lehmann and Colin Tapper (eds), *A Handbook of European Software Law*, Oxford: Oxford University Press, p. 183.

13 Article 1(1) of Directive 91/250/CEE.

14 Article 1(2) of Directive 91/250/CEE.

15 Article 2(1) of Directive 91/250/CEE; see Ubertazzi, L.C. (1994), 'Soggetti del Diritto', in Luigi C. Ubertazzi (ed.), *La Legge sul software, commentario sistematico*, Milan: Giuffrè, p. 23.

16 Article 8(1) of Directive 91/250/CEE.

17 Article 1(3) of Directive 91/250/CEE.

is not copied from another existing program),[18] attracting criticisms from several scholars who disagreed with this choice.[19]

The Directive tries to strike a fine balance between the interests of authors in an absolute right to economically exploit their creations and users' interests in employing their programs free from heavy practical constraints.[20]

On the one hand, it grants the author the exclusive right to perform (herself) or to authorize: the partial or entire, permanent or temporary reproduction of the program in whatever form;[21] acts comprising the translation, adaptation, arrangement and alteration of the program and the reproduction of the results thereof;[22] and any form of distribution to the public.[23] On the other hand, the European legislation expressly recognizes the complexities regarding the framing of the reproduction right for software programs. In particular, the Directive acknowledges the difficulties legitimate users would face if they had to negotiate further licences to perform software's basic functions, such as loading the program.[24]

---

18 See Explanatory Memorandum accompanying the first Directive Proposal, part two, §1(3), in Lehmann and Tapper, *supra* note 12. Such a thesis is further corroborated by the latter sentence of Article 1(3), which excludes the implementation of any other criteria to determine the originality level of a program.

19 Cartella, M. (1994), 'Le attività di riproduzione riservata', in Luigi C. Ubertazzi (ed.), *La Legge sul software, commentario sistematico*, Milan: Giuffrè, p. 56; Lehmann, Michael (1993), 'History of the Development and Principal Issues in the Legal Discussion', in Michael Lehmann and Colin Tapper (eds) (1993), *A Handbook of European Software Law*, Oxford: Oxford University Press, p. 169. *Contra*: Foglia, R. (1991), 'La direttiva CEE sulla tutela del software', *Foro It.*, IV, 307; Fabiani, M. (1989), 'Software: prodotto dell'ingegno in cerca di protezione', *Dir. Inf.*, 561. Both authors argue that the originality level, as defined, can allow for a comprehensive analysis of the intrinsic qualities of the program (like the presence of new elements falling outside the public domain).

20 Dreier, T. (1991), 'The Council Directive of 14 May on the Legal Protection of Computer Programs', *EIPR*, **13**, 319; Lehmann, *supra* note 19; Verstrynge, Jean-François (1993), 'Protecting Intellectual Property Rights within the New Pan-European Framework: Computer Software', in Michael Lehmann and Colin Tapper (eds) (1993), *A Handbook of European Software Law*, Oxford: Oxford University Press, p. 1.

21 Article 4(a) of Directive 91/250/CEE.

22 Article 4(b) of Directive 91/250/CEE.

23 Article 4(c) Directive 91/250/CEE.

24 In order to be enjoyed by the final consumer, software programs need to be 'read' by the computer. As everybody knows, human beings (and indeed quite a few highly specialized human beings) can read the program only when expressed in source code and not in object code, which is 'readable' – that is, executable – only by computers. Moreover, consumers are not at all interested in reading the source code of the program – which, except for programs licensed with the open-source model, is never released with the copy of the software. For computers to 'read' the program a first copy needs to be made in the permanent memory. After this first step, every time someone

For this specific purpose, the Directive expressly exempts the acts of loading, displaying, running, transmission or storage of the program from the need for additional licences from the author insofar as they are: performed by the entitled licensee, strictly necessary for the use of the computer program and in conformity with the program's 'intended purpose'.[25] The Directive further establishes that legitimate software users have the right to make a back-up copy and the right to observe, study or test the functioning of the program to determine the ideas and principles underlying each of its elements.[26] Interestingly, however, while the latter set of uses cannot be limited in any way, legitimate uses exempted by Article 5(1) (corresponding to authors' exclusive rights listed in Article 4(a)(b)) can be restricted through contractual provisions.[27]

Eventually, since the European Parliament expressed great concern, during the legislative process of adopting the Directive, about computer markets staying open and wanted to safeguard the competitiveness of EU industries, a great deal of attention was devoted to the interoperability issue and to the protection of interfaces. Accordingly, the Directive provisions exclude copyrightability of computer interfaces, recognized as the fundamental tool to afford compatibility within computer networks.[28]

2.2 *The patent paradigm*

The patentability of computer-implemented inventions has progressively evolved around the concept of the *technical character* of the *contribution* (more simply: *technical contribution*) brought about by the invention.

Because the patentability of computer programs is specifically banned by Article 52.2(c) EPC, and because such an exclusion is solely limited to programs claimed *as such* (namely: in their most abstract form), the EPO patiently undertook the job of demonstrating that software could be patentable

---

wants to use the program, the software must be 'loaded' into the computer's temporary memory. Each act of loading, running and executing the program requires a temporary copy (that is, reproduction) of the program to be made by the computer; hence for each of these activities the user would in principle need permission from the author, who has the exclusive right to authorize third parties to copy and reproduce the work.

25 In fact, Article 5(1) specifies that '*in absence of specific contractual provisions*, the acts referred to in Article 4(a) and (b) shall not require authorization by the right-holder' (emphasis added).

26 Article 5(2)(3) of Directive 91/250/CEE. Note, however, that the making of a back-up copy is allowed – and cannot be limited through contract provisions – insofar as it is necessary for the functioning of the program. The right to use, observe and test the program to discover its underlying principles and ideas is allowed only to the 'persons having a right to use a copy of a computer program', meaning that third parties who are not licensees cannot lawfully study the functioning of the program.

27 Article 5(1) of Directive 91/250/CEE.

28 Article 1(2) of Directive 91/250/CEE. See also sections 4.1 and 4.2 *infra*.

when it amounted to an invention whose contribution to society was indeed *technical*. At the very beginning, the EPO gave great importance to the technical result as well as the technical means implemented.[29] Because the greatest objection raised against software patentability concerned the fear that first inventors could steal mathematical and scientific concepts in their most disembodied forms, depriving society of the basic tools of science, the EPO probably thought that technical means would suffice to confer some concreteness on the invention, by forcing patentees to claim something tangible.[30]

Soon after, however, the EPO realized that, because all software necessarily makes use of hardware components to produce a certain result (hence, makes use of technical means), the latter requirement (the technical result rather than the technical means) needed more attention.[31] The most recent EPO case law has evolved mainly around the concept of technical contribution.[32] The EPO carefully explained that the technical contribution, which may even be *potential*,[33] could result in ameliorations internal to the functioning of the hardware,[34] hence not visible to the human eye, or in an external result that takes form and shape throughout the hardware components.[35]

---

29 In *Vicom/Computer-Related Invention*, T 208/84, [1987] EPOR 74, § 5, one of the first and most important decisions on the patentability of CIIs, the Technical Board of the EPO explained the difference between mathematical methods and a technical process. In the language of the Board: 'a mathematical method or algorithm is . . . only an abstract concept prescribing how to operate on numbers. No *direct technical result* is produced by the method as such. In contrast thereto, if a mathematical method is used in a technical process, that process is carried out on a *physical entity* (which may be a material object but equally an image stored as an electric signal) by some *technical means* implementing the method and provides as its result a certain *change* in that entity' (emphasis added).

30 Already in the *Vicom/Computer-Related Invention*, *ibid*., at § 7, the Board explains that: 'a method for digitally filtering data remains an abstract notion not distinguished from a mathematical method so long as it is not specified what physical entity is represented by the data and forms the subject of a technical process, that is a process which is susceptible of industrial application'.

31 T 26/86, *Kock & Sterzel/X-Ray Apparatus*, [1988] EPOR 72, § 3.3.

32 For a thorough reconstruction of the EPO's trend toward the patentability of computer-related inventions, see Beresford, Keith (2000), *Patenting Software under the European Patent Convention*, London: Sweet & Maxwell; Liesegang, E. (1999), 'Software Patents in Europe', *C.T.L.R.*, (5), 48.

33 *IBM/Computer Program Product*, T 1173/97, [2000] EPOR 219, § 13. In an analogous sense, see *IBM/Computer Program Product II*, T 935/97, [1999] EPOR 301.

34 *IBM/Data Processor Network*, T 06/83, [1990] EPOR 91; *Sohei/General-Purpose Management System*, T 769/92, [1996] EPOR 253; *IBM/Computer Program Product*, T 1173/97, [2000] EPOR 219, which described the invention therein as one concerning the technical functioning of a computer caused by the program running on it.

35 Case *Vicom/Computer-Related Invention*, T 208/84, [1987] EPOR 74; *Kock & Sterzel/X-Ray Apparatus*, T 26/86, [1988] EPOR 72.

Notwithstanding the efforts the EPO claims to have made in shaping an efficient regulatory framework for the protection of CIIs,[36] the scenario of software patenting in Europe is far from satisfying. On the one hand, the policy of the EPO has been said to be far too lax, especially towards business methods,[37] and biased towards granting patents rather than constraining the flood of patent applications.[38] On the other hand, patent protection in general remains a tool at the disposal of a few. According to EPO official statistics, in 2004 patent applications for 'electronics and electric communication techniques', which normally include CIIs (classification type H04 and H03), accounted for 10 per cent of overall applications filed.[39] At first, such data may seem encouraging because such a percentage is the highest among the 32 classification groups; however, at a closer glance, *European* patent applications amount to little more than one-third of the overall number. This situation is not confined to software inventions. Again referring to the above-mentioned statistics, in 2004 50 per cent of patent applications were filed by foreign applicants (26 per cent were American applications) versus 49 per cent European applications. The explanations for this phenomenon are quite easy to grasp. Patents are very costly to obtain. Drafting appropriate claims for an

---

[36] Karamanli, Theodora (2005), 'Patent Protection for Software: The European Case', presentation given at the I-Law conference organized by the Berkman Center for Internet & Society at Harvard School of Law, Turin, May 2005 (presentation on file with the authors).

[37] The Board of Appeal clarified its policy approach towards business methods in the recent case *Hitachi/Auction Method*, T 258/03, [2004] EPOR 55, where it explained that the technical character of the method can be inferred from the fact that the alleged invention implies technical means, but then it firmly relies on analysis of the technical contribution to filter out only meritorious inventions. The Board expressly admits that taking such an approach means depriving the provision contained in Article 52.2(c) EPC of any legal significance (*ibid.*, § 4.1–4.7), but it does not appear preoccupied by this outcome.

[38] It is also worth recalling that, because the EPO makes profits proportionally to the number of titles it issues, it has been accused of having a biased approach in favour of patentability. This criticism was openly addressed to the EPO by the European Parliament during the legislative process for the adoption of the Directive on CIIs: see Opinion of the Committee on Industry, External Trade, Research and Energy, 21 February 2003, for the Committee on Legal Affairs and the Internal Market on the proposal for a Directive of the European Parliament and of the Council on the patentability of computer-implemented inventions (COM(2002) 92 – C5-0082/2002 – 2002/0047(COD)), Amendment 2, Recital 7a (new), in European Parliament Report, 13 July 2003, PE 327.249, A5-0238/2003, http://www.europarl.europa.eu/sides/getDoc.do?type=REPORT&reference=A5-2003-0238&language=EN&mode=XML#title1, accessed 4 November 2007.

[39] EPO Annual Report 2004, http://www.epo.org/about-us/office/annual-reports/2004/statistics.html, accessed 4 November 2007.

invention requires a great deal of expertise and money.[40] This is especially true of patents in Europe, where the price rises depending on the number of territories where the applicant wants the patent to be issued. And after all the monetary efforts there is no guarantee that the title of protection will remain unchallenged for the whole 20-year term.

Confronted with these difficulties, European undertakings, often SMEs, prefer to stick to copyright law, whose protection (besides lasting much longer) arises with the very creation of the program, which means, as mentioned, that it requires no eligibility test, hence involves a negligible cost.

3 The protection of derivative innovations

Until now, we have analysed the protection granted to CIIs by patent and copyright law in a 'static scenario'. However, because innovation in the software industry is highly incremental and cumulative in nature, in the sense that future innovations will always be indebted, to a certain extent, to previous contributions from earlier inventors, it is significant to look at the problem from a dynamic point of view.

Therefore in evaluating which paradigm is best suited to cover computer programs, it must necessarily be taken into account how and to what extent the form of protection we choose affects follow-on innovators and/or competitors whose innovation might happen to infringe upon an existing title of protection. We must focus on the treatment each paradigm affords to dependent creations.

3.1 Derivative and dependent innovations in patent law

In today's economic environment, for an invention to be *subsequent* has become the rule rather than the exception, due to the above-mentioned cumulative character of the inventive process.

Under the broad category of subsequent inventions fall all the innovations borrowing, to a different extent and degree, knowledge from an earlier innovation. Roughly speaking, this macro-category of subsequent innovation can

---

[40] A large portion of such money is needed for translation purposes. Roughly speaking, it has been estimated that an average European patent has 17 pages of description and three pages of claims; protection is filed for eight Member States and maintenance fees are paid for 10 years. For such a patent, translation costs amount to 10 200, procedural fees are about 4300, agent fees 5500 and maintenance fees 8500 (for a total cost of 28 500). As we can easily see, translation costs are by far the highest costs patentees have to bear. More extensively on the role of translation costs in the creation of a Community patent see Bostyn, Sven (2004), 'The Unbearable Heaviness of Harmonization: SPLT and CP', in Marco Ricolfi (ed.), *I Brevetti per invenzione tra diritto europeo e diritto nazionale*, Turin: Giuffrè, p. 105, at 135 *et seq.*

be divided into two subgroups according to the different extent of their 'taking' from previous inventions. Often, such borrowing merely consists in getting 'some sort of inspiration' from the first invention. The second innovator, by learning the logical processes and functional problems tackled by the first inventor, all disclosed in the patent application, develops different competitive solutions and obtains the same type of useful result without interfering with the prior patent.[41] On this hypothesis, the innovation is *substitutive* and does not, in principle, amount to a counterfeiting of the first invention. The substitutive (second) invention will generally be deemed *autonomous* from the first in both its patentability and exploitability on the market.[42] Conversely, at other times the borrowing goes deeper, requiring actual, direct use of the earlier innovation in order to develop a second one. In this latter case subsequent inventions are usually called *derivative*.

The *patentability* of *derivative* inventions, as with any other inventions, is conditioned on the fulfillment of all patentability requirements. Hence, the right to file for patent protection and to obtaining it is 'absolute', in the sense that no authorization whatsoever is needed from the alleged first inventor. This will allow the derivative innovator to protect her own invention against any infringer (including the holder of the first patent). However, the autonomous (economic) exploitation of the derivative innovation is directly conditioned by the different extent of borrowing from the first invention.

It is generally accepted that when the second inventor achieves, through a new and original coordination of well-known technical elements and tools, a new and original solution (not realized by either the patented element or tool by itself), this invention (called a *combination invention*) will be *independent*, provided that the new and useful result goes beyond the mere sum of the combined factors.[43] Similarly, when the second invention 'transfers' a known

---

41 Ghidini, Gustavo (2006), *Intellectual Property and Competition Law: The Innovation Nexus*, Cheltenham, UK and Northampton, MA, US: Edward Elgar, pp. 25 *et seq*. and 31 *et seq*.

42 Indeed, infringement will be found only if the technical solution subsequently proposed by the second inventor is identical, or at any rate 'equivalent', to the former patented invention, due to the substantial similarity of the means used to achieve the same purpose. Ghidini, *supra* note 41, at 31.

43 Falce, Valeria (2006), *Lineamenti giuridici e profili economici della tutela dell'innovazione industriale*, Milan: Giuffrè, p. 129; Floridia, Giorgio (2005), 'Le creazioni intellettuali', in Paolo Auteri, Giorgio Floridia, Vito Mangini, Gustavo Olivieri, Marco Ricolfi and Paolo Spada (eds), *Diritto Industriale, Proprietà Intellettuale e Concorrenza*, Turin: Giappichelli, p. 235; Greco, Paolo and Paolo Vercellone (1968), *Le invenzioni e i modelli industriali*, Turin: Utet, p. 100. *Contra*: Vincenzo Di Cataldo (2005), in Adriano Vanzetti and Vincenzo Di Cataldo, *Manuale di diritto industriale*, Milan: Giuffrè, p. 342, which lists combination inventions among the dependent ones.

technical solution, formerly patented with regard to a certain sector, to a distant field of use, not thought of, and thus not mentioned in the claims of the original inventor, and reaches a useful new result, the second patent will be independent of the first in relation to its economic exploitation.[44] These latter types of derivative innovations may be called *derivative-autonomous*.[45]

Conversely, second inventions that simply follow the research path pursued by the first invention (that is, they stick to solving the same technical problem within the same technical field) and try to 'improve' upon the product's or process's performance, adding further useful features or eliminating negative features or side-effects, should typically be termed *derivative-dependent*.

The freedom to patent vis-à-vis the need for permission for the economic exploitation of the dependent patent must not be seen as a contradiction within the patent law system. Mere patent ownership, while economically inoffensive to the first patent holder, provides several advantages to a follow-on innovator, even if the first patentee refuses to grant a licence to operate the invention. Indeed, even when 'dependent' inventors cannot legally operate the derivative invention, they can use patent protection against any infringement of the second innovation (even towards the previous patentee).

The right to 'immediately' sue for infringement may further help second inventors in the not infrequent case where the first patent has already 'lost' a significant part of its time validity. In such cases, patent ownership would protect the follow-on inventor in her preparatory entrepreneurial activity, enabling her to 'jump in the market' right after the previous patent's expiration, thus preserving the segment of the market where the former patentee operated.

---

44 A different theory has been proposed for the assessment of the dependency nexus in the case of (chemical) *second use* patents, which have been considered, from a systematic point of view, as a specific type of translation invention. According to this doctrine, the evaluation of the likely dependency of these derivative inventions should take into consideration the inventive effort undertaken by the first inventor. Therefore, a (chemical) second use patent would be *autonomous* if the first patent, in turn, concerned a structurally known compound; while it would be *dependent* if the first patent covered a compound created from scratch (that is, where novelty and originality lay in the very structure of the molecule). See Di Cataldo, Vincenzo (1995), 'La problematica delle invenzioni chimiche', in Adriano Vanzetti (ed.), *I nuovi brevetti. Biotecnologie e invenzioni chimiche*, Milan: Giuffrè, p. 69; Guglielmetti, Giovanni (2004), 'Tutela "assoluta" e "relativa" del brevetto sul nuovo composto chimico, originalità dell'invenzione e dinamiche della ricerca', in *Proprietà intellettuale e concorrenza. Studi di diritto industriale in onore di Adriano Vanzetti*, Milan: Giuffrè, vol. 1, p. 765.

45 Falce, *supra* note 43, at 129; Falce, V. (2003), 'Diritto d'autore e innovazione "derivate" nelle information technologies', *Riv. Dir. Ind.*, **47**, 74, at 77; Di Cataldo, *supra* note 43, at 342.

3.2 A fast track for 'high profile' follow-on innovations

As a general rule, unless the 'dependent' inventor is granted a licence, she cannot commercially exploit her innovation. In practice, this means that former patentees can foreclose access to markets of technological *innovation* with detrimental effects for societal welfare in terms of a lesser degree of technological *competition* in the short run that will cause, in turn, a slowing of innovation progress in the long run.[46]

It could be argued that the very structure and functioning of the patent paradigm requires that, as long as protection has not expired, the right-holder is granted exclusionary rights towards unauthorized uses of the patented innovation. This is surely true, but granting an overly broad scope of protection to first patentees might prove particularly detrimental in *new economy* markets where, as stated, innovation is of a highly cumulative nature. Fortunately, the picture is not complete as yet. In order to reduce the intensity of those detrimental effects to the minimum compatible with patents' inherent excluding power, *and* in order to achieve a reasonable dynamic (pro-competitive) balance between the reward of first and second/derivative innovators, Article 31(l) TRIPS distinguishes, among the dependent inventions, those of 'ordinary' technical and economic relevance from those that represent an 'important technical advance of considerable economic significance'[47] (and thus also provides for a relevant competitive advantage). With regard to these 'high profile' derivative inventions, Article 31(l) TRIPS envisages a special regime and grants to second inventors the right to obtain a licence on the first inventor's patent. More specifically, the provision invites parties to voluntarily negotiate the licence on fair and reasonable terms and only in the case of a negative outcome from bargaining will the second inventor be entitled to a compulsory licence from the first innovator.

Of course, the duty upon first inventors to eventually grant a licence for significant improvement innovations will act somewhat as a Damocles' sword,[48] diminishing their bargaining power (as deprived of veto power) and thus encouraging fair negotiations. Indeed, the significance of this and other

---

[46] Given the hybrid nature of information as a product and a research tool, the establishment of a proprietary regime grants not only an exclusive right to commercial exploitation but also sole and unlimited access to that resource vis-à-vis further research. Benkler, Yochai (2001), 'A Political Economy of the Public Domain: Markets in Information Goods versus the Marketplaces of Ideas', in Rochelle C. Dreyfuss, Diane L. Zimmerman and Harry First (eds), *Expanding the Boundaries of Intellectual Property – Innovation Policy for the Information Society*, New York, N.Y.: Oxford University Press, p. 267.

[47] The 'economic significance' may refer to the revenues expected from the invention as well as, more generally, to a benefit for society at large.

[48] Ghidini, *supra* note 41, at 37.

types of compulsory licences lies more in the encouragement of voluntary settlements rather than in the ultimate recourse to publicly imposed solutions. On the other hand, and at the same time, Article 31(l)(ii) TRIPS provides for a reciprocal cross-licensing scheme whereby the first inventor, compelled to license, is entitled to obtain a licence on the dependent invention.

The benefits of this paradigm are substantial. On the one hand, the non-voluntary licence in favour of derivative inventors prevents the first patentee from foreclosing the market at will to derivative innovations that significantly contribute to and improve upon previous technology. On the other hand, the cross-licensing scheme avoids the risk that the first innovator – due to the reduced competitive impact of the high-profile derivative innovation – will be 'left behind', with just a 'surpassed' patented innovation (thus deprived of its commercial value: just think of an important antibiotic from which the second invention removes severe adverse effects). On the contrary, the 'duo' will be able to impart to the market the most advanced innovation with enormous benefits for consumers in terms of more product competition, lower prices and overall faster product development.

3.3 Copyright treatment of derivative innovations in general

The Berne Convention for the Protection of Literary and Artistic Works has framed a scenario whereby every 'secondary' (derivative) work – that is, a modification of any kind and to any extent of a previous copyrighted work – is also copyright-protected from the very moment of its completion;[49] nonetheless, any use of the derivative work (by the second author) that goes beyond merely private use will need the consent of the first creator in order not to be infringing.[50] Copyright for software makes no exception to this generally acknowledged principle.[51]

From this quick snapshot, copyright treatment of secondary works seems not to be so distant from that of patents. But don't trust first snapshots. Indeed, although both paradigms differentiate between the *entitlement* to exclusive

---

[49] In the wording of Article 2(3) of the Convention, any 'translations, adaptations . . . and other alterations of a literary or artistic work are to be protected without prejudice to copyright in the original work'.

[50] It is worth recalling that the Convention grants the author of a literary or artistic work the sole and exclusive right to perform and/or authorize others to perform: the translation of her work (Article 8), the reproduction thereof in any manner or form (Article 9), its public performance (Article 11), the broadcasting or the communication thereof to the public (Article 11 *bis*), its public recitation (Article 11 *ter*) and adaptations, arrangements and other alterations thereof (Article 12).

[51] Please note that copyright protection for software, although not explicitly codified in the Berne Convention, has later been inserted into Article 10(1) of the TRIPS Agreement.

protection – independent of 'first author's' consent – and industrial and commercial *exploitation*, copyright law *never* (leaving aside the pseudo-exception of 'private use') grants a fast track to derivative works unconstrained by the first author's will. Copyright law does not envision any distinction whatsoever among derivative works. They all need permission from the first author.[52]

The detrimental effect of such absolute blocking power entrusted to copyright owners is partially mitigated if one refers to the traditional, classic conception jointly concerning the 'subject matter' of copyright (that is, works capable of a purely intellectual – including an aesthetic – enjoyment), and the 'object' of protection, namely 'expression' as distinguished from 'ideas'. As is well known, on this very concept, embodied in the first version of the Berne Convention is founded the classical distinction of copyrightable from patentable subject matter – the latter referring to technical innovations satisfying practical functions and needs. Now, within the framework of the classical clear-cut 'division of labour' (all technical innovations to patents – in relation to the technical ideas provided by the inventor; all works of purely intellectual enjoyment of copyright – in relation to the expressive form provided by the author), the blocking effect on 'derivative creations' induced by the principle of 'absolute veto power' appears less troublesome – although not fully satisfactory, as we have seen with reference to translations. Indeed, in a scenario expressly reserved for intellectual and aesthetic fruition, where the legally protected value of the work lies in the 'form' (better: in a form not moulded by any technical-practical constraint) rather than in the substantive concept behind it, authors usually have infinite room for variation. They typically do not *need* to closely follow first creators' paths in order to express their own creative personality, not even to gain 'audience niches', since markets for artistic and intellectual creations tend never to get saturated. That is why, as remarked, in traditional copyright settings, the likely blocking effect on derivative creations that can arise from the author's 'absolute' veto power – and thus, the lack of any double-track mechanism of the kind envisioned for patents – normally causes much less detrimental effects.

---

52 Let us just think of translations, the basic tool of international circulation of culture. Under the current copyright paradigm (unlike those of much nineteenth-century European legislation) the simple 'no' of the author (and/or assignee) can bar vast portions of mankind from access to relevant works of literature, economics, philosophy and so on. There is an exception, however, for developing countries, which, under the conditions set forth in Articles I and II of the Appendix to the Berne Convention, can benefit under certain circumstances from a system of non-exclusive and non-transferable licences.

When the copyright paradigm is applied to a technical subject matter, however, the effects on derivative innovations become detrimental. In fact, according to the Directive, the author of the program has the exclusive right to perform or authorize not just the permanent or temporary reproduction of the program, but also the 'translation, adaptation, arrangement and any other alteration of a computer program and the reproduction of the results thereof, *without prejudice to the rights of the person who alters the program*'. This means that despite the rights that immediately arise, upon creation, in the (derivative) programs that somehow modify an existing program, the exploitation of such software will always be infringing unless an authorization is obtained from the first author.

3.4 Copyright for software: the entrapment of derivative innovation?

In 1980 the US Congress amended the Copyright Act to introduce computer programs among copyrightable subject matter, with the famous *fictio iuris* likening computer programs' language and coding to literary works.[53] The pressure to insert a parallel provision in the text of the Berne Convention failed,[54] but Europe followed the path anyway through Directive No. 91/250.

Clearly, the comparison was fallacious and misleading from both a theoretical and a practical point of view. Programs consist of a written set of instructions, but that is the end of the analogy. Despite their written form, software programs, even in their more intelligible form – that is, source code – remain codes not readable by the average human being. Moreover, program coding is extremely functional. Each individual portion of a code is dictated by technical and functional design. The choice of 'form of expression' does not depend on the aesthetic inspiration of the programmer, but rather it is technically bound by efficiency concerns, interoperability needs, consumers' preferences and so on. In other words, software code is just a set of technical ideas embedded in a binary code,[55] and it should not matter – as supporters of copyright protection for software habitually claim – that such expressions may not be 'the only ones' conceivable to write the program.[56]

---

[53] See also *Apple Computer, Inc. v. Franklin Computer Corp.*, 714 F.2d 1240 (3rd Cir. 1983).

[54] But note that, as mentioned *supra* note 51, computer programs nowadays have to be protected as literary works in the sense of the Berne Convention according to Article 10(1) TRIPS Agreement.

[55] On the technicalities of computer programs and the peculiarities of the subject matter see Keplinger, M.S. (1977), 'Computer Intellectual Property Claims: Computer Software & Database Protection', *Wash. U. L.Q.*, 461.

[56] Software being a utilitarian subject matter, it should be assimilated to industrial paradigms. For example, utility models protect every different form insofar as it confers a new utility.

Furthermore, the analogy has also proved wrong in practice. Software represents a very peculiar and hybrid subject matter in that although – like copyrightable subject matter – it appears in written form, the value of the program – like patentable subject matter – lies in its 'behaviours', that is, in the functionalities the program is able to perform.[57] However, because software 'carries know-how on its surface' competitors can well replicate software functionalities without bothering to obtain access to the source code and copy it. In other words, copyright law proved ineffective in solving the public-good problem that is generally solved through IPRs, because copyright targets the portion of the good that in this context has no value itself: namely, the writing.

American courts soon realized that cases of literal copying of software were not going to be massive and struggled to reframe copyright protection in such a way as to cover software beyond non-literal copying. After a first round of cases drawn on the so-called *abstraction-filtration-comparison test*,[58] where courts interpreted software copyright protection broadly and declared infringing each independently created program whose features resembled another one,[59] courts stepped back and severely curtailed the scope of copyright protection for computer programs.[60] In practice, American courts realized

57 Samuelson, P., R. Davis, M.D. Kapor and J.H. Reichman (1994), 'A Manifesto Concerning the Legal Protection of Computer Programs', *Col. L. Rev.*, **94**, 2308.

58 The test consists of three steps. First, the allegedly infringing program must be dissected – from the general idea behind the program till its practical functionalities – into its modules, routines and subroutines. Think, for example, of a writing program whose main function or idea is to reproduce virtually the act of writing on a typewriter. In such a case, the program will be dissected until single portions that perform small functions are isolated, such as, for example, cut and paste. The second step involves the so-called *abstraction*, namely for each portion of the program that has been dissected it is necessary to abstract the underlying idea. Eventually, the form of expression, as separated from the abstract idea, must be filtered out and compared with the presumably infringed software to see whether there is *substantial similarity*.

59 In the famous case *Whelan Associates v. Jaslow Dental Laboratory*, 797 F.2d 1222 (3rd Cir. 1986), the Federal Circuit explained: 'the purpose or functioning of a utilitarian work would be the work's idea, and everything that is not necessary to that purpose or function would be part of the expression of the idea'. It further added: 'where there are many means of achieving the desired purpose, then the particular means chosen is not necessary to the purpose; hence, there is expression, not idea'.

60 The above test has been considerably restricted in *Computer Associates International Inc. v. Altai*, 982 F.2d 693 (2nd Cir. 1992). The court explained that the so-called *filtration* is aimed at filtering out only the portions of the programs that truly involved a creative choice by the programmer. Conversely, if the form of expression is the *one and only efficient way* to express a certain idea, the latter is said to have merged with the expression, hence will not be copyrightable (the so-called *merger* doctrine). In the same way, standard programming techniques regularly used by all programmers

they had vested copyright with a sort of patent-like breadth of protection without burdening programmers with the hurdle of actually meeting patent eligibility requirements and going through the whole application process. Such a broad scope of protection for copyrighted software indeed amounted to an excessive extension of the paradigm.

4 Copyright and other forms of protection

Proof of such 'redemption' in Europe has not been found, at least not in Italy, where there is no precise judicial orientation with regard to when and to what extent non-literal copying of a program amounts to an infringement. Some courts have argued that independent creation of the program suffices as a defence against infringement; others, however, have tried to draw some boundaries, but the result is not satisfactory.[61] A likely difference in (judicial) trends creates uncertainty as to the kind of protection afforded by copyright throughout Europe regarding the originality level required for eligibility of protection, the scope of protection and, consequently, the boundaries between first and second derivative creations. Again, because copyright comes with no cost at the moment of creation (and fixation) of the work, one could argue that this difference in trends of protection should not be worth worrying about. However the very same fact that copyright is handed out basically without any filtering to everyone becomes troublesome if courts in proceedings give it a wide scope of protection. If this were to be the case, copyright protection would be much stronger and intrusive than patent protection, because it would grant strong protection with no safeguards in exchange.

---

may not be protected by copyright; nor will portions of the programs that serve interoperability purposes – that is, those necessary for the program to communicate with a certain operating system or hardware components (the so-called *scene à faire* doctrine). Finally, the court requires verification that the portion of the program does not lie in the public domain. Only program portions that have survived this deep scrutiny receive copyright protection and can then be compared with the allegedly infringed program. A few years later, the First Circuit in the last episode of the *Lotus v. Borland* saga further curtailed copyright protection for software, holding that menu-command hierarchies, method of operation and single commands of the Lotus spreadsheet program were not copyrighted portions of the software, see *Lotus Development Corporation v. Borland International Inc.*, 49 F.3d 807 (1st Cir. 1995). Cf. Reichman, J.H. (1995), 'Charting the Collapse of the Patent-Copyright Dichotomy: Premises for a Restructured International Intellectual Property System', *Cardozo Arts & Enter. L.J.*, **13**, 475; Reichman, J.H. (1994), 'Legal Hybrids between the Patent and Copyright Paradigms', *Col. L. Rev.*, **94**, 2432.

[61] See Ghidini, Gustavo, Emanuela Arezzo and Maria L. Montagnani (2006), 'Softwareschutz und Softwareverträge in einzelnen Ländern, Italien', in Hanns Ullrich and Mathias Lejeune (eds), *Der internationale Softwarevertrag*, Frankfurt am Main: Verlag Recht und Wirtschaft, p. 816.

4.1 The residual (?) role of trade secret

This picture is not complete yet. Although copyright is meant to protect software in whatever form of expression, meaning both source code and object code, it is widely known that the source code is never disclosed to the public nor, quite often, to the copyright office when a copy of the program is submitted for registration.[62] Similarly, patent law does not require the disclosure of the source code of computer-implemented inventions in the patent application. Therefore, clearly both forms of protection allow a fair degree of protection to technical information as a trade secret. Because the trade secret has acquired strong protection since its codification in Article 39 of the TRIPs Agreement,[63] demanding the protection of relevant technical information on software programs has the effect of adding another layer of protection to them, with significant anti-competitive effect for firms that need interoperability in order to compete in the same or an ancillary market.

As mentioned earlier, some scholars have rightly pointed out that because software bears know-how on its face, it is extremely easy for competitors to appropriate such know-how and embed it in an independently created program.[64] This consideration may lead us to think that, at the end of the day, access to the source code should not matter that much. After all, we have seen that even when the source code is never disclosed the innovation process goes on at a rapid pace. While this is surely true, there are still instances where access to the source code really matters. For example, in order to allow interoperability between programs or between programs and hardware components, programmers need access to that specific portion of code; a similar one

---

62 In Italy, for example, the documentation necessary to register software only comprises a copy of the program on a CD-Rom and a description of its functionalities. Such information can easily be found on the official website of the SIAE, the Italian collecting society in charge of software registration. See http://www.siae.it/olaf_sw.asp?link_page=Olaf_sw_PercheRegistrare.htm&open_menu=yes, accessed 4 November 2007. Conversely, the US Copyright Office requires, for a successful registration of the program, a perceptible copy of 'identifying portions of the program (first 25 and last 25 pages of the source code) reproduced in a form visually perceptible without the aid of a machine or device'. See Circular 61 – Copyright Registration for Computer Programs, http://www.copyright.gov/circs/circ61.pdf, accessed 4 November 2007.

63 Moreover, the Italian Industrial Property Code seems to have introduced a much stronger protection of trade secrets than the one adopted by Article 39 TRIPS because its misappropriation is no longer conditioned on the circumstances that the information is stolen by illicit means. See Vanzetti and Di Cataldo, *supra* note 43, at 447 *et seq*. The interpretation of the new provision is very controversial. In favour of a stronger protection see Floridia, G. (2005), 'Le creazioni intellettuali', *supra* note 43, at 195.

64 Samuelson *et al*., *supra* note 57.

will simply not do the work. It could be counter-argued that the Copyright Directive contains a provision allowing decompilation of software for interoperability purposes.[65] However, reverse engineering is not enough. The European *Microsoft* case is a clear example of how important access to certain code portions is in order to make programs – or a network of programs – talk to each other.[66] While copyright law is in no position to solve this fallacy of the system, patent law could easily be amended to require mandatory disclosure of the source code.[67]

4.2 The protection of software through technological measures

Furthermore, software can be protected through technical measures like digital encryption, watermarking and so on. The recourse to these means of protection is widespread, especially for software distributed online. While these measures represent quite a reliable tool of protection, surely enough to protect software against attempts coming from average-skilled internet users, European legislators have decided to provide them with extra strength by giving them special legal protection.

Interestingly, the legal protection of technological measures for computer programs was silently introduced via the Software Copyright Directive,[68] thus anticipating both the WIPO Copyright Treaty (1996)[69] and the Information

---

65 Article 6 of Directive 91/250/CEE.

66 See Commission Decision of 24 March 2004, Case COMP/C-3/37.792 – *Microsoft*, europa.eu.int/comm/competition/antitrust/cases/decisions/37792/en.pdf, accessed 4 November 2007; confirmed in substance by the CFI in Case T-201/04, *Microsoft v. Commission*, [2007] ECR II-0000 (not yet reported). Commissioner Monti ordered Microsoft to disclose the specifications of the interfaces of the Windows workgroup server operating system to competitors (especially Sun Microsystems) to enable the latter to achieve full interoperability of their server operating systems with Microsoft's, and in particular to ensure the same degree of compatibility that exists between the latter and the Windows operating systems for personal computers designed to operate within a single network of computers.

67 For example, Article 13 of the Directive 98/44/EC of the European Parliament and of the Council of 6 July 1998 on the legal protection of biotechnological inventions, OJ 1998 No. L 213, p. 13, expressly requires that 'where an invention involves the use of or concerns biological material which is not available to the public and which cannot be described in a patent application in such a manner as to enable the invention to be reproduced by a person skilled in the art, the description shall be considered inadequate for the purposes of patent law unless: (a) the biological material has been deposited no later than the date on which the patent application was filed with a recognized depositary institution . . .; (b) the application as filed contains such relevant information as is available to the applicant on the characteristics of the biological material deposited'.

68 Article 7(1)(c) of Directive 91/250/CEE.

69 See WIPO Copyright Treaty, adopted by the Diplomatic Conference on 20 December 1996, Article 11 (Obligations concerning Technological Measures).

Society Directive 2001/29[70] introducing legal protection for technical measures covering subject matter protected by copyright, neighbouring rights and the *sui generis* right provided for in Chapter III of Directive 96/9/EC.

There is no evidence that legal protection of technological measures surrounding software was ever an issue during the long legislative process that eventually led to the adoption of the Software Copyright Directive. Nor that anyone discussed the likely coexistence of such provisions with the interoperability (decompilation) exception.[71] Rather, the concept of technical measures does not even figure in the Directive's recitals, which usually clarify and explain how to interpret the normative part of a directive.[72]

It must be said that, *literally*, the legal protection afforded to technical measures by the Software Directive is smoother than that later provided by Directive 2001/29 for all remaining copyrightable subject matters. In fact, the latter provides right-holders with a twofold cause of action: against the circumvention itself of the technological measure pursued by any person who knows or has reason to know that such activity is illegal; and against the manufacture, import, distribution, sale, rental and so on of products and devices *primarily* produced and marketed for the purpose of circumventing or facilitating the circumvention of technological measures.[73]

Conversely, the older Software Copyright Directive only provides for a cause of action against 'any act of putting into circulation, or the possession for commercial purposes of, any means the sole intended purpose of which is to facilitate the unauthorized removal or circumvention of any technical device which may have been applied to protect a computer program'.[74] This should imply, at least in theory, that the mere act of circumvention of a computer program for other than business purposes should not be deemed unlawful; hence the circumvention of technological measures for interoperability purposes or to exercise any of the exceptions granted in Article 5(2) and (3) of Directive 91/250 should always be allowed.

---

70 Article 6 of Directive 2001/29/EC of the European Parliament and of the Council of 22 May 2001 on the harmonization of certain aspects of copyright and related rights in the information society, OJ 2001 No. L 167, p. 11.

71 On the contrary, the American Digital Millennium Copyright Act, 17 USCA 1201(f)(1), has expressly regulated the relation between protection of anti-circumvention measures and decompilation.

72 For an in-depth analysis of the legislative works that led to the adoption of Directive 91/250 see Vinje, Thomas (1993), 'The Legislative History of the EC Directive', in Lehmann, Michael and Colin Tapper (eds) (1993), *A Handbook of European Software Law*, Oxford: Oxford University Press, p. 183; Lehmann, *supra* note 19, p. 169.

73 Article 6(1)(2) of Directive 2001/29.

74 Article 7(1)(c) of Directive 91/250.

Article 7 of Directive 91/250 tries to somehow reconcile these provisions.[75] The wording of Article 7, however, is too vague and it is not backed by any other provisions or recitals to clarify its meaning, as was the case, for example, in Directive 2001/29, where EU legislators inserted an ad hoc provision to ensure that users of copyrighted goods would benefit from the exceptions and limitations provided for within the same Directive.[76] The uncertainty surrounding this issue has led to paradoxical results. In Italy, for example, at least two different courts have held that conduct aimed at circumventing technical measures protecting a computer program amounted to an unauthorized alteration of the software and was, therefore, infringing the copyright on the program.[77] Practically, although Italian copyright law has not introduced any norm that would punish the circumvention of technical measures (protecting software) per se, courts have endorsed a very protectionist approach, going well beyond what is established by the very same law (both national and European). The inappropriateness of such a far-reaching approach, which risks unduly shrinking fair uses granted by the software Directive, finds strong confirmation in the fact that the European legislature had the chance to broaden the protection for technical measures applied to software during the legislative process that led to the adoption of Directive 2001/29, and they decided not to. In fact, recital 50 of the latter Directive expressly states that the content of Directive 2001/29 does not affect the specific provisions on protection provided for by Directive 91/250 and that, in particular, Directive 2001/29 'should not apply to the protection of technological measures used in connection with computer programs, which is exclusively addressed in that Directive'. Moreover, the same recital clarifies the relation between technological measures protecting software and the exceptions provided in Articles 5(3) and 6 of Directive 91/250, explaining that the newly harmonized legal protection for digital copyrighted products should neither inhibit nor prevent the development or use of any means of circum-

---

75 The article begins with 'without prejudice to the provisions of Articles 4, 5 and 6'.

76 Article 6(4) of Directive 29/2001/EC provides that, absent voluntary measures taken by right-holders, Member States must take appropriate measures to ensure that a beneficiary of an exception or limitation provided for in Article 5(2)(a), (2)(c), (2)(d), (2)(e), (3)(a), (3)(b) or (3)(e) be granted the means of benefiting from that exception or limitation, provided that the beneficiary was entitled to access to the copyrighted work in the first place. This provision has not been praised for its clarity; however, it shows legislators' concerns in preserving a balance between right-holders' and users' interests.

77 Tribunale di Forlì, 5 February 2003, (2003) *AIDA* 959. Tribunale di Torino, 30 October 1997, (1999) *AIDA*, 599.

venting a technological measure when such conduct is aimed at making use of one of the above limitations.[78]

In the end, the clarifications made through Directive 2001/29 seem to show a certain willingness of the European legislature to adopt a two-tiered framework for the protection of technological measures, featuring a stronger regime for works covered by copyrights, neighbouring rights and the *sui generis* database right, and a somewhat weaker regime for measures applying to computer programs. Nonetheless, the impact of such clarification is not foreseeable and, at the moment, does not seem to be strong enough. The Italian courts' approach in the cases quoted above is surely an example of how Article 1(2)(a) and recital 50 of Directive 2001/29 have not been uniformly taken into account.

On a lighter note, a further difference remains between software technical measures and technical measures covering remaining copyright subject matters. While Directive 2001/29, like Section 1201(f) of the Digital Millenium Copyright Act (DMCA), grants protection only to *effective* technological measures, no such *caveat* is envisioned by the Directive 91/250, which simply talks about 'technical devices'. Nonetheless, Directive 2001/29 gives such a broad definition of *effective* measures[79] that many commentators have wondered whether the insertion of this parameter serves any purpose whatsoever.[80] Therefore it is not clear whether – and it seems highly unlikely that – this small difference in the wording of the provisions will actually have a significant impact.

5 Towards a broader idea of copyright: the open-source model

As we have explained, the alleged benefits of the copyright paradigm for software cannot be easily assessed. We fear that EU Member States have adopted different approaches towards copyright protection for software, varying from strong, patent-like to very weak, almost imperceptible protection.

As explained, contrary to the general belief, such uncertainty is not good for the European software industry. If, as we sense, the majority of national

---

[78] Note that the Directive, in Article 1(2)(a), clearly explains that its provisions shall leave intact and shall in no way affect the existing Community provisions relating to computer programs.

[79] Article 6(3) of Directive 2001/29, indeed, explains that technological measures are to be deemed effective where 'the use of a protected work . . . is controlled by the rightholder through application of an access control or protection process, such as encryption, scrambling or other transformation of the work or other subject-matter or a copy control mechanism, which achieves the protection objective'.

[80] De Sanctis, V.M. (2003), 'Misure tecniche di protezione e libere utilizzazioni', *Dir. Aut.*, 1.

courts still grant copyrighted software a broad scope of protection, copyright will be turned into a dangerous tool capable of hindering innovation in the software market, because copyright protection arises at the very moment of creation. Moreover, as we have just explained, copyright protection for software has brought this new form of protection for technological measures, resulting in a new, additional layer of protection for computer programs that is able to seriously undermine the feasibility of decompilation exceptions for interoperability purposes.

Having said that, it appears legitimate to ask why copyright protection for software is so deeply cherished, resulting ultimately in harsh criticism towards the PD on CII patentability. We think that a large part of this European attitude stems from the widespread acceptance and diffusion of the *open-source software* licensing model.

5.1 Copyright and open-source software

The *open-source software* movement has enjoyed a wide diffusion in Europe. It is common knowledge that the name open-source software has become a synonym for a very peculiar licensing model applied to computer programs. Roughly speaking, this licensing system uses the copyright paradigm, which inevitably covers software creations, to build a pool of technical know-how from which everyone can borrow, provided that each user is also willing to contribute. More specifically, the open-source model dissects the 'good' and the 'bad' sides of copyright: namely, the entitlement itself and the exclusive rights conferred by such entitlement. Then it forces parties willing to join the pool to give up the 'bad' side – that is, exercising exclusive rights against third parties' reproduction, alteration, translation or whatever modification of their work – while it still retains the 'good' side of copyright as a credible threat to compel those same people not to cheat on the pool, for example by patenting the derivative creation. However the great aspect of open-source licensing is that adhering members do not simply agree not to exercise their exclusive rights against the members of the pool. Open-source licensing's most salient feature is that the pool's members agree to share the 'recipe' with others; hence the name *open source*, where open stands for open access.[81] And this is not all. Often the licence agreement requires licensees to license their derivative works, granting access to their source code. This self-perpetuating mechanism that allows disclosure of the source code to extend to derivative creations has been referred to as

[81] Free like free speech and not like free beer. Stallman, Richard M. (2002), *Free Software, Free Society: Selected Essays of Richard M. Stallman*, Boston: Free Software Foundation, pp. 41 *et seq.*

open source's *viral effect*.[82] Putting it in different words, the open-source licensing scheme has been successful in curing the trade-secret problem present in both copyright and patent law and making the release of source code possible.

This licensing model has been highly appreciated by European SMEs that can easily acquire the technical knowledge and tools needed to enter the software market at a negligible cost and without the risk of producing an invention that, if marketed, would infringe a product already covered by patent, or a program already copyrighted.

5.2 Open-source software and patents

We sense that the strong leaning towards copyright as a tool to protect software and the corresponding diffidence towards patents comes substantially from the (erroneous) belief that open-source software needs copyright while patents, in turn, would kill it.

As hinted above, people have praised open source's virtue and beneficial properties and contrasted them with the alleged foreclosing effects stemming from proprietary paradigms. A flood of words has been spent on open source indeed. All possible studies and comparisons have been undertaken, from all possible angles and perspectives: sociological, economic and legal.[83] Sometimes, however, looking at the same issue from different angles can be counterproductive if the basic assumptions are not kept in mind. What we intend to say is that comparing the pace of innovation in the proprietary model and in the open-source model makes sense, surely, from an economic point of view; nonetheless, it does not make sense to try to compare, from a legal point of view, open source, which is a licensing scheme, with either copyright or patent, which are exclusive rights.

---

82 Dusollier, S. (2003), 'Open Source and Copyright: Authorship Reconsidered?', *Col. J. L. & Arts*, **26**, 281. Ghidini, G. and V. Falce (2004), 'Open source, General Public License e incentive all'innovazione', *AIDA*, 3.

83 Among the legal articles see: Nadan, C.H. (2002), 'Open Source Licensing: Virus or Virtue?', *Tex. Intell. Prop. L.J.*, **10**, 349; Satchwell, M.D. (2005), 'The Tao of Open Source: Minimum Action For Maximum Gain', *Berkeley Tech. L.J.*, **20**, 1757; Eng, J. (2005), 'From Software to Life Sciences: The Spreading of the Open Source Production to New Technological Areas', *Temp. J. Sci. Tech. & Envtl. L.*, **24**, 419. Economic and sociological analyses seem to have merged in the following article: Lerner, J. and J. Tirole (2005), 'The Scope of Open Source Licensing', *J. L. Econ. & Org.*, **21**, 20. A significant economic study about open source has been carried out by Giuri, P., G. Rocchetti and S. Torrisi (2002), *Open Source Software: From Open Science to New Marketing Models: An Inquiry into the Economics and Management of Open Source Software*, LEM Working Paper Series, http://www.lem.sssup.it/WPLem/files/2002-23.pdf, accessed 4 November 2007.

Open source simply requires a form of entitlement to fence off. As explained earlier, the entitlement is a crucial part of the whole mechanism, but the specific *nature* of the entitlement does not alter the result. Many companies nowadays endorse an 'open policy', meaning that they have spontaneously given up a huge number of intellectual property rights on software so that the open-source community can make free use of them as input to build new programs. Among these companies are IBM, Novel, Computer Associates, Sun Microsystems and RedHat. Notably, the IPRs that these companies handed over are patents. In 2005, IBM alone relinquished 500 patents on software.[84] IBM's CEO, David Kappos, has recently described IBM's interests in open policies for innovation and, at the same time, in a better tailored patent system.[85] Interestingly, notwithstanding this attention to open-source policies, IBM remains the company with the biggest patent portfolio, with 40 000 active patents worldwide.[86]

What we have just described leads us to two conclusions. First, open source and patents are not at odds, as many believe. Many initiatives have been launched recently involving patents and open sources, not only in the software industry[87] but also in the biotechnology sector.[88] Second, patents are fundamental intangible assets, and even companies that strongly advocate and call for open policies still prefer to protect software creations through patents rather than copyright. Open source supporters, fearing that patentability of

---

[84] See Shankland, S., 'IBM Offers 500 Patents for Open-source Use', 10 January 2005, http://news.com.com/IBM+offers+500+patents+for+open-source+use/2100-7344_3-5524680.html, accessed 4 November 2007.

[85] Kappos, David and Ray Strimaitis (2005), 'Collaborative Innovation and the Patent System – Replacing Friction with Facilitation', paper delivered at the Softic Symposium, Tokyo, 9 November 2005, http://www.researchoninnovation.org/swconf/IBM%20Views%20On%20Software%20Patents.pdf, accessed 4 November 2007.

[86] In 2005 alone IBM was granted 2974 patents by the US PTO, see http://www.ibm.com/ibm/licensing/patents/, accessed 4 November 2007.

[87] A 'Patent Commons Project' has been recently launched by OSDL ('Open Source Development Lab') and companies like IBM, Red Hat, Sun Microsystems, Novell and Computer Associates. The Patent Commons Project provides a central reference library and database hosted by the OSDL where patentees pledge their IP for the benefit of open-source software. More information can be found at http://www.patent-commons.org/, accessed 4 November 2007.

[88] BIOS (biological open source licences) is a licensing model that is recently attracting more and more attention. Although BIOS licensees must agree to share improvements, usually the first technology to be licensed is covered by patents and this represents another tangible proof (after the OSDL quoted above) that open source can work also in a scenario where patents are widely used. Information about the BIOS initiative can be found at www.bios.net. Also, see Mark, P. and V. Ferguson (2004/2005), 'A Change of Scenery: Open Source Licensing and its Application to the Biotech Industry', *Patent World*, (178), 22.

CIIs might put an end to open-source licensing in Europe, have fuelled a climate of distrust against software patents. In particular, they fear that patents on software will eliminate technology from the open-source commons and maybe even expose open-source developers to infringement suits. This is a possible risk, although it might just as easily come from copyright owners who have not embraced the open-source model, as indeed happened in the case *SCO Group v. IBM*.[89]

6 Conclusion

This chapter aimed to analyse the set of available tools of protection for software creations in Europe remaining after the dismissal of the Proposal for a Directive on the patentability of computer-implemented inventions.

The dismissal of the above proposal is not likely to eliminate patent protection for software-related inventions. As explained, the patentability of this kind of invention has been introduced by the European Patent Office, whose power and legitimacy is independent of the European Community's bodies and laws. There is no reason to believe that the EPO has any intention whatsoever of stepping back and erasing a patentability trend that has been developing since the end of the 1980s.

Conversely, the European Commission, Council and Parliament had the chance to take part in this legislative process, to introduce official rules binding throughout the Community and to adjust the EPO's judicial trend where they thought it was deficient. At the time of writing, the Commission seems to be unwilling to submit a new proposal for a directive, which means that the situation will remain unchanged, and patent and copyright will remain alternative or, as often happens, cumulative tools of protection. This outcome has been largely applauded by supporters of the open-source movement, whose campaign against software patentability had taken on the tones of a *Religionskrieg*. The widespread partiality towards open source as a licensing model to facilitate the creation of a technical pool of know-how and technical resources seems to have overshadowed the potential negative effects of copyright law as applied to such a utilitarian subject matter as software.

---

89 Because open-source licensing is based, as explained, on the disclosure of the source code, it may well happen that a copyright owner claims that the program covered by open-source licensing infringes on her program whose source code is secret. This actually happened in the case *SCO Group v. IBM* (Docket No. 2:03CV00294 (D. Utah)), where SCO claimed that IBM had handed to the GNU/Linux project several source code portions belonging to Unix, an operating system program that now happens to be owned by SCO, hence infringing SCO's copyrights. For an in-depth analysis of the case see Zittrain, J. (2004), 'Normative Principles for Evaluating Free and Proprietary Software', *U. Chi. L. Rev.*, **71**, 265.

As we have stressed throughout this study, it is not clear whether the EU Member States have applied copyright law to software in a restrictive and balanced way or, rather, in an overly broad manner, coming close to patent-like protection. If the latter were to be the case, the adverse effects on the innovative process would be extremely worrying because copyright protection arises at the very moment of creation, with no test whatsoever of its level of originality. Furthermore, as is well known, copyright protection lasts for the life of the author plus 70 years; therefore a great deal of time must pass before the knowledge embedded in a copyrighted program enters the public domain. In addition, when copyright protection for software was introduced, the European legislature silently inserted, through Directive 91/250/CEE, a peculiar form of protection for technological measures aimed at protecting the program. Because it looks as if the norm was not carefully thought out and debated when the Directive was adopted, such sweeping protection risks damaging the – already unsatisfactory – interoperability provisions and the other limitations and exceptions envisioned by the Directive.

In conclusion, the protection of software creations in Europe seems chaotic at best. The same piece of innovation can be subject at the same time to patent and copyright protection, trade secret and – where technological measures are present – legal protection of technological measures. Moreover, the scope of each of these rights is far from clear, and it is different in each Member State.

Patent law could offer a suitable means of protection in consideration of the utilitarian subject matter at issue. If properly tailored, patent law could bring several benefits to the software industry and could prove to be a far more efficient tool than copyright law.

Clearly the task is not an easy one, also considering the dysfunctions surrounding the EPO's internal mechanisms and the difficulties of creating a Community patent. Nonetheless, as pointed out above, because it seems inconceivable for the EPO to step back and stop granting patents on CIIs, giving up the creation of a harmonized framework does not seem a feasible solution.

15 Development of the economics of copyright*

Christian Handke, Paul Stepan and Ruth Towse

1 Introduction

Once only the preserve of a relatively small group of specialist lawyers, work on copyright is now established in a wide range of academic disciplines, as well as in interdisciplinary endeavours.[1] That is because copyright law has wide-ranging implications for many economic, social, cultural and political considerations besides legal ones. In this chapter we deal with the development of the economic analysis of copyright and its implications for competition law. In the past, there has been far more emphasis in the economic analysis of intellectual property (IP) on patents than on copyright, no doubt in part because patents were seen as a much more important vehicle for encouraging economic growth. Now that we have entered an era in which service industries are growing faster than manufacturing and there is a great deal of emphasis on the creative industries, a greater interest in the economics of copyright has developed. However, there are fundamental differences between patents and copyrights that make a separate analysis necessary: copyright is automatic and so costs the creator nothing to acquire; it applies to works that may be close substitutes and, in addition, copyright lasts much longer than a patent, depending upon the life of the author plus 70 years.

There have been previous surveys of the economics of copyright.[2]

* This chapter is a shortened and merged version of two reports commissioned by SGAE (Spanish Authors' Society) Fundación Autor. We are grateful to them for permission to adapt the reports: *Economics of Copyright Law* and *Economics of Copyright Collecting Societies*. The views expressed in it are those of the authors and do not represent those of SGAE, Fundación Autor.

1 See, for example, Frith, Simon and Lee Marshall (eds) (2004), *Music and Copyright*, 2nd ed., Edinburgh: University of Edinburgh Press; Macmillan, Fiona (ed.) (2005), *New Directions in Copyright Law*, vols 1 and 2, Cheltenham, UK and Northampton, MA, US: Edward Elgar.

2 Raskind, Leo (1998), 'Copyright', in Peter Newman (ed.), *New Palgrave Dictionary of Law and Economics*, London; Macmillan, vol. 1, p. 478; Gordon, Wendy J. and Robert Bone (1998), 'Copyright', in Boudewijn Bouckaert and Gerrit De Geest (eds), *Encyclopedia of Law and Economics*, Cheltenham, UK and Northampton, MA,

Liebowitz and Watt survey a specialized literature on copyright and the music industry[3] and Towse deals with aspects of copyright of special interest to artists – moral rights, performers' rights and artists' resale rights.[4] Copyright has also been included in more general surveys of the economics of IP by Besen and Raskind[5] as well as Menell.[6] Surveying economics of copyright is not altogether straightforward as there are several different valid analytical approaches that have been taken – welfare economics, property rights, law and economics, empirical estimates – and writers on the subject tend to interweave different approaches. This is understandable as the main goal is to explain the 'real world' of copyright's presence but it makes the task of disentangling the underlying arguments of the various strands more difficult. Furthermore, substantial changes in copying technology have taken place that made copying easier and cheaper and they alter some of the conclusions about copyright in the earlier literature.

Within the literature surveyed here, we make a distinction between the economics of copying and the economics of copyright. We also refer briefly to the law and economics analysis of copyright. While economists have a tendency to ignore the legal detail about copyright law and have been content to speak of copyright in a generic way, on the other hand, the discipline of law and economics pays considerable attention to the detailed analysis of the doctrines of copyright law (scope and duration, limitations and exceptions, derivative works, etc.) but uses a narrow range of economic analysis, mainly static welfare economics.

Economists as early as Adam Smith had made comments on copyright but it was not until Plant (1934) that there was a systematic analysis of copyright that could be called 'economics of copyright'.[7] The related economics of copying took shape in the second half of the 20th century with articles by Hurt

US: Edward Elgar, Entry 1610; Towse, Ruth and Rudi Holzhauer (2002), *Economics of Intellectual Property*, Cheltenham, UK and Northampton, MA, US: Edward Elgar.

3 Liebowitz, S.J. and R. Watt (2006), 'How Best to Ensure the Remuneration of Creators in the Market for Music? Copyright and its Alternatives', *J. Econ. Surv.*, **20**, 513.

4 Towse, Ruth (2006), 'Copyright and Artists: A View from Cultural Economics', *J. Econ. Surv.*, **20**, 567.

5 Besen, S. and L. Raskind (1991), 'An Introduction to the Law and Economics of Intellectual Property', *J. Econ. Persp.*, **5**, 3–27.

6 Menell, Peter S. (1998), 'Intellectual Property: General Theories', in Boudewijn Bouckaert and Gerrit De Geest (eds), *Encyclopedia of Law and Economics*, Cheltenham, UK and Northampton, MA, US: Edward Elgar, Entry 1600.

7 Plant, A. (1934), 'The Economic Aspect of Copyright in Books', *Economica*, **1**, 167.

and Schuchman,[8] Breyer,[9] Novos and Waldman[10] and Johnson.[11] An important article by Liebowitz started another line of discussion about the possibility of appropriating rewards through market means using price discrimination, thereby reducing the case for copyright as a necessary intervention to enable the creator to obtain a return on her effort.[12] This was known as 'indirect appropriability' and it spawned a considerable subsequent literature. Application of the Coase theorem and property rights analysis of copyright began with Merges.[13] Law and economics only began to analyse copyright in earnest with the seminal paper on the law and economics of copyright law by Landes and Posner.[14] A more specialized literature dealt with the economics of copyright collectives, starting with Peacock and Weir.[15]

2 The basic economics of copyright

Economists view copyright law as a means of providing an incentive to produce creative work. However, like any form of state intervention, it creates costs. The oldest view is that copyright is a monopoly and therefore causes prices to be higher than under competition; however, monopoly pricing is justified as it enables the fixed costs of production to be covered. Nevertheless, copyright creates access costs because higher prices exclude consumers who value the work by more than the marginal cost but less than the price being charged. This is referred to as 'under-utilisation' and its trade-off with 'underproduction' that would result without the copyright incentive is the focus of many studies. It is sometimes presented as a trade-off between consumers' and producers' interests. However, copyright can also exclude creators who are deterred from building upon prior works because they are unwilling to pay the price the copyright holder demands or incur the transaction costs of obtaining the necessary permissions. Some of these costs increase

---

8 Hurt, R.M. and R.M. Schuchman (1966), 'The Economic Rationale of Copyright', *Am. Econ. Rev. Papers & Proceedings*, **56** (2), 421.

9 Breyer, S. (1970), 'The Uneasy Case for Copyright: A Study of Copyright in Books, Photocopies and Computer Programs', *Harv. L. Rev.*, **84**(2), 281.

10 Novos, N.J. and M. Waldman (1984), 'The Effects of Increased Copyright Protection: An Analytical Approach', *J. Polit. Econ.*, **92**, 236.

11 Johnson, W.R. (1985), 'The Economics of Copying', *J. Polit. Econ.*, **93**, 158.

12 Liebowitz, S.J. (1985), 'Copying and Indirect Appropriability', *J. Polit. Econ.*, **93**, 945.

13 Merges, R.P. (1995), 'The Economic Impact of Intellectual Property Rights: An Overview and Guide', *J. Cultural Econ.*, **19**(2), 103.

14 Landes, W.M. and R.A. Posner (1989), 'An Economic Analysis of Copyright Law', *J. Leg. Stud.*, **18**, 325.

15 Peacock, A. and R. Weir (1975), *The Composer in the Marketplace*, London: Faber.

with the scope and strength of the rights and the strength of enforcement.[16] The copyright regime also causes administrative and enforcement costs that create a 'deadweight loss',[17] meaning that they use up resources without adding value.

Due to these costs, some economists have rejected copyright and focused on market solutions, such as the 'first mover' advantage, that is the strategic advantage of being first to market.[18] As copying technologies developed and became more widely available, the 'business model' solution began to seem less feasible but, ironically, now that enforcement of copyrights is becoming more and more difficult, the discussion about 'new business models' has returned, meaning ways of appropriating revenues that are not primarily based on a copyright regime.[19]

2.1 Copyright and monopoly

Adam Smith, writing in 1762, made brief observations on copyright law, which had been introduced in England in 1710, and on the copyright monopoly (or 'exclusive privilege' as he called it in his *Lectures on Jurisprudence*). Although normally a scourge of such monopolies, Smith regarded copyright (which in his day lasted for 14 years) as doing no harm and maybe even doing some good and so it was not 'altogether to be condemned'.[20] Later political economists were less charitable. During the great Patent Debates of the 19th century in Britain, copyright came in for some share of attention from Macaulay, who memorably stated: 'copyright is a tax on readers for the purposes of a bounty for writers' thus very succinctly summing up its political economic aspect. He also said in a famous quotation:[21]

---

[16] Plant, *supra* note 7; Landes, William M. (2002), 'Copyright, Borrowed Images and Appropriation Art: An Economic Approach', in Ruth Towse (ed.) (2002), *Copyright in the Cultural Industries*, Cheltenham, UK and Northampton, MA, US: Edward Elgar, p. 9.

[17] Watt, Richard (2000), *Copyright and Economic Theory: Friends or Foes?*, Cheltenham, UK and Northampton, MA, US: Edward Elgar.

[18] Plant, *supra* note 7; Hurt and Schuchman, *supra* note 8; Agarwal, R. and M. Gort (2001), 'First-mover Advantage and the Speed of Competitive Entry, 1887–1986', *J. L. & Econ.*, **44**, 161; Boldrin, M. and D. Levine (2005), 'Intellectual Property and the Efficient Allocation of Social Surplus from Creation', *RERCI*, **2** (1), 45.

[19] Varian, H. (2000), 'Buying, Sharing and Renting Information Goods', *J. Ind. Econ.*, **48**, 473.

[20] Hadfield, G.K. (1992), 'The Economics of Copyright: A Historical Perspective', *Copyright Law Symposium (ASCAP)*, **38**, 1, at 23.

[21] Quoted in Hadfield, *supra* note 20, at 29 *et seq.*

> Copyright is a monopoly and produces all the effects which the general voice of mankind attributes to monopoly . . . the effect of a monopoly is to make articles scarce, to make them dear, and to make them bad. . . . It is good that authors be remunerated; and the least exceptional way of remunerating them is by a monopoly. Yet monopoly is an evil; for the sake of good, we must submit to evil; but the evil ought not to last a day longer than is necessary for the purpose of securing the good.

Even in 1934, Plant was essentially following the same line by emphasizing monopoly, though he had several other important analytical points to make.[22] Indeed, it can be argued that Plant anticipated a great deal of present day analysis on the economics of copyright (moral hazard, rent-seeking, 'business models'), something now acknowledged by Landes and Posner.[23]

So, the earliest analysis of copyright by economists hinged on the statutory monopoly and the opportunity it affords copyright-holders (authors and others) to raise prices. Of course, that is exactly what it is supposed to do: it enables the copyright-holder to raise sufficient revenue to repay the investment in the creation of copyrightable works. The incentive to create them is thus financed through the market: the copyright monopoly allows the copyright owner to charge a price above the cost of making and marketing copies of the work until such time as the copyright expires. Thereafter, the work enters the public domain and becomes a public good in the economic sense that it is non-rival and non-excludable. Liebowitz and Watt remind us of Demsetz's insight that copyright is a system for the private finance of public goods.[24] However, what is insufficiently emphasized is that this takes place dynamically: the later social benefit comes at a private cost borne by earlier generations of consumers, the time lag depending upon the duration of the copyright term. As the copyright term increases in duration, this gets increasingly more inequitable as the present generation is always poorer than future ones.

Abhorrence of monopoly permeated early economic thinking about copyright, even though it is acknowledged that copyright monopolies are weak and conform more to Chamberlinian monopolistically competitive goods than to an actual monopoly (Yoo, 2005);[25] copyrighted works are not homogeneous but they have fairly close substitutes and there is competitive entry in the market

[22] Plant, *supra* note 7.

[23] Landes, William M. and Richard A. Posner (2003), *The Economic Structure of Intellectual Property Law*, Cambridge, MA and London, UK: The Belknap Press.

[24] Liebowitz and Watt, *supra* note 3.

[25] Yoo, Christopher S. (2005), 'Towards a Differentiated Products Theory of Copyright', in Lisa N. Takeyama, Wendy J. Gordon and Ruth Towse (eds), *Developments in Economics of Copyright Research and Analysis*, Cheltenham, UK and Northampton, MA, US: Edward Elgar, p. 103.

that drives the price below the monopoly price that would be charged by a single supplier. Consequently, the anti-monopoly stance is now regarded as simplistic and more subtle arguments for and against copyright are considered appropriate. This, of course, is consistent with changes in the economist's approach to competition law.

2.2 Monopoly and increasing returns

A contemporary way of defending copyright starts from a well-known characteristic of information goods, namely increasing returns.[26] Increasing returns means that efficiency increases as more units are produced and therefore unit costs fall. This is the case for copyrightable works, which are information goods, because the fixed cost of producing the original first copy tends to be high, while the variable costs of reproducing and marketing it are often very low. Because marginal cost is below average fixed costs, marginal cost pricing is impossible for the profit-maximizing producer. Increasing returns to scale results in 'natural monopoly', a situation in which a monopoly supplier is able to supply the market more efficiently than if there were competition; breaking up such a monopoly by competition law would result in higher prices and reduce welfare.

Government regulation can mitigate the adverse effects of a natural monopoly and even achieve an optimal result. For example, it may require the monopoly producer to introduce a two-part tariff that achieves marginal cost pricing combined with some other charge (or subsidy) covering the fixed cost. That, however, has not happened in the cultural industries dependent on copyright (except, perhaps, in the special case of broadcasting). Price discrimination could likely achieve the same result through the market, as we discuss below in relation to the economics of copying; that requires monopoly conditions in order to succeed.[27] We therefore see that there is a dual monopoly – the statutorily created copyright and the spontaneous market development of the natural monopoly in the production of information goods. There is also a dual role for the government – as creator of statutory property rights and as regulator of their effects in the market. It is an interesting question whether digitalization will alter the ratio of fixed to marginal costs and so change the significance of increasing returns in the production of copyrightable works.

Network economies are a specific form of increasing returns: by contrast with the supply-side character of technologically determined increasing

---

[26] Shapiro, Carl and Hal R. Varian (1999), *Information Rules, a Strategic Guide to the Network Economy*, Boston, MA: Harvard Business School Press.

[27] Shapiro and Varian, *supra* note 26; Boyle, J. (2000), 'Cruel, Mean or Lavish?: Economic Analysis, Price Discrimination and Digital Intellectual Property', *Vand. L. Rev.*, **53**, 2007.

returns, network economies apply to the benefits to consumers from having access to a larger number of contacts in a system of users, such as email or telephone. They also reinforce the tendency to natural monopoly. This is discussed in more detail below.

The analysis of natural monopolies is most relevant to collective rights management and to copyright-collecting societies, which may be natural monopolies, and we also discuss that later on.

3 The economics of copying and indirect appropriability

Landes and Posner made a useful distinction between the economics of copyright and the economics of copying.[28] Whereas the economics of copyright focuses on the features of copyright law, the economics of copying deals with the economic effects on markets for the 'original' due to the ability to make copies using technical means of reproduction. The two are obviously related. The possibility of unauthorized use is the *raison d'être* of copyrights and changes in copying technology affect the efficiency and significance of the copyright system. The history of the development of copying technologies is that they have made copying easier or cheaper. The economics of copying focuses on the relation between the fixed costs of creating the work in the first place and the marginal cost of making copies as introduced above.[29]

It is useful to trace the development of the economic analysis of copying because it set the terms in which later discussion took place and much of it is relevant today even under different technological conditions. Novos and Waldman (1984) considered the effect of an increase in copying as causing underproduction and the effect of an increase in copyright protection as causing underutilization.[30] In their model, consumers are indifferent between a legal and an illegal copy. They find analytical support for the underproduction hypothesis but very little support for the underutilization argument. Johnson noted that copying by consumers without compensating the creators had become easier and he analyses the economic case for restricting copying in the short run and in the long run.[31] In the short run, the determinant is the impact of restrictions on demand for authorized copies on the one hand, and their impact in terms of reducing total consumption on the other. In the long run, the justification of restrictions depends on the value placed on variety and the extent to which the number of works supplied is responsive to the presence of unauthorized copying.

---

28 Landes and Posner, *supra* note 14.

29 O'Hare, M. (1985), 'Copyright: When is Monopoly Efficient?', *J. Pol'y Anal. & Manag.*, **4**, 407; Pethig, R. (1988), 'Copyrights and Copying Costs: A New Price Theoretic Approach', *JITE*, **144**, 462.

30 Novos and Waldman, *supra* note 10.

31 Johnson, *supra* note 11.

As an alternative to legal solutions such as copyright law, Liebowitz introduced the idea of indirect appropriability.[32] He demonstrated that the supplier may sometimes overcome the adverse effects of copying on revenue through market means, in particular, by using price discrimination as a business model. Price discrimination – charging different prices for the same product – can be practised only by a monopoly supplier and only when the market can be segmented and it is not worth doing unless there are different elasticities of demand in each market segment. Liebowitz analysed the case of academic journals where publishers supply two distinct markets, that of individual subscribers and that of libraries that are willing to pay a much higher price than individual subscribers. Liebowitz examined the impact of photocopying and concluded that copying did not harm journal publishing because publishers were able to increase their revenues by using price discrimination. Although copying takes place in libraries, the higher price of library subscriptions compensated for the lost sales to individuals who would presumably otherwise have purchased the journal issue. Publishers were therefore compensated indirectly for unauthorized copying. Liebowitz provided empirical evidence that, in the case of journal publishing, these effects were strong enough to sustain publishers' revenues. Thus the market would overcome the underproduction problem without intervention. Besen utilized the idea of indirect appropriability to identify cases in which unauthorized copying leads to diverse results, depending upon the reaction of producers to the existence of private copying.[33]

Varian revived the discussion on indirect appropriability but now with file-sharing in mind.[34] He identified three circumstances in which sharing would lead to an increase in the producer's profit: first, when the transaction costs of sharing are less than the marginal costs of production; second, in the case of a limited number of uses, the firm would practise price discrimination and sell the product for a higher price; third, when there are heterogeneous preferences. Depending on the individual taste and budget, people can share or buy. Sharing enables the producer to cater for a segment of the market that otherwise would be neglected. In a later paper, Varian modelled the effects of copying on pricing decisions by a (temporary) monopolist supplier.[35] Here copying is treated like a competitor entering the market. The monopolist reacts by changing his price-setting strategy.

---

32 Liebowitz, *supra* note 12.

33 Besen, Stanley (1998), 'Intellectual Property', in Peter Newman (ed.), *New Palgrave Dictionary of Law and Economics*, vol. 2, London: Macmillan, p. 348.

34 Varian, *supra* note 19.

35 Varian, H. (2005), 'Copying and Copyright', *J. Econ. Persp.*, **19**(2), 121–38.

Takeyama analysed a related application of indirect appropriability.[36] She focused on the network externalities of unauthorized reproduction of intellectual property and their impact on social welfare. Because consumers benefit from network externalities, they are willing to pay a higher price for these benefits and producers may appropriate higher revenues. Thus, so the argument goes, producers may well be willing to tolerate unauthorized use that increases the network of users. Takeyama found that in the presence of network externalities, unauthorized copying could not only raise a firm's profit but also might cause an unambiguous Pareto improvement to social welfare.[37] She went even further, suggesting that due to network effects, there might be an increase in the social welfare even in the absence of indirect appropriability as described by Liebowitz[38] and Besen.[39] Liebowitz and Margolis later responded to this, finding the argument highly exaggerated.[40] They argued that the effects deriving from network externalities are not very well understood. They claim that most of the effects that are summarized under the term network externalities are not externalities in an economic sense – they are simply technological network effects that can be resolved by ownership and contracts or else the effects are pecuniary and therefore have no welfare implications.

In 2005, the *Review of Economic Research in Copyright Issues* (*RERCI*) published the results of a symposium on indirect appropriability, inviting Liebowitz and his contemporary writers to comment on the progress of this concept and to restate their ideas, particularly since in the interim, the advent of digitalization had changed the nature of copying. Liebowitz responded by saying that the concept seemed in retrospect to have been important in its time for showing that all copying was not necessarily damaging to producers but that it had limited application and had been taken too far by some economists.[41] Johnson and Waldman concur that the idea is limited and show that where the market is flooded by copies – as appears to have occurred with the

---

36 Takayama, L. (1994), 'The Welfare Implications of Unauthorized Reproduction of Intellectual Property in Presence of Demand Network Externalities', *J. Ind. Econ.*, **42**(2), 155.

37 See also Bensaid, B. and J.-P. Lesne (1996), 'Dynamic Monopoly Pricing with Network Externalities', *IJIO*, **14**, 837; Economides, N. (1996), 'The Economics of Networks', *IJIO*, **14**, 673.

38 Liebowitz, *supra* note 12.

39 Besen, S. (1986), 'Private Copying, Reproduction Costs, and the Supply of Intellectual Property', *Inf. Econ. & Pol'y*, **2**, 5.

40 Liebowitz, S.J. and S.E. Margolis (1995), 'Are Network Externalities a New Source of Market Failure?', *Res. in L. & Econ.*, **17**, 1.

41 Liebowitz, S.J. (2005), 'Economists' Topsy-turvy View of Piracy', *RERCI*, **2** (1), 5.

explosive growth in file-sharing and the diffusion of CD-burners – the price will be driven down to the cost of making copies; thus the market would fail to compensate creators and cover other fixed costs of production.[42] On the other hand, Johnson shows that novel pricing strategies have developed and suggests that these could help to overcome some of the problems of loss of revenue due to copying – again, a market solution that does not call for intervention.[43]

4 Specific approaches within the economics of copyright

4.1 Welfare economics and cost-benefit analysis

From the early contributions to the field one can see that the acceptance of copyright has always been somewhat ambiguous for economists. Copyright law was opposed by some on the grounds that the market could work well without it and those who accept the case for it recognize that it has both costs as well as benefits to society as a whole. Welfare economics deals with such questions and attempts to provide general solutions to these dilemmas.

A defining concept in welfare economics is Pareto optimality, a situation in which there is no possible reorganization of resources that can improve welfare for one member of the society without making another worse off. This state requires that all markets are perfectly competitive (with marginal cost pricing) and no market failure. Market failure occurs under various conditions: the presence of unpriced goods (such as public goods or externalities), monopoly and missing markets (such as the lack of insurance covering risk or forward markets). Argued in terms of Paretian welfare economics, a 'first-best solution' – an optimal allocation of resources – cannot be achieved for information goods because they are public goods; moreover, statutory creation of copyright, that 'privatizes' the public good feature, introduces a monopoly element that, while protecting the author and enabling her to obtain a reward, interferes with perfect competition, a necessary condition for Pareto optimality. Copyright is therefore a 'second-best solution' and must be judged in terms of the relative benefits and costs in the markets for copyright material rather than by a sweeping overall justification. This implies that for maximum welfare, every copyrightable work should have its own duration, something that was recognized by Landes and Posner[44] but rejected on the grounds that there must be a uniform term to minimize costs of disputes, etc. Posner (2005)

---

42 Johnson, J.P. and M. Waldman (2005), 'The Limits of Indirect Appropriability in Markets for Copiable Goods', *RERCI*, **2**(1), 19.

43 Johnson, W.R. (2005), 'Creative Pricing in Markets for Intellectual Property', *RERCI*, **2**(1), 39.

44 Landes and Posner, *supra* note 14.

states that in general the optimal term of copyright is that period of time over which the discounted future revenues from the copyrighted work are equal to the discounted future costs due to the copyright.[45]

In analysing whether copyright provides the most efficient solution available and can thus be justified in terms of social efficiency, many other writers on the economics of copyright have adopted the welfare approach, identifying the relative costs and benefits.[46] Welfare gains and losses are discussed and comparisons made to this (static) world of perfect competition in which there are constant returns to scale, marginal cost pricing, no public goods or externalities and no transaction costs. In this world, social efficiency would be achieved and, by contrast, anything that violates the underlying conditions is viewed as market failure. Market failure is seen as capable of being rectified by state intervention, in this context, by copyright law. Copyright, however, is a second-best solution and therefore, despite claims or the implication that it can do so, copyright law cannot restore the economy to first-best Pareto optimality.[47] It is also questionable whether claims that copyright law should be framed so as to minimize the deadweight loss caused by the higher price copyright monopolists charge (higher than the unobtainable perfectly competitive price) are meaningful without the prop of Paretian welfare economics. Moreover, the cost-benefit approach of balancing welfare gains and losses has little credibility unless they can be measured empirically, something that is rarely done.

The ideal-type Paretian welfare approach serves to highlight some of the theoretical stumbling blocks for the economic analysis of copyright, however. The presence of increasing returns (natural monopoly) and/or public goods characteristics – both frequently recognized as attributes of the 'information' economy – as well as transaction costs have all been regarded as causes of market failure over and above the statutory grant of monopoly itself. Each of these elements may be changed by technological developments; for example, totally secure digital technological protection measures could eliminate the

---

45 Posner, R.A. (2005), 'Intellectual Property: The Law and Economics Approach', *J. Econ. Persp.*, **19**(2), 57.

46 Novos and Waldman, *supra* note 10; Hollander, A. (1984), 'Market Structure and Performance in Intellectual Property: The Case of Copyright Collectives', *IJIO*, **2**(3), 199; Johnson, *supra* note 11; Besen, *supra* note 39; Besen, S.M. and S.N. Kirby (1989), 'Private Copying, Appropriability and Optimal Copying Royalties', *J. L. & Econ.*, **32**, 255; Koboldt, C. (1995), 'Intellectual Property and Optimal Copyright Protection', *J. Cultural Econ.*, **19**(2), 131; Bensaid and Lesne, *supra* note 37; Watt, *supra* note 17.

47 See 'Introduction' to Towse, Ruth and Rudi Holzhauer (2002), *Economics of Intellectual Property*, Cheltenham, UK and Northampton, MA, US: Edward Elgar; Landes and Posner, *supra* note 12.

non-excludability features of some goods and services currently viewed as public goods and could also reduce transaction costs. The conclusions of economists writing before digitalization, when the only means of unauthorized copying was resetting type or photocopying for printed matter or VHS and audio tapes for television and music reproduction respectively, are therefore at a considerable disadvantage when viewed in retrospect, however valid the analysis was at the time.

4.2 Public goods and property rights

Another quite different approach to the economic analysis of copyright is the property rights approach. This developed from the so-called Coase theorem, which states that, subject to the cost of transacting, property rights will be traded in a free market so as to be allocated to the most valuable use.[48] As long as property rights are established, there is no need for state intervention because any disputes can be settled by negotiation and compensatory payments or, if that fails, through the courts. This approach therefore obviates the need for social welfare analysis. It is easy to see how it led to the development of law and economics. In this scheme, copyright law 'propertizes' literary, dramatic, musical and other creative works and enables them to be used optimally.[49] The focus for efficiency therefore turns to the minimization of transaction costs, which include the costs of contracting and protecting rights.

Other writers express the problem of rewarding creators simply in terms of the economic case for property.[50] The 'Tragedy of the Commons' exemplifies the case for well-established property rights. Where property, for example land, is commonly owned, no one has an incentive to invest in its improvement. Everyone attempts to 'free ride' on the investment of others, resulting in a stalemate where no improvement can be achieved. Economic efficiency therefore requires the establishment of property rights that exclude users who do not contribute to the creation of value. Although copyright itself is a form of state intervention, in a property rights approach the emphasis tends to be more unequivocally on minimizing the need for any other type of state intervention. Copyright's merit is presented in terms of establishing property rights where they otherwise would not exist so that the market can be left to work. However, the 'Tragedy of the Commons' argument has been questioned in relation to copyright on the grounds of the non-rivalry of informa-

---

48 Merges, *supra* note 13.

49 Posner, *supra* note 45.

50 Depoorter, B. and F. Parisi (2002), 'Fair Use and Copyright Protection: A Price Theory Explanation', *Int'l Rev. L. & Econ.*, **21**, 453.

tion goods. The insight that information goods differ from tangible goods was introduced by Arrow, arguing that information goods are public goods and that non-rivalry demands free access on the grounds of economic efficiency;[51] consequently, he made the case for financing R&D through public finance. The non-rivalry of information goods in general and of copyrightable content in particular implies that the frequently argued 'Tragedy of the Commons' case for copyright law as a means of privatizing (or 'commodifying') intellectual property does not apply because there is no need to ration use in order to avoid depletion. This is the basis of the 'Creative Commons' argument against copyright. Moreover, Landes and Posner, the leading exponents of the law and economics approach to IP, also reject the argument for copyright law based on the 'Tragedy of the Commons' on the grounds that copyrightable works are non-rival.[52] This is also relevant to the question of extending copyright indefinitely.[53]

One encouraging sign in the recent debate on the extension of copyright is that it is not taking place in an empirical vacuum, as has previously been the case. Evidence on the longevity of copyrighted work in terms of their survival on the market has been brought to bear on the discussion.[54]

To sum up this section, it can be seen that there remains scepticism on the part of economists, albeit on different grounds, about the economic case for copyright and how to establish the appropriate duration. Moreover, there is no consistent view of the underlying economic justification even among those who support the case for copyright law.

5 Law and economics

In general, as explained earlier, the research agenda in law and economics is different from that in economics. The purpose of this section is to give a flavour of the discussion of basic issues rather than to review its large literature on copyright. Essentially, law and economics uses the tools of economics to understand legal doctrines. Economists working on the economics of copyright are more interested in the impact of and changes to copyright law on the

---

51 Arrow, Kenneth J. (1962), 'Economic Welfare and the Allocation of Resources for Invention', in National Bureau of Economic Research (ed.), *The Rate and Direction of Incentive Activity*, Princeton: Princeton University Press, p. 609.

52 Landes and Posner, *supra* note 23.

53 Romer, P. (2002), 'When Should we Use Intellectual Property Rights?', *Am. Econ. Rev., Papers and Proceedings*, **92**(2), 213.

54 Landes and Posner, *supra* note 23; Liebowitz, Stan. J. (2004), 'Will MP3 Downloads Annihilate the Record Industry? The Evidence So Far', in E. Boorstin (ed.), 'Advances in the Study of Entrepreneurship, Innovation, and Economic Growth', Vol. 15, Amsterdam: Elsevier, p. 229, echoing research first done by Breyer, *supra* note 9.

working of markets. The specific doctrines of copyright law to which economic analysis has been applied include the protection of expressions not ideas, the author's rights in derivative works (such as translations, musical arrangements, film scripts based on a book), work for hire doctrine, the duration of the copyright term and the exceptions and limitations to copyright for private study and research, parody, criticism, etc., known as 'fair use' in US law and 'fair dealing' in the UK.

Landes and Posner neither emphasize the monopoly aspect of copyright, nor other types of market failure, but instead place the focus on the optimal balance between the positive and negative incentives to creativity.[55] With the maximization of economic welfare as the objective in the Chicago view, the law must strike a balance between the protection of an author and the costs that that imposes on other authors, such as search costs for novel means of expression and of obtaining permission to use the copyright works of others. That balance is to be found when the cost of extra protection by copyright, which inhibits creativity by restricting access to the public domain, equals the incentive it provides to authors.

Landes and Posner's seminal model yields specific policy considerations concerning the scope and duration of copyright law and the fair use exception, which they discuss in terms of the strength of protection.[56] As noted earlier, they recognize that copyright should be discriminatory and not applied across the board and that economic efficiency indicates there should be greater copyright protection for works that have greater social value. However, a discriminatory regime has too high transaction costs and therefore the copyright term has to be uniform. The optimal level of copyright protection must take account of the higher transaction costs that it causes. The costs of tracing copyright owners increase with the duration of copyright, providing a brake on the desirable length of the copyright term. Finally, the lower the costs of administering copyright and the more authors' incentives to produce respond to it, the greater would be the optimal extent of protection. However, recently Landes and Posner have changed their view on the duration of copyright.[57] They now argue for indefinitely renewable copyright. They argue that the vast majority of copyrights would not be worth renewing and that tracing and transaction costs therefore would not be excessive. Copyright therefore can play an anal-

---

[55] Landes and Posner, *supra* note 14; Landes, *supra* note 16; Landes and Posner, *supra* note 23.

[56] Landes and Posner, *supra* note 14.

[57] Landes, William M. and Richard A. Posner (2002), 'Indefinitely Renewable Copyright', Working Paper No. 154, University of Chicago John M. Olin Law and Economics, http://www.law.uchicago.edu/Lawecon/WkngPprs_151-175/154.wml-rap.copyright.new.pdf, accessed 4 November 2007; Landes and Posner, *supra* note 23.

ogous role to trademarks, which can last indefinitely when renewed. Landes and Posner argue that indefinite renewability would also reduce rent-seeking behaviour as witnessed in the so-called Sonny Bono extension to the US copyright term for corporations (for example, by the Disney Corporation).[58] Rent-seeking – lobbying to acquire economic benefits from the state, such as stronger copyright laws that favour copyright-holders – is analysed by public choice theorists as rational economic behaviour relating to political matters; potential gainers will expend an amount of money on lobbying up to the value they expect to gain from it. If copyright were indefinitely renewable, no further extensions of the copyright term would be possible and there consequently would be no incentive for rent-seeking to change the duration of protection.

Another important topic in law and economics that has attracted a lot of attention is the 'fair use' doctrine. Though it is a specific feature of US law, it has come to be used more widely as a general term denoting that the exclusive right of authorization is limited in copyright statutes and exceptions are made for certain uses of copyrighted material without the author's consent and without payment. Gordon pioneered the application of transaction cost economics to US fair use doctrine.[59] According to Gordon, the underlying economic rationale is that a market can fail to develop (what economists call a missing market) when transaction costs exceed the value of copies to individual users. However, as Landes and Posner have argued, an excessively strong copyright regime that tolerated little fair use would raise transaction costs and copyright-based earnings, transferring rents to artists from users and raising the costs of creation to later authors.[60] An excessively weak regime, on the other hand, would not provide sufficient incentives to look for means of charging and therefore would reduce transaction costs and earnings. It would also ease what Landes and Posner called 'productive' (as compared to 'reproductive') fair use of copyright material for creating new and derivative works and benefit consumers. Fair use regulations within copyright law therefore must balance these opposite tendencies. This analysis has been important in the discussion whether or not downloading of copyrighted material from the internet by private individuals is 'fair use'.[61]

---

58 Landes and Posner, *supra* note 23.

59 Gordon, W.J. (1982), 'Fair Use as Market Failure: A Structural and Economic Analysis of the Betamax Case and its Predecessors', *Col. L. Rev.*, **82**, 1600.

60 Landes and Posner, *supra* note 14.

61 Klein, B., A. Lerner and K. Murphy (2002), 'The Economics of Copyright "Fair Use" in a Networked World', *Am. Econ. Rev., Papers and Proceedings*, **19**(2), 131.

The extent to which fair use diminishes the strength of copyright and thus the case for intervention by competition law is an interesting question. There seems to be no work specifically on that topic.

6 Technological change and dynamic analysis

In economics, the distinction between static and dynamic effects is very important, not least because many of the formal models that economists use are static, often for no better a reason than that dynamic models are very difficult to formulate.[62] Where static analysis focuses on allocative and productive efficiency in the short run, that is, with an unchanging state of technology, dynamic analysis allows for innovation and technological change over time. The distinction, however, is crucial to the understanding of the economics of copyright because the incentive that copyright law offers is a dynamic one: knowing that in the future your work will be protected is the stimulus to creating it in the present. In addition, technical progress, which we know to be altering the ability to copy and to protect the author, takes place over time and has a dynamic effect on markets. It is misleading that the effect of the copyright monopoly on a market is frequently modelled in terms of the deadweight loss of monopoly, particularly by writers on law and economics. Static and dynamic effects are easily confused.[63] In fact, many writers seem to slip all too readily from static to dynamic reasoning, as noted by Landes and Posner.[64] Many economists writing on copyright refer to the need for the dynamic incentive and justify it by using static welfare economics and market failure arguments.

The distinction between immediate effects and long-term effects of copying and copyright, first emphasized by Johnson,[65] is also important due to the speed and intensity of technological change. Structural and technological changes in the industries in which copyright plays an important role, such as publishing, film and music, go far beyond the effect of increased unauthorized copying. It is therefore necessary to address the implications of copyright law over time, for which the approach of the economic historian is perhaps the most suitable. David uses historical analysis to evaluate the economic impact of copyright in various industries and in changing technological conditions, arguing that the copyright (and patent) regime has created obstacles to technological innovation and creativity instead of assisting them.[66]

---

[62] Liebowitz, *supra* note 41; Liebowitz, S.J. (2006), 'File Sharing: Creative Destruction or just Plain Destruction?', *J. L. & Econ.*, **49**, 1,

[63] See 'Introduction' to Towse and Holzhauer, *supra* note 47.

[64] Landes and Posner, *supra* note 23.

[65] Johnson, *supra* note 11.

[66] David, Paul A. (1993), 'Intellectual Property Institutions and the Panda's

A different dynamic approach is that taken by Schumpeter[67] who coined the phrase 'creative destruction' that has been taken up by a number of recent writers on the economics of copyright.[68] Schumpeter – who incidentally did not consider copyright[69] – provides the analytical counterpart to the historical approach. His insight was that perfectly competitive firms in the static sense have neither the means nor the incentive to innovate. Therefore a growing economy must be propelled by monopolistic firms that compete in an evolutionary way through technological innovation and enjoy the fruits of their monopoly power until such time as they are pushed out by a superior innovator – hence, creative destruction. As greater understanding of the evolutionary approach to economics takes hold, we can expect less condemnation of monopoly in general. What is important from this perspective, however, is that incumbent firms are not protected from entry to their market by innovators that challenge their dominant position.

Another dynamic problem is that technological change and changes in market conditions necessitate the adaptation of copyright law. Changing circumstances mean that simply reconstructing the same protection as existed before a particular technological change may not be adequate (or may be downright impossible). What complicates this issue further is that technological changes are rarely smooth and not always fully anticipated. They can have disturbing effects on markets, as we have seen with the introduction of online distribution networks in the music industry. It is inevitable that the law will lag behind technological changes, which present difficult challenges to law-makers with respect to IP and competition law. Thus dynamic analysis highlights a number of serious economic drawbacks to copyright by contrast to the static welfare and property rights approaches which suggest copyright is basically sound and it is just a matter of getting the measurement of costs and benefits right. It may be that competition law is sometimes better at addressing the

---

Thumb: Patents, Copyrights, and Trade Secrets in Economic Theory and History', in Mitchell B. Wallerstein, Mary Ellen Mogee and Roberta A. Schoen (eds), *Global Dimensions of Intellectual Property Rights in Science and Technology*, Washington, DC: National Academy Press, p. 19; David, Paul A. (2000), 'The Digital Technology Boomerang: New Intellectual Property Rights Threaten Global "Open Science"', Working Paper, http://www.researchineurope.org/documents/paul3.pdf, accessed 4 November 2007; David, P.A. (2004), 'The End of Copyright History?', *RERCI*, 1 (2), 5.

67 Schumpeter, Joseph (1942), *Capitalism, Socialism and Democracy*, New York and London: Harper & Bros.

68 Liebowitz, *supra* note 61; Handke, C. (2006), 'Plain Destruction or Creative Destruction? Copyright Erosion and the Evolution of the Record Industry', *RERCI*, **3**(2), 29.

69 Blaug, M. (2005), 'Why did Schumpeter Neglect Intellectual Property Rights?', *RERCI*, **2**(1), 69.

effects of copyright in the market *ex post* than copyright law is at adapting to technological innovation *ex ante*.

7 Empirical studies

Empirical studies have not figured much in the economics of copyright and one reason for this is that they do not form part of the intellectual tradition of studying the law or of law and economics. In economics more generally, however, empirical studies have always occupied an important position as a means of testing theories. Recently, empirical studies of copyright have become more prominent and they fall into two distinct groups: macroeconomic studies of the size and importance of copyright-based industries and microeconomic studies of the economic effects of file-sharing networks such as Napster.

7.1 Macroeconomic studies of the size of copyright-based industries

The macroeconomic studies of copyright-based industries are straightforward in their intention to measure the contribution to the national income of those industries producing goods and services that have a strong copyright element; however, the inferences that can be drawn from them are not straightforward. For instance, the role copyright plays in stimulating production cannot be inferred from them because there is no causality implied by such measures. There are controversies about which industries to include but not about the standard measure of value-added that should be used. There have been, and still are, problems of obtaining suitable data, especially in developing countries. Unfortunately, there is a tendency to exaggerate the inferences that these figures represent and they are often used for advocacy purposes.[70] However, it is clear that the industries concerned – the cultural and software industries – now represent typically around 5 per cent of gross domestic product and are growing at around 5 per cent annually, which is faster than manufacturing; however, only the US systematically has an export surplus from international trade in copyright works. This type of study is being strongly promoted by the World Property Organization.[71] In 2004, the *Review of Economic Research on Copyright Issues* (*RERCI*) devoted its first issue to these matters.

7.2 Microeconomic studies of the economic effects of file-sharing networks

What macro studies do not measure, however, is the impact of unauthorized

[70] Towse, R. (2004), 'Number-crunching is Not just a "Neural" Activity', *RERCI*, **1**(1), 79.

[71] Gantchev, D. (2004), 'The WIPO Guide on Surveying the Economic Contribution of the Copyright Industries', *RERCI*, **1**(1), 5.

use – so-called 'piracy'. Recently, the interest in this issue has been considerable because in several major music markets – in particular the US and Germany – the explosive growth of music file-sharing networks since 1999 has coincided with substantial reductions in sales of authorized copies. For that question, micro-econometric studies are needed and there have been many of them over the last few years by economists attempting to test the effects of unauthorized use on legitimate business. We do not attempt to review them all here but instead sketch some of the issues involved.[72]

So far, economic studies have mainly focused on the question whether file-sharing harms right-holders of musical works by decreasing sales.[73] This is what Johnson would call the short-run effects of copying.[74] The specification of what constitutes harm has been a significant aspect of court cases against Napster and its successors in the US.[75] It continues to be of practical importance in the courts, for ongoing reforms of copyright legislation and for the businesses concerned.

One standard approach to analysing the question is to correlate measures of file-sharing with sales of recordings while controlling for simultaneous changes to a range of other factors that might have influenced sales. Ultimately, the observation of alternative variables attempts to develop a counter-factual idea of what sales would have been otherwise.[76] Although economists have

---

72 For a survey, see Liebowitz and Watt, *supra* note 3.

73 For a study of off-line 'piracy', see Hui, Kai-Lung and Ivan Png (2003), 'Piracy and the Legitimate Demand for Recorded Music', *B. E. J. Econ. Anal. & Pol'y*, **3**(1), Article 11, http://www.bepress.com/bejeap/contributions/vol2/iss1/art11/, accessed 4 November 2007.

74 Johnson, *supra* note 11.

75 See, for example, Fine, Michael (2000), 'Soundscan Study on Napster Use and Loss of Sales', http://www.unc.edu/~cigar/papers/FileSharing_March2004.pdf, accessed 4 November 2007.

76 Liebowitz, S.J. (2005), 'Pitfalls in Measuring the Impact of File-sharing', CEFifo Econ. Stud., **51**(2–3), 439 = http://www.utdallas.edu/~liebowit/intprop/pitfalls.pdf, accessed 4 November 2007, and Liebowitz, *supra* note 61, provides an overview of some of the literature on this issue. Studies are by Liebowitz, *supra* note 54; Liebowitz, Stan J. (2005), 'Testing File-Sharing's Impact by Examining Record Sales in Cities', Working Paper, Center for the Analysis of Property Rights and Innovation, University of Texas at Dallas, http://som.utdallas.edu/capri/Impact_file_sharing.pdf, accessed 4 November 2007; Liebowitz, *supra* note 61; Blackburn, David (2004), 'Online Piracy and Recorded Music Sales', Working Paper, Harvard University, http://www.katallaxi.se/grejer/blackburn/blackburn_fs.pdf, accessed 4 November 2007; Boorstin, E. (2004), 'Music Sales in the Age of File-Sharing', Senior thesis, Princeton University, http://www.cs.princeton.edu/~felten/boorstin-thesis.pdf, accessed 4 November 2007; Hong, Seung-Hyun (2004), 'The Effect of Napster on Recorded Music Sales: Evidence from the Consumer Expenditure Survey', SIEPR Discussion Paper No. 03-18, Stanford Institute for Economic Policy Research,

analysed different data sets using differently specified models, the consensus that has emerged is that unauthorized downloading has reduced sound carrier sales somewhat, though they differ in the extent to which they believe it is the only explanation for falling sales. The only outright denial of any significant effect of file-sharing on sales comes from Oberholzer and Strumpf.[77] And this study has been criticized by Liebowitz[78] and Zentner.[79]

There are many technical difficulties encountered in doing detailed quantitative analysis. Furthermore, data on loss of sales and unauthorized piracy supplied by industry lead-bodies such as the RIAA (Recording Industries of America Association) or the IFPI (International Federation of the Phonographic Industry) are subject to the same problems, although they never report them. They are interested parties and some researchers have voiced objections as to the validity of their data.[80]

A challenge to any of these studies might be that it is by no means clear that the record industry was in state of competitive equilibrium when file-sharing struck.[81] On the one hand, it is organized in a few major multinational firms that wield considerable market power according to most accounts.[82] On the other, the record industry appears to go through structural changes with continued merger activity among the major companies, increasing importance of media tie-ins as a source of income and authorized online services growing rapidly to name but a few volatile aspects.[83] Under such circumstances it seems particularly difficult to isolate the effect of file-sharing.

---

http://siepr.stanford.edu/Papers/pdf/03-18.pdf, accessed 4 November 2007; Michel, N.J. (2005), 'Digital File-Sharing and the Music Industry: Was there a Substitution Effect?', *RERCI*, **2**(2), 41; Peitz, M. and P. Waelbroek (2004), 'The Effect of Internet Piracy on Music Sales: Cross-section Evidence', *SERCI*, **1**(2), 71; Zentner, A. (2005), 'File-Sharing and International Sales of Copyrighted Music: An Empirical Analysis with a Panel of Countries', *Topics in Econ. Anal. & Pol'y*, **5**(1), p. 1452.

77 Oberholzer, Felix and Koleman Strumpf (2004), 'The Effect of File-Sharing on Record Sales: An Empirical Analysis', http://www.unc.edu/~cigar/papers/FileSharing_March2004.pdf, accessed 4 November 2007.

78 Liebowitz, S.J. (2005), 'Pitfalls in Measuring the Impact of File-Sharing', *supra* note 76.

79 Zentner, A. (2006), 'Measuring the Effect of Music Downloads on Music Purchases', *J. L. & Econ.*, **49**, 63.

80 Liebowitz, *supra* note 54.

81 Handke, *supra* note 67.

82 Silva, F. and G.B. Ramello (2000), 'Sound Recording Market: The Ambiguous Case of Copyright and Piracy', *Industrial and Corporate Change*, **9**, 415–42; Zentner, *supra* note 79.

83 See Alexander, P.J. (2002), 'Peer-to-peer File-Sharing: The Case of the Music Recording Industry', *Rev. Ind. Org.*, **20**(2), 151; Bockstedt, Jesse, Robert J. Kauffman and Frederick J. Riggins (2005), 'The Move to Artist-led Online Music Distribution: Explaining Structural Changes in the Digital Music Market', Proceedings of the 38th

The contentious issue of the extent to which file-sharing harms suppliers is not the end of the story, either. First, file-sharing is not the only new copying technology. CD-burners are either excluded or addressed as complementary to file-sharing networks. For example, in the German market, for which IFPI reported the most severe falls in sales in any of the major markets, mass diffusion of CD-burners and falling sales preceded file-sharing. CD-burners might sometimes merit attention in their own right. Furthermore, the effects of file-sharing might not be homogenous as between rights-holders. Blackburn finds that sales of publications by previously well-known artists are diminished as file-sharers substitute purchased copies for downloads.[84] On the other hand, file-sharing appears to boost record sales for previously unknown artists. They seem to gain more from the additional exposure of their works than they lose due to consumers substituting unauthorized downloads for the purchase of authorized copies. Last but not least, in the context of public copyright policy, consumers' interests need to be accounted for. Obviously, consumers might benefit considerably from the availability of vast catalogues of works online at very low cost.[85] Rob and Waldfogel estimate that consumers' welfare gains from file-sharing are considerably higher than producers' losses.[86] They do not take account of the long-term effects of diminished incentives to supply copyrightable works, however. Studies on the supply of works in the context of diminished copyright protection might shed some light on this important issue.

To inform copyright policy, it is thus not sufficient to establish that so-called piracy harms producers. Reasonably accurate estimates of the extent of such harm would have to be set in relation to potential welfare gains to consumers – with the important caveat that reduced appropriability could over time adversely affect supply – as well as the administration and enforcement costs of copyright protection. Whereas the majority of empirical studies suggest that file-sharing is harmful for producers, the authors of such studies are more evenly divided over the issue whether their results justify increased efforts to protect copyright. While some authors endorse the RIAA's enforcement strategy, others express doubts as to whether enforcement either makes good business sense or should be promoted by public policy.

Annual Hawaii International Conference on System Sciences (HICSS'05), http://misrc.umn.edu/workingpapers/fullpapers/2004/0422_091204.pdf, accessed 4 November 2007.

[84] Blackburn, David (2004), 'A Study of Online Piracy and Recorded Music Sales', Working Paper, Harvard University, www.economics.harvard.edu/%7Edblackbu/papers/blackburn_fs.pdf, accessed 4 November 2007.

[85] Silva and Ramello, *supra* note 82.

[86] Rob, R. and J. Waldvogel (2006), 'Piracy on the High C's: Music Downloading, Sales Displacement, and Social Welfare in a Sample of College Students', *J. L. & Econ.*, **49**, 29.

It remains to be seen whether the better data and complete coverage of recent years – so far many studies have captured only the first two or three years after Napster established file-sharing as a mass phenomenon – will resolve the issue of gauging the detrimental effects on suppliers. Michel,[87] Liebowitz,[88] Bhattacharjee *et al.*,[89] and Krishnan *et al.*[90] all suggest new approaches to this question.

Empirical studies that test predictions from theoretical models are the preferred way for economists to address this as any other economic issue. The problems encountered in doing such work demonstrate how difficult it can be to get satisfactory results, a problem that IP and competition law surely share.

8 Economics of copyright-collecting societies

Collecting societies (also called copyright collectives or their activities referred to as collective rights management) play a vital role in the administration of copyright. There is a specialized literature on the economics of collecting societies[91] and empirical work.[92] We do not review this literature in detail here but instead give a general overview of the issues covered by it.[93]

---

87 Michel, *supra* note 76.

88 Liebowitz, *supra* note 78.

89 Bhattacharjee, S., Ram D.G. and G.L. Sanders (2003), 'Digital Music and Online Sharing: Software Piracy', *Communications of the ACM*, **46**(7), 107.

90 Krishnan, R., M.D. Smith and R. Telang (2003), 'The Economics of Peer-to-peer Networks', *J. Inf. Tech. Th. & Appl.*, **5**(3), 31.

91 See Hollander, *supra* note 46; Besen, S.M., S. Kirby and S.C. Salop (1992), 'An Economic Analysis of Copyright Collectives', *Va. L. Rev.*, **78**, 383; Watt, *supra* note 17; Einhorn, Michael A. (2002), 'Music Licensing in the Digital Age', in Ruth Towse (ed.), *Copyright in the Cultural Industries*, Cheltenham, UK and Northampton, MA, US: Edward Elgar, p. 165; Liebowitz, Stan J. (2005), 'MP3s and Copyright Collectives: A Curse Worse than the Disease?', in Lisa N. Takeyama, Wendy J. Gordon and Ruth Towse (eds), *Developments in the Economics of Copyright: Research and Analysis*, Cheltenham, UK and Northampton, MA, US: Edward Elgar, p. 37.

92 See Peacock and Weir, *supra* note 15; MacQueen, H. and A. Peacock (1995), 'Implementing Performing Rights', *J. Cultural Econ.*, **19**, 157; Towse, Ruth (2001), *Creativity, Incentive and Reward*, Cheltenham, UK and Northampton, MA, US: Edward Elgar; Kretschmer, Martin (2002), 'Copyright Societies do Not Administer Individual Rights: The Incoherence of Institutional Traditions in Germany and the UK', in Ruth Towse (ed.), *Copyright in the Cultural Industries*, Cheltenham, UK and Northampton, MA, US: Edward Elgar, p. 140; Kretschmer, M. (2002), 'The Failure of Property Rules in Collective Administration: Rethinking Copyright Societies as Regulatory Instruments', *EIPR*, **24**, 126; Matsumoto, Shinji (2002), 'Performers in the Digital Era: Evidence from Japan', in Ruth Towse (ed.), *Copyright in the Cultural Industries*, Cheltenham, UK and Northampton, MA, US: Edward Elgar, p. 196.

93 Handke, C., P. Stepan and R. Towse (2007), 'Economics of Copyright Collecting Societies', *IIC*, **38**, 937.

Various features of collecting societies have interested economists: their rationale of reducing transaction costs and so enabling authors (and now performers) to exercise their rights, which they could not feasibly do individually, thus facilitating authorized use; the unintended effect that collective action by authors, undertaken in their own interests, reduces costs for users; their status as natural monopolies in addition to (in many but not all countries) a grant of monopoly by the state; the economic benefits and drawbacks of the blanket licence; determination of the rates that should be set; and the effect of digitalization on the administration of rights as a tool (digital rights management (DRM)) and the question of management of digital rights. Finally, and topically, there are policy questions whether such societies are still needed and if so, how they should be regulated. From the economic point of view, collecting societies are not easy to understand; though none of their individual features presents a challenge to economists, put altogether they are sufficiently complex to be problematic, in particular as to policy implications, such as the correct level of regulation and the future of collective rights management in a digital world.

Collecting societies are co-operative membership organizations that, depending upon their constitution, may or may not be able to act as clubs and control the size of the membership. They pool rights management for members and in so doing create a market that, for the vast majority of copyrights, would otherwise not exist. Sharing costs of licensing and monitoring uses of the works in their care reduces the cost for members and makes licensing feasible. Issuing blanket licences reduces costs to users and makes them more willing to acquire licences and online administration makes it even cheaper. The very existence of collecting societies is therefore essential to the copyright regime. Even if every copyright work were encrypted (which seems difficult to achieve for all existing copyright works and in a way that would hold up for the full 70 years of the copyright term) and even if technological protection measures were to work perfectly (which some doubt is ever possible), collective rights management would still be more efficient because it will always be easier to deal with a 'one-stop-shop' than with a multitude of copyright-holders. Moreover, cooperative agreements between societies administering similar bundles of rights are an important facilitating factor for the worldwide commercialization of copyright works. Note that these agreements, and in some cases, the origin of the societies themselves, are spontaneous market outcomes, not the result of policy or regulation.[94]

---

94 Merges, R.P. (1996), 'Contracting into Liability Rules: Intellectual Property Rights and Collective Rights Organizations', *Cal. L. Rev.*, **84**, 1293.

In economic terms, the collecting society is likely to be a natural monopoly with high set-up costs and low marginal costs and that means that a competitor is highly unlikely to enter the market spontaneously. Moreover, forcing competition by regulation would cause costs to rise in most markets. Because copyright law is national law, collecting societies usually operate in national territories. Thus national monopolies are natural monopolies (or vice versa). Most economists in general believe that a natural monopoly should be left intact but regulated.[95] That, of course, raises the question of how and how much collecting societies should be regulated, which is controversial. What is evident is that many (perhaps all) collecting societies are strongly regulated either directly or indirectly. As so often with applying economics in the 'real world', the actual numbers matter, for example, the size of the costs of the natural monopoly as compared to its benefits to the whole society.

However, some of the 'dangerous' effects of the natural monopoly are countered by the fact that the collecting society typically deals with another co-operative monopoly, such as a trade association, when setting the rate for a particular type of use. There are also monopsony users – meaning sole demanders of a particular good or service – such as the old state monopoly broadcasters, which were at one time the only purveyors of publicly performed music.[96] Another example is photocopying; universities acting in concert confront authors' and publishers' licensing societies as a virtual monopsonist of photocopying of academic journal articles.[97] The resulting 'bilateral monopoly' diminishes the effect of the monopoly power of the collecting society. This is something that should be recognized by competition authorities seeking to regulate collecting societies.

The commonest form of licence used by the collecting society is the blanket licence. While this is administratively efficient, it is not economically efficient – another trade-off. It has a number of cross-subsidy arrangements for both revenues and administrative costs, mostly for reasons of equity. It seems likely that the top stars are the ones who pay for them. However, if these members voluntarily stay in the society, then we must assume that it is regarded as offering an acceptable service to them. Although it may well contribute to solidarity, the blanket licence is essentially a solution to the high costs of individual transactions. These costs may well be very considerably reduced by digital management of rights (one aspect of digital rights management – the other being the management of digital rights) and over the life span

---

95 Watt, *supra* note 17; Baumol, William J. (2003), 'Applied Welfare Economics', in Ruth Towse (ed.), *A Handbook on Cultural Economics*, Cheltenham, UK and Northampton, MA, US: Edward Elgar, p. 20.

96 Peacock and Weir, *supra* note 15.

97 Towse, *supra* note 92.

of present-day collecting societies, various technological developments have changed users, producers and means of doing business. It will be interesting to see if DRM permits top stars to leave and go it alone, managing their own rights, as some believe they will. If so, they will undoubtedly want to charge a fee higher than the blanket licence fee, thus making users of the most popular works worse off. The only reason the fee would be lower would be if the star's costs of administering her rights were considerably lower than those of the collecting society; economists' admittedly theoretical understanding of these matters suggests that that would be unlikely. Well, let us wait and see – a natural experiment! It certainly seems that some industry users have persuaded the European Union that greater competition in the provision of rights management services would be beneficial. Our understanding of the economic literature suggests this is unlikely.

That said, there are no doubt opportunities for improving the services provided by collecting societies, particularly as digitalization becomes more widespread.[98] No doubt the distribution rules will become easier to administer. However, equity will always demand that they are seen to be fair, not just efficient. Even the bundle of rights that is efficiently administered together could change and collecting societies could merge to reduce administrative costs further – but that means even bigger monopolies.

To sum up this literature, it is clear that copyright would have considerably less value for individual content creators without collective administration of rights, even with DRM. It well demonstrates the point that it is not the copyright 'monopoly' per se that is anti-competitive but the way in which it is used, especially by enterprises with strong bargaining power and market dominance – the big media corporations and the collecting societies. The economic analysis of collecting societies therefore suggests that there is a dilemma for competition law: without them there would be no legal use of copyright but they tend towards natural monopoly and therefore exert market power. The problem is not all on the side of the collecting societies, however: the other side of the coin is the tendency to market dominance in the cultural industries whose products are copyrighted content.

9 Alternatives to copyright and rejection of copyright law

In this chapter, we have presented a range of arguments that are used to make

---

[98] See Monopolies and Merger Commission (1996), *Performing Rights*, London: HMSO, cm. 3147; Rochelandet, Fabrice (2003), 'Are Copyright Collecting Societies Efficient? An Evaluation of Collective Administration of Copyright in Europe', in Wendy J. Gordon and Richard Watt (eds), *Economics of Copyright – Developments in Research and Analysis*, Cheltenham, UK and Northampton, MA, US: Edward Elgar, p. 176; Einhorn, *supra* note 91.

the economic case for copyright law. The predominant understanding is that copyright involves various trade-offs. Whether copyright overall leads to greater social efficiency can only be determined on the basis of a careful assessment of market conditions (the economics of copying) and an assessment of specific legal doctrines (law and economics) and the administration of rights in practice. Whatever the economic rationale supporting copyright, there have always been some authors who have challenged the case for copyright law.

There have been both outright rejections of copyright law as well as suggested modifications. The 'one size fits all approach' to copyright, justified in terms of reducing transaction costs, has always been controversial on the grounds of economic efficiency and does not accord with the preferences of some authors either. 'Some rights reserved' is the buzz phrase of the development of the creative commons movement. This accepts the copyright regime but seeks to adapt it by offering the possibility to waive some rights and retain others, thus allowing a range of licences that can be utilized that suit the individual. These are increasingly easy to administer with digital rights management but may not be easy to protect. The principal idea behind it is to sell creative products on the market but to leave behind the ballast that slows creation down by asking for permissions. Some writers go further, however, taking the view that knowledge is a public good and cannot by its nature be owned by one person: free access to and use of it is an important precondition for continued innovation. A further source of concern is what has been called the 'anti commons' (the antithesis of the 'tragedy of the commons'), a situation in which property rights are so debundled and ownership or control so scattered that the transaction costs to coordinate the various right-holders become so high that it becomes virtually impossible to make use of the property.[99] Occasionally, this might be a problem with traditional 'one size fits all' copyright. Creative commons might turn out to increase the complexity even further, even though they aim to provide suppliers with greater flexibility and users with greater freedom.

The alternatives to copyright law that have been suggested are either market solutions of the 'business model' variety or transfers organized by the government. Market solutions include first-mover advantage, price discrimination, joint sale of complements, versioning[100] and indirect appropriability;[101] transfers organized by the government are taxes on blank CDs,

---

99 Depoorter and Parisi, *supra* note 50.
100 Varian, *supra* note 35.
101 Liebowitz, *supra* note 12.

computers etc.,[102] direct finance through state subsidies[103] or grants and prizes,[104] who argue that an optional reward scheme (which may also be provided privately) is more efficient than having only an intellectual property rights regime.

Boldrin and Levine argue that freedom of contract and first-mover advantage is a sufficient basis for a competitive market of ideas.[105] Although describing themselves as conservative economists, they find that well-defined property rights are less important than unhindered competition. They argue that intellectual property has come to mean not only the right to own and sell ideas but also the right to regulate their use. This creates a social inefficient monopoly and claim that what is commonly called intellectual property might be called 'intellectual monopoly'. The inefficiency comes with regulatory measures that are built into the current copyright regime. No one selling potatoes could limit their use and consequently sue the inventor or producer of chips for using potatoes without licence. This view expressed by Boldrin and Levine appears to be diametrically opposed to the Kantian *droit d'auteur* or natural rights approach in continental Europe.

Finally, there are objections that copyright does not act as an incentive for creators anyway but just protects business interests that exploit copyrights. A less strong version of this is held by Towse, who argues two points: first, that the greater economic power of corporations in comparison to that of individual artists (creators and performers) means that the artists are not likely to get a good deal; second, that artists are motivated not only (or even) by monetary reward but peer recognition, which is usually involved in prizes, and moral rights that protect the artist's reputation and the integrity of their work may also be a significant factor in the support artists gain from copyright and, more especially, authors' rights.[106] Her evidence suggests that copyright does not yield much in the way of earnings for any other than superstar artists, although the share of the 'industry' is considerably bigger.[107]

---

102 Farchy, Joelle and Rochelandet, Fabrice (2002), 'Copyright, Appropriability and New Economic Behaviour', in Ruth Towse (ed.), *Copyright in the Cultural Industries*, Cheltenham, UK and Northampton, MA, US: Edward Elgar, p. 178.

103 Plant, *supra* note 7; Hurt and Schuchman, *supra* note 8.

104 Shavell, S. and T. van Ypersele (2001), 'Rewards versus Intellectual Property Rights', *J. L. & Econ.*, **44**, 525.

105 Boldrin, M. and D. Levine (2002), 'The Case against Intellectual Property', *Am. Econ. Rev., Papers and Proceedings*, **92**, 209–12; Boldrin and Levine, *supra* note 18.

106 Towse, *supra* note 92.

107 See also Kretschmer, Martin and Philip Hardwick (2007), 'Authors' Earnings from Copyright and Non-copyright Sources: A Survey of 25 000 British and German Writers', http://www.cippm.org.UK/publications/alcs%20report.pdf, accessed 31 March 2008.

10 Conclusion

As economists have pointed out over two centuries, there are several ways that society can solve the problem of how to encourage the creators and innovators of new works: it can reward them directly by state or private patronage and/or it can leave it to the market. If the latter, some intervention is likely needed to enable creators to appropriate revenues sufficient to give them the incentive to create and disseminate works. Each system has its pros and cons and each involves some sort of trade-off. There is no Pareto optimum possible.

Research on the economics of copying is concentrated in the English-speaking world and contributions from other – mainly European – countries are frequently published in English, too. That no doubt reflects the internationalization, not only of economics as a discipline, but also of copyright itself. The focus on English and on US scholarship has resulted in several notable features. First, most of the literature deals with economic rights and there is very little literature on moral rights or on performers' rights.[108] Second, overwhelmingly more attention is paid by economists to efficiency rather than equity aspects of copyright: concern with maximizing welfare, minimizing transaction costs, property rights and so on are all efficiency issues. Equity matters, which would include the distribution of both royalties and of the costs of what we can call the copyright system – who pays for the costs of administration and of monitoring and protection (including court proceedings, tribunals and suchlike) – also the sharing of royalties and other revenues, such as remuneration schemes between authors, publishers, performers and other claimants – have been largely ignored. Even now that there is increasing interest in empirical studies, they tend to be about the effect of unauthorized use on businesses rather than on creators or artists. Where is it written that the rule of thumb according to which an author should receive a 10 per cent royalty is equitable?

The view held by those who strongly favour copyright protection is that without copyright, there would be much less production of creative content, a reduction in diversity and hardship for creators. Those who are totally opposed to copyright believe it leads to the exploitation of consumers and of creators, holds back artistic development and cultural diversity because it encourages the growth of large corporations, and inhibits freedom of expression. Most economists do not subscribe to either extreme position. There is certainly scepticism about copyright on the part of quite a few economists: the reasons range from the view that it is simply a means of rent-seeking to the view that it was useful once but that it cannot work any more with digitalization. In between are theories about its asymmetric effects on copyright 'partners', that

108 See Towse, *supra* note 4.

is, creator and distributor (author and publisher), that it really only helps commercial enterprises and not the primary creator and that over-reliance on copyright has inhibited publishers from developing new business models for charging for the use of copyright material (especially in the music business).

The most common view of copyright law held by economists is that it requires a balance of opposing economic forces: the incentive to create versus access to existing creations (meaning in terms of both pricing and granting permissions), that is, of costs and benefits. Often, a satisfactory outcome can only be established when actual numbers can be attached to the many short- and long-term effects. When it comes to specific problems, such as the effect of digitalization, abstract models do not prove very helpful and analytical techniques give way to case studies of management behaviour or economic historical experience. However, there is a general consensus that property rights are important for trade to take place in creative work and although copyright is not the only way to establish such rights, it is one that has stayed the course.

It has been suggested repeatedly over three centuries that state patronage (subsidy) or a system of prizes and awards could provide the necessary incentive to primary creators and that publishers 'lead time' or 'first mover' advantage would be sufficient protection for them to stay in business. Whether business models suited to internet commerce can yield sufficient revenues to maintain a desirable (though not necessarily optimal) supply of cultural products without copyright protection is a hard question to answer. On the one hand, the whole economic organization of the creative industries has depended for so long on copyright that it is hard to say what life would be like without it. We have 'copyright lock-in' and there would be high switching costs associated with abandoning it. This applies not only to the production and distribution by the industries but also to the system for collecting and distributing royalty revenues to individual creators. On the other hand, recent history has shown that adaptation to new business models can and does take place – witness the growth of legal online services for downloading music. The story of creative destruction is that those firms that can adapt survive. Should 'lame ducks' be propped up by statutory copyright protection (Plant's concern 70 years ago)?

Copyright law has weathered several technological storms in its 300-year existence and has adapted to the introduction of sound recording, radio and television, home recording and photocopying while maintaining much the same principles. But who the creators are, what works they produce and how they gain access to them has obviously changed a great deal over the years. Many of what are now called the creative industries developed with copyright protection from the very start. What we do not know is what historians call the counter-factual: what would they look like without copyright? Nevertheless, this is the situation that is very often evoked – the world 'with' and the world 'without' copyright. A parallel is found in competition law – the world with monopoly versus the world of perfect competition. However, one of the significant differences between copyright law and competition law is that any tendency to monopoly that is due to copyright is assisted by the state whereas competition law deals with economic organization that has come about due to market forces. Copyright is needed to get markets to work but how the markets then develop and use copyright ownership as a barrier to entry can be regulated by competition law without denying the case for copyright. As stated above, the fault mostly lies with the use of copyright and the original creator, unless she is a superstar, mostly has little bargaining power or control over use.

Progress in economics can be judged by two yardsticks: theoretical progress and empirical progress. There has been notable progress in theoretical understanding of the economic aspects of copyright law within the different approaches outlined at the beginning of this chapter. The property rights approach and contract theory have been very fruitful in providing insights into the economic organization of the creative industries which rely heavily upon copyright, as well as into the kind of royalty contracts creators make with the industries and with collecting societies that administer the rights. Even though a lot of this theorizing appears abstract and mathematical to the outsider (and also to some insiders), it has contributed to progress in understanding the difficulties. There also has been empirical progress, for example in testing the claims for the music industry that illegal downloading is what is responsible for its reduced sales revenues; and Landes and Posner (2002) make their case for indefinitely renewable copyright by using empirical analysis. There is much more to be done, however. We know very little still about what motivates creativity, how much artists and other creators earn from copyright and other sources, how much they would need to earn to continue to be creative, whether a shorter or a longer term of copyright protection would be in their interests, how important moral rights are to creators and many other points connected with the creative process as contrasted with the role of copyright in industry.

PART 6

NATIONAL IP RIGHTS AND CROSS-BORDER COMPETITION

16 Intellectual property, the internal market and competition law

Stefan Enchelmaier

1 Introduction

Intellectual property, the internal market and the Community's competition law are intertwined in several respects. The European Court of Justice's first judgment on competition law, *Consten and Grundig*,[1] is a case in point. The distribution agreement there at issue purported to grant Grundig's exclusive distributor in France, Consten, complete protection against parallel imports from other Member States (also called 'absolute territorial protection'). This was to be achieved by means of a trade mark assigned exclusively to the distributor. The Court therefore had to clarify the relationship between competition law (which was touched on by the exclusive distribution agreement), the internal market (the prevention of all non-authorized imports into France), and intellectual property law (the trademark employed to that end).

This connection between the three elements is reflected in the very wording of the EC Treaty. Article 2 EC says that the aims of the Community (a harmonious, balanced, and sustainable development of economic activities and so on) shall be achieved by establishing, among other things, a 'common market'. This end is served, according to Article 3(1) EC, by 'an internal market characterized by the abolition, as between Member States, of obstacles to the free movement of goods [and] services' (letter (c)), and by 'a system ensuring that competition in the internal market is not distorted' (letter (g)). The provisions implementing these general stipulations in the Treaty are Articles 28[2] and 49 for the free movement of goods and the freedom to provide services, on the one hand, and Articles 81 and 82 on the Community's competition law, on the other. What is more, Article 4(1) enjoins both the Community and the Member States to conduct their economic policies 'in accordance with the principle of an open market economy with free competition'.

[1] Joined Cases 56 and 58/64, *Consten and Grundig v. Commission*, [1966] ECR 299.

[2] I do not propose to discuss Article 29 EC, which has not yielded any case law with regard to intellectual property rights. All article numbers are tacitly updated to reflect the renumbering following the Treaty of Amsterdam (1997).

Article 28 laconically states that 'quantitative restrictions on imports and all measures having equivalent effect shall be prohibited between Member States'. Article 30 gives examples of such restrictions by allowing, among other things, 'the protection of industrial and commercial property' as a ground for derogating from the prohibition in Article 28.[3] As regards Article 49, the text of the Treaty contains no hint of a clash between the freedom to provide services and intellectual property or of the resolution of such a conflict. Instead, the ECJ has developed mechanisms similar to those applicable under Article 28.[4] Articles 81 and 82, in turn, declare 'incompatible with the common market' behaviour as prohibited under the two provisions. If agreements and other conduct relating to intellectual property come, in principle, within the ambit of Article 28, and if this provision and Articles 81 and 82 all serve to create a common market between Member States, one may conclude that intellectual property and competition law have some complementarity, and some conflict, too.[5]

Thus, the Court has accepted that, for example, trademarks are 'an essential element in the system of undistorted competition which the Treaty seeks to establish and maintain'.[6] There can be little doubt that this statement is true: one of the parameters for describing the state of competition in a given market is product differentiation. Patents and trademarks bring about just this. They force competitors, if they do not want to or cannot obtain a licence, to come

---

3 For simplicity's sake, the relationship between the grounds of justification contained in Article 30 and the 'mandatory requirements' recognized in the Court's jurisprudence since the judgment in Case 120/78, *Rewe Zentralverwaltung v. Bundesmonopolverwaltung für Branntwein* ('*Cassis de Dijon*'), [1979] ECR 649, cannot be explored here; see Enchelmaier, S. (2003), 'The Awkward Selling of a Good Idea, or a Traditionalist Interpretation of *Keck*', *Y.E.L*, **22**, 249, *passim*.

4 Case 62/79, *Coditel v. Ciné Vog* ('*Coditel I*'), [1980] ECR 881.

5 There is, as yet, little literature on the relationship between the rules on free movement and those on competition; see specifically on intellectual property issues Ullrich, H. (1992), 'Patents and Know-how, Free Trade, Inter-enterprise Cooperation and Competition within the Internal European Market', *IIC*, **23**, 583; more generally see, for example, Reich, Norbert (1990), 'Die Bedeutung der Binnenmarktkonzeption für die Anwendung der EWG-Wettbewerbsregeln', in Jürgen F. Baur (ed.), *Festschrift für Ernst Steindorff*, Berlin: Duncker & Humblot, p. 1065; Mortelmans, K. (2001), 'Towards Convergence in the Application of the Rules on Free Movement and on Competition?', *C.M.L. Rev.*, **38**, 613; Monti, G. (2002), 'Article 81 and Public Policy', *C.M.L. Rev.*, **39**, 1057; Stuyck, Jules (1999), 'Libre circulation et concurrence – les deux pilliers du marché commun', in Marianne Dony and Katherine de Walsche (eds), *Mélanges en hommage à Michel Waelbroeck*, Brussels: Bruylant, vol. II, p. 1477, all with further references.

6 Case C-10/89, *CNL-SUCAL v. Hag* ('*Hag II*'), [1990] ECR I-3711, para. 13; Case C-9/93, *Internationale Heiztechnik v. Ideal-Standard*, [1994] ECR I-2789, para. 45.

up with something different. As under Articles 28 and 30, problems for competition would ensue if applicants were allowed to overcome the intrinsic limitations of intellectual property rights in order to adulterate them for anti-competitive purposes.[7] In cases of conflict, however, it is for the Treaty rules on competition to determine which use made of intellectual property rights is lawful and which is not.[8]

2 Intellectual property and the internal market

Taking each of the areas of potential conflict in turn, we can begin with the relation between intellectual property and the internal market. To this end, the notion of the common market ought to be explained, as it occurs both in Articles 28 and 49 and in Articles 81 and 82.

2.1 The foundations of the internal market: Articles 12 and 14 EC

This is not the place to discuss in detail the relationship between the notions of the common market and the internal market.[9] The Treaty does not explain whether these are identical concepts, or whether the internal market is, metaphorically speaking, a smaller circle inside a bigger circle representing the Common Market. Article 95(2) EC seems to militate in favour of partial identity; Articles 2, 3 and 14(2) EC, by contrast, might be read to imply complete identity. In view of the fact that both bear some relation, however described, to the so-called Four Freedoms,[10] and that they share the quality of being means to achieve the ends of the Community as set out in Article 2, it can be ruled out that both are wholly independent notions, with at most a partial overlap (as in two intersecting circles).

---

7 Opinion of AG Léger, Case C-321/03, *Dyson v. Registrar of Trade Marks*, [2007] ECR I-693, paras 90–101 (technical features of a vacuum cleaner can only be protected as a matter of patent law, not trademark law).

8 Anderman, Steven (1998), *EC Competition Law and Intellectual Property Rights*, Oxford: Oxford University Press, p. 9. For a comprehensive treatise on the relationship between intellectual property and competition law in the European Community, see Heinemann, Andreas (2002), *Immaterialgüterschutz in der Wettbewerbsordnung*, Tübingen: Mohr Siebeck, and Stothers, Christopher (2007), *Parallel Trade in Europe – Intellectual Property, Competition and Regulatory Law*, Oxford, UK and Portland, OR, US: Hart Publishing.

9 On this, see Ehlermann, C.-D. (1987), 'The Internal Market following the Single European Act', *C.M.L. Rev.*, **24**, 361, at 363–70; Pescatore, P. (1987), 'Some Critical Remarks on the Single European Act', *C.M.L. Rev.*, **24**, 9; Gormley, L. (2002), 'Competition and Free Movement: Is the Internal Market the Same as a Common Market?', *E.B.L.R.*, **13**, 517, *passim*.

10 That is, free movement of goods (Articles 25, 28 *et seq.* EC), services (Article 49 EC), persons (Articles 39, 43 and 48 EC) and capital (Article 56 EC).

Pragmatically, therefore, the appropriate starting point for the following analysis is Article 14(2) EC, which contains the most articulated description of the internal market: 'the internal market shall comprise an area without internal frontiers in which the free movement of goods, persons, services, and capital is ensured in accordance with the provisions of this Treaty'. This is the result of, in the words of Article 3(1)(c), 'the abolition, as between Member States, of obstacles to the free movement of goods, persons, services, and capital'. The provisions of Articles 40(b) and 44(2)(c) indicate, furthermore, that 'obstacles' in the sense of Article 3(1)(c) translates into 'restrictions'; the absence of restrictions is, conversely, labelled 'freedom'. These terms are, variably, used in the provisions of Articles 28, 39, 43, 49 and 56. The internal market is created, therefore, by the removal of the restrictions mentioned in these provisions.[11] This textual analysis tallies with the jurisprudence of the Court. According to it, the Treaty, by establishing a Common Market, and by progressively approximating the economic policies of the Member States, seeks to unite national markets in a single market having the characteristics of a domestic market.[12]

There is also a general prohibition of discrimination in Article 12 EC. Its first subparagraph reads: '[w]ithin the scope of application of this Treaty, and without prejudice to any special provisions contained therein, any discrimination on grounds of nationality shall be prohibited'. This does not rule out unequal treatment per se, but only to the extent that there is no objective reason (other than nationality), pursued by proportional means, for the inequality.[13] Articles 14 and 12 are complementary:[14] Article 12, and the four

---

[11] Similarly Waelbroeck, M. (1989), 'Le rôle de la Cour de Justice dans la mise en œuvre de l'Acte Unique Européen', *C.D.E.*, **25**, 41, at 43, and Opinion of AG Geelhoed, Case C-491/01, *British American Tobacco*, [2002] ECR I-11453, paras 103–8.

[12] Case 207/83, *Commission v. United Kingdom* ('*Origin markings*'), [1985] ECR 1201, para. 17. In an earlier judgment, the Court formulated more cautiously that the aim of creating the common market was 'to merge the national markets into a single market bringing about conditions *as close as possible to those of a genuine internal market*' (emphasis added), Case 15/81, *Schul*, [1982] ECR 1409, para. 33. This latter formula reappears in Case C-41/93, *France v. Commission* ('*PCP*'), [1994] ECR I-1829, para. 19. It is taken from a judgment on competition law, namely Case 26/76, *Metro v. Commission*, [1977] ECR 1875, para. 20 ('. . . objectives of the Treaty, in particular the creation of a single market achieving conditions similar to those of a domestic market').

[13] Case C-224/00, *Commission v. Italy* ('*Road traffic offences*'), [2002] ECR I-2965, paras 19 *et seq.*; Case C-451/99, *Cura Anlagen*, [2002] ECR I-3193, para. 32. In the same sense more recently Case C-14/01, *Molkerei Wagenfeld*, [2003] ECR I-2279, paras 49–54, and earlier Case C-29/95, *Pastoors*, [1997] ECR I-285, paras 19–25.

[14] The provisions of the Treaty must always be interpreted so as to form a coher-

fundamental freedoms implementing it for their respective area, prohibit any kind of discrimination, direct or indirect. What is not covered by such a prohibition is a universal ban in a Member State of a product or service available in other Member States. Such a ban is not discriminatory: it makes it equally impossible for products of any provenance to reach the market in that Member State. To the extent, however, that the ban suppresses any market in the product or service in the Member State in question, its territory ceases to be part of the wider market common to all the Member States.

In sum, therefore, the rules on free movement prohibit two things. First, there must not be requirements in national law putting products or services from other Member States at a legal or at a merely factual disadvantage. Secondly, there must not be blanket bans on the importation of goods or the provision of services across the borders between Member States. There must, in other words, be no attempts at creating 'home markets' reserved for the established economic operators. Yet this is precisely what intellectual property rights (IPRs) would allow their proprietors, were it not for the intervention of the EC Treaty as interpreted by the ECJ.

2.2 Free movement and intellectual property

The combined effect of three provisions, Article 28 EC, on the one hand, and Articles 295 and 30 EC, on the other, governs the free movement of goods[15] in relation to which intellectual property rights exist in one or several Member States of the Community. Article 28 prohibits quantitative restrictions on imports and measures having equivalent effect between Member States. In principle, products lawfully marketed in one Member State may be marketed in any other Member State.[16] At the same time, however, Article 295 states that the EC Treaty 'in no way prejudice[s] the rules in Member States governing the system of property ownership'. Intellectual property rights are a form of property. The laws of the Member States grant the holders of such rights control over the production and marketing of products incorporating, in the way they are made or presented, the protected intellectual property.

National law can, however, grant rights only as far as the jurisdiction of the respective Member State extends. In other words, national intellectual property rights are territorial: they grant rights only for the territory of the Member

---

ent whole; see, for example, Case C-113/00, *Spain v. Commission*, [2002] ECR I-7601, paras 75–8.

[15] Similar principles apply to services, such as broadcasts, as in Case 69/79, *Coditel v. Ciné Vog* ('*Coditel I*'), [1980] ECR 881, para. 15, but the following discussion will focus exclusively on goods.

[16] Case 120/78, *Rewe Zentralverwaltung v. Bundesmonopolverwaltung für Branntwein* ('*Cassis de Dijon*'), [1979] ECR 649, para. 14.

State which has awarded them.[17] This limitation would enable the holder, were it not for the impact of Community law, to isolate the markets in the Member States from each other. The proprietor can achieve this by suing unauthorized traders if they import goods coming within the terms of the IPR into Member States where the holder has been granted the right, or even if the goods are merely transported through such states.[18] In this sense, *as early as 1966* the applicants in *Consten and Grundig* argued that this was an 'original inherent right' of the holder of the trademark from which the absolute territorial protection derived under national law.[19]

Article 30 reinforces Article 295 in that it allows prohibitions on imports or exports justified on the grounds of, among other things, the protection of 'industrial and commercial property'. The ECJ reads this to encompass IPRs such as copyright,[20] trademarks,[21] patents,[22] designs[23] and models.[24] Although prohibitions of imports or exports on this ground must not, pursuant to the second sentence of Article 30, constitute 'arbitrary discrimination or disguised restrictions on trade between Member States',[25] these restrictions nevertheless bring about the exact opposite of the free movement of goods.

The ECJ, therefore, had to strike a balance as to the extent to which IPRs could be allowed to hamper, in accordance with Article 30, the free movement of goods that is in principle guaranteed by Article 28. To this end, in the Court's interpretation, Article 30 only permits derogations from the free movement of goods where such derogations are justified for the purpose of safeguarding rights which constitute the 'specific subject matter' of this property;[26] anything else would go further than required and would thus be disproportionate. The specific subject matter of patents and all other intellectual

---

17 Case C-9/93, *Internationale Heiztechnik v. Ideal-Standard*, [1994] ECR-2789, para. 22.

18 See, for example, Case C-23/99, *Commission v. France* ('*Car parts*'), [2000] ECR I-7653, paras 10–12.

19 Joined Cases 56 and 58/64, *Grundig and Consten v. Commission*, [1966] ECR 299, at 345.

20 Case 78/70, *Deutsche Grammophon v. Metro*, [1971] ECR 487, para. 11.

21 Case 192/73, *Van Zuylen Frères v. Hag* ('*Hag I*'), [1974] ECR 731, paras 6–12.

22 Case 15/74, *Centrafarm v. Sterling Drug*, [1974] ECR 1147, paras 8 *et seq.*

23 Case 144/81, *Keurkoop v. Nancy Kean Gifts*, [1982] ECR 2853, paras 22–5.

24 Case 53/87, *CICRA v. Renault*, [1988] ECR 6039, para. 10.

25 This is but an awkwardly worded expression of the requirement that the measures taken be proportional: Case 40/82, *Commission v. United Kingdom* ('*Newcastle poultry disease*'), [1982] ECR 2793, paras 14–19; most recently Case C-114/04, *Commission v. Germany* ('*Pesticides*'), 14 July 2005, unreported (http://curia.europa.eu/en/content/juris/index.htm), para. 30.

26 Case 15/74, *Centrafarm v. Sterling Drug*, [1974] ECR 1147, para. 8.

property rights mentioned above is the same: their holder has the right to be the first to put products incorporating the protected intellectual property on the market anywhere in the Community.[27] This formula betrays the specific perspective of the free movement of goods. Within the limits set by the Treaty, the proprietor of course retains the rights national or Community law grant him, in particular the right to suppress copying[28] or counterfeiting.[29]

This way of arguing from the specific subject matter of an intellectual property right superseded the older distinction between the 'existence' of the right and its 'exercise', first employed, in the context of competition law, by the ECJ in *Consten and Grundig*,[30] and later transferred to the jurisprudence on Article 28.[31]

While the specific subject matter tells us what owners of IPRs are allowed to do based on these rights, the essential function tells us the economic or other policy reasons why the legal system allows them to do so. The essential function of a patent is, briefly, to allow an inventor temporarily an exclusive position, enabling him to recoup his development costs (which he may or may not actually achieve); of a trade mark, to guarantee the origin and quality of the product to the consumer, and to protect the right-holder against those who want to exploit his reputation without his authorization.[32]

Nevertheless, the new formula is not without problems either. It may be as necessary as before to weigh the competing interests, only this time so as to establish what the specific subject matter is. To this end, the Court asks what the 'specific function' of a given intellectual property right is; this then determines the extent of the right and thus the question of whether its specific subject matter has been exhausted in a specific case. The Court applied such

---

27 Case 187/80, *Merck v. Stephar*, [1981] ECR 2063, para. 9, for patents; Case C-10/89, *CNL-SUCAL v. Hag* (*'Hag II'*), para. 14, for trademarks. Since the coming into force of the agreement on the European Economic Area (EEA) in 1994, 'Community' must be read as 'EEA', Case C-355/96, *Silhouette*, [1998] I-4799, paras 25–31. Once the product has undergone customs clearance (see Articles 23(2) and 24 EC), it makes no difference whether it originates in the Community or in a third state: Case C-352/95, *Phyteron v. Bourdon*, [1997] ECR I-1729, para. 21.

28 Case 15/74, *Centrafarm v. Sterling Drug*, [1974] ECR 1147, para. 11; Case 144/81, *Keurkoop v. Nancy Kean Gifts*, [1982] ECR 2853, para. 22.

29 Case C-23/99, *Commission v. France*, [2000] ECR I-7653, para. 39.

30 Joined Cases 56 and 58/64, *Consten and Grundig v. Commission*, [1966] ECR 299, at 345.

31 See, for example, Case 78/70, *Deutsche Grammophon v. Metro*, [1971] ECR 1147, para. 11. At the end of this passage, however, the Court already spoke of 'safeguarding rights which constitute the specific subject-matter of such property', thus anticipating the later formula.

32 Case 187/80, *Merck v. Stephar*, [1981] ECR, 2063, para. 10, for patents; Case C-10/89, *CNL-SUCAL v. Hag* (*'Hag II'*), para. 14, for trademarks.

reasoning for instance to determine whether the sale of a videotape exhausted the right to control its rental for commercial purposes: it does not, because copyright is meant to afford the right-holder an adequate share in the fruits of the commercial exploitation of his creation. The price paid by the purchaser bears no adequate relation to the benefits that can be reaped by renting out the tape if this intention was not known at the time of the sale.[33] The Court used the same method regarding the question of whether transit through the territory of a Member State could be stopped by the right-holder,[34] or whether the use of a right had occurred 'in the course of trade' (as required by Article 5(1) Trade Mark Directive 89/104).[35]

As it happens, this way of determining the specific subject matter in light of the specific function and under the circumstances of each case makes the old notion of 'specific subject matter' well suited to the 'more economic approach' to competition law that the Commission has followed since the late 1990s.[36] Little wonder, one may say, as the Court's jurisprudence, since its beginnings,[37] declined mechanistic formulae for establishing whether a given agreement restricted competition. The 'specific function' of an IPR may be reconsidered in the light of changing facts and the different effects the exercise of an IPR would have on the market in question. In this, it meets with the new 'market-realistic' thinking of the Commission.

The reconciliation of the conflicting aims of Article 28, and of Articles 295 and 30 EC, is achieved by the doctrine of 'exhaustion': once the proprietor has put products on the market in relation to which he holds intellectual property rights, he can no longer object to these goods being exported or imported into other Member States. The right is exhausted as soon as its holder has availed himself of its specific subject matter. From then on, parallel trade in these goods is permissible: anyone may, for the purpose of resale, freely take them across the borders between any Member States. Once a product is marketed anywhere in

---

[33] Case 158/86, *Warner Brothers v. Christiansen*, [1988] ECR 2605, paras 14–16.

[34] Case C-23/99, *Commission v. France* ('*Car parts*'), [2000] ECR I-7653, para. 45; Case C-405/03, *Class International*, [2005] ECR I-8735, paras 33–49; see also Case C-115/02, *Rioglass*, [2003] ECR I-12705, para. 27. Different principles apply to the treatment of counterfeit goods under Regulation (EC) No. 3295/94, OJ 1994 No. L 341, p. 8, as amended by Regulation (EC) No. 241/1999, OJ 1999 No. L 27, p. 1, because by this Regulation, the Community has discharged an obligation under the TRIPS Agreement: Case C-383/98, *Polo/Lauren*, [2000] ECR I-2519, paras 26–9, and Case C-60/02, *X* ('*Rolex*'), [2004] ECR I-651, para. 54.

[35] C-2/00, *Hölterhoff v. Freiesleben*, [2002] ECR I-4187, paras 16 *et seq.*

[36] On this, see Drexl, Josef, Chapter 2 in this volume, section 2.1.

[37] Case 56/65, *La Technique Minière v. Maschinenbau Ulm*, [1966] ECR 235, at 248; more recently, see Case T-61/89, *Dansk Pelsdyraflerforening v. Commission*, [1992] ECR II-1931, para. 98.

the Community, its movement anywhere else in the Community can (in principle)[38] no longer be opposed by the holder of IPR in the product. Thus, the several territories of the Member States are fused, in effect, into one single market. Metaphorically speaking, the consent of the right-holder, or of his licensee, to the first marketing becomes the 'key which opens the door of the common market to [. . .] products [incorporating IPRs]'.[39] This jurisprudence of the ECJ was cast in legislative form in Article 7(1) of Directive 89/104/EEC.[40]

3 Intellectual property and competition law

In this section, the relation between intellectual property and competition law will come into focus. Again, the analysis is aided by an exposition of the basic notions. In the present context, this entails a reflection on how competition law relates to the internal market; to what extent Community competition law pursues aims of its own; and finally, how Community law reconciles the conflicting claims of intellectual property and competition law.

3.1 The internal market and competition law

As already pointed out, both Articles 81 and 82 EC label as 'incompatible with the common market' conduct in breach of their respective prohibitions.[41] The reference to the common market emphasizes that Community competition law complements the Treaty's provisions on free movement and vice versa. This is true with regard to both goods[42] and services.[43] In the same vein, the Court

---

38 An exception applies to the repackaging of goods imported by way of parallel trade; for a summary of the case law see Case C-143/00, *Boehringer Ingelheim v. Swingward*, [2002] ECR I-3759, paras 14–16, 45–52 and 61–7; Joined Cases C-71 to 73/94, *Eurim-Pharm v. Beiersdorf*, [1996] ECR I-3603, paras 42–70; Joined Cases C-427 *et al.*/93, *Bristol Myers-Squibb*, [1996] ECR I-3457, paras 44–79.

39 Opinion of AG Mancini, Case 19/84, *Pharmon v. Hoechst*, [1985] ECR 2281, p. 2288, third paragraph.

40 First Council Directive 89/104/EEC of 21 December 1988 to approximate the laws of the Member States relating to trade marks, OJ 1998 No. L 40, p. 1, as amended by Directive 92/10, [1992] OJ 1992 No. L 6, p. 35. For references to other Community Directives containing exhaustion clauses, see Opinion of AG Sharpston, Case C-479/04, *Laserdisken*, [2006] ECR I-8089, paras 18–22; Rognstad, Ole-Andreas, Chapter 17, in this volume, note 1 therein.

41 We can again do without distinguishing between the 'common' and the 'internal' market.

42 It is immaterial whether the goods affected be finished products, see Case T-62/98, *Volkswagen v. Commission*, [2000] ECR II-2707, semi-finished products such as carton board, see Case C-248/98 P, *KNP v. Commission*, [1999] ECR I-9641, or raw materials like calcium, see Joined Cases C-68/94 and C-30/95, *France v. Commission and SCPA v. Commission*, [1999] ECR I-1375.

43 Case T-213/00, *CMA CGM v. Commission*, [2003] ECR I-913.

held in *Consten and Grundig* that 'an agreement between producer and distributor which might tend to restore the national divisions in trade between Member States might be such as to frustrate the most fundamental objecti[ve]s of the Community. The Treaty, whose preamble and content aim at abolishing the barriers between states, and which in several provisions gives evidence of a stern attitude with regard to their reappearance, could not allow undertakings to reconstruct such barriers'.[44]

The connection between competition law and the law on free movement is further highlighted by the fact that the Court employs the same formula, originally devised in order to ascertain under Article 81 whether an agreement 'may affect trade between Member States', when enquiring whether a piece of national law amounts to a 'measure having equivalent effect to a quantitative restriction' in the sense of Article 28. In both cases, what counts is whether the agreement or national law is 'capable of constituting a threat, either direct or indirect, actual or potential, to freedom of trade between Member States in a manner which might harm the attainment of the objectives of a single market between states'.[45]

This is not to say that there are not important differences. For a start, Member States cannot, in their legislative capacity, invoke the *de minimis* privilege. According to this, agreements between undertakings will not be prohibited if they do not appreciably affect trade between Member States.[46] Member States cannot plead the lack of importance of measures having equivalent effects to quantitative restrictions,[47] or the small volume of trade in a

[44] Joined Cases 56 and 58/64, *Grundig and Consten v. Commission*, [1966] ECR 299, at 340. The point was later reiterated by the Commission: 'Companies should not be allowed to recreate private barriers between Member States where State barriers have been successfully abolished', Commission Notice – Guidelines on Vertical Restraints, OJ 2000 No. C 291, p. 1, para. 7.

[45] *Ibid*., at 341. Substantially the same formula is found in Case 8/74, *Dassonville*, [1974] ECR 837, para. 5, for the free movement of goods, and in Case 36/74, *Walrave and Koch*, [1974] ECR 1405, paras 17–18, for the free movement of services.

[46] The Court first so held in Case 5/69, *Völk v. Vervaecke*, [1969] ECR 295, paras 5–7; see more recently Case C-306/96, *Javico v. Yves Saint Laurent Parfums*, [1998] ECR I-1983, para. 26. See also Commission Notice on agreements of minor importance which do not appreciably restrict competition under Article 81(1) of the Treaty establishing the European Community (*de minimis*), OJ 2001 No. C 368, p. 13. '*De minimis*' is short for *de minimis non curat praetor*: 'a judge does not deal with trifling matters'.

[47] Case C-126/91, *Yves Rocher*, [1993] ECR I-2361, para. 21. It has been argued by Mortelmans, *supra* note 5, at 633 *et seq*., that the Court employs something like a *de minimis* doctrine under Article 28 when it takes 'too uncertain and indirect' hindrances out of the scope of that provision. Even if Mortelmans's interpretation of the jurisprudence were correct, however, the Court's reasoning is misguided; see Enchelmaier, *supra* note 3, at 289–92.

given category of goods between them.[48] What is more, discrimination on grounds of nationality is not of the same concern under Articles 81 and 82 as under the Treaty's provisions on free movement. Exclusionary conduct, be it under Article 81 or 82, usually targets competitors because they are competitors, not because they are foreign.[49] Often, such conduct seeks to quell unwelcome (parallel) trade in the undertaking's own products.[50] Conversely, while undertakings frequently try to isolate national markets against each other by means of absolute territorial protection,[51] import prohibitions in national law can usually be overcome by obtaining marketing authorizations,[52] registering with supervisory authorities[53] and the like. Rather than entailing prohibitions, such requirements in practice result in mere encumbrances. Undertakings, in their turn, have been known to be much more tenacious when it comes to keeping out (or keeping in) products from (or bound for) other Member States[54] – in particular, by making use of IPRs, as the cases cited above testify.

3.2 The aims of Community competition law

Here is not the place to explore in detail the various explanations offered by courts, administrative authorities and academics as to the aims of Community competition law, or of competition law and competition in general.[55] It is often

48 Case 21/84, *Commission v. France* ('*Franking machines*'), [1985] ECR 1355, para. 13.

49 See, for an example of a market-sharing agreement under Article 81, Joined Cases T-236 *et al.*/01, *Tokai Carbon v. Commission*, [2004] ECR II-1181; for discrimination under Article 82 (through fidelity rebates) see Case T-219/99, *British Airways v. Commission*, [2003] ECR II-5917, confirmed by Case C-95/04 P, *British Airways v. Commission*, [2007] ECR I-2331 (15 March 2007).

50 See Joined Cases C-2 P and 3/01 P, *Bundesverband der Arzneimittelimporteure v. Commission* ('*Bayer/Adalat*'), [2004] ECR I-23.

51 See, for example, Joined Cases 56 and 58/64, *Grundig and Consten v. Commission*, [1966] ECR 299, and more recently, Joined Cases T-236 *et al.*/01, *Tokai Carbon v. Commission*, [2004] ECR II-1181.

52 Case 124/81, *Commission v. UK* ('*UHT milk*'), [1983] ECR 203; Case C-473/98, *Toolex Alpha*, [2000] ECR I-5681, paras 36 *et seq.*; Joined Cases C-388/00 and C-429/00, *Radiosistemi*, [2002] ECR I-5845, para. 43: granting of a national mark of conformity.

53 Case C-55/94, *Gebhard*, [1995] ECR I-4165; Case C-58/98, *Corsten*, [2000] ECR I-7919; these are cases relating to establishment and services, respectively, where such requirements are commonplace.

54 For recent examples, see Case T-368/00, *General Motors Nederland v. Commission*, [2003] ECR II-4491; Case C-338/00 P, *Volkswagen v. Commission*, [2003] ECR I-9189.

55 See the text and references in Whish, Richard (2003), *Competition Law*, 5th ed., London: Butterworths, ch. 1; Bellamy, Christopher and Graham Child (2001), *European Community Law of Competition*, 5th ed., London: Sweet & Maxwell, paras

overlooked that the Treaty offers its own description, albeit in a somewhat oblique manner, of why competition enjoys the protection of Articles 81 and 82. Agreements in breach of Article 81(1) may be exempted according to Article 81(3) if, among other things, they 'contribute to improving the production or distribution of goods or to promoting technical or economic progress, while allowing consumers a fair share of the resulting benefit'.

It cannot be presumed that undistorted competition pursues one aim or set of aims, while the Treaty, exceptionally, allows trade-distorting agreements if they seek to accomplish a different aim or set of aims. Court and Commission use essentially the same criteria when the question arises of whether an allegedly abusive conduct under Article 82 is justified. The Commission has, in a recent discussion paper, expressly proposed to draw on Article 81(3) in this context.[56] This also follows from the notion of 'competition on the merits', which the Court uses in determining whether the conduct of a dominant undertaking is abusive,[57] because Article 81(3) lists the merits of unfettered competition.

Article 81(3), therefore, describes the aims of competition in general, and explains why Community law should protect it. These aims also motivate the creation of the common market. Within such a market, the Court held, 'economic interpenetration will result from a division of labour between Member States'.[58] According to traditional understanding, in the words of Adam Smith, 'the greatest improvement in the productive powers of labour, and the greater part of the skill, dexterity, and judgment with which it is any where directed or applied, seem to have been the effects of the division of labour'. From this, the desirability of a market common to several states naturally follows: '[a]s it is the power of exchanging that gives occasion to the

---

1-075 *et seq.;* Goyder, Daniel (2003), *EC Competition Law*, 4th ed., Oxford: Oxford University Press, chs 2, 12 and 13; Emmerich, Volker (2001), *Kartellrecht*, 9th ed., Munich: C.H. Beck, § 1; Bishop, Simon and Mike Walker (2002), *The Economics of EC Competition Law*, 2nd ed., London: Thomson/Sweet & Maxwell, chs 1 and 2; Schmidt, Ingo (2005), *Wettbewerbspolitik und Kartellrecht*, Stuttgart: Lucius, *passim;* Swann, Denis (2000), *The Economics of Europe*, 9th ed., London: Penguin, pp. 129–48.

[56] DG Competition Discussion Paper of December 2005 on the application of Article 82 of the Treaty to exclusionary abuses, Brussels, http://ec.europa.eu/comm/competition/antitrust/others/discpaper2005.pdf, accessed 4 November 2007, paras 84–92. The Court of First Instance, in Case T-139/98, *AAMS v. Commission*, [2001] ECR II-3413, para. 79, deployed a proportionality assessment in a similar vein.

[57] Case 322/81, *Michelin v. Commission* (*'Michelin I'*), [1983] ECR 3461, para. 70; see also Enchelmaier, Stefan (1997), *Europäische Wettbewerbspolitik im Oligopol*, Baden-Baden: Nomos, pp. 141 *et seq.*

[58] Case 207/83, *Commission v. United Kingdom* (*'Origin markings'*), [1985] ECR 1201, para. 17.

division of labour, so the extent of this division must always be limited by the extent of that power, or, in other words, by the extent of the market'.[59] This reasoning was further buttressed by the explanation of the mechanism of 'comparative advantages' by the English economist David Ricardo (1772–1823).[60] There is, hence, no conflict between the aims of economic efficiency and the aim to create a market geographically as wide as possible, although one sometimes finds these two objectives played off against each other in the literature.[61]

3.3 Intellectual property and competition law – dependent or interdependent?

IPRs pose two problems for competition law. First, there is again the problem of territoriality. It was discussed above from the point of view of the free movement of goods and services. Under the relevant provisions, the Member States come into view because they grant economic operators IPRs, and provide courts in which these rights can be enforced. National courts, however, only ever act at the behest of right-holders, most often 'undertakings' in the sense of Articles 81 and 82 who are seeking to reserve for themselves the markets for whose territories they have obtained IPRs. This becomes a problem specifically for Community competition law when an agreement purports to allow the other contracting party, in exercise of the IPR, to exclude third competitors from the contract territory. These competitors may be licensees of the right-holder, but with different territories allocated to them, as permissible under Article 4(1)(c)(v) of the Technology Transfer Block Exemption Regulation (TTBER)[62] and, as between the right-holder and his several licensees, under (ii) and (iv). This compounds the problem, as the contractual bond is a disincentive to licensees' challenging their exclusion from other licensees' territories. This disincentive will arise even where there is no express stipulation prohibiting such challenges.

---

[59] Smith, Adam (1776), *An Inquiry into the Nature and Causes of the Wealth of Nations*, reprinted in William B. Todd (ed.) (1976), *Glasgow Edition of the Works and Correspondence of Adam Smith*, vol. 1, Oxford: Oxford University Press, book I, ch. I, para. 1 (p. 13), and ch. III, para. 1 (p. 31).

[60] For a simple model of the theory of comparative advantages, see Enchelmaier, Stefan (2005), *Europäisches Wirtschaftsrecht*, Stuttgart: Kohlhammer, para. 3 (pp. 3–5).

[61] *Contra*: Korah, Valentine (2006), *Intellectual Property Rights and the EC Competition Rules*, Oxford and Portland, OR, US: Hart Publishing, paras 2.1.2 (pp. 8 *et seq.*) and 2.6 (pp. 18 *et seq.*). For a critical discussion of Korah's approach, see the book review by Enchelmaier, Stefan (2006), *GRUR Int.*, **55**, 675, at 676.

[62] Commission Regulation (EC) No. 772/2004 of 27 April 2004 on the application of Article 81(3) of the Treaty to categories of technology transfer agreements, OJ 2004 No. L 123, p. 11.

Secondly, IPRs grant exclusive control over the exploitation of the invention, reputation, design and so on. This exclusive position bears some similarity to a monopoly, a market structure that Community competition law shuns. Nonetheless, the mere holding of an IPR does not, of itself and independently of the further conditions stipulated in Article 82, amount to a dominant position,[63] nor is the exercise by a dominant undertaking of its right necessarily abusive in the sense of that provision.[64]

The problems that IPRs pose for the law on free movement within the Common Market are thus very similar to, if not identical with, those besetting Community competition law. The second sentence of Article 30 EC requires a weighing, in the framework of a proportionality assessment, of Member States' legitimate concerns marshalled against the prohibition in Article 28. As a consequence, only actions to exploit or defend the specific subject matter of an IPR can justify deviations from principles as fundamental to the Treaty as the free movement of goods or the freedom to provide services. To put it differently: what is justified under Article 30 is, to that extent, not 'incompatible with the common market'. Articles 81 and 82 contain no freedoms additional to the four freedoms,[65] together making up the common market as envisaged in Articles 3(1)(c) and 14(2) EC. Moreover, as a similar process of weighing takes place under Article 81(3), namely of the efficiency-improving and welfare-enhancing effects of an agreement against its anti-competitive consequences, the reverse is also true: what is impermissible under Article 28 and 30 will not become permissible if made the subject matter of an anti-competitive agreement.[66]

The starting point is, hence, that actions for the exploitation or defence of the specific subject matter of an IPR by its holder are not, in principle, contrary to the aims of competition law. This is either because these actions do not amount to a distortion of competition in the first place[67] – as when the proprietor takes action against illicit copying[68] – or, if they do, because the condi-

63 Case 40/70, *Sirena v. Eda*, [1971] ECR 69, para. 16; Case 78/70, *Deutsche Grammophon v. Metro-SB-Großmärkte*, [1971] ECR 487, para. 16. Action taken by the proprietor to enforce the IPR constitutes no agreement or other proscribed conduct under Article 81(1), either; see Case 24/67, *Parke, Davis v. Probel*, [1968] ECR 55, at 71.

64 Case 102/77, *Hoffmann-La Roche v. Centrapharm*, [1978] ECR 1139, para. 16.

65 See *supra* note 10.

66 European Commission of 13 December 1989, Case IV/32026 (90/38/EEC) – *Bayo-n-ox*, OJ 1990 No. L 21, p. 71, paras 60 *et seq.*

67 As the ECJ held in Case C-9/93, *Internationale Heiztechnik v. Ideal-Standard*, [1994] ECR I-2789.

68 For an example, see Case C-60/02, *X* ('*Rolex*'), [2004] ECR I-651.

tions for an exemption under Article 81(3) are fulfilled, as illustrated by the general exemption, pursuant to Article 81(3), for technology licensing granted by Article 2 TTBER. Nevertheless, the provisions on competition law are complementary and supplemental, underpinning and fortifying the role of the provisions on free movement in the creation of the Common Market.[69] Because of the different ambit of the two sets of provisions, conduct justified under Article 30 can still be illegal under Articles 81 or 82.

For example, Article 4(1) and (2) TTBER lists restrictions in licensing agreements which are within the proprietor's capacity to exploit his IPR. This is because the 'specific subject matter', in the framework of Articles 28 and 30, serves to determine whether the right-holder can oppose someone else's marketing of goods (or services, in the case of Article 49) embodying the rights. He cannot do so if he has first marketed the goods himself, or if someone else has done so with his consent. Once the right-holder has thus enjoyed the benefits of the specific subject matter, his rights are exhausted. This, however, is conditional on the first 'marketing' of the products, which, in turn, requires that the proprietor transfer to third parties the right to dispose of the goods embodying his intellectual property rights, allowing him to realize the economic value of the right. There is no marketing if, even after a physical transfer of the goods, the proprietor retains control over the goods in order in particular to ensure their quality.[70]

If, by contrast, exhaustion has occurred, the products can be traded freely between Member States. The beneficiaries of this freedom are economic operators outside the commercial organization (in the wider sense) of the licensor, so-called parallel traders. This is because supplies between licensor/producer and licensee/distributor do not exhaust the right, unless the licensor/producer has not reserved any control over the goods, in particular over the circumstances in which the licensee/distributor transfers to independent third parties the right to deal with the goods as they see fit. Nor is the licensee/distributor free to deliver the goods or provide the services wherever he likes. It is only his marketing of the goods or services, and only in the circumstances as stipulated in his agreement with the licensor/producer (as the right-holder whose

---

69 See the extract from *Consten and Grundig*, *supra* note 44.

70 Case C-16/03, *Peak Holding*, [2004] ECR I-11313, para. 42. There is no marketing in this sense either in the case of goods undergoing the external transit procedure or the customs warehousing procedure, because they are not released into free circulation unless the trader so chooses, Case C-405/03, *Class International*, [2005] ECR I-8735, paras 33–49; see also Case C-115/02, *Rioglass*, [2003] ECR I-12705, para. 27 ('transporting goods lawfully manufactured in a Member State to a non-member country by passing through one or more Member States does not involve any marketing of the goods in question').

consent is decisive), that brings about exhaustion in the first place. There are innocent explanations for such limitations, such as quality requirements or provisions on warranties differing between Member States.[71] Subsequent redeliveries to the original licensee/distributor of course remain possible. They will, however, have gone through so many hands, each adding their costs and profit margin to the price, that the licensee's engaging in parallel trade will rarely be economically viable.

For want of exhaustion, marketing restrictions in technology licensing agreements are, thus, unobjectionable under Article 28. Yet this reasoning would also allow for restrictions which limit competition to an unacceptable extent, excluding by their very presence the application of the TTBER to the whole of the agreement in which they are stipulated. The restriction of Article 4(1)(c)(v) TTBER is a case in point. That provision makes an exception to the general prohibition against market allocations between competitors for

> the restriction, in a non-reciprocal agreement, of *active* sales by the licensee into the exclusive territory or to the exclusive customer group allocated by the licensor to another licensee provided the latter was *not a competing undertaking* of the licensor at the time of the conclusion of its own licence.[72]

Presuming a licence agreement were to forbid passive sales, or the proviso were not fulfilled: in the absence of exhaustion, the provisions on the free movement of goods alone would not be an obstacle to such stipulations.

It follows that it is only a necessary, but not a sufficient condition of legality under Articles 81 and 82 that action taken for the preservation of IPRs be justified under Article 30. This is in keeping with the case law of the Court. From the beginning, namely the judgment in *Consten and Grundig*, it has condemned absolute territorial protection in a situation where export prohibitions on other (*in casu,* Grundig) distributors outside the Member State concerned would have ruled out any exhaustion, and would thus have thwarted any legal parallel trade.[73]

3.4 Should competition law determine exhaustion?

In light of the above, one might contemplate a short cut.[74] As we have seen,

---

[71] This possibility was accepted by the ECJ in Case C-349/95, *Loendersloot v. Ballantines*, [1997] ECR I-6227, paras 41 *et seq.*

[72] Emphasis added.

[73] Direct exports by Grundig into France, that is exports side-stepping Consten, would also not have led to exhaustion, because for *that* territory, Consten was the relevant proprietor whose consent to the first marketing determined whether exhaustion occurred; differentiating, albeit from a different starting point: Rognstad, *supra* note 40, at section 5.

[74] This is developed in great detail by Rognstad, *supra* note 40, at section 3.

in the end it is for competition law to determine whether limitations on competition in agreements pertaining to IPRs are acceptable; never mind that the right has not been exhausted. If that is the case, one might as well let competition law determine whether exhaustion has occurred in the first place. To allow the proprietor in every case to rely on his IPR in addition to the contractual stipulations would bolster marketing limitations acceptable under Articles 81 and 82. Conversely, if the restrictions of competition were unacceptable, there would be no need to go through the charade of invoking a non-exhausted right which would ultimately have to yield anyway. Such a 'harmonized' or 'holistic' approach would, for instance, remove an oddity regarding the importation into the Community of goods first marketed in a non-Member State: a proprietor is, in principle, allowed to keep out of the Common Market goods first marketed in third countries;[75] the same person might, however, under the provisions of Community competition law, be forced to allow these goods onto the Common Market. This would be the case if additionally (and maybe in reliance, in good faith, on his seemingly unfettered right), he had obliged his licensees or distributors not to market the products in any Member States.[76]

On reflection, however, there remain some questions about this proposal. IPRs protect intangible subject matter, but they are property nonetheless. The law of property, tangible or intangible, emphasizes legal certainty more than contract law in particular. This is because dealings in property affect third parties not privy to the transaction – any third parties, as property rights are absolute, that is, they work against the world at large. For this reason, public registers are kept to record legal relationships (ownership or security interests) concerning land, IPRs, other intangibles[77] and even chattels.[78] These registers lend publicity to rights *in rem*. As far as, for instance, Community trade marks are concerned, Article 23(1) of the Community Trade Mark Regulation[79] requires such publicity for assignments (Article 17), security interests (Article 19) and licences (Article 22) to take effect vis-à-vis third parties without notice.

75 See Case C-355/96, *Silhouette*, [1998] I-4799.

76 As in Case C-306/96, *Javico v. Yves Saint Laurent Parfums*, [1998] ECR I-1983.

77 For an example, see section 860 UK Companies Act 2006.

78 As in the English Bills of Sale Acts 1878, 1882 and 1890, whose clumsiness is these days, however, largely circumvented through devices such as floating charges (to which section 860 UK Companies Act 2006 – *supra* note 77 – apply) or retention of title ('*Romalpa*') clauses.

79 Council Regulation (EC) No. 40/94 of 20 December 1993 on the Community trade mark, OJ 1994 No. L 11, p. 1.

In this situation, to make the validity of transactions concerning IPRs conditional on their clearance under competition law would wreak havoc on the requirement of legal certainty that underpins all property law. The 'more economic approach' lays emphasis on effects over form, on repercussions on the competitive process in the markets affected and on market shares. The ensuing legal uncertainty, however one gauges it, may be an acceptable price for a flexible and realistic competition law. This is no justification, however, for exporting it to the area of property law, where it yields no countervailing benefits.

One could try to mitigate the upheaval by differentiating between, on the one hand, transactions that might affect competition among the parties or between them and third undertakings and, on the other hand, dealings in IPRs that are not likely to have such an effect. Assignments (because they bring about the disappearance of a competitor) and licences (entailing the appearance of a new competitor) would fall within the first category. Security interests, by contrast, would fall under the second heading: they become operational only if the grantor defaults on performing whatever obligation is thus secured. Nevertheless, the second category is not as straightforward as it first appears. If a competitor or an undertaking connected with it is (or by assignment becomes) a major creditor of the right-holder, this fact might influence both parties' competitive behaviour.[80] Whether or not these differentiations are workable at all, they would, in any case, reintroduce complexity that the 'harmonizing' approach sought to reduce. Regardless of this objection, what would be gained by making exhaustion a function of competition law?

There would, first, be a one-step assessment where before there were two steps. This gain would, however, be more aesthetic than substantive. It may be tedious to go through the motions under Article 30 to establish that no exhaustion had occurred, always in the knowledge that the decision about the concrete powers of the proprietor will ultimately be made under Article 81 anyway. This is, however, the sort of complexity most developed legal systems engender where separate groups of norms, guided by different policy concerns, sometimes co-exist and sometimes trump one another.

Secondly, in case no exhaustion had occurred (because competition remained undistorted or the distortion was acceptable), the licensor's rights for breach of the licence would be reinforced by its rights *in rem* as the holder of the IPR. The difference between the two is that breach of contract requires some sort of culpability whereas infringement of property rights does not (at

---

[80] This is related to the paradigm of minority shareholdings, which might in principle give rise to concerted practices between competitors; see Joined Cases 142 and 156/84, *BAT and Reynolds v. Commission*, [1987] ECR 4487, para. 44.

least not if no damages are claimed). Seeing that *ex hypothesi* the infringer of the property right is, as licensee,[81] aware of the limits of his powers and, conversely, acts in full knowledge of the licensor's remaining competences, nothing is gained by sparing the right-holder the trouble of proving intention or negligence on the part of the infringer of his property rights. This was not a problem to begin with.

In all, therefore, property law, both at Community and at Member State level, would pay a high price for an insignificant simplification of the assessment under Articles 30 and 81 EC. Courts or legislatures should think twice before adopting the proposed approach.

3.5 Article 82 EC

IPRs confer exclusive control on their proprietor, and in (only) this sense amount to what could be labelled a 'monopoly'. The exclusivity is temporary in the case of patents and copyright, as these rights expire after a specific number of years; it is, in principle, unlimited in the case of trade marks. The prerogative of the right-holder relates, however, only to the exploitation of a given intellectual property right. Whether it also amounts to a monopoly on the market for products like the one embodying the right is a question for a traditional market analysis.[82] In other words, an undertaking is not dominant in the sense of Article 82 EC merely because it holds IPRs. From this, it follows that not every act to exploit or defend the right, including a refusal to license, is per se abusive.[83] This question, too, is determined in the same way as every other allegation of abuse under Article 82. The ECJ has in recent years developed a three-pronged test with special reference to the refusal to license intellectual property rights.[84] This test has met with almost universal criticism.[85]

Guidance in devising a more convincing formula might be taken from the Court's case law on the repackaging by parallel traders of goods bearing trade marks.[86] In principle, it is for the proprietor alone to decide to which goods to

81 Different considerations apply to 'genuine' parallel traders: Joined Cases C-414–416/99, *Davidoff and Levi Strauss*, [2001] ECR I-8691, paras 45–59.

82 Case 40/70, *Sirena v. Eda*, [1971] ECR 69, para. 16.

83 Case 238/87, *Volvo v. Veng*, [1988] ECR 6211, para. 8.

84 Joined Cases C-241 and 242/91 P, *RTE and ITP v. Commission ('Magill')*, [1995] ECR I-743, paras 52–6; Case C-418/01, *IMS Health*, [2004] ECR I-5039, paras 28–9, 38, 44–6, 49.

85 In this volume alone, see the contributions by Drexl, Heinemann and Conde Gallego, each with further references.

86 A summary of the jurisprudence on repackaging can be found in Case C-143/00, *Boehringer Ingelheim v. Swingward*, [2002] ECR I-3759, paras 12–16.

affix the trade mark.[87] By marketing the same product under different marks in different Member States the proprietor could, however, deprive parallel trade of much of its attraction: for want of the familiar brand, consumers might not grasp the opportunity to obtain the same goods more cheaply. The question thus arises whether parallel traders may use the trade mark which the product bears in the Member State of importation. The ECJ allows such relabelling if a number of conditions are met. The most important one in the present context is that the right-holder's refusal to allow parallel traders to use the same mark as in the Member State of importation must not lead to an 'artificial partitioning of the market'. This would be the case if otherwise 'effective market access' would be denied; parallel traders must not merely seek to 'secure a commercial advantage' by using the mark more familiar to consumers.[88]

The details are immaterial here; the underlying principles, however, can be applied to the assessment of refusals to license under Article 82. In the case of trade marks, the power of the right-holder to exclude others from the market is not necessarily rooted in the intrinsic superiority of his product. Legally, his power stems from the protection of the brand in the trade mark Acts, and factually, from consumers' tendency to plump for what they recognize (thanks to constant advertising) and from their reservations against the unfamiliar. The power to exclude is, in that sense, extraneous and accidental. So, too, is the protection afforded by a patent that has become the industry standard. This may have occurred because the proprietor enjoyed the first-mover advantage (as in *IMS Health*),[89] because there were network effects (as in *Microsoft*)[90] or because of sheer coincidence (as, arguably, in *Video cassette recorders*[91] or

---

[87] Case 3/78, *Centrafarm v. American Home Products*, [1978] ECR 1823, paras 11–14.

[88] Case C-143/00, *Boehringer Ingelheim v. Swingward*, [2002] ECR I-3759, paras 50–3; Joined Cases C-427 *et al.*/93, *Bristol Myers-Squibb*, [1996] ECR I-3457, paras 53 and 55; Case C-443/99, *Merck, Scharp & Dohme v. Paranova*, [2002] ECR I-3703. paras 25–8; most recently, see Opinion of AG Sharpston, Case C-348/04, *Boehringer Ingelheim et al. v. Swingward and Dowelhurst* ('*Boehringer II*'), [2007] ECR I-3391, *passim*, on the conditions of repackaging.

[89] Case C-418/01, *IMS Health*, [2004] ECR I-5039.

[90] European Commission of 24 March 2004, Case COMP/C-3/37.792 – *Microsoft*, C(2004)900 final = http://ec.europa.eu/comm/competition/antitrust/cases/decisions/37792/en.pdf, accessed 4 November 2007. The decision was upheld in substance by the CFI, see Case T-201/04, *Microsoft v. Commission*, [2007] ECR II-0000 (not yet reported).

[91] European Commission of 20 December 1977, Case IV/29.151 (78/156/EEC) – *Video cassette recorders*, OJ 1978 No. L 47, p. 42: competition between Philips's 'VHS' system and Sony's 'Betamax'.

Standard-Spundfass).[92] In both cases of exclusion from the market, through trade marks or through patents (at least market-standard patents), there is – in *that* respect – no 'competition on the merits' as required by the ECJ in *Michelin*.[93] To be sure, mere dominance, rather than a monopoly (in the technical sense) conferred by the standardization, will not suffice to assume 'exclusion' in this sense, and will not be a basis for imposing an obligation to license on the undertaking.

To find such an absence of competition engenders different consequences in the case of trade marks and of patents. In the repackaging cases, exhaustion has occurred, whereas in the case of a refusal to license, it has not. Article 28 EC gives parallel traders a *right* to ship goods between Member States;[94] in the absence of exhaustion, by contrast, the licence is a *privilege* usually only granted against consideration. Without readiness to pay, it cannot be demanded.

Even if the applicant is willing to pay for it, the licence may still be refused. This will be legal if the competence of the would-be licensee were in doubt; in this case, the refusal would not hinder technical or economic progress. At the same time, the refusal would not be excessive. Furthermore, the licensing conditions, especially the fee, must not be such as to deprive consumers of the benefit of the additional offer on the market. In other words, there must not be a minimum royalty such as to match the price of the competing product with that of the licensor. Lastly, for the refusal to be legal, there must still be substitutable technologies on the market so that not all competition would be quelled and a monopoly maintained or established. These are, of course, the criteria of Article 81(3) EC. For the reasons explained above, they are applicable to Article 82 as well.[95] This might also be a way to avoid the difficulties the ECJ has created with its opaque and largely *ad hoc* criteria in *IMS Health*.

4 Conclusion

Competition law, the internal market and intellectual property are entwined in

---

92 German Federal Supreme Court (BGH), judgment of 13 July 2004, Case K ZR 40/02, *Standard-Spundfass*, (2004) *GRUR*, 966 = *Standard Tight-Head Drum*, (2005) *IIC*, **36**, 741, at 746 (English translation).

93 Case 322/81, *Michelin v. Commission* ('*Michelin I*'), [1983] ECR 3461.

94 In a similar sense, the Court has held, regarding comparative advertising, that 'an advertiser cannot be regarded as taking unfair advantage of the reputation of the distinguishing marks of his competitor if effective competition on the relevant market is conditional upon a reference to those marks'; Case C-59/05, *Siemens v. VIPA*, [2006] ECR I-2147, para. 15.

95 Text preceding and following *supra* note 56.

several ways. Both competition law and the law governing the internal market face specific similar problems when reconciling their respective, interrelated aims with the requirements of the protection of intellectual property rights. These solutions are based on the same principles, however much they differ in their details.

17 The exhaustion/competition interface in EC law – is there room for a holistic approach?

Ole-Andreas Rognstad

1 Introduction

In European Community law, there are two main instruments for preventing territorial partitioning of markets for goods and services protected by intellectual property rights (IPRs). The first of these is the exhaustion principle (or first-sale doctrine), which was developed by the European Court of Justice (ECJ) during the early 1970s on the basis of the rules on free movement of goods under Articles 30 and 36 of the EEC Treaty (now Articles 28 and 30 EC). Today the principle also finds its legal basis in various Community directives and regulations in the field of IPR.[1] The second instrument is competition law, as the concept is understood under Articles 81 and 82 EC and the case law interpreting these provisions.

Generally speaking, the exhaustion principle states that once a product is put on the market in the European Community (or, by way of the EEA Agreement, the European Economic Area, including Norway, Iceland and Liechtenstein in addition to the EC countries) with the consent of the right-holder, the IPRs in

[1] For *trade marks*, see Article 7 First Council Directive 89/104/EEC of 21 December 1988 to approximate the laws of the Member States relating to trade marks, OJ 1989 No. L 40, p. 1, and Article 13 Council Regulation (EC) No. 40/94 of 20 December 1993 on the Community trade mark, OJ 1994 No. L 11, p. 1; for *computer programs*, see Article 4(c) Council Directive 91/250/EEC of 14 May 1991 on the legal protection of computer programs, OJ 1991 L 122, p. 42; for the *distribution right of performers and phonogram producers*, see Article 9 Council Directive 92/100/EEC of 19 November 1992 on rental right and lending right and on certain rights related to copyright in the field of intellectual property, OJ 1992 No. L 346, p. 61; for *databases*, see Articles 5(c) and 7(2)(b) Directive 96/9/EC of the European Parliament and of the Council of 11 March 1996 on the legal protection of databases, OJ 1996 No. L 77, p. 20; for *designs*, see Article 15 Directive 98/71/EC of the European Parliament and of the Council of 13 October 1998 on the legal protection of designs, OJ 1998 No. L 289, p. 28, and Article 21 Council Regulation (EC) No. 6/2002 of 12 December 2001 on Community designs, OJ 2002 No. L 3, p. 1; and for the *distribution right in copyright*, see Article 4(2) Directive 2001/29/EC of the European Parliament and of the Council of 22 May 2001 on the harmonization of certain aspects of copyright and related rights in the information society, OJ 2001 No. L 167, p. 10.

question are exhausted, and the holder of those rights is no longer entitled to invoke them in order to block imports from another Member State. This principle applies to all kinds of IPRs, and thus leaves – at least on the face of it – limited room for individual assessments depending on the kind of IPR that is involved. The exhaustion principle has its limits, however: first, at least with regard to trade marks, it does not apply to cases where two or more undertakings independently own, by way of assignment, the rights to the same trade mark in different territories of the EU/EEA.[2] Second, the exhaustion principle only applies to trade within the EC/EEA, leaving imports from countries outside this territory outside the scope of the principle.[3] The various Community directives (and regulations) go even further, in that they provide for EU/EEA-wide exhaustion only, in that the Member States are not even entitled to let the rights be subject to exhaustion by the sale of products outside the territory of EC/EEA.[4] Third, in relation to copyright and related rights, the exhaustion doctrine does not apply to the rental of (physical) copies of a work or other protected subject matter.[5] And fourth, the ECJ has long confirmed that the principle of exhaustion only applies to the distribution of goods, not services,[6] and as a consequence the EC Directive on Copyright in the Information Society explicitly states that the rights to communicate a work and to make available phonograms and the like to the public are not exhausted by an exercise of those rights – which *inter alia* means that no principle of exhaustion can apply to online transmissions.[7]

The second set of rules relevant to market partitioning is the competition provisions in Articles 81 and 82 EC. It is settled that the prohibition against anti-competitive co-operation in Article 81 regulates export and resale bans in licensing and distribution agreements, as well as contract clauses that empower the assignees or licensees to invoke IPRs in order to prevent the

---

2 Case C-9/93, *Ideal-Standard*, [1994] ECR I-2789.

3 See Case 51/75, *EMI v. CBS*, [1976] ECR 811, paras 8 *et seq.*; Case 270/80, *Polydor v. Harlequin*, [1982] ECR 329, paras 15–29.

4 Regarding trade marks, see Case C-355/96, *Silhouette*, [1998] ECR I-4799, and Case C-173/98, *Sebago*, [1999] ECR I-4103. See also Joined Cases 414–416/99, *Zino Davidoff and Levi Strauss*, [2001] ECR I-8691. For copyrights, see Case C-479/04, *Laserdisken*, [2006] ECR I-8089.

5 See Article 1 of the Rental and Lending Right Directive, *supra* note 1, See Dir. 1992/100, and the case law of the ECJ, Case 158/86, *Warner Brothers v. Christiansen*, [1988] ECR 2605; Case C-200/96; Case C-61/97, *Egmont Film*, [1998] ECR I-5171; *Metronome v. Music Point*, [1998] ECR I-1953.

6 Case 72/79, *Coditel v. Ciné-Vog Coditel v. Ciné-Vog* (‘*Coditel I*’), [1980] ECR 881.

7 Article 3(3) Information Society Directive, *supra* note 1.

distribution of goods or services from other countries.[8] Similarly, the prohibition against the abuse of dominant position (Article 82) may in certain cases apply to unilateral conduct of the proprietor contributing to territorial market partitioning.[9]

It follows that both the exhaustion principle (or non-exhaustion, as the case may be) and the competition rules may be relevant to territorial partitioning of the market. This is readily apparent. Not so obvious is the answer to the question: what else is there to the relationship between the two sets of rules? The question touches upon the general issue of to what extent Community rules on free movement of goods and services converge with competition rules,[10] but also has implications beyond this issue, as the treatment of imports from countries outside the EEA in the Community directives and regulations applies to a situation that is not covered by the free-movement rules.[11] In any case the exhaustion/competition interface is a question of convergence between the scope of IPRs and IP policy on the one hand and competition rules and policy on the other. In this respect the following analysis may provide interest even beyond the context of Community law, although the discussion will concentrate on the latter.

2 The traditional approach: the 'cumulation theory'

The relationship between the exhaustion principle and the competition rules in Community law has been subject to some debate in legal scholarship through the years. The dominant view seems to be that the two sets of rules do not converge, and that the question of whether the prerequisites of the two rules have been fulfilled must be considered separately and independently – or so the argument goes.[12] Under this approach the legal consequences are to be

---

8 See, *inter alia*, Joined Cases 54 and 56/64, *Consten and Grundig v. Commission*, [1966] ECR 299; Case 40/70, *Sirena v. Eda*, [1971] ECR 69; Case 28/77, *Tepea v. Commission*, [1978] ECR 1391; Case 258/78, *Nungesser v. Commission* ('*Maize Seeds*'), [1982] ECR 2053; Case 262/81, *Coditel v. Ciné-Vog Coditel v. Ciné-Vog* ('*Coditel II*'), [1982] ECR 3381; Case C-9/93, *supra* note 2.

9 See Case 24/67, *Parke, Davis and Co. v. Probel*, [1967] ECR 55; Case 40/70, *supra* note 8; Case T-198/98, *Micro Leader v. Commission*, [1999] ECR II-3989.

10 For a general discussion of the topic, see, for example, Mortelmans, K. (2001), 'Towards Convergence in the Application of the Rules on Free Movement and on Competition?', *C.M.L. Rev.*, **38**, 613.

11 *Supra* note 3.

12 See *inter alia* Turner, Jonathan D.C. (1983), 'Competition and the Common Market after Maize Seeds', *E.L. Rev.*, **8**, 103, at 114–17; Reindl, Andreas (1993), 'The Magic of Magill: TV Program Guides as a Limit of Copyright Law', *IIC*, **23**, 60, at 69–71. This seems to be the prevailing view in German legal scholarship; see, for example, Ebenroth, Carsten Thomas and Wolfgang Hübschle (1994), *Gewerbliche*

added to – not harmonized with – each other. They are, in other words, cumulative.[13] Thus, the IPRs may be exhausted independently of the validity of the proprietor's attempt to partition the market under the competition rules. Also, conversely, the attempts to compartmentalize the market may be condemned by competition law even though the IPRs in question are not exhausted.

Several arguments have been offered in favour of this form of separate and cumulative application. First, it is maintained that the principle of exhaustion and the competition rules pursue different objectives and that taking into consideration the one set of rules while applying the other may run contrary to these objectives. Some authors claim that while the principle of exhaustion pursues the fundamental goal of market integration, the same objective is only relevant under the competition rules to the extent that it leads to the improvement of production or distribution or technical or economic progress in the sense of Article 81(3) EC.[14] Similarly, several authors consider the non-exhaustion that occurs in relation to imports from third countries to be a form of protectionism that favours Community trade over non-Community trade, a fact that runs contrary to general competition law objectives (see section 6 below).

The exhaustion principle and the competition rules also target different audiences. The exhaustion principle limits the ability of the legislature (either of the Member States or, in relation to Community rights, also of the Community itself) to determine the scope of the rights granted to right-holders. The competition rules, on the other hand, regulate the market behaviour of undertakings. According to some scholars, this distinction makes the two sets of rules incompatible, thereby requiring separate consideration and application of each rule.[15]

The fact that the exhaustion principle originates from the rules on free movement of goods in Articles 28 and 30 of the Treaty rather than from the competition provisions has also led some scholars to advocate separate treat-

---

Schutzrechte und Marktaufteilung im Binnenmarkt der Europäischen Union, Heidelberg: Verlag Recht und Wirtschaft, pp. 138–48; Ullrich, Hanns (1997), 'Gewerblicher Rechtsschutz und Urheberrecht; Gemeinsame Forschung und Entwicklung', in Ulrich Immenga and Ernst Joachim Mestmäcker (eds), *EG-Wettbewerbsrecht*, Munich: C.H. Beck, pp. 1199–202 (paras 91–5).

13 Thus also the term 'cumulation theory'; see, for example, Schödermeier, Martin (1987), 'Die Ernte der Maissaat. Einige Anmerkungen zum Verhältnis von Art. 30 und 85 EWG Vertrag', *GRUR Int*, **36**, 85.

14 See Turner (*supra* note 12), at 116; Ebenroth and Hübschle (*supra* note 12), at 147.

15 See, for example, Koch, Norbert (1986), 'Article 30 and the Exercise of Intellectual Property Rights to Block Imports', *Fordham Corporate Law Institute*, **13**, 605; Reindl (*supra* note 12), at 69 *et seq.*

ment. Article 28 EC does not provide for a *de minimis* rule, whereas Article 81 does. This means that any minor restriction on the free movement of goods may be caught by the exhaustion doctrine, whereas only market behaviour with an appreciable effect on the market is subject to the competition rules. The difference of scope in this respect has also been put forward as an argument in favour of separate and cumulative application of the exhaustion principle and the competition rules.[16]

It has also been argued that the different effects of a judgment under the two sets of rules militate towards their separate application. A finding of exhaustion means that the IPRs may not be enforced. This, it has been held, is not a question of market behaviour, but of the scope of a legal position granted by state (or Community) authorities, and a judgment on exhaustion of rights will therefore also affect the rights of third parties that have not participated in the proceedings. On the other hand, a judgment that confirms a breach of competition law only affects the specific conduct of the undertaking concerned.[17]

Furthermore, the following statement by Advocate General Gulmann in the *Magill* case on the differences between Articles 28 and 30 on the free movement of goods and the prohibition against abuse of a dominant position under Article 82, may also be considered as an argument in favour of separate application of the principle of exhaustion and the competition rules: '[a]n analysis under Articles [28 and 30] is general and applies to every case subject to the rules in question while an analysis under Article [82] only relates to a specific case in respect of which account is taken of all the special circumstances surrounding it'.[18] The same statement could be made in relation to Article 81.

Finally, there are concerns about the nature of intellectual property rights and legal predictability. As IPRs affect the position of third parties, it is alleged that making the scope of the rights dependent on the validity of contracts under the competition law would 'wreak havoc on the requirement of legal certainty that underpins all property law'.[19] Thus, it can be held that the property nature of IPRs calls for a separate and cumulative application of the exhaustion principle and the competition rules.

---

[16] See, for example, Reindl (*supra* note 12), with reference to Joined Cases 177/82 and 178/82, *Van de Haar*, [1984] ECR 1797.

[17] Reindl (*supra* note 12), at 71. For a similar point related to the different effects of the rules on free movement of goods and the competition rules, see also Ullrich (*supra* note 12), at 1197 *et seq*. (para. 92).

[18] Joined Cases C-241/91 P and 242/91 P, *RTE and ITP v. Commission*, [1995] ECR 743, para. 43.

[19] Enchelmaier, Stefan, Chapter 16, in this volume, at section 3.4, with further discussion *ibid*.

The case law of the ECJ may at least to some extent seem to support the traditional view that the question of whether the prerequisites of the two sets of rules have been fulfilled must be considered separately and independently. In the *Nungesser* (‘*Maize Seeds*’) case, the Government of the UK advanced the view that a contract between two undertakings that impeded the freedom of importers to buy maize seeds in the country of an owner of breeders’ rights to the seeds, with a view to exporting them to the country of the licensee, could not be regarded as an agreement restrictive of competition contrary to Article 81(1) EC, as the products had been marketed in the first state with the consent of the right-holder, and were therefore subject to the exhaustion rule. The Court rejected the argument, holding that this view failed to take into account that the power of the Commission to enforce Article 81 was not affected by the fact that persons or undertakings subject to such restrictions were in a position to rely upon the free-movement-of-goods provisions in order to escape such restrictions.[20] In other words: the territorial export restrictions in contracts were not necessarily contrary to the competition rules even though the breeders’ rights were exhausted and could not be used to block import of the products into the territory of the licensee. This means, at the least, that the cumulative approach would apply in the situation where the rights are exhausted by way of the sale of products in the exporting country.

Whether this decision should be read as a general embracement of the ‘cumulation theory’ may, however, be subject to discussion. Even if it could, the desirability – and the necessity – of a system built on the view that the prerequisites for the exhaustion of IPRs and the competition rules should be considered separately, with the consequence that the rules are to be applied cumulatively, may be questioned. In the following, I will examine the arguments for the cumulative approach further, with a view to considering the potential for a more harmonized or convergent interpretation of the two sets of rules.

3 The alternative: a holistic approach

As the preceding discussion demonstrates, it is indisputable that in many areas the exhaustion principle and competition rules differ in terms of objectives and scope. However, it is not obvious that the consequence to be drawn from this fact is the separate and cumulative application of the two sets of rules. At least the overall problem to be solved by both can be identified as one: to what extent should the holder of an IPR be permitted to partition the market by preventing or blocking the distribution of goods and services from one terri-

---

20 Case 258/78, *Nungesser v. Commission* (‘*Maize Seeds*’), [1982] ECR 2053, paras 62 *et seq.*

tory to the other. The question concerns whether, and to what extent, intra-brand competition should be promoted, what the impact of the restrictions is on inter-brand competition and market integration, what the consequences in terms of market efficiency are, whether the interests of the proprietors are sufficiently secured and so on. A strong argument can be put forward in favour of one policy in this respect instead of several internally inconsistent policies. The fact that the policy may pursue different objectives is no argument for accepting that these different objectives lead to inconsistent results. Thus it is not so much a question of trying to formulate 'a grand unifying theory' according to which the Treaty generally seeks to ensure 'free trade in conditions of fair competition' as one author has put it,[21] but instead a question of how different aspects of the same problem may be solved in a manner that does not create inconsistencies.

In this scenario, IPRs may at all times be considered as tools to achieve the current EC policy on territorial restrictions. To the extent that territorial restraints are considered favourable in this respect, having taken into consideration all relevant circumstances, it should be possible to invoke IPRs in order to sanction such restraints, and vice versa.

This means that the proper function of IPRs in a Community context should not only be defined by traditional IPR concepts as the reward function in patent and copyright law and the origin function in trademark law, but also under the influence of the particular Community objectives of a common competition policy and market integration. The balancing point of the various objectives should represent the actual function of the IPR in a Community context, and should consequently be decisive to the extent the right-holder may (or may not) establish territorial restrictions for the distribution of goods and services in the Common Market. The way the ECJ has handled parallel imports from countries outside of the EEA (see section 6 below) is a good example of the appropriateness of this approach. The fact that the trademark holder, as a general rule, will be in a position to prevent parallel imports from third countries, but not from other EEA states, cannot possibly be explained through traditional concepts of trademark functions (such as the guarantee of the origin of the products). The only reasonable explanation for this result – whether one agrees with the ECJ on the legitimacy of the argument or not – is that IPRs are tools for the achievement of the EC policy towards territorial restrictions.[22]

A different question involves the relationship between the goals of market integration and economic efficiency in the European Union. It may be held

---

21 Reindl (*supra* note 12), at 69.
22 See further section 6 *infra*.

that these goals do not converge, as there are other concerns at stake in favour of a fully integrated market besides just efficiency. Others, however, claim that there is no necessary conflict, as market efficiency will lead to market integration in the end.[23] This problem will not be discussed further here. For the purposes of this chapter it suffices to point out that if in fact the two goals do not converge, this should for the sake of consistency also be reflected in the EC competition policy on territorial restraints, as it is not easy to see why market integration should only be promoted through provisions aiming at state measures and not also through provisions regulating private undertakings' behaviour with the same effects. The case law of the ECJ and the attitude of the EU Commission against 'absolute territorial protection' follow at least to some extent this approach,[24] and apart from the wording of Article 81 it is hard to find support for the view that market integration is relevant under the competition rules only to the extent that it leads to the improvement of production or distribution or technical or economic progress. On the other hand, in following this 'holistic view', the same arguments that promote a move towards a more economic approach to territorial restrictions in competition law, of which there are signs in the group exemptions on vertical agreements (Regulation 2790/1999) and technology transfer (Regulation 772/2004),[25] should be reflected in the way and the extent to which IPRs may be invoked in order to prevent imports from other Member States. Whether, or to what extent, such an approach may be reconciled with the present case law of the ECJ will be further analysed in sections 4 and 5.

In any event, it is difficult to see how the differences in scope between the principle of exhaustion and the competition rules noted above militate against this approach. Even though the two sets of rules target different audiences, it is possible to consider market-integration concerns when deciding on the validity of contractual restrictions in a licensing agreement under the competition rules, and to let economic arguments determine to what extent Member States may let the holder of IPRs invoke his rights to prevent the distribution

---

23 See Enchelmaier (*supra* note 19), at sections 1 and 3.2 for references to both views.

24 See Joined Cases 54 and 56/64, *Grundig and Consten v. Commission*, [1966] ECR 299; Case 28/77, *Tepea v. Commission*, [1978] ECR 1391, and Case 258/78, *Nungesser v. Commission* ('*Maize seeds*'), [1982] ECR 2053.

25 See further Waelbroeck, Denis (2006), 'Vertical Agreements: 4 Years of Liberalisation by Regulation n. 2790/99 after 40 Years of Legal (Block) Regulation', in Hanns Ullrich (ed.), *The Evolution of European Competition Law: Whose Regulation, Which Competition?*, Cheltenham, UK, and Northampton, MA, US: Edward Elgar, p. 85. See also Drexl, Josef, chapter 2, in this volume, at section 2.1.

of goods or services from other Member States.[26] Nor does the fact that the free-movement-of-goods provision in Article 28 EC leaves no room for a *de minimis* rule, whereas Article 81(1) does, compel the separate application of the exhaustion principle and the competition rules. The lack of a *de minimis* rule in Article 28 means that any minor restriction on parallel imports that results from the non-exhaustion of IPRs will constitute a trade restriction. Still, the question will be whether this restriction is justified in order to safeguard IPR interests under Article 30 of the EC Treaty. Thus, mere reference to the different scope of Articles 28 and 81 EC does not rule out the possibility of justifying a rule whereby the IPRs are not exhausted if the goods are sold into the importing state contrary to an export ban that only restricts competition to a minor extent and therefore falls outside the scope of Article 81.

There are also reasons for questioning the relevance, and even the appropriateness, of the statement that the provisions on the free movement of goods are abstract rules that apply to every case subject to the rules in question, in contrast to the competition rules, which only relate to a specific case. To be sure, the question under the free-movement provisions is basically whether a state measure prevents the movement of goods, services or persons within the European Union and if so whether this is justified on legitimate grounds, subject to the so-called proportionality test. The answer to this question will in principle affect all persons or undertakings subjected to the state measure. However, the proportionality test may well be constructed in such a way that the outcome of the balancing between free movement and public-policy interests (such as the interest in safeguarding IPRs) will depend on the facts of each case. The exhaustion principle may thus be viewed as a generally phrased outcome of the proportionality test application of which – exactly – depends on the facts of each case. The question of whether the products were put on the market within the EEA with the consent of the right-holder cannot possibly be answered without taking due consideration of the specific facts in each case. Against this background, it is hard to see why for example the assessment of whether the right-holder actually has consented to the marketing of the products in the importing state could not depend on the validity of a contractual territorial restriction under the competition rules. It is submitted that such a method would only add to a further refinement of the proportionality test inherent in the exhaustion principle, which provides for taking competition concerns into consideration when deciding whether a territorial restriction is

---

[26] Schödermeier, *supra* note 13, argues against the cumulation theory on the ground, *inter alia*, that the free-movement provisions also target private undertakings, and that the provisions consequently have third-party effects. This argument is in my opinion untenable; see also Ullrich, *supra* note 12, at 1202 (para. 94).

justified on grounds of safeguarding IPRs. The 'decentralized' system of enforcement of EC competition law resulting from Regulation 1/2004, including the competence of national authorities to apply Article 81(3), helps set the stage for such an approach.

This leaves us with the argument that IPRs are property rights in need of legal certainty since they affect the position of third parties, and that this position cannot, or should not, be affected by the validity of an *inter partes* arrangement. The status of IPRs as property rights has been fiercely debated over the years. Irrespective of this classification problem – which, in my view rightly, has been referred to as having 'a purely symbolic character', since the nature of IPRs should be examined by way of their real features and not as a postulate[27] – it cannot be disputed that legal certainty is at stake when the scope of the rights is determined.[28] Indeed, all IPRs reflect the tension between the need for legal certainty on the one hand and the need for suitable and just rules on the other. It is therefore hardly an exaggeration to claim that it is rare to find IP regimes that provide for legal certainty in all respects when it comes to the boundaries of the rights. As far as the third-party effects of an *inter partes* arrangement are concerned, it is hard to avoid concluding that the question of whether the right-holder has consented to the marketing of the product in question to some extent will depend on contractual relations. To consider the validity of a contract under competition rules when deciding whether the right-holder has consented to the marketing of the products represents, is in my opinion, no rarity in this respect.

In sum, I find the arguments put forward in favour of a cumulative and separate application of the exhaustion principle and the competition rules not very convincing. This, however – as shown – neither means that the free-movement provisions and the competition rules converge in all respects, nor does it imply that the alternative to a separate and cumulative application necessarily is that the principle of exhaustion and the competition rules will always lead to the same results.[29] The conclusion to be drawn is merely that the case for having rules on territorial restrictions that lead to an inconsistent policy does not seem compelling.

Indeed, as pointed out above, a solution whereby the exhaustion rule to a certain extent depends on the compliance of private parties' conduct with

---

[27] Geiger, Christophe (2006), 'Constitutionalising Intellectual Property Law', *IIC*, **37**, 371, at 376.

[28] See Enchelmaier, *supra* note 19, at section 3.4.

[29] In a recent Danish dissertation, my identical viewpoints expressed with reference to the Scandinavian discussion have been misinterpreted in this respect; cf. Danielsen, Jens Hartvig (2005), *Parallelhandel og varernes frie bevægelighed*, Copenhagen: Jurist- og Økonomforbundets Forlag, pp. 495 *et seq.*

competition law does not promote a high level of legal certainty. The desirability of such a solution must therefore depend on whether this is an acceptable price to pay for achieving a consistent legal regime.[30]

The potential for inconsistency under the cumulative approach is two-sided. On the one hand, as will be pointed out, a solution providing for exhaustion of the IPRs in question though territorial restrictions in contractual arrangements surrounding the IPRs are considered to comply with the competition rules implies an inconsistent policy to the extent that the reasons for accepting the territorial restraints converge with the arguments for justifying IPRs.[31] In situations in which exhaustion does not occur following the cumulative approach, on the other hand, condemning territorial restrictions under competition rules might lead to a similar inconsistency. This consequence can, to be sure, be avoided if the competition rules are applied to the conduct of the right-holder in the importing country, with the result that the IPRs cannot be invoked in order to block imports.[32] The prerequisites for applying the competition rules in this respect will, however, not always be fulfilled, and they do not in any case always lead to the same result as if the exhaustion principle were interpreted in compliance with the competition rules.[33] Inconsistencies are therefore likely to occur under the cumulative approach even in situations where the IPRs are not subject to exhaustion. In such situations, moreover, little is gained in terms of legal certainty by choosing the cumulative approach.

To conclude, in order to achieve a more consistent policy concerning territorial protection and parallel trade, it is at least worth considering abandoning the cumulation theory in favour of a more holistic or harmonized approach. The further implications of this approach will be explained in the following sections.

4 Contractual resale restrictions in intra-Community trade

The first situation we will look at in our analysis of the room for a more holistic approach to the exhaustion/competition interface involves distribution and licensing agreements that restrict a buyer's ability to resell goods. For example,

---

30 In this respect, there might be different opinions. According to Enchelmaier, *supra* note 19, at section 3.4, 'property law . . . would pay a high price for an insignificant simplification of the assessment under Articles 30 and 81 EC' if the solution suggested here were accepted. In my opinion, however, there is more to it than an 'insignificant simplification'; see the following arguments.

31 See section 4 *infra*.

32 See Joined Cases 54 and 56/64, *Grundig and Consten v. Commission*, [1966] ECR 299; Case 40/70, *Sirena v. Eda*, [1971] ECR 69; Case 51/75, *EMI v. CBS*, [1976] ECR 811.

33 See further section 5 *infra*.

a producer and right-holder *A* and an exclusive distributor *B* may agree that the latter is banned from selling the goods outside its territory. Alternatively, a licensing agreement may require that a licensee *D* has an obligation towards the licensor *C* to enter into distribution agreements only on condition that the distributor refrain from exporting the products.

Whether and to what extent the territorial restrictions are contrary to Article 81 EC may depend on additional circumstances. For the sake of simplicity, consider the following examples taken from the group exemptions. According to Article 4(b)(i) of the Block Exemption Regulation (BER) on Vertical Agreements,[34] the restriction of active sales into the exclusive territory reserved to the supplier or allocated by the supplier to another buyer is exempted from the prohibition against anti-competitive agreements in Article 81(1), provided *inter alia* that the market share held by the buyer does not exceed 30 per cent of the relevant market (Article 3). Similarly, in technology-transfer agreements between non-competitors each holding a market share that does not exceed 30 per cent, the Technology Transfer Block Exemption Regulation (TTBER)[35] exempts provisions whereby the licensee undertakes to pass on territorial restrictions on the distributors' active sale of products produced under the licence. Thus, it is evident that certain contractual restrictions concerning distributors' resale of products in given situations may comply with the competition rules.

If we look into the reasoning for exempting territorial restrictions of this kind, recital 6 of the BER on Vertical Agreements states that on a general basis:

> [v]ertical agreements of the category defined in this Regulation can improve economic efficiency within a chain of production or distribution by facilitating better coordination between the participating undertakings; in particular they can lead to a reduction in the transaction and the distribution costs of the parties and to an optimisation of their sales and investment levels.

The corresponding statement in the TTBER (recital 5) is that technology-transfer agreements will 'usually improve economic efficiency and be pro-competitive as they can reduce duplication of research and development, strengthen the incentive for the initial research and development, spur incremental innovation, facilitate diffusion and generate product market competition'.

---

[34] Commission Regulation (EC) No. 2790/1999 of 22 December 1999 on the application of Article 81(3) of the Treaty to categories of vertical agreements and concerted practices, OJ 1999 No. L 336, p. 21.

[35] Articles 2, 3 and 4(2) of the Commission Regulation (EC) No. 772/2004 of 27 April 2004 on the application of Article 81(3) of the Treaty to categories of technology transfer agreements, OJ 2004 No. L 123, p. 4.

Considering that resale bans on the said conditions contribute to the achievement of these goals, the question then is whether this should also be reflected in the IPRs. From the holistic viewpoint presented above, the improvement of economic efficiency should be part of the essential function of IPRs, and at the same time market integration concerns should be taken into consideration when exempting certain territorial restrictions in distribution and technology transfer agreements. Pursuing this reasoning further, it could be argued that holders of IPRs should be entitled to invoke their rights against imports in breach of contractual territorial restrictions that comply with the competition rules.[36]

The present legal framework, however, leaves no room for such a solution. It is clear that the principle of exhaustion will apply in the cases mentioned above, irrespective of the contractual territorial restraints and regardless of what kinds of IPRs are involved. In both examples, the products are sold with the consent of the right-holder. The contractual restrictions apply to the resale of the products, and at that stage the rights in the state of import are already exhausted.[37] As stated above, the *Nungesser* judgment of the ECJ confirms that the present legal situation calls for a cumulative application of the principle of exhaustion and the competition rules in the resale situation.[38] Whether this solution is justified could, however, be subject to discussion. In particular with regard to 'incentive-based' intellectual property rights, such as copyright, patents and designs, the arguments for accepting territorial restrictions in contracts under the competition rules should also be relevant in determining the scope of the rights. The fact that the right-holder in the import state will not be in a position to invoke his right in order to sanction territorial restrictions in distribution and licensing agreements that are believed to improve economic efficiency and have positive implications for the incentives to innovate might be considered to be an inconsistency in the EC policy on territorial restrictions in the trade with IPR-related products. At the very least, the present solution should find its justification in arguments in favour of the *de facto* weaker territorial protection that will result from the fact that the proprietor will only be in a position to sue for breach of contract, and not IPR infringement. As put forward above, I do not find the arguments in favour of a separate application of the exhaustion principle and the competition rules entirely convincing from a policy point of view.

---

36 This question must not be confused with the question under certain national regimes of the effect of contractual restrictions in IPR licences, for example, the German doctrine of '*dinglich wirkende Beschränkungen*' (restrictions with *erga omnes* effects). Such doctrines have no relevance under Community law.

37 See in particular Case C-16/03, *Peak Holding*, [2004] ECR I-11313, paras 50–6.

38 See section 2 *supra*.

5 Direct export/import restrictions in intra-Community trade

The second type of situation involves a product imported directly from the producer and right-holder in another Member State in breach of an export ban in a licensing or an assignment agreement. Consider first the licensing situation. For example, the licensee *D*, who holds rights in State *X*, sells the products in State *Z* in conflict with its contractual obligations not to compete with licensor *C*, or alternatively licensee *E*, who holds exclusive rights in State *Z*. Export bans in licensing agreements are even more likely to comply with competition rules than bans on resale by distributors.[39] The case law of the ECJ gives no clear answer as to whether the exhaustion principle applies in situations of direct exports from the right-holder in one Member State into the territory of another. Different views prevail in the legal scholarship. In favour of exhaustion, the view has been put forward that the rights are exhausted through the granting of the licence itself,[40] despite the fact that the view is hard to reconcile with the very phrasing of the principle – that the products are put on the market with the consent of the right-holder. A different argument leading to the same result is that a contractual restriction in licensing agreements on where the products are put on the market does not conclusively determine whether the products are put on the market with the consent of the right-holder.

In favour of the solution that the rights are not exhausted in the case of direct exports/imports, some authors have maintained that the principle of exhaustion requires that the product be put on the market in the state of export.[41] A more obvious and plausible argument, in my opinion, is that the proprietors' consent to the sale is lacking in cases in which the products are sold into the territory of the licensor or a different licensee in conflict with the terms of the licensing agreement.

There is a middle solution, however, which builds its argument on the latter view, but which takes the results under the competition law into consideration in accordance with the holistic view presented above: the IPRs in question are not exhausted unless the export ban is contrary to the compe-

---

39 See again Articles 2 and 4(1)(c)(iv) and (v) and 4(2)(b)(i) and (ii) TTBER read together.

40 See, for example, Johannes, Hartmut (1976), *Industrial Property and Copyright in European Community Law*, Leyden: A.W. Sijthoff, p. 74; Hoffmann, Dieter and Orlagh O'Farrell (1984), 'The "Open Exclusive License" – Scope and Consequences', *EIPR*, **8**, 104, at 108.

41 See Reindl, Andreas (1997), 'Intellectual Property and Intra-Community Trade', *Fordham Int'l L.J.*, **20**, 819, at 839. This understanding seems, moreover, to be the prevailing interpretation in German legal scholarship.

tition rules.[42] Fundamentally, the licence agreement represents a consent to the distribution of the goods, so that the sale of the products from licensee *D* into the territory of the licensor *C* or another licensee *E* must be considered to have been carried out with the consent of the right-holder, unless there is a valid restriction concerning where the products are to be put on the market. If the export ban complies with the competition rules, for example it is covered by the group exemption of the TTBER, such a valid restriction exists whereby the goods should not be considered to have been put on the market with the consent of the right-holder. If on the contrary the export ban is in breach of and invalid under Article 81 (or 82) EC, the ground for denying consent to the sale lapses, whereby the sale contrary to the invalid export ban should be considered to have been carried out with the consent of the right-holder.

This solution provides for a consistent policy on parallel imports in the European Community (EEA). The fact that it is conceptually incorrect to speak of a conflict of norms in the relationship between the principle of exhaustion (free movement of goods) and competition rules[43] should not lead to the conclusion that it is irrelevant to take compliance of export bans with competition rules into consideration when deciding whether a product is put on the market with the consent of the right-holder. A solution whereby the right-holder in the importing state (licensor *C* or licensee *E*) may invoke its IPRs in order to prevent a sale in breach of the export ban despite the fact that this clause is invalid under the competition rules should not be considered as inconsistent on a norm level. However, the consistency of such a solution on a policy level should be questioned. Whether the ECJ will accept the approach suggested here is, however, still an open question. In the *Nungesser* case, where licensed products were put on the market with the consent of the right-holder,[44] the ECJ did opt for a supplementary application of the competition rules to export restrictions in a licensing agreement. However, this is not tantamount to the Court's refusal to take account of the same rules when considering whether the right-holder has consented to the sale of products in breach of such export restrictions.

It has been suggested that the problem of direct imports and restrictions in licensing agreements (see section 4 *supra*) could be solved by an analysis

---

42 In this direction, see Tritton, Guy (2002), *Intellectual Property in Europe*, 2nd ed., London: Sweet and Maxwell, p. 656, however, differently in Tritton, Guy (2008), *Intellectual Property in Europe*, 3rd ed., London: Sweet & Maxwell, pp. 677–8. See also Massaguer, José (1989), *Mercado Común y Patente Nacional*, Barcelona: Libreria Bosch, pp. 323 *et seq.*; Metzger, Axel (2001), 'Erschöpfung des urheberrecthlichen Verbreitungsrechts bei vertikalen Vertriebsbindungen', *GRUR*, **103**, 210, at 213 *et seq.*

43 See, for example, Ullrich, *supra* note 12, at 1199.

44 See section 2 *supra*.

similar to that used in the *Ideal-Standard* case.[45] In that case the ECJ confirmed that the exhaustion of trademark rights does not apply to a situation where the trademark (i) has been assigned (ii) within a limited territory of the Member States (iii) to an undertaking which has no economic link with the assignor and (iv) the assignor opposes the assignee's efforts to market the trademarked product in the state in which the assignor has retained its trademark rights.[46] The ECJ held that this situation had to be distinguished from the case in which the imported products come from a licensee or a subsidiary, as a contract of assignment does not give the assignor any means of controlling the quality of products that are marketed by the assignee. Thus, the Court held:[47]

> [T]he consent implicit in any assignment is not the consent required for application of the doctrine of exhaustion of rights. For that, the owner of the right in the importing State must, directly or indirectly, be able to determine the products to which the trade mark may be affixed in the exporting State and to control their quality. That power is lost if, by assignment, control over the trade mark is surrendered to a third party having no economic link with the assignor.

On the other hand, the Court also stated that 'where the undertakings independent of each other make trademark assignments following a market-sharing agreement, the prohibition of anti-competitive agreements under Article [81] applies'. This would not mean, however, that Article 81 could be applied 'mechanically' to every assignment, because it would be necessary to analyse the context, the commitments underlying the assignment, the intention of the parties and the consideration for the assignment before concluding that the assignment agreement was anti-competitive contrary to Article 81.[48]

In my opinion, there is an important distinction between applying Article 81 in the '*Ideal-Standard* situation' and applying the same provision to export bans in licensing agreements. In the *Ideal-Standard* case, the very foundation of the market-sharing arrangement would be assignment of the rights. If the assignment were found to be void under the competition rules, the holder of the rights in the importing country (Ideal-Standard GmbH) would not be in a position to block imports, as the rights in the exporting country would then be owned by the French subsidiary of the same company. The lack of compliance of export prohibitions in licensing agreements with the competition rules, on

---

45 Case C-9/93, *Ideal-Standard*, [1994] ECR I-2789.

46 *Ibid.*

47 *Ibid.*, at para. 43. Whether the same applies to assignments of other IPRs is a question not yet settled by case law.

48 *Ibid.*, at para. 59.

the other hand, would not in itself deprive the right-holder of the ability to block imports. Under the cumulative approach, this will only lead to the invalidity of the contract clause, whereas the right-holder in the importing country will still be in a position to invoke his IPRs to prevent imports from the right-holder in the exporting country, given that the IPRs are not exhausted by way of the direct sale. If the right-holder in the importing country is a licensee (*E*), it would indeed be possible to attack the licensing agreement under Article 81.[49] If, on the contrary, the licensor himself (*C*) holds the rights in the importing country, the import restriction will not be the result of an agreement, but merely of the IPR granted by the state (or the Community), whereby Article 81 is not applicable. Unless the licensor holds a dominant position in the market so that his conduct could be caught by Article 82, he would – under the cumulative approach – be in a position to invoke the IPRs to prevent the imports of products, even though the export ban would conflict with Article 81.

In conclusion, it may be alleged that only the possibility of a simultaneous application of the exhaustion principle and the competition rules – so that fulfilment of the consent criteria depends on whether the consent given complies with the competition rules – will provide for a fully consistent legal regime as far as direct imports are concerned. This solution, moreover, does not exclude the possibility of in certain cases supplementing the exhaustion rule with the competition rules, that is applying the latter with the result that the right-holder in the importing country is no longer in a position to block imports, even though the rights are not exhausted. This was the method applied by the ECJ in the *Ideal-Standard* scenario, and does not lead to policy inconsistencies.

6 Extra-territorial imports/exports

Ever since the *EMI v. CBS* case of 1976[50] and definitely since the *Polydor* case of 1982,[51] it has been clear from the case law of the ECJ that the exhaustion principle does not apply to imports from countries outside the EU, simply for the reason that the EC Treaty's rules on free movement of goods solely apply to intra-Community trade. In 1998, the ECJ went a step further in the context of the Trade Mark Directive. In the well-known *Silhouette* case, the Court held that the exhaustion rule in Article 7(1) of the Directive should be interpreted to exclude a principle of international exhaustion. National rules cannot provide for the exhaustion of trade-mark rights on products marketed outside

---

49 See, for example, Cases 54 and 56/64, *Grundig and Consten v. Commission*, [1966] ECR I-2789.

50 Case 51/75, *EMI v. CBS*, [1976] 811.

51 Case 270/80, *Polydor v. Harlequin*, [1982] ECR 329.

the EEA by the proprietor or with his consent.[52] In the recent *Laserdisken* decision, the ECJ confirmed that Article 4(2) of the Information Society Directive is to be interpreted in the same way.[53] Although the ECJ has not yet dealt with the question in the context of other IPRs, it is reasonable to assume that the similar provisions in the Design Directive (and Regulation) along with the Computer Program and Database Directives will be interpreted in the same way.[54]

Although this principle of exclusively EEA-wide exhaustion has been considered as pursuing protectionist purposes – creating a 'fortress Europe'[55] – such an approach actually finds no support in the reasoning of the ECJ. Indeed, one could question the true protectionism of a solution that puts multinational companies of non-European origin such as Microsoft or Sony in a position to prevent parallel imports from outside the EEA. The fact is, in any case, that the ECJ – interestingly enough – has proffered market-integration concerns against parallel imports from outside the EEA, stating that the principle of regional exhaustion 'is the only interpretation which is fully capable of ensuring that the purpose of the Directive is achieved, namely to safeguard the functioning of the internal market', and that 'a situation in which some Member States could provide for international exhaustion while others provided for Community exhaustion only would inevitably give rise to barriers to the free movement of goods and the freedom to provide services'.[56] The legitimacy of this statement will not be further discussed here, as our concern is the relationship between the principle of regional exhaustion and the EC competition rules.

It follows from the case law of the ECJ that export bans and territorial restrictions even in extra-Community trade may be caught by Article 81(1), as long as they are capable of affecting the trade between Member (and EEA) States to an appreciable extent. In the *Javico* judgment, decided three months prior to the *Silhouette* decision, the ECJ found that a clause in a selective distribution agreement obliging the German distributor to sell products only in

---

52 Case C-355/96, *Silhouette*, [1998] ECR I-4799; see also Cases C-173/98, *Sebago*, [1999] ECR I-4103, and Joined Cases C-414–416/99, *Dino Davidoff and Levi Strauss*, [2001] ECR I-8691.

53 Case C-479/04, *Laserdisken*, [2006] ECR I-8089.

54 In the Case of Article 4(c) of the Computer Program Directive, the outcome has been confirmed by the CFI in Case T-198/98, *Micro Leader v. Commission*, [1999] ECR II-3989, paras 34 and 54.

55 See, for example, Joller, Gallus (1998), 'Zur territorialen Reichweite des Erschöpfungsgrundsatzes im Markenrecht: Silhouette einer Zwischenbilanz', *GRUR Int*, **47**, 751, at 758 *et seq.*

56 Case C-355/96, *Silhouette*, [1998] ECR I-4799, para. 27.

territory outside the Community (Russia, Ukraine, Slovenia), did not by its very nature infringe Article 81(1), but that it nevertheless could have an anti-competitive effect. This might be the case, the Court held:[57]

> [w]here the Community market in the products in question is characterised by an oligopolistic structure or by an appreciable difference between the prices charged for the contractual product within the Community and those charged outside the Community and where, in view of the position occupied by the supplier of the products at issue and the extent of the supplier's production and sales in the Member States, the prohibition [against the re-importation of the products into the Community] entails a risk that it might have an appreciable effect on the pattern of trade between Member States such as to undermine attainment of the objectives of the common market.

The Court's attitude to (re-)export bans from outside the Community in the *Javico* judgment may possibly be considered as less restrictive than its attitude towards export bans in intra-Community trade, and it has been suggested that the decision must be read in light of the fact that the Court at that time foresaw the outcome of the *Silhouette* case. A more plausible assumption is, in my opinion, that the Court takes a more economic approach to parallel imports from outside the Community because the market-integration concerns that lie behind the stricter attitude to parallel import restrictions in intra-Community trade are not at stake here.

Considered from a different point of view, *Javico* may seem to imply a policy inconsistency vis-à-vis the outcome of *Silhouette* and *Sebago*, because it allows national and Community authorities to initiate actions to restrict parallel imports from outside the Community despite the seemingly hostile attitude to such parallel imports inherent in the principle of EEA-wide exhaustion. Again, however, the policy inconsistency depends on the relationship between the principle of (non-)exhaustion and the competition rules. If the same standpoint is taken in relation to imports from third countries as was suggested above with regard to direct imports in intra-Community trade, policy inconsistencies are avoided as this opens the way for a comprehensive solution to parallel imports from third countries. This means that sale of products contrary to export bans from third countries to the Community (EEA) that are in breach of Article 81(1) EC should be seen as having been carried out with the consent of the right-holder.

Indeed, the ECJ left limited room in the *Davidoff* judgment for a doctrine of 'implied consent' – meaning 'deemed consent' – under Article 7(1) of the Trade Mark Directive. There, the Court held that although it is sometimes

---

[57] Case C-306-96, *Javico*, [1998] ECR I-1983, paras 18–24.

acceptable to imply consent to the marketing within the EEA of products that were previously marketed outside the EEA, such as when it followed from facts and circumstances that the trade-mark proprietor had renounced her right to oppose placing the goods on the market within the EEA, consent cannot be inferred from the mere silence of the proprietor. Thus, even if the proprietor fails to communicate his opposition to the marketing of the products in the EEA to all subsequent purchasers of the goods, even if the goods carry no label warning of this marketing prohibition and even if the trade-mark proprietor does not impose any contractual reservations, these facts do not amount to sufficient evidence to prove the proprietor's consent to the marketing of the goods within the EEA.[58]

The matter dealt with here, however, is of a different nature, as the question is not whether a consent to marketing within the EEA can be implied from the behaviour of the right-holder, but rather whether an express but invalid prohibition against sales within the EEA should be considered when deciding whether the right-holder has consented to the marketing of the goods there. Consistent with the reasoning described in section 4 above, where the territorial restriction is in breach of (and therefore invalid under) the competition rules, weight should be placed on the fact that the right-holder has consented to the marketing of the goods, and not the geographical scope of this consent. The same should be the case where the distribution or licensing agreement contains no express prohibition against exports into the EEA, but the right-holder in other ways has acted in order to prevent such exports, contrary to Article 81(1). This amounts to the simultaneous application of the principle of EEA-wide exhaustion and the competition rules.

In addition, the competition rules may supplement the principle of EEA-wide exhaustion, in the sense that the right-holder's behaviour surrounding the invoking of his IPRs in order to prevent imports into the EEA may come into conflict with Articles 81 or 82 (compare sections 4 and 5 above). In the *EMI v. CBS* case from 1976, the ECJ held that the exercise of trade-mark rights might fall within the ambit of Articles 81 or 82 if it were to manifest itself as the subject, the means or the consequence of a restrictive practice. The Court stated that an agreement between traders within the Common Market and competitors in third countries that would bring about an isolation of the Common Market and reduction in the supply of products originating in third countries might affect adversely the conditions of competition within the Common Market.[59]

---

[58] Joined Cases 414–416/99, *Zino Davidoff and Levi Strauss*, [2001] ECR I-8691, paras 55–7.

[59] Case 51/75, *EMI v. CBS*, [1976] ECR 811, paras 27 *et seq*.

In its *Micro Leader* judgment of 1999,[60] the CFI confirmed the potential for supplementary application of the competition rules to the principle of EEA-wide exhaustion only, as it annulled the decision of the Commission rejecting a parallel importer's (Micro Leader's) complaint against the actions of Microsoft France and Microsoft Corporation seeking to prevent French-language editions of Microsoft software packages marketed in Canada from being imported into France. Although the CFI found that Microsoft's rights under Article 4(c) of the Computer Program Directive were not exhausted by the marketing in Canada, it held that the Commission had failed to carry out the necessary investigation of whether its market behaviour nevertheless was contrary to Article 82 of the Treaty. The Court noted that factual evidence put forward by MicroLeader indicated that Microsoft had applied lower prices in the Canadian market than in the Community market and that the Community prices were excessive. In the CFI's opinion, the Commission was therefore not right to conclude that Microsoft had merely enforced its copyright according to the Computer Program Directive since the rights were not exhausted, but should have carried out a further analysis of whether Microsoft's market behaviour – including its enforcement of copyright – constituted a breach of Article 82 under the particular circumstances of the case. The approach of the CFI is, in this author's view, undoubtedly the right one.

In conclusion, the principle of EEA-wide exhaustion does not reflect the whole picture of the EC policy of parallel imports from third countries, because it has to be considered in the context of the competition rules. It should be noted that the reasoning behind the principle of EEA-wide exhaustion does not conflict with the simultaneous and supplementary application of the competition rules. The main concern of the ECJ in the *Silhouette* and *Laserdisken* judgments was to ensure a uniform policy on parallel imports from third countries, in order to prevent restrictions on intra-Community trade as a result of different exhaustion rules in the various Member States. The simultaneous and supplementary application of the competition rules represents no threat in this respect. On the contrary, it may be asserted that the combination of the principle of non-exhaustion and the competition rules – if applied as suggested here – leaves room for a more economics-oriented approach to the parallel-import problem than is the case in intra-Community trade, where the policy to a large extent is determined by market-integration concerns. Whether the principle of EEA-wide exhaustion is compatible with market integration concerns on a more global level is a matter best left for another day.

60 Case T-198/98, *Micro Leader v. Commission*, [1999] ECR II-3989.

7 'Non-exhaustible' copyrights

As mentioned in my introductory remarks, both the case law of the ECJ and the EC Directives on copyright and neighbouring rights show that various 'rights' in this field are not subject to exhaustion. To put it differently: it is the distribution right that is subject to exhaustion, not the right of rental, the reproduction right, the right of communication to the public or the right of public performance.[61]

Also with respect to these rights, the case law of the ECJ confirms that the competition rules at least may supplement the rules of non-exhaustion. In *Coditel II*,[62] the Court opened the door to applying Article 81 EC to territorially restricted licences for the TV broadcast of films, although it had two years earlier, in *Coditel I*, found that the broadcasting right was not subject to a principle of exhaustion under the Treaty rules on free movement of services (Article 49).[63] The Court in both *Coditel* judgments emphasized that the copyright-holder in a film has a legitimate interest in calculating the fees for the actual or probable number of performances. This implies that a principle of exhaustion for TV broadcasts would run contrary to this objective. Nevertheless, the Court left open the possible application of Article 81 to the territorial partitioning of national markets for the broadcasting of films. The Court stated: 'where there are economic or legal circumstances the effect of which is to restrict film distribution to an appreciable degree or to distort competition on the cinematographic market, regard being had to the specific characteristics of the market'.[64] Similarly, the exercise of the copyright-holder's exclusive right of rental[65] is also likely to be subject to the competition rules, depending on the economic or legal circumstances of the case.[66] As regards online transmissions, the EC Commission has on several occasions initiated proceedings against 'one-stop-shop' clauses in reciprocal agreements between collecting societies, which require the clearance of multi-territorial licences in the 'country of destination' only, claiming that this system elimi-

---

61 See *supra* notes 5–7.

62 Case 262/81, *Coditel v. Ciné-Vog* ('*Coditel II*'), [1982] ECR 3381.

63 Cases 72/79, *Coditel v. Ciné-Vog Coditel v. Ciné-Vog* ('*Coditel I*'), [1980] ECR 881.

64 Case 262/81, *Coditel v. Ciné-Vog Coditel v. Ciné-Vog* ('*Coditel II*'), [1982] ECR 3381, para. 17.

65 See Article 1 of the Rental and Lending Right Directive, *supra* note 1.

66 In Case C-61/97, *Egmont Film*, [1998] ECR I-5171, para. 9, the ECJ dismissed the order for reference from the Danish court on the compatibility with Articles 81 and 82 of the exclusive right of rental under the Rental Directive on the ground that the court had failed to provide the ECJ with sufficient information as to the effect of those Articles in connection with the matters of fact and law in the main proceedings.

nates price competition between collecting societies in the European Market.[67] In this respect, the competition rules may serve as tools to ensure market integration and intra-brand competition in the market for online transmission of copyright work, despite the fact that the copyright-holder's exclusive right to such transmission (communication to the public) is not subject to any principle of exhaustion comparable to that which applies to the distribution of goods within the Common Market (EEA).[68]

8 Concluding remarks

Whether market partitioning of IPR-protected goods or services is provided for by the state granting territorial protection to IPR holders or through the market behaviour of the proprietors, the issues involved are the same. The notion of competition law and IP law as conflicting areas, and competition law as something quite apart from the free movement of goods in this respect, represents an obstacle to a comprehensive and consistent policy on territorial restrictions in the Common Market. To the extent that territorial partitioning of markets is deemed to have a positive impact after an overall consideration of the different policy issues involved, the presumption is that the proprietor should be allowed to impose such restrictions, be it through contractual arrangements, unilateral conduct or enforcement of its IPRs. Conversely, to the extent that territorial restrictions are considered to have a negative impact in this respect, the proprietor should not be given instruments for the territorial partitioning of the market.

This does not necessarily mean that a situation in which the proprietor can only enforce territorial protection by way of contract provisions, and not by its

---

[67] See European Commission Decision of 8 October 2002, Case COMP C2/38.014 – *IFPI* ('*Simulcasting*'), [2003] OJ L 107/58. In this decision the Commission granted an exemption under Article 81 EC despite the fact that the IFPI Simulcasting Agreement provides for a one-stop shop based on the country-of-destination principle for calculating royalties. However, the Commission only did so as the Agreement leaves it to the user to choose between different national societies for the grant of a licence. This creates at least some price competition with regard to administrative costs. See also the Commission's Statement of Objections to the so-called *Santiago Agreement* of 29 April 2004, COMP C2/38.126; see Press Release IP/04/586 of 3 May 2004, http://europa.eu/rapid/pressReleasesAction.do?reference=IP/04/586&format=HTML&aged=0&language=EN&guiLanguage=en, accessed 4 November 2007, resulting in the Commission's Notice pursuant to Article 27(4) of Reg. 1/2003, [2005] OJ C 200/11; and its more recent Statement of Objections against the CISAC model contract, Case COMP C2/38.698, press release MEMO/06/63 of 7 February 2006, http://europa.eu/rapid/pressReleasesAction.do?reference=MEMO/06/63&format=HTML&aged=0&language=EN&guiLanguage=en, accessed 4 November 2007.

[68] Article 3(3) of the Information Society Directive, *supra* note 1.

IPRs, implies a policy inconsistency. But the explanation for why this would be the case should lie in the breadth of the territorial protection needed in order to pursue the policy considerations at stake, and not in the different legal bases of the principle of exhaustion and the competition rules. Indeed, it is hard to see a justification for the possible situation where a proprietor's attempts to partition the market are deemed unlawful under the competition rules, whereas he is nevertheless entitled to enforce his IPRs to prevent imports from other Member States.

This approach leads to the following scheme for the overlap between the principle of exhaustion and the competition rules: in cases where the exhaustion principle applies, there should be two options. In the first, the applicability of the principle should depend on whether the goods are sold in accordance with territorial restrictions in licensing or distribution agreements, or by unilateral conduct on the part of the proprietor, both in compliance with the competition rules (entailing simultaneous application of the exhaustion principle and the competition rules). In the second option, the exhaustion occurs irrespective of the compliance of the proprietor's conduct with the competition rules, as a result of a conscious policy choice with respect to the breadth of the territorial protection desired. Similarly, in cases where the exhaustion principle does not apply, there are two options. Either the application of the non-exhaustion rule should depend on whether territorial restrictions in licensing (or assignment) agreements, or the unilateral conduct on the part of the right-holder, comply with the competition rules (simultaneous application of the exhaustion principle and the competition rules); or the proprietor's position to invoke the IPRs under the non-exhaustion rule should be subject to scrutiny under the competition rules (application of the competition rules supplementary to the non-exhaustion rule).

The holistic approach presented here suggests that for the sake of policy consistency, the principle of exhaustion and the competition rules must always be read in close context, although they are separate pieces of legislation with different conditions and ambits. Their legal consequences should be harmonized, in the sense that the one hand knows what the other hand is doing. The separate application of the two sets of rules should, according to this approach, never be the point of departure for an assessment of whether the conditions under the respective rules are fulfilled. It may well, however, be one of the possible legal consequences after a comprehensive assessment of the matter.

Even though this analysis has been carried out in the context of European Community law, it is possible to address the issue of convergence between IP and competition rules on territorial restrictions and parallel imports at a broader level. To the extent that a legal framework for dealing with these issues will be developed under WTO/TRIPS in the future, it is to be hoped that the stage is set for a more comprehensive policy in this respect than the European experience shows us.

18 Competition policy and intellectual property in the WTO: more guidance needed?

*Robert D. Anderson**

1 Introduction

Recognition of the legitimate role of competition policy vis-à-vis intellectual property rights (IPRs) and licensing practices is an important element of the overall balance embodied in the WTO Agreement on Trade-Related Intellectual Property Rights (TRIPS). The relevant provisions acknowledge that 'licensing practices or conditions pertaining to intellectual property rights which restrain competition may have adverse effects on trade and may impede the transfer and dissemination of technology' and stipulate that WTO Members 'may adopt, consistently with the other provisions of this Agreement, appropriate measures to prevent or control' practices constituting 'abuse[s] of intellectual property rights having an adverse effect on competition in the relevant market'.[1] As examples of such practices, the Agreement refers to exclusive grant-back conditions, conditions preventing challenges to validity and coercive package licensing.[2] These provisions reflect concerns regarding the potential anti-competitive effects of IPRs protected under the Agreement that were expressed particularly by developing countries during the negotiation of the Agreement in the course of the Uruguay Round of multilateral trade negotiations.[3]

* The chapter has been prepared strictly in the author's personal capacity. The views expressed must *not* be attributed to the WTO, its Secretariat, or any of its Member governments.

1 See Article 40(2) TRIPS. In addition, Article 8(2) provides that 'Appropriate measures, provided that they are consistent with the provisions of this Agreement, may be needed to prevent the abuse of intellectual property rights by right holders or the resort to practices which unreasonably restrain trade or adversely affect the international transfer of technology'. The scope and content of these provisions are discussed further, below.

2 Article 40(2) TRIPS. There is no suggestion that this list is exhaustive; on the contrary, Article 40(2) is explicitly couched in non-exhaustive terms (the Agreement states only that such practices 'may include' the practices mentioned).

3 See, for background and discussion, World Trade Organization (1997), 'Special Study on Trade and Competition Policy,' in *Annual Report of the World Trade Organization for 1997*, Geneva: WTO, chapter IV; Anderson, Robert D. (2002),

The competition-related provisions of the TRIPS Agreement, while representing an essential element of balance in the Agreement, also leave important questions unanswered. For example, they do not define the basis on which practices may be deemed to be anti-competitive – that is, the evaluative standards to be employed. The full set of practices that may be deemed anti-competitive (beyond the three examples mentioned) is left undefined. The Agreement also provides little in the way of guidance regarding the remedies that may be adopted in particular cases, beyond making clear that any measures adopted must be consistent with other provisions of the Agreement.[4]

Whether the lack of guidance provided by the TRIPS Agreement regarding these questions is a problem can be debated. Frederick Abbott, for one, argues that the broad discretion for governments in the design and implementation of competition policies vis-à-vis intellectual property that results from the wording of the current provisions serves the best interests of developed and developing countries alike and, therefore, that no amendment to the Agreement or development of parallel rules on anti-competitive practices in relation to IP is warranted.[5]

However, even if no amendment to the TRIPS Agreement as such or development of parallel binding rules is deemed to be desirable or feasible in the current circumstances, there could be merit in a policy analysis and development exercise at the multilateral level to consider the relationship between competition policy and IPRs. The question of possible guidelines – whether of a binding or non-binding nature – could be addressed in that context. Certainly, there are reasons for believing that there are costs associated with the dearth of guidance for WTO Member countries regarding the optimal application of competition policy in this area (see detailed discussion in section 3, below). In brief, the application of competition policy vis-à-vis intellectual property is one of the more complex and technically challenging sub-fields of such policy. In the absence of appropriate guidance, WTO

'Intellectual Property Rights, Competition Policy and International Trade: Reflections on the Work of the WTO Working Group on the Interaction between Trade and Competition Policy', in Thomas Cottier and Petros Mavroidis (eds), *Intellectual Property: Trade, Competition and Sustainable Development*, Ann Arbor: University of Michigan Press, chapter 17; and Abbott, Frederick M. (2004), 'Are the Competition Rules in the WTO TRIPS Agreement Adequate?', *J.I.E.L.*, **7**, 687.

4 Anderson, *supra* note 3; see also Anderson, R.D. and H. Wager (2006), 'Human Rights, Development and the WTO: The Cases of Intellectual Property Rights and Competition Policy', *J.I.E.L.*, **9**, 707.

5 Abbott, *supra* note 3; see also Abbott, Frederick M. (2005), 'The "Rule of Reason" and the Right to Health: Integrating Human Rights and Competition Principles in the Context of TRIPS', in Thomas Cottier, Joost Pauwelyn and Elisabeth Burgi Bonanomi (eds), *Human Rights and International Trade*, Oxford: Oxford University Press, p. 279. Abbott's position is discussed further, below.

Members lacking experience, particularly developing countries, may well find it difficult to implement appropriate enforcement policies in this area. In addition, as will be elaborated below, there are potential negative externalities or spillovers associated with differing national standards in this area. For example, remedies imposed in one jurisdiction may impinge on behaviour (and potentially on economic welfare) in other jurisdictions. A particularly acute example of this concern relates to situations in which remedies imposed in one jurisdiction require the sharing of proprietary information. In such cases, it may be difficult to prevent the information disclosed (or products manufactured using such information) from 'leaking' across borders.[6]

To be sure, even if it is deemed desirable to provide additional guidance for WTO Members regarding these questions, it may not be possible to agree on appropriate standards to govern all practices in all situations. Although approaches to the competition policy-intellectual property interface in major developed jurisdictions have undergone a degree of convergence in recent years and a number of useful guidelines on national enforcement policies are available for reference,[7] there remain important residual differences even between the US and the European Community.[8] In the past, even greater divergences have been evident between developed and developing countries regarding issues in this area.[9] It is important, however, not to be defeatist regarding these differences and the consequent scope for development of policies that would enhance global welfare. Even if it is not possible to agree on standards to govern all anti-competitive practices relating to IP in all cases, there could well be gains from an exchange of views on issues in this area in the context of the multilateral trading system.

---

6 See the discussion of remedies imposed in recent cases relating to practices of the Microsoft Corporation, section 3.4 *infra*.

7 See, for example, US Department of Justice and Federal Trade Commission, 'Antitrust Guidelines for the Licensing of Intellectual Property', 6 April 1995, http://www.usdoj.gov/atr/public/guidelines/0558.htm, accessed 4 November 2007; Commission Notice – Guidelines on the application of Article 81 of the EC Treaty to technology transfer agreements, OJ 2004 No. C 101, p. 2; Canadian Competition Bureau, 'Intellectual Property Enforcement Guidelines', 2000, http://strategis.ic.gc.ca/pics/ct/ipege.pdf, accessed 4 November 2007; Japanese Fair Trade Commission (1999), 'Guidelines for Patent and Know-How Licensing Agreements under the Anti-Monopoly Act', 30 July 1999, http://www.jftc.go.jp/e-page/legislation/ama/patentand-know-how.pdf, accessed 4 November 2007, and Japanese Fair Trade Commission, 'Guidelines on Standardization and Patent Pool Arrangements', 2005, http://www.jftc.go.jp/e-page/legislation/ama/Patent_Pool.pdf, accessed 4 November 2007.

8 See the discussion in section 3 *infra*.

9 See Anderson, *supra* note 3, and references cited therein.

In addition to pertinent developments at the national level, any discussion of issues concerning the interface of intellectual property and competition policy in the WTO could build effectively on developments and discussions that have already taken place in various intergovernmental fora. The interface of competition policy and intellectual property rights has been an important topic of discussion, *inter alia*, in the OECD Committee on Competition Law Policy and the UNCTAD Intergovernmental Group of Experts on Competition Law and Policy.[10]

Experience in the WTO Working Group on the Interaction between Trade and Competition Policy – which was established at the Singapore Ministerial Conference in December 1996 and met regularly in the years from 1997 through 2004 but is currently 'inactive' – is also, very much, of interest in this regard. The application of competition policy vis-à-vis IPRs was an important focus of the Group in the initial years of its work.[11] As discussed in this chapter, the record of those discussions suggests that the state of international thinking has progressed since the more extreme divergences of the past and that there may be more scope than is commonly realized for further work on fostering common approaches among WTO Member countries in this area, centred around sound economic principles.

This chapter reflects on these questions and possibilities. The intention is *not* to provide a definitive answer to the question of what kind of guidance is needed or to take particular positions on current enforcement issues, but to illuminate the need for guidance and some of the issues that would need to be addressed. The overall perspective of the chapter is that, in the long run, there will be a need for greater international coordination in this area. This reflects both the technical challenges for enforcement policy and the potential negative spillovers from a lack of international coordination that are noted above.

---

10 See, in particular, OECD, Committee on Competition Law and Policy (1998), 'Competition Policy and Intellectual Property Rights', DAFFE/CLP(98)18, http://www.oecd.org/dataoecd/34/57/1920398.pdf, accessed 4 November 2007; and UNCTAD (2002), Intergovernmental Group of Experts on Competition Law and Policy, 'Competition Policy and the Exercise of Intellectual Property Rights', TD/B/COM.2/CLP/22/Rev.1, http://www.unctad.org/en/docs//c2clp22r1.en.pdf, accessed 4 November 2007. A useful summary of past UNCTAD work in this area is provided in Heinemann, Andreas (1999), 'Intellectual Property Rights and Competition Policy: The Approach of the WTO Working Group on Trade and Competition', in Roger Zäch (ed.), *Towards WTO Competition Rules*, Berne and The Hague: Staempfli Publishers and Kluwer Law International, p. 299, at 314–17.

11 See World Trade Organization (1998), 'Report of the WTO Working Group on the Interaction between Trade and Competition Policy', WT/WGTCP/2, http://docsonline.wto.org/DDFDocuments/t/WT/WGTCP/2.doc, accessed 4 November 2007, at Section C(III)(c).

However, agreement on common standards will not be easy. In the short run, there is a need for renewed international dialogue and reflection on issues concerning the interface of competition policy and intellectual property. Such dialogue whould include but not be limited to competition specialists and should take account of recent economic learning and lessons from national enforcement experience in addition to past discussions at the international level, including in the WTO. The scope for resulting guidance and whether such guidance would be of a voluntary nature or otherwise are questions that could be assessed within the scope of such discussions.

The remainder of the chapter is organized as follows. Section 2 outlines the existing competition policy-related provisions of the TRIPS Agreement, noting in particular the questions that these provisions leave unanswered and the significance of these questions. Section 3 develops the need for a further learning and policy development exercise in this area at the multilateral level, fleshing out the points noted above. Section 4 sets out a number of particular issues on which an exchange of views and further international convergence would be desirable, noting the problems that can flow from differing national standards and approaches in this area. Section 5 reviews the discussions that took place on this topic in the early work of the WTO Working Group on the Interaction between Trade and Competition Policy, noting the main points of agreement between the participating Members. Section 6 provides concluding remarks.

2 The competition policy provisions of the TRIPS Agreement: flexibility provided and questions unanswered[12]

The area of IPRs is an important example of a sphere in which the role of competition policy is already directly reflected in an existing WTO Agreement, the Agreement on Trade-Related Intellectual Property Rights (TRIPS).[13] As already noted (note 1 *supra*), the basic right of WTO Members to take measures, consistent with the provisions of the Agreement, to prevent abuses by rights holders and the resort to practices which unreasonably restrain trade or adversely affect the international transfer of technology is recognized in broad terms in Article 8(2) of the Agreement.

In the same spirit but focusing on the specific issue of licensing practices, Article 40(1) of the Agreement notes that: 'Members agree that some licensing practices or conditions pertaining to intellectual property rights which

12 See also Anderson, *supra* note 3, and Anderson and Wager, *supra* note 4.

13 Anderson, R.D. (1998), 'The Interface Between Competition Policy and Intellectual Property in the Context of the International Trading System,' *J.I.E.L.*, **1,** 655; see also Anderson, Robert D. and Peter Holmes (2002), 'Competition Policy and the Future of the Multilateral Trading System,' *J.I.E.L.*, **5**, 531.

restrain competition may have adverse effects on trade and may impede that transfer and dissemination of new technology'.

To address this concern, Article 40(2) recognizes the right of Member governments to take measures to prevent anti-competitive abuses of intellectual property rights, provided that such measures are consistent with relevant provisions of the Agreement. Article 40(2) also contains a short illustrative list of practices which may be treated as abuses.[14] It should be noted that neither Article 8(2) nor Article 40(2) indicates that specific practices shall be treated as abuses or specifies remedial measures that must be taken. In this sense, the competition provisions of the Agreement are permissive rather than mandatory.[15]

Article 40(3) of the Agreement provides that a Member considering action against an intellectual property owner that is a national or domiciliary of another Member can seek consultations with that Member. The latter Member is required to cooperate through the supply of publicly available non-confidential information of relevance, and of other information available to that Member, subject to domestic law and to the conclusion of mutually satisfactory agreements concerning the safeguarding of its confidentiality.

Competition policy considerations are also embodied in the TRIPS Agreement provisions relating to compulsory licensing in respect of patents. Article 31 of the Agreement sets out detailed conditions that must be respected in the granting by Member states of any compulsory licences. However, paragraph (k) of Article 31 stipulates that Members are not obliged to apply certain of these conditions[16] in circumstances where the compulsory licence is granted 'to remedy a practice determined after judicial or administrative process to be anti-competitive'. In particular, requirements to show that a proposed user has made efforts to obtain voluntary authorization from the right holder on reasonable terms and conditions and that such efforts have not been successful within a reasonable period of time are not applicable in these circumstances. In addition, the requirement in Article 31(f) that authorization for use of a patent under a compulsory licence be predominantly for the supply of the domestic market of the Member authorizing such use can also be rendered inapplicable by such a finding.

The existence of the foregoing provisions reflects a concern articulated by some countries, especially developing countries, during the negotiation of the Agreement that the various commitments regarding standards of protection for

---

[14] These are exclusive grant-back conditions, conditions preventing challenges to validity and coercive package licensing.

[15] See also Anderson, *supra* note 3.

[16] Specifically, those contained in paras (b) and (f) of Article 31.

intellectual property that are embodied therein be balanced by a recognition of the right of Members to take appropriate measures to address resulting abuses.[17] They provide broad discretion to WTO Member governments to implement competition policy remedies with regard to anti-competitive licensing and other practices. As such, they represent an important aspect of the flexibility that is built into the Agreement.

As pointed out in the Introduction to this chapter, however, the foregoing provisions leave unanswered a number of important questions. For example, they do not define the basis on which practices may be deemed to be anti-competitive. Second, the full set of practices that may be deemed anti-competitive is left undefined.[18] Third, the Agreement provides no specific guidance on remedies, merely stating that any measures adopted must be consistent with other provisions of the Agreement. Presumably, one implication of the latter limitation is that the remedy of compulsory licensing cannot be imposed other than in a manner consistent with the provisions of Article 31.

3 The need for further guidance for WTO Members in this area: technical challenges, policy legitimacy, avoiding overly sweeping approaches and international coordination issues

As noted in the Introduction to this chapter, there may be advantages as well as disadvantages to the lack of guidance provided by the TRIPS Agreement on the matters identified in the preceding section. Abbott, in particular, argues that the broad discretion for governments in the design and implementation of competition policies vis-à-vis intellectual property that results from the wording of the current provisions serves the best interests of developed and developing countries alike.[19] However, even if no amendment to the TRIPS Agreement as such or development of parallel binding rules is deemed to be desirable or feasible in the current circumstances, there are reasons for believing that the current situation is not optimal, and that ways need to be found to provide additional guidance for WTO Members in this area. This part of the chapter considers these reasons. The form that further guidance would take – that is whether it might be of a binding or non-binding nature – is a question that could be addressed at a later stage.

---

17 See discussion in World Trade Organization *supra* note 3, at 72–4.

18 The latter might not be a problem if the evaluative criteria were specified. It is not uncommon, in domestic statutes, to provide an open-ended illustrative list of acts that are covered by a particular provision. However, in view of the lack of evaluative criteria and defining principles, the open-ended nature of the set of anti-competitive practices could result in arbitrary application of the authority provided in Article 40(2).

19 Abbott, *supra* note 3.

3.1 Facilitating desirable competition policy interventions vis-à-vis intellectual property licensing and other abuses

The application of competition policy vis-à-vis intellectual property is undeniably one of the more complex and technically challenging sub-fields of such policy. It has taken decades for the major jurisdictions applying competition policy in this area (principally the US, the EC, Japan, and Canada) to develop the relevant analytical tools and approaches. Therefore, while respecting the right and possible interest of developing countries to follow different approaches, it is important to recognize the practical difficulties that they face in developing and putting into place any approach at all. This is particularly so with regard to anti-competitive practices that are transnational in nature (for example, anti-competitive clauses in international licensing agreements). An obvious way forward is to examine the approaches that have been adopted in regimes with active policies in this area, in conjunction with relevant legal and economic literature, and to consider the adoption of policy approaches. A policy that simply preserves all options in this area may well be synonymous with a policy of non-intervention with regard to IP licensing and other abuses.

For greater precision, the competition authorities of the US, the EC, Canada and Japan have all adopted more or less comprehensive guidelines or other policy statements setting out the analytical and other approaches that they take toward licensing and other IP abuses.[20] Of course, each of these instruments has its own particularities reflecting its institutional and policy context. None of them purports to represent 'the final word' on the optimal application of competition policy vis-à-vis intellectual property. In fact, these instruments are all subject to occasional updates or revision to take account of new learning and policy developments. They nonetheless represent highly useful syntheses of enforcement approaches that both provide guidance to firms and facilitate policy application by responsible officials. As such, they are an essential point of reference for international reflection and for jurisdictions with less experience in this area.

3.2 Ensuring policy legitimacy

Guidelines and similar policy statements serve purposes that go beyond the pedagogical. Apart from the technical challenges involved in effective competition policy interventions vis-à-vis licensing and other IP abuses, developing countries may hesitate to apply their competition policies in this area out of fear of some kind of retaliation or other pressure.[21] A key benefit of international deliberations on a possible resulting guideline on enforcement issues in

---

20 On the US, EC, Canadian and Japanese guidelines, see *supra* note 7.

21 This possibility is recognized by Abbott, *supra* note 3.

this area could be to confer legitimacy on (well-founded) interventions by developing country competition authorities with respect to anti-competitive abuses of IPRs.

3.3 Avoiding overly sweeping or rigid enforcement approaches

Competition law and enforcement officials recognize that, in addition to under-enforcement of national competition policies vis-à-vis intellectual property rights, national economic welfare can be reduced by over-enforcement of such policies (that is, excessively sweeping or per se condemnation of practices that can, in appropriate circumstances, be welfare-enhancing). In this regard, the position articulated in the US IP Antitrust Guidelines of 1995 is to the point: [22]

> Field-of-use, territorial, and other limitations on intellectual property licenses may serve pro-competitive ends by allowing the licensor to exploit its property as efficiently and effectively as possible. These various forms of exclusivity can be used to give a licensee an incentive to invest in the commercialization and distribution of products embodying the licensed intellectual property and to develop additional applications for the licensed property. The restrictions may do so, for example, by protecting the licensee against free-riding on the licensee's investments by other licensees or by the licensor. They may also increase the licensor's incentive to license, for example, by protecting the licensor from competition in the licensor's own technology in a market niche that it prefers to keep to itself.

Recognition of the potential pro-competitive benefits of licensing and other vertical practices is not an invention of contemporary competition agencies; it is a basic tenet of modern industrial organization economics.[23]

The fact that licensing and other vertical practices can serve legitimate pro-competitive purposes cautions against excessive reliance on per se rules in regard to such practices. Recognizing this, for the past two decades or more competition agencies have progressively eschewed such rules in favour of case-by-case or 'rule of reason' treatment of such practices. Helping countries to avoid the self-inflicted harm caused by excessively rigid or sweeping rules is another possible benefit of a comparative assessment or policy development exercise encompassing these issues at the multilateral level.

---

22 US IP Antitrust Guidelines, *supra* note 7, Section 2.3. See also the thoughtful discussion of current enforcement issues in Platt Majoras, Deborah (Chairman, US Federal Trade Commission) (2006), 'A Government Perspective on IP and Antitrust Law', Speech, American Antitrust Institute Conference, The IP Grab: The Struggle Between Intellectual Property Rights and Antitrust, Washington, DC, http://www.ftc.gov/speeches/majoras/060621aai-ip.pdf, accessed 4 November 2007.

23 See, for example, Carlton, Dennis W. and Jeffrey M. Perloff (2005), *Modern Industrial Organization*, Boston, MA: Addison Wesley, 4th ed., chapter 12.

3.4 Possible negative spillovers resulting from conflicting national competition policies vis-à-vis intellectual property[24]

Independent of the concerns noted above which relate to the costs of under or over-enforcement of competition policy vis-à-vis IPRs at the national level, there are potential externalities or spillovers associated with differing national standards in this area. In some cases, the spillovers will be positive in the sense that measures taken to protect competition in one market will also benefit consumers in other markets and will have no adverse effects. However, negative spillovers can also arise. For example, remedies imposed in one jurisdiction may impinge on behaviour (and potentially on economic welfare) in other jurisdictions. A particularly acute example of this concern relates to situations in which remedies imposed in one jurisdiction require the sharing of proprietary information. In such cases, it may be difficult to prevent the information disclosed (or products manufactured using such information) from 'leaking' across borders.

The recent example of remedies implemented by various jurisdictions in respect of practices of the Microsoft Corporation illustrates this concern. As is well known, in the course of a number of related cases the competition authorities of the United States and the European Communities have taken different positions – in some respects, only subtly different – regarding aspects of Microsoft's conduct. Although these cases have typically been framed in terms of abuse of dominant position or monopolization rather than abusive licensing practices as such, the two areas are intimately connected.[25] In reviewing a 2004 decision of the European Commission in one such case, the Antitrust Division of the US Department of Justice issued a press release stating as follows:[26]

> The U.S. experience tells us that the best antitrust remedies eliminate impediments to the healthy functioning of competitive markets without hindering successful competitors or imposing burdens on third parties, which may result from the EC's remedy. [. . .] Sound antitrust policy must avoid chilling innovation and competi-

[24] This section of the chapter draws on material in Anderson, Robert D. and Alberto Heimler (2007), 'Abuse of Dominant Position: Enforcement Issues and Approaches for Developing Countries', in Vinod Dhall (ed.), *Competition Law Today: Concepts, Issues and the Law in Practice*, New Delhi: Oxford University Press, chapter 2.

[25] Cases of anti-competitive abuse of intellectual property rights will often be framed as abuses of a dominant position. See, for example, Canadian IP Enforcement Guidelines, *supra* note 7.

[26] 'US Department of Justice, Assistant Attorney-General for Antitrust, R. Hewitt Pate, Issues Statement on the EC's Decision in its Microsoft Investigation', Press Release, 24 March 2004; http://www.usdoj.gov/opa/pr/2004/March/04_at_184.htm, accessed 4 November 2007.

> tion even by 'dominant' companies. A contrary approach risks protecting competitors, not competition, in ways that may ultimately harm innovation and the consumers that benefit from it. It is significant that the U.S. district court considered and rejected a . . . remedy [similar to that imposed by the EC] in the U.S. litigation.

As a further (perhaps even more stark) illustration, in early December 2005, the Fair Trade Commission of Korea made public an order requiring Microsoft to sell in Korea a version of its Windows operating system that includes neither Windows Media Player nor Windows Messenger functionality, requiring Microsoft to facilitate consumer downloads of third-party media player and messenger products selected by the Commission, and prohibiting Microsoft from selling in Korea a version of its server software that includes Windows Media Services. In response, the Antitrust Division of the US Department of Justice issued a press release stating as follows:[27]

> The Antitrust Division believes that Korea's remedy goes beyond what is necessary or appropriate to protect consumers, as it requires the removal of products that consumers may prefer. The Division continues to believe that imposing 'code removal' remedies that strip out functionality can ultimately harm innovation and the consumers that benefit from it. We had previously consulted with the Commission on its Microsoft case and encouraged the Commission to develop a balanced resolution that addressed its concerns without imposing unnecessary restrictions. Sound antitrust policy should protect competition, not competitors, and must avoid chilling innovation and competition even by 'dominant' companies.

Without taking any position on the substantive merits of the approaches taken in the three jurisdictions (the US, the EC and Korea), the foregoing exchanges illustrate clearly the potential for conflicts where different jurisdictions take different approaches in addressing transnational abuses of a dominant position (or abuses of intellectual property rights). A minimum requirement to avoid conflicts in such cases is adherence to the well-known principle of national treatment (one of the founding principles of the WTO), which broadly requires that countries not impose burdens on foreign producers or products that they do not impose on their own firms or products.[28]

---

[27] 'Statement of Deputy Assistant Attorney-General J. Bruce McDonald Regarding Korean Fair Trade Commission's Decision in its *Microsoft* Case', Press Release, 7 December 2005, http://www.usdoj.gov/atr/public/press_releases/2005/213562.htm, accessed 4 November 2007.

[28] The application of the principle of national treatment in the WTO varies as between relevant agreements. See World Trade Organization (1999), 'The Fundamental WTO Principles of Transparency and Non-discrimination', WT/WGTCP/W/114, 14 April 1999, http://docsonline.wto.org/DDFDocuments/t/WT/WGTCP/W114.DOC, accessed 4 November 2007.

However, it is not clear that this, by itself, will answer all possible concerns, particularly where differences in the remedies imposed by particular jurisdictions result not from discrimination as such but from substantive differences in enforcement philosophies and approaches. There may, indeed, be no simple solution. Possibly, the answers can be found in further international discussions aimed at fostering intellectual consensus on the substantive issues involved. However, the potential for conflict in cases of abuses of intellectual property rights (or abuses of a dominant position involving intellectual property rights, particularly as a remedy) at least raises the possibility that something more than this – meaning a system of international coordination, whether voluntary or otherwise – will eventually be needed.

4 Issues that might be addressed in a possible international guideline/policy-making exercise

This section of the chapter sets out some specific issues on which international reflection and (possibly) coordination may be desirable. The list of issues derives from the guidelines that have been issued by the competition authorities of the major jurisdictions having experience in this area, and related enforcement experience and jurisprudence. Some of the issues noted concern the basic approach and coverage of competition law vis-à-vis intellectual property; others involve particular practices of current interest. Where possible, an effort is made to identify international coordination problems that may arise in relation to the issues and categories of conduct discussed in addition to the basic questions of enforcement policy. The potential international coordination problems identified (particularly in regard to the treatment of licensing issues, pooling, anti-competitive patent settlements and refusals to license) reinforce the case for further discussion of these issues in appropriate international fora.

4.1 The basic role of competition policy vis-à-vis intellectual property rights

A premise common to the guidelines of major jurisdictions with experience in this area is that, at least at a broad level, the protection of IPRs per se is not inconsistent with the goals of competition policy. Rather, if properly designed and administered, IPRs strengthen competition in the long run by providing incentives for the development and production of new products and production processes and by facilitating technology transfer.[29] Furthermore, in most

[29] The US IP Antitrust Guidelines, *supra* note 7, Section 1.0, describe the basic relationship between intellectual property and competition law as follows: 'The intellectual property laws and the antitrust laws share the common purpose of promoting

(not all) cases, substitutes are available for products that are protected by IPRs. This implies that the mere existence of IP rights, by itself, should not be seen as proof of the existence of market power.[30] The latter view has now been adopted in US Supreme Court jurisprudence in addition to relevant enforcement guidelines.[31]

Notwithstanding this overall relationship of complementarity, experience has made clear that IPRs can indeed give rise to significant market power in particular cases and that the exercise of such rights can conflict with the content and/or the objectives of competition law in a variety of ways. Four basic categories of practices which can and do give rise to conflicts with competition law in particular cases are the following: (i) the acquisition of IPRs, for example through mergers or simply the assignment of IPRs; (ii) technology licensing arrangements (whether domestic or international); (iii) cooperative arrangements among innovating firms, including patent pools; and (iv) anti-competitive settlements in patent infringement cases that deter entry by generic competitors. These specific aspects of competition law enforcement would constitute important elements of any international policy-development exercise or guideline in this area and are discussed further below.

---

innovation and enhancing consumer welfare. The intellectual property laws provide incentives for innovation and its dissemination and commercialization by establishing enforceable property rights for the creators of new and useful products, more efficient processes, and original works of expression. In the absence of intellectual property rights, imitators could more rapidly exploit the efforts of innovators and investors without compensation. Rapid imitation would reduce the commercial value of innovation and erode incentives to invest, ultimately to the detriment of consumers. The antitrust laws promote innovation and consumer welfare by prohibiting certain actions that may harm competition with respect to either existing or new ways of serving consumers.'

30 Anderson, Robert D. and Nancy Gallini (1998), 'Introduction to the Issues', in Robert D. Anderson and Nancy Gallini (eds), *Competition Policy and Intellectual Property Rights in the Knowledge-based Economy*, Calgary: University of Calgary Press, p. 1.

31 See *Illinois Tool Works, Inc. v. Independent Ink, Inc.*, 126 S.Ct. 1281 (2006). In the past, competition law in the US was guided by the presumption that the mere existence of patents or copyrights gives rise to the existence of market power, which in turn was an important threshold condition for the application of 'per se rules' (rules embodying a blanket prohibition of relevant practices) in regard to practices such as tying arrangements. See *Jefferson Parish Hospital District No. 2 v. Hyde*, 466 US 2 (US Supreme Court), and past precedents cited therein. However, economic analysis and Guidelines adopted by the US Department of Justice and Federal Trade Commission in 1995 called this view into question, pointing out the availability of substitutes for many protected works or technologies. Acceding to this approach, the US Supreme Court, in its decision in *Illinois Tool Works, Inc. v. Independent Ink, Inc.*, struck down the old presumption, accepting the conclusion that patents do not necessarily confer market power. On this decision see also Jones, Clifford A., Chapter 10, in this volume; and Grimes, Warren, Chapter 11, in this volume.

Consideration is also given to an issue on which there is no international consensus – namely the treatment of refusals to license – and to the transcending importance of competition advocacy.

4.2 Competition issues regarding the acquisition of intellectual property rights

An important 'threshold' issue that could be addressed in an international guideline or policy-making exercise concerns the basic applicability of competition law to acquisitions of IPRs. IRPs may be acquired either by themselves or as a consequence of a merger of corporate entities owning such rights. It is of critical importance that acquisitions of IPRs, like other forms of property, be subject to the constraints of competition law. This principle is recognized in the guidelines of major jurisdictions with active enforcement programmes in this area and in some relevant judicial decisions.[32]

4.3 The treatment of licensing and related practices

The treatment of licensing practices is a central issue at the interface of competition law and intellectual property rights. Licensing practices that may, in particular cases, have anti-competitive effects include grant-backs, exclusive dealing requirements, tie-ins, territorial market limitations, field-of-use restrictions and price-maintenance clauses. The overall trend in competition-law jurisprudence internationally is to treat such practices on a case-by-case or 'rule of reason' basis.[33] As noted above, economic learning is supportive of such an approach in that it makes clear that these practices can, at least in some circumstances, serve legitimate pro-competitive functions.[34]

---

[32] Some time ago, the Canadian Competition Bureau found it necessary to make an intervention in a case before the Federal Court of Appeal, *Apotex Inc. v. Eli Lilly and Company*, A-579-04, 2005 CAF 361, on the question of whether the assignment of a patent could constitute an agreement or arrangement to lessen competition unduly, contrary to the conspiracy provision of the Canadian Competition Act. In its decision, the Court adopted the Bureau's position, holding that Canada's patent legislation 'does not immunize an agreement to assign a patent from section 45 of the Competition Act when the assignment increases the assignee's market power in excess of that inherent in the patent rights assigned'. See, for details and further background, Scott, Sheridan (Commission of Competition, Canada) (2006), 'Competition Law and Intellectual Property Law: Getting the Balance "Just Right"', Address to the University of Victoria Faculty of Law International Intellectual Property Law Symposium, 15 July 2006, http://www.competitionbureau.gc.ca/internet/index.cfm?itemID=2146&lg=e, accessed 4 November 2007.

[33] There are, nonetheless, important residual differences in the treatment of licensing practices among jurisdictions, perhaps particularly between the US and the European Community.

[34] See text accompanying *supra* note 23. The central importance of economic

Under this approach, licensing arrangements are assessed on the basis of factors such as the following:

- the extent and availability of substitutes for the products and (existing or future) technologies in question (a basic determinant of market power);
- implications of the arrangements in question for market power, coordination of pricing or output, and foreclosure of access to inputs;
- the extent to which they impose exclusivity;
- the extent of rivalry and the pace of innovation in the markets affected;
- possible efficiencies resulting from the arrangement.[35]

A case-by-case approach to the treatment of licensing practices may strike some as unduly permissive or lenient.[36] In the past, some developing countries have advocated a stricter approach. An unduly strict or per se approach is likely, however, to be self-defeating. Sweeping prohibition of restrictive practices in international licensing agreements would raise the costs and/or reduce the incentives for technology owners to enter into voluntary arrangements that are generally pro-competitive and are an important vehicle for international technology transfer. This does not, however, imply that restrictive licensing arrangements should be immune from scrutiny; rather, the suggestion is simply that such scrutiny should be carried out using the market power and other screens and tests that are suggested by relevant economic literature and case experience.[37]

Where licensing arrangements are international in scope, the application of competition law in this area can clearly give rise to international coordination problems. In the absence of 'comity' or similar considerations, where a particular licensing arrangement is subject to the competition laws of two or more jurisdictions, the arrangement could be deemed illegal under laws of the jurisdiction taking the 'strictest' approach notwithstanding that it would be tolerated or even deemed desirable under the approach of the other jurisdiction.

---

learning as the basis for sound competition rules and related analysis is stressed in Kovacic, W.E. (2004), 'The Modern Evolution of U.S. Competition Policy Enforcement Norms', *Antitrust L.J.*, **71**, 377.

35 See also Anderson and Heimler, *supra* note 24.

36 Abbott, in particular, emphasizes that, in his view, Section 40 of the TRIPS Agreement permits per se prohibition of licensing practices. Abbott, *supra* note 3.

37 See, for further discussion, US IP Antitrust Guidelines, *supra* note 7; and the various essays in Anderson and Gallini, *supra* note 30.

4.4 Issues concerning patent thickets and pooling

Another important issue meriting attention in any international policy development exercise or guideline is that of patent thickets and pooling. Patent thickets are situations in which an overlapping set of patent rights requires firms seeking to commercialize new technology to obtain licences from multiple patentees. For example, a single semiconductor product can be potentially subject to hundreds or *thousands* of patents. The impact of patent thickets is heightened by the risk of 'hold-ups' – that is, the danger that new products will inadvertently infringe on patents issued after the products have been designed.[38]

Patent pools and/or cross-licensing can be an efficient response to these phenomena in many cases, although they can also raise antitrust concerns. A key insight in this regard is that pools combining complementary patents are generally efficiency-enhancing; whereas pools comprised of substitute patents can indeed create market power and are a legitimate focus of antitrust concern.[39] Why might it eventually prove necessary to treat the issue of patent thickets and pooling in an international guideline or policy development exercise, as opposed to merely addressing it at the national level? The answer is that pools raise, potentially in acute form, the international coordination issues flagged above. If particular pools or cross-licensing arrangements are permitted in one jurisdiction but not in another, spillovers are likely to arise.

4.5 The treatment of patent settlements

Another important issue that is highlighted by recent enforcement experience in developed jurisdictions concerns anti-competitive 'settlements' in patent infringement cases that thwart entry by generic competitors. This possibility is likely to be of particular concern in situations where public policy seeks to facilitate entry by generic competitors. As Majoras explains, under the relevant US legislation:[40]

> In nearly any case in which generic entry is contemplated, the profit that the generic anticipates will be much less than the profit the brand-name drug company would make from the same sales. Consequently, it will often be more profitable for the branded manufacturer to buy off generics.

---

38 Majoras, *supra* note 22.

39 Shapiro, Carl (2001), 'Navigating the Patent Thicket: Cross Licenses, Patent Pools, and Standard-setting', in Adam Jaffe, Joshua Lerner and Scott Stern (eds), *Innovation Policy and the Economy*, vol. 1, Cambridge, MA: MIT Press, p. 119; see also Ullrich, Hanns, Chapter 6, in this volume.

40 Majoras, *supra* note 22.

Of course, 'buying off' potential generic competitors is likely to be strongly contrary to the interests of consumers.

As part of the global response to current public health emergencies, recently the TRIPS Agreement has been amended to facilitate generic production of pharmaceutical medicines for countries affected by such crises.[41] It is important that this policy not be undercut by anti-competitive settlements between brand-name and generic drug companies. Accordingly, this issue could be an important focus of international deliberations regarding the interface of competition policy and intellectual property.

4.6 Refusals to license

An additional issue on which it may be difficult to achieve full convergence is that of refusals to license IPRs. In the EU, the *Magill*[42] and *IMS Health*[43] cases have made clear that such refusals can indeed violate relevant competition law provisions, depending on the circumstances and, in particular, on whether they impede the development of new products. On the other hand, in the US, there is a strong or, in the view of many commentators, absolute presumption that patent holders are entitled to refuse to license their patented inventions (the situation is less clear with regard to copyright).[44] Independent of views concerning which side in this debate is 'right', the treatment of refusals clearly poses stark problems of international policy coordination: where technology is made available by compulsory licence in one jurisdiction (despite possible opposing views in another jurisdiction), it will be difficult to prevent it from 'leaking' across borders.[45]

4.7 Competition advocacy in relation to intellectual property rights

Recent experience also underlines the importance of advocacy activities by competition agencies aimed at ensuring that patents and other forms of intellectual property rights are not awarded unnecessarily or cast in overly broad

---

[41] See, for details, Anderson and Wager, *supra* note 4.

[42] Joined Cases C-241 and 242/91 P, *RTE and IRP v. Commission* ('*Magill*'), [1995] ECR I-743.

[43] Case C-481/01, *IMS Health*, [2004] ECR I-5039.

[44] See, for example, Delrahim, Makan (US Deputy Assistant Attorney-General for Antitrust) (2004), 'Forcing Firms to Share the Sandbox: Compulsory Licensing of Intellectual Property Rights and Antitrust', Remarks before the British Institute of International and Comparative Law, London, UK, http://www.usdoj.gov/atr/public/speeches/203627.htm, accessed 4 November 2007.

[45] Such concerns would appear to underlie the concerns voiced by the US Department of Justice in regard to the remedy imposed by the Korean Fair Trade Commission in its recent *Microsoft* decision, referred to *supra* in note 27 and accompanying text.

terms.[46] Such activities can include public education activities, studies and research undertaken to document the need for market-opening measures, formal appearances before legislative committees or other government bodies in public proceedings or behind-the-scenes lobbying within government.[47] An important and highly pertinent example of a competition policy advocacy activity in the specific area of intellectual property is the 2003 report of the US Federal Trade Commission entitled 'To Promote Innovation: The Proper Balance of Competition and Patent Law and Policy'.[48] This report provides a penetrating discussion of the harmful effects on competition that can flow from the awarding of unjustified patents (or patents that are cast in overly broad terms), and puts forward a range of proposals to address these problems. Affirming the importance of such activities in relation to intellectual property could be another valuable contribution of an international guideline or policy-development exercise relating to competition policy and intellectual property at the multilateral level.[49]

5 Past discussions in the WTO Working Group on the interaction between trade and competition policy as a point of reference for further policy development work at the international level[50]

At the 1996 Singapore Ministerial Conference, WTO Ministers established a Working Group on the Interaction between Trade and Competition Policy (WGTCP). The mandate given to the Working Group at that time was to consider issues raised by Members relating to the interaction of the two policy fields, including anti-competitive practices, and to identify any areas that might merit further consideration in the WTO framework.[51] Between 1997

46 Majoras, *supra* note 22; see also Kovacic, W.E. (2004), 'The Future of US Competition Policy', *The Antitrust Source*, September 2004, http://www.ftc.gov/speeches/kovacic/kovacicreplytokolasky.pdf, accessed 4 November 2007.

47 See generally Anderson, Robert D. and Frédéric Jenny (2005), 'Competition Policy, Economic Development and the Possible Role of a Multilateral Framework on Competition Policy: Insights from the WTO Working Group on Trade and Competition Policy', in Erlinda Medalla (ed.), *Competition Policy in East Asia*, London: Routledge–Curzon, p. 61.

48 'To Promote Innovation: The Proper Balance of Competition and Patent Law and Policy', Report by the Federal Trade Commission, October 2003, http://www.ftc.gov/os/2003/10/innovationrpt.pdf, accessed 4 November 2007.

49 The importance of competition-advocacy activities vis-à-vis intellectual property policy is also emphasized in Canada's IP Enforcement Guidelines, *supra* note 7.

50 This section of the paper draws on material in Anderson, *supra* note 3. A complementary discussion is provided in Heinemann, *supra* note 10.

51 Singapore Ministerial Declaration, Adopted on 13 December 1996, http://www.wto.org/English/thewto_e/minist_e/min96_e/wtodec_e.htm, accessed 4 November 2007, para. 20.

and 2003, a wide-ranging examination of the relationships between trade and competition policy, and between competition policy and economic development, was carried out in the WTO Working Group. As is well known, the exploratory work of the Working Group led eventually to a protracted debate, in the Group and outside, of the merits and demerits of a possible 'multilateral framework on competition policy'. At the WTO Ministerial Conference in Cancún, Mexico, in September 2003, it was not possible to reach a consensus on the launching of negotiations on a multilateral framework on competition policy as had been proposed by the European Community and various other WTO Members in the run-up to the conference. Subsequently, the General Council of the WTO decided, as part of the so-called July package of 2004, that no further work would be undertaken toward negotiations on competition policy (or on the separate issues of investment and transparency in government procurement) for the duration of the Doha Round.[52]

Notwithstanding the failure thus far to reach agreement on the launching of negotiations, the work of the Working Group on the Interaction between Trade and Competition Policy remains an important point of reference for discussions on international competition policy. For most WTO Members, the opposition to negotiations did not reflect a view that the issue of competition policy had no relevance to the goals of the multilateral trading system. Indeed, although without yielding a consensus on negotiations, preparatory work in the WTO Working Group catalogued a variety of ways in which anti-competitive practices can adversely impinge on the objectives of the system, and a number of possible synergies between the system and the work of national competition authorities.[53] Even participants who have been openly sceptical of the desirability of negotiations on competition policy in the WTO have noted the usefulness of the work done in the Working Group in promoting positive interest in the subject and wider understanding of competition policy concepts and tools.[54]

---

[52] Decision Adopted by the General Council on 1 August 2004, WT/L/579, http://www.wto.org/english/tratop_e/dda_e/draft_text_gc_dg_31july04_e.htm, accessed 4 November 2007. See, for related discussion, Anderson and Wager, *supra* note 4 and Anderson and Jenny, *supra* note 47.

[53] See, for details, World Trade Organizsation (1998–2003), 'Annual Report of the WTO Working Group on the Interaction between Trade and Competition Policy to the General Council', WT/WGTCP/2-8, available at http://www.wto.org/english-tratop_e/ comp_e/wgtcp_docs_e.htm, accessed 4 November 2007.

[54] For example, William Kolasky, then US Deputy Assistant Attorney-General for Antitrust and by no means an advocate of WTO competition rules, has stated as follows: 'Over the years, we have been told that our WTO papers – dealing with issues like technical assistance, building a culture of competition, and establishing antitrust priorities – have been of enormous help to countries that are in the process

The subject of the relationship between IPRs and competition policy was an important focus of the WTO Working Group in the early years of its work. The debates on this issue contain many elements relevant to possible further work in this subject-area at the multilateral level. For example, the discussion took as a point of departure the recognition that competition policy can be an important factor in balancing the rights of producers under intellectual property legislation, and in counteracting particular abuses thereof. The debate recognized both the costs entailed by overly strict enforcement policies and regulations in the area of technology licensing and the dangers of an overly lax approach. The Working Group also took note of the evolution that has taken place in the enforcement policies of WTO Members with experience in this area, and attached importance to this as a basis for further analysis.[55]

Some additional highlights of the Working Group's deliberations on this subject are as follows:

- There was wide acknowledgement that competition laws are necessary to prevent abusive practices and ensure that interfirm rivalry is not restricted to an extent beyond that intended by the intellectual property laws, and thereby that the market assigns a fair and efficient value to such property.[56]
- The discussion in the Working Group recognized that the availability of substitutes for goods and technologies covered by IPRs is an empirical question to be determined on a case-by-case basis.[57] As noted above, this is a base-line assumption of economics-based approaches to antitrust analysis in this area.[58] Further, even if the intellectual property right concerned generates market power, the right holder's behaviour might not necessarily constitute an abuse of dominance.
- There was a general recognition that licensing arrangements are normally pro-competitive and are an important vehicle for technology transfer. Where an individual licensing practice needs to be examined, this should normally be done on a case-by-case or 'rule of reason' basis by which the pro-competitive benefits are weighed against anti-competitive effects.[59]

---

of establishing an antitrust regime'. See Kolasky, William J. (2002), 'Global Competition Convergence and Co-operation: Looking Back and Looking Ahead', Remarks to the American Bar Association Fall Forum, Washington, DC, http://www.usdoj.gov/atr/ public/speeches/200442.htm, accessed 4 November 2007.

55 See, for a more comprehensive discussion, Anderson, *supra* note 3.

56 World Trade Organization (1998), *supra* note 11, para. 113.

57 World Trade Organization (1998), *supra* note 11, para. 115.

58 See text accompanying notes 30 and 31, *supra*.

59 World Trade Organization (1998), *supra* note 11, para. 116.

- Consistent with the above, the point was made that the proper application of competition law should avoid both excessively stringent enforcement approaches, which can lessen innovation, and the weak or ineffective application of such law, leading to the abuse of market power. Either approach can have an adverse effect on output as well as an inhibiting effect on trade.[60]
- The view was also expressed that more attention should be paid to ensuring that the intellectual property rights themselves are underpinned by sound competition principles and that they promote global welfare. Over-protection of intellectual property rights can contribute to the entrenchment of horizontal and vertical restraints, for example through patent pooling among competitors and the restriction of parallel imports. Some Members suggested, further, that future negotiations in the area of IPRs should give equal weight to recognizing the risks of both under- and over-protection of such rights. Under this approach, advocates of higher levels of protection would be required to demonstrate empirically that the changes they proposed are likely to increase global welfare.[61]
- The point was made that the TRIPS Agreement itself reflects the view that regimes for the protection of intellectual property rights should be balanced by safeguards intended to restrain anti-competitive practices involving the use of intellectual property rights. Some Members stated explicitly that the relevant provisions of TRIPS provide insufficient guidance on the practices that should be treated as abuses and the remedies that would be appropriate, and that more guidance in this area would be useful.[62]

In sum, the discussion of the interface between competition policy and IPRs in the WTO Working Group on the Interaction between Trade and Competition Policy was both wide-ranging and penetrating. The discussion delved into matters such as the objectives of IP laws and their relation to those of competition policy; the potential efficiency benefits of 'restrictive' licensing arrangements; the evolution of Member states' competition-enforcement policies in this area and the reasons for such evolution; and the implications for economic welfare of the practice of international market segmentation through IPRs. In key respects, the discussion in the Working Group paralleled the evolution of scholarly thinking in this area. As such, it

---

60 World Trade Organization (1998), *supra* note 11, para. 117.
61 World Trade Organization (1998), *supra* note 11, para. 118.
62 World Trade Organization (1998), *supra* note 11, para. 119.

may provide more of a basis for further work in this area than has hitherto been recognized.[63]

6 Concluding remarks

Recognition of the legitimate role of competition policy vis-à-vis intellectual property rights (IPRs) and licensing practices is an important element of the overall balance embodied in the WTO Agreement on Trade-Related Intellectual Property Rights (TRIPS). The relevant provisions reflect concerns regarding the potential anti-competitive effects of IPRs protected under the Agreement that were expressed particularly by developing countries during the negotiation of the Agreement in the course of the Uruguay Round of multilateral trade negotiations.

The competition-related provisions of the TRIPS Agreement, while representing an essential element of balance in the Agreement, also leave important questions unanswered, particularly on evaluative standards of assessment, on the full range of practices that may be deemed anti-competitive and on the specific remedies that may be adopted in particular cases. These gaps heighten the technical challenges for WTO Members in putting the provisions to good use and also raise potential international coordination problems. For example, remedies imposed in one jurisdiction may impinge or be felt to impinge on behaviour and on economic welfare in other jurisdictions. The potential for such problems has already been seen in international tensions relating to remedies imposed in the various *Microsoft* cases. Even if no amendment to the TRIPS Agreement as such or development of parallel binding rules is deemed to be called for to address these issues, there could be merit in a policy analysis and development exercise at the multilateral level to consider the relationship between competition policy and intellectual property rights.

Of course, even if it is deemed desirable to provide additional guidance for WTO Members regarding these questions, it may not be possible to agree on appropriate standards to govern all practices in all situations. Despite the recent convergence of the approaches to the competition policy–intellectual property interface in major developed jurisdictions, there are still differences, particularly between the US and the EC. Still there is no cause to be defeatist regarding these differences. Even if it is not possible to agree on standards to govern all anti-competitive practices relating to IP in all cases, there could well be gains from a further exchange of views on issues in this area, in an appropriate international forum.

Experience in the WTO Working Group on the Interaction between Trade and Competition Policy is of interest in this regard. The application of compe-

---

63 See, for a more comprehensive discussion, Anderson, *supra* note 3.

tition policy vis-à-vis IPRs was an important focus of the Group in the initial years of its work. As discussed in this chapter, the record of those discussions suggests that the state of international thinking has progressed since the more extreme divergences of the past and that there may be more scope than is commonly realized for further work on fostering common approaches among WTO Member countries in this area, centred around sound economic principles.

In any event, for all the reasons discussed in this chapter, it seems likely that issues at the interface of IPRs and competition policy will be a growing source of interest and possible international tensions in the years to come. Consequently, what today may seem impossible, namely a renewed discussion of these issues in the WTO, might yet come to pass.

Index